POTOMAC ARCHAEOLOGY

Based on Collections of and Assistance from
Charles W. Merry (Rockville, Maryland) and Spencer O. Geasey (Myersville, Maryland)

Wm Jack Hranicky, RPA
Director
Virginia Rockart Survey

Potomac River Fall Line and Gorge

Virginia Academic Press
Alexandria, Virginia
2016

This publication is dedicated to the memory of William H. Holmes (1846-1933), Smithsonian Institution, who introduced middle Potomac River valley archaeology to the world.

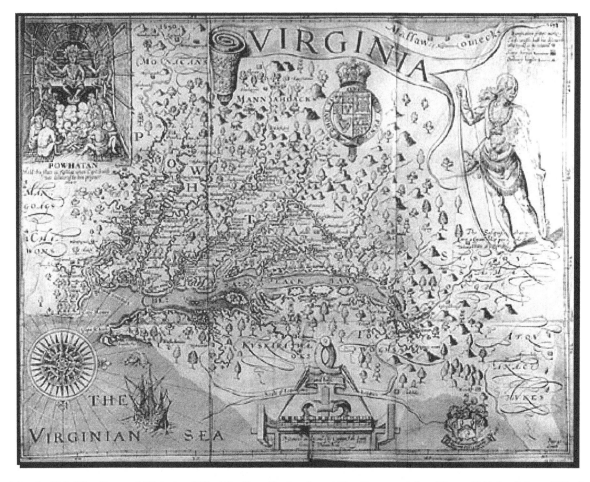

From: John Smith's The Generall Historie of Virginia, New-England, and The Summer Isles. I.D. and I.H. for Edward Blackmore, 1632. It was published a year after Smith's death and is a slightly different version than the famous 1612 map.

Copyright: 2016 Virginia Academic Press
Version 3

ISBN-13: 978-1537704500

Acknowledgments

The author thanks the following for allowing private and museum collections to be photographed, providing information about collections and sites, and discussing general information for the text. They are: Charles W. Merry, Howard A. MacCord, Sr., Michael F. Johnson, Tyler Bastian (see Chronology section), the late Charles A. Pettit, Vic Jenkins, Scott Silsby (see Experimental Archaeology section), James Sorenson, Elizabeth Vance and Larry Vance, Doug Dillinger, Dennis C. Curry, Kathy Butts, Jeffrey P. Tottenham, Stephen Isreal, Mark S. Kelly, Dan Isgrig, W. C. Nye, John and Violet Eicholtz, Harry A. Jaeger, Theodore R. Reinhart, William A. Thompson, Jr., Garland Stanton, Brian Station, Bart Quillin, David Dickson, Steve Lavagnino, Clinton Gurley, Jerry and Sandy Sherman, John M. Selmer, F. Kirk Drier, Errett Callahan and Daniel Abbott, (see Experimental Archaeology section), Jeffry Tottenham (see Bifaces and Knives section) Patrick Keefe, Michael E. Barber, Edward Bottoms, Bernard Means, Michael D. Petraglia, Jack Cresson (see Experimental Archaeology section), Barry C. Kent, D. J. Winkler and Jerome H. Winkler, Spencer Geasey, Ambassador George McGhee, the late John Nichols, Ronald G. Orr, Teresa Preston (and her father George Erwin Bray), Isabella Brown (Pamunkey Museum), Dan Guzy, and R. C. Printz.

Special thanks to Rodney M. Peck who has provided information for several books. He has been of tremendous assistance on the Paleoindian Period, especially providing Cumberland points and information for publication.

As part of this study, Gary Fogelman (Indian Artifact Magazine) provided broken bannerstones from Pennsylvania. See Miscellaneous Tools/Implements section.

For ethnographic data and artifacts, thanks to Raymond K. Dabbs, Sonny Wells, John Selmer, Thomas Zane Summers, George E. Bray, and Eugene M. Hayes, Jr.

Keith Egloff formerly of Virginia's Department of Historic Resources provided DHR radiocarbon files and numerous sources of archaeological information that helped make this publication possible. Also, Paul Inashima's publication provided the radiometrics for the projectile point section. Thanks to them and the DHR.

Dan Guzy, an engineer by profession, has made a study of MPRV fish weirs and his comments for this publication were greatly appreciated.

Special thanks to local state and county agencies and local museums. These are: Fairfax County Archaeological Survey, Alexandria Archaeology Museum, Smithsonian Institution, Fairfax County Park Authority, and Virginia Department of Historic Cultural Resources.

And, thanks to the able and most helpful assistance of various members of the Archeological Society of Maryland, Inc., Archeological Society of Virginia, Council of Virginia Archaeologists, and West Virginia Archeological Society. Numerous amateur archaeologists and local artifact collectors have assisted the author during the last 25 years in promoting site recording, artifact identifications, and other scholarly research on the prehistory of the Potomac River valley of Maryland, West Virginia, and Virginia. These efforts were truly appreciated by the author.

The Fairfax Archaeological Survey collections were used to supplement the study collections. Their field surveys were performed by Michael F. Johnson and in some cases, volunteers of the Archeological of Virginia. Access to these collections is greatly appreciated by the author. Another contribution to this study was made by Ambassador George McGhee of Middleburg, Virginia. He provided the author with a point collection that will eventually be housed in the Alexandria Archaeology Museum in Alexandria, Virginia.

Special thanks to Ronald G. Orr of the Maryland Archaeological Conservation Laboratory located at the Jefferson Patterson Park and Museum in Calvert County, Maryland. He provided an insight to Maryland's archaeological collections, including helping in recording artifacts for this publication. The Spencer Geasey and Charles Pettit collections are located there, and some of their artifacts were used in this study. Pettit numbered all his artifacts and maintained a log of where each artifact was found. His collection now belongs to the Maryland Historic Trust.

R. C. Printz left is collection on display at the Herndon Historical Society. It now is housed at the Fairfax County Archaeological Survey. Numerous specimens from his collection are presented. Another source is the collections of Hugh V. Stabler. He worked with Smithsonian archaeologists during the 1930-50s on sites in the Potomac River valley, and even made trips to the Plains states to do volunteer work.

Of special assistance were Robert A. George, John Nugen, Harry Spencer, and Stephen Miller of the Armed Forces Radiobiology Research Laboratory (AFRRI) in Bethesda, Maryland. The irradiation of jasper and rhyolite samples provided insights into lithic distributions and usage. Special thanks to Isabelle Brown at the Pamunkey Museum for showing the author their collections. And, Daniel Abbott (Nanticoke) for providing insights to *Native American ways*.

Of special thanks to Charles McNett who provided early academic training, Robert Stephenson who fostered an archaeological interest in the area, and Howard MacCord who provided opportunities to work in the area and elsewhere in Virginia. They have passed on from the archaeology world.

Pamunkey Museum, King William County, Virginia.

In dedication to:
   Charlie (Buddy) Merry and Spencer Geasey. Both were great friends; we walked many a field together over the years. They have since passed away.

Cover: Two jasper Paleoindian artifacts found by Charlie Merry on the Maryland side of the Potomac River. He is holding the artifacts.

Because students of American Indian life have been unable to interpret the uses to which these (implements) were put, and further on account of the apparent value attached to such objects by the native Americans, they have been the subject of much speculation (Warren K. Moorehead 1917).

Foreword

Interest in the prehistoric inhabitants of the Potomac River Valley goes back centuries. The first known European to ascend the river any distance, Captain John Smith, was in part interested in collecting information on native lifeways along the river. And the prehistoric stone artifacts littering the river's floodplain piqued the curiosity of the region's settlers since at least the seventeenth century. This interest in the Potomac's prehistoric past continues today, and Wm. Jack Hranicky's (2003) earlier volume, ***Lithic Technology in the Middle Potomac River Valley of Maryland and Virginia***, was a welcome addition to the small but now growing corpus of published literature on the study area. In this brief forward I would like to try and put this new revised publication in the context of our collective thinking, both past and present, on the archaeology of the Potomac River Valley.

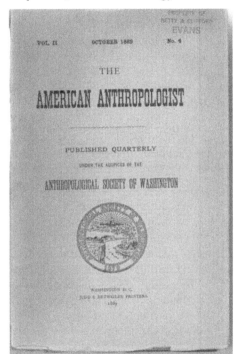

This new version joins a greater stream of thought on the prehistory of the Potomac River Valley. The earliest scholarly endeavors to uncover this past date to the last two decades of the nineteenth century. Around that time individuals working out of the Smithsonian Institution and a sister agency, the Bureau of American Ethnology, along with other nonprofessional archaeologists residing in or near that city began to collaborate on creating an understanding of Potomac Valley prehistory. The newly formed Anthropological Society of Washington often served as a venue for such deliberation on local prehistory. A symposium held by that organization in 1889 probably represents the first systematic effort to describe the then known prehistoric past of the region.

Early issue (Vol. II, No. 4, 1889) of the American Anthropologist that was published monthly by the Anthropological Society of Washington. Now it is published by the American Anthropological Association.

Out of this early interest came the research question that would thrust the Potomac River Valley onto the national stage. Thomas Wilson, of the Smithsonian Institution's Department of Antiquities, had suggested a link between artifacts being recovered in the District of Columbia along a tributary of the Potomac River and what were then purported to be Paleolithic implements simultaneously being recovered in other parts of the country. William Henry Holmes of the Bureau of Ethnology would use these same implements from within Washington, DC to effectively crush the notion of such a deep antiquity both here and elsewhere. His research on this issue eventually produced the first published book focusing for the most part on the Potomac River Valley. That 1897 publication, carrying the *imprimatur* of the Fifteenth Annual Report of the Bureau of American Ethnology, would become a landmark in both local and national archaeology.

As many of these early pioneers in Potomac archaeology passed on or turned to other interests at the turn of the twentieth century, another new and active cadre of archaeologists stepped in to further our knowledge of local prehistory. The honor roll is long, including such dedicated souls as David Bushnell, Alice Ferguson, William Graham, Karl Schmitt, Robert Stephenson, T. Dale Stewart, Howard MacCord, Art Johnson, Carl Manson, Richard Slattery, and Richard Stearns, just to name a few. It was these individuals and others like them that would begin the task of patiently expanding our knowledge of regional prehistory. A very few of these individuals made a living at that task. Recompense for most was little more than a chance to make a contribution to our knowledge of the river's former inhabitants. To this day regional archaeology remains dependent on the perseverance of such folks.

More help, however, soon arrived as two local universities retained archaeologists on their faculties who developed an interest in Potomac Valley archaeology. William Gardner and Charles W. McNett, Jr., of Catholic University and American University respectively, formed the Potomac River Archaeology Survey in the late 1960s to further our knowledge of local prehistory. They set out to survey existing collections and trained a corps of graduate students as they excavated at a number of sites along the river's shore. These efforts, along with the labor of a host of other individuals and the Archeological Societies of both Virginia and Maryland, moved us toward an even better understanding of the past.

As we approached the last quarter of the twentieth century, however, change was on the horizon. It is sad that interest in Potomac prehistory for a while seemed to wane somewhat. Many archaeologists who had once worked here turned to other interests. Historical archaeology, the archaeology of the colonial and post-Revolutionary past, at the same time expanded greatly. The rectangular trowels of the historical archaeologists quickly began to outnumber the pointed variety of Marshalltown still preferred by prehistorians. And as a result, research on the Potomac's prehistoric past seemed to slow near the end of this last century.

I am happy to report this stagnation now appears to be lessening. We, in fact, appear to be seeing a renaissance of sorts in the study of Potomac Valley prehistory. Stephen Potter's book on the region was a welcome addition. American University conducted multi-year excavations at a late prehistoric site in the Potomac Piedmont. William Gardner undertook some interesting studies on or near Selden Island in this same part of the river. The Maryland Historic Trust along with the Archeological Society of Maryland undertook important excavations in the western watershed. Bob Wall continues his excavations in the upper Potomac Valley. Various other research undertaken by cultural resource management firms along the Washington, DC waterfront is likewise bringing new data to light. Their recovery of a very unique Middle Woodland burial and new information about the local ceramic sequence is of particular note. Charles McNett even reports he is in the final stages of revising his long awaited manuscript on Potomac Valley prehistory.

Professor Joe Dent working on a square at the Cactus Hill Site in Virginia. He was Fieldschool Director for American University summer 2000 archaeology studies, which included work at the site

And now we also have Hranicky's new book on the archaeology of the Potomac River Valley. The strengths of this book will be immediately evident to all who turn its pages. The volume is artifact based, focusing on the lithic technology of what is labeled the Middle Potomac River Valley (MPRV). This study area stretches from the confluence of the Shenandoah and the Potomac River to the west downstream to Occoquan Creek on the Coastal Plain. Great use is made of various private artifact collections along with those housed in local repositories. This is supplemented with the author's vast personal experience working in the region. In the process interesting new ideas are offered on the interpretation of the lithic technology. Another strong point of the book is that it crosses modern political boundaries. It is one of the few volumes today that is not focused on only one side of the Potomac River. Readers who once worked in the Potomac River Valley, or who still do, will find a refreshing *family album* sort of feel to its pages. All the characters are there (including the book's author) who have worked so hard to bring the region's past to light. I invite you to come and join him for another look at an old friend – Potomac River Valley prehistory.

Richard J. Dent
Director, Potomac River Archaeology Survey
American University, Washington, DC.

Preface

The author back in highschool was fascinated with de Soto's meeting with various southeastern Native Americans. Later, Catlin's travels sparked the interest of what it must have been like to meet Native Americans before the European invasion that nearly destroyed thousands of cultures. The study of early explorers led to the author's life-time study of prehistory, namely the American Indian's history.

Based on this interest, the following publication is a study of lithic technology as found in the Middle Potomac River Valley (MPRV). The archaeological focus of a single geographical area offers an opportunity to present projectile point typology as a microtechnology even though some of the types have widespread distributions. As for macrotechnology, the area is an ideal study opportunity for new large tool data because of the lack of published data. The MPRV presents a physical artifact collection for lifeways in a snap-shot view of prehistory. Or, in other words, what technology(s) did the Native Americans use while living in the valley along the Potomac River's fall line. Their toolkit contained numerous tools, including the projectile point, axe, celt, drill, and knife implements; of which, some are unique; others are Panindian.

Concern with history (past experiences) may be a genetic code in the human race – one that is directly used for survival and is stored in an individual's subconscious memory; all individuals remember their past experiences – their history. It is frequently related to survival. This memory, when shared in a social group or society, is called the collective memory and is often manifested in prehistoric societies as folklore, traditions, ceremonies, etc. Contemporary, as well as nonliterate, societies frequently use the collective memory as *social norms* or acceptable behaviors, or simply justification for the rationale and control of various human activities. Another way of describing a collective memory is history (oral traditions), which is a set of known events in time and space for any given society. Consequences of specific local events are basically irrelevant in the total history of humanity. Of course, some historians would argue consequences cause changes in historical directions for societies, but these are frequently based on subjective appraisals and personal value systems of researchers. For prehistory, we translate the Native Americans traditional past as uncovered archaeologically. For lithic technology, these traditions and behaviors are manifested in their toolkits and the ways they used them.

Wm Jack Hranicky – Measuring Artifacts at the Jefferson Patterson Park and Museum in Calvert County, Maryland. As shown, always wear latex gloves when handling museum specimens.

This publication is the result of the author's work, investigation, artifact recording, and general archaeological research in the Middle Potomac River Valley (MPRV) over the last 40 years. This study of stone tools and implements was performed to:

*Update the current knowledge base of MPRV archaeology
*Provide new data and interpretations on MPRV lithic technology
*Provide a single-source for published MPRV references
*But mainly, provide a study on:
- History of MPRV archaeology (people and sites)
- MPRV environmental influences (Native American utilization)
- Basic MPRV artifacts (classification and typology)
- Tool usage by Native Americans (living archaeology).

This publication presents a sample of MPRV artifacts from the arrowhead to the axe. It shows lithic usage for these tools and illustrates how they were used in the Native Americans' society. These tools are organized chronologically and contrasted to various artifacts and time periods found elsewhere. All of which leave this publication as a humble beginning for the 21st century in Potomac River valley archaeology.

Three principal stones were used in the MPRV, namely quartz, quartzite, greenstone, and rhyolite. These materials were tested scientifically in the study with methods that are suggested as making lithic identifications and comparisons easier. They provide the means for standardization in archaeology.

A chronological framework is presented for the MPRV that is based on the Classic Paleoindian – Archaic – Woodland (PAW) model used by eastern archaeologists. The PAW is discussed with technology as its major focus. The framework is also used in the Projectile Point section that incorporates environmental conditions from the MPRV's prehistory.

Example of Potomac River Valley Urbanization. MPRV archaeological site are rapidly disappearing; many of them have had little or no archaeological investigations.

Overall, the classification of points and tools is based on empirical observation from which analyses were subject to the author's experience with the prehistoric cultural framework of the Potomac River valley. Typology is presented as a morphological standard based on a collection of physical attributes that are found on MPRV points.

Prehistorically, the Middle Potomac River valley is disappearing. Housing, shopping malls, colleges, industrial complexes, and numerous other urbanization projects have destroyed, and are continuing to destroy prehistoric sites. Some sites do get excavated, but most never see an archaeologist's trowel.

Claude Moore Colonial Farm Reconstruction on Turkey Run, Fairfax County, Virginia

This study captures MPRV archaeology as it existed during the late 20th century. It presents a summary of current archaeological knowledge with the expectation that more work will be done.

While most important, Native American history dates over 10,000 years. They left the area more-or-less as they found it. The Colonial Period sees the beginnings of a super culture, which until recently exploited the earth's resources with little care about the future. The history of the river valley comes from the past and belongs to the future. Hopefully, the landscape can survive humanity.

Potomac View of Rosslyn, Virginia. The modern age, 2000 version, stands on prehistoric sites along the Potomac River – a consequence of history. The 2100 version will stand on these historic sites, a consequence of history and so forth... We are our history and modernization is overwriting prehistory...

Wm Jack Hranicky
Registry of Professional Archaeologists (RPA)

Table of Contents

Introduction 1
MPRV Environment 38
Prehistoric MPRV Chronology 64
Toolmaking Technology 99
Projectile Point Typology 135
Projectile Points 153
    MPRV Paleoindian Period 154
    MPRV Archaic Period 160
    MPRV Woodland Period 187
MPRV Flakes as Tools 202
Bifaces as Knives 211
Artifact Caches 228
MPRV Prehistoric Pottery 241
MPRV Rockart 244
Miscellaneous Tools/Implements 247
Experimental Archaeology 292
Appendix A – Broadspear Examples 315
Appendix B - Tribute to William Henry Holmes 317
Appendix C – Potomac Crossroads Projectile Points 320
Appendix D Potomac Valley Clovis Site 322
References 335

From those ancient fires of the past . . .
(Formerly a Monacan Display at Natural Bridge, Virginia)

The beginnings of Smithsonian history ...

After reading this book, the reader will either agree or disagree with the author, have learned something about the Potomac River Valley Native Americans, seen archaeology at work, for places where there is volunteerism, understanding of prehistory, learn to identify lithic artifacts, and discovered where contributions to prehistoric knowledge can be made. This archaeological overview is only a modest study of the American Indian's history in the Potomac River valley. And mentioning one major player in the study of Native Americans everywhere, but especially here in the Potomac River valley, is the Smithsonian Institution in Washington, DC.

We look to the 19th century for the beginnings of prehistoric studies. From those efforts, we have built a history of the American Indian in the Potomac River valley. This history involves numerous individuals who come into play as amateur and professional archaeologists, collectors, historians, ethnographers, and, of course, Native Americans. Among these people is James Smithson (1765-1829).

Smithson's personal books.

He was an English scientist who provided funds for the founding of the Smithsonian Institution in Washington, DC. In his times, he was a well-known chemist and mineralogist; he published 27 major works. His substantial inherited wealth allowed him to pursue scientific studies. Upon his death, his entire estate went to the United States of America for *an establishment for the increase and diffusion of knowledge*. In 1904, Smithson's remains were brought to the U.S. under escort, including Alexander Graham Bell, and were interred in the original Smithsonian building – called the Castle.

Although John C. Calhoun and other congressmen said that the federal government could not accept Smithson's bequeath, John Quincy Adams in 1846 helped establish it by congressional act. The Smithsonian is governed by a Board of Regents, namely the Vice President, Chief Justice, three senators, three representatives, and six at large individuals.

Throughout the 19th and 20th centuries, the Smithsonian Institution has maintained the standards and provided the focus for archaeological research in the MPRV and all the world.

**James Smithson Tomb at the Smithsonian.
Born of English royalty, he wanted his name remembered over his ancestral family members, dukes and kings.
He succeeded, as the Smithsonian is the most famous museum in the New World.**

Introduction
(Overview to the Potomac Native Americans' Stoneage)

The fall line of the Potomac River in Maryland and Virginia was home to countless prehistoric Native Americans who left us evidences of their lifeways. It is a rich area archaeologically, and, in many ways, it is a complicated area to produce a history covering the Native Americans' 10,000+ years of occupation, which ranges from temporary campsites to long-term villages. This area was sparsely occupied during the early human history and heavily occupied at the time Captain John Smith visited the Potomac in 1608 (Potter 1993). The river's name is derived from the Patawomeke tribe that once lived in what is now Stafford County, Virginia (McCary 1957). Or as: *The 16 of June [1608], we fell with the River Patowomek* (Captain John Smith as in Haile 1998). The first Native Americans that Captain Smith met in the MRPV area were the Doeg, later changed to the Dogue (Johnson 1996).

For late prehistory, the entire Potomac River basin, including West Virginia's mountains and the Shenandoah River valley, saw different tribes that spoke Siouan, Algonquian, and Iroquoian languages. Algonquian is the principal language for the area under study. Most tribal chiefs were multilingual and could easily communicate with their neighbors. The arrival of Smith marked *what became* the end of the Powhatan chiefdom, especially for the upper Potomac River valley. From this time forward, the Native Americans eventually would be pushed out of the valley. At least Smith recorded the tribes living in the area, namely Pamunkeys, Piscataways, Tauxenents, and Nacotchtanks, which provides limited ethnographic data for the area (Potter 1993).

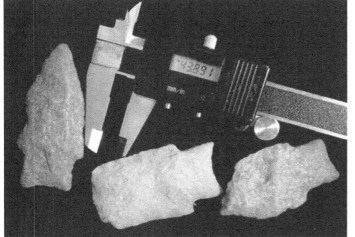

Lithic technology ...
the science of prehistoric stone tools and their usage.

As a geological feature, the river's fall line offered a crossing place throughout most of prehistory, provided crystalline stones for tools, supplied water including anadromous fish, had fertile areas for growing crops, and forests for hunting game. As an archaeological focus, it has extensive prehistoric cultural resources. From 9500 BC (11,500 BP) (Years Before Present = BP) to Contact, pre-Contact Native Americans occupied the river basin and left countless millions of their artifacts. After Contact we called the period (1600s) the protohistoric, which is not presented here archaeologically. For an ethnographic discussion of Virginia Native Americans, see Speck (1928), Haile (1998), Swanton (1946 and 1952), Hudson (1976), Wood, Waselkov, and Hatley (1989), Rountree (1989), Gallivan (2016), and Potter (1993). For various population and tool estimates, see Hancock (1927), Mooney (1928), Dobyns (1966), Feest (1973), Ubelacker (1974), Turner (1978 and 1989), Hranicky and McCary (1996), Klein and Klatka (1991), and Johnson (1996). For settlement patterns, see Potter (1983), Custer (1990), and Brombery (1987). For coastal Algonquian studies, see Flannery (1939) and Doddard (1978), and for Woodland Period mortuary practices, see Bushnell (1920), Curry (1999 and 2000), and Gold (2000). Algonquian and Iroquoian languages are the principal spoken words, see Goddard (1978), Loundsburg (1978), Siebert (1975), and Feest (1978). All of the Native Americans' ethnographic histories are briefly presented, but the main focus is lithic technology. For early protohistory, Campbell (1906) offers an overview of missions in Maryland. Finally, as an overview of the archaeology in the area, see Dent (1995); his publication has an excellent summary of Chesapeake Bay area prehistory, and in the opposite direction. Carr and Moeller (2015) provide northern information from Pennsylvania, and Gingerich (2013) provides an overview of paleostudies for the east coast.. Holland (1960) offers perspectives from northwest Virginia. For local prehistories, see Arlington (Rose 1966), Fairfax (Johnson 1996), and Washington, DC (Humphrey and Chambers 1977). Finally, Porter (1979) offers a bibliographic overview; however, it needs updating. A lengthy bibliography for the river valley is presented in the reference section. And, the lithic technology of the Potomac River valley starts with the work of Holmes' (1897) ***Stone Implements of the Potomac-Chesapeake Tidewater Province***, published by the Bureau of American Ethnology in Washington, DC.

Another early classic is *Archeology Chronology of the Middle Atlantic* States (Schmitt 1952) which is in *Archaeology of Eastern United States* by James B. Griffin (1952). Also, the radiometrics are based on Inashima's (2008) *Establishing a Radiocarbon Date Based Framework for Virginia Archaeology*.

In the 1860 Annual Report of the Smithsonian Institution in Washington City, A. Morlot of Lausanne, Switzerland wrote:

> Not long ago we should have smiled at the idea of reconstructing the bygone days of our race previous to the beginning of history properly so called. The void was partly filled up by representing that ante-historical antiquity as have been only of short duration, and partly by exaggerating the value and the age of those vague and confused notions which constitute tradition ... consider the antiquarian as a geologist, applying his method to reconstruct the first ages of mankind previous to all recollection, and to work out what may be termed pre-historical history.

The above references start the study of prehistory, and over the years, American archaeologists have developed their science of the study of humanity – called prehistoric archaeology.

The study of archaeology started in the Potomac River valley over 100 years ago. This publication is one of many past, present, and surely future studies on the river's former inhabitants called prehistoric Native Americans. This study attempts a five-fold goal that is representative of all contemporary American archaeology:

- Reconstruct culture in a chronological order in local, regional, and national contexts.
- Reconstruct past lifeways of how people obtained their daily livelihood, in this case with lithics for tools.
- Achieve an understanding of how and why human societies have changed over time.
- Identify social/religious controls for tool change and maintenance.
- Explain how people adapted to particular environments, especially changing ecologies over time.

This archaeological overview is the underlying philosophy for this publication. Information and data for this goal come from many sources.

Figure 1 – Held in Trust – 1999 Virginia Archaeology Month Poster. It featured archaeology in Alexandria.

From the Hands of the Past to the Hands of the Future

We may find it amazing that Mother Nature has preserved prehistoric artifacts for thousands of years, and mankind can destroy them in a matter of minutes. At least, through care, concern, and commitment of some Americans, the hands of the past have passed their artifacts and history on to us, from which we will pass them on to future citizens who share our concerns about the past. Knowledge of the past – where we come from – is universal among humanity. Perhaps history and passing it to our offspring is what separates us from the rest of the animal kingdom.

We are temporary custodians of both public and private prehistoric artifacts; however, the future depends on us to pass them forward in time. As a responsibility of archaeology, the discipline has developed outreach programs to take archaeology from the site and museum to the general public – show the past to the present in order to better safeguard it for the future.

Americans can trust that the past will be transferred to the future (Figure 1). One group of specialists will ensure that this happens – people who are trained and/or have an active interest in archaeology are, of course, amateur and professional archaeologists. Throughout this publication, hands holding the past are presented – antiquity has that feeling of touching ancient people. For some, holding the past is electrifying or simply feeling the karma (previous prehistoric owner) of an object. Collecting these objects becomes a passion of processing antiquity. Study becomes a quest for knowing and understanding the past.

Will prehistoric artifacts be part of the public trust? Probably, but the main question as we move through the 21st century is – whose trust: Native Americans? Collectors? Politicians? Archaeologists? All?

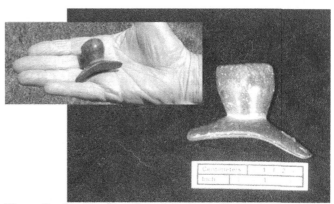

Figure 2 – Steatite Pipe Found by Hugh Stabler in the 1930s Along the Potomac River Beach at Lowes Island. The platform pipe's dimensions are L = 56, W = 27, H = 38 mm, and bowl diameter is 21 mm. It is saved for the future, as it will be turned over to Virginia for museum curation.

From an archaeological perspective, we can ensure the accumulation and transfer of prehistory simply by collecting data from all prehistoric resources before they are destroyed or simply lost because of careless public servants, indifferent citizens, or dealers of antiquities (Figure 2). We cannot keep everything from the past, but representative samples can be used as the evidence of the past and tell the artifacts' cultural histories.

Regardless of the source, let archaeology have the data; perhaps, let the Native Americans have the artifacts. Knowledge should be the primary goal in the study of humanity, past and present; and, most importantly, across cultural boundaries. While their oral traditions are perfectly acceptable as a knowledge base of history, the science of archaeology offers an unbiased objectivity about history. Both have something to offer for those who *like history*. We will never know the complete history of mankind, but a sample as told from all viewpoints is a starting place for the future.

Study Overview

This study presents lithic projectile point and micro-marcrotool technologies that were used by pre-Contact Native Americans. It includes major published references for tool technologies, industries, classes, and types in the area called here – the Middle Potomac River Valley (MPRV) provenance. The MPRV fits into what archaeologists call the Middle Atlantic Culture Area (MACA). This culture area is only one of numerous culture areas; namely, the northeast and southeast are proximity culture areas. All United States/Mexico/Canada culture areas were established by Krober's (1939) Cultural and Natural Areas of Native North America that is a principal influence in the publication.

Note: Some archaeologists consider old publications as passé and refuse to use them. Most elders in archaeology's golden days have presented artifact identifications and classifications, methods, and interpretations that were reasonably correct; so why re-invent the *prehistoric wheel*? Of course, there are new discoveries and techniques that provide new interpretations about the past. But, as a demand, all graduate students must read the old literature ... maybe even use some of it.

As a total picture of eastern Native American history, MACA does not always standalone as a culture area; in fact, many times it shows southern influences, such as Morrow Mountain and Savannah River technologies; other times northern influences, such as Lamoka, Koens-Crispin-Lehigh, and Orient technologies; and even western influences, such as Adena and Hopewell technologies. These technological influences are the result of migrational patterns, trade associations, political controls (intracultural relations), and/or language and kinship relations. The Native American's total technological universe (macrotechnology) in the eastern U.S. woodlands and the middle Atlantic seaboard are found in the MPRV; however, a microtechnology exists which identifies the MPRV's material culturally. This publication is a presentation of MPRV artifacts, but for *comparative examples*, artifacts from all the Middle Atlantic States (and other states) are used. Tools or implements are divided into the following classes:

1 – Microtools (projectile points, drills, scrapers, etc.)
2 – Marcotools (axes, celts, mauls, splitters, etc.).

Further, microtools are subdivided into the following classes:

1 – Points
2 – Axes
3 – Celts
4 – Knives
5 – Drills
6 – Scrapers
7 – Adzes
8 – And more classes.

Of all the cultural remains left by the past inhabitants, lithic flakes are the most common and, at the same time, are the most diagnostic items recovered in archaeological contexts. Flakes are the ***signatures of prehistoric knappers***; and, if only analyzed by using tool production methodologies, flakes provide a tremendous amount of data. In some cases, flakes can be refitted back into cores or bifaces that give an insight into the toolmaker's logic and method of producing a tool.

Figure 3 – Sample of a Local Point MPRV Collection Used in This Study. The major focus was to find representative specimens of all tool industries. As an estimate, nearly 60% of the collections represented tool types that either could not be typed or represented types that remain to be identified. The major problem with this study approach is the lack of archaeological contexts for the collections. Broken tools were included and used for obtaining descriptive and distributional data. They are used in illustrations where appropriate; broken and expended tools represent the norm in field-collected and site-produced artifacts. Or as a parallel from another time:

I do not, however, desire to deal with these collections specifically, to describe them or review their history, but to present an analysis of the group of phenomena to which they belong (Holmes 1894).

When tools and implements are classified and grouped, namely physical shapes, materials, sources, activities, stratigraphically, chronologically, etc., they provide one basis for interpreting Native American prehistory. Naturally, other cultural remains make up the archaeological record. It was a lithic world, and these people, especially in early prehistory, depended on stone materials for tools with which they secured their daily livelihood. As such, MPRV stone studies are presented throughout this publication with a focus of being highly significant in culture. This stone study offers methological examples for other archaeological investigations. Culture and technology are not synonymous; they are different. Technology does not necessarily drive culture or cause culture change; but, it is a product of culture.

Basic MPRV Cultural Focus

As in Hranicky (2015), the generalized MPRV overview is:

> **Piedmont Valley Region.** This region seems to show a long-time, in-place cultural development by a relatively sparse population. Some influences from other regions were accepted, e.g., a few burial mounds, similar to those in upper western Virginia. The Potomac valley shows many influences from Regions to the north (Pennsylvania, New York, etc.). Inhabitants of the James and Rappahannock valleys in 400 YBP were Siouan-speaking Monacan and Manahoac groups. Projectile point typology tends to be oriented towards southeastern and northeastern types. Paleoindian and Archaic points tend to be macrotypic; Woodland points tend to be microtypic. Environmentally, the region has a piedmont and partly coastal focus. The major lithic stone for microtools is quartzite and rhyolite. The first bowls were made from steatite. The earliest pottery is the Marcy creek type.

Artifact Study Basis

This point typology and tool study was based on private and public collections in the MPRV. It consisted of over 30,000 specimens, which included all tool industries, but mostly broken projectile points. Most of the artifacts were recorded by county provenance and were found within a mile of the Potomac River.

These study collections consisted of field-collected artifacts. While over the years some artifacts were collected from archaeological sites, none of the artifacts were *dug* from archaeological sites (Figure 3). Table 1 lists the major site in the upper Potomac River valley. Approximately 40% of these collections contained broken, quartzite Savannah River or Late Archaic materials, or miscellaneous, nontypeable bifaces. Thus, the remainder was used to produce the basic study data. Also, Late Archaic bifaces from broken specimens are presented.

A major objective of this study is to include as many formerly unpublished artifacts as possible and expand current MPRV projectile point typology. And, because major private collections are disappearing, an objective of this study was to record and document some of them before they disappeared. Private collections often contain a representative selection of artifacts for the entire prehistoric chronology for a region. The Trittipoe site (Hranicky and MacCord 2000) and Fisher site (MacCord and Hranicky 1983) collections were also used in this study. The Pamunkey Museum provided ethnographic specimens for this study. Of course. The Merry and Geasey collections were used.

Table 1 – Major Prehistoric Sites in the Potomac Riverine	
Maryland	Virginia
<ul><li>Conococheoque</li><li>Devilibiss</li><li>Biggs Ford</li><li>Rosenstoce</li><li>Shepard Barrack</li><li>Shepard</li><li>Hughes</li><li>Winslow</li></ul>	<ul><li>Fisher</li><li>Seldon Island</li><li>Fry</li><li>Barlow</li><li>Kerns</li><li>Cabin Run</li><li>Keyser</li><li>Trittipoe</li></ul>

Publishing artifacts from all these sources adds to our knowledge of artifact type distributions, stylistic variations, and usage and overall human behavior. Each collection that was used was recorded, analyzed, and photographed; sample artifacts were then chosen for this study. Those points and tools generally best represent points and tools for that classification. They are average specimens that are found in the MPRV; however, in some cases, better quality materials are shown. All illustrated points and implements are from the MPRV unless noted otherwise. Georeferencing by county is not used for the MPRV. Daily mobility of these ancient people precludes specific local provenances. Thus, a generalized reference to artifact geography is used. There are examples from other geographies that are used for comparative specimens which are marked by county and state. The projectile point types that were selected are based on type publications of Ritchie (1961), Coe (1964), Broyles (1971), Hranicky (1994 and 2015), Kent (1970), and based on archaeological surveys and general artifact collection analyses. New point types are presented based on the study collections. The large tool types and classes are based on Hranicky (1995) and numerous society bulletins and journals. Two previous Maryland artifact studies that were used as early collections studies are Steponatis (1980) and Wanser (1982).

This publication is divided into:

- **Introduction**
- **MPRV Environment**
- **Prehistoric MPRV Chronology**
- **Toolmaking Technology**
- **Projectile Point Typology**
- **Projectile Points**
- **MPRV Flakes as Tools**

MPRV = Middle Potomac River Valley

- Bifaces as Knives
- Artifact Caches
- Miscellaneous Tools/Implements
- Experimental Archaeology
- MPRV Pottery
- MPRV Rockart
- References.

This publication is the result of the author's work, investigation, artifact recording, and general archaeological research of two MPRV collections. This study of stone artifacts and implements was performed to present a public artifact record that includes:

- History of MPRV archaeology (people and sites)
- Environmental influences (Native American resource utilization)
- Tool materials and manufacture (procedures and production)
- MPRV artifacts (classification and typology)
- Native American oral histories (social and religious factors)
- Tool usage by the Native Americans (living archaeology).

The overall approach for this study was to attempt to place all study artifacts into an environmental setting, namely ecoscenes and watersheds, and then analyze all artifacts using a structural-functional approach. All of this is discussed in a chronological framework with various social manifestations, such as economics, migrations, political organizations, local resource exploitations, climatic influences, and linguistic groupings. Of course, use of these factors varies by time period.

MPRV Timeframe

The Middle Atlantic area's prehistory is classically divided into:

1 – Paleoindian Period (12,500 to 8500-8000 BP)
2 – Archaic Period (9000 to 4000 BP)
3 – Woodland Period (3000-1000 BP to 400 BP).

While references to pre-Paleoindian and post-Woodland (Contact) Periods are made, the basic framework for this study is the above list. See Prehistoric MPRV Chronology Section.

Early Collectors in the MPRV

Three early-day collectors in the MPRV are Judge William J. Graham, Titus Ulke, and S. V. Proudfit. Graham was a judge for the U.S. Court of Customs and Patent Appeals. He died in 1937, and his collection is now at the Smithsonian. Ulke lived in the Georgetown area. His collection is also at the Smithsonian. Proudfit collected in the 1880-90s and published *Ancient Village Sites and Aboriginal Workshops in the District of Columbia* in the newly formed Anthropological Society's American Anthropologist in 1889. These men walked fields when open farm land made up the MPRV. They collected and published, but most importantly, their artifact collections are in the public realm. Other collections, most are now in the public realm, are illustrated and discussed throughout this publication.

Study Collections

This study would not have been possible without the kindly and cooperative assistance of two MPRV collectors. These collectors used here have maintained their collections in a scientific manner that permitted easy access to the artifacts and, more importantly, their data. Repeating, the purpose of archaeology is to collect data about antiquities – not artifacts.

This study followed what is an old concept in science, namely, the 1822 Scientific Congress of Carlsruhe's (Grand Dutchy of Baden which became part of Germany) Rule 10:

> The association shall process neither collections nor property of any sort. An object presented at any of the settings shall be returned to its owner. The accruing expense shall be provided for by an assessment made with the consent of the members present.

Note: The history of science is not a focus here; only its implications on the modern practice of it.

Once upon a time, collectors regularly attended state and local archaeological meetings and brought their recent discoveries. Due to various reasons, this is no longer the practice. Now, it is necessary to go to them to study their artifacts. Private artifact collections are numerous in any part of the U.S.

Figure 4 – Ronald G. Orr working on collection records at the Jefferson-Patterson Museum in Maryland. He was extremely helpful in showing collections for this study.

Most collectors are knowledgeable about prehistory and respond to research questions with valuable answers.

Those collectors used in this study are very active in talking to local schools, contributing to local and state archaeological societies, reporting sites they find, and most importantly, publishing their finds. Serious collectors do not dig on archaeological sites, but restrict their field activities to farm-field, surface finds. In many cases, these collections end up in the public domain. For example, one other collection used in this study are Charles A. Pettit (see his references). There are numerous collections that are now at the Jefferson-Patterson archaeological park in Maryland (Figure 4). Also, see Pettit quote in the Miscellaneous Tool/Implements section.

Figure 5 – The Buried World of Material Culture is Subject to Many Viewpoints ... archaeologists, historians, relic dealers, collectors, writers, politicians, Native Americans, etc. (Arrows are modern replications; see Experimental Archaeology Section.)

Amateur archaeologists also made this study possible. An example is Paul Cresthull who was editor of Maryland Archaeology for years. His interest and contributions are extensive (see his references). And for a Virginia amateur, Lanier Rogers has years of study and work at the Thunderbird site in Warren County, Virginia (see Prehistoric Chronology section and his references). Of course, there are members of the professional archaeological community who say collectors, amateurs, knappers are "... and ..., etc." (Figure 5). Contributions are not always restricted to artifacts. Scott Silsby is a well-known naturalist and flintknapper. His work is shown in the Experimental Archaeology section, and he contributed greatly to this presentation for his understanding tool chassis, lithic materials, and tool usage.

Romantically, every collector may dream of obtaining antiquities for safekeeping for the future of humanity. But, most assume some growth in the monetary value of their objects d' historia. As was said of George Gustav Heye (as in the Heye Foundation):

He accomplished something of enduring significance in his life of focused accumulation, though our contemporary sensibilities may not be entirely comfortable with an individual who appropriated, on a massive scale, the evidence of cultures not his. Some may even see in Heye's action a bloodless reenactment of earlier great wrongs. And yet, in his unstoppable course, Heye saved an irreplaceable living record that might otherwise have gone to oblivion. (November 2000, Lawrence M. Small, Secretary, Smithsonian Institution, Washington, DC).

We may never know the value of collectors of Native American artifacts; we can only appreciate what we have and ensure that archaeology is the only means to the science of studying the past. Trustingly, part of the private collections will end up in the public domain.

In the real world of archaeology, history, and possibly anthropology, we have a wide range of interests and practices that affect antiquities. For the world of archaeology, we find the following people in mainstream archaeology (Hranicky 1996):

1 - ***Collector*** - anyone who accumulates specific objects; one who usually has considerable knowledge about this topic. Any person who has one or more Native American artifacts.

2 - ***Looters*** - anyone who willfully destroys a (pre-)historical context (site) to obtain artifacts for profit or personal gain.

3 - ***Pothunters*** - see looter. Term generally is used to refer to someone who digs on an archaeological site without archaeological training, archaeological certification, or permission to dig.

4 - ***Relic Hunters*** - usually means hunting on archaeological sites with a metal detector.

5 - ***Treasure Hunters*** - anyone who hunts lost gold mines, sunken ships, the Fountain of Youth, Atlantis, or other noble fantasies.

6 - ***Relic Miners*** - one who pays for a square area on a site in which he digs for artifacts and keeps what is found.

Note: Even if records are kept, relic mining is never archaeology.

7 - ***Historian*** - scholar who studies paper, oral, or magnetic forms of documentation about history. Usually not involved in material culture except above-ground structures or places where events happened.

8 - ***Amateur Archaeologist (AA)*** - anyone who participates in scientific archaeology by working with professional archaeologists; mainstream of the American archaeological community.

9 - ***Paraprofessional Archaeologist (PPA)*** - anyone who has training in archaeology without the extensive college course work; training in amateur certification programs; advanced-experienced amateur.

10 - ***Professional Archaeologist (PA)*** - anyone who has studied college-level archaeology with an advanced degree in anthropology, has years of field experience, has expert competence in identifying artifacts, and has been certified as a PA by an accredited agency or association. For American archaeology, the certifying organization is the Registry of Professional Archaeologists (RPA).

11 - *Arm-Chair Listener* - person who is interested in every aspect of archaeology but does not actively participate in archaeological field or laboratory activities.

12 - *Museumologist* - someone with museum training who actively supports and participates in field and laboratory archaeology and public artifact acquisitions.

And, mostly,

13 - *Native Americans* - people who have direct reference in American prehistoric archaeology; many of them actively participate in all archaeological activities.

Study Basics

This study makes four major assumptions that affect the overall analysis and interpretation of the study MRPV collections:

1 – This study assumes that there were environmental, climatical, and geological conditions that attracted and/or affected the MPRV inhabitants at various times in prehistory. The overall approach presents the MPRV as a set of ecosystems (uplands, piedmont, and tidewater) from which the Native Americans exploited natural resources and led relatively successful lives in an environment that supported procreation.

2 – This study assumes a Panindian nature (technological continuum) of all tool and implement classes and industries; most of which had their origins in the Paleoindian Period which has an Old World legacy. All Native American societies were aware of the total universe of tool technology and elected to use (not use) various parts of it.

3 – This study assumes that Native Americans maintain oral histories that can be applied to the understanding and classification of their prehistoric lithic tools. The study relied on limited ethnographic information for the MPRV.

4 – This study assumes that the size of the artifact population overcomes sampling biases. This proposition is reasonably true for the projectile point part of the study collections; however, the remaining macrotools are truly biased and the only effort to offset the bias was to suggest artifact classes that should be in the collections. These suggestions are based on Hranicky (1994 and 1995) and Dent (1995) and MPRV site reports.

A major factor that was exploited by the Native Americans, especially during the Late Archaic and Early Woodland Periods, was the area's abundance of crystalline rocks, from which numerous tool types were made. The primary focus is geology's relationship to the Native American's tool technology. MPRV's basic geology and environment are presented in the MPRV Environment section.

The major technology that is discussed is the projectile point. But within the scope of prehistoric lithic technology, the point is involved in almost every facet of microtechnology, and in some cases, a factor in macrotechnology. Consequently, this publication covers all stone tool classes, not just projectile point typology.

Watershed Approach

While basically an environmental approach was used for this study, human behavior was the primary concern in the study. As such, human beings were viewed as part of the environment and subject to the dominance nature has over its human inhabitants. The human population lived in the MPRV throughout prehistory with various climatical, technological, and cultural changes which affected their habitation and lifeways. Based on the basic human need for water, the MPRV allowed movement throughout the area; therefore, there were no barriers, except cultural, that restricted MPRV occupation. As such, the watershed approach was used to interpret the artifact collections. The MPRV is viewed as one among many rivers in the interriverine geosystems of the Atlantic coast. Fairfax County's publication ***Stream Protection Strategy – Baseline Study*** (Rose 2001) was of tremendous assistance in using a watershed approach. It provides an environmental approach to resource utilization.

The fall line Potomac allowed north/south population migrations. Also, the river provided water travel into the upperlands and the Shenandoah River valley.

Romance of Archaeology

Few learned disciplines receive overall acceptance and interest by the general public, as does archaeology. It is always viewed as the scientific approach to acquiring history and the best way to preserve our past is in our museums. The ancient past has an attraction, romance if you wish, for demonstrating where we came from and who we are. The American public generally understands the role of archaeology, but what the role actually is varies. Ramos and Duganne's (2000) survey of what the word archaeology means to the public, includes: (overall) digging (22%), additionally, digging for bones or artifacts (37%), etc., (specific) history, heritage, and antiquity (12%), objects from the past (11%), dinosaurs/bones (10%), digging up bones (9%), artifacts (8%), past cultures, ancient societies, and civilizations (8%), etc. What is important, less than 1% mentioned Native Americans. This low percentage says that Americans do not generally see the relationships between Native Americans and archaeologists.

And as a consequence of public opinion, everybody seems to be an amateur archaeologist offering viewpoints and opinions about prehistoric artifacts and other antiquities. This places a lot of misinformation into the general knowledge pool about prehistory. The Internet simply compounds the problem. Even within the professional community of archaeology, talent and professionalism varies which causes conflicting prehistorical interpretations. There is no attempt to resolve the problem in this publication, only suggesting to the reader that *most-all* archaeology is based on opinion from individuals who use what we call collectively the scientific method. Experience for these opinions is based on academia and spending a few years working with the opinion topic. Naturally, publishing a book or two helps professional credibility.

Note: In the Old World, the term amateur has reverence and respect. And, collectors are principal resources for microtool studies.

Collecting is, perhaps, a result/consequence of this romance. Collecting both pre-Contact and ethnographic artifacts consumes a major past time and is a major economic factor in the U.S. As such, the collector (total) holds the world of prehistory which is, in many cases, available for study – but many professional archaeologists will not use the resource. In a recent paper, The **Romance of Collecting** by Rodney Peck (2001), he suggests:

... collectors, who probably outnumber archaeologists a thousand to one, can offer the archaeologist extraordinary artifacts that he probably never recovered intact. ... Both the collector and archaeologist are learning that each has much to offer.

As suggested (Hranicky 1996), this romance is what got most archaeologists into archaeology in the first place; it keeps some amateur archaeologists in archaeology for a lifetime (Figure 6).

And as mentioned, the American public has a basic concept as to what archaeologists do, but often collecting dinosaur fossils is conceived as part of their duties. For others, the romance of archaeology comes from the British and their Old World investigations, leaving the Americanist as being somewhat distantly removed from *real archaeology*. Regardless of the viewpoint, most people find old artifacts fascinating, and somehow by touching it – they touch the past. Figure 7 may portray what some view as an archaeologist, but noteworthy, William A. Ritchie, former New York State Archaeologist, played a major role in the creation of American archaeology.

Figure 6 – Spencer Geasey at the 2000 Oregon Ridge Knapp-In, Maryland. He always maintained his collection (by sites), which now belongs to the Maryland Historic Trust. His artifacts are used throughout this publication. He is an excellent example of an amateur archaeologist who has spent a life time studying and working in and on American prehistory, which has meant major contributions to Maryland and Virginia archaeology. With the assistance of the author, Geasey turned his several-thousand-piece collection over to Maryland. He published several papers on his artifacts.

Amateur Archaeological Societies

At one time in eastern America, amateur archaeological societies were the only groups actively working in most states. Their early work laid foundations for the *wave* of professional archaeologists who would follow. These societies fostered and promoted preservation and reported investigations of cultural resources via publications. They participate in professionally-sponsored field activities and perform archaeological services with varying degrees of expertise. Additionally, there were major museums, several federal agencies (for example, U.S. Park Service), and colleges/universities working; but the bulk of archaeology in the various states was conducted by amateur archaeologists. While most societies no longer excavate sites independently of the professional community, this was the practice in the early days of American archaeology.

As a special note, Hugh Stabler, R. Gates Slattery, and David Hughes started the Potomac Valley Archeology Club in 1932 or 1933. It was short-lived, but it probably can be considered the earliest amateur archaeological society in the MPRV.

Figure 7 – The Uniform from Ancient Days in Archaeology. This is a photograph of William A. Ritchie who's *A Typology and Nomenclature for New York Projectile Points* is among the most quoted publications in U.S. archaeology. His types are used throughout this publication. Photograph was taken during 1950s at the Bates site in New York.

Even today with the tremendous growth of professional archaeology programs and people (contract firms, academia, and state-federal agencies), the state amateur society still continues to provide services, support, and outlets for the practice of archaeology.

Figure 8 – Hands-on Experience and Amateur Certification. ASV Members working on certification: Left-to-right is Ann Wood, Steve Cerny, Michael Johnson (instructor/site director, retired Fairfax County archaeologist), and Wilther Santanmaria at the Cactus Hill Site in Virginia. They are learning archaeology and at the same time contributing to the excavation of Virginia prehistory. Lower photograph: Albert J. Pfeffer III (center) receiving the ASV's first of the new century Amateur Certification diplomas. Left is Michael B. Barber and right is Harry A. Jaeger, past ASV presidents, respectively.

The three archaeological societies that cover the MPRV are:

1 – Archeological Society of Virginia (ASV)
2 – Archeological Society of Maryland, Inc. (ASM)
3 – West Virginia Archeological Society (WVAS).

Each year, the ASV presents the Howard MacCord Lecture at its Annual Banquet. The ASM presents the Richard E. Stearns Memorial Lecture at its Annual Spring Symposium. Both are tributes to people for outstanding archaeological contributions, especially working with amateur archaeologists. See volunteers in the Prehistoric Chronology sections. Also, the ASV presents annual awards for professional and amateur archaeologists to its members who have made major contributions to the archaeology of Virginia; and, the ASV has a Hall of Fame for Virginia Archaeologists. All three societies provide training, but the ASV has an Amateur Certification Program (Figure 8). For an example of certification requirements, see Hranicky (1985).

Society membership is open to anyone, and these societies offer journals, newsletters, and other publications. There are field activities in which to participate, and tours to archaeological sites that are available to members. Society addresses can be obtained from anthropology departments at universities or state archaeological offices.

The MPRV area is represented by two professional agencies:

- Fairfax County Archaeology Laboratory
- Alexandria Archaeology Laboratory.

There are county and city archaeologists, namely in Alexandria, Fairfax, Loudoun, and Prince William governments.

Figure 9 – Joffre L. Coe. His work at the Hardaway site in North Carolina produced the standard projectile point sequence for the Middle Atlantic area. His publication –*The Formative Cultures of the Carolina Piedmont* - is a classic reference in American archaeology. Also, he influenced the author's lithic continuum philosophy.

The Archaeological Excavation

While cigar boxes filled with field finds offer an interesting past-time, it is not the major concern in American archaeology – the excavation is the major focus. Not down playing surface finds too much, archaeology is concerned with surface distributions and records them simply as archaeological surveys. Field-collected artifacts are loosely tied to space and remotely tied to time. Even then, vast amounts of data are acquired from these activities. However, the archaeological site offers the vertical element, namely the time factor called stratigraphic chronology. The site fixes artifacts in time and space, which are then compared to other site excavations. Altogether, sites build a picture of the past. This study is based on two major site excavations, namely the Hardaway site in North Carolina (Coe 1964) and St Albans site in West Virginia (Broyles 1972). Coe's (1964) Carolina Sequence, which is based on the Hardaway site, is probably the most frequently quoted publication in American archaeology (Figure 9).

The excavation is a scientific enterprise that involves removing dirt from archaeological remains in such a manner that every recovered artifact is mapped to its exact location within the site context. This aspect of archaeology is not applicable to this study other than excavational contexts used in artifact analysis and interpretations. For the readers who may wish to follow up with actual participation in field archaeology, contact state archaeological societies.

Do We Need Artifacts?

At least one great archaeological philosopher once said that archaeology is the study of artifacts. While this may be a practical reality about the profession, the enterprise, like physics, chemistry, geology, history, sociology, economics, is an intellectual specialty of which the main product is information based on field-collected data. Naturally, the physical objects come along with their study, such as old papers and deeds (history), rocks (geology), elements (chemistry), or artifacts (archaeology). However, when we view other specialties, what is their primary focus? It is knowledge. As for archaeology, once studied after their initial discovery, old papers and deeds, Native American artifacts, etc. go to museums. They are, indeed, evidences of knowledge, but they become secondary or even forgotten focuses of scientific inquiries, as the basic quest is for new knowledge.

Prehistoric artifacts tend to become redundant, for example the Savannah River (SR) projectile point. We could easily dam the Potomac River with all of them that have been found. Even with tens-of-thousands of SR points, new ones are being discovered, studied, and added to museum collections. How many do we need until the collections become *enough* of them. After all, we have the records of their discoveries, contexts, analyses, and interpretations (Figure 10). Therefore, archaeology is really the knowledge of the past; not the accumulation of the past.

Study of Artifacts

All artifacts are the result of human behavior; however, behavior can be interpreted and classified in numerous ways, such as scientifically, economically, environmentally, politically, religiously, etc. Archaeologically, behavior generally is viewed as having created material culture from which inferences are made about the total social system. Operationally, this is a practical means of studying the past. But unfortunately, or fortunately to keep archaeologists working, we never present a true accurate picture of prehistory. One reading prehistoric descriptions and interpretations about prehistory should recognize that human behavior is:

1 – Partly innate physical activities
2 – Partly learned from within a specific society
3 – Mostly random events
4 – Based on different values, beliefs, talents, etc.
And,
5 – Using stone tool knowledge that is quasi universal for mankind
6 – Using scientific measurements which are assumed to be related to the prehistoric world.

Figure 10 – A Lone Big Sandy Projectile Point Found in a MPRV Field. It is the evidence of the past; it shows its age by heavy patination, which has all but removed the flake scars. Some place, at some time, the Native American who owned this point stopped in the field and, for one of many reasons, but probably tool expention, laid the point down – 9000 years later, someone picked it up. We have a brief contact with the past, but move on to the next discovery.

Then, one might recognize why archaeology is an artifact-oriented discipline, which is used to obtain knowledge about prehistory. Artifacts are concrete objects in known time and space. They came into being by human behavior; but more importantly, they are objects that are confined to the Laws of Nature and reflect environmental factors in their creation. As such, archaeologists tend to spend more time on them with laboratory physical science tools than studies with ethnographic comparisons and social/anthropological theory. A mixture of both methods may provide a consensus about ancient people.

Figure 11 – Rhyolite Debitage from the Manufacture of Stone Tools. These materials represent a short-term campsite where the Native Americans primarily replenished their toolkits. Also, other social-living activities were performed at the site.

With this viewpoint, this study follows a physical science approach, almost a G. W. F. Hegel's Natural Law philosophy. And, it follows a technological continuum for prehistoric stone tools; this will be discussed. Additionally, the presentation assumes a *psychic unity* as seen metaphorically in artifacts – naturalistic view of artifact structure and a cultural view of function (as in Hranicky 1973, Ortman 2000, and Shore 1996), or as a cognitive perspective in archaeology (as in Tilley 1999 and Renfrew and Zubrow 1994). The basic argument is a Panindian lithic technology continuum from which local societies modified tools to fit their social agenda. Full development of this approach will be developed in another place as this publication provides essentially a naturalistic approach (basic morphology) to the study of MPRV artifacts. As a special note: Assuming there is a technological continuum, then there is a cultural continuum in the Americas. The Native Americans believe this; here again, this is another story, time, and place.

Artifacts and Their Deposition

As mentioned, this study is based on surface collections and, as such, it has a built-in bias – nonrecovery of deeply buried artifacts in the MPRV, especially near the river. Geologically, the river has overflowed its banks hundreds of times during prehistory. This has resulted in soil build-up over cultural remains. River erosion has exposed artifacts, but the major source of field artifacts has been from the freezing and thawing that grades artifacts upwards to the surface. Farming activities, such as plowing, cause artifacts to surface. However, the river is old and in some areas, build-up can be over 10 meters thick for the Holocene. The average soil freezing depth for the MPRV is 105 cm (Waters 1992). Artifacts below this depth remain in a relatively stable environment. This is called a paleosurface of stability. As a consequence, Early Archaic artifacts are not coming to the surface. Their absence gives the effect of nonoccupation. There is no way to overcome the problem; this study assumes normal distributions for artifacts for all of the Middle Atlantic area.

Figure 12 – Debitage of Finalizing Shapes for Tools. These artifacts are discards; their useable implements were carried off to be used in their daily activities.

MPRV site locations have one focus from upland through coastal habitation. Within each area, site locations have three possible focuses, namely alluvial (flood plains), first and second terraces, and highlands (nonriverbed areas). Within the areas, lithic stratigraphic units vary in thickness; thus, depth measurements must be collocated to time of other geographies. Numerous models have been developed in archaeology to address settlement of these areas throughout prehistory. One factor rarely addressed in these models is the moisture index. Naturally, soil composition, vegetation, and animals are major settlement factors.

Figure 13 – Finally, Points do at Least Tell Who and Perhaps When the Area was used. These tools are part of the tool lifecycle as these were discarded, and new tools were made to replace them. These technologies appear to have been made by Late Archaic Native Americans.

As mentioned, this study basically does not deal with site locations; data that are presented are based on surface sampling, and distributions are assumed to be skewed.

It Starts with Native American Discards

The study of American prehistoric archaeology starts with artifacts, the so-called *material culture* that the Native Americans discarded, namely expended tools, discarded food remains, post molds of former housing, broken pot sherds from once useable containers; all of which still tell a story about people who left no written record of their history. Their history lies buried for archaeologists to discover and analyze. As this publication deals with lithic technology, the following shows what can be learned from Native American debitage. Figures 11, 12, and 13 show debitage from surface finds near Harmony, Frederick County, Maryland.

The MPRV does not always show finely-made arrowheads, axes, and pottery. Tools show a wide-range of craftsmanship and are often found broken. The real world of archaeology is basically putting the Native Americans' debitage back together. It is a reconstruction of the broken artifacts back into the culture of those people who originally made them. From these material cultural remains, archaeological inferences are made about the total cultural picture of the Native Americans' societies.

Figure 14 – Quartz Projectile Point with Tourmaline Crystals. It may represent an intended artform by the maker or simply be unusual material that was convenient to the maker.

Tools as an Artform

Some tools that are found throughout prehistory exhibit workmanship that is considered an artform (see Hranicky 1985). Art does not exist in a vacuum; it is related to activities in the social system that created it. Based on the normal distribution of a type, these tools are the unusual, but sometimes, there are well-made tools that probably served a special purpose or at least identified the user in the prehistoric society as having a special role. Figure 14 shows such a point (tool) that can be classified as an artform; for its social setting, it may have been a prestige or status item.

Some technologies, such as Clovis, Adena, and Susquehanna, always exhibit well-made points. Other points, such as Monocacy, Bear Island, or Poplar Island, generally show expedient workmanship – they are perhaps the ghetto of MPRV prehistory. Art is sometimes restricted to specific technologies, but all societies have it – we just do not see it.

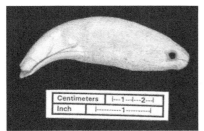

Figure 15 – MPRV Bear Canine Tooth. It is drilled for stringing on a necklace.

Other than non-MPRV comparative examples, this publication does not generally include organic or ceramic artifacts. An organic artifact was preserved at the site, now destroyed, on the Virginia side of the confluence of the Potomac and Monocacy Rivers. Figure 15 shows a drilled bear canine tooth, which presumably was part of a necklace. Other organic artifacts are illustrated and discussed throughout the text.

Another piece of prehistoric art is an effigy of an animal head (Figure 16). It appears to be a bear's head. This form of art shows specialization for a society's ideological-religious or political needs for high-status goods and implements. It may have had a color appliqué. The use of color on artifacts has not been studied archaeologically to prove how extensive it was.

Figure 16 – Effigy Head (L = 109, W = 72, T = 23 mm, 10 oz) Stone is a flint with impurities, which give it a striped-like appearance. It was found on the Loudoun side of the Potomac River.

We can assume that wooden tool handles were carved with artwork (decorations) that added prestige to the tools' owner. Art was an everyday experience, but it probably had social status associated with it. See Moore (1994) for art at the Rosenstock site (18FR18) in Frederick County. And for artifact decorations, see Isreal (1995 and 1996) and the Experimental Archaeology section.

Another form of art is engraving symbols and designs on shells (Figure 17). The earliest study of shell art is Holmes (1883). This artform is late in prehistory and probably has its art sources in the Mississippian cultures of the Southeast. Also, see wooden mask in Prehistoric Chronology section. The Native Americans also used copper items; however, none were observed in the study collections. For a summary of Engraved shell mask, see Smith and Smith (1989).

Figure 17 – Shell mask was found near the village of the Patawomeke on the Potomac River, Stafford County, Virginia. It dates from 1609-1638 AD. (Chase-Dunn and Hall 1999; Smithsonian Institution photograph). The mask was used on Virginia's 1990 Archaeology Month Poster.

Native American Sacred Places

Without written or even oral histories, Native American sacred places in the MPRV are totally unknown. We can assume, based on ethnographic data from other areas, namely the Southeast, that Native Americans had special places for ceremonies, etc. For example, Natural Bridge in western Virginia was a gift from their god, which saved the Monacans from pursuing Mohawks, and Lenapes to the north of what became Virginia (Figure 18). Another Monacan sacred place is their homeland on Bear Mountain, Amherst County, Virginia.

Figure 18 – Natural Bridge, Virginia. It is worshiped as the Bridge of Mohomny by the Monacans.

For the MPRV, Difficult Run (Hranicky 2001) and Bald Friar (Cresthull 1974) rockart sites suggest sacred areas. Another possibility is geological features that are unusual or associated with villages, quarries, hunting areas, and other social practices (Figure 19). While these will never be proven, Native American land use and appreciation were factors that provided what can be called Native American attachments which are successful occupations, and justified long-term habitations.

Gulliford's (2000) *Sacred Objects and Sacred Places – Preserving Tribal Traditions* provides a model for identifying and preserving sacred objects and places. Archaeology needs to work on this aspect, which is often a consequence of excavations and museum curations. Numerous oral histories from Native American tribes could fill this need.

Technology Continuum

Technology is presented here as a continuum, of which most components were originated in the Paleoindian Period and became Panindian throughout prehistory. Or, as MacCord (1999) agues Cultural transitions. In part, it follows Hantman's (1990) argument:

> *Processual archaeology, with its paradigmatic emphasis on gradualism and continuity, and its rejectile of the projectile point style equals culture model, rebelled against the population replacement model...*

Figure 19 – Waterfalls on Little Catoctin Creek, Frederick County, Maryland. While a natural phenomenon, the falls happen to be in the middle of one of the largest rhyolite quarry areas in Maryland. Numerous prehistoric artifacts were found around it.

The continuum is viewed as technology maintenance over time, and tool change/additions come into local societies via a Panindian knowledge base, not necessarily a movement of people. Naturally, prehistoric migrations did occur. The best example is the widespread occurrence of Clovis points.

MacCord (1999) offers a cultural continuum for Virginia, which applies to the MPRV and this study as:

1- Humans are generally conservative, resisting innovation until a new idea is proven, is imposed by command, or is adopted and applied by a respected leader or person in the group.
2- Cultural change can involve technologies, art, daily/seasonal routines, diet, beliefs, and social organization, either separately or in conjunction with other changes.
3- Changes are reflected in the archeological record by new or different artifacts, changes in dietary refuse, changed or mixed burial practices, new residential or community patterns, and elaboration of art motifs.
4- Cultural changes result from three major trends or causes:
   a. *Cultural drift, or internal, random experimentation or accidents, with general adoption of the fittest ideas.*
   b. *External influences, which stimulate or induce change by example or through curiosity, with or without the application of force.*
   c. *Migrations, invasions (en masse or by infiltration), or conquest.*

These concepts are used where appropriate, especially where they can be incorporated with lithic technology presentation.

A technological continuum is basically a study of toolkit production, maintenance, and useability over time and space. The basic Native American lithic toolkit consists of axes/celts, choppers, points/knives, scrapers/gravers, punches/drills, and other miscellaneous tools. Change or variation is often a temporary local variation and, while numerous basic tool designs date to the Paleoindian Period, toolkit additions occur throughout prehistory. For example, the axe, celt, and bannerstone were added after the Paleoindian period. The bow and arrow is a late manifestation of Panindian technology; whereas, the atlatl was brought into the New World (Hranicky 2002b).

While the approach here is not truly a processual analysis, it does follow that general philosophy and maintains that toolkit adjustments are the result of reactions to ecological variations. Naturally, experimental designs and ideological factors play roles in change and variation on the basic toolkit. Variation then becomes a basic cross-culture approach (as in McNett 1979 and Murdock 1949). As a practical method, most researchers cannot avoid comparing artifacts from one area to another, even on a world-wide basis. Obviously, these comparisons should be used cautiously.

Change based on ecological influences becomes the justification for the variation (Hranicky 2002a). For some justified arguments, environmental factors cause technological changes. However, for any given time period and geographical locations, tool maintenance (tradition), not change, is the normal practice in prehistory (Figures 20a and 20b).

From the notebook ...

There are still millions of Native American artifacts that remain to be studied and published. Each tells a piece of Native American history. Report your artifact/site discoveries to you state archaeological agencies.

Throughout this publication "From the notebook ..." topics are used to fill-out pages.

that are based on technology. There is more to interpretations based on technological analyses; it includes interpretation of social ways and kinship, technological achievements, ideological worldviews, and environmental livability.

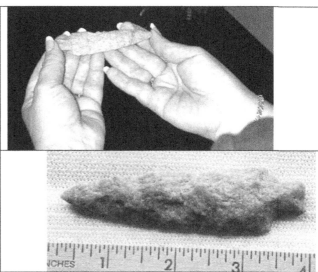

Figure 20b – Classic Lowes Island Point. It was found at Presley Creek and the Potomac River in Northumberland County, Virginia. This type is named here. See Projectile Point section. Upper photograph is the hands of the present that will pass this point on to the future. The stone is the *technology carrier* for Native American tool manufacture.

Figure 20a – Pair of Lowes Island Points. They were found side-by-side in a test pit at 11.5 cm on a bluff overlooking the Maryland side of the Potomac River. The style of both points indicates a technological consistency (or maintenance) of the type. This recovery of artifacts becomes what is known as the archaeological record.

All social systems operate in an environment in which the system adapts to, adjusts with, and is modified by the overall (long- and short-term) ecology. Thus, prehistory is a system of cultures, by curations, and catchment utilizations at particular times and places in U.S. prehistory (Hranicky 2002a). Archaeologically, these social systems are viewed as site contexts, and local land (perhaps regional) cultures

The following pages (Plates 1 and 2) contain sample points that show some of the excellent workmanship of the MPRV prehistoric Native Americans. These points represent archaeological time from the Paleoindian to Woodland times, and they can easily be called artforms from culture technology. These point types are discussed in the Projectile Point section.

From private prehistoric collections:
- **What constitutes data?**
- **What constitutes information?**
- **What constitutes preservation?**
- **What constitutes curation?**
- **What constitutes site lose?**
- **What does a single artifact find mean?**

Text continued on page 18.

Pros and Cons of the Artifact among Professional Archaeologists and Collectors

Who has the artifact is the most hotly debated topic in American archaeology: Who has and owns prehistoric artifacts, and how they were acquired. The entire issue of the SAA's 2015 *Archaeological Record* (Volume 15, Number 5) was devoted to the pros and cons of the collector in prehistoric archaeology. One factor among the papers in this publication was collaboration among all parties in prehistoric endeavors. Perhaps as a middle ground between professionals and collectors is Shott and Pitblado's (2015) paper which suggests for collectors:

- Do not loot, or buy or sell artifacts for the sake of possession or profit.
- Agree to maintain reasonable documentary standards (even if they did not before we reached out to them).
- Freely open their collections and documentation for study and recording
- And, collectors make some type of arrangement for permanent curation
- Obtain written permission to surface hunt on private property *
- Report large surface clusters to state agencies. *

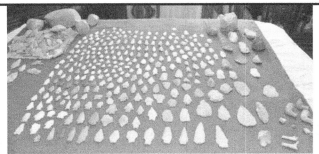

Jeffry Hart Showing his Collection to the Author for Analysis

Alfred Willis' Collection by Site (Location) Storage

Naturally or consequently, many professionals will never consult collectors which is, maybe, part of the problem with the collector world. For those interested in knowledge from artifacts, the collector world is a valuable resource. With jillions of 10,000 years of artifacts, we still do not have a complete prehistoric record. Additionally, many amateur archaeologists are against any form of artifact collecting.

One must remember that the sources for private collections are disappearing with new urban landscapes, modern highway systems, and changing agriculture practices; thus, in the next few years, field-collected artifacts cannot be found as they once were. Collectors offer state-wide coverage of prehistoric artifacts.

Private collections offer the best examples of the horizontal distribution of artifacts which was the basis for this publication. Next, these collectors offer free storage which has become a major factor for museums and archaeological agencies. On the negative side, these collections tend to disappear without notice; monitoring is needed. Thirdly, there is the private rights to property with artifacts; naturally, public lands control artifact acquisition by authorized people.

If we are to preserve cultural materials for the future, it is imperative that archaeologists investigate all possible artifact curations in the private world. They are disappearing at an alarming rate in Virginia.

Reference:
Shot, Michael J. and Bonnie Pitblado
(2015) *Introduction to the Theme "Pros and Cons of Consulting Collectors."* The SAA Archaeological Record, Vol. 15, No. 5, pp. 11-13.

** Added by the author.

Plate 1 – Classic MPRV Projectile Points *
Charles W. Merry Collection
Rockville, Maryland

 Clovis	 Holmes	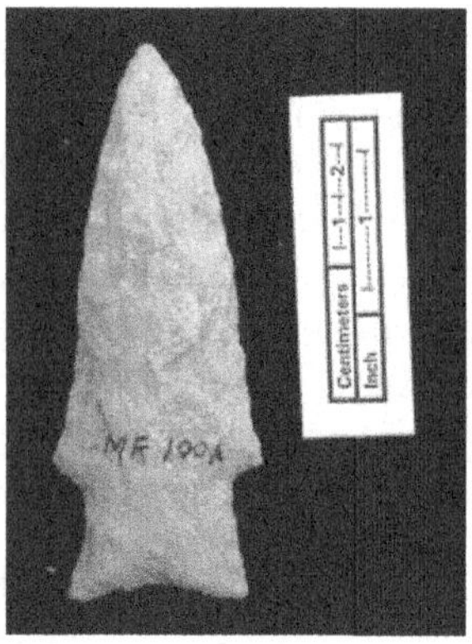 Patuxent	 Lowes Island
 Savannah River	 Genesee	 Morrow Mountain	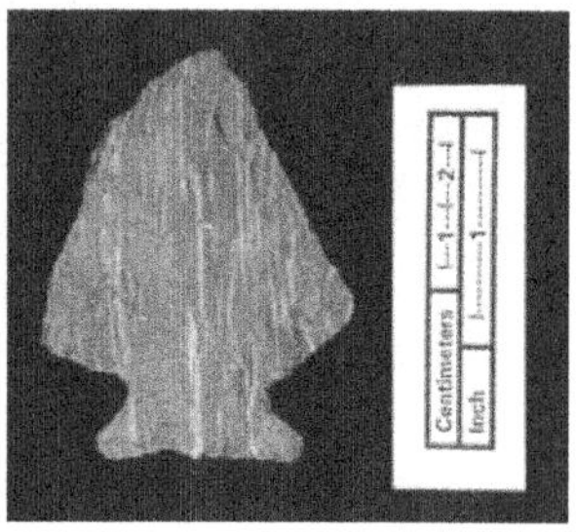 Susquehanna
 Whites Ferry	 Snyder	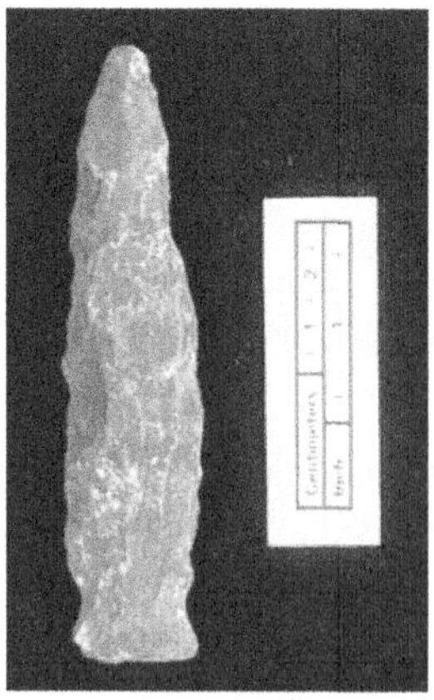 Halifax	 Clovis

The projectile points represent human reactions and adaptations to various environments (ecoscenes) and climates in the MPRV; all of which covers 10,000+ years of Native American occupation. These points are part of the Native Americans' toolkit. Their toolkits were composed of macrotools (axes, celts, adzes, hoes, etc.) and microtools (points, drills, scrapers, knives, etc.).

* These point types are described in the Projectile Points section.

Plate 2 – Classic MPRV Projectile Points *
Spencer O. Geasey Collection
Myersville, Maryland

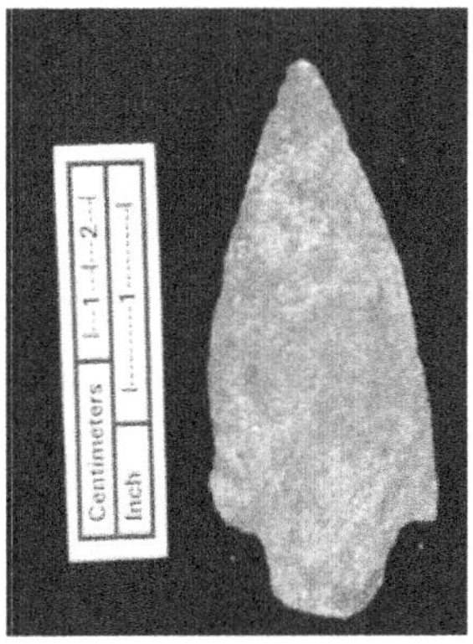 Adena	 Bare Island	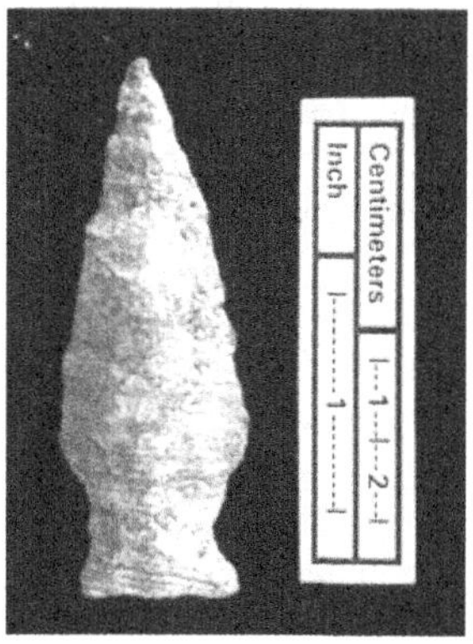 Halifax	 Whites Ferry
 Lowes Island	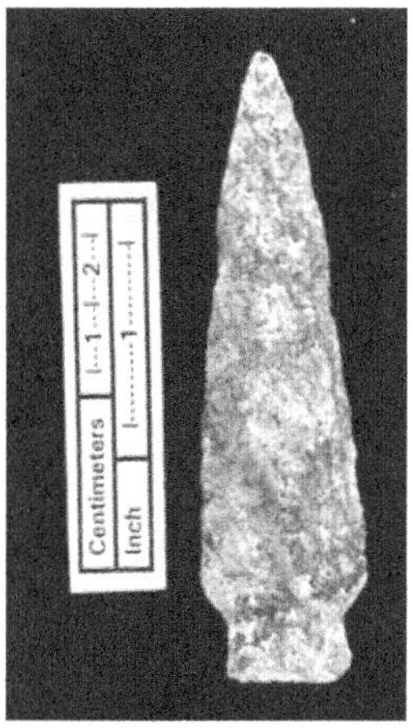 Duncan's Island	 Fox Creek	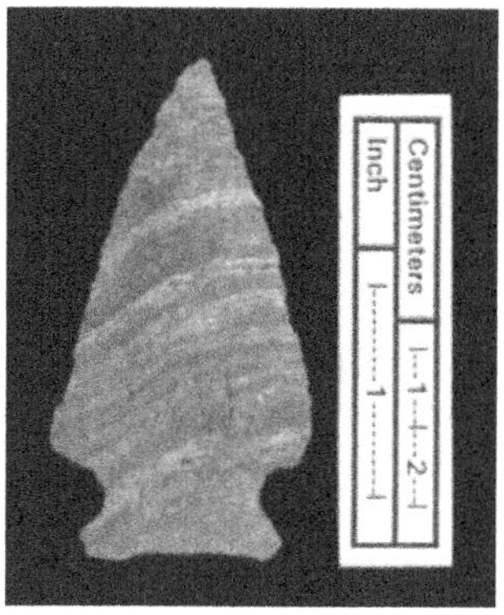 Susquehanna
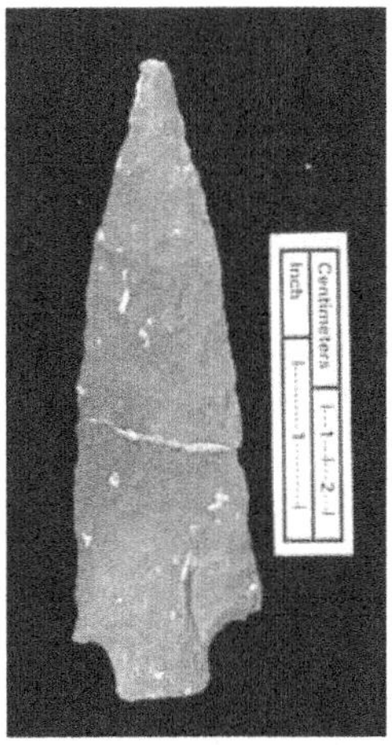 Lowes Island	 Pequea	 Savannah River	 Big Sandy

The projectile point best represents the lithic technology continuum for pre-Contact Native Americans' toolkit. This toolkit changed in its contents over time and in response to changing natural environments in which the MPRV was only a minor part of the total Native American history.

* These point types are described in the Projectile Point section.

Ethnographic Sources for Technology

Fortunately for archaeology, there are countless documents describing the post-Contact (or slightly pre-Contact) Native American ways of creating and using technology. The ideal present day source for Native American ethnography is the Smithsonian's 20 volume series ***Handbook of North American Indians*** with William C. Sturtevant as its general editor.

While many historic ethnographers fail to comprehend the true nature of toolmaking, many give us a basic understanding of Native American techniques. When these techniques are tested in the field and laboratory (experimental archaeology or tests on field data), the picture becomes clearer for stone tool technology. Briefly, several examples are presented; others were used throughout this publication and are listed in the References section.

As an example, Mason (1895) recalls:

... both Indians and white men pound a small piece of jasper into excellent shape for an arrow-head with a small pebble of quartz alone ... to effect this, take a thin chip of any conchoidal stone between the left thumb and forefinger. With an elongated pebble of hard stone strike a series of quick, light, elastic blows along one margin of the chip, barely touching it. The nearer one comes to missing the edge the better. The blow is better struck downward and slightly under.

For its day, this description is reasonably accurate. Powell's (1895) study of Viards Indians of California is another example:

A fragment held in one hand, protected by a piece of untanned elk skin, was wrought with a hammer in the other hand.

The T-shaped crutch method would probably be unknown if not for an early description by Sellers (1885):

Large blocks of obsidian or any easily flaked stones were held between the feet of the operator while sitting on the ground, the "impulsive pressure" being given to the tool grasped in both hands, a cross-piece on the upper end resting against his chest, the bone end against the stone in a slight indentation previously prepared, to give the proper angle and to prevent slipping.

And probably the earliest recording of flintknapping is Torquemada (1615, translated in Tylor 1861):

One of these Indian workmen sits down upon the ground and takes a piece of this black stone ... about eight inches long ... and as thick as one's leg ... and cylindrical; they have a stick as large as the shaft of a lance ...

Nelson's (1916) famous study of Ishi, a Yahi Indian, offers:

Ishi holds a water-worn bowlder in the right hand and a lump of obsidian in the left, and ... to break up the latter or to dislodge flakes from it by means of repeated direct blows.

While not exactly conducive to the modern study of lithic technology, these and numerous other ethnographic descriptions offer a flavor of Panindian toolmaking in the Americas. There are insights to be gained from the early studies.

Lithic Technology Overview

<u>**Lithic technology**</u> - was controllable in prehistory; classifiable and definable in archaeology, which overall is:

...processes and procedures for making stone tools; human quality of toolmaking; skills in tool production; tool usage in a social setting; sum total of manufacturing knowledge in prehistory. It is the social process of taking form and style and turning them into lithic implements.

The major focus is Native American flintknapping, such as making blades and bifaces, but it includes all stone industries. Modern experimental archaeology contributes to the basic understanding of tool production and usage. This focus is presented, described, and illustrated (or at least attempted) in the Experimental Archaeology section. As lithic technology grows as a science, we can assume so will its scope, terminology, and diversity. It is quickly becoming a philosophy within archaeology which justifies its existence. Basically, the overall philosophy follows (Hodson, et al. 1970):

The prehistoric archeologists start from material remains and attempt to interpret them in terms of the life and development of early man. Although not often explicitly stated, the method of proceeding from relevant raw material to a useful interpretation depends on the basic, simple axiom that patterns or regularities in material remains may be expected to reflect patterns in the agency that produced them. The basic tasks of the prehistorian, then, are to recognize and interpret regularities in the known surviving material relevant to his field of study.

And furthering lithic technology philosophy from Crabtree (1970):

Prehistoric lithic technology is the science of systematic knowledge of forming stone into useful cutting, chopping, and other functional implements. But lithic technology comprises two factors - the method and the technique.

The method is in the mind; the technique is in the hands. Method is the logical manner of systematic and orderly flaking process, or preconceived plan of chipping action and based on rules, mechanics, order, and procedure. Method verifies historians' theories that flintknapping was not a haphazard art but, rather, a carefully planned process of making stone tools to suit a specific functional purpose. The shape, length, width, thickness, form, and technique of applied force to fashion the tool was predetermined by the toolmaker before the initial fracture of raw material.

The technique represents the application of the method by the worker with a suitable fabricator to form the stone into his mental conception; each technique produces distinct flaking character and technological attributes. Manner is part of the flaking technique and is the model or characteristic style of preparation and application of forces to form the artifact by a definite method. Manner is the determined angle and application of force – whether percussion by the straight line or curved blow, pressure by pressing or snapping, indirect force by percussion or pressure, etc. Technique is the ultimate result of the method applied in a predetermined manner.

Basic Principles for MPRV Artifact Analyses

This study presents tool analyses as a physics orientation that examines:

1 – Workend
2 – Chassis (hafting)
3 – Use Wear
4 – Replication
5 – Lifecycle
6 – Technique.

The first principal focus in the study of any prehistoric lithic tool is its *workend*, which is defined as:

Workend as a Principle – end or margin of a tool that does the cutting, chopping, grinding, scraping, etc. Tool area where the energy forced into the tool leaves it into another object (target). It is the functional work area of any tool. Major workend factors are:

1 – Operational edge (bit or share)
2 – Functional axis (direction of tool's work)
3 – Applied force into the tools.

The second principal focus is the *chassis* mounting of the tool, which is defined as:

Chassis (Hafting) as a Principle - mounting technique(s) for stone implements; hafting a tool to a shaft or handle. Chassis design is directly related to work and tool efficiency. The following are chassis factors:

1 – Tool dimension (flat or imbedded) - type of tool determines the way that the stone is hafted.

2 – Haft dimension (sinew, slot, or glue) - way the tool is secured to a shaft or handle determines its durability.

3 – Reinforcement (extra glue, sinew, etc. or pieces of bone/wood) - increase in the normal way of rehafting or fixing worn out hafting.

4 – Toughness (fasteners) - strength of the hafting elements to secure the tool to the shaft or handle.

5 – Load (structural design) - shape of the tool composite for adequate support of the load of stone in the tool.

6 – Workend (directional force) - tool shape as to best use the stone workend. Also, its ease of resharpening is a factor.

7 – Leverage (normal handling) - shape of the composite so that it can be used efficiently.

8 – Carrier (technology) – basic or primary material used for the tool; material vary in all of the above factors.

While many tools were successful implements, we can assume a small percentage were not. Hafting is the primary factor in successful tools. Thus, chassis failure is the result of:

1 – Using the tool for a purpose not intended by the maker

2 – Over or excessive use which exceeds normal usage

3 – Excessive use of force into the tool

4 – Poor mounting design for tool size and shape

5 – Normal wear out.

As an estimate, a macrotool chassis probably has a five-year life span, and a microtool chassis has less than a two-year span. Both were resharpened periodically throughout the tool's lifecycle. In some cases, large macrotools, such as axes, may have lasted a lifetime; most were rehafted numerous times.

Figure 21 shows an early effort at tool replication by Fred Morgan, a past ASV president. Following in the Experimental Archaeology section, numerous tool replications are used to illustrate and offer possible explanations for Native American tool usage. Also, see Bifaces as Knives section.

The third principal focus in the study of any prehistoric lithic tool is its use wear, which is defined as:

Use Wear as a Principle - wear that is produced during tool usage and causes polish, striations, and chippage on the edge. All tool usage leaves wear patterns, which can be observed microscopically. According to Edmonds (1996):

The use of stone artefacts for different tasks can often be identified by the close inspection of tool edges. At a macroscopic level, use wear traces include small scars and scratches (sometimes referred to as utilization damage). With the aid of a microscope, it is also possible to identify microwear traces - alterations to the surface of the tool including striations, polishes, and even residues. Experimental research has shown that the character, density, and distribution of these traces can be used to identify both how a certain tool was used, and upon what materials.

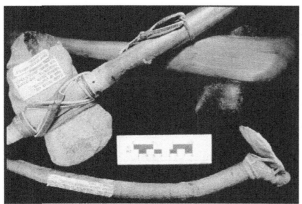

Figure 21 – Replication Macrotools by Fred Morgan in the 1950s. He was a past ASV president and collector; most of his collection is now in the public realm. Over the years, numerous amateur archaeologists have made presentations on how Native American artifacts were made and used.

The forth principal focus in the study of any prehistoric lithic tool is its *replication*, which is defined as:

Replication as a Principle – scientifically making a stone tool based on archaeological and ethnographical studies of Native American artifacts. It serves as a method of studying the entire toolkit, from initial quarrying to expended tools. By using tool replications, lifecycles can be determined for prehistoric tools. Replication provides a means for testing prehistoric tools by using them in actual living situations. Replication is based on typology; thus, it implies that tool shape/design is consistent in Native American toolmaking. It becomes a scientific technique of replicating data from contexts containing a type.

The fifth principal focus in the study of any prehistoric lithic tool is its *lifecycle*, which is defined as:

Lifecycle as a Principle – every prehistoric tool has a lifecycle that started with its creation and ends with its expention (discard). Lifecycle is dependent on the tool's design shape, industry membership, intended function, input force and output energy, work-usage, task accomplishment time, chassis mounting, and material. It is a major factor in a society's tool replenishment activities. It includes:

1 – Curation activities
2 – Tool initiation for future work
3 – Social operation of the tool
4 – Expention and tool discard.

The final principle applies to the entire tool production process, which is *technique*. It is defined as:

Technique as a Principle – human behavior via a learned method of producing a specific tool. Technique can be equated with tradition, but mostly, it is a focus on a specific production process. Or as Crabtree (1970) states:

Technique is the ultimate result of the method applied in a predetermined manner.

Technique is the observable procedures and methods as viewed from the stone tool. It can vary among individuals, but overall, technique is culturally driven, such as fluting, grinding, polishing, notching, etc. Technique can be observed in artifacts and their debris.

These principles are used here as the basic philosophy for describing, analyzing, and interpreting the study collections and MPRV artifacts in general. With these principles and other archaeological tools, any lithic technology study can:

1 – Discover and interpret Native American ways of stone tool production

2 – Understand Native American cognitive and behavioral approach to using stone tools

3 – Native American methods and operations for tool replacement.

Archaeological Methods in the Study

Overall, the basic archaeological procedures follow Joukowsky (1980), Bahn, (1991) and Purdy (1996). Table 1 shows the basic methods of collecting data from which information about the MPRV artifacts is presented. Naturally, objectivity was attempted, but different researchers might view the data differently and present different interpretations. Since the study is based on a random sample of artifacts, it is not all-inclusive of the total prehistoric world of the MPRV.

Study sources and recommended publications on field archaeology are: Martha Joukowsky's (1980) *A Complete Manual of Field Archaeology* and, Barbara Purdy's (1996) *How to Do Archaeology the Right Way*.

Table 1 – Analytical Approach to Studying MPRV Prehistory

Analytical Unit	Description	Example
Influence	Tradition or social ways.	Savannah River point is a broadspear.
Distribution	Geography where the artifact found.	The Dalton point is found all over the eastern U.S.
Technoculture	Specific set of attributes for a tool typology that is found over a large area and over a long period of time.	Clovis, Kirk, Morrow Mountain, and Savannah River points make up technocultures.
Timemarker	Key artifacts that have reliable dates (Hranicky 1987) and known distributions which can be used to identify archaeological contexts. It includes lithic points and pottery.	Clovis, Kirk, Morrow Mountain, and Savannah River points make up technocultures.
Environment	Landscape where the artifact was manufactured and used.	The Morrow Mountain point is found in the upland, piedmont, and coastal environments.
Ecology	Artifact-human interface for a specific geography.	Hoe is used for horticulture.
Cimatology	Temperature, sunlight, winds, moisture, etc.	Change from paleo-to-archaic environments as reflected in the presence or absence of rock-lined fireplaces.
Procedure	Performing an activity was performed with an artifact.	Properly placing a spear on an atlatl and launching it and hitting a target.
Process	Artifact application in social activity.	Using a knife in the butchering process.
Curation	Material acquisition and tool manufacture.	Methods for making an axe.
Structure	Parts and shape of the artifact.	Lanceolate point with fluting.
Function	Operation of the artifact in an activity.	Hafted tools with cutting edge.
Concept	Why do they have the artifact and what did it mean to an activity.	Tool offers a mechanical advantage over nature.
Archaeological Fact	Specific statements about the artifact.	Point measures L = 55, W = 27, and T = 12 mm.
Archaeological Time	Time period for the cultural activity.	Paleoindian period dates around 9500 BC.
Classification/ Typology	Grouping of artifacts.	Clovis, Kirk, Halifax, etc. types.
Lifecycle	Estimating the normal usage of the tool in a social setting.	Average basalt axe lasted five years.
Useability	Defining how the tool was actually used in a social setting.	Way to use an axe on a tree.
Modality	The operation of a tool by users.	The projectile point is a multifunctional tool.
Expention	Methods of discarding expended tools and starting toolmaking all over.	Clovis points are usually expended when length = <50 mm.
Language	Linguistic areas where dialects of a parent language are spoken, for example Algonquian speakers.	Virginia has four major linguistic families: Iroquoian, Siouan, and Algonquian, (SW Virginia) Muskogian. Maryland has Iroquoian and Algonquian families. (Based on Krober 1939)
Statistics	The metric system is recommended for any measurements in lithic technology. As a note for scientific measurements, the metric system has no counterpart in the Native Americans' concept of space and/or dimension; it is purely a modern concept of measuring.	Regardless of the method used in measuring artifacts, there is an error factor present in collecting numbers (see Shott 2000).

Archaeological Terms

Terms and concepts that are used are from Hranicky (2002a), some of which are discussed here. Marcotool definitions are presented in the Miscellaneous Tools/Implements section.

Acutus – tip of a knife/blade as formed by the share (cutting edge) and bank (back) of the blade.

Band – group of socially-related members who number approximately 50 people. Some type of leadership is assumed. Any group under 50 members is arbitrarily set as a small band; over 50 members is a large band. Band assumes all age groups and both sexes. Specialized bands may exist, but the term *party* better refers to it. Bands were probably subdivided into clans.

Biface – any stone object that has flakes removed from both sides. It is the basic form in stone reduction by percussion or pressure flaking.

Bit – cutting edge on a macrotool; workend; sharp end of a blade. It is the opposite end of the poll on a macrotool.

Blade – any long narrow stone piece removed from a core. It constitutes uniface technology and probably predates biface technology in the Americas. It is also used to refer to the workend of a knife or projectile point.

Catchment – physical geography around a site or occupation territory where there are physical and living resources that can be exploited by human beings. It implies a socially-known territory.

Chippage – knapping method of using a hard hammerstone to chip (chipping) lightly along a blade edge to resharpen it. Practice was common among broadspear pointmakers. Note: It should not be used as a method of manufacture. The chipped axe is a misnomer; however, it is an old term and still used.

Core – any stone piece that has flakes removed from it to produce a tool or implement.

Curation – social processes that exploit a catchment for survival resources.

Decortation – procedure of removing the cortex from a cobble before continuing to reduce it into a useable or workable biface. Decort is a stone surface without cortex.

Expention – end of a tool's lifecycle; the discard is not a simple throw away, but involves tool replacement. It refers to the entire ending process of using, including its maintenance, a tool after which it is discarded. It involves toolkit replenishment operations. Its main cause is blade attrition. In some cases, expended tools are the furthest from their source.

Flake – any piece of stone produced by the process of stone reduction into a tool or implement.

Frank – cutting blade edge; part of the blade that functions as the cutting part of a tool. It is the part of the blade that extends from the tip (edge) to the top of the blade. Frank process is to cut into the target area from the edge to the top of the blade. Frank is usually measured as the angle from the tip to the top part of the blade.

Function – purpose for which the tool was made; result of design. It is part of the Native Americans' design and is assumed to be part of the structural plan. Function is always culturally determined and may not always be obvious on the tool or in the archaeological context.

Implement – any human-made object that has a purpose in a social setting. It lacks the specific work operation of a tool. It is used as a generalized reference for a culturally-made object; nonfunctional artifact. However, tool and implement are used interchangeably.

Knapping – any reference to flaking stone into a tool. It is a general reference to any way of manufacturing a stone tool. It is another term for flintknapping.

Lithics – generalized reference to lithic technology as practiced at a particular time and place in prehistory. It is a short term for lithic technology.

Macrotool - large heavy duty, nonprojectile tool which may or may not have been hafted and was used to apply massive amounts of energy into an object. It is usually made from coarse-grain or fine-grain materials, which exhibit brittle fracture properties. This tool was made to withstand constant battering against other materials. It was resharpened frequently and had possibly a five-year plus tool lifecycle. Examples are the axe, celt, adze, gouge, maul, or hoe. Major parts are:

1 - Hafting area
2 - Poll
3 - Body
4 - Tressel
5 - Wedge-shaped bit.

Macrotool lengths (generalized) are:

1 - Small = <100 mm
2 - Medium = 101 - 200 mm
3 - Large = >201 mm
4 - Ceremonial = >400 mm.

Microtool - small, usually hafted tool, which was used to apply specific amounts of energy into an object or target area. It is usually made from fine-grain materials that exhibit brittle fracture properties. Tool was not made to withstand massive battering but was made for sharp cutting edges. It was resharpened frequently. Examples are the knife, projectile point, drill, graver, or scraper.

Microtool lengths (generalized) are:

1 - Small = <25 mm
2 - Medium = 26 - 50 mm
3 - Large = >51 mm
4 - Ceremonial = >150 mm.

In terms of useability, macrotools tend to be generalized tools that required little, if any, training; whereas, microtools tend to be specialized tools that required training. Useability is discussed in the Toolmaking Technology section.

Mobility - capability of a band to maintain daily food and water during migrations. It involves tool production, transportation, and usage. Mobil units usually have portable toolkits. Cowan (1999) argues costs and benefits of tool production strategies as they relate to mobility. Mobility is assumed for early MPRV populations.

Modality – tool operation as a behavior of the user. Toolmaker's intended tool use for a specific task. Modality implies human behavior of the user and ranges from unitask to multitask operations. See Projectile Point Typology section.

Point – general term for any bifacially-flaked, pointed object. It is a casual reference for projectile and more formal than arrowhead. See Projectile Point section.

Poll – back end of a macrotool; nonworkend. It is the top (distal) end of blade on an axe, celt, adz, chisel, or maul.

Process (Technology) – means by which people act (behave) to established procedures, methods, and traditions to produce tools which are used for desired end results.

Projectile Point – any lithic object that is bifacially- or unifacially-flaked, has a pointed end, two cutting edges, and a shaft-mounting area, and the term can be synonymous with lanceolate blade, biface, and knife (Hranicky 1991). Moorehead (1910) was the first to define projectile points as a tool class.

Share – knife blade edge; actual knife edge that performs cutting.

Social System – cultural practices and behavior by group of (usually related) people at a particular time and place in prehistory.

Stone - another term for lithic material; piece of rock; tool composition. For lithic technology, it generally means material that is predominantly used for tools in specific contexts.

Stone is a nonorganic material of an earthy nature. It is the basic element (construct) for prehistoric tools and implements. It is a generalized reference to the lithic material used in knapping. The basic archaeological varieties are granite, marble, limestone, sandstone, quartzite, rhyolite, quartz, flints, and basalt. Petrographically, these variety names have an exact significance, but, technically, they are often used very loosely. Thus, any light-colored, hard, igneous rock with a texture resembling that of granite is often called granite in archaeology, regardless of whether it is a true granite or more properly a syenite or porphyry. Greenstone and argillite also have a variety of names and descriptions in archaeology. In the same way, limestone is used to include dolomite, and marble to include serpentine. Chalcedony is often classified as flint. In other words, stone means many things in archaeology.

Structure (Point) - physical design or observable feature of a projectile point; designed for a specific use. It is the deliberate design of a tool or implement by the Native Americans. Design always assumes a planned function for a tool, even if it becomes multifunctional. Structure is always subject to the Laws of Nature in the manufacturing process.

Target – work area; any place on an object where energy was applied via a tool. Work is the mechanical process by a human of applying energy into a target area to accomplish a specific task.

Technology – application of knowledge to fashion tools and implements. It is knowledge in a prehistoric society that enabled them to fashion stone (or organic) implements from material(s) they extracted from nature. For lithic technology, it incorporates:

1 - Structure of products from technology
2 - Function/purpose of the products
3 - Useability in a social setting
4 - Cultural mythology or worldview of nature
5 – Useability based on industry.

Technology cannot exist solely in the material culture world; it is always part of and interacts with the social system. Technology can be unknown, such as the mechanical screw in American prehistory. But once known, technology becomes common knowledge among the social members. In other words, technology is treated as Panindian in this study. Technology as procedures and processes depends on compatibility with the natural environment and the state of the social system at the time it is found archaeologically. Technology is present in the archaeological record as:

1 - Concentration of specialized lithic debris; specialized activity area

2 - Tools that are replicated in inter- and intrasite associations or contexts; tool traditions

3 - Presence of material procurement for tool production; presence of quarry blanks, special clays, or any nonlocal material

4 - Increased utilization of local environmental foodstuffs based on increased tool usage; extended curation

5 - Trade or exchange of materials and/or production items; indications of surplus

6 - Specialization in production and/or tool usage; status tools

7 - Transportation of tools from one location to another; future tool usage.

Tools represent a prehistoric technological continuum, and divisions of the continuum are arbitrary on the part of the archaeological community. Since technology represents only one aspect of a culture, placing value on it over other culture attributes, such as economics, religion, sociokinship, or politics, skews the total appraisal of the culture under study. Unfortunately, the archaeological study of prehistory involves what remains, material culture of which technology is a highly visible entity. Even here, archaeology's viewpoint is oriented toward lithic materials because these items are usually the only materials that survive the tenures of time. If we assume the continuum philosophy, one might ask where does it start in prehistoric America? Does the Paleoindian toolkit come to the archaeological scene fully developed? Assuming this as a starting place, we move along the tool/implement development to the small triangular point of the late periods, which reflects the invention and use of the bow and arrow. We can assume that all people living in North-to-South America during the last 10,000 (or more) years shared in some way the prehistoric technology of the Native Americans. One supporting argument for the continuum theory is that a point type is frequently found among different cultures, for example the widespread use of corner- or side-notched, stemmed, lanceolate, bifurcate, and triangle points. While minor differences do occur, these basic styles have been identified and dated throughout prehistory. This philosophy does make it difficult to practice typology and could be construed to suggest that types only exist in the laboratory. As lithic concepts:

1 - Body of methods and materials used (past and present) to manufacture stone tools. According to Crabtree (1972):

The study of techniques. Science of studying and interpreting the combined or distinct attributes of individual techniques. Implies a systematic control of minute and distinguishable detail.

2 - Body of knowledge and practices that were used to design and manufacture implements, including necessary skills and acquisition of lithic materials.

Lithic technology exists in American prehistory for a long period of time. Remarkably, most technologies show very little change over their history.

Technology Carrier – the basic element on which technological elements are built, such as stone for a projectile point or axe, or wood for an axe. The carrier is the basic unit of efficiency; carrier choice quality was known to the Native Americans. The carrier can be graded by durability, workability (as in Callahan 1979), and efficiency.

Tool – any object used to perform a human task or work. Tools are classified by style and function within classes and industries.

Tool Assembly – any combination of tools or collection of tool parts that are assembled collectively to perform a single function (Figure 22), such as spear and atlatl, bow and arrow, or axe. Assembly can also refer to parts needed to make a tool, such as grooving, fluting, grinding, etc.

Toolmaking – curation and process used to produce a tool in a specific society.

Work – controlled expended energy to accomplish a specific task. For lithic technology, work is performed with a tool. Work is applied to a target area on an object.

o o o o o

Figure 22 – Rockart at Difficult Run Petroglyph Site (44FX2380). Ethnographic example of a tool assembly of the atlatl (hook and board) and spear (point and shaft). For a site report, see Hranicky (2001). Rockart sites are another example of Native American sacred places. See Rockart section.

Geoarchaeology Focus

The overall approach, even a requirement, in this study is the effects that the MPRV environment had on human occupation, and how the Native Americans reacted to them. This focus considers geology, biology, archaeology, anthropology (ethnology), and a number of other sciences in the evaluation of tools in the MPRV's prehistory. The basic scientific philosophy is:

Geoarchaeology - archaeological geology; application of concepts and methods of the geosciences to archaeological research and methods. It uses techniques and approaches from geomorphology (physical geology), crystal/chemical structures (mineral composition), sedimentology (alluvial deposits), pedology (soil formation), stratigraphy (layers and artifacts), and geochronology (dating) to interpret sites, artifactual contexts, and their environmental conditions; it is the application of geological principles to solve archaeological problems (Hranicky 2002a).

Overall, geoarchaeology is a total environmental approach to the study of prehistoric artifacts (see Waters 1992). According to Rapp and Hill (1998):

The present distribution and visibility of archaeological sites are based initially on the environmental conditions which existed at the time of human occupation. These conditions made a particular functional activity possible and provided the circumstances which later transformed or preserved the artifactual evidence of human behavior. Many functional activities that take place at a site are related to the landscape context or habitat setting and the resources available at that location. Certain types of activities are restricted to the availability or distribution of resources across a landscape. Specific types of archaeological manifestations are likely to be associated with these landscape patterns. Perhaps the most obvious of these are locations related to the availability of a spatially restricted resource or activity context. For instance, procurement activities associated with stone and mineral sources in the location of quarry sites near sources of raw materials. Similarly, campsites and butchery sites can be expected in settings connected with animal migration routes or near water-related resources.

Within this viewpoint, the MPRV study examines lithic technology, namely micro- and macrotools, as part of the Potomac River's ecological systems to which the Native Americans adapted and lived. Ecology is based on deBlij and Muller (1998) and Turekian (1996). Geology is based on Foster (1988), Frye (1990), and Ladoo and Myers (1951).

Potomac Estuary Basin

The Wisconsin glaciation did not reach what was to become the Potomac River basin. Most of the area from upper New Jersey northward was covered with ice during the maximum extent of the Ice Age. As the glaciation retreated, gameherds, vegetation, and Paleoindians migrated following the retreat. MPRV had periglacial factors that included permafrost, and coastal areas were extended with the continental shelf. Native Americans occupied this area at various times. Now water-covered, this area had lagoons, estuaries, and barrier islands, much like North Carolina's coast today. It extended the coastal plain approximately 11 miles. There are Paleoindian sites on the continental shelf.

Figure 23 – Potomac River above the Fall Line. Maryland is on the left and Virginia to the right. This ecoscene is a riverine environment in which all tool classes were used to exploit its resources.

The Potomac River is not a true river; it is an estuary (Figure 23). True rivers flow continuously downstream, but an estuary is subject to rise and fall of ocean tides. The Potomac River has fresh water at its headwaters and varying degrees of brackishness toward the end of it. This factor offers marshes that create tremendous food sources, especially during seasonal migrations of geese and fish. Its flood plains and terraces made excellent camp and village locations from which the Native Americans exploited the river valley's resources.

Figure 24 – Forest Conditions at Mason Neck State Park, Virginia. The forested environment constitutes the majority of the MPRV area. The principal adaptive tool for it was the axe.

The Potomac River dates to and has its origins in the Wisconsin glacial period. Water runoff from it started between 18 and 14,000 years ago. By 9,000 years ago, most of the glaciation was gone from the continental United States. The basin occupies 14,670 square miles. Figures 24 and 25 show various ecoscenes in the MPRV study area.

The Potomac River is canoeable except through the gorge, where the Native Americans dismounted and carried their canoes around it. This and other river travel by canoe make up the communication system in prehistory (Franklin 1979). The Seneca rapids are navigable. There are numerous islands in the river from the fall line to the Shenandoah River. These islands were inhabited throughout prehistory, especially during the Woodland Period.

Figure 25 – Potomac River Marsh at Mason Neck State Park, Virginia. The principal adaptive tool may have been the bola; other necessary tools for the marsh environment remain to be defined.

The Potomac River is part of the Atlantic Coastal Plain region by its providing rain and spring runoffs to the Chesapeake Bay. The Plain is a lowland which does not exceed 300 feet above sea level. The mountainous areas are the source of bedrock decomposition from which rocks and soil move downward. For general purposes of this study, the river basin is divided into primary ecoscenes of uplands (mountainous), piedmont, and coastal regions.

The headwaters (North Branch) of the Potomac River are located in the western Allegheny Mountains near Fairfax Stone, a monument at the Maryland-West Virginia state lines. The mouth is located at Point Lookout, Maryland and Smith Point, Virginia. This confluence with the Chesapeake Bay is 38° 00' N (latitude) and 76° 15' W (longitude).

The river is approximately 400 miles long. Its width at Point Smith, Virginia is 11 miles. The deepest point at the tidal portion at Washington, DC is 107 feet.

The major tributaries are the North and South Branch, Savage, Shenandoah, Monocacy, Occoquan, Anacostia, and Cacapon Rivers. The Antietam and Conococheague Creeks are also tributaries.

These rivers and creeks composed the watershed, which was occupied at various times during prehistory. They see at least two types of populations: 1) migratory bands and 2) nonmigratory villagers. While the MPRV can be divided into ecoscenes and studied in terms of settlement and adaptive processes, this study identifies and uses these perspectives but mainly presents lithic artifacts as products of this environment.

The entire river lies in five physiographic provenances:

1 – Coastal Plain
2 – Piedmont Plateau
3 – Blue Ridge
4 – Valley and Ridge
5 – Appalachian Plateau.

Figure 26 – Difficult Run, Fairfax County, Virginia. Streams were a food source of various fish. Stream gradient varies by ecozone.

Basically, the piedmont is the focus of this study; however, all provenances are relevant in the Native Americans' occupation of the valley. The Ridge and Valley area is the Shenandoah River valley. This land is hilly to mountainous with frequent lithic outcroppings in the higher elevations. From Harpers Ferry to the west of Washington, DC, the area has low rolling hills and is usually forested (Late Holocene). West of the Blue Ridge, the rockbeds are foliated sedimentary layers of limestone, dolomite, sandstone, and shale. From the Blue Ridge to Washington, DC, the rockbeds are metamorphic (mainly crystalline) and some igneous formations. The rockbeds in the piedmont offered good lithic sources for the Archaic Period Native Americans. From Washington, DC to the river's mouth, there is an alluvium layer of sedimentary materials from the uplands. The coastal area offered good horticulture soils and a long growing season for the Woodland Period Native Americans. MPRV physiological factors are discussed in the MPRV Environment section.

The average rainfall is 36 to 45 inches, but this amount varied throughout prehistory. In prehistoric times, river flooding was common. Most of the river has a flood plain with a second terrace paralleling the river. Generally, late occupations were on this terrace.

Figure 27 – Small Swamp in the Piedmont of the Potomac River Valley. These swamps occur in the forested floodplain of the river. Occasionally, during flooding, the swamp contains trapped fish. They are often a short-term food source of frogs/toads, snakes, and turtles.

Watershed Stream System

The Potomac River watershed is composed of hundreds of streams (runs). There are two types of resources: streams/runs (Figure 26) and swamps (Figure 27). One is replenished, including water; the other is a short-term water resource that is easily exploited until it dries up. We have fish inventories today (Rose 2001), but reconstructing a species list for the prehistoric MPRV remained to be done from archaeological excavations. The Native American technologies utilized to exploit water resources are pole and line/hook, fishtraps, nets, fish line, spear/bow/arrow, and harpoon. These techniques are based on ethnographic data and are not easily observed in archaeological contexts.

There is a statistical relationship between the drainage imperviousness and the biological quality of the stream (Klein 1979 and Booth 1991). Each stream consists of a biological and habitat integrity that still exists today. We do not know the human effect on a stream other than the assumption of Native Americans utilizing its resources. There is a possible correlation among the vitality of ecological resources, quality of life, and continued habitation of a geographical area.

These resources are factors in Native American settlement patterns. For example, when a society establishes a village on the confluence of a stream and the Potomac River or one of its major tributaries, there is a limited time period until the village exploits the local non-river water resources. Continuous fishing and catching snakes/turtles depletes a stream, marsh, or swamp. As a consequence, the villagers have to travel further for these food sources. With dwelling deterioration and sanitary conditions, the village is moved.

Figure 28 – Original Building for the Smithsonian Institution as Seen in winter, Washington, DC. The museum has been and still is a primary organization in the investigation of the MPRV's archaeology. William Holmes spent numerous years working in this building. See Clifford Evans in the pottery section.

Early MPRV Archaeology

For the MPRV, the Smithsonian Institution has played an important role in the last two centuries for the study on prehistoric Native Americans and their cultural remains (Figure 28). While the following applies to the entire U.S., it can be used to start the prehistoric MPRV research.

> **Circular No. 36** - issued by the Smithsonian in January 1888 for information concerning prehistoric implements:
>
> Question 1. How many of these rude implements have you in your collection?
>
> Question 2. Of what material are they made?
>
> Question 3. Where have they been found?
> (1) As to locality.
> (2) Position, condition and association with what objects.
> (3) Whether on or under the surface, and if so, at what depth, and in what kind of geologic formation.
> (4) Where they found in mounds, tombs, or other ancient structures.

(5) Were any other implements found with them, and if so, of what kind.
(6) Did their deposit seem to be accidental or intentional.
(7) Have they been described in any publication, and if so, in what, and where can it be obtained.
(8) Can you forward specimens (as many as possible) to this Museum in exchange for publications or duplicate specimens.

Response to this questionnaire basically started national prehistoric collections at the national museum. Countywide, other museums started prehistoric collections; all of these collections easily exceed a billion prehistoric artifacts.

While numerous publications occur around and after the Smithsonian's call, namely Holmes (1891, 1890, 1897 and 1919), Fowke (1894), Mooney (1890, 1889, and 1907), Brunner (1987) Procedifit (1889), Reynolds (1880 and 1893), and Wikson (1888 and 1889), the First Woodland Conference (Woodland Conference 1943) started formalizing the East into archaeological regions (culture areas). More recently, Byers (1959), Fitghugh (1972), Ford and Webb (1956), Johnson (1964), Kinsey (1977), Lewis and Lewis (1961), Logan (1952), Luchterland (1970), Munson (1966), and Sears (1948) can be considered the base works for contemporary eastern archaeology. Within the eastern realm, the Middle Atlantic area comes into existence (archaeologically speaking) with the founding of the Middle Atlantic Archaeological Conference in the early 1970s.

From the notebook . . .

Front/back side (historic drill bit board):

Back/front side (prehistoric artifact display):

Collectors often mount high-quality specimens on boards (formerly Loy Carter collection). While this method makes them easy to view, this often destroys one face and/or edges of points (Hranicky 1989). Some glues are next to impossible to dissolve for removing the points. These specimens are probably from Mecklenburg County, Virginia.

The following is a summary of archaeologists who have made major contributions to our knowledge of MPRV prehistory as seen in projectile point typology and all lithic technology. As a note, for years the basic library was Griffin (1945), Ritchie (1961), Coe (1964), Broyles (1971), and ASM and ASV bulletins for archaeological sources.

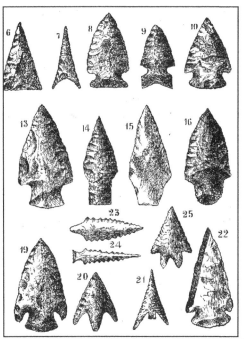

Figure 29 – An Example of Early Projectile Point Publication (Wilson 1888) – knives or spear-heads?

While not totally applicable to the MPRV, Wilson (1888) was among the first to publish stone tools in the U.S. His Smithsonian publication, ***Chipped Stone Classification***, was a how-to book in prehistoric anthropology. He used the term anthropology for the study of stone tools; this would become archaeology shortly thereafter (Figure 29). For this figure, his questions are whether they are *arrows or spear-heads or knives*. This discussion continues today. At approximately this same time, Fowke (1894) was conducting archaeological surveys of the Potomac and James Rivers that started producing artifacts and archaeological data.

Holmes (1897) refers to the MPRV area as being in Virginia's tidewater. However, the elevation on the MPRV averages over 300 feet above sea level, and the current geological focus is to call the area the *piedmont*. His publication ***Handbook of Aboriginal American Antiquities*** (1919) is considered the bible of American archaeology, even though there is less use of it today than there was in the 20th century.

During the 1920s, Bushnell did survey and ethnographic work in Virginia's piedmont. His major contributions are monographs on the Monacan (Bushnell 1930) and the Manacan (Bushnell 1935). Also, he named the Elys Ford point (Bushnell 1935).

<u>Note</u>: William H. Holmes, David I. Bushnell, and Carl F. Miller are members of the ASV's Hall of Fame for Archeology.

Ritchie (1932) probably established the term *archaic* in archaeological chronologies. He used it in reference to the Lamoka culture in New York. Griffin (1946) added the divisions Paleoindians, Archaic, Early Woodland, Middle Woodland, and Late Woodland (Mississippian) to the eastern Archaeological calendar for prehistory.

Another early work occurring in the MPRV is William J. Graham (1935) publication on Port Tobacco Indians in Maryland (Figure 31). T. Dale Stewart also made MPRV contributions starting with *Excavation of the Indian Village of Patawomeke (Potomac)* in 1939.

Figure 30 – James B. Griffin (University of Michigan). He was among the first to publish in 1952 a synthesis on the East. *Archeology of Eastern United States*, which included the MPRV, is a classic book in American archaeology, but he is perhaps best known for his Fort Ancient studies.

Griffin (1945) published a summary assessment of artifact collections from Virginia and North Carolina (Figure 30). He was examining the coastal plain with reference to the Ohio River valley.

Another early work was William J. Graham's (1935) publication on Port Tobacco Indians in Maryland (Figure 31).

Schmitt (in Griffin 1952) published one of the first chronologies of the Middle Atlantic area. He used both the concept of component and culture, and he was the first to expand the Koens-Crispin and fishtail points in the area. While others failed at identifying the bannerstone, he discussed it (Figure 31).

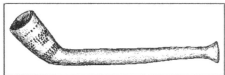

Figure 31 – Late Woodland Pipe Showing Dentate-Stamped Decoration (After Graham 1935)

Evans (1955) set up the pottery analysis schema for Virginia. While not a lithic presentation per se, Clifford Evans' 1955 *A Ceramic Study of Virginia Archeology* is a major contribution to MPRV archaeology. It was the first major pottery synthesis for the Commonwealth. Most of his pottery types are still used today.

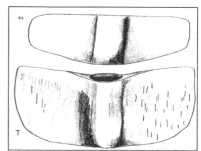

Figure 32 – Middle Atlantic Area Bannerstones as Published by Karl Schmitt (1952)

Ritchie's (1961) typology of New York has widespread acceptance in eastern archaeology as the standard point typology. He set up *a convenient classification and nomenclature* to replace awkward phraseology in archaeology at that time. This publication became the standard and justification for typology everywhere.

Stephenson and both Fergusons' (1963) work at the Accokeek Creek site in Maryland near Washington, DC has become a standard reference in MPRV archaeology (Figure 33). The pottery analysis has been proven to be incorrect, but the lithic tools are established types and used here. Stephenson attributed Popes Creek pottery to the Early Woodland; now it has been assigned to the Middle Woodland (Mouer 1990). Ms. Ferguson, who worked along with her husband and with Stephenson, introduced the term *previllage*, but it failed to catch on in archaeology.

Coe's (1964) publication of his Carolina sequence has become the *bible* for Middle Atlantic and southeastern archaeology. It established point types in a chronological order that have withstood the test of time and are used exclusively as time markers and cultural indicators. The principal site was the Hardaway site, which carries the point name.

Figure 33 – Robert Stephenson and Lewis R. Binford at the 1975 Society for Historic Archaeology's 8th Annual Meeting in Charleston, South Carolina. Stephenson was responsible for the Accokeek site in Maryland's publication. Dr. Binford started his career in southern Virginia.

McNett (1979) at American University was influential in the archaeology of the MPRV; working with students and William Gardner of Catholic Univekrsity, his pottery studies helped establish ceramic sequences in the area. He was among the first to recognize the value of the computer in archaeology. Many of his students, including the author, spent many hours doing factor analyses on pottery rims.

MacCord's (1944 to 1996) investigations have contributed greatly to the understanding of MPRV prehistory (Figure 34). His Middle Atlantic area work, especially in Virginia, ranks among the best in American archaeology and has contributed tremendously to our understanding of MPRV prehistory. His work helped establish the Montgomery focus as a basic framework for MPRV prehistory. Additionally, he obtained a Virginia appropriation of $80,000 for analyses and publication of 50+ unreported sites during the last part of the 20th century. It became known as the ASV Backlog Project. For a site list, see Hranicky (1997).

Kinsey (1971) was among the first to publish arguments (pro and con) for establishing the Middle Atlantic Culture Area. This same year saw a meeting at American University, Washington, DC that started the Middle Atlantic Archaeological Conference (MAAC). It has met every year since.

Plate 3 shows three more early archaeologists working in the MPRV.

Charles (Buddy) W. Merry with his Collection in Rockville, Maryland (1990s)
He collected in Virginia and Maryland.

Figure 34 – Howard A. MacCord Washing Pottery. Photograph was taken in April 1969.

Text continued on page 32.

Charlie Merry with his collection after moving to Virginia
After his death, his son sold his collection; provenance was somewhat maintained.

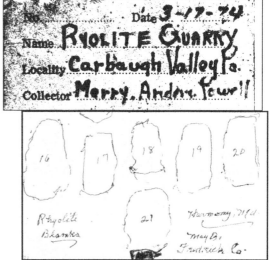
Sample of Charlie Merry's Notes

Plate 3 - From those yesterdays of MPRV archaeology....

Top: **Carl Manson** searching a Maryland cave on the Potomac River.
He is remembered for his work at the Marcy Creek site.

Photographs by Hugh V. Stabler (below, 50+ years later) who took them in the late 1940s.

Bottom: **Gates Slattery** and a FBI agent (name not known) shovel testing in a Maryland cave. He is remembered for his Montgomery Focus.

Hugh V. Stabler Showing Potomac Creek Site Beads (Shown in Text). His artifacts are used throughout this publication.

Broyles' (1971) publication on her work at the St Albans site in Kanawha County, West Virginia is a standard and is used for the MPRV (Figure 35). The work at the site was started in June 1964 and continued periodically to 1968. The St Albans bifurcate is named after the site; the bifurcate sequence of MacCorkle, St Albans, LeCroy, and Kanawha was established from the excavation.

Figure 35 – Bettye Broyles at the 1975 Society for Historic Archaeology's 8th Annual Meeting in Charleston, South Carolina. Broyles was the principal investigator at the St Albans site in Kanawha County, West Virginia. Her stratigraphic evidences set the cultural sequences for the Potomac River valley and the Middle Atlantic area.

Gardner (1978) introduced to the Cultural Resources Management (CRM) world the idea that floodplains were not the only place to look for sites (Figure 36). His *Idealized Transect* offered a new philosophy in determining cultural resources and their settlement patterns. His major contribution is the work at the Thunderbird site (Gardner 1974, 1977, 1983, and 1985).

Figure 36 – Richard J. Dent (American University) and William M. Gardner (Catholic University) at 2000 Eastern States Archeological Federation meeting at Solomons, Maryland

Numerous Ph.D. dissertations and Masters Theses from Catholic, American, and George Washington universities have made contributions to MPRV prehistory. They are quoted where appropriate and listed in the References section.

The Indian/archaeologists relationships in the Middle Atlantic area have always been excellent and cooperative (Figure 37). However, the profession must realize that archaeology in the 20th century was, for the most part, based on a white, male, middle class value system (Hranicky 2002a). Native American ways and support are very important to the 21st century archaeology. The archaeological profession needs to become more involved in Native American activities concerning their history; a mutual understanding of methods would be beneficial to both groups. The Native American oral histories and their application to archaeology are discussed throughout this publication. For an excellent discussion of Native American oral traditions, see Mason (2000).

Figure 37 – 1977 Photograph of Chief Turkey Tayac, formerly of the Piscataway and from Mechanicsville, Maryland, at the White House in Washington, DC. He always attended both Maryland and Virginia archaeological meetings and activities. He was a regular guest at the Annual Banquet of the Eastern States Archeological Federation. For tributes to him, see Jones (1966) and Hurley (1980). He is buried on the Accokeek site in Maryland.

Major MPRV Sites

The following list presents the major archaeological sites in the MPRV and a summary of the work performed on them. Naturally, other site work has been performed, but it is impossible to list all of them.

Accokeek Site (18PR8) – It is located on the Maryland side of the Potomac River near the creek and was occupied from the Archaic through Woodland Periods. It has Marcy Creek, Pope's Creek, Accokeek, Mockly, and Potomac Creek components, all of which reflect a Middle Atlantic seaboard cultural provenance (Stephenson, et al. 1963). Major point types are: Piscataway, Calvert, Vernon, and Clagett.

Catoctin Creek Site – It is located on the Virginia side of the Potomac River. It has yielded two fluted points, spokeshaves, back knife, side- and endscrapers, cores, cobble tools, and hammerstones (Dent 1991 and 1993). Materials were made from local jasper, which is probably from the Point-of-Rocks area.

Everhart Rockshelter Site (18FR4) – It is located five miles upstream from the Potomac River on the Catoctin Creek (Maryland) and represents an uplands focus. It was excavated by Geasey (1974) who found almost the complete range of prehistoric pottery.

Fisher Site (44LD4) – It is a palisaded village on the Potomac River near the mouth of Broad Run. The site was tested by Richard Slattery and Hugh Stabler in the 1930s and again by Howard MacCord and Jack Hranicky in 1983 (in Slattery and Woodward 1992). It yielded the Shepard variety of Albemarle pottery. Site dates around 700 BP. Figure 38 shows a modern reconstruction of a palisade.

Gore Site (18MO20) – Also known as the Walker site and Selden Island site No. 1, it presents evidence of palisading during the Late Woodland Period.

Figure 38 – Monacan Village Reconstruction at Natural Bridge, Virginia. It shows an example of a palisade for a village. Style dates approximately 1700 AD. Display is no longer maintained.

Hughes Site (18MO1) – Maryland site that has been heavily pot-hunted. It was excavated by Sterms (1940). It is a circular village with no palisade. It has shell tempered pottery that is similar to Keyser ware in the Luray Focus. Site dates around 1600 but has no trade goods.

More work has been performed at the site by Dent and Jirikowic (1999), who worked as the Potomac River Archaeological Survey at American University, Washington, DC. They re-excavated parts of the site during the 1990, 1991, and 1994 seasons.

Jeffrey Rockshelter (44LD17) – Site was excavated by ASV Northern Virginia chapter (1960s and 70s) under the direction of ASV past president Arthur Johnson. A published report can be found by Klein, et al. (1997), which is part of the ASV Backlog Project (Hranicky 1997), and senior thesis by Fischler (1978). It is probably the only MPRV site to produce a Hardaway-Dalton projectile point. Additionally, the site has a range of point types, Palmer, Kirk, LeCroy, MacCorkle, Stanly, Morrow Mountain, Brewerton, Lamoka, Orient, Meadowood, Otter Creek, Adena, Holmes, Koens-Crispin, Savannah River, Susquehanna, Snook Kill, Piscataway, Potts, Teardrop, Fox Creek, Levanna, and Madison. All of which make it one of the MPRV's s important lithic sites. It is also known as the Jeffrey-Harris Rockshelter.

Marcy Creek – It is an Early Woodland site located at the creek and the Potomac River. Excavated by Carl Manson (1948), it produced pottery that was tempered with steatite; initially called Washington steatite-tempered ware. The pottery is now called after the site and refers to the first pottery in the MPRV (Evans 1955). Pottery is followed by the Selden Island ware as defined by Slattery (1946).

Kerns Site (44CK3) – It is located in the Shenandoah Valley, but related to the Montgomery Focus of the MPRV (Slattery and Woodward 1992). It has the Levanna point type and produced excellent pipe examples.

Mason Island Site (18MO13) – It was tested by Kathryn A. Franklin and was reported to the Maryland Geological Survey in March 1974. It contained shell-tempered pottery which overlaid limestone and quartz tempered sherds. Below them were steatite-tempered pottery.

Plum Nelly (44NB128) – It was excavated by Stephen Potter (Potter 1982). It has an excellent range of projectile points from Savannah River to Levanna points.

Shepard Site (18MO3) – A published report is found in MacCord, Schmitt, and Slattery (1957). Initially, the site was known for its Shepard cord-marked pottery (Schmitt 1952); however, this became the Albemarle series (Evans 1955). Additionally, the site has numerous other pottery types. It was not palisaded and the village layout is circular. It contained a very good compliment of lithic artifacts, especially the Levanna projectile point.

Trittipoe Site (44LD10) – Site was excavated by the ASV Northern Virginia chapter (1968-70) and finally analyzed and published by Hranicky and MacCord (2000), which is part of the ASV Backlog Project (Hranicky 1997). It is a multicomponent site with major occupations attributable to the Montgomery and Mason Island focuses (800-400 BP). A large part of the site is extant, but is suffering from plowing. This site collection was used in this study.

Winslow Site (18MO9) – It was tested by Richard Slattery and Hugh Stabler during 1940-41. It contained Selden Island steatite- and sand-tempered pottery and Marcy Creek steatite-tempered pottery. It was one of the first sites to yield pottery data on vessel shape for the MPRV. Pots were round and pointed-base vessels. It established decorated clay pipes for the Early Woodland Period. It has large triangle points, which must be assigned to later Woodland periods. It has the Holmes point which may be attributed to the Early Woodland occupation.

Clark's Branch Site – a multicompenant site that is located on a narrow floodplain in Fairfax County. It has Potomac Creek pottery and a wide range of Archaic through Woodland projectile point (Inashima 2012). Figure 39 shows a small sample of the site's points. The site produced the following radiocarbon dates:

- Palmer (10,880-10,130 cal BP)
- LeCroy (9560-9030 cal BP)
- Fort Nottoway (10,230-9560 cal)
- St Albans (10,660-8770 cal BP)
- Hardaway (12,000-11,200 cal BP).

Figure 39 – Sample of Clark's Branch Points (After: Inashima 2012)

An excellent overview of some of these sites can be found in Slattery and Woodward (1992) and MacCord (1985). These sites are listed to show their importance in MPRV archaeology.

Current MPRV Research and Investigations

Like most areas of the U.S., the MPRV has offered archaeological investigations in response to growth and development of Potomac River cities. The area has been transformed from a generally rural to a specifically urban area. The MPRV is home to Washington, DC (a global city of importance) and as such, offers an excellent place to live and work, which causes a major increase in urbanization. This process threatens all prehistoric resources. Some sites are being saved by state and federal park agencies, but most sites are going to be destroyed by building projects within the next 20 years. The archaeological community must take action that is needed to gain as much artifactual evidence and data as possible before these sites are lost. Research and excavation can preserve this part of America's past. Also, large private prehistoric collections are disappearing. With farmers using no-till planting, field artifacts are not turning up as they did in the early days of collecting. As a consequence or benefit to archaeology, private collections are not being made, and even then, land becomes homesteads with no immediate artifact recovery for archaeology. Prehistoric knowledge increases are on hold.

Prehistoric Artifact Repositories

A major threat to Archaeological Resources Management (ARM) is the loss of private collections. An ARM can be established at local universities, museums, and/or archaeological agencies to receive and curate donated prehistoric artifact collections. It helps maintain local resources by keeping them in the area in which they were found. The MacCallum More Museum and Gardens in Case City, Virginia is an excellent example. The museum houses the prehistoric collection of Arthur Robinson, a founding father and past ASV president.

In addition to the Smithsonian Institution in Washington, DC, the Jefferson-Patterson is a major repository in the Potomac River valley. As mentioned, it was a major data/artifact source for this publication.

Figure 40 – Chipped Axe Copy of a Metal Axe. Metal tool technology did not transfer to Native American stone technology; thus, trade for metal tools became an important concern with the Native Americans.

End of Prehistory

While Captain John Smith's visit to the fall line of the Potomac River is the basis for ending MPRV prehistory, Native American relations during the 17th and early 18th centuries see a major technological adjustment in their toolkits. This publication does not address this aspect of history, only to offer someone's long-time ago attempt to bridge European technology with his Native American technology. Figure 40 shows a rhyolite axe that copies the European design; perhaps he was trying to borrow the efficiency of metal technology and, by magic, place it in Native American technology.

Copying metal technology in stone was common in the Middle Atlantic area. Eventually, European trade replaced this Native American practice with metal tools. See Hranicky (2002b) for a discussion on Native American toolmakers copying metal tools in stone. Arrowheads made from brass, iron, and glass also reflect this transition by the Native Americans.

As a side note about Virginia Native Americans, the Mattaponi have paid for over 350 years an annual tribute of pelts or game to Virginia's governor. Chief Custalow, at this writing, was 88 years young and had participated in the ceremony for 80 years. The Mattaponi 155-acre reservation is in King William County. The tribute is per Treaty and is in lieu of taxes – a worthy trade.

The Native American Stone Age ends with the so-called European invasion of new people, but more importantly, a new form of technology. Of course, there were other consequences of the culture conflicts and assimilations. Figure 41 shows the metal age of the bow and arrow. For a study of Contact research, see Hodges (1993). For studying metal tool usage by the Native Americans, the classic study *Metallic Implements of the New York Indians* by W. M. Beauchanys (1902). It is based on ethnographic examples and data.

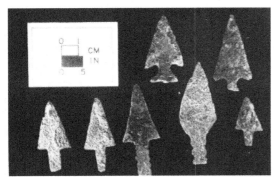

Figure 41 – Various North American Metal Arrowheads. Early metal arrowhead designs varied but were mainly influenced by the European makers who imposed their designs on the Native Americans.

This technology age for the Native American cultures is offered in Gilbert (1943):

Arrow pointing was done by cutting triangular bits of brass, copper, and bone and inserting them into the end of split-reed arrows. Deer sinew was wound around the split end and drawn through a small hole in the head and then the sinew was moistened. The wood of the bow was dipped in bear's oil and then fire seasoned. Bear's gut was used for the string.

Urban Archaeology in the MPRV

The MPRV is basically under asphalt - Washington, DC. Most of the area has seen prehistoric sites obliterated by urbanization. Road construction, housing developments, and high-rise office complexes have had a major impact on prehistoric archaeology. As an example of geography, Loudoun County, Virginia during the 1990s had a 100% growth in population, including housing, roads, etc. Within this century, most of the prehistoric sites will disappear; hopefully, they will receive archaeological investigations. One of the major highway projects is the building of a new Woodrow Wilson bridge across the Potomac River. Figure 42 shows a sample of artifacts that were recovered in testing for the bridge's impact on cultural resources. Figure 43 shows highschool students participating in the test excavation at Jones Point, Virginia. Numerous prehistoric sites were destroyed during the construction of the Capital Beltway. As for the rest of the MPRV area, farming has given way to housing projects and shopping malls. Like the Native Americans, prehistory has almost disappeared.

Figure 42 – Sample of Jones Point (Alexandria, Virginia) Artifacts. These artifacts were recovered during testing for the environmental assessment for the Woodrow Wilson bridge replacement on the Potomac River. The Federal Highway Administration and the Virginia Department of Transportation funded this project.

Living Archaeology

If archaeology is the dead space for storage of museum boxes, dust, and cobwebs, then why attempt to educate, inform, and keep the public alive with the romance of historical heritages and living histories? Because, archaeology is the only key to the past and artifact recovery gives an insight to the physical world of – long past peoples.

Figure 43 – Highschool Volunteers Screening at the Jones Point Excavation, Alexandria, Virginia. Student is holding an artifact that she found in screening. Photograph courtesy of the Alexandria Archaeology Museum, the Federal Highway Administration, and the Virginia Department of Transportation.

Archaeology provides the means for getting from the artifact to historical recreations regardless of whether they are in display cases or public enactments on the lawn of the museum. Reenactments are common place in America today because they permit the public to relive the past. This is called *living archaeology*, or perhaps living history. The difference between the two demonstrations is the science of archaeology versus the social nature of history books. Both have their values in presenting historical interpretation, but archaeology's methodology offers an objective approach to presenting the past; whereas, history is always a subjective presentation. Archaeological contexts are testable, historical contexts rely more on paper trails in archives, documents, and old books.

Another aspect of living archaeology is the study in nonliterate societies or so-called primitive societies. This study is partly possible in the U.S., but most Native American tribes have become modernized and only maintain cultural ways of dance, folklore, dress, and religion (Figure 44). Their technology has become totally a toolkit of metal tools. In this respect, the definition is:

> **Living Archaeology** - examining human behavior in relation to materials and material residues as a means of discovering relationships within contemporary societies that allow him/her to specify when and under what circumstances certain kinds of behavior may have been important in relation to overall processes of human adaptation (Gould 1980). Technique usually involves living in contemporary semi-prehistoric societies and studying their material usage and discard deposition. It is especially valuable in studying tool field conditions and usage. It is also called ethnoarchaeology.

Figure 44 – **Living Culture History as a Way of Life**. Dance by the Plains Native Americans at 1970s Smithsonian Folk Festival, Washington, DC. A premise of this publication is that the American prehistoric lithic tool continuum is based on Native American traditions.

Living archaeology is dependent on experimental archaeology and Native American traditions. This method involves taking actual (preferably excavated) artifacts (tools and implements) and replicating them, and finally, using replicated tools and testing them in living situations and environments pertaining to specific Native Americans and time periods. Once tested experimentally, tools can be used as authentic reproductions for actual demonstrations. The approach also includes the Native Americans' folklore, methods, and traditions for tool production and usage; the experimental factor becomes not only interesting, but also beneficial experiments in social interactions and processes. See Experimental Archaeology section for replication and reproduction methods.

As suggested above, living archaeology is a concern of this study; it is called experimental archaeology and provides insights into the Native Americans' actual stone tool usage. Or, as Gould (1980) states:

...the more clearly one can show the interrelatedness of human behavior to the biological and physical requirements for human life in any given area, the more securely one can make uniformitarian assumptions about that behavior, given similar circumstances, may have operated in the past...the ecological connection.

Collecting Prehistoric Artifacts

While a few (or most) professional archaeologists frown on the practice of privately collecting Native American artifacts, some find it a contribution to the study of prehistory. Recently, Gramly (1997) published prehistoric points from the Douglas Sirkin collection. The book shows some of the finest projectile points ever made by the Native Americans, but at the same time, most archaeologists would cringe at the thought that these museum quality specimens are not in the public realm. But, this collection has little consequence on the total artifact collection left behind by Native Americans. Any point in the collection can be replicated a thousand times over. What is important, the collection was published? Regardless of the consequences in and to American archaeology, private collections contain data and specimens that must be recorded and published (Figure 45).

Figure 45 – **Display Tray in the Arthur Robertson Collection now Housed at the MacCallum More Museum in Chase City, Virginia**. While popular in yesteryear, never glue artifacts to boards. Keep each artifact separately and mark it with its provenance.

When collectors maintain accurate records, report sites, and study local prehistory, their data and knowledge are beneficial; they save a lot of ground-walking field work for the professional archaeological community (Hranicky 1996 and 1989). If you collect, maintain your collection as if you have a scientific archaeological laboratory (Hranicky 1989); all archaeological data are important. Never dig in an archaeological site and report all your sites to the appropriate state agencies.

Too often, artifacts are maintained in paper bags or cigar boxes that causes damage to points. However, even then, there is still scientific data – but they are data only if reported to archaeologists who would record them.

Literally, tens of thousands of people have *a few* prehistoric Native American artifacts. The major problem is the after-life for the artifacts after the collector dies (Figure 46). It is amazing that Mother Nature can protect prehistoric artifacts for thousands of years, but humankind can destroy them in a few seconds. Some collectors' families try to place their collections in the public realm, but most collections are placed on the relic market. Always contact a professional archaeologist to examine your family's collection before disposing of it.

Figure 46 – Another Example of Artifact Storage. It is a home-made box probably dating prior to the 1930s (George Erwin Bray Collection, Northumberland County, Virginia).

Artifact Collections and their Impact on Archaeology

As mentioned, most archaeologists find little value or tolerance for collectors (Hranicky 1996). There is a fine line between picking up a random field-found artifact and a field-associated site artifact. If anyone digs in the above fields (into sites), there is no valid argument against site destruction, even if the land is privately owned. But one additional factor is a consequence of digging – the burial rights of Native Americans. The ethical question is: When do private property rights become an ethical (and moral) question in the American society? The overall justification is a simple one – any destruction of history (digging sites) is a violation of a society's right to its history. No private landowner has the right to allow the destruction of history by allowing nonscientific activities on private lands. The collector has a moral and ethical obligation to protect history. If site destruction is preform without regard to protecting history, then this activity becomes a criminal intent for personal gained and should merit a jail term. Without doubt from the author, any activity on Native American burial sites is a gross violation against humanity (Figure 47) – a time crime.

Ethnographic Data and Inferences

Ethnographic data come from people who first contacted and observed Native Americans and then wrote chronicles of their accounts. Based on these writings, we can recreate the social life-ways, world-views, traditions, and material culture of the Native Americans. Following a Panindian technological approach to prehistoric studies, we can reconstruct the societies that once inhabited the Potomac River valley. For an overview of the early ethnography, see Rountree (1989, 1990, and 1993). Where appropriate throughout the text, ethnographic sources and data are used. Early James River references also contribute to our understanding of MPRV Native Americans' prehistory (see Haile 1998).

Figure 47 – 1991 Owensboro Relic Show in Kentucky. Left: view of the showroom and display tables. Center; Native American protest for the show outside the show. Right: table display of complete pottery vessels that may have been illegally removed from mounds in the Mississippi River valley. There are too many unbroken specimens (assuming that they are not fakes). If true (most likely), are the Native Americans justified in protesting the show? As a note, the show organizer served time for digging on an Native American mound in Indiana. Regardless of the viewpoints, this is not American archaeology. The entire circumstances for relic shows and collectors who purchase prehistoric artifacts become a moral concern for the good of the American society.

Figure 48 – Chevron Bead (L = 48, D = 37 mm). It is in the George Erwin Bray Collection, Northumberland County, Virginia. It was a common trade bead of the Jesuit missionaries.

Occasionally, private collections contain unique and/or important ethnographic items. The chevron trade bead in Figure 48 may date 450 to 400 BP; it was found near the Potomac River in Northumberland County, Virginia. This trade bead type has been found in Contact sites of the Susquehannocks (Fogelman 1991 and Karklins 1982).

It has the classic 7 layers of color and 12 facets at the ends. It is one of the largest beads found in Virginia and probably indicates pre-Jamestown contact with the Potomac Native Americans. Unfortunately, there is no site context for the artifact. This bead form is still manufactured today; however, they generally are about a 1/2 inch (12 mm) in length. Even as a surface find, it still offers suggestions for field investigations – namely, early contact with Native Americans.

Expention (Expended)

If the reader checks his/her dictionary, the word **expention** is not found. Nevertheless, it is the process for a tool user when the tool is near or at the end of its lifecycle (Hranicky 2002a). Every culture has a process or set of procedures when a tool is to be discarded. The Native Americans knew when to throw away a tool and replace it with a new one. As a suggestion, the Paleoindian discarded Clovis points when the point's length was reduced to approximately 50 mm. Figure 49 shows an expended axe, but it could have been resharpened for more service. For axes and celts, broken (badly chipped) bits usually meant discard. Another example, the expention process for bifurcates is discard at 25 mm. Their expention process was to use the point until the blade was resharpened until no blade remained. Other point users had different lengths; for example, the Halifax point expention is approximately 35 mm. This assumption is - the *function of tool length* is a major aspect in this study of stone tools. We can assume:

1 – All tools have a length function that is relatable to workends
2 – All tool lengths are quantifiable
3 – All tool lengths have qualifying factors
4 – All tool lengths are subject to their industry
5 – All tool lengths have a relationship to workend angles
6 – All tool lengths are not necessarily intentional by the toolmaker
7 – When found, most tool lengths represent expention.

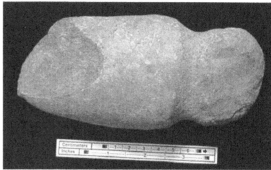

Figure 49 – Expended Axe. It has heavy bit damage, but could have been resharpened. The Native American elected to discard it because resharpening would have altered the cutting angle of the bit.

Tools were valuable assets in the Native American world. While misuse did occur, proper tool handling was directly related to raw material availability, skill and talent to make tools, expected tool longevity, and other factors; all of which were known to the Native Americans as part of their daily survival. As a focus of this perspective, this study offers examples for tools:

1 – Sourcing raw materials
2 – Function and structure
3 – Classification
4 – Maintenance
5 – Useability and lifecycles
6 – Expention.

Each of these focuses is discussed throughout the publication, and, constitutes the basis of the study collections and analyses.

MPRV Environment
(Native American Prehistoric Living Conditions)

No prehistoric society escaped its physical environment while it was living in it. Until the Late Archaic and Woodland Periods, Native Americans migrated from climate to climate and from physical geography to geography. Widespread nomadic migrations and short-term campsites were common throughout the East. After which, the MPRV saw relatively permanent populations. In addition to the Native American's adaptation to each environment, the climate and physical landscape were also changing through prehistory.

Nature's cycle goes on ... turkey vulture on the rockart boulder overlooking Difficult Run in Virginia.

As an archaeological consequence (or challenge), these various human conditions on the various landscapes present archaeologically a 10,000-year+ occupation for investigation, study, and analysis in order to produce a Native American history. These various environmental conditions are classified as research factors, and while they differ all over the U.S., there are commonalities in archaeological research that are used throughout the discipline. The environment is presented as a controlling ecology that varied throughout the total human occupation.

This section provides an overview of the MPRV's physical environment that existed from the Paleoindian to Woodland Periods. It includes the geology, especially lithic resources, and biology, especially edible foodstuffs and material used for general habitation, and finally, climate for living conditions during all archaeological periods. All these factors affected lithic technology that was used by the pre-Contact Native Americans. Where appropriate, or where data are available, all tool discussions are viewed in an ecological setting of the MPRV.

Environment

An abiotic framework is needed to describe and interpret the various prehistoric cultures that lived in the MPRV area. This section attempts such a presentation which combines natural resources and their human usage. As a focus, the living resources (aquatic, terrestrial, and human) had a spatial organization that was imposed by natural events, such as climate, edible foodstuffs, resources, and their availability. The framework includes surficial and bedrock geology, topography, vegetation, soils, and wildlife. The use of resources and the dispersion of effluents' natural processes define the quality and viability of the lifestyle(s) among the MPRV inhabitants. The MPRV was a frontier that unfolded to the Native Americans that started as uninhabited geography and climaxed in territories that were known to specific groups. This occupation represents a sustained use of natural resources by the Native Americans for over 10,000 years.

Looking at the MPRV's geology over the last 10,000+ years, many aspects of it are relatively constant, such as minerals and hydrology, while other factors, such as game, climate, and landscape, have changed over time.

When the human element is superimposed on this environment, social/material change basically comes as:

1 – New populations moving into it

2 – Political/religious factors adjust to their cognitive perception of a changing environment

3 – Physiological consequences caused by a changing environment, namely foodstuff and temperature.

In most cases, number 2 overcame pressures or causes from environmental changes – probably best described as a psychic-unity modification for a society. Regardless of the social adjustments, social/religious properties in artifact changes are very difficult to see archaeologically. Each of the above factors is used throughout this publication with the environmental approach being the dominant analytical form. These social/religious factors are discussed where appropriate, or most likely, when data are available.

Plate 4 – MPRV Rhyolite Projectile Points
Charles W. Merry Collection
Rockville, Maryland

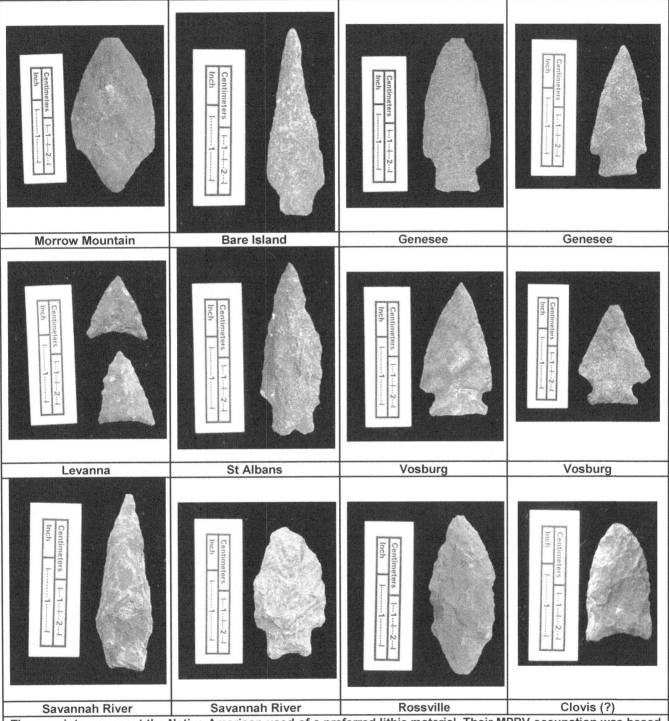

Morrow Mountain	Bare Island	Genesee	Genesee
Levanna	St Albans	Vosburg	Vosburg
Savannah River	Savannah River	Rossville	Clovis (?)

These points represent the Native American used of a preferred lithic material. Their MPRV occupation was based on this aspect of the Potomac River valley's natural resources. While predominant during certain time periods, rhyolite was not the only stone that was utilized. Other groups preferred quartzite, quartz, and jasper for their microtools.

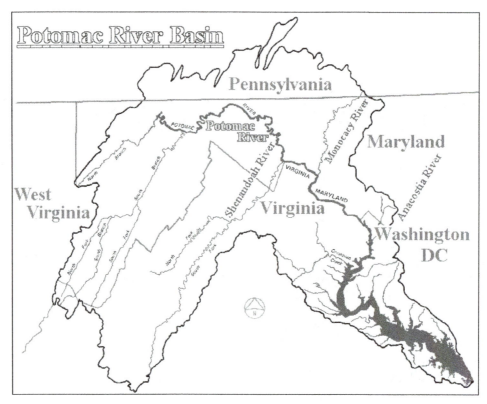

Figure 1 – Map of the Potomac River Basin. It shows the MPRV Watershed.

As an example of MPRV stone usage, projectile points from the Charles Merry collection are shown in Plate 4. These points are from Loudoun County, Virginia and Montgomery County, Maryland. They are made from MPRV rhyolite and date from the Late Archaic through Woodland Periods. Other rhyolite points and bifaces are shown throughout this publication.

The use of an environmental approach is not a recent method of investigation and analysis in archaeology. Gilbert (1943) in his study of Eastern Cherokees comments:

The natural environment of a people is divisible into several sets of influences, depending on the type of material concerned. The terrain, climate, minerals, plants, and animals are all conceivable as types of unified influences helping to give order to a people's culture. The factors arising from the terrain comprise such characteristics as the surface configuration of the land, the distribution of surface water in rivers, lakes, or ponds, the sites of settlements, trails, and the human orbit of activities.

Two approaches are used to describe the Native American habitation of the MPRV, which are:

1 – Ecoscene (ecoregion) approach, in which the MPRV is delineated as a geography that has similarity of geology, climate, soils, biota, and hydrology.

2 – Watershed approach, in which the ecoregion is delineated as a hydrologic system that has physical boundaries; a natural drainage system from tributaries to streams to rivers. In this case, the Potomac River is a subsidiary of the Chesapeake Bay drainage system.

While not presented as a model per se, this study is based on Bormann and Likens' long-term Hubbard Brook Ecosystem Study (Bormann and Likens 1994), geophysical applications (as in Boyce-Ballweber 1988), and environmental archaeology (as in Butzer 1971). It offers a contrast to the traditional settlement pattern methods in archaeology in that resources, not the physiography (see Meggers 1954), determine human behavior and occupation. The sociopolitical structure in a society governs its resource utilization. The basic assumption for the MPRV is that everything the Native Americans needed was available to them.

Holocene: Its Beginning

Until recently with the discovery of pre-Clovis sites in the eastern Atlantic seaboard, the need to know the beginning of the Holocene has not been a factor in eastern archaeology. For many scholars, such as Martin and Klein, et al. (1984), the beginning of the Holocene is the end of the Pleistocene, or quite generally, 11,000 BP (Wendland 1974). This date generally coincides with Clovis technology, but Clovis does not constitute the beginning of the Holocene. Other geological factors are more important, namely climate. Butzer (1971) suggests that the Llano tradition, dating 11,600-10,900 BP, reflects a shift from hunting mammoth to bison, which is contemporary with the Valders readvance in glaciation; the subsequent Folsom dates to the subsequent retreat. These dates are marking a climatical change, which if only for the West, marks the beginning of the Holocene. Can these dates be used in the East, or for that matter, worldwide? The answer is yes. Additionally, the Holocene, not the Pleistocene, was responsible for agriculture and animal domestication; although, it would take many thousands of years before the Native Americans would discover it.

Using oxygen isotopes trapped in the ice on Greenland, world-wide climate conditions can be calculated. The Pleistocene has ending dry-warm and dry-cold fluctuations around 11,000 BP, but this time period marks a decrease in $*^{18}O$ which is correlated with the Younger Dryas of northern Europe and in a study of oxygen isotypes in the Gulf of California (Haynes 1993). The Holocene begins at 10,750 +50 –150 years BP (Stromberg 1985).

MPRV Area

Figure 1 shows the Potomac River Basin watershed area. It includes the Shenandoah, Monocacy, Occoquan, and Anacostia Rivers. For West Virginia, it includes the North and South Branches of the Shenandoah River. The MPRV is defined as the area lying between the confluence of the Shenandoah and Occoquan Rivers. Ecologically, the MPRV ecoscenes are defined here as a piedmont environment that consists of low rolling hills, grasslands, and forest, depending on the geological time table for the area. Basically, MPRV lies between the erosional mountains and depositional plains of Maryland and Virginia. While predominantly piedmont, the MPRV is divided, as in Kroeber (1939), into these geological (ecoscenes) divisions that are classified as:

1 – Coastal plain (lowlands)
2 – Piedmont
3 – Ridge and valley (Uplands).

Note: Schmitt (1952) referred to the area west of the fall line as being a mountain provenance, but this has generally been replaced by an upland focus.

Each of these environments is used in the Projectile Point and Miscellaneous Tools/Implements sections to describe the general operating environment of the point or tool. The Great Valley between the Valley and Ridge and Blue Ridge provenances is classified here as an upland environment. The general MPRV environment is a temperate climate with yearly temperate averages being comfortable in which societies can easily survive. Of course, climate varied throughout antiquity.

As a watershed focus, the Potomac River is the *main street* of the MPRV with the Shenandoah, Monocacy, and Anacostia Rivers being major tributaries. The Anacostia River focus is not well defined here because of its high occupation in the 20th century – few fields near the Potomac River junction could be collected. The Monocacy River occupations provide the majority of the artifacts in this study. This river junction includes the Virginia side of the river.

The use of a watershed approach depended on extensive data of the drainage and/or estuary complexes. High topographic relief combined with shallow, impervious bedrock formations make the MPRV an excellent area for this type of study. The correlations between nutrients and sediments with respect to Native American land uses, rock types, and living resources can be composed into a habitation (not settlement) model. In other words, with all resources available, sites can be located anywhere, except for the usual restrictions for water access. Artifact distributions can be correlated to watershed drainage patterns; especially where water resources are utilized. However, this scope is beyond this study. As a start, see Langland, et al. (1995).

Surface collections lend themselves to studies of land use via watersheds. Most MPRV sites are located within 1000 meters of the river/stream ways in the Potomac River valley. More surface data are needed to determine actual waterway usage; however, for most tool industries, they are found in the entire MPRV watershed.

The MPRV watershed provided canoe transportation systems as the Potomac River was a connection to both the uplands (especially to the Ohio River valley) and lowlands (especially to coastal areas in the upper Southeast). Technology follows riverways, which can be used as technology focuses in prehistory, for example, the Mississippi, Ohio, Missouri Rivers and more regionally, the James, Susquehanna, and Potomac Rivers. Any particular location can be viewed as microtechnology centers which practice some or all parts of the Panindian technology. For the Woodland/Mississippian late periods, watersheds became the domain of political centers. Riverways were probably not a major factor during the Paleoindian Period; their focus was open grasslands. For the Archaic Period, the East was more of an intra-riverways system of population movement. For the Woodland, the rivers become basic (nonmigration) centers for habitation.

The ecoscene and watershed approach is used here to analyze the MPRV's humans and their artifact distributions. The MPRV is treated as a ground metrics of stream, trail, and river courses for Native American usage and settlement. This focus includes intraregional pathways. When mixed with natural resource procurement, the occupation becomes a social/physical network, which allowed survival by working any area, not just floodplains. The so-called floodplain models generally incorporate settlement exceptions, such as quarry sourcing, terrace or inland occupations, or political boundaries. This approach is hampered by the lack of stratigraphic site data in this study.

Ecologically, the MPRV's fall line divides the area into: 1) eastern deciduous forest and 2) coastal plain grasslands, forest, and marshes. The following offers a brief discussion of inorganic and organic factors as they apply to human habitation.

The main lithic focus of the MPRV environment is the cultural use of rhyolite and minor, but for the early time period, is the use of jasper. Quartzite is the secondary focus, especially for the Middle and Late Archaic Periods.

MPRV Geology

The MPRV geological formations are divided broadly into:

1 – Unconsolidated formations
2 – Carbonate formations
3 – Siliciclastic formations
4 – Crystalline formations.

Each formation is a factor in MPRV lithic analyses and is used where appropriate in lithic sources. Table 1 presents the lithic composition of the river basin. While the Native Americans did not utilize all of the MPRV's lithic materials, many of them were used in their technology. The table is based mainly on USGS (1967) and includes references quoted in the table. The MPRV geology was exploited for stones which were used for both microtools and macrotools. Another aspect of MPRV geology is soils that played a factor during the Woodland Period's horticulture technology. We might assume that village life was a result of living in a forested environment; naturally, the shift to a cooler climate was a factor.

Table 1 – MPRV Lithography *			
Material or Formations	**MRPV Distribution**	**Artifacts**	**Comments**
Biotite-quartz-feldspar gneiss	Uplands, piedmont	Bannerstones	Rarely used.
Amphibolite, epidote, and metamorphosed gabbro	Uplands	Axes	It was a popular stone in the American Southwest, but was rarely used in the East.
Layered gneiss	Piedmont	Pottery	Shows up in tempering.
Gabbro	Uplands	Axes	
Diorite, quartz, and gabbro	Uplands, piedmont	Axes Points	White quartz is a common projectile material.
Diabase	Uplands	Axes Hammerstones Mauls.	After greenstone, this was the most common stone for heavy duty macrotools.
Quartz	Uplands, piedmont, tidewater	Points Pottery temper	Colors are white, rose, and clear.
Quartzite (Also, Prelnite)	Uplands, piedmont, tidewater	Points	Major stone for Archaic projectile points.
Granitic rocks	Uplands	Axes	
Serpentinite	Piedmont	Not observed.	No evidence of usage, but bannerstones and pipes are possible.
Steatite, and ultramafic rocks	Uplands, piedmont	Vessels Pottery, Bannerstones	Beginning focus for pottery.
Anorthosite	Uplands		No evidence of usage.
Quartzite, w/bedded conglomerate, schist, and gneiss	Uplands, piedmont		Generally, not used, but pendants occur.
Marble, crystalline limestone, and dolomite	Uplands, piedmont	Gamestones, Magicstones Pottery Whetstone	Limestone used as temper and whetstones.
Coarse- and fine-grain mica schist and mica gneiss	Uplands, piedmont	Pottery	Used in form of clays containing schist.
Fine-grain mica schist, chlorite schist, and phyllite w/bedded quartzose rocks	Piedmont	Pottery, Pipes Bannerstones	Used in form of clays containing schist.
Gneiss and schist, massive and granitic in appearance	Piedmont	Bannerstones	Usually well made; appearance is a factor.
Argillite, siliceous shale, slaty shale, slate, phyllite.	Uplands, piedmont	Knives Gorgets	Good cutting shears.

Greenstone and green schist	Uplands, piedmont	Axes Celts	Most common material for macrotools.
Volcanic rocks	Uplands	Axes Celts	Hardstone preference.
Sandstone and shale	Piedmont	Abraders Gorgets	Some usage as knives and projectile points.
Conglomerate	Piedmont	Points	Rarely used.
Red shale	Piedmont	?	Not used, no explanation; red shale areas are void of artifacts and sites.
Mudstone	Piedmont, tidewater		Rarely used.
Red sandstone, shale, and conglomerate	Piedmont		Generally, not used.
Basaltic rocks	Uplands	Axes, Bannerstones	After greenstone, it is common for axes.
Clay	Uplands, piedmont, tidewater	Pottery Polishing materials Paints	Basic material for pottery. It is used for abrasive actions.
Metagraywacke	Uplands and piedmont	Clays for pottery	Not a preference.
Magnitite	Uplands and piedmont	Red paint (?)	Probable usage.
Chalcopyrite	Piedmont	Blue paint (?)	Probable usage.

*Geology based on: Jonas and Stose (1938), Jonas (1928), Hopson (1964), Cloos and Cooke (1953), Cloos and Broedle (1940), Calver (1963), Orndroff, Epstien, McDowell (1999), Drake, Southworth, and Lee (1999), Fleming, Drake, and McCartan (1994), Southworth (1991, 1994, and 1995), and USGS (1967).

MPRV Geologic Summaries

The following paragraphs present an overview of the physical world that the Native Americans lived-out in MPRV prehistory. These summaries present the area as it existed from Late Archaic to Contact. In other words, its prehistoric view is much like it was today. However, prior to this woodland eoscene, the MPRV area was a grassland with minor occurrences of wooded areas. These two eoscenes generally represent a nomadic versus sedentary way of pre-Contact life in the MPRV. We might assume that village life was a result of living in a forested environment; naturally, the shift to a colder climate was a factor

Overview of Basic Geological Settings

For the Potomac River valley, geological structures are:

1 – Alluvial - deposits which were transported by flowing water. For the MPRV, this is a factor below the fall line. This was a factor for the Woodland Period, namely soils for horticulture. It is a factor in the entire MPRV floodplain.

2 – Eolian - wind blown dunes and loess. This is a coastal factor and does not apply directly to the MPRV. This factor is the key to understanding deposition at Cactus Hill site in southern Virginia.

3 – Spring - sediments accumulate at the point where groundwater emerges. It is primarily an upland factor and remains to be studied archaeologically for the MPRV. Springs do occur in the MPRV Piedmont and Uplands areas.

4 – Lacustrine - sediments in and around standing bodies of water such as swamps, lakes, and bogs. It is a factor in the Potomac estuary, especially at junctions of streams below the fall line. It is a factor in riverine occupations during the Late Archaic and Woodland Periods.

5 – Culluvial - sediments are deposited by gravitational actions in uplands and mountainous areas. It is based on slopes and is more of a consequence in water runoffs than rock movement in the MPRV. Igneous rocks are factors in macrotool production and tool usage; their source is always the uplands.

6 – Glacial - sediments are not present in the MPRV, but are present in areas to the north of the MPRV. Permafrost limits are MPRV factors for the Paleoindian Period.

7 – Rockshelter - sediments transported by water and gravity that were trapped in rock overhangs, eaves, and shelters. Shelter utilization is a major factor during the Paleoindian and Early Archaic Periods, but they were *livable* throughout prehistory (Figure 2). Shelters were occupied during the Early Woodland, but habitation starts towards village sites after this period. The Clipper Mill Road Rockshelter in Baltimore County offers evidence of this type of occupation sequence (Isreal 1998). Shelter

occupation is not common during the Middle Archaic Period. Neidley (1996) provides a study of three Goose Creek rockshelters in Virginia.

8 – Coastal - sediments accumulated by wave and tidal actions along shores (also, alluvial deposits in coastal plains). It is a factor in areas below the MPRV fall line, especially for Woodland Period people and their needs for resources, namely salt.

Each of these structures goes into the various makeups of the MPRV ecoscenes; where appropriate, they are discussed in text as factors in lithic technology and human adaptive processes.

Figure 2 – Rockshelter at the Little Catoctin Creek Rhyolite Area of Frederick County, Maryland (see Geasey and Ballweber 1992). Most of the excavated biface-points were made of rhyolite.

Lithic Materials

Raw materials are the key to understanding the MPRV settlement and the understanding of natural (flora and fauna) elements, and cultural/social (lifeways) of people who settled pre-Contact times. The economy was based on local materials to meet needs of toolmaking as it affects the total society. Obviously, this focus cannot be applied to all people who have lived in the MPRV because of differing technological organizations. However, rhyolite and quartzite usage are in essence – a form of lithic determinism. Answers to why these materials, especially rhyolite, remain for future studies and will not be attempted here. But, did lithic materials draw the inhabitants into the MPRV?

Raw materials according to Meeks (2000):
Because both the availability and accessibility of lithic raw materials determine the types of tools that can be produced within the constraints of a lithic technology, the basis for understanding the potential effects of raw material costs on the use and function of stone tools requires an understanding of the lithic resources that were both potentially exploitable as well as those that were utilized by a population. That is, the reconstruction and explanation of any aspect of a given technological system cannot be divorced from the role of lithic raw materials within the system, for stone provides the medium from which materials may have had on stone function, technological strategies, and raw material utilization has only recently been explored in any detail.

Lithic material definitions are based on the geology of the MPRV and pertain to tools found in the area. Occasionally, tools made from different materials were made elsewhere and carried into the MPRV. For example, Ohio gray flints are sometimes found in the MPRV. However, the overall toolmakage is from local materials. The major sources are river cobbles that are transported downstream by the Potomac River, and various outcrops that were quarried by the Native Americans for tool materials.

Attempts at defining geological stones are not new in archaeology as Howell's (1939) **Comment Concerning Certain Mineralogical Terminology** offers an early attempt at standardizing stone definitions. Lithic terminology is found in Hranicky (2002).

The following is a summary of the major stone types used in this study. Lithic identification is based on crystal structure and size (Figure 3). With electronic microscopes, lithic structure is readily viewable.

Microtool Lithography

For small tools, the Native Americans used the following stones in the MPRV area. These stones are used throughout the publication and in the Projectile Points section.

Agate (Onyx) = Varieties: sardonyx, onyx, careolonyx. Quartz group. Hardness 7. Specific gravity 2.5-2.7. Color variable. Opaque. Dull sheen or matte. Flat conchoidal fracture. On a fractured or polished surface horizontal or concentric lines of different colors visible. Texture sometimes mossy. No jointing. Sharp, thin edges in fracture. Latent fibrous crystalline structure under microscope. It is common in early and late prehistory.

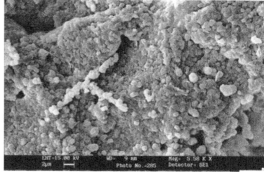

Figure 3 – Crystal Structure of Quartzite

Argillite = Clastic sedimentary rock. Rock that consists of particles that are between particles for shale and slate. It has some recrystalline, is usually coarse grain, and does not have good cleavage (Figure 4). Colors are gray, black, red, or green. Argillite is not used here because of its difficulty of distinguishing it from rhyolite (see Didier 1975). Like rhyolite, it has numerous descriptions in the geological literature. The material tends to be a coastal formation.

Figure 4 – Argillite Examples from Frederick County, Maryland.

Chalcedony = Varieties: chrysoprase, carnelian, quartzite, and sapphirine. Quartz group. Hardness 7. Specific gravity 2.5-2.65. Color variable: white, tan, yellow, brown, blue. Opaque, thin section transparent. Edge in fracture very sharp and thin. No jointing. Latent fibrous crystalline structure under microscope. It is common in eastern Paleoindian, and used throughout the Early Archaic. Based on the study collections, it probably has an uplands focus (Figure 5). Chalcedony is rare in the MPRV, but points and implements made from it are usually well made.

Figure 5 – Big Sandy Point Made from Chalcedony. It is a thin, well-made point. The nomenclature for this type is discussed in the Projectile Point section. Above is a curve (20 mm) also made from chalcedony. Its purpose is unknown.

Chert = Quartz group. Hardness 7.0-6.0. Contains structural impurities. Green to gray in color. Fracture rough conchoidal, rough flakes. Flakes tend to be smaller than flint because of its structure. Used throughout the U.S. prehistory. It is found as nodules in limestone.

Felsite - see Rhyolite.

Flint = Quartz group. Hardness 7. Specific gravity 2.37-2.67. Besides SiO_2 (95%) contains traces of sand, clay, and other materials. Black, tan, or brown color. Opaque. Conchoidal fracture. Dull or greasy sheen in fracture. Flint can be subdivided into: 1) opal-chalcedony (gezites), 2) chalcedony (silexes), 3) quartz-chalcedony flints (silexites), and 4) fresh-water flints produced in gypsums. The best flaking flints have a chalcedony relationship. Chalk flints were used in the Old World Paleolithic and Neolithic. Major U.S. types are Mercer, Flint Ridge, Dover, and Edwards. Both gray and black flint colors occur in the MPRV.

Jasper = Quartz group. Hardness 6.6-6.0. Contains 70-73% pure quartz with the remainder being clay and iron oxides (hematite) which give it color. Yellow, white, brown, red, green, and gray colors. Fracture is rough conchoidal, matte surface. Flakes irregular as compared to flint. It is used throughout the U.S. prehistory. Note: Jasper outcrops did occur at Point of Rocks, Maryland; however, they disappeared due to urbanization. Jasper tends to be a Paleoindian material and is not common in the MPRV.

Limonite = Also bog iron and ironstone. Porous sedentary stone containing iron oxide. It is principally a northeast stone; several specimens were observed in the MPRV. For a study of this stone, see Ward (1988).

Quartz Crystal = Quartz group. Hardness 7. Specific gravity 2.5-2.8. Watery transparent in color. Glassy luster. Fracture flat conchoidal. Ill-knit jointing. Brittle. Crystalline forms, hexagonal terminating in hexagonal pyramids. Large crystals occur in rock fissures or on surface. Used in all prehistoric periods. Impure specimens occur, such as gray (smoky) and rose quartz. Milky, rose, amethyst, and smoky quartz do not have well-developed crystals. Quartz crystal artifacts occur, but the most common quartz form is white quartz. Clear quartz microtools are rare in the MPRV, but in southern Virginia, the use is not uncommon (Figure 6).

Figure 6 – Clear Quartz Points from Southeastern Virginia (Formerly Floyd Painter Collection). All are early points with right two points being Hardaway and Dalton points, respectively.

Quartzite = Quartz group (silicified sandstone). Hardness 7. Specific gravity 2.5-2.8. Gray, black, tan, brown, and white colors. Dull, glassy luster. Rough conchoidal fracture. Fracture surface granular, slightly lumpy. Quartzite is a metamorphosed sandstone. Frequently the individual grains of sand have been cemented by the introduction of secondary silica, producing a rock stronger than the original. While rare in Paleoindian times, it is frequently used for knives and other microtools, especially in the Late Archaic Period. Quartzite for this study is named after the Weverton formation; it is a light tan granular rock. Quartzite tends to be a Middle through Late Archaic Period material.

Obsidian = Not found in the MPRV. It is mentioned because of it occurring in the East (for Virginia, see McCary 1968 and for New Jersey, see Bello and Cresson 1998).

Rhodolite = Reddish-brown quartzite-like material that comes from North Carolina and upper Maryland. Few specimens were observed and because of difficulty identifying it, the stone type was not used.

Rhyolite = Quartz group. Hardness 6.3-6.7. Specific gravity 3.1-3.3. Green, gray, and black colors. It is classified here as a cryptocrystalline stone with excellent workability for microtools. Fracture surface is granular. It has smaller grain structure than quartzite. Rhyolite tends to be Late Archaic through Early Woodland Period material. Depending on the geological expert, there are five to nine varieties in the East. The principal locations are Massachusetts, Pennsylvania, Maryland, Virginia, and North Carolina.

Macrotool Lithography

For large tools in the MPRV, the Native Americans used the following stones. These stones are used throughout the publication and in the Miscellaneous Tools/Implements section.

Andesite = Mesocratic with an aphanitic-porphyritic texture. Colors are brown, greenish, and dark gray. Hardness is 5.0-6.0. After basalt, andesite is the most abundant volcanic rock. It usually has phenocrysts. Material is not well identified in the East.

Basalt = Pyroxene group. Hardness 6-6.5. Specific gravity 2.6-3.11. Black or dark gray color. Dull sheen. Rough or uneven fracture. Basalt is a very fine-grained, dark-colored igneous rock consisting essentially of plagioclase feldspar and augite. Basalt and other similar fine-grained, dark-colored, igneous rocks are known commercially as *trap*. It is frequently used for macrotools, especially for hammerstones.

Chlorite = Group name. Hardness is 2.0 – 2.5, cleavage is perfect, specific gravity is 2.6 to 3.3, fracture is scaly, earthy, not elastic, is transparent to translucent, and color is green, black, and pearly. Generally, chlorite only occurs in bannerstones.

Conglomerate = Similar to sandstone in origin and composition, but is made up of cemented gravel, pebbles, and even large boulders instead of sand. It is sometimes used for high-quality (ceremonial) macrotools.

Diabase = Igneous rock that is dark in color from orangish brown to blackish-brown. Upland forms are grayish brown. Texture is porphyritic. Its chemistry is mafic. Its main eastern formation is the Triassic basin in Pennsylvania and New Jersey; it occurs in MPRV sills and dikes. Diabase is common in heavy-duty hammerstones; it is a rare material for MPRV axes.

Diorite (greenstone) = Feldspar group. Hardness 6-5.5.0. Specific gravity 2.8-2.85. Contains little or no quartz and is 75% feldspar with hornblende and sometimes mica. Gray, green, and brown colors. Conchoidal fracture and rough surface with fine or small grains. It is a major stone for American macrotools.

Gabbro = Pyroxene group. It is mafic; melanocratic with a texture similar to granite. Colors are dark green, dark gray, and almost black. Texture is phaneritic; structure is massive but may exhibit a layered structure. Hardness is above 5.5. It is not common in the continental crust, but large exposures occur in Minnesota.

Gneiss = Crystalline, more or less banded rock formed from granite or related rocks by intense pressure and heat. This process is known as *metamorphism*. It is sometimes used for bannerstones.

Granite = Quartz or feldspar group. Hardness 6.0-6.5. Specific gravity 2.5. Fracture surface granular. It is commonly phaneritic, medium-to-coarse, occasionally porphyritic with phenocrysts of well-formed crystals of potash feldspars. Granite is an igneous, completely crystalline rock of fairly uniform texture, containing distinctly visible grains. It consists essentially of quartz and feldspar, but also usually contains mica or hornblende and numerous minor accessory minerals. The texture varies from fine to coarse grained. It is frequently used for macrotools.

Note: Granite is commonly used as a collective term for a number of related leucocratic, plutonic rocks that have similar chemical and mineralogical compositions, such as syenite, monzonite, pegmatite, and granodiorite.

Hornfel = Dense, granoblastic material. It is very compact and massive which fractures with a splintery to conchoidal fracture. Colors are dark gray to black, has a dull luster, and hardness is 6.0-7.0. It is a metamorphism of argillaceous sediments. Hornfel weathers quickly, even Woodland Period points do not show flake scars. It is poorly identified for Middle Atlantic area tools; more data are needed.

Limestone = When pure, it consists of calcium carbonate. It often grades into dolomite (calcium-magnesium carbonate) and also usually contains more or fewer impurities such as sand and clay. Sometimes the structure of shells and other marine organisms from which the limestone was derived is more or less preserved in the limestone. It is frequently used for abraders and polishers. It is also used for temper in pottery.

Marble = Crystalline rock formed by the metamorphism of limestone or dolomite. It is sometimes used for ceremonial implements.

Peridotite = Quartz or feldspar group. It is leucocratic with an uneven granular, coarse-grained structure. Colors are variable, but it is similar to granite. It has a glassy luster. It occurs below the surface and is not common except where rivers have cut deep into the bedrock. Hardness is approximately 6.0.

Quartzite = see Microtool Lithography.

Sandstone = Sedimentary rock consisting essentially of grains of quartz sand, cemented more or less firmly together with clay, silica, calcium carbonate, or iron oxide. Sandstones with a silica cement are usually the strongest and most desired for structural purposes. Some sandstones also contain feldspar (arkose) and mica. It is frequently used for abraders and polishers. In the Northeast, barstones were made from sandstone; however, igneous rocks were the preferred material.

Schists = Finely banded, foliated metamorphic rocks. In the MPRV, it contains mica. It is rarely used; however, ornamental objects are made from it.

Shale = Quartz group. Hardness 4.5-5.5. Specific gravity 3.1-3.5. Colors are brown, gray, and tan. It is a fine-grain material. Fracture surface is granular. It is common in the southeast Atlantic coast and was used throughout prehistory.

Slate = Fine-grain metamorphic rock characterized by one-directional cleavage, varied colors, and a variety of chemical compositions. It often contains mica, chlorite, quartz, hematite, and rutile. Colors are gray, red, green, purple, yellowish brown, and buff. Luster varies from dull to highly micaceous. Specific gravity is 2.7 or 2.8.

Steatite (Talc) = Soft massive rock of which the chief mineral component is talc. It is also called soapstone. Colors are greenish gray, gray white, gray black, and brown. Hardness is 1.0 to 3.5. Specific gravity is 2.6 to 2.8. Luster is greasy to pearly. Cleavage in crystalline varieties. Fracture is irregular and tenacity is sectile to nearly brittle. Transparency is translucent to opaque. It always feels greasy. Steatite is the material used for Late Archaic – Early Woodland Period bowls and pipes. For a steatite irradiation study, see Truncer (1989).

Syenite = Quartz or feldspar group. It is leucocratic with a phaneritic texture. Colors are pink, white, light gray, pale green, and pale brown. Hardness is 5.5-6.0. It is similar to granite but has little quartz in it. It sometimes occurs adjacent to limestone masses.

Trachyte = Quartz or feldspar group. It is leucocrative with mostly light-colored minerals as phenocrysts. Hardness is 5.5-6.0. Fractures by splitting easily. It is formed when magma of syenitic composition is erupted as a lava flow; rapid cooling accounts for the development of small crystals. Colors are light-to-medium gray, pink, green, or tan; occasionally dark gray.

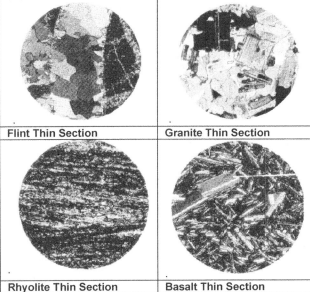

Figure 7 – Geological Thin Section Examples. Thin sections provide visual inspections of stone composition which, with practice, can be used to identify stones, and in some cases, source the materials.

Thin Sections of Geology Specimens

The preparation of microscopic thin sections for lithic materials used by the Native Americans has not received wide-spread attention in the archaeological community. The method allows actual observation of the physical structure of stones' crystal structures. Some experimentation with the technique was performed, but this study relies on irradiation of samples for chemical analyses and general geologic methods for identifying stones. Use of thin section lithic interpretations needs more study for the method to become a practical application in American archaeology. Figure 7 shows thin sections of major MPRV materials. Thin sections of lithic materials should be a standard practice for local or riverine prehistoric archaeology. If performed and catalogued, visual inspection of lithic materials would lead to better geologic assessments of archaeological materials. Petraglia (1994) makes excellent use of the method in his study of quartzite. As has been argued, lithic classification is still the cornerstone of archaeological methodology (Odell 1981 and Andrefsky 1998). As a rule, thin sections offer visual differences among stones which at least causes the archaeologists to note stone differences, such as argillite and rhyolite have different grain structures.

Lithic thin sections provide a visual inspection of:

1 – Knapper's choice of materials
2 – Stone identification in toolmaking areas of a site
3 – Inter- and intrasite stone comparisons
4 – Visual records of site stones.

Figures 8a and 8b provide graphics example of quartzite and rhyolite samples. A thin section catalog for various archaeological regions needs to be started. This practice is well established in geology.

Lithic composition within a geological formation may vary within a few meters; as such, lithic thin sections should be used cautiously.

Figure 8a – Quartzite Thin Section. It is basically a sandstone that has been converted into solid quartz rock. When struck, quartzite breaks around grains that produce a rough surface. Quartzite frequently has numerous mineral inclusions, which affect texture and color. The major MPRV colors are brown and tan. As its granular structure varies, it is sometimes called greywacke and metaquartzite. It is resistant to weathering and, as such, numerous outcrops are found in the MPRV. This thin section is a crystalline specimen. It has numerous colors, but the MPRV varieties are generally tan and gray.

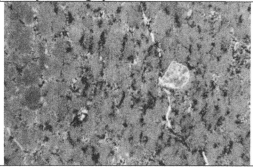

MPRV Rhyolite – Frederick County, Maryland (Organist Petrographic Laboratory, Delaware)

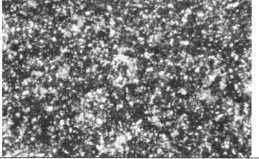

MRPV Rhyolite – Loudoun County, Virginia (Organist Petrographic Laboratory, Delaware)

Figure 8b – Sample of Rhyolite Thin Sections Used in This Study. Rhyolite is basically composed of silica with sodium, quartz, feldspar, biotite, and potassium molecules. The word comes from the Greek word *rhyax* meaning stream (lava flows). For the MPRV, it is found in banded, particle inclusions, and pure forms.

Radioisotope Identification as a Means for Lithic Material Sourcing

There are numerous techniques in archaeology and geology for determining the source of lithic materials that the Native Americans used for their tools. The basic approach is matching the elemental composition of stone from quarries or upland outcrops to local site or survey-found artifacts. Irradiation provides lithic source mapping, identification of workstations from quarry sites, and mapping migration patterns and geographies.

Lithic sourcing involves chemical (nuclear) analysis of stones to determine their exact origins geographically. While chemical composition for stone will vary within a few meters, trace elements tend to be homogeneous within a formation for larger areas. Thus, trace elements can be used for fingerprinting stone. Isotope ratios are key to identifying stone composition for tracing sources.

The following is a summary of geochemical techniques for analyzing stone. Each technique offers different results. This is followed by two case studies:

1 – Rhyolite study
2 – Jasper study.

Note: These studies are presented as examples and do not reflect true stone distributions for the MPRV.

X-Ray Fluorescence Spectrometry (XRFS)

XRFS technique evaluates the surface of a specimen (200 microns). As such, small flakes can be analyzed. The sample is irradiated with an X-ray beam. Excited electrons give off wavelengths that determine the various elements in the sample. For an archaeological use of the technique, see Warahina (1992).

X-Ray Emission Analysis (XREA)

XREA technique uses X-rays to induce particles or protons to identify sample elements. For an archaeological use of the technique, see Parkes (1986).

Neutron Activation Analysis (NAA)

NAA technique uses a nuclear reactor to bombard a sample with neutrons, which causes elements to breakdown into radioactive isotopes. The wavelength and radioactive emission frequencies are used to determine the various elements. Approximately 50 elements can be identified with the technique. For an archaeological use of the technique, see Church (1994). This technique was used here for testing rhyolite, steatite, and jasper samples.

Note: Be cautious using the NAA technique on artifacts. For example, upon irradiating jasper specimens, the iron (Fe) becomes radioactive and must be maintained in a nuclear storage laboratory for 55 years.

Electron Microprobe Analysis (EMPA)

EMPA technique is an electron probe technique to analyze crystal structure in specimens. The sample is scanned with an electron beam which emits secondary X-rays for element identification. For an archaeological use of the technique, see Kempe and Templeman (1983) and Black and Wilson (1999).

Plasma Emission Spectroscopy (PES)

PES technique heats the sample until it becomes a plasma (6000°C). A stream of argon is pasted over the sample through a radio coil, which yields trace elements. For an archaeological use of the technique, see Kempe and Templeman (1983).

Atomic Absorption Spectroscopy (AAS)

AAS technique is a flame photometry technique, which causes the elements to dissociate themselves into constituent atoms. It is often used for gross mineral contents (McLaughlin 1977).

For an in-depth summary of all these methods, see Andrefsky (1998). Each of these methods offers different types of data for lithic analyses; collectively, they are the new sciences that are used for stone and mineral studies

Figure 9 – Armed Forces Radiobiology Research Institute, Bethesda, Maryland. NAA data in this study was irradiated there.

MPRV Lithic Samples

All MPRV lithic material contains various heavy elements (Lanthanide and Actinide series). By creating isotopes of these elements, they can be detected and used to produce a radioisotopic fingerprint of a particular lithic material that was used by the Native Americans. For this study, actual flaked materials are used and, as a control, non-Native American materials from the same area are used. Sample size was in some cases < 1 gram. The Armed Forces Radiobiology Research Institute (AFRRI) was asked to perform irradiation on the collected samples under their public assistance programs. AFRRI has a TRIGA reactor located at National Institutes of Health, Bethesda,

Maryland (Figure 9). The reactor produced radioactive isotopes, which were used to classify (identify) each sample. This technique is called the NAA method.

A neutron activator containing a uranium-235 core was used. When ^{235}U absorbs protons, it gives off a tremendous amount of energy, namely more protons and gamma rays. To control the emission, boron carbide (boron-10) is used to absorb the protons and power level. The lithic specimen is irradiated which produces isotopes. The process allows for precise identification of materials within an irradiated specimen and has applications ranging from dating works of art to forensic analysis of criminal evidence. For lithic technology, the process identifies trace elements which can be used to fingerprint a piece of lithic material. Trace element combinations are often compared to other similar or related material. If their combinations differ, then the two samples are considered different.

Atoms of the same type, such as carbon-12, uranium-92, etc. are not always identical. If two or more atoms have identical numbers of protons but different numbers of neutrons, they are called isotopes. Isotopes are not stable atoms and generally decay back to the normal atom, for example:

$$C14 \Rightarrow C12$$

This decay is measured in half-lives. These half-lives have become very useful for dating tools in archaeology, namely the radiocarbon. The following isotopes (and half-lives) can occur in archaeological materials:

Na-22 (2.605 yr)   **Na-24 (14.96 hr)**
Mg-27 (9.45 min)   **Al-28 (2.25 min)**
Cl-38 (37.2 min)   **Ar-41 (1.82 hr)**
K-42 (12.36 hr)   **Cr-51 (27.7 day)**
Mn-54 (312.2 day)   **Mn-56 (2.578 hr)**
Co-58 (9.1 hr or 70.88 day)
Fe-59 (44.5 day)   **Co-60 (5.27 yr)**
Zn-65 (243.8 day)   **Se-75 (119.8 day)**
As-76 (26.3 hr)   **Zr-95 (64 day)**
Te-123 (119.7 day).

Note: Some isotopes are members of decay chains and are not considered here as valid trace elements; for example, magnesium (Mn-54) is a member of the aluminum decay chain. As such, Cobalt (Co-58), Iron (Fe-59), and Samarium (Sm-153) are not valid indicators.

These isotopes are measured by examining their spectra and counting parts per million (ppm). Isotropic refers to lithic material whose properties do not vary among its crystallographic direction. For lithic technology, it means workable versus nonworkable materials for knapping. Cubic crystals and amorphous substances are usually isotropic. The opposite is anisotropic.

As an initial testing radioisotopic example, chert from the Williamson Paleoindian site in Dinwiddie County, Virginia was tested (see Table 2). A quartzite sample from the site was used for control and comparison.

Table 2 – Irradiated Chert Samples from the Williamson Site, Dinwiddie County, Virginia			
Isotope	Chert #1	Chert #2	Quartzite #3
Atomic Mass Unit (AMU)	Wt: .31700 g Count	Wt: .14065 g Count	Wt: . 4297 g Count
Na-24	0.24	0.22	2.4
Mg-27	0.12		
Al-28	35.0	34.0	
K			1.1
Mn-56	0.11	0.08	
Co-60			0.0015
Br-82			0.014
Sb-122	0.037	0.01	0.003
Sm-153	0.056	0.03	0.29
Dy-165q	0.8	0.44	

The Williamson test example shows one isotope, dysprosium (Dy) that could be used to identify lithic materials that are found elsewhere as being from the Williamson site quarry. Williamson material has been reported over 300 miles away from the source; neutron or proton activation can identify the source for these way-out specimens. An example of rhyolite found several hundred miles from its source is shown in Figure 10. Irradiation test, thin section comparisons, and simple visual inspections are some of the ways to source artifact stone.

Note: No Williamson chalcedony was observed in the MPRV. This material was used during the Paleoindian Period and probably does not occur north of the James River.

Figure 10 – Rhyolite Biface Found on the Dime Site (44SK92), which is located in the James River Drainage of Virginia. It measures L = 90, W = 58, T = 17 mm. This biface material comes from Frederick County, Maryland. It offers a visual example of tracing artifact materials. Most specimens are not this easy to source.

Sourcing Rhyolite - As a test of analytical procedures and scientific methods, rhyolite samples were collected from numerous quarries and sites from Pennsylvania to North Carolina, the major focus in the MPRV rhyolite usage. Table 3 (end of section) presents the results of the irradiation tests.

While testing is limited in this study, Virginia rhyolite has a high percentage of tantalum (Ta) and low percentage of europium (Eu); whereas, in North Carolina, these percentages are reversed (Bondar 2000). Other heavy elements which can be used in sourcing rhyolite are: lanthanum (La), neodymium (Nd), hafnium (Hf), ytterbium (Yb), uranium (U), and thorium (Th). However, La percentages are used to define rhyolites in Maryland, Virginia, and North Carolina.

Based on testing for this study, a rhyolite usage map is proposed (Figure 11). The Early Archaic Period rhyolite is found in the Carolinas and southern Virginia. The Middle Archaic Period continues from the early period, but also see an upland focus. The Later Archaic Period usage of rhyolite moves the Potomac River-Susquehanna River drainage areas. By the Late Woodland Period, rhyolite is not the dominant material for the MPRV. Naturally, there are overlaps for area and chronology distributions.

Sourcing Jasper - Jasper is abundant in Warren County, Virginia outcrops. It was utilized extensively by Paleoindians, especially along the Shenandoah River. For the MPRV, the source for the jasper is Point of Rocks, Maryland. While its occurrence frequency is very low, jasper artifacts do occur. The question is the sources – did the Native Americans get the materials from Warren County in Virginia, local materials, or nearby Pennsylvania? And, are the materials different? As a study source, see Blackman's (1976) geochemical analysis of Delaware and Pennsylvania jaspers.

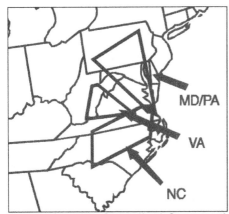

Figure 11 – Map Showing Generalized Concentration Based on Quarry Sources. Virginia's (VA) primary source is Mt Rogers, North Carolina's (NC) source is Uwharrie Mountains, and Maryland and Pennsylvania (MD/PA) have numerous deposits that were used for quarries.

One of the few known Point of Rocks jasper artifacts is shown in Figure 12. This material was used throughout early and late prehistory, as a Paleoindian knife is shown in text, and a Levanna triangle point was found in the Wilson project. It dates to the Late Woodland Period. The outcrop was formerly located near highway Routes 15 and 464; the area now has townhouses. To provide at least a small record, irradiated data are presented in Table 3.

Jasper samples were irradiated to determine the rare elements and the amount of iron (Fe) in samples from Virginia and Pennsylvania. Tables 4 and 5 (end of section) present the results.

Table 3 – Irradiated Jasper Samples from Point of Rocks – TRIGA Reactor		
Weight = 0.03721 gram		
Isotope	Light	Heavy
Na-24	0.12370	3.32438
Mn-54	0.00027	0.00713
Co-57	0.00016	0.00418
Fe-59	0.00284	0.07640
As-76	0.01115	0.29953
Sb-122	0.00200	0.05373
Te-132	0.00046	0.01228
Xe-133	0.00050	0.01333
La-140	0.00121	0.03251

Note: Additional samples are in the Spencer Geasey collection at the Jefferson-Patterson Museum in Maryland.

These are not the only jasper outcrops for prehistoric Native Americans who were using it. Arnold Valley near Lexington, Virginia has an outcrop, but it contains impurities that prevent it from being used for large biface production. The recently found Brook Run site (Culpeper County, Virginia) is a quarry where the Native Americans dug for jasper. It is over 14 feet deep. Digging for stone was discussed for rhyolite and occurs for steatite; it is also presented in Hranicky (2002). This site's ecoscene is the Rapidan or Rappahannock rivers. It has high quality jasper; the quarry dates 10,500 to 11,500 years ago, and has produced over 700,000 artifacts.

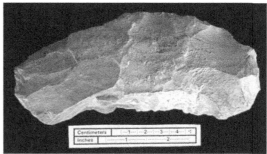

Figure 12 – Unusual Biface Made from Point of Rocks Jasper (L = 145, W = 60, T = 21 mm). It was published in Geasey and Ballweber (1999). It may date to the Pleistocene era.

Front Royal jasper has been found by the author on the Rappahannock River (Figure 13). It is a large spall that was serving as a knife. It has lateral retouch on both lateral margins. Moving to the uplands, Figure 14 shows a jasper biface found in Shenandoah County, Virginia.

Figure 13 – Jasper Spall Found in Spotsylvania County, Virginia (L = 123, W = 83, T = 21 mm). It has a large quarry bulb scar, and thin-section slides show it comes from Front Royal in Warren County, Virginia. It has serrations on edges. This specimen is classified as a Pleistocene era blade-flake artifact.

One jasper study has been published, but this study does not directly cover the MPRV (see Blackman 1976). An experimental study of jasper is in Petraglia, et al. (1998). It demonstrates problems in working jasper, namely:

1 – Lithic homogeneity within outcrops as a factor in workability

2 – Lithic fracture as in good-to-poor conchoidal flaking

3 – Lithic useability of working large spalls and flakes.

Figure 14 – Jasper Biface (L = 84, W = 51, T = 10 mm) from Shenandoah County, Virginia. Breakage is post-Native American. It is well-made and thin suggesting that it is a Paleoindian specimen. Surface is heavily weathered.

All of which are factors in the Native Americans' choice of the stone for bifacial tools. Additionally, jasper is a hard stone, and hinging and splitting are frequently seen in archaeological contexts. See broken Clovis points in the Projectile Point section.

Sourcing lithic materials will sometimes yield the sources that the Native Americans traveled to for the stone. The material was frequently shaped into transportable quarry spalls or worked into quarry bifaces (Stage 1). Stage 1 bifaces were carried to lithic workstations and reduced further into smaller bifaces or into finished tools (Figure 15). There are five stages – from spall to finished preform – used in this publication. Biface stages are discussed in the Toolmaking Technology section.

Figure 15 – Jasper Stage 1 Biface from Chester County, Pennsylvania (L = 160, W = 86, T = 22 mm; D/P Index = .706). It was a large quarry spall that was worked into a biface for transport. Note: lower right indentation is post-Native American. This quarry method was common throughout prehistory for flints and jaspers. Basic jasper sources for the MPRV remain open.

Jasper may be the only material in the Potomac River valley that can be attributed to technology traditions, namely Clovis, Palmer, and St Charles. Figure 16 shows a well-made jasper biface that was probably made by one of these early pointmakers in the MPRV. It has a flat distal/proximal (D/P) profile which was the result of the knapper's final flaking to finish the biface. Careful and corrective flaking is performed so that the knapper controls the surface in order to maintain evenness across each face. See Toolmaking Technology section.

Figure 16 – Jasper Stage 4 Biface. It is a well-made biface but has minor areas of cortex remaining (L = 127, W = 51, T=10 mm). It is from the R. C. Printz collection that is now housed at the Fairfax Archaeological Survey in Falls Church, Virginia.

MPRV Quarries

Holmes (1897) was the first archaeologist to study MPRV quarrying. Many of his sites are gone, but they include the following sample list:

Dunbarton Heights	Naval Observatory
Great Falls	Cabin John Bridge
Little Falls	Anacostia Valley
Zakiah Creek	Mount Vernon
Clifton steatite quarry	Connecticut Avenue
Thompson quarry site	Brown quarry
Wilson quarry	Olney – Fair Hill.

The MPRV has numerous quarry sites; however, that survey is not part of this study. Quarry studies are a major factor in tracing prehistoric stone usage; for the MPRV, they need to be made as urbanization is destroying them.

Quarry Processes

Quarry stone is the Native American's preference for stone tools. While field pickup and streambed cobbles are available, the entire prehistory for tools shows a tendency for the Native Americans to use local quarry stones or travel distances to acquire them. In Virginia, quarry sites at Thunderbird, Warren County and Williamson, Dinwiddie County, Virginia were used extensively in the Paleoindian Period; they illustrate stone preferences for specific groups in prehistory.

This practice is often called lithic determinism in archaeology. This school of thought is not always valid in determining social behavior in a whole population at a specific time period. *Why is a certain stone?* A valid question in archaeology.

The primary reason for quarrying is stone workability – quarried stone has more moisture and flakes better. This type of material is often called *fresh* stone. One argument in modern flintknapping is soaking stone for several days enhances it workability. False, workable stones do not have the permeability to absorb moisture. However, recent experimentation by Callahan (2001) of wetting the striking platform seems to improve flaking.

Figure 17 – Original Rhyolite Hardaway Points Excavated by Joffre L. Coe That Appear in His Carolina Sequence Publication. Coe published his points with the tip down; thus, to this day, all theses and dissertations at the University of North Carolina follow the practice/

In addition to earlier periods, Native Americans used quarries through to the end of the Woodland Period. An excellent example is the high-quality rhyolite found in North Carolina's Uwarria Mountain. See Daniel (2001) for a material availability study. Figures 17, 18, and 19 show views of the extensiveness on Native American procurement of the material. These quarries were used extensively; so much that archaeological cuts through the debitage go down 30+ meters (via a North Carolina state excavation) and still do not reach the bottom. For Virginia, this rhyolite is found in the lower coastal area, especially around the Dismal Swamp. It is occasionally found up to the James River.

Quarry Analyses

The refuse from a quarry site can be tremendous. Without too much detail, Strauss and Hermes (1996) offer basic analytical units for quarry materials, which are:

1 – Tabular forms
2 – Blocky forms
3 – Core and fragments
4 – Angular waste
5 – Flake-like items
6 – Flakes
7 – Unifaces.

Number 7 may be difficult to discern from flakes, and microflakes should be added for the small nondescript items. Since flakes were readily available in several study collections, they were studied, especially if they were made into tools. See Flakes as Tools section.

As a quarry practice, most work shows breaking up boulders into smaller pieces (spalls) which were then carried to another area for bifacial reduction activities. Campsites are rare at the quarry but are common at the reduction area. Eastman, et al. (1998) comments on a North Carolina workshop:

Site 31DH616 served primarily as a workshop, or lthic reduction site, where large cores quarried from the stone outcrop were worked into smaller flake blanks. Some biface blanks and preforms were produced, as were finished tools; however, for most part the lithic material left the site as flake blanks, to be worked into finished tools elsewhere.

Quarry - source of lithic materials for the manufacture of projectile points and other implements. Major types are (Hranicky 2002a):

1 – Type 1 - no digging, stone removal from outcrops

2 – Type 2 - outcrop removal plus shallow digging

3 – Type 3 - outcrop removal plus intensive digging

4 – Type 4 - outcrop removal and large pits plus undercutting of beds or creation of shelter/caves by digging.

Types 1 to 3 were practiced extensively in the MPRV. Quarry sites have disappeared due to urbanization.

Figure 18 – Uwharrie Mountains in North Carolina. It shows an archaeological cut through spalls, flakes and debris by 10,000 years of Native Americans' removal of rhyolite. It shows a tour for the 1999 Uwharrie Lithics Conference attendees.

Numerous quarry pits occur in the Catoctin range of Maryland and Pennsylvania. They range from 5 to 15 meters in diameter and are seldom more than a meter deep. For unknown reasons, they are often back filled. As a hypothesis, pits were used to extract banded rhyolite. Where banded rhyolite occurs in projectile points, the bands are diagonal at 45°. This practice may be significant culturally; specific groups (clans) are using this material form of rhyolite.

Extraction of stone for tool production involves:

1 – Stone location - finding the stone source that is acceptable in toolmaking

2 – Stone milling - testing a stone source for its best depositional layer or location

3 – Stone processing - actual block/chunk removal of stone for use in the manufacture/production process

4 – Stone benification - working stone into useable or moveable pieces for tool production

5 – Stone refinement - actual working stone into desired tools.

Figure 19 – Close up of the archaeological cut in the Uwharrie Mountains, North Carolina. The entire mountain has tens of millions of spalls, flakes, and general debris left by the Native Americans over the past 10,000 years.

For quarry extraction process, which is based on the Little Catoctin Creek quarry area in Frederick County, Maryland, major work for lithic processing is:

1 – Block/boulder removal
2 – Next, chunk and trim into manageable pieces
3 – Reduction with waste flakes
4 – Biface preparation
5 – Tool finalizing.

Mounds of reduction flakes are the most prominent feature for most quarries and associated workstations. Depending on the quarry as an initializing to finished biface production area, flakes can be classified as:

1 – Primary flake - full cortex remaining on one face
2 – Secondary flake - some cortex remaining
3 – Tertiary flake - no cortex remaining.

Note: Extremely large igneous hammerstones cause well-pronounced ripples in the surface of broken pieces.

Quarry Rejects - lithic material that remains at the quarry site after procurement activities (Figure 20). Debris can be classified by:

1 – Man-made fractures
2 – Geological fractures
3 – Edge malformations
4 – Spall thickness
5 – Hinge fractures
6 – Impurities in material
7 – Irregular-miscellaneous pieces.

Each of the above factors can be attributed to human behavior and human reaction to the physical environment and its properties. The Native Americans knew these factors, and how to overcome them; there are millions of well-made prehistoric tools in the MPRV.

Figure 20 – Quarry Spalls (left-to-right) Frederick County, Maryland, Pulaski County, Virginia, and Conover Valley, Pennsylvania. They are probably quarry rejects; otherwise, they would have been made into tools.

Quarry Testing – with variation in lithic quality, the Native Americans tested outcrops for their purity – workability. Cobbles and boulder faces frequently have a large flake removed which enabled the Native American knapper to examine the surface under the weathered cortex.

Quarry Tool – variety of pointed, massive implement used to break up stone at a lithic outcrop. It was usually hafted. The quarry always offered fresh stone for toolmaking. The most common material is basalt and quartzite.

Another quarry tool is the digging tool. It is a hoe-like implement which was hafted. In contrast to the above tool, the digging tool did not function as a crushing or large scale breaking tool. It is mentioned, not illustrated, in the Miscellaneous Tools/Implements section because it is not reported in the literature. Thus, comparative or simply basic examples are not available.

Quarry Spall – basic lithic removal piece that is transported to another workstation for final reduction into workable bifaces. These bifaces are then transported to another workstation usually some distance from the quarry for final manufacture into tools and implements (Figure 21).

Figure 21 – General Reduction Sequence for Susquehanna Knife; from Spall to Point (Knife)

Quarry Transport Biface

Large crudely-worked bifaces made of rhyolite have been found long distances from quarry sources. They are generally found outside site contexts and do not constitute caches. They suggest a quarry process of producing pieces for carrying (and trading) them to distant locations or maintaining them for future toolkit replenishments.

Quarry Refitting Studies

Refitting is the technique of reassembling flakes back into their original core or biface; genesis of a lithic reduction station. Putting flakes back together to reform the original biface or bulk material offers an insight into the knapper's strategy for toolmaking. According to Morrow (1996):

...technique of backtracking from debitage to the initial core. It attempts to reconstruct the knapping process for a tool or implement.

Since this study relies on field-collected materials, the chance of refitting flakes, etc. was not a practical reality; thus, no material was refitted for the collections. However, it is a major aspect of experimental archaeology. Petraglia (1994) provides a Potomac River basin quarry study – *reassembling the quarry*.

Frederick County, Maryland Rhyolite Quarries

Frederick County has numerous rhyolite outcrops that were utilized extensively by the Native Americans (Figures 22 and 23). As mentioned, the quarries in the Little Catoctin Creek were used for this study (Geasey 1974), for rhyolite processing (Ballweber 1999 and Geasey and Ballweber 1999). It covers approximately 500 acres and judging by its projectile point types, it was used for the entire MPRV time period. For a Blue Ridge rhyolite overview, see Geasey and Ballweber (1991 and 1999). For Pennsylvania and Maryland, see Stewart (1987).

Figure 22 – Quarry Spalls form the Rhyolite Outcrops in Frederick County, Maryland

Lithic extraction involved breaking surface boulders with heavy diabase hammerstones. Diabase as opposed to basalt may be the preferred stone for the quarry maul; this remains to be proven. These hammerstones may have Pennsylvania origins. This quarry area has associated workstations where spalls were shaped into bifaces. The bifaces were transported to all MPRV habitation areas.

In the workstations, quartzite hammerstones were used to shape the spalls into bifaces. There was some antler billeting. Since points and other tools have been found, some workstations were used for living sites. At present, there is no data available for the time periods, number of quarry workers, amount of curation, or length of time at the quarry.

Figure 23 – Rhyolite Quarry Processing Area in Frederick County, Maryland. This area is covered with rhyolite debitage and workstations. The principal adaptive tools from this area are the maul and pick, which are used here for quarrying raw materials.

Small, transportable bifaces were used in some habitation sites as tools, and then they were manufactured into tools. However, low flake counts suggest the habitation site was for:

1 – Quarry spalls (storage)
2 – Biface shaping
3 – Biface reduction (set-up biface or preform)
4 – Shaping into tools.

Quartz and Quartzite

White and sometimes clear quartz is the third most popular stone used by the MPRV Native Americans. Its usage starts with the Paleoindian Period and continues to Late Woodland times. The bifurcate, Halifax, Lamoka, Piscataway, and Potomac pointmakers made extensive use of it. During the Late Woodland Period, white quartz usage for microtools exceeded 65% of the total stone material counts. Stephenson, et al. (1963) shows a high quartz percentage for points, namely in the Calvert, Piscataway, Vernon, and Potomac types.

Quartz usage, especially for religious practices and projectile points, extends into the historic period, as Beverly (1705) includes a quote:

Twelve miles from the Falls [James River], there is a Chrystal Rock, wherein the Indians do head many of their Arrows.

Also for the Middle Archaic Period, use of quartz was minimal. Israel and Davis (1992) report a quartz workshop that may be used for an MPRV overview. Toward the end of this period, a new technology becomes popular. It is the use of quartz for microtools which was the manufacture of points by the bipolar reduction technique. See Toolmaking Technology section.

Figure 24 – Quartz Boulder in Frederick County, Maryland. It has associated quartz points. Native Americans once camped around this boulder from which they worked spalls off for tool production. Quartz points have been found near the boulder.

The MPRV Native Americans had two primary quartz sources: pickup field and stream cobbles and boulder outcrops. Boulder outcrops are more common on the Maryland side of the Potomac River (Figure 24). Virginia's quartz is often brittle with numerous fractures that make the workability very poor. However, pure, fine-grain quartz does occur in accessible outcrops (Figure 25). The Halifax pointmakers were the most consistent users of quartz, namely through the bipolar reduction technique. Figure 26 shows a sample of quartz MPRV points. See Toolmaking Technology section.

The collections in this study have a high frequency of quartz points and implements. However, this material was not studied because of the major focus on rhyolite, quartzite, and jasper.

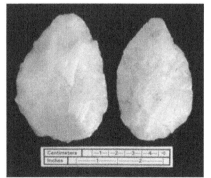

Figure 25 – MPRV Quartz Bifaces Bipolar Method)

Quartz points during the Late Woodland Period tend to be small (<50 mm) notched and stemmed varieties. Other areas in the Middle Atlantic area have quartz points exceeding 100 mm. The assumption here is that most Late Woodland Period points are made from pick-up quartz cobbles.

Figure 26 – Sample of MPRV Quartz Points. Examples of high-quality quartz that was used for various point types.

Quartzite is the most popular stone in prehistoric Virginia. It constitutes tools and implements from the paleo era to Contact. Figure 27 shows a typical point example.

Figure 27 – MPRV Quartzite Specimen
(L = 96, W = 45, T = 10 mm)

Additional Quarry Examples

In southwestern Virginia, the Native Americans used Buck Mountain near Roanoke extensively for quartzite. Its earliest mining appears to be with the Big Sandy pointmakers. Figures 28 and 29 show a site located on a ridge outcrop and in situ flakes that were produced there in tool production. Quarry materials, probably preforms, were carried to other nearby campsites. These sites are usually near streams and rivers. The hammerstone was quartzite. Some small bifaces remain on the sites as well as lithic knapping tools. The site (several miles of quarrying) has not been published. It offers these observations:

1 – Travel to quarry areas for materials
2 – Short-term occupation to process stone
3 – Preference for particular stone materials.

These inferences are present in the MPRV and are factors in stone tool analyses.

Figure 28 – Quartzite Quarry Debris at Buck Mountain, Roanoke County, Virginia showing spalls, flakes, and general debris. The material is fine-grain and appears to have been used during the Early Archaic Period.

Another quarry source that is well-known in Virginia is the quarry at the Williamson site in Dinwiddie County, Virginia. This site was exploited by Paleoindians around 9500 BC. The chert is called the Cattail Creek chalcedony. Figure 30 shows a discard spall from the site and a comparative rhyolite spall from Maryland. Study of this quarry site has applications for the analyses of MPRV jasper quarries that were utilized during the Paleoindian Period. However, no comparisons were made in this study. See Hranicky and McCary (1995) for discussions on Williamson quarrying.

Figure 29 – Examples of Quartzite Quarry Materials at Buck Mountainquarry site. It dates to the Big Sandy era; however, subsequent pointmakers probably used material from the area. Left>Right: Scraper, point, biface, utilized flake, and blade core.

Quarry Sources

The drainage of the watershed of the Potomac River basin offered the Native Americans numerous lithic materials from which to choose. Most of these materials were simply pick-up rocks from fields and riverbeds. However, pure material was often the preferred choice, so the Native Americans quarried it. Quarry sourcing and lithic mapping remains a priority in MPRV archaeology. Unfortunately, with the area divided by two states, coordinated efforts remain to be done. Lithic procurement and utilization by the Native Americans of the MPRV area still remain to be studied further; the stone *arrowhead* story is not complete.

As a published resource, Holmes (1897) presents research on MPRV quarries.

| Discard Chalcedony Quarry Spall Found on the Williamson Paleoindian Site in Dinwiddie County, Virginia. The piece has a deep side fracture which made reduction nearly impossible. | Discard Rhyolite Quarry Spall found in the Catoctin Quarry area of Frederick County, Maryland. This piece has several hinges and a flat back side which made reduction nearly impossible. |

Figure 30 – Two Quarry Spalls: Left is Paleoindian and Right is Late Archaic. Also, they are too thick, most knappers prefer flatter pieces. With more material available, why try these; get another spall to work. They are 7000 years apart, but working stone is the same.

Table 6 – MPRV Living Habitat		
Trees:	**Animals**:	**Birds**:
Hickory	Deer	Turkey
Oak	Raccoon	Goose
Chestnut	Muskrat	Duck
Red Cedar	Opossum	Swans
Black Locust		Cranes
Walnut	*Also:	Herons
Hackberry	Squirrel	Pigeon
Maple/Birch	Fox	
Mulberry	Skunk	*Also:
Persimmon	Woodchuck	Woodcock
Osage	Beaver	Grouse
Pine	Weasel	Dove
Elm	Mink	Quail
Grape	Otter	Hawk
	Rabbit	Eagle
*Also:	Bear	Owl
Rose	Bobcat	Osprey
Birch	Chipmunk	Buzzard
Beech	Rat/mice	
Magnolia	Voles/moles	
Rhododendron	Skrew	
	Bat	
	Pigeon	
	*Possibly:	
	Buffalo**	
	Elk	
	Wolves	
	Boar	
	Mink	
	Porcupine	
	Fisher	
Plants:	*****Fish**:	**Snakes**:
Bean	Gar	Rat
Maize	Sucker	Pine
Squash	Bass	King
Pigweed	Catfish	Water
Graminae	Perch	Milk
		Hognose
*Also:	*Also:	Green
Strawberry	Trout	Garter
Blackberry	Sunfish	Ribbon
Raspberry	Picheral	Copperhead
Tobacco	Bullhead	Rattlesnake
Cherry		
Barley (?)	**Reptiles**:	***Miscellaneous**:
Sunflower	Box turtle	Clams
Hazelnut	Water turtle	Snail
Hackberry	Slider/cooter	Oysters
Wild onion	Snapping	Blue crab
Cabbage	Turtle	Mussels
Ginger	Frog	
Tuckahoe		***Insect**:
		Grasshopper
		Beatle

* Added here, but not based on archaeological remains.
** Buffalo is mentioned twice by Gilbert (1943) in his reference to Cherokees.
*** See Introduction section.

Foodstuff data are lacking in the MPRV because archaeological analyses of food remains have not been performed due primarily to the lack of skilled archaeologists in paleoecology. Other sciences must also be consulted because they offer skills and data to give insights to archaeological contexts. Ethnographic and archaeological excavational data do suggest a wide variety of foods for prehistoric Native Americans (Figure 31).

An immunological analytical technique has been perfected. It is called cross-over electrophoresis (CIEP) as in Newman (1994) and Petraglia (1998). Their testing identified rabbit or hare and wolf, coyote, fox, or dog. This method has been challenged; see Fiedel (1995). Another study is in Inashima (1992) and offers affirmation of the technique.

As a procurement method for meat, Speck (1928) describes driving deer and rabbits by fire and dogs. The method was needed when populations increase as seen in village life.

Figure 31 – Ethnographic Food Suggestion. Engraving based on John White's 1588 watercolors of North Carolina Native Americans. Fish and berry/acorns appear as a diet staple; there is ethnographic data for Native American diet.

Paleoethnobotany does not present theories that can be utilized on archaeological data, but many of its techniques can be used (as in Ford 1979). Archaeology has increasingly recovered more plant and animal remains, and forthcoming 21st century analyses will offer significant contributions in the study of Native American economies. Plants are considered here as weeds when they interfere with human activities or wellbeing. The Weed Science Society of America (1966) published 1775 weeds in the U.S. While many of these are not native to the U.S., a large percentage are native, and we do not know how the Native Americans used or did not utilize them. The U.S. Department of Agriculture (USDA 1971) provides a working list of weeds, which includes basic botanical data. The prehistoric botany of the MPRV remains to be studied (for example, see Blake and Cutler 2001). Petrides (1958) provided the overall identification of plants and trees for this study.

The ultimate goal of archaeology is ecosystem-settlement patterns based on geology, biology, culture, time, climate, etc. This focus provides analyses of the natural MPRV environment that offered Native Americans:

1 – Medicine
2 – Tools and weapons
3 – Food and drink
4 – Housing and wind breaks
5 – Clothing
6 – Food containers
7 – Fire and heating

And based on the above,

8 – Ideological symbols and social practices.

Food sourcing and processing is not discussed other than reference to tool function. For animal resources in the MPRV, see Moore (1994). For a comparative study on anadromous fish, see Barber (1980). The MPRV has fish and water life in abundance; thus, this aspect was an attraction for prehistoric settlers. These were presented in Table 6.

Another environmental factor is the use of it for medical practices by priests or shamans. The woodland environment was a significant resource and played a major role in site locations which probably had priest needs in selection. However, it is difficult to prove archaeologically (see Frink 1996). Excellent sources for Native American medical resources are Moerman (1968) and Weiner (1972). Plants and weeds played an important role in shaman practices.

The basic focus here is that the environment had an influence on point typology, and general tool useability and lifecycles.

MPRV Water

Obviously, water is the primary factor for watershed compositions. But archaeologically, types of water as influences on behavior have not been studied. For that matter, this factor is basically open for interpretation in contemporary societies.

The MPRV water supply was dependent on rivers and streams. The type of rock in the watershed determines the run-off water, such as limestones yield hard, alkaline waters; black shale, carbonaceous schists yield oxygen-poor waters. Quartzose sediments and rocks have little capacity to neutralize acid in waters.

Frederick County (Maryland) and Frederick County (Virginia) limestones have the highest acid neutralizing capacity. The Catoctin metabasalt with phyllite and quartzite are essentially nonreactive with acidic stream water. East of the Chesapeake Bay, unweathered greensand, as in Kent County, Maryland, reduces and eliminates nitrates. The pH varies across the MPRV.

The differences in water may be effectual on the social processes, especially habitation decisions. The argument here is there is a stress/anxiety factor in water acidity. This factor, if important and provable, remains to be studied.

MPRV Shorelines

Rise and fall of sea levels as well as coastal erosions for the MPRV are available in geological studies, but are totally lacking in archaeological studies, especially erosional effects on coastal sites. Lowery (2001) provides a study for the eastern shore. The continental shelf was occupied during the Pleistocene and early Holocene (Hranicky 2007).

MPRV Climate

The relationships and timetable of geological/environmental conditions to archaeological classifications of culture remain speculative at best, but nevertheless, attemptable (see Carbon 1982). Table 7 presents a combination of these types of information, based on MPRV geological and archaeological data. For generalized purposes, the MPRV can be divided into environments of:

1 – Glacial – Early American, Paleoindian, and Early Archaic Periods
2 – Postglacial – Middle Archaic Period to Contact.

Table 7 – Relationship Among Geological and Archaeological Calendars *			
Geologic Divisions and General Environment	Years	Specific MPRV Climatic Conditions	Archaeological Divisions
Late Holocene	400 BP		Woodland Period:
	800 BP	Neoboreal	Late Woodland
(Atlantic Environment)	1000 BP	Neoatlantic (Medithermal)	Middle Woodland
	1800 BP		
	0 AD	Scandic	
			Early Woodland
	3000 BP	Subatlantic	
Middle Holocene	4000 BP	Subboreal (Altlthermal)	Archaic Period:
	5000 BP		Late Archaic
(Boreal Environment)	7000 BP	Atlantic (Hypothermal)	Middle Archaic
	9000 BP	Boreal (Anathermal)	Early Archaic
Early Holocene	10,000 BP	Boreal (Anathermal)	Paleoindian Period:
(Savannah Environment)			All periods or phases.**
	11,000 BP	Preboreal	
Terminal Pleistocene		Late Glacial	Preclovis – Early Man ***

*Based on Rapp and Hill (1998), Wendland and Bryon (1974), and Turekian (1996).
** Gardner (1989) suggests there are three periods or phases; however, they do not appear to be equated with climatical divisions.
*** No Preclovis MPRV occupation is assumed.

These climatical conditions are correlated to projectile point typology in the MPRV Prehistoric Chronology and Projectile Points sections. The general climate references are used in the Miscellaneous Tools/Implements section because of the difficulty or correlating climate and tool invention/borrowing and its continual usage over time.

The MPRV's Late Woodland Period has approximately 219 days a year of sunshine; in January the average variation on mean temperature is 2 degrees; in July the average variation on mean temperature is 26 degrees (Donn 1975). For the grassland period, the climate is subhumid and for the forest period, the climate is humid. Earlier periods saw variation in climate which remain to be documented archaeologically as in the above daily scale.

Paleoclimatology

It is the study of climate and the interactions of humans within it. The study of climate formations and change through time for specific geographies includes atmospheric compositions, ocean currents, trade winds and jet streams, weather trends and periods, and weather comparisons (see Cronin 1999). Climate modeling offers an environmental history that provides an explanation on human behavior and adaptation (see Washington and Parkinson 1986). When coupled with archaeological data, climate and human habitation data form a picture of human occupations and their associated technologies.

Within the human habitation zone of 0E to 40EC, there are numerous ecoscenes ranging from desert to swamp lands. In many cases, the land as viewed today differs from the same land in prehistory. The local climate, whether now or past, is subject to complicated geological events that are triggered by other nonrelated fluctuating events. The basis of which lies in some type of energy balance model to define climate periods, and in the case of today's weather, predict climate. Archaeology offers data for long-term predictions. Basic climatologic factors are manifested in:

Physical:
1 – Land space (mostly grasslands and woodlands with marshes)
2 – Atmosphere (basically warm and cool)
3 – Land (three basic forms)
4 – Ocean (nearby to the MPRV).

Processes:
1 – Absorption (intake by plants/animals)
2 – Precipitation (moisture)
3 – Solar radiation (sunlight)
4 – Condensation (atmospheric variation)
5 – Air motion (seasons).

While fauna, flora, and evolutionary changes have been assumed in anthropology and paleontology, no archaeological method had been developed to measure the amount of change, duration, etc. based on climate. Does climate cause social change? Was it a factor in human migrations? A method called transfer functions uses data relating to some physical variables by means of regression formulas. A regression coefficient can infer past environments. Additionally, climate modeling has offered the study of patterns and *what-if* scenarios to climate studies. Most of these techniques are based on core drillings and organic population numbers in the core. Other factors are the remains (trapped or changes) for elements in the atmosphere, such as oxygen, carbon dioxide, nitrogen, and ozone. Varying amounts of any of them cause changes in weather. Social change, if based on climatical changes, would have to be based on seasonal variations tied to annual time periods (see Custer 1984). These cause/effect factors are difficult to determine archaeologically.

As a possible hypothesis, the climatical and geographical factors affecting human occupation of the eastern U.S. occur at the time when deglaciation stops and most of the ice-covered areas are gone. This time is around 8000 BP (based on Crowley and North 1991). Additionally, during 11 to 10,000 BP, there is a rapid reduction in ice-covered area. By 6000 BP, most of the northern ice-cap has retreated to present day Greenland. During this deglaciation, the jet streams followed different paths, including split jet streams for the eastern U.S. Thus, ground conditions had different temperature ranges and moistures. A first warming phase comes around 13 to 12,000 BP (Atkinson, et al. 1987). The major wind change factor is shown on eolian features in North America as shifting from ice-age northwesterly to present day southwesterly (Wells 1983). This has a drastic effect on precipitation and moisture levels in soils, lakes, and rivers. The warming phase that occurs around 8000 BP leaves the East with climate much like today's climate. With few exceptions, most of the planet was drier during the Ice Age because most of the water was locked in glaciation. At this point in time, deglaciation has passed the Hudson Strait (Mix and Ruddiman 1986). Two key issues are 1) the change in fauna and flora and 2) consequences to human occupations. Research shows that there were large changes of climate in areas bordering the ice sheets (see Watts 1983 and Wright 1987). Tundra extended southward from ice margins, which was replaced by a spruce-pine boreal forest. Further south, oak-hickory forest, local grasslands, and shallow lakes provided the environment that would follow deglaciation (see Brush 1982).

Rainfall as a climatical factor is not discussed for the MPRV because of the lack of geological data (see Knox 1983). It is assumed to be a factor in watershed analysis. Generally for the MPRV's prehistory, the area is drier in the early years and eventually towards Contact has an annual rain/snow fall of >35 inches.

Prehistoric technology shows the inventions (borrowing) of the axe and broadspear in the Middle Atlantic area. Is there a cause/effect climatical relationship? The answer is a major environmental shift causes Native American technology to adjust to it. The axe does not have to be present in all societies, as the broadspear can cut down small trees equally well. The most noted broadspear is the appearance of the Morrow Mountain, and disappearance of small notched and stemmed points. These two technologies are found in areas away from the middle Atlantic coastal provenance and suggest woodland as opposed to grassland environments.

MPRV Soils

Soils are not part of lithic technology in this study but are included as a suggested factor in settlement patterns. For a soils overview, see Birkeland (1984) or go to the basic source for soil theory in Bjerrum, Casagrande, Peck, and Skempton's (1960) tribute to Kark Terzaghi, who is considered the father of soil mechanics. He suggested factors that could be investigated archaeologically, namely:

1 – Elasticity of clays
2 – Water capacity
3 – Soil viscosity
4 – Swelling of wetted clays
5 – And perhaps, atmospheric pressure.

Figure 32 – Terrain in the Ridge and Valley Provenance (USGS). The area at various times was open grassland.

These factors could be used in (non-)occupation of low areas, pottery, water retention and run offs, vegetation patterns, human factors, etc. An archaeological study of the physics of colloidal matter?

Soil studies are incorporated into the study of horticulture for the Woodland Period. As a suggestion, soils play a role in Late Woodland horticulture and settlement patterns. MPRV soils can be identified as:

1 – Pleistocene
2 – Early Holocene
3 – Middle Holocene
4 – Late Holocene.

Most MPRV areas have all four types of deposits, especially where streams enter the Potomac River. Deposition is not uniform throughout the MPRV; thus, identifying cultural deposits is sometimes difficult. These levels parallel the MPRV's chronology somewhat and can be used to find habitations based on soil analysis. One of the first soil studies was performed at the Thunderbird project in Warren County, Virginia (see Gardner 1977 and 1982).

As an untested hypothesis, soils containing Barium-56 date to the Late Pleistocene and Early Holocene; whereas, soils containing Strontium-38 date to Middle and Late Holocene Periods. These elements appear to be mutually exclusive; however, flooding has mixed them in soils.

The coastal plain soils were the best of the three provenances for Native American horticulture. They contain at least 50% quartz with some feldspar. Micas, iron (Fe) oxides, heavy minerals (illmenite, rutile, titanium), and clay minerals compose the remaining percentages. The piedmont soils are derived from igneous (gabbro) and metamorphic (gneiss) rocks. Mica schist is the primary parent rock. The weathered version is sometimes called saprolite (rotten rock). Again, clays and iron (Fe) oxides are found, especially for the Virginia side of the Potomac River, such as red shales in the Leesburg area. Geologists classify types of soils, mafic (fertile) and felsic (less fertile). Distribution of these soils should be a factor in settlement patterns. The Valley and Ridge soils were formed from sedimentary rocks from the surrounding mountains, namely sandstones, limestones, and shales (Figure 32). While the Blue Ridge is not considered part of the MPRV study area, it offers contrasting data. The higher elevations strongly influence soil morphology. Soils are much colder than those in lower elevations. Soil often has a thick upper horizon of organic material. This pattern reduces soil formation to thin layers.

Note: The coastal plain for Maryland and Virginia can further be divided into inner and outer plains with the amount of clay and sand differentiating the separation.

****

Table 8 and 9 list radiation data.

Table 8 – Irradiated Rhyolite Samples *				
Sample	Isotope	Light	Heavy	Percentage of Lanthanum to Sample
MPRV 0.05523 g	La-140	0.01056	0.19115	11.50
	K-42	4.22784	76.54970	
MPRV 0.04532 g	La-140	0.00908	0.20040	12.06
	K-42	4.66808	103.00265	
MPRV 0.05106 g	La-140	0.01554	0.30433	18.31
	K=42	4.40346	86.24081	
	Co-57	0.00052	0.01009	
MPRV 0.01469 g	None	0.0	0.0	0.0
	K-42	1.15735	78.78489	
Frederick County, MD 0.10464 g	La-140	0.04727	0.45171	27.18
	K-42	11.22260	107.24962	
Frederick County, MD 0.06102 g	La-140	0.01031	0.16891	10.16
	K-42	11.22940	184.02819	
Frederick County, MD 0.11372 g	La-140	0.01242	0.10921	6.57
	K-42	18.6440	163.94654	
	Br-82	0.03166	0.27836	
	Xe-133	0.00152	0.01335	
Hardaway Site, Stanly County, NC 0.07898 g	None	0.0	0.0	0.0
	K-42	1.79891	22.77678	
Hardaway Mountain, Stanly	La-140	0.00302	0.08580	5.16

County, NC 0.03518 g	K-42	1.39176	39.56111	
Hardaway Mountain, Stanly County, NC 0.04540	None K-42	0.0 1.19910	0.0 26.41189	0.0
Hardaway Site, Stanly County, NC 0.10337 g	La-140 K-42	0.00813 7.15036	0.07836 68.90585	4.71
Grayson County, VA 0.02166 g	None K-42	0.0 2.49520	0.0 115.19852	0.0
Montgomery County, NC 0.01414 g	None	0.0	0.0	0.0
Randolph County, NC 0.03498 g	La-140	0.00253	0.07234	4.35

* Irradiated for 10 minutes at 500 KW and counted for 10 minutes.

Comments: Lanthanum (La) is the best across the rhyolite sample population that can be used in sourcing. It is absent in samples from southwestern Virginia rhyolites and has the highest concentrations in Maryland samples.

Geologic Note: Rhyolite is formed by flowing bands; thus, variation occurs both horizontally and vertically within deposits. The above is limited sampling and was not performed to document rhyolite formations. These data are used to confirm the technique; thousands of samples are needed to map sources.

Table 9 – Jasper Irradiated Samples

How Nuked	lt6/hrd6	lt7/hrd6	lt7/hrd6	lt7/hrd6	lt7/hrd6	lt9/hrd6	lt8/hrd6	lt8/hrd6	lt8/hrd6
Track #	Hran0010	Hran0011	Hran0012	Hran0013	Hran0014	Hran0015	Hran0016	Hran0017	Hran0018
Sample Source	Shoop Site	Warren Cty	Warren Cty	Warren Cty	Warren Cty	Thunderbird Site	Pennsylvania	Pennsylvania	Pennsylvania
Weight	0.7103 gram	3.775 gram	1.114 gram	2.976 gram	0.6667 gram	4.018 gram	6.415 gram	2.714 gram	0.4091 gram
Isotope									
Not (Na-22)	6.2	4.18	4.35	2.885	4.4375	39.445	2.475	4.25	8.25
Na-24 (hrd)	0.1065	0.0393	0.054	0.04225	0.04511	0.0505	0.145	0.1122	0.18885
Mg-27 (lt)	1.37	0.73	0.51						
Al-28 (lt)	1920	785	1470	961.5	1713	1296.5	531	1408	3301.5
K-42 (hrd)									
Mn-54 (hrd)		0.000089	0.000107	0.000109	0.000088	0.000024	0.000062	0.000065	0.000066
Mn-56 (lt)	0.517	0.71	0.82	2.895	0.41725	6.7	12.145	17.755	19.75
Fe-59 (hrd)		0.000885	0.001065	0.001048	0.000874	0.000219	0.000621	0.000652	0.000759
Co-60 (hrd)							0.000021	0.000019	0.000021
Zn-65 (hrd)							0.000069	0.000081	0.00008
As-76 (hrd)	***					0.004316	0.035535	0.030195	0.03859
Br-82 (hrd)									
Sb-122 (hrd)	0.001875		0.000665			0.000364	0.000449	0.000479	0.000663
Sm-153 (hrd)	0.00101	0.000385		0.002122	0.000313	0.000174	0.028275	0.019085	0.04683
Dy-165 (lt)							2.6115	6.545	4.9715
Au-198 (hrd)						0.000046			

Notes: lt = light nuke (0.02 Mw), hrd = hard nuked (20 Mw), Flux = 1e13/cm2/sec at 1 Mw. * = may exist.

Comments: The major differences in jasper sources produce varying compositional elements and variations in the amounts of each element. By creating radioactive isotopes, these elements can be measured. Numerous elements are produced by this technique, but they cannot be observed because of their extremely short half-lives. The heavier elements create observable isotopes, but more importantly, these elements are rare and offer better lithic fingerprinting based on statistical presentations of lithic composition. The obvious differences in this table for samples are the absence of cobalt (Co) and zinc (Zn) in Warren County specimens and the higher composition of iron (Fe) and manganese (Mn) in the Warren County specimens. Also, all specimens contain sodium (Na) that is the result of handling the specimens before placing them in the laboratory. The Shoop (PA) sample is simply a control item for ensuring statistical differences.

Note: lt = light radiation and hrd = hard radiation.

Results: While statistical relationships can be established for this set of tests, AU only occurs at Thunderbird. More testing would be needed; but it essentially argues that not all jasper at the Thunderbird site came from Warren County, Virginia. Thunderbird is located in that county.

Geologic Note: Jasper is a sedimentary formation that varies by the surface contents that form the deposits. As such, it can vary both horizontally and vertically. These data are not intended to map jasper deposits in the MPRV. These data are used to confirm the technique; thousands of samples are needed to map sources.

Prehistoric MPRV Chronology
(Native American History in the Potomac River Valley)

The prehistory of Maryland and Virginia's human history starts around 12,500 BP with a tool technology that is called Clovis after the 1930s lanceolate projectile point found near Clovis, New Mexico. The Thunderbird Paloindian site complex in the Shenandoah River valley initializes MPRV prehistory for the Potomac River valley. MPRV prehistory ends with the European contact in the middle 1500s to the early 1600s. The classic reference to European Contact is the 1608 visit of Captain John Smith which is Smith's First Bay Expedition June 2 to July 21 (see McCary 1957). This visit resulted in subsequent ethnographic recordings of Virginia's Native Americans. However, the Spanish and French were very active in Virginia waters during the last half of the 16th century; and they, not the English, were most likely to have been the first Europeans in the area (Lewis and Loomie 1953, Haile 1998, and Hranicky 1979).

Left: Smithsonian simulation display of Captain John Smith meeting MPRV Native Americans.

Archaeologists divide Virginia prehistoric chronology into Paleoindian, Archaic, and Woodland (PAW) Periods. The PAW model is based on Middle Atlantic archaeological site excavations and general research investigations, which include work in geographies above and below the MPRV. As an overview based on the Chesapeake Bay area, Dent (1995) presents an excellent picture of all three periods. Dates used here are based on Hranicky (1987 and 1994), Justice (1987), Carr and Haas (1996), and Maslowski, Niquette, and Wingfield (1995). All radiocarbon dates are calibrated dates unless otherwise indicated. The main source of radiocarbon dates is from the Virginia Department of Historic Resources' Virginia Radiocarbon Database (Egloff 1999). Hantman, Wood, and Shields (2000) offer an ethnographic example of connecting the Native Americans to the past. Swanton's (1946) ***The Indians of the Southeastern United States*** is used for basic ethnographic data.

For prehistory, time is a positional factor and not necessarily the same across geographies (synchronic versus diachronic). For example, coastal Virginia and Maryland see the use of pottery several hundreds of years before the western uplands Native Americans have it. As such, time becomes a precarious indicator of technology. Few artifacts, other than point types, are indicators of time. As an entity, technology is not a good time set when applied to large geographical areas. Unless, of course, you have Clovis or pottery technologies represented. This brings up time as an archaeological method that covers a range of years – never a specific year. Time is relative to both time and space; essentially, it is a generalized cultural sequence indicator.

Search for First Virginians and Marylanders

Sometime during the termination of the last Ice Age, the Middle Atlantic area sees the first human beings come into the area. The date for this arrival remains speculative, but 22,000 BP is being used in the archaeological community. This early date for the MPRV has not been proven, even though early sites, namely Cactus Hill (Virginia) (Figure 1), Topper (South Carolina) and Meadowcroft (Pennsylvania), are on both north and south geographies outside the MPRV and have approximately this early radiocarbon date for each site. South America has early dates and, if proven, may have a consequence on North American prehistory. For an early American prehistoric overview, see Dillehay (2000), Tankersley (2000), Parfit (2000), and Nemecek (2000).

These early American wayfarers saw the end of the Pleistocene and consequently, the extinction of approximately 30 separate genera. They are often accused of causing this extinction – so-called overkill theory. This is called the human-wave theory, which is still popular today (see Redman 1999). The extinction process arguments are suggested in Martin and Klein (1984).

The first MPRV inhabitants are the Paleoindians of which there is no radiometric date. The 9900 BP from the Thunderbird site in Warren County is used. It is based on Gardner (1974 and 1977). Prior to this date the area was probably void of any human populations.

Figure 1 – Cactus Hill points from the site in Sussex County, Virginia. The site dates 16,000 years ago. This site was the first archaeological proof of people in Virginia before Clovis. Photograph by Mike Johnson.

It is probably not (most likely) an environmental consequence but (and) most likely (not) a human-caused extinction; author's mix on words, causes, and blame. Or, as Ehrlich and Ehrlich (1981) comment:

Species are not all equally likely to disappear under the pressure of environmental change. The vulnerability of a species depends on a wide variety of such factors as its total population size, geographical distribution, reproductive ability, ecological relations with other species, and genetic characteristics.

Whichever, they played roles in the MPRV natural economies and subsequent ecologies. The toolmaking process is present (even perhaps initiated) here and is the primary role in culture throughout prehistory.

The major question archaeologically for the eastern U.S. is: did the first immigrants have the lanceolate technology? Were they simply using a simple blade technology? Questions and future research were presented at the Clovis and Beyond conference in Santa Fe, New Mexico in October 1999. The pre-Clovis questions are still a premiere interest; but for the moment, a more traditional MPRV prehistory is presented – Clovis pointmakers were the first people to come into the MPRV. And, based on nationally-collected fluted point data (U.S. National Park Service), including Virginia and North Carolina point data, the lower Middle Atlantic area has the largest concentration of fluted points found in the U.S. The southeast, probably the Carolinas, is the initializing source for Clovis technology (Hranicky and McCary 1995). This point type may be the lithic continuum of the Simpson and Suwannee types of Florida.

Middle Atlantic Timemarkers

While most point types represent calendar dates, some are used to indicate specific lifeways. Once a type becomes kind-of a symbol for a particular lifeway, it can become a timemarker in archaeology. The following types are good timemarkers for the Middle Atlantic area and make excellent MPRV timemarkers.

> **Clovis** = Paleoindian
> **Dalton** = Paleoindian to Archaic Transition
> **Hardaway** = Early Archaic
> **All Bifurcates** = Early to Middle Archaic
> **Morrow Mountain** = Middle Archaic
> **Halifax** = Late Archaic
> **Lamoka** = Late Archaic
> **Savannah River** = Late Archaic
> **Koens-Crispin** = Late Archaic
> **Meadowood** = Meadowood Phase
> **Susquehanna** = Late Archaic and Early Pottery
> **Adena** = Adena Culture, Early Woodland
> **Snyders** = Hopewell
> **Madison** = Middle Woodland
> **Clarksville/Potomac** = Late Woodland.

These points are discussed in the Projectile Point section and are used throughout this section. As with any type, there is variation within the basic morphology; however, most archaeologists recognize these types in the field and laboratory.

MPRV Technology Divisions

While many archaeologists assume cultural divisions for eastern prehistory, namely Paleoindian, Archaic, and Woodland Periods, the actual culture of people living during these periods has no designation other than pre-Contact Native Americans or for a short description - Indian. While some languages can be argued via glottochronology, any tribal associations are usually out of the question for archaeology. The Algonuian language is assumed at least back to 1000 year ago (see Harrington 1955, Bloomfield 1946, and Siebert 1975). Many Native American groups claim identification and association with these early archaeological periods, but they too cannot prove it. The Woodland Period probably has some tribal association for the entire period, but migrations still play a role in eastern occupations.

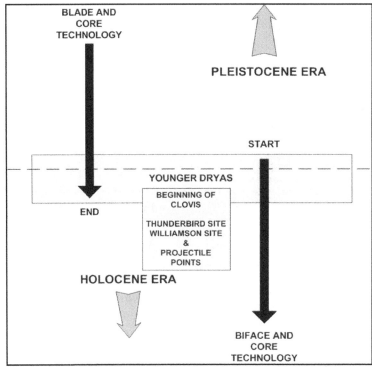
Basic Model for Human Occupation of Virginia with Early Sites

The Middle Atlantic area has nine Pleistocene dates. These generalized are:

**#1 = Meadowcroft (PA) [16,000 YBP]
#2 = Topper (SC) [50,000+ YBP]
#3 = Arkfeld (VA) [presently, no date]
#4 = Spout Run (VA) [10,000+YBP]
#5 = Saltville (VA) [16,000 YBP]
#6 = Cactus Hill (VA) [16,000 YBP]
#7 = Cinmar (VA) [22,000 YBP]
#8 = Brook Run (VA) [13,000 YBP]
#9 = Miles Point (MD) [20,000 YBP].**

As to a better reference to early Americans, the periods are equated with major technology, as:

- **Early American Period = time of the first entry of people into Virginia (blade technology). Also, it is called the Pleistocene era occupations.**

- **Paleoindian Period = Clovis (biface and blade) technology with atlatl. Start of "arrowhead" technology in Virginia.**

- **Archaic Period = Multiple technologies (bifaces and polished macrotools)**

- **Woodland Period = Ceramic and horticulture technology (village life) with bow and arrow.**

Technology does not drive history; there is no technology determinism in the Native American social systems. And, it is not evolutionism (Darwinianism or Spencerianism) as a means of change based on technology. As stated and repeating, technology is a continuum that is superimposed on all human societies. How much of a factor it was on social behavior remains in current archaeology – more-or-less – a speculative orientation.

Even with the above forms of technology, the projectile point is still the basic timemarker. For example, Figure 2 shows Adena points from the Ohio River valley found in Maryland. These points have a distinctive style and easily mark the Early Woodland Period. See Projectile Point section for discussion of the Adena point. The above framework constitutes the basic philosophy of the study.

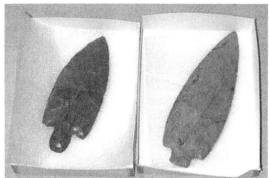

Figure 2 – Two Flint Adena Points from Maryland's Eastern Shore. For the Woodland Period, the Adena type is one of the best-made points in the Eastern U.S. (Jefferson-Patterson Park and Museum).

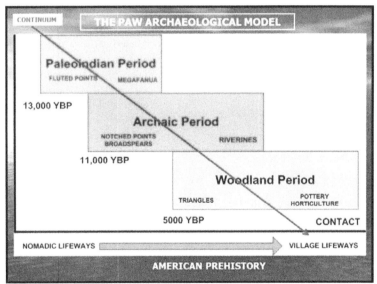

Figure 3 - Classic Presentation: Paleoindian (P), Archaic (A), and Woodland (W) – the PAW Model

Culture Chronology

As a special note, the above archaeological periods are academic and do not necessarily translate into ground-buried resources (Figure 3). This framework provides a laboratory division on materials collected from the past. These divisions have changed with each generation of archaeologists, for example the Paleoindian and Archaic Transition Periods, Midwestern system, etc. Archaeological classifications remain – the best guess of professional and amateur archaeologists working at this time with the antiquities in hand and with those artifacts recovered from previous investigations. There is always something new to be discovered which, may or may not, change our present interpretations of prehistory.

Basically known as the PAW model, lithics for these archaeological periods in the MRPV are:

Paleoindian Period - *Thin sections of jasper tend to suggest a single source for stone used by the Paleoindians. This practice has been classified as lithic determinism in archaeology; however, lithics do not necessarily control the*

overall social constitution in prehistoric societies. It still implies travel to specific quarry areas which affect hunting/gathering practices and habitation locations. Travel to quarries sometimes involved hundreds of miles. The period generally date 13,000 to 11,000 BP.

<u>Archaic Period</u> - Quartzite thin sections suggest wide-spread acquisition for the stone which is the most common used during the Archaic Period. Quartzite is readily available throughout Maryland and Virginia, especially in outcrops surrounding river basins. The pick-up cobble is also a primary source for the Indians. Quarrying, especially in the uplands, is the secondary source. The Early Archaic Period is a carryover of cryptocrystalline stones from the Paleoindian Period, namely flint and jasper usage. The period generally dates 11,000 to 5000 BP.

<u>Woodland Period</u> - Thin sections tend to show local acquisition of stones, but foreign stones do occur. The variety of stones used by the Indians also suggests that stone preference was not a major concern. There is an increase in lithic artforms where high quality and exotic stones were preferred. The MPRV sees stone, usually flints and cherts, coming in occasionally from the Northeast and Ohio River valley. The principal stones were quartzite, rhyolite, and quartz. The period general dates 5000 to Contact.

Demographics

The MPRV has the approximately the same demographics as the Middle Atlantic area (Figure 4). However, few studies exist and the following are presented as a starting place for future research. The following charts was influenced by Hancock (1927), Mooney (1928ohnson (1999), Dobyns (1966), Feest (1973), Ubelacker (1974), Turner (1978 and 1989), Hranicky and McCary (1996), and Klein and Klatka (1991). A classic model for demographics is Hassan's (1981) ***Demographic Archaeology***.

Based on the MPRV environment at various times, ethnographic data, and experiences derived from experimental archaeology and generalized hour counting, the Native Americans spent:

Paleoindian Period (80% of day light time in food procurement)

Middle Archaic Period (90% of day light time in food procurement)

Late Archaic Period (75% of day light time in food procurement) Beginning of a settled way of life.

Late Woodland Period (55% of day light time in food procurement) Horticulture produced most the daily needs for food.

Figure 4 – Generalized Population Estimate for the MPRV. During the Paleoindian and Early Archaic Periods, there were times when there were no Native Americans in Virginia and Maryland.

These percentages are untested but argue that lifeways became more efficient toward the Contact era. Figure 3 suggests population numbers during the pre-Contact era, but again, it is only a suggestion as a starting point for future research. Based on a 316 skeletal study by the author at the Smithsonian (Hranicky 1975), the ages of the average prehistoric group were:

Lifespans:
Years:	0-12	13-20	21-35	36-55	56+
No:	119	33	78	75	11

Based on biological principles, a survivable population needs to have 300+ members. The average band or village had at least this number of individuals.

Estimates for pre-Contact Virginia vary with little consensus; however, as a suggestion, the indigenous population numbered over 30,000 individuals. For population estimates see Feest (1973). Also, see MacCord's (2001) ***How Crowded Was Virginia in A.D. 1607?***

Table on the Powhatan
Thomas Jefferson's Notes on Virginia

Based on Hassan (1981) and Butzer (1971), the following premises are assumed for the general Native American population (growth and settlement) in the MPRV:

- Food production for the Archaic/Woodland Periods became possible because wild

progenitors for both plants and animals already existed in the MPRV.
- Shelters and seasonal clothing were developed early in prehistory.
- Native Americans of the Late Archaic Period were harvesting the wildlife that led to a food producing society.
- Populations were becoming riverine-based societies during the Late Archaic Period.
- Overall, the Holocene forced changes is subsistence, namely forest-oriented foodstuffs.
- Seasonal maturation of fruits and berries, bird and fish migrations, and stationary game herds offered predictable food supplies.
- Technology was a continuum that originated in the Paleoindian Period and was modified through time to meet changing needs in habitation.
- Native American ancestry is traceable to the first inhabitants of the MPRV.
- Native American adaptive strategies produced food surpluses.

Of course, these premises are only applied to lithic technology. Even then, they are suggestions for cause-effect arguments for MPRV occupations and resource utilizations. Overall, MPRV archaeology has a *long way* to go before we have a complete picture of Native American history in the Potomac River valley.

PAW Summary

This publication presents a traditional summary of the PAW periods in the MPRV. It is based on current research and interpretations by archaeologists working in the MPRV. For early MPRV-Middle Atlantic syntheses, Hranicky (1974) offered **A Framework for Virginia Prehistory** and Thomas (1974) offered **A Brief Survey of Prehistoric Man on the Delmarva Peninsula**. Following these summaries, others followed, such as Custer (1996 and 1984), Dent (1995), Wittkoski and Reinhart (1989), Curry and Custer (1982), and Reinhart and Hodges (1990, 1991, and 1992). For a summary in Frederick County, Virginia's Opequon Creek, see Geier and Hofstra (1999).

The prehistory of the Middle Atlantic area could not be written without the assistance of volunteers, especially those belonging to organizations like the Archeological Society of Virginia (ASV) and the Archeological Society of Maryland, Inc (ASM). These volunteers, usually called amateur archaeologists, have contributed countless hours to all phases of American archaeology, namely hours in excavations, hours in laboratory work, and hours in hunting and recording archaeological sites. The following two pages show examples of site excavations with volunteers (Plates 5 and 6).

Tables 1 and 2 present an overview of point and tool industries, chronology, and technology for the MPRV. MPRV radiocarbon dates are found in Egloff (1999). More dates, especially for pottery, are located in Potter (1993), and points in Reeve (1992) and Petraglia and Knepper (1996). Related Blue Ridge dates are in Inashima (1992). Plate 7 shows MPRV fluted points.

While well entrenched in Middle Atlantic archaeology and suggested above, the PAW divisions may be the greatest arbitrary decision ever made in American archaeology. And, defining it may obscure the true nature of the occupation of Virginia and Maryland by Native Americans. Few archaeologists agree on the end of the Paleoindian Period other than the discontinuance of the Clovis point. For years, a transition period was argued for Paleoindian-Archaic Periods. This resulted in the Dalton, and for some archaeologists, the Hardaway points being placed in the Paleoindian Period. Next toward the end of the Archaic Period, few agree when and what constitutes the start of the Woodland Period other than the absence or presence of pottery. Even today, the term *Terminal Archaic* is used; perhaps it does imply the end to a cultural way(s).

The use of archaeological periods is perhaps what Stewart (1992) calls a heuristic device that permits archaeologists to communicate. Another viewpoint is Mouer's (1991) *Formative Transition*. Reference here to any period is relative and assumes extensive overlap among periods. Reference to early, middle, and late are generalized time references within each period. This publication tries to avoid the archaeological magic of the number *3* (Hranicky 1983); an imposed tripartite on culture does not work. Mouer (1990) notes this history of dividing prehistory into *three* parts.

MPRV prehistory is viewed here as a technological continuum. Various classes/types were modified to meet local social and ideological preferences, but the overall Native Americans toolkit remained essentially the same (Panindian) for all triparts of prehistory. Culture is viewed here as collective social behavior based on survival via lithic technology. A society is a group of people who have chosen not to live in scattered isolation, but live as a social unit where members submit to norms, traditions, and values which are established by the whole group. The technological continuum parallels or is intertwined among interacting groups who exchanged ideas, beliefs, information, etc. These interactions constitute the knowledge base, in this case, toolmaking. Over time, this interaction created the Panindian nature of technology.

When technology is viewed as a continuum from whatever was brought into the New World to what is found at Contact, events of inventions, innovations, adoptions, and borrowing technological methods or approaches do not readily present major periods of prehistory. For example, the projectile point technology is used throughout prehistory. Why should the invention of the notch constitute a new time period when all other elements in the toolkit remain the same? Does the invention of pottery, or for the MPRV borrowing it, change a time period? Naturally, purists assume such, but the fact is that bowls are found previously; natural food resources were utilized throughout prehistory; political and social practices were developed earlier with sociolinguistical divisions based on linguistic heritages and families. All of which leaves pottery a single event in the history of Native Americans. Horticulture is nothing more than localized control of plants. Wild plants and fruits are still available. Justification for a Woodland Period is a game that archaeologists play with pottery – pottery does not equal culture alone. In fact, technology is only one aspect of culture; unfortunately, it is what is found most often archaeologically.

Text continued on page 77.

Archeological Society of Maryland 1978 Fieldschool at Nolands Ferry Site. Archaeologist and Fieldschool Director Tyler Bastian working with amateur archaeologists William and Muriel Lynch. The Maryland Annual Fieldschool draws over a hundred amateur archaeologists each year. The fieldschool provides training as well as opportunities to work in real archaeology – digging into the past in Maryland.

Table 1 – Major Toolkit Classes in MPRV Prehistory		
Paleoindian Period	**Archaic Period**	**Woodland Period**
Basic Toolkit:	**Toolkit Additions:**	**Toolkit Additions:**
Abrader	Axe**	Adz*
Chopper	Bannerstone	Bow and Arrow
Drill	Birdstone	Chisel
Flaking tool	Blade Serration	Fishhook
Graver	Boatstone	Hoe
Hammerstone	Boilingstone	Mortar
Knife	Bola	Netsinker
Perforator	Celt	Pendant
Projectile Point	Gorget	Pestle
Saw	Holestone	Pipe
Scraper	Container***	Pottery
Sharpener		Splitter
Spokeshave	**Toolkit Deletion:**	
Wedge	Saw	
	Wedge	⇑ Post-2000 BC (4000 YBP)
⇑ Post-9500 BC (11,500 YBP)****	⇑ Post-8500 BC (10,500 YBP)	
Old World Carryover:		
Atlatl		
Blade Tools (?)		

* Adz is classified as a Woodland Period invention.

** Axe is added as a response to the forest environment which began in the Archaic period; the 3/4 groove axe is considered here as a Late Archaic Period invention; 4/4 grooving starts in the Middle Archaic Period.

*** Stone containers are made from steatite and ceramic containers have fiber tempering.

**** Recent archaeological investigations at the Cactus Hill site in Sussex County, Virginia has yielded evidence that Native Americans were in Virginia as early as 16,000 years ago (Johnson 2000). This time does not apply to MPRV chronology.

Plate 5 – Volunteers at the Fisher Site (44LD4) Loudoun County, Virginia (1981)

Fisher Site Directors - Howard MacCord and Jack Hranicky An invitation to help with an excavation usually draws amateur archaeologists from all over the state. Examples of their work are shown on this and the next page.	Washing artifacts, artifacts, artifacts; and showing an excavated artifact to other volunteers.

From site lay out to back filling the site after the excavation.	Field instruction on how to excavate a feature; field training is common in Virginia and Maryland archaeology.

Volunteers working in main trench across the site; learning by doing.	Howard MacCord and Michael Johnson (Right) – Johnson is site director on the Taft site on next page.

Plate 6 – Volunteers at the Taft Site (44FX70), Fairfax County, Virginia (1986)

Finishing an excavation square for mapping, recordkeeping, and photography.

Volunteer measuring the precise location of an artifact and in background another volunteer continues to excavate.

Laying out a site square for excavation and screening (washing) dirt from an excavated square.

Field laboratory instruction for processing artifacts; artifacts were processed daily.

Archaeology frequently draws the news media; it is popular with the American public.

Archaeologist's toolkit...Every archaeologist has a personal set of tools that he/she always uses in the field.

This is the world of volunteer archaeology...

1986 Fieldschool at the Taft site; some of these volunteers were working on Amateur Certification. Michael Johnson was Site Director, and Jack Hranicky was Fieldschool Coordinator.

Table 2 – MPRV Technology Overview

Years	Archaeological Period	Lifeways and Environment	Major Starting Technology	Comments BC/AD Dates
400 BP (Note 1)	Late Woodland ↓ Period II (Note 5)	Regional political organizations. Space is closed and wooded. Soils = settlement patterns. Occupied all ecoscenes.	Potomac Hoe Splitters Copper ornaments	Prehistory ends and the protohistory for the MPRV starts with Capt. John Smith's visit in 1609. Major pottery types are Townsend (1000 – 1700 AD), Page (1250 – 1400 AD), Keyser (1300 – 1500 AD), Rappahannock (950 - 1550 AD), and Potomac Creek (1360 - 1600 AD) (Note: 16). Palisaded villages start >1400 AD. Copper and shell gorgets are added to material culture. Language is Algonquian. Decorated and effigy pipes are found. General domestication of maize (1300 AD), squash, and bean (900 AD) plants; hoe is added to the toolkit.
500 BP Chieftain (Note 13)				
Potomac Native Americans				Origins of the Native Americans as the Europeans found them in the 17th century (Note 12).
1000 BP		Large villages, established horticulture practices	Levanna Madison Gouge Chisel Bow/Arrow	Generalized time for starting the Late Woodland. Major pottery types are Mockley (200 – 750 AD), Culpeper (0-800 AD) (Note: 17), and Shepard (750 – 1300 AD). The Middle Atlantic area sees the introduction of the large triangle point as the dominant point form.
2000 BP	Middle Woodland ↓ Period I (Note 5)	Small villages Occupied all ecoscenes.	Piscataway Potts Warratan Jacks Reef Snyders	Generalized time for starting the Middle Woodland. Beginnings of established villages. Major pottery is Popes Creek (650 BC – 200 AD). Corn (maize) is introduced around 200 AD (Note 14).
3000 BP		Start of hamlets and horticulture (slash & burn) (Note 4)	Bare Island Meadowood Adena Adz Bowls	Small bands of hunter/gatherers still occur with small hamlets. Major pottery types are Marcy Creek (1350 – 1100 BC), Bushnell (1350 BC) and Selden Island (1250 – 900 BC). Pipe probably occurs here. Food storage pits and mortar/pestle become common. Triangle point technology moves into the MPRV area (Note 9). This time basically ends the broadspear tradition.
4000 BP	Early Woodland ↑ Period I (Note 5)	Local riverine, long term occupations; beginning of horticulture versus their former foraging ways.	Susquehanna Lamoka Koens-Crispin Savannah River 3/4 groove axe	Archaic Period ends around 2000 BC for the MPRV (Note 6). Savannah River and Susquehanna points are associated with steatite bowls. It marks the beginning of domesticated plant seeds. Around 1600 BC, fiber-tempered pottery comes into Virginia's coastal plain from the coastal Southeast.
Plant/seed domesticated; start of horticulture (Note 15).				
5000 BP	Late Archaic ↓↑	General foraging/ nomadic bands. Occupied all ecoscenes.	Halifax Chipped axe	Probably represents the beginning of bipolar flaking method. This time starts the narrowspear tradition. The 3/4 groove axe first appears.
6000 BP		Space is mostly wooded.	Guilford	MPRV may periodically be void of human occupation.
7000 BP	Middle Archaic ↓	Space is mixed grasslands and woods.	Morrow Mountain II and Morrow Mountain I	Generalized time for the Middle Archaic Period. Time starts the broadspear technology (tradition) in the Middle Atlantic area (Note 3).

Years	Archaeological Period	Lifeways and Environment	Major Starting Technology	Comments BC/AD Dates
			Stanly (Note 10) Mortar/Pestle	
8000 BP		Occupied all ecoscenes.	Kirk Stemmed	Axe technology comes into Virginia and Maryland around this time. Beginning of bannerstones (Note 7). Stemmed point technology is added to the prehistoric toolkit.
9000 BP		Small band occupation of all ecoscenes.	LeCroy St Albans MacCorkle Big Sandy	Less reliance on quarried materials for tools; fields and stream beds become sources for lithic materials. Start of hunting small game, such as deer, rabbit.
10,000 BP	Early Archaic ↓	Wide-spread, nomadic migration. Space is open with grasslands. Occupied all ecoscenes.	Kirk Notched Big Sandy Palmer St Charles (Note 11) Hardaway Celt	Starts the Early Archaic Period. Paleoindian Period ends around 8500 BC. Corner/side notching becomes the dominant point technology, but bifurcate technology is also present and used by highly migratory populations. Marks the beginning of quartzite as the predominant material. Boat technology is probably a carryover from the Paleoindian.
10,500 BP		Start of side-notched technology and regional cultures.	Hardaway-Dalton Dalton	Post-Pleistocene environment.
11,000 BP	Paleoindian ↓↑	Hunter/gatherer bands tied to game migrations or sources. High mobility tied to cryptocrystalline lithics. ↑	Clovis Atlatl Blades Wedges	Atlatl is used for spear throwing; borrowed or brought into Virginia and Maryland that is used throughout prehistory. Human-built shelters as demonstrated at the Thunderbird site. Staged bifaces in tool production (Note 8). The lanceolate is the only point in the MPRV.
13,000 BP (Note 2)				No site evidence that any human occupation occurs in the MPRV prior to 11,000 BP. For the lower eastern Atlantic coastal plain, it is basically a lithic preprojectile point era; blade technology.

Note 1: Population estimates can be found in Feest (1973), Klein and Klatka (1991), and Randolph (1978).
Note 2: During the early prehistory, there were times in Virginia that were devoid of Native Americans (Hranicky and McCary 1996).
Note 3: Broadspear technology may represent a new wave of Native Americans coming into Virginia, even for the East. Coe (1964) refers
      to the Stanly type as the beginning or the Broadspear Tradition.
Note 4: Slash and burn horticulture and villages (see Potter 1993).
Note 5: Based on Custer (1984).
Note 6: Based on pottery dates by Waselkov (1982) and steatite association for Savannah River points.
Note 7: Based on Coe (1964). No Virginia or Maryland dates have been obtained.
Note 8: Custer (1990).
Note 9: Triangle points date to 5-3000 BP in the Northeast (Brennan 1984). However, the triangle biface occurs throughout
      prehistory; its usage as a tool remains to be established technologically.
Note 10: Stanly points are rare in the MPRV.
Note 11: St Charles has a technological relationship with the Hardaway pointmakers.
Note 12: Potomac valley Native Americans probably have an earlier, continuous history, but the MPRV suggests at least three
      language families.
Note 13: Potter (1993) suggests starting date for chieftain organization in the MPRV.
Note 14: Based on Smith (1993).
Note 15: Meggers (1954) suggests horticulture as criteria for the beginning of the Woodland (ceramic ear) Period.
Note 16: Early date of 1160 is based on Dent (2000).
Note 17: Triassic sandstone-tempered ware, based on Johnson (2000).

Table 3 – McCary Fluted Point Survey Data for the MPRV

Point #	Length	Flute 1	Flute 2	Width	Thickness	Material	County
318 *	54	50	32	32	6	Chert	Prince William
391	73	17		29	8	Rhyolite	Loudoun
471 *	25	16	14	22	4	Greenstone	Fairfax
688	60	22	49	24	6	Rhyolite	Fairfax
852 #	95	22.5	9	30	10	Quartz	Fairfax
853	74	35	40	28	8	Chert	Fairfax
854	60	50	36	25	7	Chert	Fairfax
855 *	25	22	13	28	6	Chert	Fairfax
856 *	12	12	11	20	5	Quartz	Fairfax
857 *#	79	20		29	10	Jasper	Warren
858 *#	74.5	29	20	33	8	Jasper	Warren
859 *#	94.5	28	26	33	9	Jasper	Warren
860 *#	74	25	23	31	8	Jasper	Warren
861 #	84.5	33	31	32	7.5	Jasper	Warren
862 *	43	40	33	32	7,5	Jasper	Warren
863 *	42	38	10	34	10	Jasper	Warren
864 *	30	13	12	22	6	Jasper	Warren
865	27.5	24	22	19	5	Chert	Warren
866 *#	42	18	17	27.5	7	Jasper	Warren
867 *#	64	22.5	19	26	8.5	Jasper	Warren
872	46			31	6,5	Jasper	Loudoun
880 *	45	12	8	20	7	Quartzite	Warren
882	32	14	12	21	8	Quartz	Prince William
933 *	33	4	7	25	7	Chalcedony	Warren
945	46	12	20	24.5	7	Jasper	Loudoun
946 *	34			30	5.5	?	Loudoun
949	45	14.5		20	12	Quartz	Loudoun
Averages	52.37	23.74	21.09	26.96	7.39		
Virginia Specimen Averages (Hranicky and McCary 1995)							
	50.7	21.0	14.0	25.5	6.5		
Thunderbird Specimen Average (Hranicky and McCary 1995)							
	61.2	N/A	N/A	29.6	8.0		
**Comparative Sample from Darke County, Ohio (Holzapfel 2001)						Based on 36 points.	
Averages	58.7	21.3		25.6	6.5		

* Broken points
\# Points shown in the Projectile Point section
(See Hranicky 1989 for McCary Survey description and contribution).
** Randomly selected sample to show consistency in Clovis points

Plate 7 - McCary Survey Clovis Points

Note: These points were included as comparative examples. For more information, see Hranicky and McCary (1995).

MC 984	MC 391	MC 392	MC 442	MC 471
Jasper	Rhyolite	Chert	Shale	Greenstone
33-20-5 mm	73-29-8 mm	91-33-9 mm	85-34-9 mm	x-22-4 mm
Fairfax Co.	Loudoun Co.	Fauquier Co.	Prince George Co.	Fairfax Co.

MC 853 Chert 74-28-8 mm Fairfax Co.	MC 854 Chert 60-25-7 mm Fort Belvoir	MC 855 Chert x-28-6 mm Fairfax Co.	MC 856 Quartz x-20-5 mm Fairfax Co.	MC 857 Jasper 79-30-10 mm Warren Co.
MC 858 Jasper 75-33-8 mm Warren Co.	MC 859 Jasper 95-33-9 mm Warren Co.	MC 860 Jasper 74-31-8 mm Warren Co.	MC 861 Jasper 85-32-8 Warren Co.	MC 862 Jasper x-32-8 mm Warren Co.
MC 863 Jasper x-34-10 mm Warren Co.	MC 864 Agate 30-22-6 mm Warren Co.	MC 865 Black Jasper 28-19-5 mm Warren Co.	MC 866 Jasper 42-28-7 mm Warren Co.	MC 867 Jasper 64-26-9 mm Warren Co.
MC 872 Jasper x-31-7 mm Loudoun Co.	MC 873 Jasper 46-31-7 mm Loudoun Co.	MC 880 Quartzite 46-20-7 mm Warren Co.	MC 945 Jasper 46-25-7 mm Loudoun Co.	MC 949 Quartz 45-20-12 mm Loudoun Co.

Paleoindian Culture Summary

The MPRV Paleoindian Period dates to the first arrival of the Native Americans into Virginia and Maryland and ends at various places between 12,500 and 9000 BP. It is characterized by the presence of the Clovis point and a well-developed toolkit. For the present, there is no ancestry in the MPRV for this technology. The basic environment is terminal Pleistocene of grasslands and sparse boreal forests. The Native Americans hunted megafauna and herd animals as well as being general food collectors. However, no megafauna kills have been identified with archaeological certainty in Virginia or Maryland. Overall, the general living conditions were in a Boreal environment. For a classic publication, see Newman and Salwen's (1977) *Amerinds and Their Paleoenvironment in Northeastern North America* for a comprehensive study of major sites, including the Thunderbird site, in environmental settings and influences on occupations.

Paleoindian artifacts occur throughout the MPRV's watershed, but the highest occupation is in the upper Piedmont, namely Warren County along the Shenandoah River. Jasper resources were primarily obtained from local quarry sites in the county. Other jasper sources were used, such as the Point of Rocks jasper. This utilization may have been after the Thunderbird Native Americans left the MPRV area. While Paleoindian occupations occur in other areas of the MPRV, no specific part of the watershed stands out as a Paleoindian choice.

The McCary Fluted Point Survey data for the MPRV suggest Thunderbird influences into the MPRV; however, a few points were made from local stones as opposed to jasper from Warren County. One point in the survey (#471) was made from greenstone; this material is brittle and difficult to knap. The general cultural pattern for the MPRV habitation and technology for the Paleoindian Period is the Thunderbird site.

As presented, the initializing MPRV tool technology is the Clovis pointmakers (Figures 5 and 6). Table 4 provides a summary of Paleoindian point data for the MPRV Paleoindian Period. The MPRV is closer to the normal Clovis distribution as computed from Virginia; however, the Thunderbird points are thicker (6.5 to 8.0 mm). Thunderbird point thickness is probably due to biface breakage (before final thinning) by unskilled or inexperienced knappers, but the actual stone could be the factor for thickness. A recently published fluted point survey (Holzapfel 2001) has point dimensions similar to the MPRV population. These data in the above table suggest consistency in Clovis technology.

Figure 5 – Virginia Longest Clovis Point. The Clovis point is regarded as the best point technology of all American point types. It is McCary Fluted Survey Point Number 748 and is called the Loy Carter point, who was instrumental in preserving it.

The Indian society during the Paleoindian Period was a simple equalitarian form with small groups of nuclear or extended families. The band was an aggregation of families or possibly clans which were under a single political control. Band size numbered between 50 and 75 people. The family may have been matralocal and was an extended family consisting of kinship members, including children and elderly members. Periodically, the band broke into small units which were task-oriented, such as hunting or quarrying. Religious or ideological beliefs were based on magic and their conceived spirit worlds. Technologically, the toolkit was well-developed, multifunctional, and adequate for daily survival. It consisted of biface, blade, and hammer (chopper) tool industries.

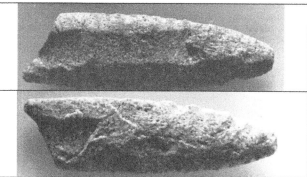

Figure 6 – Broken Clovis Point from Montgomery County, Maryland (Both Faces). As mentioned in the Introduction section, most archaeological remains are discarded items from the past; however, all these objects are useful in reconstructing history. This point was snapped during usage and was discarded a long time ago (photograph supplied by James Sorenson).

The MPRV Clovis point style/definitions are based on the Williamson and Thunderbird sites. Even then, they more closely resemble northeastern Clovis points than any other area (Johnson 1989). However, this may be reflective of a time gap and change over time, which is probably indicative of the Native Americans following northern migration of game herds. Hranicky (2001 and 2002) attempts to argue that the Simpson and Suwannee Paleoindian points predate Clovis. Both types are found in

Virginia and possibly further north along the coastal plain. Following this logic, the Williamson site is older than Thunderbird (Hranicky and McCary 1996). Technoclovisly, Williamson people did not move to the Thunderbird site and area; there is a stylistic difference between their points. The Thunderbird site has become the model for Maryland/Virginia Paleoindian studies (Figure 7). Consequently, it is not necessarily representative for southern Virginia and the Carolinas.

The Clovis point is basically bimodal (operation) tool as it served as a knife and projectile point. During the Clovis/Dalton stage, the point becomes trimodal as the drill function was added to the blade. Shortly thereafter, the scraper function was added. This appears to be unusual since the hand-held scraper was so common. The exact date for these technologies remains to be established. From this point in time, most projectile points are multimodal. Modal functions are discussed in the Toolmaking Technology section.

Figure 7 – Excavation at Thunderbird Site, Warren County, Virginia During the 1973 Season. William A. Gardner was the site director. Most of the site has been purchased and is now in the public realm.

Clovis is a biface technology; however, it is frequently associated with uniface (preferably called blade technology). The Williamson site offers proof of this association. While hard to prove, some Clovis points were made off a blade. The blade was worked bifacially. This technique works in experimental archaeology and remains to be documented in a site context.

In addition to the famous Clovis point, their toolkit consisted of the abrader, anvil, chopper, drill, flaking tool, graver, hammerstone, knife, perforator, projectile point, scraper, spokeshave, and wedge (see Dent 1991 and 1995). Most of these classes were initiated in the Paleoindian Period and continued to Contact. The wedge served as a felling tool (Hranicky 2002a). By holding it next to a tree trunk and striking its poll, the bark and wood can be cut, eventually downing the tree. It probably served as an ancestral form of technology for the axe and celt.

Their clothing was animal skins, which was not essentially needed in the paleoenvironment. The shelter was simple post supported dwellings which primarily served as wind and rain protectors. At these sites, there were no forms of food storage as the food supply was readily available. The habitation sites were not locations where Native Americans made their tools. Paleosites tend to show workstation locations near quarry sites.

As mentioned, the Paleoindian technology consisted of both biface and blade technologies with the latter predating Clovis technology. The distribution of Clovis points includes the entire U.S. and could imply a single, large population moving all over during a 7-800-year period. For their general population, groups split off and became regional populations with their specific technologies. Overall archaeologically, the Clovis point originated in the Southeast (Anderson 1990 and Hranicky and McCary 1996). Blade technology tends to follow the Clovis point distribution in North America.

There are deep bogs at the Thunderbird site that remain to be investigated that may contain earlier evidence of human occupation (Figure 8). The inference here is that the MPRV contains numerous deeply buried sites for the early parts of prehistory.

Figure 8 – Lanier Rodgers (August 1973) working on a ladder which reached down (5+ meters) to an ancient bog at the Thunderbird Site, Warren County, Virginia. He carried mud up to the surface one bucket at a time. In later years, he received the Archeological Society of Virginia's Amateur of the Year Award and is an outstanding example of amateur archaeology in America.

The main subsistence was meat because during Boreal conditions there was a lack of edible plants. As megafauna were random migratory herds; the Native Americans were too. With breaks to replenish toolkits with specific lithic materials, the Native Americans followed them. This can be classified as what Binford (1980) calls specialized foragers settlement pattern. Overall, Paleoindian sites reflect what Boyd (1989) calls:

...sameness and ...they practiced a high-quality hunting specific technology.

In other words, they were general foragers and scavengers who hunted large game, but also killed small animals and ate plants, berries, grubs, and roots. Their diet was multinutritional and adequate and remains basically the same until the Woodland Period when more specialized plants were added to their diet.

The study of early MPRV Native Americans is handicapped because there has not been a final report on the excavations at Thunderbird in Warren County, Virginia. Research is limited to partial site reports of Gardner (1974, 1977, 1978, 1981, 1983, 1985, 1986, 1989) and Gardner and Verrey (1979). This is a major site in Virginia, and it needs to have a final report. See Speiden (2000) for summary of the site purchase placing it into the public realm. Table 4 presents a general summary of the Paleoindian Period.

Table 4 – Paleoindian Period Summary
• **Game-specific hunting**
• **Single lithic preferences**
• **Absence of rock-lined hearths**
• **End of Clovis point technology**
• **Established toolkit**
• **Change to smaller points**
• **End of high-quality knapping**
• **Atlatl and spear technology**
• **Wide-spread mobility**
• **Boat technology**
• **Bands start subdividing**
• **Open grassland ecology**
• **Savannah environment**
• **Occupation in a stable environment**

Archaic Culture Summary

The Archaic Period, if for many archaeological purposes in theory and concepts, only serves as the *middle ages* between the Paloindian and Woodland Period Native Americans. It occupies the greatest amount of time during prehistory. The MPRV Archaic Period dates from 9500-8000 to 2000-1000 BP with overlaps for the pre- and succeeding periods. It is not particularly a popular focus for archaeological investigations. And after its initiation, site densities and populations become more of a scatter of lithic debris by very small groups of people. With some exceptions, it is a period of short-term campsites by Native Americans with the hearth as the principal archaeological feature. The environment ranges from a Boreal to Atlantic conditions. It does mark the end of the Pleistocene and the beginning of the Holocene for the Middle Atlantic area. Evidence of this change is probably reflected in the need for continuous fires; the fire-cracked rock becomes common in sites after the Paleoindian Period. These rocks are the result of rock-lined hearths that also indicated a change in cooking methods and foods. See MPRV Environment section.

As a time period, Egloff and McAvoy (1990) suggest (and modified here) the period represents basically:

- Post-Pleistocene environment for the Native Americans
- Shift from hunting megafauna and large herd animals to smaller forest game
- Introduction of new projectile point technologies
- General population increases
- Increased use of the multifunctional tool
- Development of the macrotool.

The period is generally divided into:

1 – Early Archaic (8500-8000 to 5000 BC)
2 – Middle Archaic (5000 to 3500 BC)
3 – Late Archaic (3500 to 2000-1000 BC).

All watersheds appear to have been occupied. The watershed sees small campsites along the minor rivers and second terraces of the Potomac River. The occupations do not have settlement preferences. The MPRV watershed was an extension of coastal aquatic Native American habitation which had its beginnings in the Paleoindian Period (see Snow 1980, Claassen 1991, or Waselkov 1987). This economical affection on tools remains to be studied and is not attempted here.

Probably the most significant watershed event is one that is geological – the formation of the Potomac estuary. The actual river dates earlier to the Pleistocene and was formed from runoff from northern glaciation. At the beginning of the Archaic Period, the landscape and ecology starts changing for the MPRV; both of which are usually the only focus of archaeological publications. As they tend to suggest, trees march across the MPRV at 30 meters per year which becomes the forested ecology of the Woodland Period.

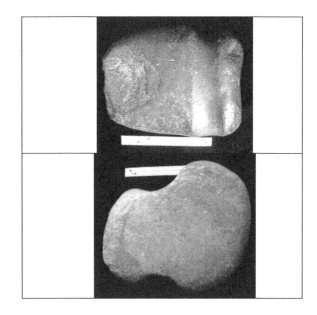

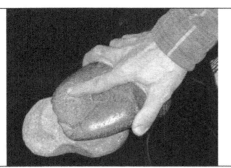

Figure 9 – Hands-on the Late Archaic Period. The period sees the Invention of the Flat Bottom (Tressel) Axe. Top photograph is a 3/4 groove, greenstone axe (L = 152, W = 113, T = 53 mm, wgt: 130 Kg, and groove averages 27 mm in width). Middle photograph is an associated quartzite whetstone (L = 116 mm, W = 133, T = 57 mm) with greenstone still remaining on its surface. Lower photograph shows a simulation of the axe resharpening process and using the actual whetstone.

For the early part of the Archaic Period, the Native American lifeways followed as a Paleoindian lifeway, with the exception of the large lanceolate point. The early Native Americans still preferred high quality lithic materials but were becoming increasingly use to picking up field and riverbed cobbles for their lithic sources (Hranicky 1986).

With the large game herds gone, the Native Americans started hunting smaller animals and continued a general foraging economy. The grasslands were disappearing and were being replaced with forest, which also modified their migrational patterns. They were staying closer to rivers. Also, the climate was becoming colder, and the Native Americans were now starting to be affected by winters. We can assume that shelters (natural and human-built) were present during the latter parts of the Archaic Period.

The most notable factor for the Early Archaic Period is the exploitation of uplands, ridge and valleys, and mountains of the entire eastern U.S. (see Purrington 1983). By the Middle Archaic Period, Archaic artifacts are everywhere in Virginia and Maryland.

During the Middle Archaic Period, the post-Clovis technologies, such as Palmer and Kirk pointmaking, were moving into southern environments. The Middle Atlantic area sees the migration of a more-forested oriented population. The axe was added to the toolkit to accommodate the new living conditions which required shelters. The origin for the axe is probably the middle Mississippi River valley (Hranicky 1995). The MPRV axe probably dates back to 8000 BP (Figure 9); however, 3/4 groove axes date to the Late Archaic or later.

The axe is a larger, more massive form of the celt. However, celts in southwestern Virginia have been found exceeding 200 mm in length (Hranicky 1995). These tools are the result of living in a forest environment, as they are used chiefly for felling trees. As mentioned, the axe and celt were the replacements for the wedge (Hranicky 2002a). The axe is an example of a process whereby the Native Americans used the wedge and its principal to create a new tool to meet new environmental conditions.

The basic tool technology is the broadspear which probably has its origins in the Ohio-Mississippi River valleys. The main Middle Archaic Period point technology is the Morrow Mountain technology. The tool material is a major shift from the cryptocrystline technologies of the earlier periods to general crystalline stones, such as quartzite and rhyolite. Another minor group is the bifurcate point makers. These people were highly migratory and covered most of the eastern U.S.

The social unit was still the band, but it was probably smaller than earlier period groups, and it was not coordinated with associated local bands. Group intrasocial behavior was more remote. Populations were heterogeneous, in that bands existed that were not biologically related. However, various bands did trade with neighboring groups and some long-distance trade occurs.

The end of the Archaic Period archaeologically is the use of containers, but horticulture is a better technology to end the period and start the Woodland Period.

Technologically, the MPRV Archaic Period follows Coe's (1964) North Carolina sequence and Broyles' (1971) West Virginia sequence. At the Thunderbird site, the break between lanceolate to notched points occurs at 10,000 BP (Gardner 1989). However, there is no Dalton, Hardaway, or St Charles component at the site, which may demonstrate an absence of human occupation after the Paleoindian Period. The Dalton and Hardaway points do occur in the MPRV, but their frequency is low. The frequency of the St Charles point is adequate for the time period. Gardner compliments this by arguing the Paleoindian extended to 9000 BP. The site does offer an early sequence for the MPRV; it has Clovis, Palmer, Kirk, Charleston, and LeCroy technologies represented.

The major MPRV point technologies are bifurcates, Morrow Mountain, Guilford, Halifax, Lamoka, Koens-Crispin, Savannah River, and Susquehanna points. The Archaic Period sees the addition of the axe, bannerstone, boatstone, bola, celt, gorget, holestone and stone container to the basic toolkit (previously, Table 1). The starting date for the celt is probably the Early Archaic Period, and it originated in the Mississippi River valley (Hranicky 1995).

A flintknapping bad day ...

Most riverbeds are lined with usable cobbles. The Holmes Run (Virginia) streambed contained numerous lithic materials. As an experiment, a quartzite hammerstone was selected; then a workable piece of quartzite was selected.

Using the quartzite hammerstone, several flakes were removed from the cobble; it was too chalky. At this point, the piece was considered a reject.

But, with a little more work, it was at least decorted. This author cannot use a hammerstone to thin a quartzite preform. It resulted in several flakes hinging out, crushed platform, and the sides are too thick. A bad day is a bad day, but the point of working riverbed cobbles has been made.

An Indian bad day at knapping...

This Savannah River biface was rejected by a knapper 4000 years ago. The above face was satisfactory; however, the reverse face (below) was a total failure. The arrow shows attempts along that margin to remove flakes that would travel across the face and remove the cortex.

Figure 10 – River Cobble Tradition (see Hranicky 1986)

The scraper and wedge are dropped from the toolkit but reappear in the Late Archaic and Woodland Periods. The Middle Archaic broadspear may be the beginning of the single multifunctional tool process (stage) in the Middle Atlantic area. In addition to these tools, one new tool finds its way into the Native Americans' toolkit. This is the slab mortar and pestle, which is a response to the increase in nut-bearing trees in the Middle Atlantic area.

For the Archaic Period, one method of lithic procurement is initiated as a regular practice; this is the river cobble tradition (Hranicky 1986). It started in the Early Archaic. Instead of traveling to a quarry location, knappers walked riverbeds to find lithic materials (Figure 10). No tools were needed, but most knappers carried personal implements for making tools. In many cases, especially for upland rivers, basalt or diabase cobbles can be found and used as hammerstones. As shown in the figure, quartzite hammerstones can be used. Any riverbed in the MPRV contains quartzite cobbles. All types, from Clovis to the Potomac point, are made from quartzite. The suggestion is that riverbed procurement was used extensively.

There are two types of cobbles: 1) field cobbles which have their origins from direct parent rocks (gravitational action) in the uplands and 2) streambed cobbles which have been transported by river actions and are from rocks in different uplands (valleys). Field cobbles tend to be more homogeneous in stone composition, but at the same time, have less moisture.

As time moves from Early to Middle Archaic to Late Archaic, there are major changes in the Native Americans' choice of lithic materials. As with the Paleoindians, the Hardaway, St Charles, and Palmer pointmakers continued to use cryptocrystalline materials, namely flint, chert, rhyolite, and jasper. Towards the Middle Archaic, a projectile point with a broad blade becomes the dominant form and quartzite becomes the dominant material. For example, the Morrow Mountain is characteristically made from quartzite. A narrow point, the Guilford, also appears and is unrelated to the Morrow Mountain style. These points may be adjustments to climate changes, namely the Atlantic Episode, and/or the results of new people moving into the area. Basically, the Middle Archaic Period is a drier and warmer climate than today.

The appearance of the Morrow Mountain point type starts the Middle Archaic Period as a technological focus. This type is suggested as a broadspear, as Virginia specimens exceed 100 mm in width (Hranicky 1994).

Generally, the Morrow Mountain point suddenly appears as a major type and does not have an ancestral technology in Middle Atlantic archaeology unless, it is the Eva point technology.

The so-called Broadspear Tradition is a false assumption based only on blade size; it should include reduction technology and tool function. See Toolmaking Technology section for a discussion of the broadspear technology.

There is another misconception in eastern archaeology that the broadspear starts with the Savannah River point, which may be the influence of Turnbaugh (1975), who suggested the *earliest dated incidence of the classic broadspear*. Turnbaugh (1975) attempted to define the broadspear as a culture. He failed to show temporal connectivity, intercultural commonness of material culture, and maritime versus upland economies. The Turnbaugh culture concept was disproved by Cook (1976) and others. It still has merit as a technoculture, which is discussed below.

Figure 11 – Left: Koens-Crispin Point and Right: Savannah River Point; both are example of broadspears.

While the Late Archaic broadspears, namely Savannah River, Koens-Crispin, and Susquehanna types, do receive more attention in archaeological investigations and the resultant literature, the broadspear starts with the Stanly type as viewed from North Carolina (Figure 11). Coe (1964:123) states:

For the Late Archaic Savannah River…, In North Carolina this period began as a continuation of the earlier Stanly Complex, and it continued the development of a broad-bladed, broad-stemmed point tradition along with polished atlatl weights and grooved axes.

Hranicky (2002) by inference to manufacturing technique similarity included the Morrow Mountain I broad-bladed type as a broadspear. The Stanly is probably a continuation of the Kirk stemmed type. The assumption here is that the Kirk has a southeastern origin. From these two point types, the broad-bladed point continues into the Woodland Period where it disappears. It was replaced essentially with the triangular point. As Coe (1964) argued a continuum from the Stanly to the Savannah River, it is assumed here (Figure 12). However, part of the continuum is missing in the MPRV because of the low frequency of occurrence for the Stanly point. The transition occurs elsewhere in the Southeast.

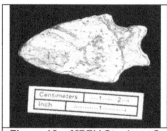

Figure 12 – MPRV Stanly or Savannah River Point? These two types represent a technological continuum. Both are heavily patinated. The suggestion: Kanawha, Stanly, and Savannah River points constitute a technological continuum for the lower Middle Atlantic area.

The broadspear technology is a percussion-flaked large thick point which has a function of a knife (see Cook 1976). Even resharpening is performed by percussion. This technology is difficult to argue as a technological continuum, but the appearance of duplicate broadspear technologies is an interesting argument, especially for typologists. A tapering round stem becoming tapered straight-sided, then with an indented base, which is subsequently followed by an expanding stem is a sequence most archaeologists are not willing to accept. All of which have one commonality – large flake percussion flaking out of quartzite or rhyolite. The broadspear includes the Stanly, Eva, Morrow Mountain I, Saratoga, Savannah River, Patuxent, Koens-Crispin, Perkiomen, and Susquehanna points. Around 2000 BC, various stages of those point technologies inhabit the entire Atlantic coastal plain and piedmont (Turnbaugh 1975 and Hranicky 1994).

Numerous arguments have been published as to whether the broadspear was actually a spear. Callahan (1979) seems to have settled it as being both a knife and spearpoint. This is a false conclusion as the wide-bladed Morrow Mountain and the later Savannah River points are not flyable as spearpoints. Almost all projectile points, starting with Clovis, served both of these functions. However, the broadspear does represent a new technology into the Middle Atlantic, namely cobble-sourced tools. Large cobbles were worked into wide-bladed points. The earlier-period corner-notched pointmakers depended on quarry sources for their lithic materials, and this technology moves out of the Middle Atlantic area. Cobbles freed the need to travel to quarries; thus, field and streambed sources offered greater freedom from fixed lithic procurements. Thus, the beginnings of longer occupations – perhaps territories – could have been a nonquarry factor. The use of local stones, even quarried stones, becomes the normal source for the Middle Archaic Period and continues into the Woodland Period.

The broadspear is probably associated with the invention of winged bannerstone and three-quarter grooved axes (Sears 1954). This bannerstone is probably associated with the atlatl; thus, the projectile point was probably a bone or antler point. The broadspear was a knife or a multiple hand-held, hafted tool. Figure 13 shows a generalized distribution for broadspears.

Based on Witthoft (1953), Mouer (1990), Painter (1988), and Custer (1984), the MPRV in the Late Archaic was part of a large broadspear technology that has the following regional complexes (technocultures):

I. Central Pennsylvania, namely Perkiomen-Susquehanna points (Witthoft 1953)

II. Delaware Valley, namely Koens-Crispin points (Hawks and Linton 1916)

III. Potomac Valley, namely Savannah River and Susquehanna points (Witthoft 1953 and Coe 1964)

IV. Central Virginia, namely Savannah River points (Coe 1964)

V. Southeastern Virginia, namely Perkiomen and Dismal Swamp points (Painter 1963)

VI. Southwestern Virginia – Tennessee Valley, namely Savannah River (Coe 1964), and Saratoga Winters (1967), Pickwick (DeJarnette, et al. 1962), and Ledbetter (Kneburg 1956) points.

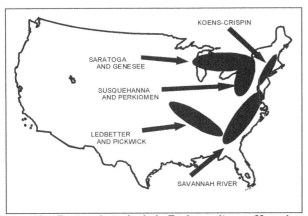

Figure 13 – Eastern Late Archaic Technocultures. Map shows basic distribution of Koens-Crispin, Saratoga and Genesee, Susquehanna and Perkiomen, Ledbetter and Pickwick, and Savannah River projectile point types.

If projectile point technology is viewed regionally in the East, there are obvious point distributions that can be called technocultures (Hranicky 2002a). A technoculture may imply territory or a preferred environment (climate or ecoscene). The Middle Atlantic point distribution for the Late Archaic Period does not show preferences for the physical geography, such as uplands, piedmont, coastal, etc.

Each of these point technology categories occurs which is indicating large geographic cultural regions; perhaps even culture areas. They are major watershed macrotechnologies which show overlaps in other river basins. For the moment, these areas are suggested as limits for technoculture migrations.

A Broadspear Model is shown in Figure 14. It basically shows the quarry as the primary source for Native American broadspear bifaces. Large spalls/flakes are a major reduction factor. For a further discussion of this model, see Cresson (1990). Once again, it is a technology, not a culture. It is viewed here as a technoculture in much the same way the computer is viewed today. Technology is a factor in all aspects of culture. While it may be the dominating factor, it is usually subject to the wishes of the whole culture of a society. Technoculture is ideologically controlled in most societies. The model coincides with the biface procedures and methods described in the Toolmaking Technology section.

As a possible explanation for the southeastern Virginia isolate of the Perkiomen technology, Painter (1963) maintained that the Dismal Swamp type was similar, probably related to the Perkiomen point, but was not the same technology (Hranicky and Painter 1988). These pointmakers may have been part of the Perkiomen band group, but were cut off by invading Savannah River pointmakers. Dismal Swamp could be a trailer to a northward movement of Perkiomen; this isolate may never be explained. As a note: both point types have asymmetrical blades that are not found on other Middle Atlantic points. The Perkiomen type was not observed in the MPRV study collections.

Kirk and bifurcate points have been found with wide blades; even wider than the Stanly point's blade. This leads to technology being the focus, not tool size. Of course, the only *baby point* in early Middle Atlantic and Southeast prehistory is the Palmer. The technology linage for the Early Archaic Period (Hardaway, St Charles, Palmer, Kirk sequence of fine-grain lithic points) disappears at the beginning of the broadspear period in the MPRV. Palmer is a continuation (or part of) the St Charles technology that is found all over the lower eastern U.S.

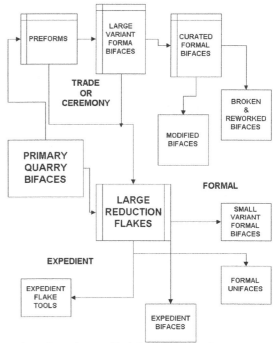

Figure 14 – Broadspear Model (Based on: Cresson 1990). It represents a technology process that can be viewed as a long-term stage in the tool continuum.

The Early Archaic Period towards its end sees the introduction of the bifurcate point (approximately 8300 BP). Its origins are most likely North Carolina and manifested in the point technologies called the Nottoway River (Painter 1970) and Quad (Soday 1954). This technology continued in the East down to 5500 BP where it disappears, or the people who were making them migrated west. The major MPRV bifurcates are the MacCorkle (Broyles 1971), St Albans (Broyles 1971), LeCroy (Kneberg 1956), Susquehanna Valley (Hranicky 1994), and Culpepper (Hranicky and Painter 1989). Figures 15a and 15b shows the major types. Identification of bifurcates is based solely on the lobes (Hranicky and Painter 1988). This point style represents the lithic technology continuum better than any other point style. The Kanawha point may represent the end of the bifurcate technology in the Middle Atlantic area. As a <u>note</u>, the classic bifucate studies are Chapman (1975) and Broyles (1971).

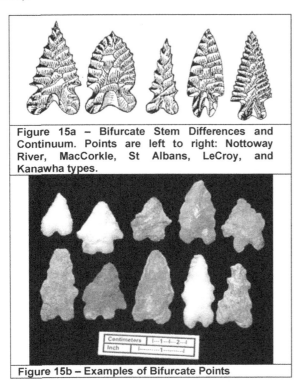

Figure 15a – Bifurcate Stem Differences and Continuum. Points are left to right: Nottoway River, MacCorkle, St Albans, LeCroy, and Kanawha types.

Figure 15b – Examples of Bifurcate Points

A small point appears around 5500 BP called the Halifax (Coe 1964). It represents the start of the bipolar flaking method which is the first shift in toolmaking technology and introduces the Late Archaic Period. The broadspear is a biface reduction method using spalls from quarries (lithic outcrops) and large cobbles. Thus, other than size, tool manufacturing techniques remain basically the same, but the dominant technology is the broadspear. The bipolar technique for the Late Archaic Period is discussed in the Toolmaking Technology section.

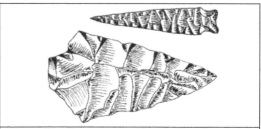

Figure 16 – Narrowspear Versus Broadspear Technology. Points are top: Halifax and bottom: Koens-Crispin types.

The Late Archaic Period probably does not exist in the Native Americans' world. If only one aspect can be attributed to the Native Americans, it is the semipermanent habitation of river valleys. Along with a climatical change occurring around 3000 BC, most archaeologists attempt to start the transition to the Woodland Period here. As mentioned, the term *Terminal Archaic* (1700-700 BC) has also been used, but archaeologically, its popularity is disappearing. See Snow (1980). The term Transitional Archaic is a carryover from Witthoft (1953), but it too has essentially had its great days in archaeology. At least it provided the acceptance of riverine occupations (Mouer 1990 and 1991).

The so-called narrowspear tradition (Ritchie 1969, Dincauze 1971, and Dent 1995) is also a misnomer tradition because it fails to define all lithic technologies (associated toolkits, etc.) being used to make points, namely the Lamoka and Halifax types. Figure 16 shows a narrowspear versus broadspear shape. If the tradition is assigned the bipolar method, then, like its counterpart, a specialized technology can be examined. Assuming no resharpening on either broad/narrow points, the narrow blade offers a functional contrast between the two forms. The basic argument is hunting verses cutting implements and Dent (1995) suggests both were multifunctional tools. For one aspect of morphology, the L*W/T ratio is different suggesting functional differences which may not have been practiced by the Native Americans. This is a major variation between the two forms as measured in tip-axis-stem angles. As such, the Savannah River point, even if attached to a spear, has little penetrating capacity; narrow-bladed points are the opposite. The size/angle difference implies a different functional axis for tools; even if cutting, a different approach to the task. The complicating factor is: there are narrow-bladed Savannah River points.

The dominant projectile point technology during the Late Archaic Period is the Savannah River. In terms of point numbers, Halifax comes in second and appears to occupy the same general terrain, and both pointmaker groups follow a general, foraging subsistence pattern. The next page shows Virginia broadspear specimens (Plate 7 – see Appendix A). No broadspears were found in the study collections that matched the blade width of the Virginia broadspear specimens; however, they must have existed.

The discovery and use of steatite, commonly called soapstone, may have been the key change in all Native Americans' social practices and population movements. Use of it for bowls allowed heating foods, but more importantly, semipermanent habitation as steatite bowls are heavy and difficult to transport. The steatite bowl was a copy of wooden bowls that were in use. The wooden bowl probably dates back to the Paleoindian Period.

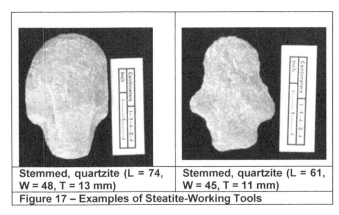

| Stemmed, quartzite (L = 74, W = 48, T = 13 mm) | Stemmed, quartzite (L = 61, W = 45, T = 11 mm) |

Figure 17 – Examples of Steatite-Working Tools

Note: Holmes (1897) was the first to publish these tools that he called scrapers.

A steatite provenance study has been performed (see Truncer 1998). The study involves analysis of 22 to 31 samples from eight prehistoric quarry sites (Pennsylvania to Virginia). The Virginia quarries are the Clifton quarry (Holmes 1897), Chula quarry (Baird 1879), and Lawrenceville quarry. The samples were irradiated at the Missouri University Research Reactor. All steatite samples showed a high degree of chemical consistency. Dysprosium (Dy), Chromium (Cr), and Cerium (Ce) are good provenance indicators.

Figure 18 – Virginia Example of Steatite Bowl Fragment from Prince George County (Formerly Fred Morgan Collection). Tool scraping/cutting marks can be seen on the material. Example shows a lug handle.

Steatite's first usage is generally credited to the Savannah River and Susquehanna pointmakers with preference here being given to the former as the inventors of the stone bowl. The Savannah River toolkit was modified to accommodate the new technology. Figure 17 shows suggested tool styles for processing steatite (Hranicky 1990 and 1993). Figure 18 shows examples of broken steatite vessel walls. Figure 19 shows the manufacturing sequence for steatite bowls in the MPRV. Holmes (1897) comments:

Steatite (or soapstone) was used somewhat extensively by the natives of the tidewater country in the manufacture of pots, dishes, and cups, as well as of smaller articles, such as pipes and ornaments It was obtained along the western border of the tidewater country, either from the surface or by quarrying, and the articles made are scattered over the entire province, occurring somewhat less frequently as we pass outward toward the Atlantic shore-line.

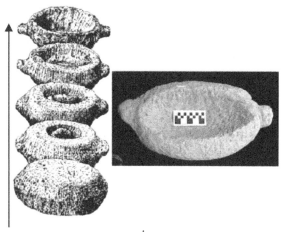

Figure 19 – Sequence for Manufacturing a Steatite Bowl (From: Holmes 1897). Steatite bowls are contemperous with Savannah River and Susquehanna points. Bowl example is from Mecklenburg County, Virginia.

The Archaic Native Americans inhabited all ecoscenes in Virginia. There were seasonal visitations for the maturation of various nuts, fruit, and berries, but this remains to be proven with archaeological site data. Ethnographic inferences as to settlement patterns are difficult to access for migratory populations that leave lithic scatters along obvious sources of water and foodstuffs locations. Upland and lowland bands practicing the same technology may never have seen each other in their times. Thus, the multicomponent site is difficult to discern archaeologically. Settlement patterns become clearer in the succeeding Woodland Period. Settled life in terms of refuse gives a better picture of curation, tool useability, and trade.

The Late Archaic Period sees plant seed domestication becoming Panindian throughout the eastern U.S. For the Middle Atlantic area, plant domestication is suggested here as starting around 4000 BP which is also the suggested starting date for the Woodland Period. For an overview of planting and harvesting seven indigenous seed plants (chenopod, marsh elder, squash, sunflower, erect knotweed, little barley, and maygrass), see Smith (1989). During the period between 4000 and 3200 BP and at various parts of the ecoscenes (uplands, piedmont, and coastal plain), there is an end to general foraging and a switch the cultigens as a livelihood in the MPRV. Aside from the Savannah River toolmakers, other societies were small were becoming sedentary populations. The cultural change affected the technology process, namely the container.

As mentioned, the wooden, skin, cane-woven container probably dates to the Paleoindian Period; it became manifested in stone during the Late Archaic Period that is more durable in archaeological contexts. Does plant domestication cause this change; this dietary question remains to be answered.

Table 5 provides a summary of the end of the Archaic Period. Sanders (1991) offers an excellent overview of the Late Archaic and Early Woodland Periods.

One aspect of lithic technology is the cache. Usually bifaces the buried cache starts with the Paleoindians and continues to the Woodland Period. The purpose of the cache is open to many interpretations; none of which adequately explain the phenomena. See Artifact Caches section.

Table 5 – Archaic Period Summary
• **Start using stone cooking container**
• **Presence of rock-lined hearths**
• **Start of domesticated plant seed usage**
• **Single riverine occupation**
• **Storage pits**
• **Axe and celt technology**
• **Large biface percussion flaking method**
• **Boat technology**
• **Polished macrotools**
• **Increase exploitation of uplands**
• **Increase in woodworking tools**
• **Open/closed semi-grassland/forest**
• **Boreal environment**
• **Occupation in a changing environment**

Woodland Culture Summary

The MPRV Woodland Period dates from 5000-1000 BP to 400 BP depending on whose viewpoint is used in archaeology. There is a wide range of environments, namely Subatlantic, Scandic, Neoatlantic and finally, Neoborael conditions, which are factors on habitation and social change.

The watershed occupation is primarily the opposite of the Paleoindian Periods; in that, the coastal plain, especially near the Potomac River or at least minor rivers, has the highest occupations. The fall line plays a role in settlement, but remains open for an archaeological assessment here. Potomac islands and flood plains were occupied for horticultural practices. The inland areas of the watershed were exploited for flora and fauna resources, which were returned to originating village.

This period is characterized by hamlet and village life for the Native Americans, including the domestication of plants. Traditionally, the Woodland Period begins with the invention of stone containers, or what Smith (1986) calls the *Container Revolution*. Stone/pottery containers affected the mobility of the Native Americans; thus, more permanent campsites resulted, which eventually became hamlets and then villages.

One aspect of the container revolution remains that contradicts the proposition which is:

Ceramic bowls predate steatite bowls...

Jenkins, et al. (1986) argue a date range of 4500-4000 BP for ceramics in the Savannah River and Chattahoochee Rivers' drainages.

Based on the argument of the Panindian nature of technology, one might conclude that pottery influenced stone bowl usage. Fiber-tempered pottery dates 4000+ BP in Florida and has its origins in South America (Hranicky 1981). For the east coast, it spread up from Florida rather slowly and reaches the Virginia coastal plain around 1600 BC. Both the Susquehanna and Savannah River point types in the MPRV have only been found in association with steatite vessels. However, this study reports two MPRV Broad River points, which, in Georgia, are associated with fiber-tempered wares (Michie 1970 and Elliott and Sassaman 1995). This point type is shown in the Projectile Point section.

Figure 20 – Potsherds. Beginning of the Pottery Technoculture – Marcy Creek Steatite-Tempered Ware. See pottery section.

For most archaeological discussions, the Woodland Period begins with MPRV's Marcy Creek pottery (Figure 20) that is steatite-tempered (Evans 1955). Manson (1948) and Gardner and McNett (1977) offer studies on early pottery. However, initially pottery may have been a slow intrusion into existing MPRV cultures. Stewart (1998) argues:

...the initial impact of ceramic technology on native society was not always revolutionary, nor equally shared by groups across the region.

Pottery types are not discussed other than their listing in Table 2 shown previously. See Kavanagh (2001) for an overview of Late Woodland Period types as found along the Monocacy River in Maryland.

Pottery as a replacement for organic containers already in place in the Native American's technology is a factor in cultural change and economics. True, it allowed a change in food preparation, caused less mobility, and started experimentation with tempers and manufacturing methods, such as coil construction. As Steward (1998) suggests, pottery does not become a dominant social factor until the Middle Woodland Period. See Pottery section.

The Early MPRV Woodland Period, including both sides of the Potomac River, may have seen food shortages. This may have resulted from over exploiting local environments because of the decrease in population mobility. As a consequence, population stress occurred, which may have caused an increase in ceremonialism. A counter argument is made, sedimentarism provided surplus time that was not needed in collecting/hunting foods. This time was used to organize and establish ceremonies and higher-level religious practices (priest versus shaman).

As suggested in Hantman, Wood, and Shields' (2000) study of the Monacans, archaeology must start equating the archaeological record with the ethnographic record. While technology is not a good indicator of culture because of its Panindian nature, other factors in excavated contexts are pottery, art, or settlement patterns that offer collaborative evidences for tribal associations. Basically, the Native Americans as the Europeans found them in the Potomac River valley have a continuous cultural history starting at least by 1000 AD. Earlier times see outside influences, namely Hopewell, Adena, and Mississippian, which suggest different cultures. The major problem with historical identification of modern Native Americans to the archaeological past is migrations.

Archaeology provides the means for Native Americans to establish their cultural identity in prehistory. Archaeological sites frequently reviles evidences that translate into histories. However, this form of documentation is rejected by a few Native Americans. Also, there are the so-called invisible Native Americans who have been mis-identified in history. For example, there was a time in Virginia when all Native Americans were recorded as *free blacks*. Then compounding this soceohistory is the grass roots movement of people who want to become Native Americans.

Continuing and as stated, pottery is archaeology's definition of the Woodland Period or basic division between the Archaic and Woodland Periods. Even with ceramics, divisions are based on a temper sequence, namely fiber, steatite, quartz, limestone, and shell. These tempers keep Native American pottery throughout the Woodland Period as poor quality vessels which have thick vessel walls. Pottery firing never reached sufficient temperatures to fuse the clay and temper into a hard ceramic; again referring to the quality of Native American pottery.

Ceramic change is a major topic in the Woodland Period archaeology. This topic is avoided here, but recommends Loney (2000) as an excellent discussion of archaeology's ceramic change concepts.

Figure 21 – MPRV Woodland Triangles. Left-to-right: Potomac, Madison, Capron, Carderock, and Levanna Types.

Custer (1984 and 2001) offers a projectile point chronology from the Delaware River valley that was used for comparison to construct the MPRV's sequence for the Late Archaic and Woodland Periods.

The major MPRV Woodland Period point technologies are represented by Savannah River (end of), Susquehanna (end of), Piscataway, Meadowood, Jacks Reef, Warratan-Potts, Madison, Levanna, and Potomac points. While the stemmed point is present, the predominate point style is the triangle (Figure 21). Woodland Period Native Americans add the adz, bow and arrow, chisel, fishhook, hoe, mortar, netsinker, pendant, pestle, pipe, pottery, and scraper to their basic toolkit. The bow and arrow technology is the major tool invention for the Woodland Period.

Note: Most archaeologists would argue that the adz was developed during the Archaic Period. There is a fine line distinction among the bits of adz, chisel, and splitter tools.

Numerous organic tools were introduced or carried over from previous cultural periods (Figures 22, 23, and 24). Organic artifacts are rare in the MPRV; examples from outside the MPRV show representative ethnographic comparisons. More examples are presented below. Excavated materials suggest that some of these organic tools may have considerable antiquity, such as the fishhook and awl. The major technological invention is the bow and arrow that probably originated in the Southeast. The blow tube for launching darts could have been present in the MPRV, but this remains to be proven archaeologically. The major cultural focus is the creation of hamlets or villages (Figure 23).

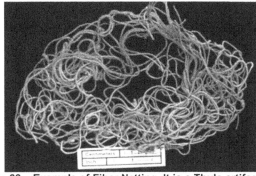

Figure 22 – Example of Fiber Netting. It is a Thule artifact from Lovelock, Nevada. It was found in August 1941.

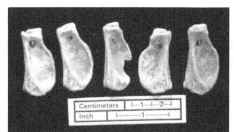

Figure 23 – Drilled Squirrel Scapulas (Washington County, Virginia). They were strung together as a necklace.

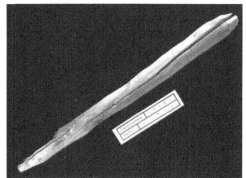

Figure 24 – Example of a Wooden Awl. It is a Thule artifact from Lovelock, Nevada. It was found in August 1941.

Figure 25 – Replication – Wolf Creek Native American Village, Bastain, Virginia. The view shows a small garden associated with the village. The village reconstruction includes a palisade. (See Plate 8 below).

Returning back to the MPRV, Errett Callahan reconstructed a Contact period house at St Mary's County, Maryland (Figure 26). Like the Native American toolkit for a dwelling, he used the celt as his basic tool. This dwelling is based on excavated post molds. Jamestown Festival Park also has displayed an Native American hamlet (Figure 27). These examples present experimental constructions that yield a generalized picture of how the Native American shelter may have appeared in prehistory.

Figure 26 – Dwelling Reconstruction (St Mary's County, Maryland). It assumes an open space environment.

Rountree (1989) notes that the Powhatan house was called yi>hakan, not a wigwam; thus, following that lead, the terms **house** and **dwelling** are used here.

Callahan's (1981) experiment of building a Pamunkey house showed that red maple, red cedar, and black locust made good woods for housebuilding.

Houses had interior hearths and storage pits. There were bunks for sleeping (some sleeping was on the ground, as in the summertime) and racks for clothing. The shelter was divided for sleep, storage, and domestic activities. The shelter has earthen floors and narrow doorways. In winter months, doorways would be covered with thatch. Placement of shelters appears to be random within the village. The average shelter was approximately 25 feet in diameter. Swanton (1952) suggests that each shelter may have had a hovel made like an oven in which they stored maize.

Gilbert (1943) based on Bartram (1853) describes the Cherokee:

These dwellings were plastered inside and out with grass-tempered clay and were roofed with chestnut-tree bark or long board shingles. In the roof a smoke hole was left... Within the ordinary dwelling there was little furniture aside from beds consisting of a few boards spread with bear skins.

While this description may or may not apply to MRPV dwellings, it is a consideration for interpreting the archaeological patters in village sites. The average prehistoric village lasted for 15 years, but many were probably occupied for less years. Figure 28 shows structural design for a Monacan dwelling.

Figure 27 – Reconstruction of a Native American Hamlet at Jamestown, Virginia. It assumes a closed space (forest) environment.

Village activities included ceremonies, games, and general social life. Their belief system included magic and a spirit pantheon. Mortuary practices included human burials within the village and group burials (see Bushnell 1920 and Curry 1999). For single burials, the individual was interred in a flexed position with or without grave goods. Bundle burials (collection of human bones) do occur.

Figure 28 – Monacan Village Reconstruction at Natural Bridge, Virginia. It shows an example of a dwelling being built using the branch framing technique. Style dates approximately 1700 AD. Display is no longer maintained.

Figure 29 shows a reed and mat covering for a hamlet. Figures 30 and 31 show an ethnographic example of a piece of mat.

Figure 29 – Reed and Mat Type of Covering for a Native American Hamlet (2000 State Fair Indian Exhibit, Richmond, Virginia). The village replication was the work of Daniel Abbott, who is a Naticoke descendant. Lodge is based on archaeological site data. Powhatan house covering was either bark or mats (Rountree 1989).

The prehistoric demography of the MPRV is represented in the excavated skeletal population and provides a life table for the former inhabitants. See Demographics at beginning of this section. The studies are incomplete and the skeletons are being reburied. Sex and aging along with pathology provide a population make up. Basically, this research is left to physical anthropologists who perform demographic analyses based on dental calcification and eruption (as in Ubelaker 1989), closure of long bones (as in Bass 1987 and Krogman 1978). For mature adults, endocrinal suture closures are used (as in Krogman 1978).

Figure 30 – Thule Matting from a Cave near Lovelock, Nevada. It was found in August 1941. It offers an example of reed and mat covering for dwellings. It was common for Algonquian speaking groups.

Age groups are usually assigned to infant <1 year, and various divisions which conclude with senior adults >55 years (Hranicky 1975). As with most nonliterate societies, the highest death rate is for the youngest and oldest parts of the population.

The Native Americans have an extensive collection of ceremonies, mythologies, belief systems, religious experiences; all of which were manifested in their material culture. These social practices have their origins during the Early Woodland (or perhaps earlier), but were manifested into high order priestly functions at the beginning of the Late Woodland. Ceremony encompassed every phase of their lives and all daily activities. Social correctness involved separation ceremonies, rites of passage ceremonies, mortuary ceremonies, purification ceremonies, conjury and witchcraft ceremonies, divination ceremonies, horticultural ceremonies, and more. Additionally, society life includes art, music, dance, and other recreational activities. For an excellent presentation of the aspect of Native American life, see Hudson (1976).

Plate 8 shows ethnographic examples of dress and personal decoration. More dress examples are discussed in the Experimental Archaeology sections.

Figure 31 – Modern Example of Matting by the Monacans. Formerly, a Village Reconstruction at Natural Bridge, Virginia.

Southern Native Americans were skilled wood carvers; de Soto chroniclers recorded religious structures filled with high quality wooden statuaries. Since made of wood, their preservation is rare, but fortunately specimens did survive. While mainly a lithic focus for this book, a recent discovery in Virginia yields a small insight into art and ceremony for the Native Americans in the Middle Atlantic area – the discovery of a wooden post mask.

The Buckingham County Mask of Virginia provides art from the past (Figure 32). It could be associated with ceremonies. However, it is argued here that it was probably a territory marker for marking the north/south trail (now Route 15) through Virginia. Other high quality socio-religious art forms occur in the Southeast, namely monolithic axes, engraved shell gorgets, stone disk, stone effigy pipes and statues, mica and copper forms, just to name a few items.

Plate 9 shows the recreation of Wolf Creek village in Bland County, Virginia. The village is based on the Brown-Johnson site (44BD1) that was excavated by MacCord (1971). This village recreation presents a typical way the Native Americans lived during the Late Woodland Period in the uplands. It has relevance to the MPRV.

Text continued on page 93.

From the Notebook...

The following table lists state curation standards for the Department of Historic Resources (DHR) of Virginia. The DHR maintains the State Curation Facility in Richmond, Virginia. These are minimal requirements for turning over private collections to the DHR.

1. All artifacts should be cleaned, except for special chemical analyses.
2. All artifacts should be labeled with site number and/or provenance with ink and writing sealed.
3. All artifacts should be placed in polyethylene, zip-locked bags or in Ricker mounts (butterfly cases).
4. All materials should be archaically stable.
5. All materials, bags, cases, etc., should be boxed.
6. All transport boxes should be labeled with names, sites, and provenance.

All collections should have documentation, including owner, catalog, publications, fieldnotes, photographs, maps, etc.

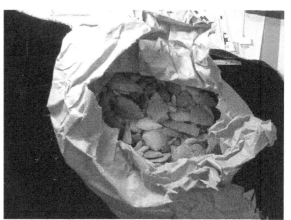

Bag of Field-collected MPRV Projectile Points (R. C. Printz Collection, Herndon area, Virginia). It represents MPRV field-collected artifacts but lacks detailed provenance. Even then, these specimens still contribute to the study of MPRV prehistory.

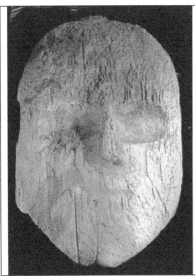  

Figure 32 – Wooden Mask from Buckingham County, Virginia. It was found in the 1980s on the James River. It was made from chestnut and measures: Face height = 39.0, Face width = 19.3, and mask depth = 10.7 cm. Back side has a support ring in the middle in which a shaft was placed extending into a notch near the top. The face probably represents a former chief or possibly a spirit. During its Native American usage, it was painted. It probably dates to the late 1700s to early 1800s (before Native American removal from the East). Tribal affiliation is probably Cherokee. Displaying the face on a pole could have marked a ceremonial place within the village; however, this face does not have a village context when it was found. As such, it probably was a territory marker on a north-south Native American trail that paralleled the piedmont.

The right watercolor was painted by John White's published 1590 engravings. It shows posts which have faces carved into the top end. (Digital copy of the original in the British Museum.)

Plate 8 - Personal Appearance Examples Based on John White Drawings (de Bry 1590 Engravings)

These drawings are based on North Carolina (Algonquian) Native Americans at the time when Sir Richard Grenville attempted to found a colony in North America. There was a summer and winter dress. Also, noted in the drawings is the extensive use of body tattooing. The clothing also has an appearance of being influenced by European dress. This observation could simply be an artist's liberty of John White.

Plate 9 – Wolf Creek Indian Village (Replication), Bastain, Virginia

The riverine environment offered numerous natural resources for daily life, but most importantly, there was an abundance of aquatic foodstuffs, namely fish, clams, and turtles. Fish weirs are discussed in the Miscellaneous Tools/Implements section. Jordan (1906) offers an early weir study. Bone fishhooks are common in excavated contexts. Tools and implements needed for these activities are not readily available in the archaeological record because a high percentage of these items were made from organic materials; their poor preservation is the fault of Nature. By using ethnographic data from other areas of the U.S., a picture can be composed of Native American ways to utilize these resources. As an example, the slash-and-burn method of horticulture was probably practiced in the late MPRV.

Walker (2000) uses wide-spread sources for defining cultural aquatic activities in coastal southwest Florida. While this area is a maritime provenance, the MPRV has parallels that were probably present in societies bordering the Potomac River. Fishing tools and implements included the netsinker, fish weir, canoe anchor, fish hook, trolling equipment, fish net, bone harpoon, and fish trap basket. Figure 33 shows an example of a western U.S. netsinker. See Miscellaneous Tool/Implements section.

Figure 33 – Netsinker with Twine Attached. It was found in a cave near Lovelock, Nevada in August 1941.

Storage pits were an essential part of village life. Fall frost stopped horticulture and winter snows covered nuts and edible roots; all of which ceased wild food supplies until spring. Thus, Native Americans needed to save surpluses, and it was accomplished by digging storage pits. There is no basic style that can be equated with storage contents or shape of the storage pit. Archaeologically, storage pits shapes are bowl-, saucer-, silo-, U- or belled-shaped. The excavation at Fletcher's Boat House in Georgetown yielded several unusual pits. This was a partial excavation by the National Park Service that uncovered 7 large pits, averaging 2 meters in diameter and 4 meters in depth. The site occupants knew the pits were there, but their basic purpose – surplus and trade, tribute, etc. - remains unknown.

Food storage pits were probably used during the Archaic Period, but few exist archaeologically. They are common in the Early Woodland Period and are the results of food surpluses and increased sedimentarism. The pit(s) was within the shelter or around its perimeter. After the pit's contents were utilized, the pit was often used as a refuse depository. Probably the most common use of the pit was for the nutmeat storage, namely chestnuts, acorns, pecans, beechnuts, chinquapins, and hickory nuts.

Their domestic plant foods were maize, beans, squash, sunflowers, pumpkins, maypops, and gourds. Popularly called corn, maize was not well developed as a staple food; its ears were small, and any adequate supply would have required large acreage (Figure 34). It arrives around 1800 BP, but does not become poplar until 800 AD (see Smith 1993)

Bullen (1958) provides an early discovery of a corn cob in Florida. It was found at the Jim Woodruff Reservoir area project. It measures: W = 78, H = 30, D = 15 mm. Cupules per 100 mm is 47. It had 10 rows. It dates 2250 +/- 250 BP. The New Mexico ear in Figure 29 measures L = 106, W = 23, T = 19 mm. It has 12 rows.

The horticulture acreage was approximately two acres per lodge. Corn must have been a surplus as:

The 10th of December [1607], Master Smyth went up the river of the Chechohomynaies to trade for corn (quote in Haile 1998).

For the Virginia and Maryland uplands, maize was wide spread in the Late Woodland. This is based on Trimble's (1996) C4-istope analysis of 130 Virginia skeletons.

Other vegetal sources were wild grass seeds, some fungi, fruits, berries, honey, and edible roots. Bird and reptile eggs were also included in their diet. Social food activities included group hunting, trapping, snaring, net fishing and spearing, and vegetal gathering. Animals were listed in the MPRV Environmental section.

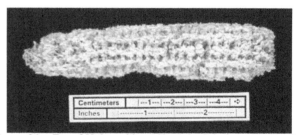

Figure 34 – Ear of Maize without Kernels. It is from the Pueblo III culture of New Mexico. Ear dates around 1300 AD. When maize was first domesticated, ears were less than 30 mm, but over time, ears became over 160+ mm.

Wright (1959) first argued for dividing the Late Woodland into three periods; these divisions have survived to date and are used here. This is followed by Custer (1982 and 1984) dividing the Woodland into two periods based largely on climatical conditions, starting the Woodland Period at 5000 BP for Woodland I, and Woodland II at 1000 BP. These periods (I and II) are used in the MPRV technology overview table shown previously; however, they are not correlated to any technology here. This violated the traditional argument of pottery being the initializing technology for the Woodland. In maintaining a climatical focus, this time coincides with a Middle Atlantic shift from a boreal to Atlantic environment. Technology is still maintaining nontriangle points, but the triangle point apparently has its invention around 4000 BP or perhaps as early as 5000 BP in the Northeast and spreads throughout the Middle Atlantic coastal plain and piedmont. Thus the triangle, not pottery, could be used to initialize the Woodland Period; however, other factors also must be used. The triangle technology is not exclusive, as points such as Rossville, Adena, Fox Creek, Warratan-Potts, and Jacks Reef are found at various times in the Woodland epoch.

Population and band size also start increasing as the Archaic phase is closing (Custer 1984). Less nonriverine occupation is found, and long distance migrations are being discontinued. Bands are becoming more territorially localized. Foodstuff procurements also become more seasonal and local environments are extensively utilized for support resources, such as lithic materials (as in Cleland 1976). The riverine systems became bases and subsequent long-term settlements. The river provided transportation avenues and communication among various settlements (Figure 35). See Experimental Archaeology section for discussion of replication versus reproduction of prehistoric objects; the canoe is used as an example.

Aside from pottery technology, the first technology intrusion into the MPRV is the Adena point starting around 700 BC. Numerous artifacts made from Ohio flints sporadically occur here and northward into the Delaware River valley (as in Custer 1984). Also, the lower tidewater of Virginia has the same intrusion as gray Ohio flints are common. The middle part of Virginia, James to Rappahannock Rivers, sees very little of the Adena materials. The Adena influences are to the North of the MPRV (see Ford 1976). Also, during this time period, projectile point types become more site-specific with a variety of stemmed points. There is an increase in exotic materials, such as slates, pipestones, copper, and what may be called extensive mortuary practices.

Figure 35 – Birch-Bark Canoe. The canoe was the principal means of transportation via the extensive river systems. This transportation provided communications and trade among various cultures. The birch-bark canoe is a Woodland invention; early canoes were dug-out canoes.

This canoe is 14 feet in length. It dates before 1896 and comes from the White Earth Agency in Minnesota. It now belongs to the Smithsonian Institution. The prow-piece is made from cedar, and the spruce greenwale lacing was done with spruce root. The warts are spruce and ribs are white cedar. Finally, the calking was done with spruce gum.

Next is the minor occurrence of the Snyders point. For whatever reasons, some archaeologists are unwilling to accept Hopewell influences in the MPRV, namely the Snyders point (Figure 36). It dates 2200 BP to 1600 BP. This type is diagnostic of the early Middle Woodland period and appears in the Ohio River valley's Hopewell ceremonialism. It was first reported typologically in Virginia in Hranicky (1991). While it is almost exclusively a flint technology in Ohio, it occurs in local MPRV materials. The type disappears in the MPRV but may have been replaced by the Chesser or Potts point.

Another technology that is characteristic of the MPRV Woodland Period is horticulture, namely crop fields. The association to the village site pattern remains to be established archaeologically. For the MPRV, this question may never be answered because few MPRV sites exist that could be investigated with a crop-field research design.

Above the fall line, sites still utilize quarried lithics, where below the fall line, lithics become pickup field and riverbed stones or travel to quarry sources. Trade probably continued among local groups as well as interculturally; however, the degree of this exchange has not been established archaeologically and is not argued here. Soils for horticulture are not discussed here. See Curry and Custer (1982), Birkeland (1984), and MPRV Environment section.

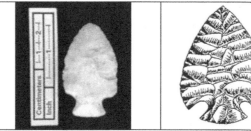

Figure 36 – Snyders Projectile Points. Point is made from Native Americana chert indicating the distance it traveled before in was discarded in the MPRV. Drawing is based on Virginia specimens (Hranicky and Painter 1989). When found in an archaeological context, these points indicate Hopewell (Ohio River valley) influences and/or contact.

One technological factor that occurs in the Late Archaic and continues to at least the Middle Woodland Period is the appearance of small white quartz points (<30 mm). They occur as notched and stemmed forms, and function appears to be projectiling. As a suggestion, these points may represent small-migratory bands that live outside the village pattern. In the study collections, there are literally thousands of them. Their correlation to the Woodland Period is an assumption based on field observations by the author.

Figure 37 – Cherokee Wooden Hoes (Smithsonian Institution, Washington, DC). The hoe is a diagnostic implement for the Woodland Period.

If the Middle Woodland can be identified and classified in Virginia/Maryland's prehistory, it offers an examination of culture in the early stages of a political society; perhaps a pre-Mississippian society(s). There is an increase in territoriality (Blanton 1992). This may translate to becoming a hamlet organization according to class, status, etc. But most importantly for technology, specialists in crafts are beginning to occur. For example, trade of lithic implements and perhaps pottery is starting to become common. MPRV pottery types are found elsewhere in the Middle Atlantic. The village society is becoming totally dependent on horticulture and local fauna resources, namely deer. The hoe is a major implement, but due to wooden hoe usage, the tool is not frequent in archaeological inventories (Figure 37). It has a widespread distribution and is found in many different styles (Figure 38). For the Woodland Period, it can easily be called the most utilitarian tool in the Indian toolkit.

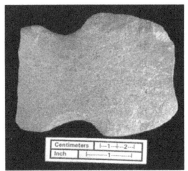

Figure 38 – Greenstone Hoe from Long Island, New York (L = 79, W = 52, T = 17 mm). It was made off a flat cobble and has a polished indentation on the bit. It was found in the early 1940s. (Formerly in the Geasey collection, now in the Southold Indian Museum in New York.)

Change from Middle into Late Woodland Period in the piedmont marks the use of flood plains for horticulture (as in Hantman and Klein 1992). We may be looking at the beginnings of riverine political/linguistic territories, namely the Maryland (Patuxent, Patapaco, Nanticoke, Choptank Rivers) and Virginia (Dan, James, Rappahannock, Potomac Rivers) *riverine cultures*. This would be opposed to MacCord's (1989) Intermontane Culture or Slattery, Tidwell, and Woodard's (1966) Montgomery Focus. Soil differences as discussed in the MPRV Environment section were known and probably played a role in MPRV settlement as subsequent politics.

Major pottery focuses have been identified in the Middle Atlantic area, which can be called technocultures. See Technocultures previously shown. Numerous cultural attributes can be attributed to Late Woodland MPRV Native Americans, which may have origins or at least influences from the Owasco from the north, Luray focus from the west, and eastern shore influences. Most of these influences involve pottery and village layout, not lithic technology.

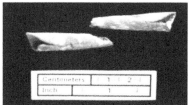

Figure 39 – Copper Cones from Chilhowie, Smyth County, Virginia.

Around 1000 BP, the climate is a Subatlantic and the MPRV point technology becomes almost exclusively the triangle point, namely the Levanna, Madison, and Potomac points. During the period several centuries before Contact, the eastern U.S. goes into a mini-Ice Age (Crowley and North 1991). Winters were more severe and the palisade offered protection from blowing wind and snow. There are no technological inferences here other than the palisade appears, which was probably used as a wind and snow barrier rather than a defensive structure for a village. However, Iroquois and Cherokee warfare was present after 1500 in the western parts of Virginia and Maryland.

Figure 40 – Cherokee Wooden Mortar and Pestle (Smithsonian Institution, Washington, DC)

Based on the Potomac Creek site (Blanton, et al. 1999), the palisaded village for the Potomac River valley probably starts around 700 BP, but may date back to 900 BP.

The Gore site, also known as the Walker site, on Selden Island is one of three known Virginia MPRV sites with a palisade. It is a Montgomery focus site (Slattery, Tidwell, and Woodward 1966). Fisher, Shepard, and Winslow sites could have been palisaded, but the archaeological evidence is not conclusive. Other palisaded sites are the C&O Canal-Moore Village near Oldtown, Maryland (Pousson 1983) and Accokeek site in Maryland.

Figure 41 – Example of Miscellaneous Containers. Village Reconstruction at Natural Bridge, Virginia. Modern example shows possible space utilization within a village. Cognitive factors on space organization in villages have not been studied.

During the Late Woodland Period (post-1400), there is a political transition to the chiefdom form of political control (see Potter 1993). The power of authority becomes a dominant form of social control that is probably a regional copy of the Mississippian social organization. Mississippian axes are found in the MPRV area.

During the Late Woodland Period, the Native Americans add copper to their cultural inventory (see Potter 1993). However, no copper artifacts were observed in the study collections. The Native American use of copper has been known since the 1830s; and, copper spearpoints (Figure 39) are known (Abbott 1885). Rountree (1989) provides an excellent study of copper usage among the Powhatan and Swanton (1946) suggests a source of copper was from the Nottoway Native Americans. Abbott (1885) provides a study of copper among the Delaware Native Americans.

Figure 42 – Cherokee Baskets (Smithsonian Institution, Washington, DC). Rarely are they preserved in buried archaeological contexts.

The final projectile point technology for the Late Woodland is the use of the small triangle point. It coincides with the MPRV Native American contact with Captain John Smith in 1608 that archaeologically terminates prehistory and starts a protohistoric period. For further information on this period, see Potter (1993), Dent (1995), and Rountree (1989).

Archaeologically, the Woodland Period sites do not generally yield organic artifacts, such as baskets, wooden knives, wooden mortars, clothing, dwelling materials, and other nonlithic artifacts (Figures 40, 41, and 42).

Consequently, lithics and ceramics skew the materialistic view of prehistory. Ethnographic data provide missing artifacts from the archaeological inventories, but here too, inferences may skew the nonlithic/ceramic materialistic interpretations. These activities present divisions of labor, name male/female and old/young. For example, Gilbert's (1943) study of the Cherokee states:

... boys are taught ... for success in hunting and ... girls are taught to make baskets, pottery, and perform household tasks.

Basket making is discussed in the Experimental Archaeology section.

All local foodstuffs were utilized with the deer becoming the stable meat. Clothing remained essentially deerskins. The canoe was a form of transportation system that augmented trade and social exchange (marriage) between groups. The domesticated dog was present in the Woodland Period; a dog skeleton was found at the Accokeek Creek site (Stephenson, et al. 1963). The date for the domestication remains to be established, but probably dates the people who first entered the New World.

Potter (1993) and MacCord (2001) provide maps with shows Native American villages as found around 1800 in the Patuxent, Potomac, and Rappahannock Rivers, which are:

Tauxenents	Acqintanacsucks
Nacotchtanks	Pissasecks
Piscataways	Nandtanghtacunds
Pamunkeys	Rappahannocks
Nanjemoys	Yaocomacos
Potapacos	Onawmanients
Patawomexes	Cekakawons
Cuttatawomens	Wicocomocos
Potapacos	Moraughtacunds
Mattapanients	Opiscopanks
Patuxents	

While decedents of the villages have survived, these villages slowly disappeared. We did not have an accurate population count (only estimates) for the post-Contact period. Based on MacCord (2001), we can assume: *population for the MPRV was low and there were extensive empty areas between small concentrations of people.*

Plate 10 shows John Whites' 1590 published drawings of North Carolina that are used for comparative examples for MPRV villages Table 6 provides a summary of the end of the Woodland Period (see Stevens 1991).

Table 6 – Woodland Period Summary
• **Chiefdom political organization**
• **Trade and exchange networks**
• **Food surpluses**
• **Fish weirs**
• **Containers (bowls and baskets)**
• **Food storage**

- Villages with territories
- Horticulture and tools
- Food processing tools
- Craft specialists
- Village ceremonial areas
- Year divisions; seasons
- Established ceremonies and rituals
- Metal usage – copper and mica
- Status burials; mortuary practices
- Pipe and tobacco
- Bow and arrow technology
- Exclusive use of triangle points
- Atlantic environment
- Closed forest ecology
- Occupation in a changing environment

In Summation

In many ways, the Native American society was not much different than the European society that replaced it. For example, diet included a wide variety of plants and animals (see Yanovsky 1936), they had art, song, and dance, well-developed religious practices and beliefs, oral traditions and histories, education for children, medicines (see Vogel 1970), well-developed technology (baskets, pottery, traps, fish weirs, snow shoes, stone tools, etc.), shelters and food storage methods, clothing, transportation systems, political leaders, trade/surplus/ economics, and family/kinship systems. Basic health was in many ways better than today's society in that heart diseases, arteriosclerosis, and cancer were rare; clean air and water were the norm, and they had few viral and bacterial ailments. They even had medicine for the common headache. One problem that was never solved was they did have a high level of infant mortality (Hranicky 1975). General physical health and condition permitted individuals to perform tasks that many contemporary Americans would quickly tire in performing. Goodchild (1999) provides an excellent overview of Indian survival.

From the notebook...

Labeling Artifacts - collectors, amateur archaeologists, general lay public (or any combination of interest and specialty with/without artifacts) should always maintain a log of where artifacts are found. An ideal practice is to record this information directly on the artifact as follows:

- Paint a small area on the worst face using whiteout (Liquid Paper).

- Using a fine-point pen and India ink, write the location, catalog number, date found on the whiteout area.

- Let the ink dry.

- Paint over the ink using a clear paint - clear fingernail polish.

- Maintain the point in a butterfly display case.

- Record point number and data in a log book.

See below for an example on marking/numbering artifacts. Most collectors record numbers on all artifacts and maintain records of their finds and acquisitions. While the pen/ink method is preferred by the author, several new pens have come on the market which can be used. One pen that produces very fine letters and does not clog-up is MICRON's PIGMA pen. The ink is waterproof and does not fade.

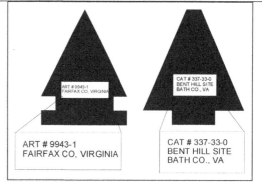

Labeling Artifacts. By using whiteout as a background ink-in the artifact number, site, and county in small letters.

Plate 10 – Ethnographic Engravings and Village Replication

Engravings based on John White's 1588 watercolors of North Carolina Villages. Upper drawing shows the palisaded village of Pomeiooc. He shows a "temple" in the upper right area. Right drawing shows the nonpalisaded village of Secota. It shows a ceremonial area in the lower right part of the drawing (Hranicky 1996). Below, the recreation of the Wolf Creek Indian village, based on MacCord (1971).

- 98 -

Toolmaking Technology
(Native American Ways of Making Stone Tools)

Perhaps the principal concern in lithic technology is Native American **flintknapping**, which admittedly cannot be used as a *catch-all* term for procurement, production, and usage for all technological objects in prehistory. It is a general term for making bifacially-flaked tools. Tool production, knapping, and/or manufacture are better terms. Native American tools and implements range from an artform to crude utilitarian tool production and have almost an endless number of styles in all kinds of lithic materials. All of which are classified and are the bases for material culture interpretations by archaeologists. As a general lithic focus, knapping is another general term for the toolmaking process that produces the material culture from prehistory and, minimally, always includes material procurement, skill in production, and tool usage. Usually, knapping (flaking) is restricted to microtool production; manufacturing (or production) usually refers to macrotool production.

Quarry procurement and processing drawing
from Heizer and Treganza (1944).

For large tools, the term manufacturing or tool production is used interchangeably. While this toolmaking process is easier to perform, it is a time consuming task that does produce tools with long lifecycles. The method creates crucial tools needed for daily living, and most of them are Panindian with consistent styles and classes. All tools are basically divided into microtools and macrotools; these tool divisions are discussed as they pertain to particular ways of toolmaking.

Skill is used here for both the individual and society in prehistory. However, unless a range of superior-to-poor quality tools is found in a social setting (or site context), it does not exist. It is only evaluated as a skill by the culture containing it. In other words, badly-made tools may be viewed in a prehistoric setting as good tools; the value judgment is socially determined. Basically for a society, it is a value judgment based on survival needs. Archaeologically, skill cannot be evaluated in a prehistoric setting based on contemporary knapping; it must be a comparison of inter- and intrasite tools and implements during a particular time period. Skill can be translated as a normative level of tool production in a society – a standard for knappers living in the society. In other words, anyone can make a stone tool, but a skilled knapper makes a better stone tool and usually more efficiently as viewed by the society in which they were made. Naturally, there is a subjective evaluation by archaeologists as to tool quality. Established styles or traditions are attributed to skill levels in specific societies. All-in-all, skill is always present, reflects learned behavior, and produces socially-acceptable tools.

Toolmaking

Material culture as viewed archaeologically is a consequence of toolmaking and human survival in prehistory. While many parts of material culture are not in the toolmaking process, the tool complex comprises over three-fourths of the physical remains from yesterday. **Toolmaking** is defined as:

...the *art of making stone tools. Process of taking stone and working (flaking, grinding, and polishing) it into tools and implements; manufacture of stone tools. It is a lithic reduction technique whereby a <u>knapper</u> removes flakes or blades from a core, preform, or biface, which eventually becomes a tool or implement. And/or where a <u>manufacturer</u> pecks, grinds, chips, and polishes stone into the shape of established tools.*

Emic versus Etic Toolmaking Methods

Kenneth Pike (1954) coined the terms **emic** (phonemic) and **etic** (phonetic). The terms (concepts) are important, if only to give the reader an understanding of how tools are interpreted archaeologically and by Native Americans.

While Harris (1968) spent pages making the distinction in anthropological theory, it comes out as *emic* equals the Native Americans' view of toolmaking versus *etic* equals the archaeologists' observation and view of Native American toolmaking. What is important here is the Native Americans viewpoint which is often based on oral traditions – their inner psychological states, concerns, and beliefs. Whereas, from the archaeological perspectives, the oral traditions become a question of semantics and acceptance on histories not made be original Native Americans.

Mason (2000) provides a discussion on archaeology and Native American oral traditions with notable two pro-arguments:

1 – Oral traditions are as valid as any other kind of information

2 – Who best can talk about their tools than Native Americans (basic emic viewpoint).

While these arguments may hold a certain amount of validity for the Woodland Period, real time depth becomes questionable to most archaeologists. Echo-Hawk (2000) addresses this issue in archaeology, especially how time depth pertains to burials. He comments:

The historical record helps to explain North American social settings as the product of traceable processes rather than as an expression of a timelessly rigid "ethnographic present." Oral traditions and the archaeological record both reveal the workings of these processes, both provide important knowledge about the ancient past. Archaeology is inherently multidisciplinary, so the study of oral literature should exist as one more realm of legitimate inquiry, featuring analytical approaches, standards, and techniques that can be employed to add useful oral information to our models of human history. Following this procedure, Indian tribes and museums can more effectively trace connections among populations extending far back into the past.

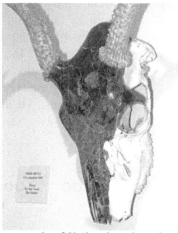

Figure 1 – An example of Native American Art. Tools used to make the object are latent operations of which only the Native American who made it knows. Are his methods truly Native American, even with metal tools? Art was made by John Black Feather Jeffries.

As such, this is an overview to a *kind of* New Lithic Technology from which broader interpretations can be made by both the Native Americans and archaeologists. By using a technological continuum and assuming the Panindian nature of tools, basic toolmaking processes become less of a technology forces cultural interpretation(s); it becomes an understanding of detailed circumstances of past cultures. For those archaeologists who might think this is a recent issue, Lowie's (1917) **Oral Tradition and History** may make interesting reading. The reader must bear in mind – there are numerous viewpoints on how the Native Americans made and used their tools (Figure 1).

Mechanical Advantage of Tools

Stone tools presented the Native Americans with a Mechanical Advantage (MA) over nature. But this knowledge took thousands of years to accumulate and become lithic traditions for their toolkits. Most of the basic toolmaking knowledge was brought into the New World, namely blade and biface reduction methodologies. Once mastered for any society, toolmaking became a technological continuum in which minor variations, innovations, and inventions occurred at various times and places (Figure 2).

As lithic scientists, we examine technology as it was used to work stone. It involves the American version of humanity's knowledge of relevant forces in nature, sources of materials, mechanics of tool construction, and the ability (skill) to use the appropriate tools and implements for daily survival. Additionally, the term **Native American prehistoric technology** means prehistoric skills of knowing and performing tool manufacture; but of greater importance, it means they had the ability to reason the MA of tools and predict future tool usage and social needs.

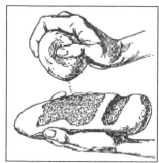

Figure 2 – One of Many Ways - Pecking a Cobble into an Axe. The axe is shaped into a final form by repeatedly striking its surface with a hammerstone.

The Native Americans understood principles of structure and function in toolmaking; all of which were incorporated into an infinite variety of tools. For lithic archaeology, technology is an abstract study with an emphasis on application – the study of technological processes in manufacturing, natural forces, chemistry of natural stones, and cultural aspects of all lithic objects. In other words, finding how the Native Americans made and used their stone tools.

Processes in Technology

Processes in technology are the means by which people act (behave) to established procedures, methods, and traditions to produce tools which are used for desired end results. It is a system of goals that are task-oriented to meet survival needs and living conditions (Figure 3). As a <u>note</u>: numbers in the following list pertain to this figure.

Tool (and nonmaterial behavior) processes are replicated from generation to generation. Overall, it is a continuum that:

1 – Starts initially from simple food curation for daily survival (basic scavenger society, New World populations were past this stage). Processes involve manufacturing clothing, shelter, and simple tools **(1)**.

2 – Becomes established methods and procedures which are replicated in the social context (basic hunting/gathering society – hunting implies procedures). Processes involve manufacturing specialty tools for food curation **(2)**.

3 – Planning activities to react to environmental conditions and influences. Processes involve tool manufacturing as a reaction to environmental situations **(3)**.

4 – Processes become specialty activities practiced by trained (skilled) individuals. Processes involved specific tool manufacturing, such as traditions.

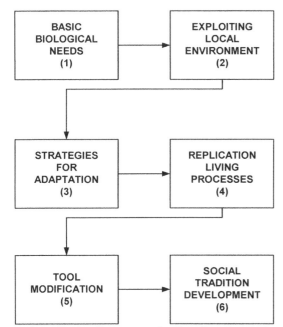

Figure 3 – Basic Processes in the Development of a Toolmaking Society

5 – Processes become regional (basic sedentary societies without major outside influences).

6 – Storage of resources for future use. Processes involve long-term planning and strategies **(4)**.

7 – Becomes multifunctional processes and procedures. Begins basic plant domestication, nonlithic processes become secondary procedures or behavior **(5)**.

8 – Processes become integration with other societies. Basic regional social systems, such as political controls.

9 – Processes produce surpluses which become trade, exchange, or tribute systems **(6)**.

Basically, process is the controlling factor in both tool structure and function, and plays a major role in style. It is observable in behavior and is manifested archaeologically in artifactual contexts. These contexts are the result of a series of actions, events, stages, procedures, ceremonies, or traditions to make, change, destroy objects in a social setting at a specific time and place. For stone tools, the process starts with lithic curation and ends with tool expention.

Design Elements in Native American Toolmaking

Regardless of the tribe and at any time period, no toolmaking operation was a course of random events. Each tool that was replicated in prehistory had a set of procedures and processes for tool manufacture and usage. If the technological continuum is acceptable, these processes (procedures) are more-or-less the same throughout prehistory. Any tool has a basic design, perhaps called a tradition in the society, but mental image exists for someone to make the tool. Thus, design leads to structure, the physical properties of any tool. Tools were not made for fun-play things. They were work-oriented and thus structure must perform a task, its function. Once a functional tool was produced, it served an individual or social group. This aspect is the tool's useability. Useability related to how the tool was used, maintained, and finally expended it. This time period is the tool's lifecycle. The end process of the lifecycle is the expention period where the user decides that the tool's useful life is exhausted, and the use starts the process and procedures all over for the next replacement tool.

For tool analyses, structure (morphology) generally means the form of archaeological classifications (typology). As a general comment, most of the archaeological record contains reasonably accurate tool classifications; however, the difficulty comes from inaccurate tool functional assessments. Collectively, both structure and function are the key to tool analyses; they cannot be separated as distinct categories. Function is structure-dependent and cannot be used as a standalone factor in human behavior. Tool operations (within industries), such as cutting, chopping, abrading, can be used as behavioral elements. As stated, structure is function-dependent, but function is not always observable in the archaeological record. Thus, the classification of tools is often based on archaeological methodologies, not necessarily the real world on Native Americans. Quite simply, we may never know the true nature of how the Native Americans considered their tools for their various tasks.

This publication was not intended to argue the above propositions; however, a brief summary of structure and function as analytical concepts is presented at the end of this section and defined in the Projectile Point Typology section.

General Tool Classifications

Each topic that is discussed below follows a general toolmaking discussion, namely macrotools (axes, celts, adzes, etc.) and microtools (points, drills, scrapers, etc.). Basics of lithic tool analyses are also discussed. The major difference between the two groups is their method of manufacture. Macrotools generally involve some flaking (chipping) but mostly pecking and grinding to shape the tool.

Microtools generally involve blade and flake reduction technologies. These tools are flaked into shape. Microtools predate macrotools in the Americas. Conversely, macrotools were invented here as a response to America's changing environment during the Archaic Period. Interestingly, the axe was invented here; other people in the world have the same tool. Is the axe a worldwide continuum or a consequence in technology that any group of people would eventually discover?

Examples of these two groups are shown in the Miscellaneous Tools/Implements, Bifaces as Knives, and Projectile Points sections.

Lithic Identification for Tools

Stones used for tools by the MPRV Native Americans were basically local materials. Occasionally, nonlocal stones are found, but they usually represent tools that were brought into the MPRV by Native Americans who migrated long distances, came in for trade, political discourse, etc. However, for early MPRV Native Americans, long distance travel for specific stones was common. The MPRV Environment section discusses stone availability and sources. Additionally, Gall and Steponaitis' (2001) study of greenstone at the Moundville site in Alabama provides an excellent model for macrotool lithic distribution based on chemical composition. The major problem in identifying stones, especially for macrotools, is polishing. For both tool classes, patination often hides the interior stone structure. Basic geological knowledge is a prerequisite for identification of stones used by the Native Americans. The following discusses two broad tool divisions:

1 – Macrotoolmaking
2 – Microtoolmaking.

Figure 4 – Possible Heat-Treated Jasper. It was found with other flakes that have a reddish color. This specimen shows potlids from excessive heating. While found with nontreated flakes, it still could be the results of a prehistoric forest fire.

Stone Modification – Thermal Alteration

Various arguments over the years in archaeology have played on the assumption that Native Americans heat-treated their stone to improve workability. At the same time, prehistoric and modern knappers worked most stones into high quality tools. Lithic skill (and talent) provides the knowledge to work stone; therefore, the argument remains speculative without qualified field-tested results. Site 44LD124 is a quarry site in Loudoun County, Virginia. Fifteen flakes show evidence of heat treatment (Petraglia 1994), which is a possible strategy for stone reduction. It is the proof archaeologically that is questionable (Figure 4) on how does heat treatment improve knappability.

As a different technique, Ellis (1957) was among the first to publish experimental results on heated stone. His conclusion was:

Experimental pressure flaking with such heated stones, however, failed to show that chips could be removed with any greater ease than they could when the tools were cold.

Quality controlled experiments are needed that are based on calorie distribution through stone and per mole, crystal structure and lattice variation, exact heat (Δ) measurements and controls, moisture indices, precise flaking methods (energy inputs and outputs), stone volume and mass, surface energy absorption or release rates, comparative data for all workable stones, and/or scientifically controlled laboratory environments for testing. These are just some of the factors needed in studying heat treatment, let alone identifying thermal altered stones in prehistoric contexts. Obviously, some prehistoric materials appear to have been heat treated, but … ancient forest or camp fires could be the answer to that question of origin. Thermal alteration was not a focus in this study. See Experimental Archaeology section.

Unusual Flaking Techniques

In studying an area such as the MPRV, ethnographic data are usually lacking and a basic assumption on flaking/manufacturing techniques lies with the researcher.

Generally, toolmaking techniques for the area under study are based on other stone tool studies. Parallels are assumed; thus, the researcher's interpretation. However, numerous ethnographic reports contain errors, especially recordings by people who are not well-informed on toolmaking. Probably the best example is Eames (1915) and Godsal (1915) reports observations of dropping cold water on hot flint to remove flakes. However, this does not construe that all unusual methods are false methods. For example, this unusual method survives (Sellers 1885):

... flattened root makes a firm seat for the stone, a notch cut into the body of a tree the fulcrum for the lever; either a pointed stick is placed on the point of the stone where the flake is to be split from it, its upper end resting against the under side of the lever, or a bone or horn point let into and secured to the lever takes the place of this stick. When the pressure is brought to bear, by the weight of the operation, on the long end of the lever, a second man with a stone, mall, or heavy club strikes a blow on the side of the lever, directly over the pointed stick or horn-point, and the flake is thrown off.

Unfortunately, he does not name the Native American cultures, but other ethnographic evidence establishes the lever and fulcrum as one of the techniques used by them. A possible hypothesis for the technique's usage is that elderly knappers used it to flake stone. Regardless of the techniques reported by early ethnographers, they must be replicated experimentally and examples recovered in site contexts.

1 – Macrotoolmaking

Macrotool manufacture produced numerous large tools, namely axe, celt, adz, chisel, gouge, etc. The axe is described, but these methods frequently apply to other macrotools. For general macrotools manufacture, see Hranicky (1995, 2001, and 2002).

Native Americans used three primary methods in lithic axe manufacture, which are the pecked-polished, flat-cobble, and chipped stone methods. There are differences among them in both manufacturing time as well as their prehistoric chronology. Axe (and celt, gouge, splitter, etc.) manufacturing techniques are:

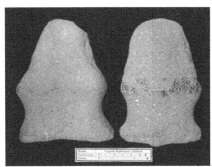

Figure 5 – Mississippian Axes from (left) Montgomery County, Virginia and (right) Spotsylvania County, Virginia. Both axes are made from rhyolite; left axe was made from a river cobble and the other axe material was quarried. The key to their differences is patination. Both axes were made by the pecking and polishing method.

1 – Pecked-polished - made by pecking a stone into the desired shape (Figure 5). There is evidence of baton-chipping (hammerstone), but this is difficult to discern because of subsequent pecking and polishing. If chipping occurred, it was probably the hard stone doing the pecking. Then the axe was ground smooth. It is usually made from heavy dense lithic materials and well made. Lithic material could have been quarried, but certainly most of the material was picked up in field/forest areas or riverbeds. Examples are shown in the Miscellaneous Tools/Implements section.

2 – Flat-cobble - usually small and made by using a thin cobble and removing small flakes off or grinding it into the desired shape. Some original cortex frequently remains. It makes up the quick and easy method of axe manufacturing. Lithic material was obtained from field/forest areas or riverbeds. Figure 6 shows an example of a full grooved axe. Examples are shown in the Miscellaneous Tools/Implements section.

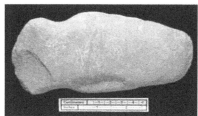

Figure 6 – Quartzite Example of a Flat-Cobble Axe from Spotsylvania County, Virginia (L = 144, W = 69, T = 21 mm). The cobble axe is the easiest form to make, and as such, it is quite common in the Middle Atlantic area. Also, the cobble was a material source for the peck/polish method; however, these axes are better made. This specimen is flat and still has cortex remaining.

3 – Chipped stone - made by removing large flakes to form the desired shape (Figure 7). This axe is sometimes called the Guilford chipped axe technique, and it has no surface treatment, such as grinding or polishing. Lithic materials were either quarried or picked in field/forest areas or riverbeds. These axes are generally poorly made. And for the Late Archaic, this style is the most common axe form in the Middle Atlantic area. Flaking (chipping) may have been a preparatory stage for pecked/polished axes. Examples are shown in the Miscellaneous Tools/Implements section.

Figure 7 – Quartzite Chipped Axe from Spotsylvania County, Virginia (L = 141, W = 70, T = 38 mm). It has a reddish color that may be due to heat-treating the material before flaking.

All groove styles occur in the MPRV except the diagonal groove. The diagonal groove, a Southwestern U.S. type, does occur in southwestern Virginia (Hranicky 1995). Grooving is a hafting setup for an axe. The MPRV axes tend to be cruder and smaller than specimens found elsewhere, especially the Southeast. The materials are local stones with a few basalts and diabase stones being used. For the MPRV, the most common axe-celt material is greenstone. Pole battering is common and recovered specimens usually have sharp bits.

Figure 8 – Macrotool Bits. Left starts with axe bits and ends on right with a splitter. Photograph shows basic blade differences for macrotools.

Macrotool Classification

Classification of macrotool bits is open to research in American archaeology. Figure 8 shows a range of bit styles and angles on Virginia macrotools. Figure 9 shows basic shapes as in Hranicky (1995, 2001, and 2002). These shapes were used here to classify macrotools in this study. We can assume that bit style equals the prehistoric function for the tool. There is no published data on site-specific bit angles of macrotools; thus, any attempt at contrasting/comparing bit angles cross culturally is impossible.

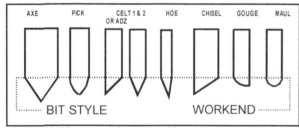

Figure 9 – Macrotool Bit Styles (From Hranicky 1995)

The bit (workend) design is a correlation of function, but for the moment, functions are not easily measured. Bit angles offer one factor for functional determinations. The basic angle measurement is from the bit/blade edge to the junction of the frank and shoulder as measured off the center (horizontal) plane of the blade (Hranicky 2002a). Table 1 presents suggested bit angles. As a hypothesis, the more symmetrical the bit is - the more vertical the striking action. Conversely, off-center bit angles have more of a horizontal action for usage. This design factor was known by the Native Americans and was correlated to tool function. The use of tools constitutes a tool modality that is discussed in the Projectile Point Typology section.

Table 1 Macrotool Bit Angles*	
Axe	>35° & <50°
Celt	>25° & <40°
Adz	>20° & <35°
Maul **	>40°
Pick	>30°
Chisel	>20° & <35°
Chopper	>20° & <50°
Gouge	>20° & <30°
Splitter	>15° & <30°
Hoe	>30° & <40°

* Based on Virginia specimens in Hranicky (1995)
** Bit is usually round.

Macrotool Resharpening

Most macrotools that are recovered from systematic surveys, surface finds, or in archaeological site contexts are generally expended implements. They were resharpened until the bit reached expention and then discarded. Hranicky (1995) has axes and celts exceeding 150 mm that suggest the basic Final Manufacture Stage (FMS) form had a blade over 100 mm. This length provided long-term lifecycles (5+ years). Due to having to examine and record macrotools in collectors' homes, bit resharpening was not studied and bit angles were not measured.

Bit degrading depends on the material that an axe or celt was used against and the length of chopping time. Once dull, an abrasive stone, such as quartzite or sandstone was used to replace bit sharpness. The most common form of bit wear down is from cutting wood. Hayden (1987) notes:

It became clear that in every major culture area in the world where edge-grinding adzes and axes had become important, wood cutting requirements were usually high.

2 – Microtoolmaking

For toolmaking or manufacturing, we assume *regularity* which is reflected in the archaeological record; whatever is recovered from the past reflects behavior in a social setting. Any manufactured item represents an event in prehistory where a Native American made an implement based on socially-accepted methods, specific materials, and learned behavior. Naturally, skill and talent are involved. While toolmaking is not unique to human beings, it is a global phenomenal habit that demonstrates a material form of culture.

For prehistory, toolmaking represents a process from a cultural sequence from initializing social organization through to its disbandment or absorption into another group. Technology as practiced by this unit is stable in the social setting where the group is successful in acquiring foodstuff and materials for daily living. Toolmaking is related to this daily activity and process; however, change in production methods is a consequence of other factors, such as population pressures, political strife, weather influences, and raw material availability. Therefore, toolmaking cannot be assumed to be a constant in any society.

The following paragraphs discuss various aspects of microtoolmaking.

Cores

Quarry and basic core processing was discussed in the MPRV Environment section. The core is the initializing stage for producing microtools. One type of core occurs that has not received notice of its importance in archaeology. This is the flake core. It is sometimes called the Levallois core technique which was primarily used to remove blades for tool production. The flake core was used to obtain large flakes which were further reduced to tools. This type of core may have been used to transport lithic material from its source to a workstation some distance away. Also, it is a quarry setup piece which then was used to produce workable flakes. Figures 10 and 11 show examples of flake cores.

Text continued after flowchart.

Figure 10 – Expended Rhyolite Flake Core from Southeastern Virginia

Figure 11 – Jasper Flake Core from Warren County, Virginia. It represents the basic flake core at or near Paleoindian quarry sites.

Biface Principles

Numerous procedures have been published on basic biface reduction procedures. Callahan (1979) is considered here as the classic set of procedures. Chart 1 on the next page presents biface basics according to Callahan (1979). Chart text is as follows.

Chart 1 – Principles of Basic Flintknapping – the basics of flintknapping according to Callahan (1979):

Stage 1 – BLANK – created by obtaining a blank (unmodified) piece of raw material. A blank may be a spall, nodule, irregular chunk, cobble, or any other form suitable for the end product. Action may vary from simply picking up a suitable piece to systematic flaking of a suitable spall from a core. Edges may vary from thin and sharp to thick and squared. Shape is irrelevant.

Stage 2 – ROUGH OUT – creates a circumferential, roughly centered edge, which is neither too sharp nor too blunt (ideally between about 55°-75°). Work should focus on the outer zone with little or no attention being paid to the central zone, cross-section, or shape. Shape and width-thickness ratios may vary in the extreme. The edge should end up being roughly centered and bi-convex, without such concavities, convexities, steps, squared edges, or other irregularities as would hinder successful execution in the next stage.

Stage 3 – PRIMARY PREFORM – creates a symmetrical handaxe-like outline with generous, lenticular cross-sections and a straight and centered, bi-convex edge. Width-thickness ratios should fall between roughly 3.00 to 4.00 while edge-angles should fall between about 40°-60°. Focus on the middle zone without losing control of the outer zone. Principal flakes should generally just contact or overlap in the middle zone, except on thin pieces, and be without such concavities, convexities, steps, or other irregularities as would hinder successful execution in the next stage.

Stage 4 – SECONDARY PREFORM – creates a symmetrical outline with flattened, lenticular cross-sections and a straight and centered, bi-convex edge. Thickness should gradually diminish during reduction so that width-thickness ratios end up falling between roughly 4.00 to 5.00 or more. Edge-angles should fall between about 25°-45°. Focus on the middle zone without losing control of the outer zone. Principal flakes should generally overlap, often considerably, in the middle zone. Generalization of the final shape may start now and patterned flake removals may be implemented. The resultant piece should be without significant concavities, convexities, steps, or irregularities as would hinder successful execution in the next stage.

Stage 5 – FINAL PREFORM – creates a symmetrical, more-or-less parallel-sided outline (if final shape is to be parallel-sided) of specific shape, with appropriately flattened, lenticular cross-sections, and a straight and centered, bi-convex edge. The outline and thickness should be within one set of principal flake removals from the final product (i.e., within about 2-4 mm at either edge). Patterned flake removals may be employed, with flake terminations being feathered. Principal flake scars in the middle zone may or may not overlap those of the previous stage. Width-thickness ratios and edge-angles should be about the same as on the final product, which may (or may not) be greater than the secondary preform. Focus on the middle zone while giving special attention to outer zone regularity. The resultant piece should be without such concavities, convexities, steps, or irregularities as would hinder successful execution in the next stage.

Stage 6 *– FLAKED IMPLEMENT – creates an implement of specific, symmetrical shape, cross-sections, width-thickness ratios, thickness and contours with a particular flake removal sequence and flake scar appearance, as appropriate to the type or anticipated function. The edge should be more or less straight but without final retouch and alignment, if needed. The focus should be upon the outer zone, with the flake scars penetrating into the middle zone as appropriate to the type or function. Fluting, if applicable, is done at this time.*

Stage 7 *– RETOUCHED IMPLEMENT – creates a finished implement, with edges and hafting elements being retouched as appropriate to the type or anticipated function. Focus on the outer zone only so as to create a sharp, very straight and centered edge, not prepared in anticipation of another set of flake removals but for function. Execute basal hafting or finishing elements such as notching, shouldering, stitching, etc. Lateral notching sequences, if applicable, are applied at this time. Basal abrasion may also be done now, as appropriate.*

A flintknapping flowchart is presented on next page; Text continued on page 106.

From the notebook…

Powhatan's Mantle

Deerskin with shell beads which is supposed to have belonged to Chief Powhatan (Wood, Waselkov, and Hatley 1989). They describe it as concentric rings, a human figure, and two deer.

It measures 233 by 150 cm and is in the Ashmolean Museum in Oxford, England. The two figures could be panthers. Note fingers on the animal glyphs. Similar glyphs occur at Paint Lick Mountain (44Tz13), Tazewell County and at the Harrison County Petroglyph site (46H51) in West Virginia (Hranicky and Collins 1997). It probably represents a human-animal figure in their mythology. The symbol is Panindian in the East.

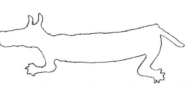

Harrison County Glyph (1 of 3 at the site)

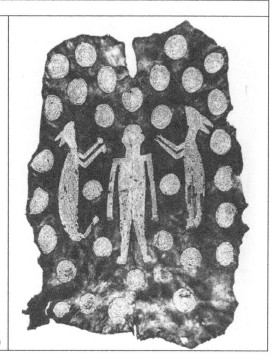

From the notebook …

Rhyolite Sample of Quarry Debris from Little Catoctin Creek area, Frederick County, Maryland

Rhyolite Biface Shaping Sample from above the Potomac's Fall Line

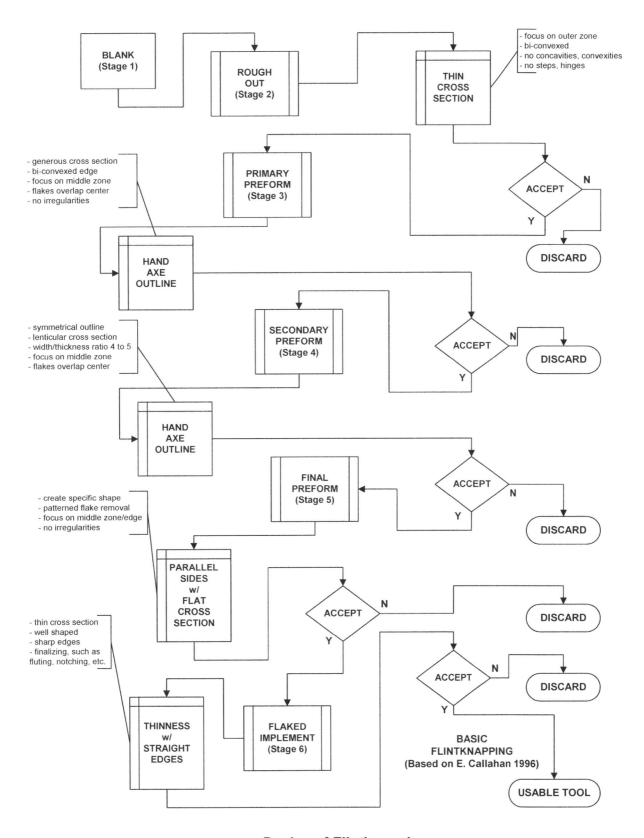

Basics of Flintknapping

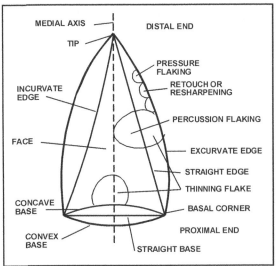

Figure 12 – Parts of the Biface. This is a simplified form; there are numerous shapes for Native American bifaces.

Biface Nomenclature

Excluding minor occurrences of blade and flake tools, most microtools involve stone reduction to a biface. This biface takes many shapes, but generally, the knapper's biface is headed toward a specific tool. Bifaces can be considered intentional forms for producing a functional tool. Figure 12 shows the parts of a biface. Some aspects apply to unifaces. Other than considering flake modification a uniface tool, uniface technology was rarely used in the MPRV, with the exception of Paleoindian jasper blade technology. Flat-sided (uniface) microtools do occur in the MPRV.

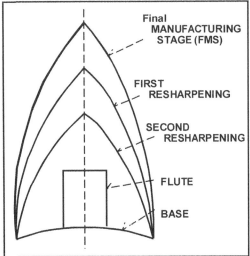

Figure 13 – Maintenance of Point Symmetry. Symmetry is a universal aspect of tools. This tool manufacture process may be an individual's genetic control for humans – symmetry. Regardless, it is a toolmaking phenomenon that occurs worldwide.

Tool Modification

Tool modification is any tool alteration after its Final Manufacture Stage (FMS), including rehafting (retrofitting). FMS is the stage in toolmaking where the tool is placed into service. It includes any hafting processes. Generally, subsequent modification involves blade (workend) resharpening. Any form of tool modification is a reduction of the tool's lifecycle and may alter basic (or intended) function. Archaeologically, tool modification form or usage is always assumed to be in and as a consequence of cultural contexts and at specific time periods. Bearing this in mind, this entire publication uses it as a basic analytical premise. Tools are rarely found in FMS condition.

Symmetry Maintenance

Generally, all prehistoric tools maintain a culturally-perceived symmetry in tool design and manufacture (Hranicky and McCary 1995). Usually, tools have a mirror image of opposite edges (lateral margins) as viewed from the medial axis. Tool usage via breakage, retrofitting, and reshapening tend to skew this symmetrical shape. This practice started in the Paleoindian period, namely Clovis technology and continues to the Woodland times, namely the Levanna point type. However, the Woodland Period has some breakdown in the practice, such as the Potomac point which, triangularly-shaped, is not generally a symmetrical point. It does maintain the wedge-advantage of the triangle. Figure 13 shows the balance of symmetry, and Figure 14 shows examples which violate symmetry. Off-centered stems are generally the result of uneven blade resharpening (Figure 15). Tool symmetry was practiced on macrotools, also.

Figure 14 – Examples of Violating Point Symmetry

Figure 15 – Heavily Patinated Point with Off-Center Blade Resharpening. Point probably functioned as a knife; it is not made of local material and cannot be typed.

Tool Retrofitting

In addition to resharpening, one major projectile point modification was retrofitting broken points back into service. Broken blades were refitted with haftable stems. These points frequently show snapped bases. Excavated data do not yield evidences to determine who the people were. Did the society who broke them refit them? Or, are these refitted points the result of people who picked them up in later times and made a *quick* projectile point?

Figure 16 – Snap-Base Points. Points may be produced by core-setup to remove flakes (usually points have no bulb scar) or most likely, points are retrofitted from large broken blade tips.

The snap-base point, called the Faison type (Painter 1991), is based on surface finds and currently does not have a date range; however, it is probably Late Archaic into the Woodland Period (Figure 16). This practice occurs all over the eastern U.S. See Projectile Points section.

Figure 17 – Distal End of a Point Blade where the Knapper Attempted to Make a Notched Point. Only one pressure flake was removed for each notch; experimental notching by the knapper?

Figure 17 shows the retrofitting of a quartzite distal end of a thin, well-made projectile point blade. It was snapped during usage, and the user (or subsequent prehistoric owner) attempted to notch the proximal margin. The notching (shallow) was not satisfactory to the knapper; thus, it was discarded.

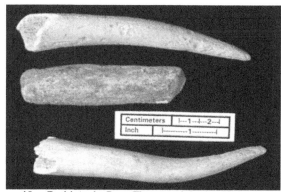

Figure 18 – Prehistoric Deer Tines and Antler Midsection – All Showing Usage. In addition to flakers, tines are also used for knife handles.

Tools for Making Tools

Figure 18 shows deer antler tools, which are only part of the possibilities for tools that the Native Americans used. The Experimental Archaeology section describes the flintknapper's toolkit. Basically, the toolkit includes:

1 – Hammerstones
2 – Peckingstones
3 – Billets (flakers)
4 – Anvilstones
5 – Abraders.

The combination and varieties of each tool group are dependent on the toolmaking task and the Native American performing the task. There were preferences in making tools as well as the material that was used and, of course, the *social* way of using them.

Stone Sources for Production

As discussed previously, there are numerous ways the Native Americans procured their stone. Large slabs of desirable stone were processed by breaking off workable spalls (Figure 19). Basically, stone is found as:

1 – Boulders and outcrops – quarrying stone
2 – Field and riverbed cobbles – pickup stones

For MPRV stone identification and rock types, see MPRV Environment section.

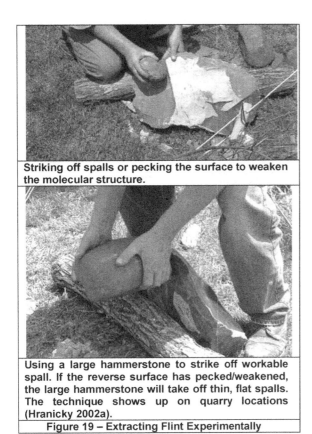

Striking off spalls or pecking the surface to weaken the molecular structure.

Using a large hammerstone to strike off workable spall. If the reverse surface has pecked/weakened, the large hammerstone will take off thin, flat spalls. The technique shows up on quarry locations (Hranicky 2002a).

Figure 19 – Extracting Flint Experimentally

Stone Reduction into Tools

In analyzing tools for typology and classification, a set of standards is needed for tool manufacture. This study is based on flintknapping methods (standards) that are defined in Ellis (1957), Crabtree (1972), Callahan (1979), Whittaker (1994), and Hranicky (2002). The Native American procedure(s) for producing tools is similar for the entire eastern U.S. and these standard references amplify, describe, and clarify methods. Generally, it is a stone reduction process that turns raw stone into finished tools via established Native American ways. The process is initialized by acquiring stone, either by quarrying it or pick-up stones in fields or riverbeds. The end product is a tool or implement that is ready to be put into service by the Native Americans. Tool production was probably a male occupation in Native American prehistory and shared among societal members. A personal toolkit is also assumed because several Virginia Native American burials have toolkits associated with male burials.

The reduction process always involves:

1 – Procurement – finding the correct stone
2 – Processing – shaping stone into tools
3 – Operations – using stone tools
4 – Expention – discarding depleted stone tools
5 – Replacement – replenishing tools.

These factors are further amplified in the following model. This is the basic approach used throughout this publication, and the model's factors are discussed later under billet flaking. See Experimental Archaeology section.

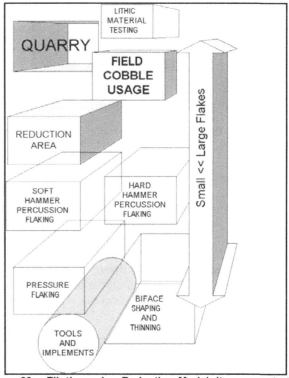

Figure 20 – Flintknapping Reduction Model. It represents the general tool production sequence from the quarry to the tool. While stages are difficult to prove archaeologically, this model implies production stages or phases in tool production. Additionally, model implies that large through to small flakes indicate a reduction or process method for lithic flaked tools.

Figure 20 shows the Reduction Model, which presents basic MPRV tool production. It involves:

1 – Location of lithic material - is basically quarrying of outcrops or field or streambed stone pickups. Once located, material is tested to determine its workability.

Note: Quarrying stone always offered fresh stone; whereas, pickup stones have moisture in the internal part of the cobble. Also, the stone has begun to decay and this affects its knappability. Cobbles often have internal fracture lines or brittleness that affects knappability.

2 – Reduction area – in convenient location, usually near the stone source, starting the reduction sequence of getting the stone into workable pieces.

3 – Hammering stone – usually starting with hard hammerstone to work large pieces, then using a smaller soft hammerstone to shape these pieces.

4 – Pressure flaking – using small flakers to finalize the piece.

5 – Hafting – if not a hand-held tool, mounting the tool in a handle or shaft (chassis mounting).

6 – Tool usage – starts the tool's lifecycle that ends with expention.

This model assumes a stone preferred by the Native Americans. As with the Paleoindians, travel to *choose* quarries often involved hundreds of miles; whereas, Late Archaic/Woodland Native Americans settled near *adequate* quarry sources. Additionally, trade for stone was common. The basic stone processing in the model is fairly constant throughout American prehistory.

Cortex Removal

Decortation is a basic toolmaking practice among all North American Indians. Cortex is removed because it is usually a weathered surface and therefore not as stable as the interior area. Because the cortex surface is usually rough, it is subject to shattering or affecting flake formation. Cortex will collapse when struck and does not rebound the way interior material does. Figures 21a and 21b show failure by Native American knappers to remove all the cortex. Cortex sometimes remains on projectile points and other tools; however, this is rare.

Note: Small boulders in and near quarry and habitation sites will frequently have one or two flakes removed. This is lithic testing by the Native Americans to determine the workability of the stone. The discard probably meant that it was unsatisfactory.

Figure 21a – Top Knife Face with Cortex (see back side below); lower point has had all cortex removed.

Figure 21b – Top knife cortex-backed knife (see front face above); lower reverse side of knife. As a general rule, all cortex was removed from knives. Both tools show usage, which probably indicates short-term usage. These two knives were made off a large flake with semibifacial reduction.

Manufacturing Methods

Tool manufacturing involves three stoneworking techniques:

1 – Hard hammer flaking (stone, etc.)
2 – Soft hammer flaking (antler, etc.)
3 – Pecking, grinding, and polishing (stone, etc.).

Generally, hard and soft hammers are used for flaking microtools. Pecking and grinding applies to the manufacture of marcotools; however, some macrotools are flaked implements. The macrotool pecking/polishing technique was discussed previously.

The hammerstone has always been the basic tool for fracturing stone. It is used to produce spalls that can be further refined into tools and implements. Hammerstone and billets (flakers, etc.) produce distinctive flakes. For each flake removal method, there are three basic flake types:

1 – Feather
2 – Hinge
3 – Step.

Flake types and analyses are discussed below.

Figure 22 – Rhyolite Biface from Adams County, Pennsylvania (L = 188, W = 58, T = 19 mm; D/P Index = .769). It probably represents a transport piece which was intended for trade or a future tool. The D/P ratio is 0.795 which is a relatively flat profile.

D/P Index for Bifaces

The Distal/Proximal (D/P) index is a measurement of the flatness of a biface (Figure 22). The index is calculated by taking a thickness measurement at each end (usually 5 mm in from the end). Then, divide the proximal measurement into the distal measurement. Perfect flatness is D/P = 1.0.

Figure 23 – Hard Hammer Percussion Quartzite Flakes. Chalk lines show the percussion bulb.

Hard Hammer Percussion

The use of a hard hammerstone for flaking is usually found on larger preforms where shaping is not as crucial as flaking in later stages. The flakes produced by this method usually have large pronounced flake bulbs (Figure 23). The primary stone for MPRV microtool bifaces is quartzite; however, basalt and diabase are frequently used for macrotools preforms.

As a method, Ellis (1957) illustrates the hafted, hard hammerstone in flaking. This method has not been demonstrated at American knapp-ins but has possibilities, namely applying more precisely-controlled energy into stone. As per usual, more testing is needed.

Stages in Soft Hammer Percussion

Billet flaking is the technique of using a club-like tool to strike flakes off a blank, core, or large flake. The process involves the following stages - a lithic reduction continuum. As discussed previously in the Reduction Model, flaking is a major part of microtool making. The following describes the method and presents flaking factors that are used to identify and classify tools, from Callahan (1979), Bradley (1975), and Whittaker (1994), who defines stages in terms of finished products that resulted from goal and techniques within each stage as in the following stages. Callahan (1979) also follows a similar procedure for making bifaces. Theses stages can be used in modern experimental knapping and prehistoric biface analyses. Native American knappers reported in this publication follow these stages, which suggests the validity of them. Since these stages can be found in archaeological contexts throughout prehistory, the basic process described here represents a technology continuum for the Americas.

Figure 24 – Large Quartzite Biface (L = 127, W = 94, T = 39 mm). It may be a quarry transfer piece, but the size indicates the knapper intended to make a wide biface. It is Stage 0 biface.

Stage 0: Raw Material and Blank (Based on: Callahan 1979 and Whittaker 1994): Both the Native Americans and modern knappers start by choosing a suitable piece of material. Ideally, a large nodule is used. Bifaces are (and were) often made from flattish nodules or tabular pieces of material. A large flake is also good, and usually has sharp edges that provide an easy beginning point. In thinning a biface, the knapper loses a lot of width. The blank should have no cortex and should be a relatively thin biface (Figures 24 and 25).

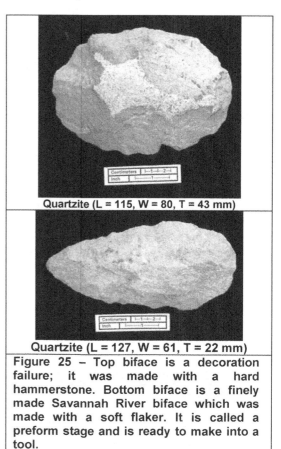

Quartzite (L = 115, W = 80, T = 43 mm)

Quartzite (L = 127, W = 61, T = 22 mm)

Figure 25 – Top biface is a decoration failure; it was made with a hard hammerstone. Bottom biface is a finely made Savannah River biface which was made with a soft flaker. It is called a preform stage and is ready to make into a tool.

Stage 1: Edged Blank (Based on: Callahan 1979 and Whittaker 1994): The primary objective is to produce a blank with bifacial edges to allow further working. Archaeologically, this is the earliest stage that can be reliably defined, and even after some working, it is still difficult for an archaeologist to know what the knapper intended to make, unless a complete sequence of worked and unfinished pieces is found with examples of the finished product (Figure 26). There definitely should not be any cortex remaining.

Figure 26 – Stage 0 or 1 Quartzite Bifaces. They are rejects or failures, but indicate basic shaping. Left: L = 91, W = 59. T = 28, middle; L = 99, W = 59, T = 31 mm; right: L = 105, W = 65, T = 20 mm. These bifaces are Stage 1 bifaces.

As Whittaker (1994) suggests:

In the first stage of bifacing, begin at a spot where a suitable platform exists and turn the edge as described earlier, working both sides alternately to remove unsuitable platforms and leave a sharp, wavy, bifacial edge with suitable platforms all around the blank. A flake with sharp, feathered edges offers lots of easy places to begin bifacing, but you should start by dulling the edge with your hammerstone, since the thin feather edge is not a good platform and gives you an excellent opportunity to cut your holding hand.

Initial bifacing can be done with either a hard or soft hammer. Unless replicating a particular technology, both are often used. The hard hammer is good for thick platforms on tough material, and the soft hammer is versatile, good for blows on platform surfaces in turning thick edges and for blows on thinner edges that turn the edge and begin thinning at the same time.

The blank at this stage is fairly thick, with width-thickness ratios around 2.00. The edge must be bifacially worked all around and suitable for further reduction. Because of the thickness, the edges should form relatively steep angles, 50 to 80 degrees or so. An edged blank is similar to some early handaxes.

Stage 2: Preform (Based on: Whittaker 1994): The objective of this stage is primary thinning. According to Whittaker (1994):

This is most easily done with a relatively large billet. Instead of removing short flakes at the edges, you are now attempting to make the flakes run across the faces of the biface, at least to the middle, and to remove the major irregularities of the faces. Get rid of as many problems as you can, concentrating on removing bad hinges and steps, major humps and knots, and cortex or other exterior surfaces.

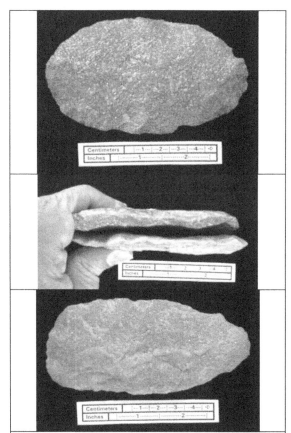

Figure 27 – Examples of Stage 2 Quartzite Bifaces with Cross Sections. Specimens were probably unsatisfactory to the Native American knappers, but they show basic workmanship in quartzite.

This biface should be a smoothly biconvex or lenticular cross-sectioned piece with fairly straight and centered edges with angles between about 40 and 60 degrees (Figure 27). It will still be relatively thick, with a width-thickness ratio of about 3.00 to 4.00. Most importantly, it should have regular faces without major flaws, or further thinning and refinement are difficult.

Stage 3: Refined Biface (Based on: Whittaker 1994): According to Whittaker (1979):

Once the piece is fairly regular and looks as if it may be worth refining, concentrate on removing large, flat flakes that run past the middle of the face, and thin the biface faster than it loses width. It is also important that you avoid major errors and keep the faces regular. You are still removing large flakes, which means stressing the biface, which is getting thinner and more fragile. All this means that you must pay careful attention to platforms and surface contours. As the biface gets smaller, you may want to shift to smaller hammers too, and be careful to give the biface adequate support (Figure 28). At the same time as you are concentrating on thinning, do not forget to work toward the outline shape you want.

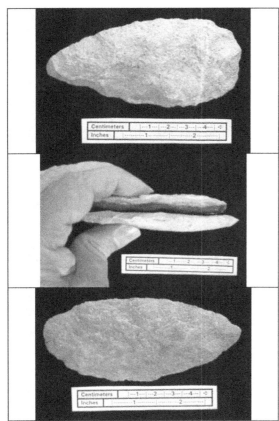

Figure 28 – Examples of Stage 3 Quartzite Bifaces with Cross Sections. Specimens could be thinner, but they are typical of MPRV workmanship in quartzite. Both bifaces still need edge trimming.

At the end of this stage, the biface should have a flattened cross-section, a width-thickness ratio of 4.00 or above, and thin edges with angles around 25 to 45 degrees. The Distal/Proximal (D/P) Index should equal 1 +/- 10%.

The snapped biface is common in later stages because of material impurities or the knapper overstrikes a platform (Figure 29).

Figure 29 – Not All Bifaces Are Successful – Broken ones are common. These breakages are the result of flexing (bending) fractures caused by knapping blows. They were not properly supported or were the result of excessive striking blows. Striking blows may have been too high on the set-up platform.

Stage 4: Finished Biface (Based on: Whittaker 1994):
According to Whittaker (1994):

Finishing a refined biface can be simple or complicated. The knapper may refine the form only a little by trimming off jagged edges and old platform remnants. Or he may want to modify the base for hafting with notches, or serrate the edge. Folsom and Clovis points at this stage underwent several more episodes of preparation and fluting, which could also be considered separate stages. A variety of techniques can be used in finishing. Either careful percussion with the soft hammer or pressure flaking are common. The major goal of the knapper seems to have been a thin piece of regular shape.

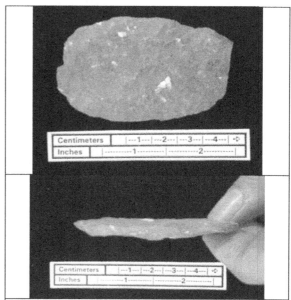

Figure 30 – Example of Stage 4 Rhyolite Biface with Cross Section. It is broken on the distal end which probably accounts for the discard; it is extremely thin (9 mm).

Figure 30 shows the thinness of a finished biface. The type of workmanship is typical of the Susquehanna pointmakers. These stages amplify the basic reduction model shown previously. The Distal/Proximal (D/P) Index should equal 1 +/- 10%.

Circular Bifaces

Most prehistoric bifaces have an elongated shape (longer than wide) that dates back to the Paleoindian Period (Figure 31).

A recent paper (Deller and Ellis 2001) reports large ovate bifaces in the Paleoindian Caradoc site of Ontario. This site has a high percentage of broken tools, which may imply deliberate breakage for ceremonial purposes – a sacred ritual. A single unfluted point was found on the site. The chert material for the bifaces occurs some 175 km away.

Furthermore, starting at the end of the Late Archaic Period, the (semi- or) circular bifaces occur. It corresponds to the introduction of the bipolar technique. This may simply be the reduction of a cobble; however, some circular bifaces are extremely thin (<10 mm) which suggests they were made by the basic (nonpolar) method of reduction. They occur in quartzite and are rarely made from rhyolite. The white quartz bifaces probably represent the Halifax or Lamoka technologies.

Figure 31 – Semicircular Quartzite Biface (L = 81, W = 54, T = 14 mm). It has long, well-developed flake scars indicating a craftsman toolmaker.

One early reported form circular form was the North point/blade (Perino 1969). He argued that it was a Hopewell form, and that it has a mortuary context. While not tested via site contexts, the circular quartzite biface is suggested as being Hopewell; thus, a Middle Woodland Period date and technology. For the MPRV, the Snyder point represents this technology.

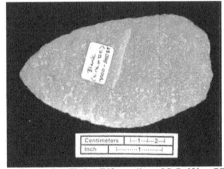

Figure 32 – Quartzite Flake Biface (L = 98.5, W = 55, T = 8.5 mm), Amherst County, Virginia. It has flat spots and a major hinge. Few bifaces have its D/P Index of 1.0.

Large Flake Bifaces

While most quartzite reduction methods involve cobble reduction, reduction from quarry spalls do occur (Figure 32). This method is a shortcut to the finished biface, but usually has two built-in flaws. First, the distal/proximal (D/P) profile (index) (side view) is curved rather than flat. Secondly, it has a taper from what becomes the base to the tip. And, it often has flat areas on the inside flake face. There are no studies to determine how common the technique was in prehistory. It closely resembles blade technology where flakes are removed from both faces. The technique can be classified as a third reduction method, as:

1 – Blade
2 – Biface
3 – Flake.

Preparatory Biface

A preparatory biface (as in Hranicky 1995), set-up biface, or preform is a flaked piece that the knapper has worked up to the point that it can be made into a tool. It has style and intentional form (shape) from which a specific tool is made. When this biface is found archaeologically, it is usually a discard that is due to a knapping error, namely broken in half, hinge fractures, and/or center humps. Fortunately, some well-made preforms have survived, which yield data about the knapper's intentions when making it (Figure 33). Thickness (thinness) is not a prerequisite for preparatory bifaces because the nature of the intended tool determines thickness and other dimensions.

Figure 33 – Preparatory Bifaces Cannot Always Be Assigned to A Tool Type or Industry – Large, weathered rhyolite biface (L = 127, W = 99, T = 18 mm) with bold flake scars. It shows no usage evidence.

The preparatory (preform) bifaces have several forms that occur in prehistory, which are:

1 – Circular shaped
2 – Lanceolate shaped
3 – Triangular shaped
4 – Leaf shaped.

These basic shapes overlap typologies and because they are not common in site and field collections, it is difficult to determine the tool that the knappers were intending to make from them, such as points, knives, drills, etc. Most prehistoric bifaces were successfully made into tools; consequently, we do not see this process archaeologically.

The next page presents quartzite biface examples for style and variation (Plate 11). Following those pages, rhyolite bifaces are shown (Plate 12). Several jasper preparatory bifaces were shown in the MPRV Environment section.

Text continued on page 122.

Plate 11 – MPRV Biface Style and Variation in Quartzite

These quartzite Stage 4 bifaces show various styles (shapes) that Native American knappers had in manufacturing. These specimens are only a small sample, and there are numerous other shapes used by them. At present, these broken bifaces were ready to be made into tools; however, knapping errors prevented it. Had breakage not occurred, we would not have them today. For this sample, the style reflects straight and excurvate sides and concave, straight, and convex bases. The bifaces were made with a deer or probably a moose antler fabricator. Minor edge trim was probably done with a deer fabricator and flaker.

The biface on the right has an attribute (characteristic) called a flat profile (Hranicky 2002a). It has a constant thickness from distal to proximal ends (D/P Profile). The sign of experienced knapping is the flat profile, but additionally, the D/P may indicate the knapper's intended function. This profile can be measured. Using a digital caliper, the biface measures L = 82.65, W = 50.52, T = 11.30 mm. Taking a measurement at 5 mm on each end at the medial axis: distal = 10.66 and proximal = 10.41 mm. By using the D/P as a ratio, a well-made biface should always equal 1.0; in this case, D/P = 1.0240. This number indicates the minor rise in the biface's center.

Another indicator for the biface is its width/thickness (W/T) ratio. The higher the number, the better made it is and/or it shows higher skill in thinning it. The ratio for the biface shown is 4.470, which is well above the average for percussion/pressure flaked quartzite bifaces.

Flintknapping techniques for these bifaces are discussed in the Toolmaking Technology section. Numbers 17 through 19 come from a Paleoindian campsite on the Potomac and Monocacy Rivers (Virginia second terrace overlooking the river junction).

Stage 4 Biface

<u>Note</u>: **Small marginal indentation is post-Native American.**

A Paleo Workstation on the Potomac…

The following examples have descriptions that reflect knapping errors, but they have knapping excellence also. They have evidence of pressure flaking, but mostly percussion flaking. These specimens are all site-surface finds, and are Paleoindian. The major errors in all knapping are bending and perverse fractures, hinges, and thinning errors. These artifacts were published in Hranicky (2015). They were found together on Virginia terrace near the Potomac River. They are debitage from a paleo workstation for refurbishing toolkits.

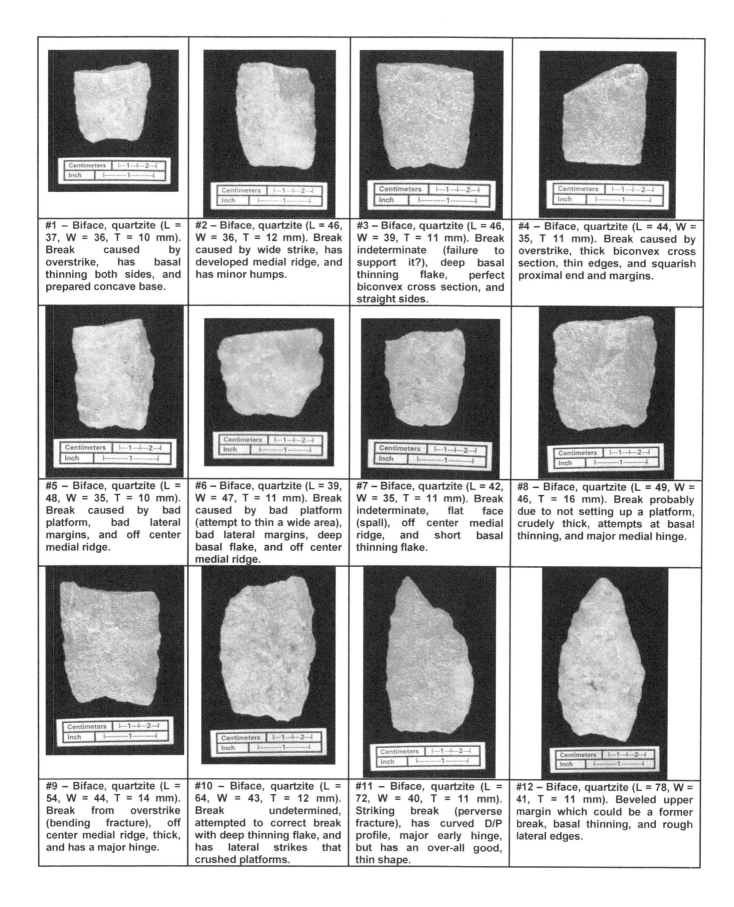

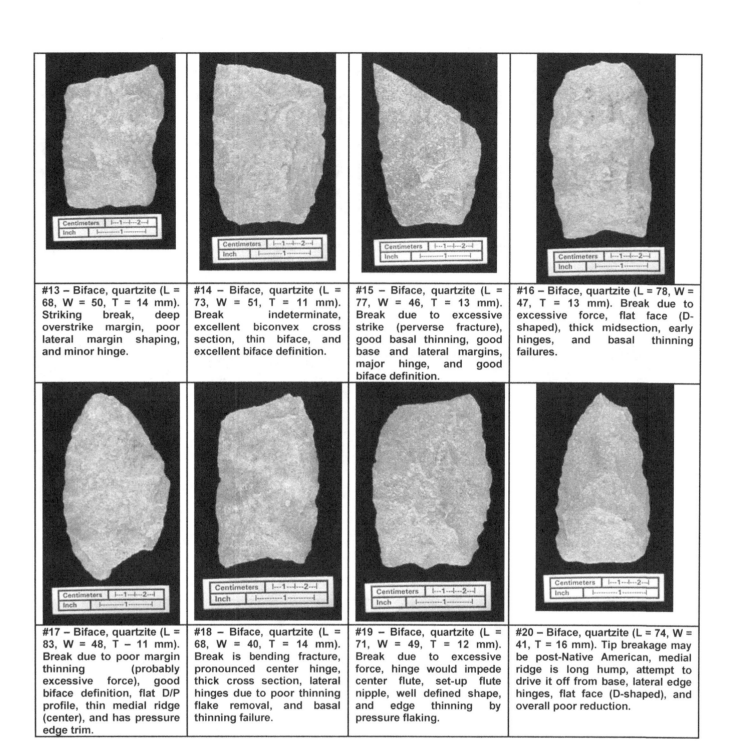

#13 – Biface, quartzite (L = 68, W = 50, T = 14 mm). Striking break, deep overstrike margin, poor lateral margin shaping, and minor hinge.	#14 – Biface, quartzite (L = 73, W = 51, T = 11 mm). Break indeterminate, excellent biconvex cross section, thin biface, and excellent biface definition.	#15 – Biface, quartzite (L = 77, W = 46, T = 13 mm). Break due to excessive strike (perverse fracture), good basal thinning, good base and lateral margins, major hinge, and good biface definition.	#16 – Biface, quartzite (L = 78, W = 47, T = 13 mm). Break due to excessive force, flat face (D-shaped), thick midsection, early hinges, and basal thinning failures.
#17 – Biface, quartzite (L = 83, W = 48, T – 11 mm). Break due to poor margin thinning (probably excessive force), good biface definition, flat D/P profile, thin medial ridge (center), and has pressure edge trim.	#18 – Biface, quartzite (L = 68, W = 40, T = 14 mm). Break is bending fracture, pronounced center hinge, thick cross section, lateral hinges due to poor thinning flake removal, and basal thinning failure.	#19 – Biface, quartzite (L = 71, W = 49, T = 12 mm). Break due to excessive force, hinge would impede center flute, set-up flute nipple, well defined shape, and edge thinning by pressure flaking.	#20 – Biface, quartzite (L = 74, W = 41, T = 16 mm). Tip breakage may be post-Native American, medial ridge is long hump, attempt to drive it off from base, lateral edge hinges, flat face (D-shaped), and overall poor reduction.

#21 – Biface, quartzite (L = 74.5, W = 46, T = 15 mm). After distal break, biface was made into a saw-like tool. It has several major hinges; otherwise, it is a fair biface.	#22 – Biface, quartzite (L = 58, W = 40, T = 13 mm). Break due to thinning lateral margin which has a long flat edge. D/P is flat, and it has excellent flaking.	#23 – Biface, quartzite (L = 46, W = 54, T = 14 mm). Snap breaks at both ends. It has two hinges, and aside from the breaks, it appears to have been well made. It has an even biconvex cross section.	#24 – Biface, quartzite (L = 51.5, W = 48, T = 10 mm). Break across the distal end and has minor hinges. D/P is flat, and it is especially thin.

	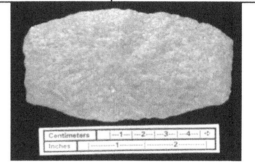
#25 – Biface, quartzite (L = 85, W = 47, T = 13 mm). Edge margin has overstrikes. Base is well defined; broken tip could have been corrected. It has deep, long flake scarps.	#26 – Biface, quartzite (L = 88, W = 47, T = 13 mm). It is well made and has distal end snap fracture. Base is well defined. It has a flat D/P profile and has a minor hinge.

What caused lithic preferences in prehistory?

When we examine the stones used during the Paleoindian era, we find flints and chalcedonies. While present in the Early Archaic, these stones are basically replaced with quartzite. However, we do find quartzite usage in the earlier era and throughout prehistory. And with minor usage earlier, the Late Archaic sees the use of white quartz. At some time during the Late Archaic, there is a change to rhyolite which probably lasted for one thousand years. Once the Woodland arises, we see all these stones. What caused the various changes in stone preferences? Perhaps, we are dealing with totally different populations?

Plate 12 – MPRV Biface Style and Variation in Rhyolite

As with the previous quartzite bifaces, these rhyolite bifaces show style and variation. These specimens are only a sample of the numerous ways the they shaped bifaces. They reflect early stages of biface manufacture and probably were made with a wooden billet, which probably reflects the Fox Creek or Woodland Period long-narrow point styles in the MPRV. Edge trim was probably made with a deer antler flaker.

With digital calipers, the biface on the right measures L = 92.08, W = 42.29, T = 11.89. It has a characteristic called a flat D/P profile. At 5 mm on each end's medial axis, it measures D = 8.12 and P = 9.67 mm; its D/P ratio is .840 which indicates a slight taper from base to tip. Its width/thickness (W/T) ratio is 3.557.

While needing testing, the biface taper indicates a projectile point form; whereas, nontaper indicates a knife or nonprojectile form. The D/P ratio can be used to determine (estimate) the Native American's intended function (Hranicky 2002a).

The following examples have descriptions that not only reflect knapping errors, but knapping excellence also. They have evidence of pressure flaking. These specimens are all surface finds, and no time depth inferences are made.

Stage 4 Rhyolite Biface
Note: Tip breakage is post-Native American.

#1 – Biface, rhyolite (L = 102, W = 36, T = 12 mm).

#2 – Bifaces, rhyolite (no measurements).

#3 – Spall, rhyolite (L = 81, W = 49, T = 14 mm)

#4 – Bifaces, rhyolite (Top: L= 99, W = 40, T = 18 mm; bottom: L = 72, W = 35, T = 14 mm).

#5 – Bifaces, rhyolite (Top: L = 96, W = 36, T = 13 mm; bottom: L = 90, W = 39, T = 15 mm).

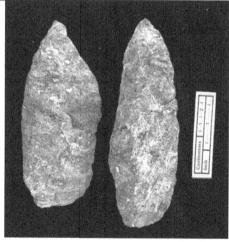

#6 – Bifaces, rhyolite (Left: L = 64, W = 27, T = 8 mm; right: L = 74, W = 16, T = 7 mm).

#7 – Bifaces, rhyolite (L>R: L = 93, W = 26, T = 19 mm; L = 98, W = 29, T = 13 mm; L = 104, W = 31, T = 18 mm; L = 83, W 35, T = 18 mm). From: Tuscarora Rockshelter, Frederick County, Maryland.

#8 – Points, rhyolite (miscellaneous styles made from long bifaces). From: Tuscarora Rockshelter, Frederick County, Maryland.

Maryland Rockshelter, Frederick County (Geasey 1975)

#9 – Tuscarora Rockshelter site (see Geasey 1971). It was occupied from Early Archaic Period to the end of the Woodland Period.

#10 – Interior Ledge of the Tuscarora Rockshelter. Shelter is located at 1600 feet above sea level and faces southeast.

#11 – Miscellaneous Rhyolite Points from the Shelter

#12 – Miscellaneous Rhyolite Points from the Shelter

#13 – Miscellaneous Rhyolite Points from the Shelter

#14 – Miscellaneous Rhyolite Points from the Shelter

Fluting a Biface

Fluting a biface was a technique that was invented by the Paleoindians and has become archaeologically their trademark attribute – namely Clovis technology (Figure 34). Few archaeologists agree on the primary or *main way* that the Paleoindians used for fluting. Experimentally, the flute can be removed using a punch, free-hand striking with a flaker, using an anvil, vice-grips, and probably methods that remain to be discovered.

Waldorf (1987) in regards to fluting:

First of all, the reason for fluting was to thin and taper the longitudinal cross-section of the base and provide channels into which the split shaft could be fitted, thus when glued and lashed, the haft would be quite stable. The Indian may have been aware of not one, but several ways to achieve this end, because some Clovis points have single flutes on one face and multiples on the other. With such flexibility of technique he would be able to overcome variability in both preform and raw material.

The basic method suggested here is using a deer flaker to remove the flute. For discussion on fluting, see Callahan (1979) and Whittaker (1994).

Figure 34 – Clovis Fluting in Quartzite. Since the base is not ground, the specimen was broken during manufacture. Fluting is often assumed to be the last step in reduction by flaking.

Tool Chassis (Hafting Process)

Chassis mounting is the process of hafting a newly-made tool to a handle or shaft. There are numerous possibilities, many of which are not preserved in archaeological contexts. Mountings are shown in the Bifaces as Knives section. Figure 35 shows various ways different point tools can have similar hafting technique. See Experimental Archaeology section for other hafting examples. Hafting does not necessarily mean to a handle. For example, an ethnographic specimen dating 1899-1903 from the Maidu Native Americans of California is shown in Taylor and Sturtevant (2000). It is a lance-shaped obsidian biface which is side notched. A deer hide string was wrapped around the notch-end, and it was worn around the neck. A shaman in curing practices used it. We have no way of knowing how (un-)popular the technique was for general carrying knives.

Hafting and Glues

Captain John Smith (in Arber 1910) was among the first to describe chassis materials:

With the sinews of Deare, and the tops of Deare hornes boiled to a jelly, they make a glew that will not dissolve in cold water.

Deer hooves and hides also make excellent glues. Another popular glue was pine tar. The most common method was to use animal sinew to wrap the tool's base to a slot-cut wooden handle. Experimental archaeology will provide more data about glues and their practical applications. These studies will be especially useful in lifecycle measurements or usage determinations. Proper use of the tool ensures a longer lifecycle. For example, knife holding is discussed in the Bifaces as Knives section.

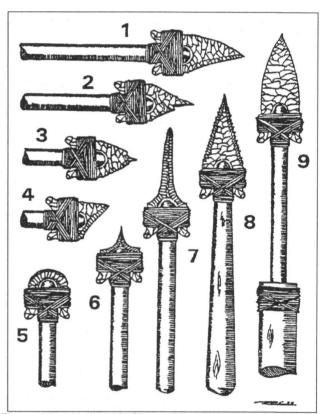

Figure 35 – Various Haftings: 1 = Sidescraper, 2 = Burin Graver, 3 = Needle Graver, 4 = Sidescraper, 5 = Endscraper, 6 = Needle Graver/Spokeshave, 7 = Drill, 8 = Saw-Knife, 9 = Knife and Spearhead (Hranicky and Painter 1988)

Sinew and Rawhide

For lithic tools, the most important cordage was the use of sinew, and for the MPRV, it was deer sinew. It was usually taken from the legs and back of deer and other large animals. It was treated by splitting it into long strands and then soaking it or lightly beating it into form. Then, it was allowed to dry.

It could be twisted into long cords, such as would be used as a bow string. Obviously, it was a strong cord. When used to haft tools to shafts, it is applied wet and as it dries, it shrinks. And, it contains a glue which aids in securing the tool to the shaft. It is usually fastened without tying a knot. The final end is tucked under the wrapping and when it dries, the binding is secure.

Rawhide was made by cutting strips from hides. It does not work well for microtool hafting, but works well on large macrotools. Glue was used to strengthen the hafting. Rawhide was better used for clothing straps, etc.

Shaft and Socket Mounting

The shaft and socket method of mounting projectile points started in the Paleoindian Period and continued through to the Woodland period (Figure 36).

Figure 36 – Experimental Hafted Clovis Points by Michael F. Johnson, Fairfax County Archaeologist. These points were mounted on short wooden shafts.

There is no proof other than by inference that the technique was used in the MPRV. However, the shaft/socket has widespread usage (Figure 37). There are two basic types of sockets:

1 – Drilled hole in which the tool was usually glued and inserted

2 – Split shaft where the center of the hafting shaft was cut as a V- or U-shaped area in which the tool was inserted. The tool was glued and wrapped with sinew.

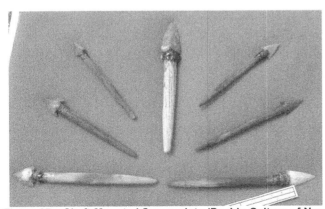

Figure 37 – Shaft-Mounted Spearpoints (Pueblo Culture of New Mexico). The shafts are wooden and points are sinew wrapped to the shaft. A single spear shaft was carried and the short shaft was inserted into it.

Knapping Errors

All flintknappers, past and present, make mistakes in the stone reduction process (Figures 38 and 39 on following pages). Most biface discards show knapping errors. Poorly-made or improperly-flaked bifaces are examples of knapping errors, especially for the Savannah River pointmakers who primarily used quartzite. If these pieces had been flaked successfully, we would not have found them; in other words, they would have been found as expended tools. As a caution, Native American knapping errors tend to skew biface data, and researchers evaluate the artifacts as constituting the normal distribution, which obviously is not usually the case. Nonflake debris always is a bias representation.

Text continued on page 125.

From the notebook . . .
Robertson Stemmed Projectile Point
The Robertson projectile point was named after Arthur Roberson, first ASV president. The points shown are from the Robertson collection at the MacCallum More Museum and Gardens in Chase City, Virginia. Rather than being a projectile point, it is probably a knife that was made the same way that points were. Or, what is sometimes called a hafted biface. This type is discussed in the Projectile Point section and typology methods in the Projectile Point Typology section.
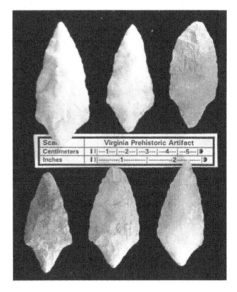
The type is usually made from white quartz and is relatively consistent in size. The cross section is biconvex. It has a distribution throughout the coastal areas of the Middle Atlantic states. Type is tentatively assigned to the Woodland Period. Technology is similar to the Piscataway point type dating 0 AD. These specimens are from Mecklenburg County, Virginia.

Figure 38 – Examples of Savannah River Quartzite Biface Mistakes. These are examples of breakage during knapping, poor initial shaping, but mostly hinge fractures which caused the biface failure. If using these as flintknapping examples, see Callahan (1979) for knapping procedures to correct or avoid these mistakes. For analytical purposes, these examples serve as ancient flintknapping failures and rejects.

These biface types are generally found because they are discards. Successful bifaces were made into tools. These bifaces are probably Late Archaic Savannah River materials. The errors are: poor initial shaping, thick bifaces, failure to get edge flaking to continue into and past the center axis, hinges, and general stone failures.

The ratio between discarded and successful bifaces cannot be determined by archaeological contexts; however, the suggestion here is that 4 out of 5 bifaces were successfully made into tools. If true, the error rate in biface production was the highest of all toolmaking groups. Two factors may account for this: 1) the high population density accounting for large numbers of broken bifaces, and/or 2) most likely, the difficulty in working quartzite.

From the notebook . . .

Potter's (1993) **Commoners, Tribute, and Chiefs – The Development of Algonquian Culture in the Potomac Valley** discusses culture clash between the Europeans and Native Americans living in the Potomac River valley. As he said: Opening years of the seventeenth century were turbulent times for the native peoples of the Potomac Valley, a prelude to ever darker times to come.

This publication is an excellent source for protohistoric MPRV Native Americans.

Engraving from Matthew Merien's Histoiae Americanae (1634). Japazaws holds a copper kettle and assist in the kidnapping of Pocahontas by enticing her aboard an English ship. Drawing courtesy of the Virginia Historical Society, Richmond, Virginia.

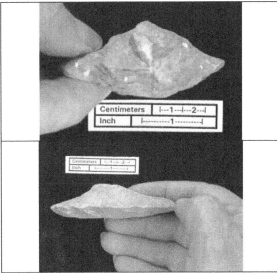

Figure 39 – Biface Hump is a Common Knapping Error. Flake removal by the knapper failed to reach the center of the biface; thus, a hump remained. There is a good argument that this form of biface was deliberate – the hump makes a good finger rest to use it as a knife. It is considered here a knapping failure. This hump is also called stacked hinges. The top specimen is made from rhyolite and the lower is made from quartzite.

Point/Knife Serrations and Beveled Edges

For the MPRV, the point and knife collections did not show serrations on blades; however, numerous point types do show blade serrations. This indicates a functional difference between what is being classified as a knife and that of a point. The most prominent serrated blade edges are those found on Kirk stemmed points, which date to the Early Archaic Period.

A serrated blade edge is suggested here as being used for cutting meats and soft materials. Using a serrated blade on hard materials removes the serrations rather quickly. Also, the serrated blade makes an excellent spearpoint which complicated functional analyses. The analogy is that nonserrated blade edges were used as projectile points; then after the kill, the blade edge was serrated for butchering.

The beveled edge on a projectile point functions differently than a serrated edge. This edge is more durable and requires less resharpening. These edge treatments are basically Early Archaic Period techniques and disappear with the introduction of the broadspear. Beveling is extremely rare in the MPRV.

Basics of Lithic Tool Analysis

Lithic analysis is the principal activity in American prehistoric archaeology, and there are numerous scientific methods and procedures for identifying and classifying stone debris and tools. Carr and Bradbury (2000) rationalize with:

...there is not a single "best" method of flake debris (or tool) analysis, but a suite of approaches that can be tailored to the analysis of a particular assemblage.

Some of the published techniques are: Ahler (1998), Bradbury and Franklin (2000), Patterson (1990), Blanton, et al. (1999), Shott (1994 and 1996), Magne (1985), Sullivan and Rozen (1985), Bradbury and Carr (1999), Ingbar (1989), Petraglia (1994), and Petraglia, et al. (1998).

Analytical techniques are presented throughout this publication; the following presents a general overview of lithic analyses that are used in archaeology and the above references. Generally, they are based on tool manufacture and usage, which are amplified by ethnographic data.

Four forms of lithic technology are seen in every facet of stone tool production, which are:

1 – Blade technology
2 – Flake technology
3 – Biface technology
4 – Broadspear technology
5 – Flake debris
6 – Bipolar technology
7 – Peck and grind technology.

Item 6 is discussed elsewhere, so is item number 7 which refers to macrotool production. These methods are the basis for this study as well as for others working with Native American stone toolmaking. Each of these techniques is manifested in all prehistoric contexts. And, all artifacts and debris are stages or events in these technologies. Analysis is the art of placing lithic pieces and specimens into a lithic technoculture so as to identify them archaeologically. The following discusses some of the basics in lithic tool analyses.

Blade technology - flake or blade with a cutting and/or sharpened edge, workend, or bit. Technically, it refers to a long narrow item that was struck from a core. According to Edmonds (1996):

... parallel-sided flakes with a length-to-width ratio of more than 2:1.

Generically, it refers to any piece struck from stone. It has:

1 – Cutting Edge and angle (share)
2 – Frank (blade edge shoulder)
3 – Tip (distal end, acutus)
4 – Base (proximal end)
5 – Cutting Axis.

Blade technology is not representative of the MPRV study collections. Blade absence was more of a factor in field collections, in that, flakes and blades are not generally collected by private collectors. Elsewhere, the Clovis, Hopewell/Adena, and Aztec toolmakers made use of blade technology (Figure 40).

Flake technology – technique of using flakes to make tool. It involved removing flakes from a core or what can be called a flake spall from a quarry site. Large flakes are often worked into bifaces. This technology is probably represented in the uniface point (Hranicky 1995). Flake tools start in the Early Archaic Period and continue through to the end of the Woodland Period. They are classified as expedient tools with short lifecycles. This technology is discussed below and see MPRV Flakes as Tools section.

Hopwell prismatic blades struck from cores made of Flintridge flint (Licking County, Ohio). See Converse (1963).

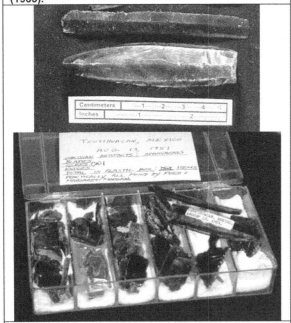

Aztec Obsidian Core, Blade, and Bladettes. These are classic core forms where long, narrow blades have been removed (formerly Fred Morgan Collection).

Figure 40 – Blade Technology Examples

Biface technology - tool or artifact with flakes removed from both sides. The major parts are:

1 – Edge
2 – Tip (distal)
3 – Base (proximal)
4 – Medial axis
5 – Flake scars.

As most archaeologists would agree, the vast majority of bifaces found in archaeological site contexts are rejects. They show knapping errors and were deemed unfinishable by the Native Americans who made them.

Bifaces can be divided into:

1 – Fragments
2 – Preforms
3 – Cores
4 – Implements.

These represent various tool stages of manufacture and breakage. Formally, a biface is:
...any thin stone piece that has had flakes removed from both faces, has sharp edges, and has been shaped into a usable preform or implement.

And, according to Edmonds (1996):
An artefact with invasive retouch on both of its principal faces, such as a leaf-shaped arrowhead or discoidal knife. The pattern of flaking required to produce these and similar artefacts is sometimes referred to as bifacial working.

Biface technology has the following production and tool attributes:

1 – Raw material	2 – Joint plane
3 – Type of preform	4 – Cortex remnants
5 – Length	6 – Width
7 – Thickness	8 – Flake removal type
9 – Platform setups	10 – Edge angles
11 – Failure pattern	12 – Recycling
13 – Modified edge	14 – Use edge type
15 – Base grinding	16 – Lateral grinding
17 – Basal thinning	18 – Cross section type
19 – General outline	20 – Profile
21 – Flakes p/cm	22 – Retouch.
23 – Style.	

Each/all are used diagnostically in any archaeological study which leads to formal explanations for their existence. They always identify a culture when analyzed correctly. See Bifaces as Knives and Projectile Points sections.

Broadspear technology – for the Middle Atlantic area, large bifacially-made spears/knives are the most common lithic tool remains. These bifaces are made by percussion flaking and are usually made from rhyolite and quartzite. Flakes are massive and have pronounced bulb scars. As a consequence of their large size, debitage is often extensive. This technology best represents the so-called lithic scatter sites and temporary campsites, which are quite common in riverine terraces and bottoms. These sites are usually accompanied with a hearth, but otherwise, have little cultural remains. Sources for the broadspear include both quarrying (outcrops) and pick-up field and riverbed cobbles. Both sources were large flat pieces that allowed the flaking of wide blades.

Broadspears do not show constant resharpening as do early point types. One of the primary broadspear materials is quartzite, which has a rejuvenate nature to edge wear.

Cobble modification (bipolar flaking) - probably first to make bipolar flaking study popular in the U.S. was Lewis Binford and George Quimby (1963), which was based on lithic materials from northern Michigan. Holmes (1919) discussed Argentina's prehistoric use of the bipolar technique. It is another example of the Panindian nature of lithic technology. The technique is a method of placing a stone on an anvil and striking it with a precursor. Force is induced from both the anvil and the precursor, which causes cones of force at both ends of the cobble. Method can be used on a cobble regardless of the cobble's axis; however, the longest axis is usually preferred. Bipolar flakes with cortex remaining may indicate the initiating axis of the cobble. According to Kobayashi (1975):

The method of flaking bipolar flakes is as follows: A worker sits down or squats on the ground. If he sits down, an anvil is placed between his knees. This method is used when bipolar flakes are removed from small cores. When big bipolar flakes are wanted, then squatting is more useful. A core is held in the left hand (for a right-handed person) and is rested on an anvil. Then direct percussion is applied to the striking platform of the core from right angles, using a hammerstone held in the right hand. In this case, the most important things are as follows:

1. When direct percussion is applied, the core rested on the anvil should be held firmly in the left hand. If this is not done, the core will slip on the anvil and bipolar flakes cannot be successfully removed.

2. The direct percussion must be applied vertically on the striking platform of the core. When a core tapers toward the distal end or an anvil with a convex surface is used, it is necessary to tap the platform lightly to see if the force is aligned with the end of the core where it contacts the anvil.

3. When the direct percussion is applied, the hammerstone must be used as if it were pressed against the striking platform of the core.

4. The size and weight of a hammerstone are also important. These factors determine the size and thickness of flakes removed from cores. To remove thin, tiny bipolar flakes, a lightweight hammerstone is used and the best results can be expected when the convex head of a hammerstone is used. When large, thick bipolar flakes are to be removed, a heavy hammerstone must be used. It is desirable to have a hammerstone with a straight edge and a U-shaped cross-section.

The surface and thickness of an anvil are also important. A flat surface is much better than a convex one. When the flaking is done, a core resting on a convex surface is apt to slip on the anvil. The more convex the surface of an anvil, the more the shattering at the distal end of a core increases. In general, the thicker the anvil the better.

All their tools can be traced to one of the above methods. Another basic analytical method is the study of flakes. The classic form of study is dividing flakes by lithic materials; however, archaeologically, the analysis involves more methods. See MPRV Flakes as Tools section.

Lithic Debitage

Anything not *an arrowhead* is considered by some archaeologists and collectors as debitage. But, there is information in this trash. For that matter, most of a site's contents is debitage. The buildup cultural materials on a site is enormous especially where it is a large village. Whether or not debitage can be correlated to population numbers remains to be proven archaeologically. Figure 42 shows a modern lithic debitage build up within a few hours. Figure 43 shows flake utilization examples.

Figure 43 – Utilized Flakes from the Fox Site, Southampton County, Virginia (formerly Floyd Painter Collection). They are made from siliceous slate which does not have the quality that rhyolite and quartzite have, but nonetheless, it was a popular material in southern Virginia and the Carolinas. See Flakes as Tools section

Debitage Classification - during any reduction process, the amount of cortex-backed flakes and chips is produced according to the flaking method that was utilized by the knapper. As a definition, Collins (1999) offers:

Debitage *- a term borrowed from the French and used in English as a noun to refer to all of the byproducts of knapping, especially flakes, but also blades, cores, chunks, chips, shatter, and debris; in French, the term is a verb referring to the act of knapping.*

Using the production process, the debitage can be classified, as:

> Level 1 – Debitage (Flakage)
>   A - Flakes with platforms
>   B - Chips or small broken flakes
>   C - Irregular flakes
> Level 2 – Cortex-Back Flakes
>   A - Testing
>   B - Initializing
>   C - Shaping
>   D - Finalizing
> Level 3 – Bipolar Flakes
>   A - Cortex remaining
>   B - Large platforms
>   C - Curved flakes
> Level 4 – Platform Flakes
>   A - Cortex platform
>   B - Single facet flakes
>   C - Multiple facet flakes
> Level 5 – Final with cortex remaining
>   A - Cortex on medial ridges
>   B - Lateral edges
>   C - Base
> Level 6 – Implements
>   A - Various tool classes
>   B - Various tool industries.

Triangular Biface

The triangular biface is difficult to make because of the distance the base flakes have to go into the biface during their removal. This often causes humps or stacked hinges (Figure 44). This biface form is intended to make a triangular point or knife. It follows the basic principles of the wedge and makes an ideal implement for penetrating or splitting functions. This biface is not common in the Middle Atlantic area and is often classified as a Baden point (see Coe 1964 and MacCord and Hranicky 1979). The triangle biface is not necessarily a preform for the triangle point; it is a knife form.

Figure 44 – Triangular Bifaces to Make Triangle Points or Knives

From the Notebook ...

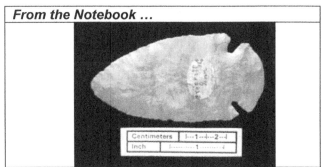

Flint Dovetail from Crockett County, Tennessee. Note the fine flaking needed to produce the notches.

Final Manufacture Stage (FMS)

As mentioned elsewhere, the initializing form for the Native American's toolkit is called Final Manufacture Stage (FMS) which is an extremely important stage in toolmaking. This is the stage in which the flintknapper places the tool into service. Hafting is a FSM factor. It starts the tool's lifecycle; as an opposite, the last usage of a tool's cycle is called the Final Usage Stage (FUS). The initial finalizing process starts with the setup, preform, or preparatory biface. It is then shaped into a specific tool. Once placed into service, the tool performs work and during this action, the tool breaks (damaged), becomes dull (resharpened), or wears out (expended). In some of these stages, the tool needs to be retrofitted and placed back into service. Expention or breakage ends all tool lifecycles.

Notching Points

Notching in the MPRV throughout prehistory was not a knapping art although the procedure is tedious. Small notching is not common in the MPRV but examples do occur (Figure 45). Fine corner notching is usually performed on flint points.

Figure 45 – MPRV Notched Points, Left: Two Flint and Right: Two Quartzite Points

The reason that the major MPRV lithic materials, quartzite and rhyolite, do not lend themselves to high-quality notching is because of their granular structures. However, skillful knappers can accomplish fine notching in quartzite and rhyolite.

Notching is accomplished by pressure flaking using a fine-pointed antler or a beaver tooth or tusk tool. It requires fine, bifacial flaking. Deep notching channels require special skills by experienced knappers. The punch technique is also used for notching. Points in the Early Archaic, namely the St Charles and Big Sandy points, show evidence of the knappers removing a concoilal flake and then pressure flaking from the reverse side to produce the notch. From Virginia and Maryland, notching disappears during the Middle Archaic Period. See Experimental Archaeology section.

Broken Points

Broken points are more common than unbroken points in surface surveys and archaeological site contexts; a human course based on actual usage that can be considered normal for prehistoric societies.

Figure 46 – Broken Points. These points were broken during manufacture, not subsequent usage as a tool. Breakage was probably caused by blows that were excessive or overbites on the striking platform. The major cause of Savannah River point breakage in manufacture was not properly supporting the biface when striking the biface with a billet.

Once past the preform stages, shaping points requires additional flaking. Knapping mistakes occur, which cause premature fractures. If blade breakage occurs, the knapper can sometimes overcome it. However, this breakage type is usually a discard and is common in field debitage collections (Figures 46 and 47).

Figure 47 – Broken Tips. Examples of knapping mistakes working quartzite. These tips are Late Archaic and cannot be assigned to any type. These tips show tool usage before breakage.

Broken points always have:

1 – Evidence of breakage during manufacture

or else,

2 – Evidence of breakage during usage

otherwise,

3 – Nonbreakage evidences of usage, of which expention is the end of its normal usage.

Tool Lifecycle

The lifecycle of a projectile point (any tool) starts when the FMS is completed and ends when the point is discarded. Naturally, some points are lost which automatically ends the lifecycle. One major question – how long is the lifecycle of all tools? As a postulate based on experimental archaeology:

**Macrotools > 5 and <10 years (retrofitting needed)
Microtools < 3 years (extensive resharpening needed).**

Lifecycle is dependent on the technology carrier (material) of the item that contains the workend. We can assume that different carriers have different lifecycles.

Knives and drills may be exceptions, but more testing on tool longevity is needed. Lifecycles determined the number of tools needed per population, need for materials acquisition, trade, if applicable, and creating specific toolmaking activities.

Expended Points

By far, the most common form for projectile points that are recovered is the expended point. Naturally, broken points constitute a major part of the recovery. Both forms represent the end of the Native American's usage of the tool. Basic expention types are:

1 – Loss of tool; accidental discard

2 – Breakage of tool, which ends tool's lifecycle, unless retrofitted

3 – Expended blade which ends tool's useability

4 – Chassis breakdown, which means tool must be rehafted or discarded

5 – Discard at a certain time or use in a tool's lifecycle.

Tool expention starts in the archaeological record of Clovis and continues through the end of the Woodland period. Deliberate expention may have been practiced where a tool proved to be bad magic. Many early projectile points show deliberate breakage (killing). While possible in snap breaks, points in Figure 48 have unusual breaks.

Figure 48 – Projectile Point Chassis and Tip Breakage: Top (left to right) breakages are impact fracture, impact, stem fracture, stem fracture. Bottom (left to right) impact, stem fracture, stem fracture, and snap fracture.

Tool usage dulls blade edges, and creates the need to rejuvenate it. The Native American used a pointed antler flaker and reflaked the cutting (workend) edge. Repeated resharpenings caused tool expention. For example, the expended forms of both St Albans and LeCroy points are approximately 25 mm. This length is assumed to have been the normal length in which these tool users were willing to discard it. For Clovis, the discard length is between 50 and 60 mm. The discard usually occurred in time (or on location for lithic materials) for toolkit replenishment.

Archaeologically, some projectile points are always found in a small expention form, namely Palmer, St Albans, LeCroy, Piscataway, and some triangles. This presents difficulty in attempting to reconstruct the manufacturing stages. As a consequence, expention measurements are presented in the Projectile Points section to aid future researchers with this problem.

Useability

Useability is the degree to which tools were used for daily livelihood. It involves the structure of a tool which assists the user in completing a task, and function of a tool being used in a prehistoric work setting (see Binford 1973, 1977, and 1979). Generally, it is a consideration of how successful a tool is. For example, the Native Americans knew that an axe bit with an angle of 40° bites into wood better than an angle of 50°. Obviously, they did not know angles, but the bit shape was known as well as the chassis assembly. Tool usages are:

1 – Getting the job done - it performed its required function

2 – Maintaining the tool - how well and how long a tool can be used; can it be retooled or resharpened

3 – Making proper use of the tool - does the tool's function make sense to the average user

4 – Learning its use - is it intuitive or easily learned

5 – Remembering its operation - can the user reuse the tool without having to relearn its usage?

6 – Performing an operation well - is the tool efficient

7 – Operating the tool - are there catastrophic or reasonable errors in using the tool.

Useability is a product of tool industries from which a tool's operation is its function. In other words, the use of a tool is determined by its industry membership; for example, an axe performing as a chopping industry tool. Bearing this in mind, how can the concept be used on the MPRV collections? Until further study is performed, macrotools are classified as:

1 – Generalized usage - no specialized training is needed to use the tool

2 – Specialized usage - training is needed in order to use the tool.

Note: These divisions are basically a subjective appraisal and are used in the Miscellaneous Tools/Implements section.

Projectile point blade configurations also suggest differences for point functions and useability (Figure 49). With the complexity of function in structure as used by the Native Americans. As such, projectile point useability will be discussed in later publications. See Projectile Points and Bifaces as Knives sections.

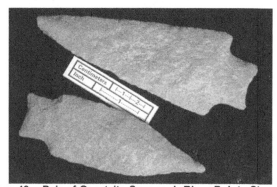

Figure 49 – Pair of Quartzite Savannah River Points Showing Different Blade Configurations. The lower point has a mucronate tip (Hranicky 2002a).

All tools have a position in their lifecycle in which the Native American considered the tool to be no longer usable. If length is used, as:

Expention = $\int L$

whereas:
$\int$ = function of length
L = length.

Length is assumed to be a function of blade usage. Then blade reduction would reach some point on the tool that would cause the Native American to discard it. While a recovered tool may appear to have more useful life, something caused it to be discarded. Thus,

Tool Blade <1 is a discard

As such, any value >1 has a useful life in the Native American world. All of which would be a mathematical model of $\int L$.

Useability testing is a method of determining whether and how a tool was used by the Native Americans. Once determined that it is not a fresh tool, testing involves:

1 – Wear pattern analysis
2 – Breakage/damage analysis
3 – Lifecycle usage rates
4 – Material durability.

Again, a mathematical model of $\int L$. As an approach, Hranicky and McCary (1995) use regression testing to establish the expention length for Virginia Clovis points. This approach allowed estimating the original length of a Clovis point. Other statistical methods are acceptable – based on length. The function of length $\int L$ is the basis for all prehistoric tool analyses.

Note: Wear patterns are used for determining the tool's basic function, such as residue remains in wear scars. This type of testing was not available in this study.

Testing also includes efficiency ratings for tools (see Jeske 1992). All tools are assumed to have been manufactured for a purpose, namely some type of work. The purpose range of work can be divided into:

1 – Cosmetic - tool is made as a pleasant-to-use style (customary tool) and reflects an artform to utilitarian shape.

2 – Catastrophic - tool is made as a survival tool; failure to accomplish specific work is a major problem or concern in the user's society.

Each of the above factors can be addressed as a minor or major problem within that range. Tool breakage is always considered as a catastrophic event. At present, there are no published studies of Native American usage of tools for specific tasks. Most tool analyses are based on wear patterns - not efficiency, easy to use, error factors, breakage, etc. by the Native Americans. The following are suggestions for studies which are basically heuristic:

1 – Normal usage (description of)
2 – Measurement of usage (heuristic)
3 – Tool environments (living conditions)
4 – Physical degradation of tools (lifecycle)
5 – Quality (form versus efficiency)
6 – Work efficiency (multiusage)
7 – Tool Efficiency (failure/success)
8 – Time (task completion)
9 – Technology carrier (basic element, such as stone, wood, shell, etc.

In this day of modern scientific instrumentation, precise measurements are possible. As such, stone tool efficiency can be measured. Two variables are present that complicate the calculation, which are chassis mounting and bit sharpness. If they are assumed as constants, efficiency can be calculated as:

$$E_f = Output/Input * 100$$

whereas:
   E = efficiency.

Note: The technology carrier is not a constant and varies by stone.

Output is the number of pounds applied to the tool and input into a target area (work). Input is measured by defining work, such as number of mm a blade cuts into with one blow of an axe or celt. Stone tools rarely have more than 50% efficiency because the total loss is partly the result of the transfer of energy that does no work. When an axe blade strikes a wooden target, part of the energy being transferred is lost as heat and noise. What is left can be classified as work. As mentioned, chassis design and bit sharpness contribute to energy loss.

Even with these complications, experimental axes and celts can be tested for efficiency with inferences for prehistoric tools. These data offer cross-culture comparisons for tool designs and their practical applications. Due to the nature of the collections, mainly surface finds, efficiency measurements were not attempted. The method is offered for future MPRV research.

| Table 2 – Tool Functional Angles* ||
Tool	Functional Angle Range
Abrader	170° to 180°
Adz	60° to 75°
Anvilstone	85° to 100°
Arrow/spear	120° to 180°
Atlatl	45° to 180°
Axe	90° to 180°
Bannerstone	45° to 180°
Bola	To be determined.
Burin	To be determined.
Chisel	90° to 145°
Celt	90° to 180°
Chopper	80° to 110°
Crescent	180° ?
Drill	80° to 110°
Gouge	30° to 65°
Graver	To be determined.
Hammerstone	20° to 150°
Hoe	85° to 100°
Knife	60° to 150°
Maul	90° to 180°
Mortar	90° to 100°
Peckingstone	85° to 95°

Perforator	Open
Pestle	80° to 100°
Pick	90° to 180°
Planer	170° to 180°
Saw	170° to 180°
Splitter	80° to 100°
Scraper	0° to 30°
Spokeshave	To be determined.
Ulu	To be determined.
Wedge	Open

* Base: Horizontal plane = 180°

Functional Angle and Axis

Each tool class has its designed (or inherent) ways of using its tools. It is the range or specific way to hold the tool to perform a specific task (Figure 50 and Tables 2 and 3). The angle (tool on target object) is called the functional axis. For example, there are numerous possible ways of holding and using the abrader (Figure 51).

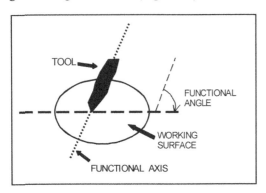

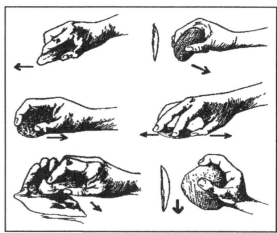

Figure 50 – Tool Functional Axis and Angle. This angle applies to all tool classes; each tool has a primary functional angle from which work efficiency is the highest.

Figure 51- – Examples of Using an Abrader. There are various ways to hold the abrader, many of which are culturally determined.

Tool function for work task is partly determined by cultural practices and traditions, but is mainly determined by the Laws of Nature. Tool usage is not always according to the best way, especially for prehistoric societies. But given the range of work tasks, the prehistoric toolkit has a high degree of efficiency and versatility. As a suggestion, each tool industry should be classified archaeologically by the functional axis of its tools. Functional angles are calculated for each tool class in the Tools/Implements section.

Table 3 – Macrotool Function and Primary Axis				
Tool	Modality *	Axis	Operation	Useability **
Axe	Unimodality	Angle	Hafted	Specific
Celt	Bimodality	Various	Hafted	General
Adz	Unimodality	Angle	Hafted	Specific
Hoe	Unimodality	None	Hafted	General
Maul	Unimodality	Various	Hafted	Specific
Pick	Bimodality	Various	Hafted	Specific
Chopper	Multimodality	None	Hand-held	General
Gouge	Unimodality	Horizontal;	Hand-held	Specific
Chisel	Unimodality	Various	Hand-held	Specific
Hammerstone	Multimodality	Various	Hand-held	General
Peckingstone	Bimodality	Various	Hand-held	Specific
Splitter	Unimodality	Vertical	Hand-held	Specific
Mortar	Unimodality	Vertical	Hand-held	General

* Modality is presented in the Projectile Point Typology section.
** Ability of any society member to use the tool.

Wear Patterns

Tool usage in prehistory provides an insight to the lifeways of Native Americans. Each time a tool was used to perform a task, microscopic scratches and chipping occurred on the tool's workend (Figure 52). Lawrence Keeley's (1980) ***Experimental Determination of Stone Tool Uses*** is among the first studies to apply wear patterns to archaeological tool interpretations. While analog microscopy systems (stereomicroscopes) have produced usable results in wear patterns, as in Odell (1975), Brose (1975), Bordes (1970), Davis (1975), Frison (1968), Gould, et al. (1971), Hester, et al. (1973), Wilmsen (1968), and others, the use of digital photography has greater potential in future research. Microtechniques are presented in the Experimental Archaeology section.

Analytically, tool workend scratches (striations) are called wear patterns, which can be used to classify the work target that leaves the impressions. Wear pattern striations vary by material; however, a general catalog can be compiled for identification. The technique requires a binocular microscope with lens greater >60X. Also, the tool must have been used on the target over an hour before enough striations are impressed (scratched) in the tool's share or bit.

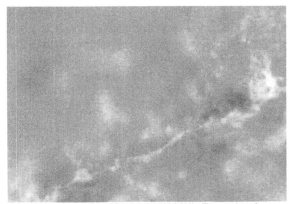

Figure 52 – Striation on Quartzite (200X). Top edge is ragged on all materials, but especially quartzite. It explains the rejuvenation nature of quartzite edges. The base of the striation is V-shaped and sometimes contains residues from its prehistoric usage.

Polish is a wear pattern. It is caused by continuously rubbing a workend on a soft surface, such as hides and woods. Figure 53 shows polish on a tanningstone (flesher).

Each type of material leaves distinctive striations. The number of striations is dependent on the amount of time and hardness of the stone. Once identifiable striations appear on the stone, a polish line is established. This line usually parallels the cutting edge and can be used to identify the major work-task of the tool. Naturally, multiple polish lines complicate functional determinations.

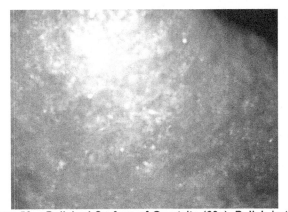

Figure 53 – Polished Surface of Quartzite (60x). Polish is the smoothing of ragged edges of the crystalline structure. Even though quartzite is granular, it can be rubbed smooth.

Wear patterns offer a possibility of establishing a task/time table for each tool class by material. Additionally, the table can be correlated by time period, which, collectively, would give an idea of tool/Indian efficiency. Microscopic scratch or wear channel analyses make it possible for measurements that were not possible until now. Prehistoric tool's workend – fresh versus used (work) - has a tremendous future in analytical archaeology.

This workend factor will probably be available in the near future; it could be called Striation Deposition Analysis (SDA). Each striation contains microscopic deposits of the surface that the tool was used on. These deposits can (will) be identified; thus, ancient work activities by the Native Americans can be identified. In this case, the hands of the past will open new doors in archaeological research.

Finally, Figure 54 shows a hypothetical polish time-line needed for various materials; all of which would be based on lithic hardness. It suggests typical tool targets that would be found on most lithic cultural remains. Because of the randomness of the collections, no wear pattern analyses were attempted in the study.

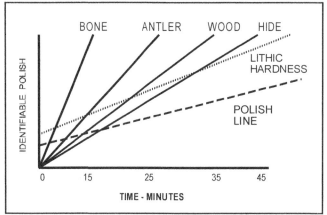

Figure 54 – Time Versus Material for Wear Pattern Analysis. Data are based on experimental bifaces made of flint. Polish increases by material and time, which is also controlled by lithic hardness. Ratios can be established.

Potomac Crossroads...

Assuming that the projectile points were cultural indicators, the Late Archaic and Early Woodland eras had an extremely high diversity of types/styles along the Potomac fall line. The following points are not typed, but they do show points styles that were not found in large number in local collections. The argument is: the fall line offered a Potomac walk-around for coastal populations migrating north and south on the coastal plain. These specimens are surface-collected points within 15 miles of the Potomac's fall line. They probably represent the last field collected artifacts as this area in mostly covered by shopping centers, groomed homes, streets and roads, etc. In other words, field distributions are no longer obtainable among collectors and archaeologists. This the largest number of single area projectile points ever published. This sample should easily demonistrate the difficulty in typing projectile points.

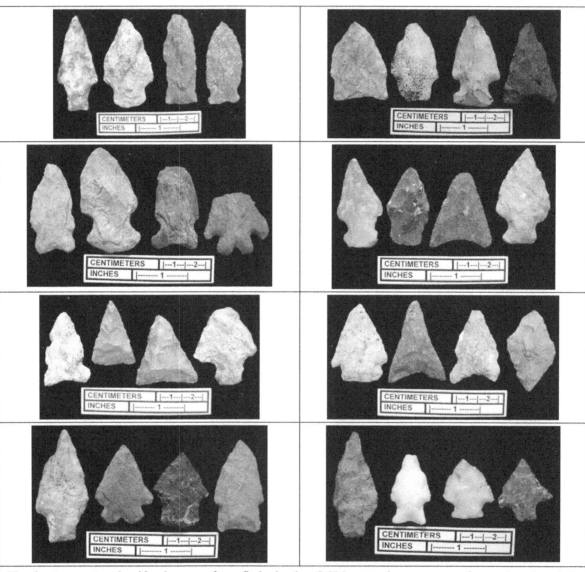

The best way to classify these surface finds is the QCM procedure on grouping points by their morphological shapes. They have no cultural contexts which can be analyzed archaeologically. These points reflect stone usage and resharpening. Somewhere where these points were found is toolkit replenishment...renewal replacement of expended tools. Do they have merit in MPRV archaeology? They do seem to always have a collector value. This sample is small; it represents the field world of millions of points. Archaeology cannot keep all of them. More specimens are shown in Appendix C.

Projectile Point Typology
[Tool Structure and Function]
(Classifying Native American Traditions for Projectile Points)

Projectile point typology may be the weave that produces all archaeological interpretation in American prehistory. No single facet of the Native American's culture has received more attention than the Native American's frequently called *arrowhead*. Of course, the arrowhead was only one part of technology used by the Native Americans; others were the all-important *spearpoint*, which makes up 80 percent of their lithic tool history. For this and other reasons, the arrowhead is called a *projectile point*, which is usually a pointed biface. The projectile

point was a multifunctional tool that was used for knives, drills, scrapers, arrowheads, spearpoints, and other purposes. Other than flakes and not counting broken pottery sherds found by archaeologists, the projectile point is the most common artifact that is found in surface finds, private collections, and excavated site contents. It is the most diagnostic item among Native American tools because of special shapes that they employed in making them. The shapes or styles can be classified morphologically into archaeological types.

The romance of American prehistoric archaeology lies with this point ... Clovis.

Reference to projectile point classification methodology is often referred to as a lumpers and splitters technique of sorting and identifying points. Lumpers tend to generalize attributes and classify points based on subjective appraisals. Whereas, splitters tend to classify points based on fine details and are more objective about attribute definitions. Frequently, splitters have a basic understanding of flintknapping and know all the minute parts of points. Lumpers should leave lithic technology alone. Neither method is totally correct nor wrong; perhaps after all, an arrowhead is only an arrowhead. Typology is perhaps ... a mechanistic viewpoint about stone tools and is not restricted to projectile points. For example, the Mississippian axe is a major archaeological southeastern type, but to what culture. Additionally, typology involves structural and functional analyses that often lead to types. As such, function and structure are discussed as they pertain to all tools, especially projectile points.

On the other side of science, technology is like fixing a watch; if you do not know what the pieces look like or know when they are worn out, you cannot correct the problem and put it together, let alone make it run. Typology is more than classification based on morphology. It is a study of the way Native Americans made and used projectile points. Broken and expended points are what archaeologists put back together in order to present a picture of prehistory. Idealistically, every projectile point fits into a type ... realistically, most projectile points are not typeable. However, typology is always assumed to represent prehistoric behavior in toolmaking.

Typology

Typology is the identification of artifacts sharing generalized attributes, which are not necessarily associated with a particular culture (Panindian attributes/traits), such as fluting, grooving, or notching. Furthermore, a type is a recognizable artifact that reflects a certain behavioral form or toolmaking style in prehistory. According to Kluckhohn (1960), an anthropological viewpoint of typology is:

...a classification that has an intent, that is, has a direction. The ways one may classify things are limitless and therefore any number of classifications may be conceived, but a typology has an explicit theoretical basis and the typologist is interested in using a given classification in order to shed light upon the reasons beneath the occurrence of some observable phenomena. . . . A classification is no more than a set (or sets) of empirical groupings established for convenience. A typology, however, is a theoretically oriented classification that is directed toward the solution of some problem or problems.

Figure 1 – The Projectile Point is the Most Diagnostic Implement in American Prehistory. Or, as Holmes (1897) said: *Their number is beyond estimate. Their most important characteristic is their general shape, nearly all being referable to origin through the leaf-shape blade.*

Regardless of a point's origin, the projectile point still remains the prima facia evidence for most of the work in prehistoric archaeology (Figure 1).

Traditionally, most typologists have been and currently are descriptive-historical methodologists. This approach is also called the classificatory-historical philosophy in archaeology, which essentially means creating and using chronological systems for artifact explanations. The physical nature of projectile points (or any tools) in terms of their long-term association with both professional and amateur archaeologists have made them ideal candidates for these approaches. Additionally, the majority of projectile points in both public and private collections are the result of ground-surface discoveries rather than the site-specific excavated materials that many archaeologists consider the only means to legitimate archaeology.

One, who practices typing, especially projectile point typing, may be called a typologist. This person is a scientific specialist in archaeology who is object-oriented in his/her investigations of material culture. A typologist studies specific classes of artifacts and their associations with specific times and cultures.

While some might argue that classification schema are not 21st century basic goals for archaeology, classification is still the most persistent issue in the field, especially for the typologist. There is a carryover from the 20th century which will be in place for the new age of archaeology – classification as a primary analytical priority. As Joukowsky (1980) argues:

The morphological and chronological study of all artifacts is important not only for the understanding of their evolutionary relationships but also for our interpretation of past cultural traditions. Typologists, artifact analysts, and professional specialists patiently study every feature of the object. They have their own approaches and deal with the specific problems of analysis and interpretation in light of past research that has been presented. Without their expertise, the archeologist can mistakenly develop a totally corrupt understanding of past traditions.

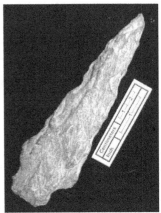

Figure 2 – This Rhyolite Point can be lumped or split, but it is still not typeable. It probably dates to the Archaic Period. It has one shallow side notch.

Lumper and Splitter Classification

Lumpers and splitters have been a classification argument since the 1940s. Lumpers tend to be very generalized with artifact attributes; whereas, splitters tend to be very specific with artifact attributes. The basic dispute over typing methodology has its beginning in southwestern pottery classifications, namely the so-called Pecos system. Taylor (1948) suggested that differences in the methods produced discipline conveniences versus culture elucidation. Or, the so-called empirical types and cultural types. The basic argument lies in the writings of Brew (1946), Judd (1940), Kidder (1936), Rinaldo and Martin (1941), and Reiter (1938). The rule of typology has never been satisfied. While it started with pottery, lumper/splitter techniques persist today with projectile points. Basically, going with Taylor (1948):

... from the viewpoint of archeological reporting, it is of the utmost importance to grant the archeologist freedom to recognize and record all those similarities and differences which, with his experience and a cultural frame of reference, seem significant to him. The publication of his empirical descriptions, named for convenience of handling and usually called types, serve to acquaint his colleagues of his findings, to elicit from them the antithetic or corroborative information urgently required, and to provide the general literature with comparative material with which to lend depth and significance to other finds from other sites.

This publication provides point and tool classification based on observations, a cultural framework, Laws of Nature, and simple opinion based on the author's experience. No type is final; no type is perfect (Figure 2). Regardless of the scientific focus, typology must identify the Native American toolmaking process. Typology is an archaeological tool; like many tools, there are numerous ways to use them.

Multiple Typologies

The major question – does a single type equal a particular society at a specific time? In other words, if a type is a social indicator, why do multiple types occur in single archaeological contexts? Answers to these questions may never be answered in archaeology; for that matter, they may not even be valid questions. Assuming archaeological methods can separate archaeological contexts, multiple types must be a social preference. Perhaps a type represents a clan or usage function, all of which most likely will never be known.

Custer (2001) and Justice (1987) argue projectile point clustering. Their premises are similar point styles are related; it is a Panindian viewpoint of technology. However, it is a form of technoclutures that has been has been argued elsewhere in this publication.

Technology as a Culture or Type

Within a culture or society, methods, procedures, and processes to produce tools, housing, clothing, etc. are needed to maintain life in a particular environment. A prehistoric society must have known the local environment and its resources, including the lithic resources, in order to exploit it successfully. For tools, it is a process of obtaining raw materials and turning them into tools. It is a cultural way to survival via tools. Some technological aspects are local procedures and inventions, even innovations. Others are Panindian borrowing from what can be called a universal knowledge base. All prehistoric societies through social intraaction had a working knowledge of all possible tool industries; they did not always elect to use every tool class within various industries. Most of the tool classes are found worldwide, such as the axe, celt, knife, atlatl, bow/arrow, etc.

For archaeological analyses, social factors in technology are extremely important in discovering cultural ways and interpreting material culture (Figure 3). Based on this, typology always involves the analysis of:

1 – Culture
2 – Design
3 – Structure
4 – Function
5 – Usage
6 – Material
7 – Use
8 – Maintenance
9 – Environment
10 – And perhaps, ceremonial/art.

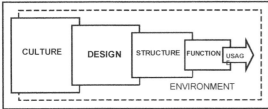

Figure 3 – Tool Production within Environment. Design is the style factor in tool production. Structure and function are consequences of design. This is a basic process flow for any toolmaking society. Basically, all tools are culturally-determined implements; but to a degree, most tools are part of universal industries.

Within the totality of the Native Americans' toolkit, the projectile point is a redundant, duplicative instrument that must serve some form of social prominence that identifies users. The projectile point is a badge of a social indicator, much like totems. It represents a social cohesiveness, karma, or technological superiority for the social unit. The point identifies the technology, such as the Palmer and Savannah River pointmakers. Technology always assumes culture, but can have specific aspects represent particular cultures. Too often archaeologists force technological cultures, such as Clovis people or Potomac Creek pottery people. The most notable example is Turnbaugh's (1975) Broadspear Model as being a culture. Any form of technology, via archaeological material evidences, always involves all aspects of culture, namely kinship relations, political controls, economic and environmental conditions, spoken language, religious beliefs, and oral histories and artforms.

Figure 4 – Fox Creek Point and Knife from King and Queen County, Virginia. They show extensive distribution of MPRV rhyolite; but more importantly, they were flaked with a wooden billet. The Fox Creek manufacture process distinguishes it from Clovis points. The tip on the Fox Creek point is called a mucronate (drill-like blade tip) point (Hranicky 2002a).

Technology is used here to refer to the Native Americans' manufacture of projectile points that consistently met the requirements of a particular society. Uniformity in production is what constitutes a projectile point (and other tools) type. Examination of any point identifies the technology that produced it, such as billet types and other flaking methods. Specific methods, such as percussion and pressure flaking, also go into all point manufacture. The billet, material, and skill are factors that determine a typed point as viewed archaeologically (Figure 4).

As a basic rule in typology:
The manufacturing process for a projectile point is more important than its attributional composition.

Perhaps technology can become a culture, such as the Clovis culture, but this would imply that technology is the dominant factor within a social unit. As such, technology can be viewed as a way to daily livelihoods, but not a contributing factor to other facets of culture like religion, politics, and language. Too much of lithic technology is Panindian and, therefore, not attributable to specific societies. Consequently, technology is not culture – never a culture.

Next, structure and function are used to determine a type; even then, all points are not typeable (Figures 5a, 5b, 5c, and 5d). Lithic technology provides standards that are used to identify and classify stone tools; they are not concrete processes. It constitutes what is called professional archaeology and the ethics of scientific research and interpretation. It is the resultant form of professionalism needed to make archaeology a science.

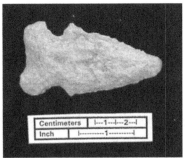

Figure 5a – Points are not always typeable – Is this MPRV quartzite point a Big Sandy or MacCorkle; perhaps it is a Transition Point?

Figure 5b – One find of a particular style is Interesting; two finds start an investigation; three finds start looking like a type. The top point is from the MPRV, and the lower flint point is from Mecklenburg County, Virginia. The point is tentatively called the Lucketts point after the area where it was first observed. The basic proposition for a type – each point has one square and one round stem corner.

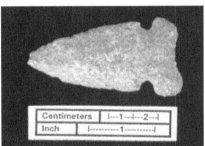

Figure 5c – An Indiana Specimen with a Round and Square Tang. This specimen has a beveled blade and is made from a fine grain quartzite.

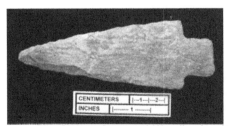

Figure 6d – The Square Stemmed Woodland point is quite common; it is difficult to type. Rhyolite, L =135, W = 48. T = 9 mm, Dorchester County, Maryland

Three principles should be followed in point typology:

1 – Same Native American point technologies do not necessarily mean that they are related in time or space. For example, all lanceolate points are not always Clovis points.

2 – Technology carriers (stone material) are not a primary factor in typology. They carrier can be an attribute, but for most cases, material was based on local utilization of material.

3 – Point type name usage should go to the first person who published a point type name and description. For example, Ritchie (1961), Coe (1964), and Broyles (1971) are the basic typologies for the MPRV. All of whom first described and named numerous eastern point types. Their types have become standard time markers for both field surveys and site excavations. Their publications are found beyond the hands of the amateur and professional archaeologists.

Type Validity (Points)

The following scale is suggested and was devised by Hranicky (1991 and 1994). It is used here for MPRV types, which may vary elsewhere. Validity is intended as a type consistency factor and usually demonstrates knapping skill. As a note: Skill may not be a social/technological factor in the Native Americans' world as we see it archaeologically.

1 – **Traditional Point** - absolute type where all manufacturing sequences, time elements, and geographic provenances are known, and the type description probably comes close to what the Native American had in mind when he made these points. Only Clovis, Cumberland, and Folsom points are in this category.

2 – **Distinctive Point** - easily provable and recognizable type with known temporal and geographical distributions. However, general morphology may be found in other types.

3 – **Positive Point** - recognizable type that does not have solid evidence for temporal and geographical distributions, but it appears to be justified for future study. It can have extensive variation in morphological attributes, but the basic style is recognizable.

4 – **Conditional Point** - usually a new type where there is enough evidence to distinguish it from other points, but it needs more research to establish it.

5 - **Site Specific Point** - particular group of points from a site that collectively show evidences for being a type, but frequently this type does not extend beyond the site's cultural boundaries.

6 – **Negative Point** - poorly defined and unrecognizable type that has little archaeological evidence to support it as a type. Types with multiple technologies within the basic description, for example describing a type with stemmed and notched points as part of the basic type description. This category also includes untypeable points.

7 – **False Point** - type that does not exist or points which were falsely assigned to a point category.

8 – **Isolate Point** - single point that does not conform to any known point type. It can also be classified as an anomaly or a unique occurrence.

9 – **Unique Point** – single point that does not appear to have been regularly manufactured; an anomaly, but well made.

Type validity is used in the Projectile Point section. It is an analytical assessment for establishing a type and provides a comparative method for communicating types in the archaeological practice and literature.

Figure 6 – Heavy Patination on a Rhyolite Morrow Mountain or perhaps a Cattle Run Point. Patination has almost removed all evidence of flake scars. Rhyolite surfaces break down quickly (prehistorically speaking) as compared to other lithic materials. As opposed to most classifying, the bit is on the right end.

Patination

Patination is the result of the aging process of stone tools. It varies by material and by geographical locations (Figures 6, 7, and 8). It is frequently an indicator of age, especially for rhyolite. However, tools made from quartz and quartzite seldom reflect heavy patinations even on Clovis points. Caution is needed for using patination as an age indicator (Hranicky 1992). A heavily patinated point could be young, and it survived in a recent acidic environment.

Another caution is irradiation (proton or neutron) analysis of stone, the patination process absorbs elements from the environment around the stone; thus, it may skew this type of analysis with foreign elements. This can be a factor in determining an artifact's burial environment. A high possibility exists for determining funerary objects.

The patination process is (Hranicky 2002a):

...surface changes colors and has a build up as a result of chemicals in the soil and atmosphere. It is the local aging condition for an artifact. Aging process varies by region -- even within several hundred feet. Thus, patination dating is an argumentative technique. For buried artifacts, patination has up/down sides; patination varies according to buried position.

As a concept, patination has been studied for years, as Sollas (1924) suggests:

The patina has this importance; if the several flaked surfaces which form the exterior of a flint have all produced at the same time, as they will have been in the case of a genuine implement, they will as a general rule all bear the same patina; but if they have been formed at different times, as may happen if they are due to natural agencies, this fact will almost certainly be betrayed by a difference in the patination...flints of each industry will often possess a distinctive patina...

During this century, artifact patination will:

1 – Be used to determine the artifact's age
2 – Be used to illustrate the artifacts burial environment.

Figure 7 – Surface (60x) of Natural Weathering Jasper. Patination flakes off leaving a rough surface. This process is common to most cryptocrystalline materials.

See Experimental Archaeology section for another discussion on patination.

Figure 8 – Broken Points Found in Different Archaeological Levels in Tuscarora Rockshelter in Frederick County, Maryland. These points fit back together and show differences in patination due to different environments.

Projectile Point Shapes

Projectile points can be classified by their generalized shapes; their basic morphology. There are numerous ways to divide them, such as by blade style, stem shape, material, or size. The Quantum Classification Method (QCM) divides all projectile points (Hranicky 1987) into:

1 – Lanceolate forms
2 – Notched forms
3 – Stemmed forms
4 – Bifurcate forms
5 – Triangle forms.

These five divisions are used throughout this publication as the basic morphology schema for any projectile point. See Projectile Points section.

The QCM is based on a basic design principle that went into each point when it was knapped (Figure 9). While the pointmaker may or may not have been aware of all the possible styles that he could select from for making his point, the American Indians, for the most part, used one of the above five basic shapes for projectile points, which are described as:

Lanceolate Form - reference to a large parallel-edged point that does not have waisting, notching, or shouldering. QCM examples are: Clovis, Golondrina, Hell Gap, Hi-Lo, Agate Basin, Beaver Lake, Nebo Hill, Pee Dee, Pelican, Copena, Cumberland, Folsom, Guilford, Quad, and Plainview. The lanceolate form points are usually long slender points with no proximal area that shows any hafting designs. For the MPRV, the major lanceolate forms are the Clovis, Whites Ferry, and Fox Creek types.

Notched Form - reference to point that has circular indentations cut into the lower edges or corners. QCM examples are: Hardaway, Besant, Big Creek, all Turkey- and Dove-tail points, Cache River, Cupp, Desert, Cahokia, Lost Lake, Palmer, Pine Tree, Big Sandy, and Dalton. The notched point is usually a medium triangular-shaped point that has notches cut into the side or corner areas of the proximal end of the point. For the MPRV, the major notched forms are the Big Sandy, Vosburg, Susquehanna, St Charles, Snyders, and Kirk types.

Stemmed Form - reference to a point that has a downward extension from the blade at the proximal end. QCM examples are: Cotaco Creek, Duncan, Eden, Flint Creek, Godar, Holland, Morrow Mountain, Pryor, Johnson, Kramer, Pontchartrain, Rio Grande, Stanly, Alberta, Dallas, Kirk, LeCroy, Adena, Savannah River, Sandia, and Scottsbluff. The stemmed point has an obvious extension at the base of the point, which makes the stemmed area noticeably different from the blade part of the point. For the MPRV, the major stemmed forms are Morrow Mountain, Adena, Savannah River, Snook Kill, Bare Island, and Koens-Crispin types.

Bifurcate Form - reference to a point that has bilobes. QCM examples are Nottoway River, St Albans, LeCroy, Fox Valley, Susquehanna Valley, and Rice. The larger the lobes, probably the older the point. Points are often found as expended points (less than 25 mm). The bifurcate probably was invented in the Carolinas and reflects a technological continuum of the Hardaway and Quad technologies. For the MPRV, the major bifurcate forms are St Albans, Culpeper, and LeCroy.

Triangle Form - reference to a point that has all three straight sides. QCM examples are: Madison, Clarksville, Garza, Levanna, Yadkin, Fort Ancient, Frazier, Fresno, Hamilton, Maud, Talco, and Tortugas. The triangle point is a medium to small point that does not have a stemmed area and does not have any notching. The sides are usually straight, and the base width is usually the same as the blade's length. For the MPRV, the major triangle forms are the Madison, Levanna, and Potomac types.

<u>Note</u>: The QCM is used here for the entire U.S. and types listed are not necessarily found in the MPRV.

From the notebook...

Powhatan – his Native American name is unknown. Monument is located on the Pamunkey Reservation, King William County, Virginia. For an overview of the Pamunkey, see Speck (1928). Note western head dress.

From the notebook...

Proclamation for Maryland Archeology Month 2000. Most states set aside one month for archaeology. Generally, it has special exhibits, lectures, site tours, open houses, and numerous public-oriented activities. The Month has become a classic form of an archaeology outreach program. This one was signed by Governor Paris Glendening.

* Notebook inserts are filler items and not necessarily related to the text.

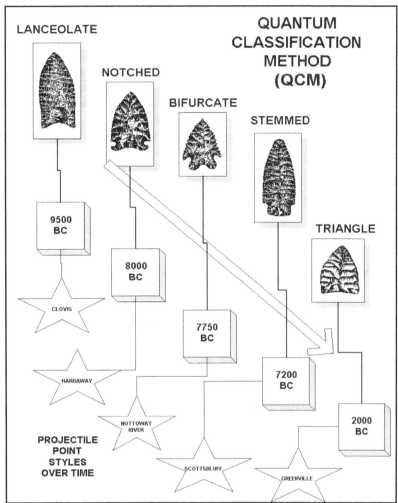

Figure 9 – Quantum Classification Method (QCM) (Hranicky 1987). <u>Note</u>: points shown are representative of American archaeology, not necessarily the MPRV. The generalized forms are lanceolate, notched, bifurcate, stemmed, and triangle styles.

Point Distributions

Projectile points are viewed as having horizontal and vertical distribution in prehistory. However, they are rarely studied in terms of technological or cultural distributions. One reason for this absence is the Panindian nature of tool technology. For example, a set of Paleoindian descriptive standards for toolmaking has not been established. As such, the migration of a culture or society depends on other archaeological tools for identification and distributions. The projectile point because of its unique form (within various style) offers horizontal and vertical studies as a unit of study. While most point forms are site-specific, numerous types have extremely wide-spread distributions, especially in early prehistory. This type of distribution is either a large area of technological borrowing or population movements. The distribution of a projectile point involves:

1 – Distribution of the technology
2 – Migration of the culture

3 – Time period of the occupation.

From a watershed perspective, the following two distributions have riverines as a common factor. But, a macrotypic distribution always has an interriverine (watershed) and, most importantly, intrariverine (regional) distributions. The following terms are used for types in this publication (Hranicky 1991 and 2001):

Macrotypic Point Distribution - type with a distribution inside and outside a state and one that usually covers a very large geographical area (at least several states). It may be subject to local modifications, but generally it still resembles the widespread type.

Microtypic Point Distribution - type with a local distribution, which is usually confined to a river and/or ecological system. The microtypic points are frequently a subtype of a major macrotypic type

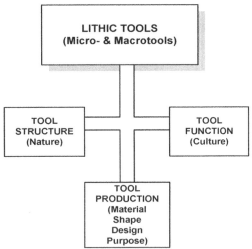

Figure 10 – Basic Factors for All Prehistoric Lithic Tools

Note: Tool production is discussed in the Toolmaking Technology section.

Both point distributions are used as a type identifier in the Projectile Point section. This approach is especially useful in analyzing collections from field/surface surveys.

Structure and Function Concepts for Tools

Structure and function are basic concepts in analytical archaeology and are used to separate and classify tools (Figure 10). The following discusses the concepts and shows relationships between the two concepts. For typology, structure is always the primary concern; function is secondary and is often used to amplify structural analysis. These concepts are presented as:

1 – Tool Structure
2 – Tool Function.

1 – <u>Tool Structure</u>

Structural analysis (morphology) is a major approach in archaeology. Structure always dictates function, but culture selects the design which is a factor in structure. All in all, these two concepts (structure and function) are interlocked to a degree that they cannot be easily separated into analytical categories. Function is assumed here to be the property (domain) of work and performing tasks; whereas, structure is assumed to be the mechanics (physics) of operating the tool or implement in performance of work tasks. Even though structure can be culturally determined, it must conform to the Laws of Nature. On the other side, function does not have any restrictive properties and always is evaluated as successful or a failure in tool performance. Without restrictions, any tool can be used for any function.

In essence, function is a behavioral property; but for that matter, so is structure. Functional wear patterns on tools reveal the total usage inventory, which permits an insight into prehistoric economies. Also, this insight can offer data that may have had a direct influence on prehistoric choices of stone material for specific tasks.

The shape of the blade determines function, but blade angles and shape have overlaps that allow them to be multifunctional tools (Figure 11). Behaviorally, the user determines tool function, even if the function fails to perform a desired task. The blade's frank angle is the best determinant for measuring the blade-use qualities of a tool. After which, blade length and thickness become more of a descriptive feature rather than functional attributes. Blade width is a factor in tool efficiency, but it depends on the frank angle for true efficiency. The frank angle should be measured off a plane, such as the medial axis. See Bifaces as Knives section for frank description.

Efficiency is directly related to chassis mounts and share (blade) sharpness, but it does assume proper usage and tool maintenance. Efficiency is a factor in work. Work can only be appraised as task accomplishment, not number of tasks, hours, etc. For the moment, experimental archaeology data provide an insight into tool efficiency. The value of efficiency is socially-determined in prehistory and does not necessarily correlate to modern archaeological analysis.

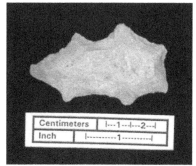

Figure 11 – Multifunctional Quartzite Point (L = 49, W = 30, T = 8 mm). It served as a hafted double spokeshave tool.

Tool function may always be a subjective interpretation on its usage for prehistoric societies. We do not have a reliable set of physical properties that move the tool into and out of the work environment based on specific task functions. A factor introduced here is tool behavior. Even with similar tool manufactures, haftings, and usage, each tool behaves differently, of which analysis is usually a subjective opinion for its operation, but one that can be based on structure and the type of work. If tool behavior varies, then the correct analysis of structure and especially function also vary. When tool behavior is coupled with skill and useability, tool lifecycle is also affected. In other words, operationally, no two tools are the same.

**Tool structure has dimensions
and tool function has rationale;
both have to be compatible.**

One aspect of structure/design is what role does language play in designing a tool, or the famous Whorfian hypothesis of linguistic relativity. How many words occur in various Native American languages for knife? Whorf (1956) was a chemical engineer and studied North American Native American languages as a hobby (another one of those amateurs). His major conclusion was that different languages emphasize in their structure different aspects of the physical (and perhaps spiritual) world. The cognitive process of using language is a factor in how tools are designed - the so-called mental template. Research on the cognitive processes of tool production offers tremendous possibilities in the study of Native American tools (see Young and Bonnichsen 1984 for an example).

In addition to the cognitive process, tool design is universal in that every stone tool, excluding pounders, incorporates the concept of the wedge. It is the basic principle of the first chopper and continues today. The wedge is a natural mental process to separate something into two or more parts. Using the wedge as a principal design, form dictates function due to the placement of the wedge in the tool's structure (Figure 12). The basic principle of wedge placement (bit and angle) determines the physical function of a macrotool.

The basic shape of a projectile point can accomplish all microtool functions. Obviously, macrotool functions, such as pounding and felling (via axes and celts) are not generally possible with the projectile point. Consequently, the projectile point has always been a hafted multifunctional tool with limited functionality in the Paleoindian Period (knife and point) through to the Woodland Period (point, scraper, drill, knife, punch, perforator, awl, burin, spokeshave and more). What is interesting is that any QMC style can perform all these functions.

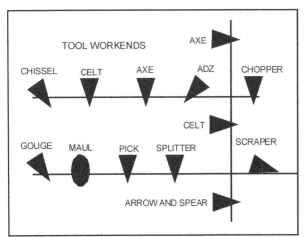

Figure 12 – Tool Examples of the Wedge Principle of Energy Transfer for Micro- and Macrotools. The black lines represent the target area into which work (energy) is applied.

Regardless of the approach to studying cultural materials, structure and function analyses are part of the investigation. Each researcher sets or justifies the rules and parameters and starts with excavational data of artifact relationships, then determines cultural factors in tool design (style) and usage, and finally, publishes an explanatory interpretation of the investigation. Obviously, structure is always present, but function may not always be present or observable in the archaeological record. Again, structure best relates to natural processes; whereas, function best relates to cultural processes.

Tool function, especially blade function of a tool, is the key to tool classification and typological divisions. It justifies archaeological tool classes. While obvious on most tools, few archaeological reports discuss tool mechanics, namely blade degrees, shape/angles, etc. Most do include resharpening which is a result of function (and a consequence of structure) and, while important, is not a major concern of functional analyses. The expended tool rarely shows blade setups and should be limited to hafting quality studies. Resharpening is, however, a factor in material durability and the tool's lifecycle. Function is relatable to useability (lifecycle) and tool efficiency, but in totality, function is most likely culture bound in prehistory -- many different usages for tools with specific functions. A tool could be multifunctional, but if a local society only used it for a single purpose, the dual nature remains to be proven archaeologically. As such, a single tool for a single function is maintained here, if only for tool identification, analysis, and classification, namely projectile points, axes, celts, drills, knives, etc. All tools have one or more of the following operational (industry) functions:

```
1 – Cutting      2 – Chopping
3 – Pounding     4 – Abrading
5 – Throwing     6 – Hunting
7 – Fishing      8 – Gaming
9 – Sewing       10 – Recording
11 – Grinding    12 – Hewing
13 – Drilling    14 – Scraping
15 – Felling     16 – Sinking
17 – Engraving   18 – Decorating
19 – Smoking     20 – Containing
21 – Caching     22 – Splitting
23 – Carving     24 – Sawing
25 – Planing     26 – Grooving
27 – Writing.
```

These operational functions are used in the Miscellaneous Tools/Implements section, and tool modality is discussed later. And repeating, some tools are multifunctional implements; thus, they are basically not typeable. As a note: Can function exist without culture?

A tool's functional axis is its physical property that can be measured and compared to various tool industries. For example, planing is almost a horizontal cut across a target area; whereas, chopping is almost a perpendicular action on a target area. In theory, each tool function has a functional work axis, which identifies the function. One aspect of function is how the tool was held by the user. Numerous functions have varying hand-held operations, which affect functional analyses. These holding patterns can be classified as subsets of function and tested on tools. Structure and function are the essence of this lithic technology presentation. See Toolmaking Technology section.

Figure 13 – Stem Differences between (Left) Koens-Crispin and (Right) Morrow Mountain II Types. Both points are made from rhyolite and are from King and Queen County, Virginia. The rhyolite source is probably the MPRV. The patination difference is due to lithic source: river cobble (left) versus quarried stone. River submersion causes the difference in stone chemistry as a physical adjustment to the molecular structure; there is a difference in knappability.

Tool structure, especially the chassis elements (hafting), is also a key to tool classification (Figure 13). Structure is related to designing a tool to perform a particular function. The most consistent part (set of attributes) of a point for typing is the stem. The stem is a structure consequence; whereas, blade is a functional consequence. Structure can easily constitute types or classes, and at the same time present a historical hierarchy of stylistic change over time.

Archaeologists have developed many ways to classify and define prehistoric tool specifications. But, they have not developed any systematic or even pragmatic way to describe the requirements for a chassis interface, namely the basic tool and hafting assembly. Additionally, the discipline has not discovered the interface between tool chassis and human interfaces. Naturally, some ethnographic data are available, but the eventual interface may be discovered by experimental archaeology. Added to these scientific deficiencies, there are no practical measurements of prehistoric tool performance. Archaeology is still looking at functional designs as basic tool structures in some type of empirically-based research methodologies. As suggested, structure does not always imply a particular function as it was used in the Native American world; however, structure always has a physical operation which can be assigned to a function.

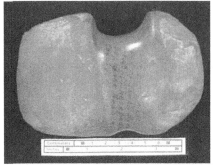

Figure 14a – Diabase Axe (L = 131. W = 89, T = 45 mm) from Anne Arundel County, Maryland. It has the classic 4/4 grooving and round poll, but the groove is unusually wide and highly polished. It was probably a long axe when it was first manufactured. There is some raised grooving. Everything is basically there for this axe type, but the form has minor differences with other 4/4 grooved axes. Since there are no archaeological standards for axe analysis, this tool can only look different – a form that does not hamper its function.

Figure 14b – Greenstone Axe (L = 113, W = 83, T = 33 mm) from Northumberland County, Virginia. Like the Maryland specimen, it has a 3/4 wide groove, and its overall shape is similar enough that an axe type may be suggested.

As argued, tool structure is the physical shape of the tool. It must conform to the Laws of Nature in order to operate as a tool. What could be called a tool's form is the cultural look of a tool design as seen in its structure (Figures 14a and 14b). Both specimens show heavy-duty hafting processes. The Native Americans viewpoint may not necessarily be the same as the archaeologist's: do tools present the same usage to each individual?

Structure as a technology is the tool's physical assembly or design; variables brought together to produce a product. Physical properties, attributes, or traits are seen empirically in an object that can be combined as a particular function, such as knife structure for cutting, drill structure for drilling, etc. Structure has four properties that affect analyses:

1 – Surface: observable physical shapes; common perception of anyone viewing the artifact. It conforms to the physical properties of Nature. It is a factor in typology.

2 – Latent: intrinsic physical shape only known to the person who made it, but is possibly observable to those who are familiar with socially acceptable shapes. It conforms to the rules of a society and is a factor in function.

3 – Learner: shape as the results of someone learning to make a particular style point or tool. Unless found in an archaeological context, these properties are difficult to discern. It is a factor of cognitive behavior.

4 – Meaning: particular modification to suit tool meaning or personalization of a point or tool. Variations are observable but cannot be appreciated as to tool adjustments for function – or meaning. For example, notch adjustments because the point will work in a certain way. In other words, a particular tool was meant to perform a certain operation (modality). It is a factor in tools that are classified as artforms.

All these properties are culture-bound and can be changed or modified within any given population especially over time. These relationships among changes, modifications, or continued shape maintenance may not always be observable in an archaeological analysis.

Theoretical Structure and Function

Analytically, structure is a reference to design, physical shape, or combination of attributes to form shape of which basic data are tabulated to provide an interpretation of the tool in a social setting. Data can be collected to a specific way tool parts are put together, arrangement of attributes, or the manner in which the item was made. In other words, any hafted tool has two sets (often overlapping) of attributes, namely:

1 – Functional attributes relatable to work and user behavior

2 – Structural attributes relatable to form and shape.

Theoretically, |**Structure + Function**| - absolute concept in lithic technology that structure and function cannot exist separately. Together, they equal the whole, as:

|structure + function| = 1

As a premise, structure generally causes function; function causes usage. Tool structure requires functional attributes, as

S_T I FA_1, FA_2..., Fn_n

whereas:
I = function of
S_T = structure
FA_1 = functional attribute

Or, structure is theoretically a collection of functional possibilities. Additionally, a functional attribute must be present in a tool's structure in order for the tool to be used in that functional capacity. A tool can have any number of functional attributes (Figure 15).

Figure 15 – Another Multifunctional Quartzite Tool (L = 71, W = 32, T = 9 mm). Tool that is almost impossible to classify. The structure suggests a drill/perforator, spokeshave, and knife functions. If hafted, the chassis area is on the right end.

The above discussion provides ideas for the analysis of projectile points. There are numerous scientific techniques and methods available in archaeology for projectile point analysis (see Hranicky 2002). The Projectile Point section uses function and structure among numerous methods and concepts, which collectively identify the type archaeologically.

Style versus Function versus Structure

Style is a cultural process of designing a tool to perform a particular function. It differs from structure in that style can overlap tool industries and classes. It is an areal unit or factor in tool design that represents social norms (sharing) or ways of producing, using, and decorating artifacts (Hranicky 2002a). This factor is present in all tools, but not necessarily recordable by modern archaeological methods. Essentially, style is a factor of:

1 – Time and space
2 – Culture
3 – Technology.

Figure 16 – Quartzite Form from Charles County, Maryland (L = 105, W = 48, T = 11.5 mm). The basic structure suggests a knife or perhaps celt form. However, the bit is smoothed (see arrow) suggesting it was used as a hoe for planting or flesher to tan hides.

Each factor is an element in all tools and constitutes attributes that are relatable to functional and structural classifications. We can assume that style changes over time and space and within any culture. Style can be attributed to specific technologies, such as Clovis and Adena tools. Even then, it is a difficult abstraction for a specific technology.

If function is assumed a ratio of structural analysis, then wear patterns can be back tracked to function. For example, using a tool to cut wood (saw function) versus rubbing hide (tanning function); all of which are observable microscopically.

Style probably equaled specific work for a tool; but since it can be transferred to another tool, style remains elusive in archaeology. Thus, it is often avoided as an analytical concept. Can style be correlated with tool operations? For example, is there a stylistic relationship to a projectile point that has a spokeshave cut into its blade? Style is analogous to variation, but variation is usually confined to class. Figure 16 presents an example of style and variation on what would normally be a knife class.

For this specimen, structure can be identified, function is not obvious, and its usage is out of range for the normal shape of the implement. Style remains an abstract quality that probably is in the mind of the toolmaker; but when used, the reality offers different circumstances – the tool served the function that was needed. The basic style here is a hand-held, hafted tool that functioned for the immediate task. Apparently, this specimen in the figure was discarded after usage; it has useful life remaining.

Figure 17 shows a North Dakota comparative example of thumbnail scrapers that are identical in style to those found in the Middle Atlantic area. These specimens illustrate a widespread Panindian use of a particular scraper style. Plate 14 shows style and variation in a sample of Late Archaic rhyolite points.

Figure 17 – Expended Paleoindian Scrapers for North Dakota. Lower left specimens are made from Ohio flint and Indiana chert, respectively. The others are made from Knife River flint which the Native Americans were willing to travel a great distance to obtain. They are made on blades that is the same technique used at the Thunderbird and Williamson sites in Virginia – a wide-spread example of the lithic technological continuum.

Function in Culture

As an addition to function, culture plays a role, but only superficially. For example, a change in technology is not necessarily a culture change. When metal was introduced into the Indian society, a change was made in the *technology carrier* – metal was substituted for stone (Figure 18). Function remained the same; efficiency was the new product, which might be argued that it caused behavioral changes … to be continued in another publication.

Figure 18 – Metal Axes. Ray Olachia, an Apache from Texas, explaining the introduction of metal tools at the 2001 Boy Scouts of America's Jamboree at Camp A. P. Hill in Virginia. He is a well-known expert on Native American tools and weapons.

Text continued on page 148.

From the notebook . . .

Artifacts - Hands on for a Boy Scout Merit Badge in Archaeology. Nicholas Cook (Left) and Nicholas Gill (Virginia Beach, Virginia) at the 2001 Boy Scout of America's Jamboree at Camp A. P. Hill in Virginia. They are examining projectile points from Mecklenburg, Virginia. The Boy Scout Merit Badge is an excellent example of an outreach program in American archaeology.

Plate 14 – Late Archaic Rhyolite Points: Style and Variation

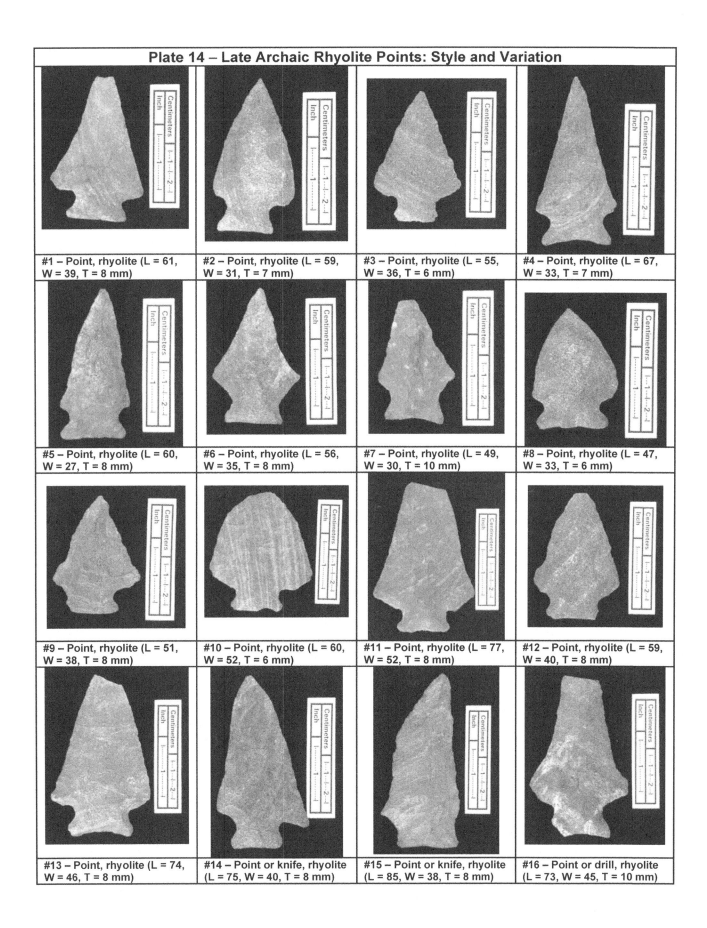

#1 – Point, rhyolite (L = 61, W = 39, T = 8 mm)

#2 – Point, rhyolite (L = 59, W = 31, T = 7 mm)

#3 – Point, rhyolite (L = 55, W = 36, T = 6 mm)

#4 – Point, rhyolite (L = 67, W = 33, T = 7 mm)

#5 – Point, rhyolite (L = 60, W = 27, T = 8 mm)

#6 – Point, rhyolite (L = 56, W = 35, T = 8 mm)

#7 – Point, rhyolite (L = 49, W = 30, T = 10 mm)

#8 – Point, rhyolite (L = 47, W = 33, T = 6 mm)

#9 – Point, rhyolite (L = 51, W = 38, T = 8 mm)

#10 – Point, rhyolite (L = 60, W = 52, T = 6 mm)

#11 – Point, rhyolite (L = 77, W = 52, T = 8 mm)

#12 – Point, rhyolite (L = 59, W = 40, T = 8 mm)

#13 – Point, rhyolite (L = 74, W = 46, T = 8 mm)

#14 – Point or knife, rhyolite (L = 75, W = 40, T = 8 mm)

#15 – Point or knife, rhyolite (L = 85, W = 38, T = 8 mm)

#16 – Point or drill, rhyolite (L = 73, W = 45, T = 10 mm)

Style and Variation in Point Typology

Style is the established normal way that the Native Americans created a specific tool that the archaeologists have identified as a type. Variation is an assessment of how far a tool can vary before it is no longer a member of a type. This is always a subjective assessment by archaeologists and will never be resolved. Specimens that are shown represent established MPRV types but, at the same time, have overlapping type attributes. See Projectile Point section and Hranicky (2015).

There is variation in lithic tools because:

1 – Material (varies even with same material) – varies in knappability and can be used for different purposes, for example obsidian for knives, basalt for hammerstone, etc.

2 – Technology (different ways of achieving the same tool) – limits the kinds of tools that can be made from stone

3 – Function (tool was made for different purposes) – use of a tool determines its shape

4 – Individual preferences (talent and skill varies) – no two tools are exactly alike

5 – Social style (acceptable tools and methods) – different ways to make the same tool; personal choices of knapping methods

6 – Skill (range of a learner to a skilled craftsman) – individual ability in toolmaking varies widely.

7 – Social history – the culture has always used a certain stone for their practical reasons or magical properties.

Note: There is an assumption in lithic technology that all tool using members in a society could make tools – contrast is a toolmaking specialist, thus, more uniformity.

As a final caution, if types do not exist in the native's mind, the variation becomes an analytical nightmare from which, tool identification and analysis is no-more archaeology than sorting tools by weight and size.

2 – **Tool Function**

Tool function is the key to identification and classification of stone tools. Function varies chronologically and culturally but can be considered a constant in the overall development of the prehistoric toolkit. It is dependent on the tool's workend and is always related to tool structure, material, and chassis. The MPRV tool study uses function as the basic determinant in the interpretation of all tools presented here. Function always implies a specific usage, but again it is always dependent on structure, design, and material's capability to perform that function. Functions can be plural actions (modality), but analytically, searching for total functionality is difficult in archaeological investigations.

For typology, a tool can have only one cognitive function; in this case, function is an abstraction of work. While different empirical functions, such as cutting, projectiling, and scraping, are different functions, they perform similar modifications to a target area. Target modification is the commonality-operation, not cutting, projectiling, or scraping operation. This example offers the mental concept of function as performed by an individual using the tool. Archaeology is not ready for a true-basic cognitive (innate) approach to tool analysis.

Function is an action or operation of lithic implements for an intended purpose or activity. It is a deliberate tool manufacture for a specific purpose(s) and has a relationship between structure and usage in that tool change (modification) always modifies function. As suggested, function, not structure, constitutes tool efficiency. Structure is the carrier of function, and design does contribute somewhat to efficiency. But proper usage of a tool's function has the highest percentage of tool efficiency tests.

For examples of ethnographic observation of tool usage, Gould (1968) offers a conclusion on function that the Ngatatjara of Australia treat the working edge as the basis for tool function. Likewise, the Dani of New Guinea, as argued by Andrefsky (1998), suggest archaeologists often misclassify function.

Analysis involves studying the Native American's purpose and use of tools. This aspect of tool usage is not always apparent to archaeological collections. While it is true that some tools/points have been found imbedded in game animal and human skeletons, the use or function of many artifacts can only be obtained by microscopic inspection, cross-cultural comparisons, and analytical insights based on experimental archaeology. For example, the projectile point probably functioned as a spear, arrow, dart, scraper, drill, punch, or knife. Figure 19 shows a tool where its basic function is not obvious. Basically, each tool is unique and defies classification unless, of course, archaeological criteria are imposed (lumpers/splitters argument).

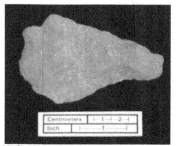

Figure 19 – Hafted quartzite perforator (?) (L = 71, W = 46, T = 10 mm). The lower left share has retouch and wear. The tip is broken, but suggests a perforator function. The left end suggests hafting. Collectively, the tool should be classified as a multifunctional tool with a basic perforator structure.

Modality Operations

Tool operation is viewed here by its modality, which is presumably based on function. The basic premise is all tools have a primary mode of operation. However, most archaeologists argue multifunctional operations for most tools. Within this context, tools are:

1 – **Unimodality**: single functional operation which is always the same each time the tool is used, for example, the bow-launched arrow or hand-held chopper. Tool is used for a single task, and everyone in the social unit would use it the same way.

2 – **Bimodality**: dual functional operations which have two different functions, for example, a drill/perforator or scraper/planner. Tool is used for a single task with two different operations, and everyone in the social unit would use it the same way.

3 – **Trimodality**: same as above but with three distinct operations. Tool is used for multiple tasks, and everyone in the social unit may or may not use it the same way.

4 – **Multimodality**: numerous functional operations, for example, the projectile point, which can be used as a knife, drill, scraper, point, etc. Tool is used for multiple tasks, and everyone in the social unit would use it differently.

The modality operation is a cognitive process of the tool user and is based on his perception of cultural ways, procedures, etc. for using the tool. As mentioned, this does not translate easily into archaeological concepts of function and tool operations.

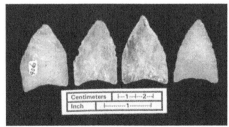

Figure 20 – **Expended Virginia Clovis Points Made from Clear Quartz.** Tool resharpening started in the Paleoindian Period, and the practice continued to the end of the Woodland Period.

Tool Resharpening

All prehistoric tools' blades during usage became dull and were resharpened by the Native Americans (Figure 20). Occasionally, the tool's chassis assembly needed retrofitting to place the tool back in service. All of which are called tool maintenance. Resharpening is performed as:

1 – Percussion chipping along a lateral margin to resharpen the edge

2 – Pressure flaking along the margin and removing microchips to resharpen

3 – Abrading an edge (beveled) to resharpen; technique is used mainly on marcotools.

One question that has not been answered – how many work-hours did a Native American get from flint, rhyolite, and quartzite knife edges before having to resharpen them? The answer depended on the nature of the work, type of target, amount of pressure applied to the tool, and the functional angle of holding the tool. Based on casual tests, five hours for basalt edges and one hour for flint edges are postulated here; proverbially, more testing is needed.

As a typological note, any projectile point blade that has been modified to any other function than projectiling is no longer a member of the basic type. For example, a burinated Dalton is no longer a Dalton point type; a point type assumes a projectiling function.

Blade Modification

Within all point types, there are evidences that function was modified after its initial manufacture. The blade was modified to perform a different task, such as scraper, graver, drill, punch, knife, spokeshave, etc. Figure 21 shows a sample of blade-modified points from the MPRV. The following page (Plate 15) contains projectile points with blade modifications.

These specimens suggest that the projectile point was a multifunctional tool and was probably the primary implement in the Native American's toolkit. While knives are dominant in prehistoric inventories, the projectile point easily served numerous functions, including the knife. This blade modification process starts with Clovis points and continues to the Woodland triangle. As an example, Clovis points are found in Virginia that have their blades modified into drills. By analogy with points always being hafted, these tools (drills, punches, etc.) are assumed here as always being hafted.

Figure 21 – **Patuxent and Bear Island Points with Spokeshaves in Blades.** If this function is restructured to these points, then we possibly can assume several hafted projectile points in each Native American toolkit. Was each of them a specialty item?

From the notebook...

Labeling Artifacts - collectors, amateur archaeologists, general lay public (or any combination of interest and specialty with/without artifacts) should always maintain a log of where artifacts are found. An ideal practice is to record this information directly on the artifact as follows:

- Paint a small area on the worst face using whiteout (Liquid Paper).

- Using a fine-point pen and India ink, write the location, catalog number, date found on the whiteout area.

- Let the ink dry.

- Paint over the ink using a clear paint - clear fingernail polish.

- Maintain the point in a butterfly display case.

- Record point number and data in a log book.

See below for an example on marking/numbering artifacts. Most collectors record numbers on all artifacts and maintain records of their finds and acquisitions. While the pen/ink method is preferred by the author, several new pens have come on the market which can be used. One pen that produces very fine letters and does not clog-up is MICRON's PIGMA pen. The ink is waterproof and does not fade.

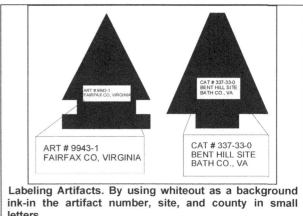

Labeling Artifacts. By using whiteout as a background ink-in the artifact number, site, and county in small letters.

From the Notebook* - Don Crabtree's 1972 An Introduction to Flintknapping...

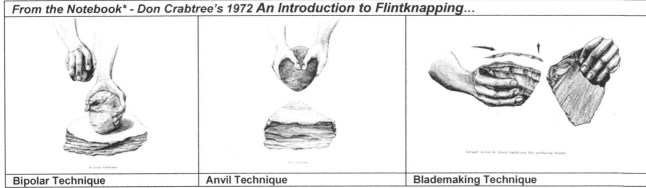

| Bipolar Technique | Anvil Technique | Blademaking Technique |

**Notebook items are fillers to control page breaks for paragraphs and chapters.

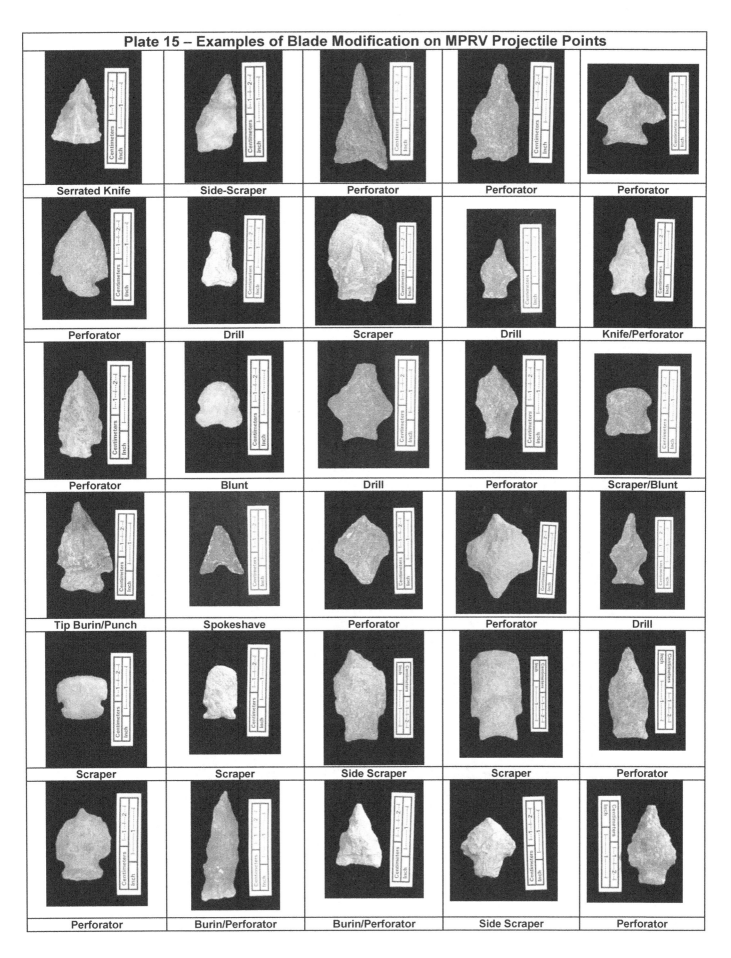

Nontypeable Microtools

Typology probably does not occur in prehistory in such a manner that the Native American would describe the point in the same way as the typologist. Native American technology for tools met their standards and, more importantly, their traditions. All projectile point types should be based on chassis mounting (QCM stem system). These point styles are easily recognizable as archaeological types. If the stem does not occur, most archaeologists argue that the point cannot be analyzed for type classification. This is a false assumption in the archaeological community. Numerous types have particular blade angles, materials, and flaking methods that can be used to identify broken blades. For example, a serrated blade may indicate a Kirk stemmed point. It is simply a matter of learning flaking technologies. Naturally, blade identification as a type is not as accurate as stem identification.

Structure and function are present in any Native American tool; they do not necessarily translate into archaeological interpretations. Artifacts in Figure 22 show a range of tools that are not generally typeable. They are probably Late Archaic Period tools that served functions that were different than the stemmed forms. If these tools represent function, then chassis-types are not adequately explained in the archaeological literature. Or, these tools, which were probably hafted, represent a simple form of a multipurpose implement. The chassis (stem) still remains a major element in typology.

Figure 22 – Untypeable Points. All are MPRV rhyolite points, whose attributes do not meet standard types. However, many archaeologists would force them into specific types.

Medium Bifaces

The MPRV has a high coincidence of medium bifaces (35 – 55 mm) which are usually made from quartz, quartzite, and rhyolite (Figure 23). They exhibit various shapes, but the suggestion here is that they are single, hand-held implements that are used for multifunctional tasks, namely scraping, perforating, and cutting. For the present, they are assigned to the Woodland Period. They cannot be typed because they (as a group) violate the QCM standard styles discussed previously.

Figure 23 – Small MPRV Tools that are not Typeable. Like flake tools shown previously, small multishaped bifaces served numerous functions. They do not follow established structure, such as projectile points. These implements served as spokeshaves, punches, and knives. Because of their weight, they were not used as spearpoints. The Late Archaic Period through to the Middle Woodland Period ecoscenes are full of these implements. Based on surface finds, these tools are nonvillage implements; they are probably tools for small microbands that are not practicing toolmaking of classic point types in the MPRV. They are assumed to be expended or discarded tools.

Projectile Points
(Middle Potomac River Valley Native American Pointed Bifaces)

All point types that have been referenced in the literature as occurring in the MPRV are listed with explanations for usage or nonusage. Types that are marked with 📖 are timemarkers for the Middle Atlantic area. Duplicate names are listed with the preferred type name being suggested. Usually, the first published name is the only name that a type should be called.

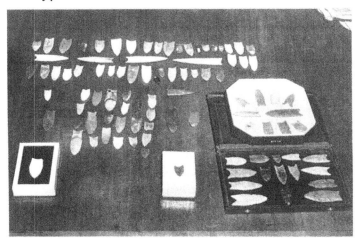

Photograph of Clovis points taken at an early meeting of the Archeological Society of Virginia (ASV). It is signed by E. B. Sacrey (October 29, 1941), who was the first ASV Secretary. This Folsom/Clovis interest would eventually become the McCary Fluted Point Survey of Virginia.

Each point type that is considered as having MPRV validity has the type namer, manufacture techniques, lithic materials, expention dimension, physical ratios description, comments, ecology, and list of similar types. Illustrations are representative of average points as found in the MPRV. Types are presented in PAW order, starting with the oldest (for example, Clovis type) and ending with the youngest (for example, Potomac type) points. All points are from the MPRV area unless otherwise indicated. Classic Middle Atlantic type forms have been presented previously and, where appropriate, repeated here with descriptions. There are numerous types found in the Middle Atlantic area that are not found in the MPRV. This absence is partly due to sampling bias and/or mostly prehistoric Native Americans' reasons for not occupying the MPRV. Types that are presented represent the basic MPRV point population; other types do occur but were not observed in the study collections. New types are defined in this listing.

Note: all Middle Atlantic types (names) were studied, and those considered but not used, are listed as "**not used**." A type chronology was initially suggested by Hranicky 1987); followed as all dates are based on Insashima (1999).

Overview

This section contains 80 point types which have illustrations along with comprehensive descriptions. For each type, the primary type reference is given; however, the reader may consult Justice (1987), Perino (1991 and 1985), and Hranicky (1991 and 1994) for additional information. The basic MPRV point references are Coe (1964), Ritchie (1961), Stephenson, et al. (1963), and Broyles (1971). Additionally, the Jeffery Rockshelter in Loudoun County, Virginia offers the basic MPRV point typology (Fischler 1978).

Most projectile point types have established descriptive nomenclatures and conform to QCM standards that are used by archaeologists and are discussed throughout this publication. Figure 1 shows the basic nomenclature.

Most prehistoric points when first put into service were well-made and demonstrated high-quality knapping. While being used by the Native Americans, points became dull and were resharpened; thus, the point size was reduced finally to a nonuseable tool. Others were broken during their usage. Both categories constitute discards; these make up 75% of the prehistoric collections in the U.S.

The environmental and climatic assessments are discussed in the Environment section and are presented as a factor for each type. The overall typology methods are discussed in the Projectile Point Typology section and Hranicky (1991 and 1994) and Justice (1988). Various radiocarbon dates on file with state agencies were used. All of these sources provided a date range, and dates are subject to change as more data are collected. The basic chronology and PAW framework are based on the Prehistoric Chronology section. Basic point manufacture methods are found in the Toolmaking Technology section.

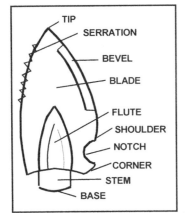

Figure 1 – Basic Projectile Point Nomenclature

Lithic Identification for Tools

Projectile points have the greatest stone diversity of any other class of prehistoric tools. They often represent preferred quarry (source) sites of the Native Americans or preferred lithic materials found in pick-up stones. These tools often have widespread distributions that make precise identification difficult. Additionally, patination often hides the crystal structure of the stone that makes identification difficult. All stones used in this section were discussed in the MPRV Environment section. Basic knowledge for stone identification requires a geological expertise. Most prehistoric archaeologists include this type of study in college and are reasonably accurate in stone identification.

Basic Assumptions Used for Point Typing

The basic assumption (theoretical orientation) for types is generally:

1 – Points have a consistent shape and style of manufacture

2 – Points represent human activities in food curation and consumption

3 – Points are multifunctional implements

4 – Points are the result of environmental factors on societies that produced them

5 – Points were made from specified raw materials that were preferred by the society that made them

6 – Points have a spatial distribution that corresponds to settlement patterns or occupation areas of specific societies

7 – Points represent a technological continuum from which regional societies adopted parts of it

8 – Point usage reflects behavior within a social setting

9 – Points reflect certain QCM styles; all of which were part of the Panindian lithic technology.

Point types, especially QCM styles, probably existed in prehistoric toolmakers' minds. The prehistoric world does not overlap or underlay the archaeologists' world. There is still work to be done in typology and its basis for interpretation about pre-Contact Native Americans.

MPRV point distributions are based on microtypic and macrotypic concepts and ecology based on the watershed method.

Point Type Identification

The following type descriptions are presented as a guide to projectile point identification. Each type is listed with basic description, chronology, lithic composition, basic measurements, and a primary reference; all of which are used to identify a point. As a caution – all points are not necessarily typeable and numerous types have stylistic overlaps because all projectile points are part of the Native Americans' technological continuum for lithic tools. Identifying points from surface collections is the most difficult because they lack archaeological contexts. They do offer data for study of large geographical areas. On the other hand, the archaeological site offers the best way to identify them because distribution and age are fixed in specific cultural contexts.

Even with the analytical factors presented in this and other publications, sound typology depends on personal opinions and years of classification experience.

MPRV Paleoindian Period

The following points represent the MPRV Paleoindian Period, which dates approximately 9500 to 8500-8000 BC. The primary type for this period is the Clovis point. Each type is illustrated with specimens that closely match published type descriptions. Types are included that have been published as occurring in the MPRV, but were not used for various reasons as discussed. The following types are presented in BC years:

- Clovis Lanceolate Point (10,500-9000 BC)
- Dalton Lanceolate Point (9200-8500 BC)
- Hardaway Notched Point (8300-7800 BC)
- Hardaway-Dalton Lanceolate Point (8500-8300 BC)
- Elys Ford Lanceolate Point (8500-7500 BC)
- Hardaway Notched Point (8500-7500 BC).

A Classic Clovis Point from Spotsylvania County, Virginia. The point has numerous shapes, especially after the Native American's resharpening (see McCary 1947). This point was among the first Clovis points in the McCary Fluted Point Survey. Presently, it is privately held in Texas.

MPRV Clovis Point. Formerly, it was part of the Charles E. Merry collection.

📖 **Clovis** – first reported by Howard (1935) and as described in Wormington (1957), it was named after the city in New Mexico. Numerous Clovis points have been found in the study area (Hranicky 1984 and 1987; and Hranicky and McCary 1996). There is a predominant usage of jasper, which comes either from Warren and Culpeper Counties, Virginia, Point of Rocks, Maryland, or numerous outcrops in Pennsylvania. The Potomac River valley points tend not to have the pronounced indentation along the lateral base as do specimens occurring further north. This is probably due to northeastern influences, namely Debert, Shoop, Bull Brook, and Vail sites.

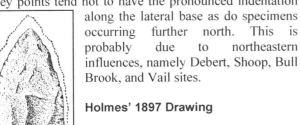

Holmes' 1897 Drawing

Type is manufactured with bifacial antler percussion flaking with pressure flaking to finalize the point. Pressure flaking is used to resharpen a point. MPRV materials are flint, chert, jasper, quartzite, rhyolite, and quartz. It is a macrotypic type, and type validity is traditional. Expention length; 49 mm (Hranicky and McCary 1995); general L/W*T ratio: 12.92 (Hranicky and McCary 1995). ***Basic Description***: Lanceolate; it is a small-to-large lanceolate point with a fluting that is usually short-to-long in length. Base is concave. Grinding is found on the base and lower lateral sides. Lateral sides are parallel to excurvate. Type dates 9300 to 12,500 BP and is found all over the U.S.

According to Wormington (1957), the Clovis point is:

Fluted lanceolate points with parallel or slightly convex sides and concave bases. They range in length from one and a half to five inches but are usually some three inches or more in length and fairly heavy. The flutes sometimes extend almost the full length of the point but usually they extend no more than half way from the base to the tip. Normally, one face will have a longer flute than the other. The fluting was generally produced by the removal of multiple flakes. In most instances the edges of the basal portion show evidence of smoothing by grinding. Certain fluted points found in the eastern United States resemble the Clovis type, but they have a constriction at the base which produces a fish-tailed effect. These have sometimes been called Ohio points or Cumberland points. Many of these tend to be somewhat narrower relative to their length than other fluted points. The earliest published Clovis (drawing) point in the MPRV is Holmes (1897). **Modality**: Its primary functions are a knife and spearpoint. **Comments**: The Clovis point is essentially a recent addition to the MPRV point catalog, as Schmitt's *Archeological Chronology of the Middle Atlantic States* (in Griffin 1952) discussion of the Middle Atlantic does not mention a Paleoindian occupation. The type becomes highly prominent when Gardner (1974) started excavations at the Thunderbird Complex in Warren County, Virginia. (Hranicky 1995). **User Lifeways**: Large bands with hunter/gatherer strategies. **User Ecology**: Occupied all environments during a preboreal climate. **Comparative Types**: Cumberland (Lewis 1954), Folsom (Figgins 1927), Debert (McDonald 1968), and Ross County (Prufer 1963). **Reference**: Howard, Edgar B. (1935) *Evidence of Early Man in North America*. Museum Journal, Vol. 24, pp. 2-3, University of Pennsylvania Museum.

Note: the book cover shows one of the finest Clovis points found in the MPRV study.

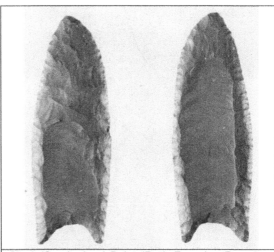

Clovis/Cumberland Point (Both Faces) – Found during the 1950 or 60s at Point of Rocks, Maryland. It is possibly made from Point of

> Rocks jasper and has one full-face flute. It is probably the finest Paleoindian point ever found in the MPRV. Photograph has no scale but the point is over 75 mm. The current owner is unknown. Photograph belongs to Spencer O. Geasey who saved a record of it. This type of fluting has, in the past, suggested the Folsom type in the East (see Hranicky and Painter 1988). The McCary Fluted Point Survey was initially called the Folsom Survey (McCary 1947).

The following pages contain Clovis points from the MPRV and other areas within the Middle Atlantic region. After which, an Archaic point section followed by a Woodland point section are presented.

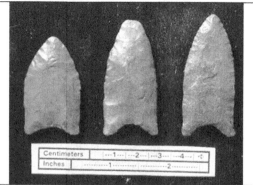

Jasper Clovis points from the Eastern Shore. Left: L = 43, W = 25, T = 7 mm, Worcester County, Maryland; Center: L 52, W = 34, T = 5.5 mm, Somerset County, Virginia; Right: L = 57, W = 22, T 6 mm, Worcester County, Maryland.

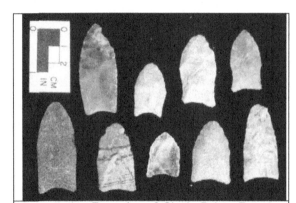

Comparative Examples of Clovis Points Found on the Williamson Paleoindian Site in Dinwiddie County, Virginia (College of William and Mary). The Williamson site has produced more Clovis points (300+) than any other Paleoindian site in North America.

Note: Some archaeologists have suggested that a pre-Clovis lanceolate form exists. This lanceolate is neither fluted nor has basal grinding. This form remains to be established archaeologically.

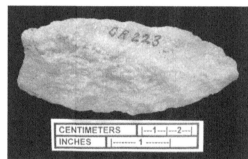

Quartzite, Montgomery County, Maryland
(Charlie Merry Collection)

For a MPRV Clovis site Collection, see Appendix D.

Plate 15 shows a major Clovis collection.

Plate 15 - The Arthur Robertson Collection

The Robertson Collection is among the best private collections ever assembled in Virginia that reached the public realm. It is housed at the MacCallum More Museum and Gardens in Chase City and at the Department of Historic Resources in Richmond, Virginia. Many of his Clovis points are in the McCary Fluted Point Survey. Robertson was a collector and active in the early days of the ASV.

Clovis Points in the Arthur Robertson Collection at the MacCallum More Museum and Gardens, Chase City, Virginia. Parts of the collection are used as study materials for highschool and college students.

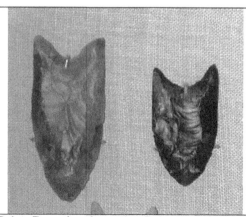

Clovis Point Examples from the Robertson Collection. The museum is the home for the collection that contains over 50 Clovis points, all of which are the first points listed in the McCary Fluted Point Survey.

Arthur Robertson's Notes. He kept meticulous notes on all his finds. He helped organize and was the first president of the Archeological Society of Virginia.

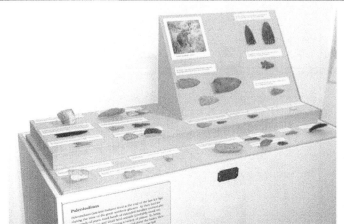
Paleoindian Display at the MacCallum More Museum and Gardens in Chase City, Virginia

Based on a state-wide sample of 1000 typeable projectile points, the following chart shows a distribution that was obtained.

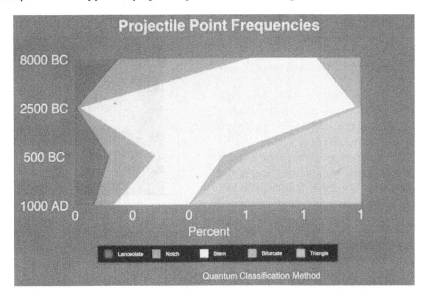

1972 Excavation at the Thunderbird Site, Warren County, Virginia

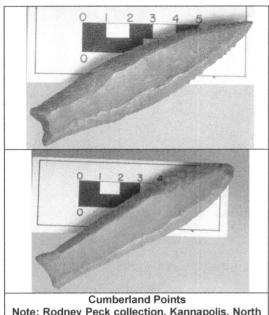

Cumberland Points
Note: Rodney Peck collection, Kannapolis, North Carolina. He is an expert on the type and runs the North Carolina Fluted Point Survey.

Cumberland – first identified by Lewis (1954). This type has not been reported in the MPRV. However, it is found in all areas north, south, and west of the study area. This type probably has only an upland focus, which may account for its absence in the MPRV. It is a macrotypic point, which has a northward distribution of at least New Hampshire (Spiess and Hedden 2000). It is illustrated but not used. It is the product of highly mobile bands; thus, they probably never occupied the MPRV.

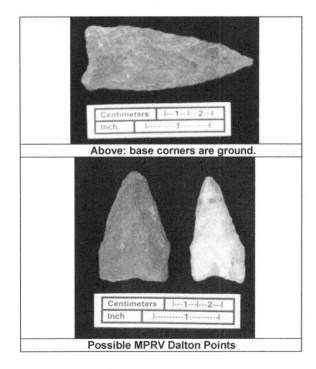

Above: base corners are ground.

Possible MPRV Dalton Points

📖 **Dalton (Hardaway-Dalton)** – first identified by Chapman (1948) after S. P. Dalton, who had a large collection of them. It is a macrotypic type, and the Middle Atlantic area appears to be its northern extent. Type dates 8500 to 11,200 BP. **Comments**: As a major note: the classic Dalton (as in Chapman 1975) does not occur in North Carolina, Virginia, and Maryland. Coe (1964) does not use the main type but uses the Hardaway-Dalton type. See Hranicky (2001). Hranicky (1994) reports central Virginia as being the northern type limit. However, since that publication, Custer (1996) reports the type in Pennsylvania, and Stanzeski (1996) reports them in New Jersey. Apparently, there is a northern upland-to-coastal occupation for the type. The rarity of the Hardaway and Hardaway-Dalton types indicates that during Early Archaic the MPRV was lightly occupied. Only two specimens were observed. Both illustrated specimens are ground and have short flutes. **Reference**: Chapman, Carl H. (1948) *A Preliminary Survey of Missouri Archaeology*. Missouri Archaeologist, Vol. 10, Pt. 4, pp. 135-164.

MPRV Elys Ford Points (?)

Elys Ford – first identified by Bushnell (1935) and named after the ford in Virginia. It is the oldest named type in Virginia. It is always well-made and very thin, usually under 5 mm in thickness. It is probably made off a blade (or flake), but blade-shaping is probably the technique that was used. Native Americans are using quarry-sourced materials with some pickup stones. MPRV material is rhyolite only; slate specimens occur in the southern part of Virginia. It is a microtypic point, and type validity is positive. Expention length = 29 mm, study number = 3; general L/W*T ratio: 7.25. *Basic Description*: Pentagonal; it is a medium-to-large, very thin pentagonal point. Type dates 10,500 to 9500 BP and is found in Virginia and North Carolina. **Modality**: Its primary function is a knife. **Comments**: The Elys Ford point has escaped site recovery, as only surface finds are known. It is classified as Paleoindian (Hranicky 1991), but this remains to be proven as it could be a form of technology that is similar to the Jacks Reef and Pee Dee types. The type is typically made from flint or shale, which distinguished it from the Pee Dee or Jacks Reef types which are predominantly made from jasper. The classic Elys Ford is the thinnest projectile point found in the eastern U.S. **User Lifeways**: Small bands with hunter/gatherer strategies. **User Ecology**: Occupied piedmont environments during a boreal climate. **Comparative Types**: Jacks Reef (Ritchie 1961) and

Pee Dee (Coe 1964). **Reference**: Bushnell, D. I. (1935) The Manahoac Tribes in Virginia, 1608. Smithsonian Miscellaneous Collections, No. 94(8), Washington, DC.

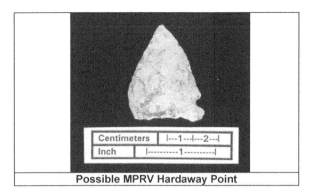

Possible MPRV Hardaway Point

Hardaway – first identified by Coe (1964), named after the site in North Carolina, and discussion by Hranicky (1986). Type is based on the Hardaway site excavation. Type dates 9000 to 10,500 BP which is suggested for the MPRV. This type has not been reported adequately in MPRV. However, a specimen was recovered in Warren County, New Jersey (Staats 1998) which suggests it should be present in the MPRV. These specimens should reflect the northern limit for the type. It is a macrotypic type; a point is shown. Figure 3 shows a classic Hardaway point **Reference**: Coe, Joffre L. (1964) *The Formative Cultures of the Carolina Piedmont*. Transactions of the American Philosophical Society, New Series, Vol. 54, Part 5, Philadelphia, PA.

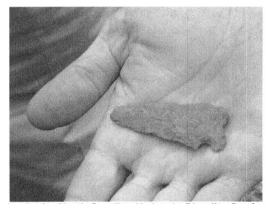

Figure 3 – At the North Carolina Uwharrie Rhyolite Conference in February 1999, a tour was provided of the Hardaway site. A recent storm had felled a tree and upon examining the roots, this Hardaway point was discovered. It was turned over to the state archaeological agency.

Hardaway-Dalton – first identified by Coe (1964) and is based on the Hardaway site excavation. This type has been reported in the MPRV at the Jeffrey Rockshelter in Loudoun County, Virginia. The suggested date is 9000 to 11,000 BP. It is a macrotypic type and because of one specimen unexamined by the author, it is not used.

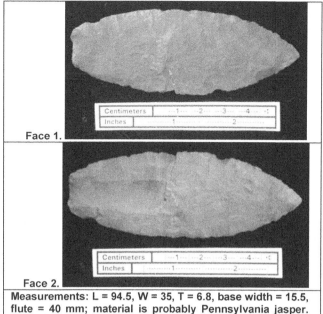

Measurements: L = 94.5, W = 35, T = 6.8, base width = 15.5, flute = 40 mm; material is probably Pennsylvania jasper. D/P ratio = 1.25. Specimen provided by Mark Kelley.

MPRV Northumberland Point

Northumberland – first identified by Hranicky (1994) and is based on the report by McCary (1982). It was named in Wm Jack Hranicky and Gary Fogleman (Hranicky 1994). It is a medium-to-large point with a single flute on one face (Figure 4). The cross section is biconvex. Point is well-made with parallel flaking. Base is usually straight. Tip is often dull which reflects its function as a knife. This type has not been reported and described previously in the MPRV, but one specimen was recorded. It occurs in Virginia, namely Madison County, Maryland, Kentucky, and Pennsylvania. Type dates to the Late Paleoindian Period. It is sometimes incorrectly referred to as the Crowfield point of Canada (as in Custer 2001). It is a macrotypic type. **Reference**: Hranicky, Wm Jack (1994) *Middle Atlantic Projectile Point Typology and Nomenclature*. ASV Special Publication Number 33.

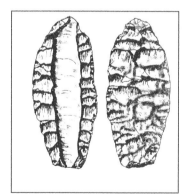

Figure 4 – Drawing of the Northumberland Knife

Simpson – named by Bullen (1968) after the collection at the Florida State Museum. The type may be a pre-Clovis point type. The type occurs in Virginia; for example, McCary Fluted Point Survey number 319 is a Simpson point. For lack of Virginia data and because it was not observed in the MPRV, type is not used.

Suwannee – named by Bullen (1968) after the river in Florida. The type may be a pre-Clovis point type. The type occurs in Virginia; for example, McCary Fluted Point Survey number 52 is a Suwannee point. For lack of Virginia data and because it was not observed in the MPRV, type is not used.

MPRV Archaic Period

The following points represent the MPRV Archaic Period, which dates approximately 10,500-8000 to 4000-1000 BP. It is subdivided into the Early Archaic (Palmer, Kirk, and Big Sandy main types), Middle Archaic (Morrow Mountain main type), and Late Archaic (Halifax, Lamoka, Savannah River, Holmes, and Susquehanna main types). Each type is illustrated with specimens that closely match published type descriptions. Types are included that have been published as occurring in the MPRV, but were not used for various reasons as discussed. Overall, the Early Archaic Period projectile point distribution is based, but not exclusively, on Gardner (1987). The remaining part(s) of the period is based on Ritchie (1963), Coe (1961), Broyles (1971), and Hranicky (1994). The following types are presented in BC years:

- Bare Island Stemmed Point (2500-500 BC)
- Big Sandy Notched (8000-6000 BC)
- Cattle Run (2000-1000 BC)
- Charleston Notched Point (7900-6500 BC)
- Chesapeake Stemmed Point (Archaic)
- Chuchatuck Notched Point (7000-6000 BC)
- Clagett Notched Point (1700-1300 BC)
- Culpeper Bifurcate Point (no date)
- Excelsor Stemmed Point (3500-2500 BC)
- Faison Mixed-Stemmed Point (3000-500 BC)
- Genesee Stemmed Point (2500-1500 BC)
- Guilford Lanceolate Point (3500-2500 BC)
- Halifax Notched Point (3500-2500 BC)
- Holmes Stemmed Point (1000-800 BC)
- Kanawha Bifurcate Point (6500-5500 BC)
- Kessell Notched Point (8500-7500 BC)
- Kirk Stem/Notch Point (7500-6000 BC)
- Koens-Crispin Stemmed Point (1800-1200 BC)
- Lackawaxan (Late Archaic)
- Lamoka Stem/Notch Point (3500-2500 BC)
- LeCroy Bifurcate Point (6500-6000 BC)
- Limeton Bifurcate Point (no date)
- Loudoun Stemmed Point (no date)
- MacCorkle Bifurcate Point (7200-6500 BC)
- Macpherson Notched Point (2500-1700 BC)
- Mason Neck Stemmed Point (3500-2200 BC)
- Monocacy Stemmed Point (Late Archaic)
- Monrovia Notched Point (2000-500 BC)
- Morrow Mountain Stemmed Point (5000-3500 BC)
- Moyock Stemmed Point (3500-2500 BC)
- Normanskill Notched Point (1700-1300 BC)
- Occoquan Stemmed Point (no date)
- Orient Fishtail Point (1200-700 BC)
- Otter Creek Notched Point (4000-3000 BC)
- Palmer Notched Point (7700-6900 BC)
- Patuxent Stemmed Point (1700-1400 BC)
- Pequea Stemmed Point (no date)
- Perkiomen Broadspear Point (1600-1400 BC)
- Piney Island Point (2200-1800 BC)
- Poplar Island Stemmed Point (1200-900 BC)
- Rappahannock River Stemmed Point (2500-1500 BC)
- Savannah River Broadspear Point (3000-800 BC)
- Snook Kill Stemmed Point (1800-1300 BC)
- Southampton Stemmed Point (5000-4000 BC)
- St Albans Bifurcate Point (7000-6500 BC)
- St Charles Notched Point (8500-7000 BC)
- Stanly Stemmed Point (6200-4000 BC)
- Susquehanna Broadspear Point (1650-700 BC)
- Susquehanna Valley Bifurcate Point (6000-5000 BC)
- Vosburg Notched Point (3200-2500 BC)
- Zekiah Swamp Stemmed Point (2000-1000 BC).

VIRGINIA'S MIDDLE ARCHAIC PROJECTILE POINTS

12,000 YBP	**Kirk Stemmed** — END OF EARLY ARCHAIC IN VIRGINIA	
10,000 YBP		**MacCorkle-Nottoway River**
8000 YBP	**Morow Mountain I**	**St Albans**
7000 YBP / 6000 YBP	**Morrow Mountain II**	**LeCroy**
	Guilford	
		Kanawha
4000 YBP	END OF MIDDLE ARCHAIC IN VIRGINIA	**Halifax**

- 161 -

Amos – first identified by Broyles (1971) and is based on surface finds at the Amos Power Plant, Putnam County in West Virginia. Dates are 6400-7750 BP. Type is probably not valid and should be included with the Charleston type. It is not used.

Ashtabula – first identified by Mayer-Oakes (1955). It is part of the Susquehanna's technological history. This type probably occurs in MPRV (Hranicky 1991). However, unless made from a high quality flint, it is difficult to discern from the Susquehanna type. It is a macrotypic point and not used.

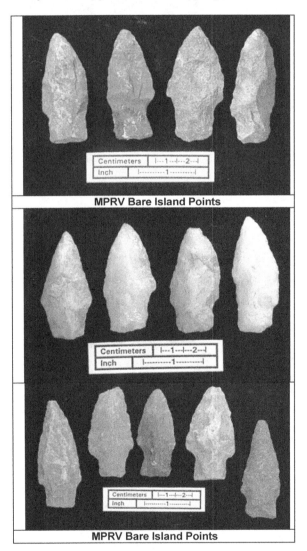

MPRV Bare Island Points

📖 **Bare Island** – first identified by Kinsey (1959) and named after the site in Pennsylvania, and as described in Ritchie (1961). It is classified as a narrow-bladed type. Type is manufactured with bifacial antler percussion flaking with pressure flaking to finalize the point. Pressure flaking is used to resharpen a point. Native Americans are using field or streambed cobbles as their lithic sources. MPRV materials are mainly rhyolite, argillite, white quartz, and quartzite, with rare occurrences of flint. It is a macrotypic point, and type validity is distinct. Expention length = 55 mm, study number = 42; general L/W*T ratio: 23.57. **_Basic Description_**: Stemmed; it is a narrow point with asymmetrical, crisp shoulders, which are pointed or rounded. Stem sides are parallel, and base is straight or slightly convex. Cross section is biconvex. Tips are pointed and always located on the medial axis. Type dates 5000 to 3600 BP and is found in the northeast and middle Atlantic areas. **Modality**: Its primary function is a knife (Hranicky 1988). **User Lifeways**: Bands with general forging strategies. **User Ecology**: Occupied piedmont environments during a subboreal climate. **Comments**: Bare Island point often has an asymmetrical blade suggesting its function is a knife. It rarely shows an impact fracture. Type is relatively common in the MPRV, especially on the Maryland side of the river (Hranicky 1988). **Comparative Types**: Kent (Suhm, Krieger, and Jelks 1954), Piney Island (Kent 1970), Kramer (Munson 1966), McWhinney (Vickery 1972), and Wading River (Ritchie 1961). **Reference**: Kinsey, W. Fred (1959) **_Recent Excavations on Bare Island in Pennsylvania: The Kent-Hally Site_**. Pennsylvania Archaeologist, Vol. 29, Nos. 3-4.

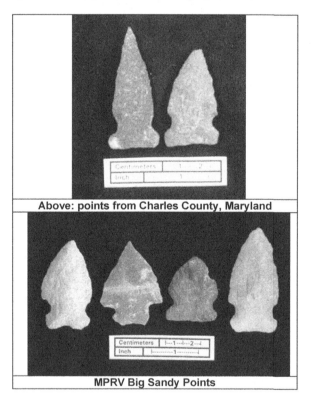

Above: points from Charles County, Maryland

MPRV Big Sandy Points

📖 **Big Sandy** – first identified by Kneburg (1956). Type is manufactured with bifacial antler percussion flaking with pressure flaking to finalize the point. Pressure flaking is used to resharpen a point. Native Americans are using quarry-sourced materials with some pickup stones. MPRV material is primarily flint, but when not available, pointmakers used local materials, such as quartzite and rhyolite. It is a macrotypic point, and type validity is traditional. Expention length = 43 mm, study number = 6; general L/W*T ratio: 9.70. **_Basic Description_**: Side-notched; it is a medium point with a triangular blade. Base is straight or concave and is usually ground. Cross section is biconvex, plano convex, or rhomboid shaped. Notch has a Y-pattern (Justice 1988). Type dates 10,000 to 8000 BP and is found in all eastern states. **Modality**: Its primary function is a spearpoint. **Comments**: The Big Sandy point is evidence of the earliest people to come into the MPRV after the Paleoindians left the river basin. The type is related to the St Charles technology and is probably the antecedent to the Kirk notch technology. Type has numerous names: Hemphill, Graham Cave, Godar, Cache River, Raddatz, Osceola, Kessell, and Taylor. While each type has a stem-area variation, they all exhibit a side-notching technology. Distribution for the early form is all over the U.S. except the Southwest; the Northwest has a 5000 BP form called the Cold Springs type (Butler 1961). If the Big Sandy is a pure technology, its primary distribution source is the Tennessee River valley. **User Lifeways**: Large, highly mobile bands with hunter/gatherer strategies. **User Ecology**: Occupied uplands environments during a boreal climate. **Comparative Types**: Cache River (Cloud 1969), Graham Cave (Logan 1952), Hemphill (Scully 1951), Taylor (Michie 1966), Kessell (Broyles 1971), Charleston (Broyles 1971), and Northern (Gruhn 1961). **Reference**: Kneburg, Madeline (1956) *Some Important Projectile Point Types Found in the Tennessee Area*. Tennessee Archaeologist, Vol. XII, No. 1, pp. 17-28.

Non-MPRV Big Sandy Auriculate Point Examples Showing Big Sandy Relationships, Right Point is a Classic Auriculate

Big Sandy Auriculate – named by Claflin (1931). It probably occurs in the MPRV, but remains to be studied as an identifiable type. It is illustrated but not used. **Reference**: Chaflin, William H. (1931) *The Stallings Island Mound, Columbia County, Georgia*. Papers of the Peabody Museum of American Archaeology and Ethnology, Vol. 14, No. 1, Cambridge, MA.

Big Sandy II – first described by Baker (1995). It is a false type if only because it implies a type I point. Unless named by the original types, no new designation should be made. Technologically, it has not been proven and is considered a false type. Type is not used.

Bottle Neck – first identified in Virginia by Hranicky and Painter (1988). Type name is a reference to morphology and fits numerous eastern point types. For description, see Converse (1963). It is probably the same type as the Ashtabula (Mayer-Oakes 1955) and is not used. Also, it is called the Catoctin point in Hranicky (2001).

MPRV Broad River Points

Broad River – named by Michie (1970) after the river in South Carolina. Type has not been defined in Virginia (Hranicky and Painter 1988 and 1989; Hranicky 1991 and 1994); thus, a tentative distribution for the MPRV. Since fiber-tempered pottery is found in the MPRV, the Broad River type is significant because elsewhere, namely Georgia, it is associated with fiber-tempered pottery (Michie 1970 and Elliott and Sassaman 1995). It is illustrated but not used. Based on pottery, the type center-dates around 3600 BP. **Comparative Types**: Genesee (Ritchie 1961), Savannah River (Coe 1964), **Reference**: Michie, James L. (1970) *The Broad River Point*. Chesopiean, Vol. 8, No. 1.

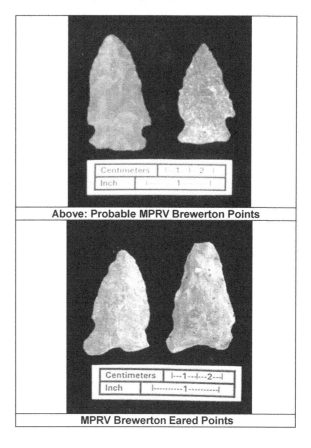

Above: Probable MPRV Brewerton Points

MPRV Brewerton Eared Points

📖 **Brewerton** – first identified by Ritchie (1961). This type is difficult to identify as a point type because it includes an eared, triangular, and corner notched style. Perino (1985) suggests that the eared variety is the result of reshapening. For the corner-notched variety, it is a technological continuum of the Vosburg type. The remaining varieties may be expended forms of the base style, which is the notched form. The type is traditionally made from Onondaga gray flint, and flint should be a factor in defining the type. The type represents the Laurentian and Frontenac complexes of New York, which have southern influences to at least the Potomac River valley. Type should be easily recognizable in archaeological site materials because of context, but is not easily recognizable in surface finds when made from local materials. There are four basic types:

- Corner Notched 4300-4700 BP
- Eared 2800-5600 BP
- Triangle 4200 BP
- Side Notched 3600-5600 BP.

<u>Reference</u>: Ritchie, William A. (1961) *A Typology and Nomenclature for New York Projectile Points*. Bulletin 384, New York State Museum and Science Service, Albany, NY.

Buggs Island – named in Hranicky (1994) after the island in southern Virginia. Type is the same as Neville (Dincuaze 1976) and Zekiah Swamp. Type is not used. See Zekiah Swamp. Keel (1976) argues for a Woodland Period version.

MPRV Cattle Run Point

MPRV Cattle Run Point

Cattle Run – named by Geier (1996) after a waterway in Virginia. Type may have Koens-Crispin relationships; but for this publication, it is a standalone type that has an association with the Savannah River type.. Type is manufactured with bifacial antler percussion flaking with pressure flaking to finalize the point. Percussion flaking is used to resharpen a point. Native Americans are using pickup field or riverbed stones. MPRV material is primarily quartzite with some local rhyolite. It is a macrotypic point, and type validity is conditional. Expention length = 82 mm, study number = 2; general L/W*T ratio: 22.77. ***Basic Description***: Stemmed, it is a medium-to-large weak rounded stem that has a slightly convex base. Shoulders are pronounced. Type dates 4000 to 3000 BP and is found in the Virginias, Carolinas, and Maryland. **Modality**: Its primary function is a knife. <u>User Lifeways</u>: Large bands of hunter/gatherers basically occupying riverines of the coastal plain. <u>User Ecology</u>: Occupied coastal environments during a subboreal climate.

Cattle Run Type (Geier (1996)

<u>Comment</u>: This type is probably what Holland (1960) calls Type P. He suggests it is found right at the preceramic-ceramic levels in Northwestern Virginia. Additionally, this type is confusing with the Morrow Mountain I type, but is later and unrelated. The Morrow Mountain is a thicker point and the Cattle Run is better made. The flaking pattern is consistent with the Savannah River percussion flaking method. Hranicky and Painter (1988) considered the type's validity, but could not date it; they named the point the Norfolk type, but did not publish it. Figure shows a drawing by Geier (1996) to help identify the point type. **Comparative Types**: Koens-Crispin (Hawkes and Linton 1916). **Reference**: Geier, Clarence R. (1996) *The Cattle Run Variant of the Savannah River Projectile Point Type*. Quarterly Bulletin, Archeological Society of Virginia, Vol. 51, No. 4, pp. 154-177.

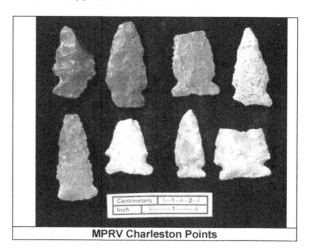

MPRV Charleston Points

Charleston – first identified by Broyles (1971), is based on the St Albans site excavation, and named after the city. Type is manufactured with bifacial antler percussion flaking with pressure flaking to finalize the point. Pressure flaking is used to resharpen a point. Native Americans are using quarry-sourced materials with some pickup stones. MPRV material is primarily flint, with some local usage of other materials. It is a macrotypic point, and type validity is distinct. Expention length = 52 mm, study number = 4; general L/W*T ratio: 12.06. ***Basic Description***: Corner-notched; it is a medium well-made point with a straight base.

Notches are small and extend upward into the point to nearly the shoulder. Stem corners are rounded. Type dates 9900 to 8500 BP and is found in the Virginias, Carolinas, Maryland, Ohio, and Kentucky. **Modality**: Its primary function is a spearpoint. **User Lifeways**: Small bands using hunter/gatherer strategies. **User Ecology**: Occupied uplands environments during a boreal climate. **Comments**: The Charleston point is among the oldest form of a true corner-notched point. See Palmer, St Charles, and Kessell discussions. If this is true, then its antecedents remain elusive. On average, it is much larger than the Palmer type. The point is probably the same technology as the Pine Tree type (Cambron 1957), Lost Lake (DeJarnette, Kurjack, and Cambron 1962), or is at least a northern relative of it; all of which are probably a continuum of the Big Sandy type. The Kirk relationship also must be considered in using and/or placing the type in prehistory, but for the present, it is earlier than the Kirk notched type. The type represents the invention of a true side-notched form of hafting. **Comparative Types**: Pine Tree (Cambron (1956), Kirk (Coe 1964), Amos (Broyles 1971), Lost Lake (DeJarnette, Kujack, and Cambrom 1962), and Cypress Creek (Lewis and Kneberg 1960). **Reference**: Broyles, Bettye (1971) *The St Albans Site, Kanawha County, West Virginia*. West Virginia Geological Survey, Report of Archaeological Investigations, Morgantown, WV.

MPRV Chesapeake Points

Chesapeake – first identified by Hranicky and Painter (1988). Type is manufactured with bifacial antler percussion flaking with pressure flaking to finalize the point. Pressure flaking is used to resharpen a point. Native Americans are using field or streambed cobbles as their lithic sources. MPRV materials are rhyolite and quartzite, with slate being used in southern Virginia. It is a macrotypic point, and type validity is distinct. Expention length = 38 mm, study number = 19; general L/W*T ratio: 10.23. *Basic Description*: Knife; it is a diamond-shaped knife that was used on all four sides. Often one point-tip is broken. Type dates to the Archaic and is found in the lower middle Atlantic area. **Modality**: Its primary function is a knife. **Comments**: The Chesapeake point is a diamond-shaped knife. It was probably hand-held because its form has no suggestion for hafting. The type may be the same as the Rossville. It was named after tidewater specimens, not MPRV specimens. Its association with other cultural materials has not been established archaeologically. **User Lifeways**: Bands with general foraging strategies. **User Ecology**: Occupied coastal and piedmont environments during a subboreal climate. **Comparative Types**: Rossville (Ritchie 1961). **Reference**: Hranicky, Wm Jack and Floyd Painter (1988) *Projectile Point Types in Virginia and Neighboring Areas*. Special Publication Number 16, Archeological Society of Virginia.

MPRV Chuchatuck Points

Chuchatuck – named by Bottoms (1986). Materials are all local stones, namely quartzite and rhyolite. For Virginia, it is found in regions 3, 4, 5, 6, and 7. It is a macrotypic point, and type validity is distinct. Expention length = 38 mm, study number = 6; general L/W*T ratio: 8.91. *Basic Description*: Notched; it is a small-to-medium point with round stem corners and a concave base. Shoulders sometimes hang giving the impression of corner notching. Its primary function is a spearpoint. Type dates 9000 to 8000 BP and is found in the Middle Atlantic area. **Modality**: Its primary function is a knife. **Comments**: The Chuchatuck point is an early usage of rhyolite. It is part of a technological sequence between the Potomac River valley side-notched points to bifurcates. Type probably occurs in flint, but none were observed. While classified as a notched point, the type could be an ancestor to bifurcate technology. **User Lifeways**: Bands with general foraging strategies. **User Ecology**: Occupied all environments during a boreal climate. **Comparative Types**: Big Sandy (Kneberg 1956). **Reference**: Bottoms, Edward (1986) *The Chuckatuck Projectile Point: A Late Paleoindian Type in Eastern Virginia*. Chesopiean, Vol. 24, No. 2, pp. 17-20.

MPRV Clagett Points

Clagett – first identified by Stephenson, et al. (1963). Type is manufactured with bifacial antler percussion flaking with pressure flaking to finalize the point. Pressure flaking is used to resharpen a point. Native Americans are using field or streambed cobbles as their lithic sources. MPRV materials are quartz and quartzite. It is a microtypic point, and type validity is positive or site-specific. Expention length = 37 mm, study number = 27; general L/W*T ratio: 16.44. **_Basic Description_**: Notched (or stemmed); it is a long, narrow, thick point with a constricted stem that expands at the base. Base is slightly convex, concave, or straight. Type dates 2700 to 2300 BP and is found in Maryland and Virginia. **Modality**: Its primary function is a spearpoint. **Comments**: The Clagett point is crudely made which makes it difficult to identify. **User Lifeways**: General foraging. **User Ecology**: Occupied piedmont environments during a subboreal climate. **Comparative Types**: Bare Island (Ritchie 1961) and Monocracy (Kent 1970). **Reference**: Stephenson, R. L., L. L. Ferguson, and G. H. Ferguson (1963) *The Accokeek Creek Site: A Middle Atlantic Seaboard Culture Sequence*. Anthropological Papers No. 20, Museum of Anthropology, University of Michigan, Ann Arbor, MI.

Condoquinet – named by Kent (1970). False type; it is the same technology as the Koens-Crispin, Snook Kill, and Lehigh types and not used.

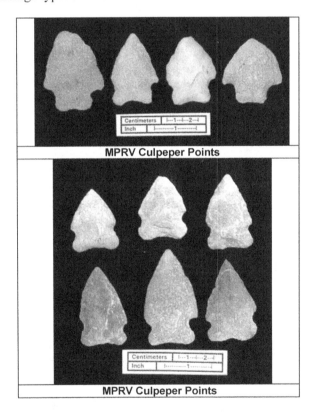

MPRV Culpeper Points

MPRV Culpeper Points

Culpeper first identified by Hranicky (in Hranicky and Painter 1988) and named after the county in Virginia. Type name spelling is changed here. Type is manufactured with bifacial antler percussion flaking with pressure flaking to finalize the point. Pressure flaking is used to resharpen a point. Native Americans are using field or streambed cobbles as their lithic sources. MPRV material is primarily white quartz with utilization of some local materials. It is a microtypic point, and type validity is conditional. Expention length = 42 mm, study number = 4; general L/W*T ratio: 10.13. Date is probably 7500 BP. **_Basic Description_**:

Bifurcate; it is a medium, thick point usually with a single barbed shoulder. Blade edges are excurvate. Lobes are sometimes ground. Type dates remain open (Middle Archaic or Woodland Period?), and it is found in the Middle Atlantic area. **Modality**: Its primary function is a knife. **Comments**: The Culpeper point technology may be part of a bifurcate continuum for the East (Hranicky and Painter 1988). The bifurcate technology ranges over time from the Nottoway River, MacCorkle, Culpeper, St Albans, LeCroy, Susquehanna Valley, Lake Erie, and Kanawha types; however, its extension remains to be established. Based on surface associations, this type may have a Woodland Period focus. **User Lifeways**: Small bands general foraging strategies. **User Ecology**: Occupied piedmont environments during a boreal climate. **Comparative Types**: MacCorkle (Broyles 1971), LeCroy (Kneberg 1956), St Albans (Broyles 1971), and Nottoway River (Painter 1970). **Reference**: Hranicky, Wm Jack (1991) *Projectile Point Typology and Nomenclature for Maryland, Virginia, West Virginia, and North/South Carolina*. ASV Special Publication Number 26.

Drybrook – first identified by Werner (1972). It is a fishtailed technology and is the same as the Orient type. It is not used.

Eva – first identified by Lewis and Kneberg (1947) and named after the site in Kentucky. Type was described initially as a Type I and II point. Specimens are found in the Delaware valley (Custer 1996) and Pennsylvania (Fogelman 1988); thus, this area distribution is assumed. All double base notching is the primary attribute of the type. If the type occurs in MPRV, it is rare; thus, it is not used.

Erb - name formalized by Fogleman (1988). Type was expected as a basally-notched point in the MPRV, but none were observed. Type is not used.

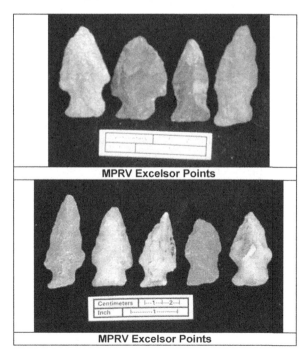

MPRV Excelsor Points

MPRV Excelsor Points

Excelsor – named by Brennan (1970). MPRV material is all local stones, namely quartzite and rhyolite. It is a marcotypic point, and type validity is distinct. Expention length = 40 mm, study number = 41; general L/W*T ratio: 14.00. *Basic Description*: Stemmed; it is a medium point with a straight or slightly concave base. One stem corner flares outward (toed). Type dates 5000 to 5500 BP and is found in the Middle Atlantic area. **Modality**: Its primary function is a spearpoint. **Comments**: The Excelsor is a common type in the MPRV; however, stem design may not have been intentional by the Native American knappers. Otherwise, type meets narrow-bladed point requirements for the Lake Archaic Period. **User Lifeways**: Bands with general foraging strategies. It dates 5000 BP. **User Ecology:** Occupied all environments during a subboreal climate. **Comparative Types**: Halifax (Coe 1964) and Lamoka (Ritchie 1961). **Reference**: Brennan, Louis A. (1970) *The Twombly Landing Site*. Bulletin, New York State Archaeological Association, No. 49.

MPRV Genesee Points
Note: Top center is not a Genesee point.

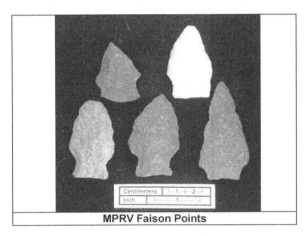

MPRV Faison Points

Faison – named by Painter (1991) after a farmer in southern Virginia. MPRV material is all local stones, namely quartzite and rhyolite. It is a macrotypic point, and type validity is distinct. Expention length = 44 mm, study number = 39; general L/W*T ratio: 14.66. *Basic Description*: Stemmed; it is a medium point with a straight or slightly concave base. Type date 5000 BP and is found in the Middle Atlantic area. **Modality**: Its primary function is a spearpoint. **Comments**: The Faison point may simply be retrofitting broken blades into service. The snapped-base point is common in the MPRV as well as the Southeast. **User Lifeways**: Band with general foraging strategies. **User Ecology:** Occupied all environments during a subboreal climate. **Comparative Types**: Elora (Cambron and Hulse 1968). **Reference**: Painter, Floyd (1991) *The Faison Projectile Point*. Chesopiean, Vol. 29, No. 1, pp. 22-25.

Fox Valley – first identified by Robert E. Ritzenthaler (1961). This type was found at the St Albans site; Broyles (1971) mislabeled it as a Kanawha type. It may be part of the technological continuum of Stanly, Kanawha, Fox Valley, Lake Erie types. Point may occur in the MPRV, but it is not used.

Genesee – as in Ritchie (1961). Type is manufactured with bifacial antler percussion flaking with pressure flaking to finalize the point. Pressure and percussion flaking are used to resharpen a point. Native Americans are using large field or streambed cobbles as their lithic sources. MPRV material is the gray Onondaga chert, but local rhyolite, quartz, and quartzite are used. It is a macrotypic point, and type validity is distinct. Expention length = 63 mm, study number = 52; general L/W*T ratio: 20.99. *Basic Description*: Stemmed; it is a large, narrow, triangularly-bladed point with a rectangular, broad stem. Point is thick. It has pronounced shoulders and a straight base. Cross section is biconvex. Some specimens have basal grinding. Type dates 4500 to 3500 BP and is found in the middle Atlantic area. **Modality**: Its primary function is a knife or perhaps spearpoint. **Comments**: The Genesee point is a Laurentian and Frontenac focus technology of the Northeast (Ritchie 1945). This technology is similar to the Kays type (Kneberg 1956), but most favors the Denton (Connaway 1957) and Kramer (Munson 1966) types. Technologically, this stem form is found all over the eastern U.S. and probably becomes an Adena subtype. After the Savannah River type, it is the most common medium-to-large point in the MPRV. Ritchie (1940 and 1945) referred to the type as stemmed and broad stemmed. However, it is maintained here as a square stemmed point. Type may have relationship with the Bare Island type and/or be an ancestral type for the smaller square-stemmed points in the Woodland Period. **User Lifeways**: Bands with general foraging strategies. **User Ecology**: Occupied piedmont and coastal environments during a subboreal climate. **Comparative Types**: Denton (Connaway 1957), Kramer (Munson 1966), and Kays (Kneberg 1956). **Reference**: Ritchie, William A. (1961) *A Typology and Nomenclature for New York Projectile Points*. Bulletin 384, New York State Museum and Science Service, Albany, NY.

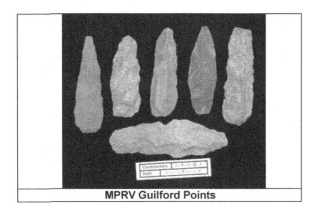

MPRV Guilford Points

📖 **Guilford** – first identified by Coe (1964) and is based on the Hardaway site excavation. It was named after a county in North Carolina. Type is percussion flaked. Native Americans are using field or streambed cobbles as their lithic sources. MPRV material is all local stones, namely quartzite and rhyolite. It is a marcotypic point, and type validity is distinct. Expention length = 68 mm, study number = 18; general L/W*T ratio: 34.23. The expended form averages 90 mm (based on Coe 1964). ***Basic Description***: Lanceolate; it is a long, narrow point with a round or indented base. Blade edges are usually straight. Cross section is usually biconvex, but squarish specimens occur. Type dates 5000 to 4500 BP and is found in Maryland, Virginia, Carolinas, and Georgia. **Modality**: Its primary function is a spearpoint. **Comments**: The Guilford point is generally a crudely made point, even though Coe (1964) comments well made. However, these crude forms may be perforators or punches and not even be part of the type. For the Carolinas, this type has a very high frequency, especially for points made from slate. The Guilford at the Doerschuck site in North Carolina contained chipped axes, giving name to the Guilford axe (Coe 1964). Well-made, thin versions are classified as Lerma points; however, context dates need verifying (Painter and Hranicky 1989). **User Lifeways**: Bands with general foraging strategies. **User Ecology:** Occupied all environments during a subboreal climate. **Comparative Types**: Lerma (as in Painter and Hranicky 1988). **Reference**: Coe, Joffre L. (1964) *The Formative Cultures of the Carolina Piedmont*. Transactions of the American Philosophical Society, New Series, Vol. 54, Part 5, Philadelphia, PA.

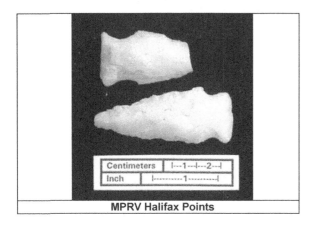

MPRV Halifax Points

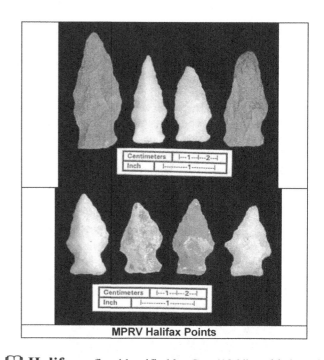

MPRV Halifax Points

📖 **Halifax** – first identified by Coe (1964) and is based on the Gaston site excavation. It was named after a county in North Carolina. It is a common point and the MPRV is the northern limit for the type; it is the classic narrow-blade point for the Late Archaic Period. Type is manufactured by the bipolar method with bifacial antler percussion flaking and pressure flaking to finalize the point. Pressure flaking is used to resharpen a point. Native Americans are using small field or streambed cobbles as their lithic sources. MPRV material is characteristically made from white quartz, but quartzite and rhyolite are used. It is a macrotypic point, and type validity is traditional. Expention length = 41 mm, study number = 63; general L/W*T ratio: 20.50. The expended form averages 44 mm (Coe 1964). ***Basic Description***: Side-notched; it is a small-to-large point with triangular blade. Notches are shallow but wide. Blade edges are straight with both incurvate and excurvate styles. Bases are usually straight or slightly concave. Base and notches are usually ground. Base is narrower than the blade. Type dates 4200 to 5500 BP and is found in the Middle Atlantic and Southeastern states. **Modality**: Its primary function is a spearpoint. **Comments**: The Halifax point may be the Lamoka point of the Southeast, or it is a southern version of the northern Excelsor type. They both have same similar time periods. These points were made as narrow points, as no wide-bladed specimens have been found. And, both types show the introduction of a new pointmaking technology – bipolar flaking. It represents a definite shift from shale and rhyolite usage in early points in North Carolina. The Halifax pointmakers may be the first Native Americans that exploited exclusively riverines, but always camped on high river terraces. This type is not generally found in the uplands. However, the Halifax point is not common in the MPRV. Also, white quartz is not the dominant material. **User Lifeways**: Large bands with general foraging strategies. **User Ecology**: Occupied piedmont and coastal environments during a subboreal climate. **Comparative Types**: Lamoka (Ritchie 1961). **Reference**: Coe, Joffre L. (1964) *The*

Formative Cultures of the Carolina Piedmont. Transactions of the American Philosophical Society, New Series, Vol. 54, Part 5, Philadelphia, PA.

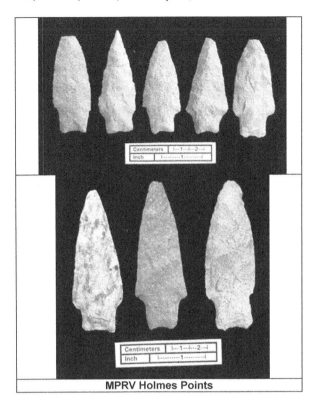

MPRV Holmes Points

MPRV Kanawha Points

📖 **Holmes** – as defined in Hranicky (1991). Point was named by Charles W. McNett of American University in Washington, DC. It was named to honor the first archaeologist working in the area. It is a classic narrow-bladed point. Type is manufactured with bifacial antler percussion flaking with pressure (or perhaps percussion) flaking to finalize the point. Pressure flaking is used to resharpen a point. Native Americans are using field or streambed cobbles as their lithic sources. MPRV materials are quartzite, rhyolite, and white quartz. It is a microtypic point, and type validity is distinct (upgraded from Hranicky 1994). Expention length = 68 mm, study number = 47; general L/W*T ratio: 2.91. *Basic Description*: Stemmed; it is a medium point with straight to slightly expanding or contracting stem, concave base, and narrow triangular blade. Type dates 3500 to 4100 BP and is found in Virginia and Maryland. **User Lifeways**: Semipermanent bands with general foraging strategies. **User Ecology**: Occupied piedmont environments during a subboreal climate. **Modality**: Its primary function is a spearpoint. **Comments**: The Holmes point is a variety of Savannah River technology or may be an independent invention of its stem technology. The Rappahannock River type may be its antecedent form. The type occupies a broadspear area but has a narrow blade technology. The type (not named) was published in Holmes (1897). **Comparative Types**: Savannah River (Coe 1964) and Bare Island (Ritchie 1961) **Reference**: Hranicky, Wm Jack (1991) *Projectile Point Typology and Nomenclature for Maryland, Virginia, West Virginia, and North/South Carolina*. ASV Special Publication Number 26.

Kanawha – first identified by Broyles (1971) and is based on the St Albans site excavation. It was named after the river in West Virginia. Type is manufactured with bifacial antler percussion flaking with pressure flaking to finalize the point. Pressure flaking is used to resharpen a point. Native Americans are using small field or streambed cobbles as their lithic sources. MPRV material is primarily flint, but local rhyolite and quartzite are used. It is a macrotypic point, and type validity is conditional. Expention length = 42 mm, study number = 3; general L/W*T ratio: 12.60. *Basic Description*: Bifurcate; it is a medium, narrow point with poorly defined lobes. Type dates 8800 to 5700 BP and is found in West Virginia, Virginia, Maryland, Kentucky, and North Carolina. **Modality**: Its primary function is a knife. **Comments**: The Kanawha point technology is part of a bifurcate continuum for the East (Hranicky and Painter 1988). The bifurcate technology ranges over time from the Nottoway River, MacCorkle, Culpeper, St Albans, LeCroy, Susquehanna Valley, Lake Erie, and Kanawha types. Coe (1964) suggests the type is ancestral to the Stanly. Each represents a technological stage in the continuum time period (7000 to 8250 BP). This type is difficult to discern from some Stanly points. It is generally made from high quality flints and probably only has an upland focus. It does occur in the MPRV. Broyles (1971) has trouble defining the type by her photographs. She includes a wide range of stem types, including the Fox Valley type (as in Ritzenthaler 1961). This may not be a valid type, or it certainly needs redefining. Because it is problematic, it was not used in Hranicky (1994), but it is used here to bring order to the type, if any exists. **User Lifeways**: Bands with general foraging strategies. **User Ecology**: Occupied all environments during a boreal climate. **Comparative Types**: Stanly (Coe 1964). **Reference**: Broyles, Bettye (1971) *The St Albans Site, Kanawha County, West Virginia*. West Virginia Geological Survey, Report of Archaeological Investigations, Morgantown, WV.

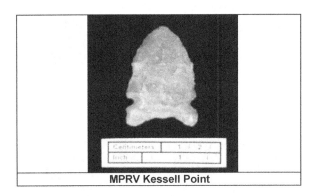

MPRV Kessell Point

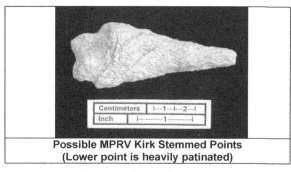

**Possible MPRV Kirk Stemmed Points
(Lower point is heavily patinated)**

Kessell – first identified by Broyles (1971) and is based on the St Albans site excavation. Type is manufactured with bifacial antler percussion flaking with pressure flaking to finalize the point. Pressure flaking is used to resharpen a point. Native Americans are using field or streambed cobbles as their lithic sources. MPRV materials are flint and quartz with local materials being utilized. It is a microtypic point, and type validity is positive. Expention length = 43 mm, study number = 1; general L/W*T ratio: 11.09. The expended form averages 35 mm (Broyles 1971). ***Basic Description***: Side-notched; it is a well-made point with a slightly to a deeply concave base. It has small U-shaped notches. Basal thinning is common. Type dates 9650 to 9800 BP and is found in West Virginia, Virginia, Maryland, and Kentucky. **Modality**: Its primary function is a spearpoint. **Comments**: The Kessell point is a technological relative of the St Charles type. Also, the type is the same as the Cache River type (Perino 1985). Generally, expended forms are recovered; thus, the original blade shapes are not truly known. If this St Charles relationship is false, the relationship between this type and the Big Sandy must occur. However, the Kessell type appears to be earlier (Brolyes 1971) than the Big Sandy type. The expended form averages 35 mm. **User Lifeways**: Small bands with hunter/gatherer strategies. **User Ecology**: Occupied uplands environments during a boreal climate. **Comparative Types**: Charleston (Broyles, Kirk and Palmer (Coe 1964), and Big Sandy (Kneberg 1956). **Reference**: Broyles, Bettye (1971) ***The St Albans Site, Kanawha County, West Virginia***. West Virginia Geological Survey, Report of Archaeological Investigations, Morgantown, WV.

MPRV Kirk Notched Points

Figure 6 - Hand in the Past. Troweling at the Kirk level at Cactus Hill (Sussex County), Virginia. Michael F, Johnson is Site Director.

MPRV Kirk Notched Points

📖 **Kirk** – first identified by Coe (1964) and is based on the Hardaway site excavation. This type occurs in two forms: notched and stemmed points. The former is the older and has numerous relatives, such as the Pine Tree, Lost Lake, Thebes, and Calf Creek types (as in Justice 1987). It is similar to the Palmer, but it has more robustness and occurs in larger sizes. Both Coe (1964) and Broyles (1971) maintain a Kirk Serrated type, which is only a special blade treatment within the type. This serration continues into the stemmed version, which justifies its being called a Kirk (Coe 1964). It is not a common point in the MPRV. Type is manufactured with bifacial antler percussion flaking with pressure flaking to finalize the point. Pressure flaking is used to resharpen a point. Native Americans are using quarry-sourced materials with some pickup stones. MPRV material primarily flint, but all other local materials are used. The Thunderbird site has stemmed Kirks made from high percentages of cryptocrystalline and rhyolite materials (Gardner 1989). It is a macrotypic point, and type validity is traditional. Expention (notched) length = 58 mm, study number = 4; general point (notched) ratio: 16.71. Expention (stemmed) length = 47 mm, study number = 10; general point (stemmed) ratio: 14.08. **Basic Description**: Corner-notched point; it is a robust point with a straight base. Stemmed: it is a robust point with a square stem and has a straight base. Base is often wider than the blade, but this is the result of resharpening. The blade was normally serrated. Base is rarely ground. Type dates for notched 7100 to 9850 BP and for stemmed 8900 to 7000 BP and is found in the eastern U.S. **Modality**: Its primary function is a spearpoint (notched) and knife (stemmed); however, specimens for archaeological contexts indicate the notched form is a technological continuum into the stemmed form. **Comments**: The Kirk point may be related to the Cypress Creek type as defined in Lewis and Kneberg (1961). The St Albans site contains both styles and offers an insight to the forms in the MPRV. The shape of the base and squareness of some corners may suggest that the Kirk notched is a continuation of the Big Sandy and Palmer technologies. This is based on specimens illustrated by Broyles (1971). Also, the Kirk type has stratigraphic position at the Cactus Hill site (Figure 6). For the present, the Kirk stemmed technology has no antecedents other than the Kirk technology itself (notched to stem forms). The Palmer-Kirk relationship needs more proof archaeologically. Kirk points have been found in excess of 150 mm; however, the expended form averages 50 mm. **User Lifeways**: Bands with hunter/gatherer strategies. **User Ecology**: Occupied all environments during a boreal climate. **Comparative Types**: Pine Tree (Cambron (1956), Amos and Charleston (Broyles 1971), Lost Lake (DeJarnette, Kujack, and Cambrom 1962), and Bolen (Neill 1963). **Reference**: Coe, Joffre L. (1964) *The Formative Cultures of the Carolina Piedmont*. Transactions of the American Philosophical Society, New Series, Vol. 54, Part 5, Philadelphia, PA.

MPRV Koens-Crispin Points

MPRV Koens-Crispin Points

MPRV Koens-Crispin Points

📖 **Koens-Crispin (Lehigh)** – basic shape was first identified by Hawks and Linton (1916). This is among the oldest named types in the East. It is a classic broadspear. This stem style occurs all over the East Coast and is known by numerous names, such as Koens, Newman, Ledbetter, Crispin, and Lehigh. Type is manufactured with bifacial antler percussion flaking with percussion (perhaps some pressure) flaking to finalize the point. Pressure and percussion flaking are used to resharpen a point. Native Americans are using large field or streambed cobbles as their lithic sources. The material is primarily quartzite for the Northeast but rhyolite is used extensively for the MPRV. It is a macrotypic point, and type validity is distinct. Expention length = 71.34 mm, study number = 12; general L/W*T ratio: 16.22. **Basic Description**: Broadspear; it is a large point with a wide, tapering stem. Base is straight. Blade is broad and has a trianguloid shape. Shoulders are broad and angular. Type dates 3200 to 3800 BP and is found along the upper Atlantic Coast. **Modality**: Its primary functions are a knife and spearpoint. **Comments**: The Koens-Crispin point has survived numerous northeast style namings. Its constricting stem offers a technology that starts around 4500 BP and continues into the Woodland. It has a distribution of the entire eastern U.S. The Lehigh type (Witthoff 1953) is the same technology and is not used here. Type has steatite bowl associations. **User Lifeways**: Large bands with general foraging strategies. **User Ecology**: Occupied piedmont and coastal environments during a subboreal climate. **Comparative Types**: Hale (1956), Long (Custer and Mellin 1986), Maples (Cambron 1962), Newnan and Hillsboro (Bullen 1968), Condoquinet (Kent 1970), Otarre (Keel 1972), Swatara (Kent 1970), and Westo (Bullen 1968). **Reference**: Hawkes, E. W. and Ralph Linton (1916) *A Pre-Lenape Site in New Jersey.* Anthropological Publications, University Museum, University of Pennsylvania, Vol. 6, No. 3, Philadelphia, PA.

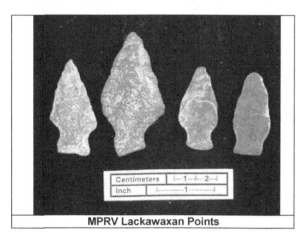

MPRV Lackawaxan Points

Lackawaxan – first identified by White (1967). It is used here for any slate point, even though this violates good typing principles (Hranicky 2001). It is always a crudely made point. Type is manufactured with bifacial antler percussion flaking with pressure flaking to finalize the point. Pressure flaking is used to resharpen a point. Native Americans are using quarry-sourced materials. MPRV material is shale or slate. It is a macrotypic point, and type validity is distinct. Expention length = 39 mm, study number = 4; general L/W*T ratio: 8.21. Type dates 2700 to 4600 BP. **Basic Description**: Stemmed; it is a crudely-made medium point with a variety of stem shapes. Type dates Late Archaic and is found in Pennsylvania, Maryland, and Virginia. **Modality**: Its primary function is a knife. **Comments**: The Lackawaxan point represents the usage of slate for points in the Northeast. The MPRV is probably the southern boundary for this type. Material is always Pennsylvania stone. **User Lifeways**: Bands with general foraging strategies. **User Ecology**: Occupied piedmont environments during a subboreal climate. **Comparative Types**: Lamoka (Ritchie 1961) and Milanville (1967). **Reference**: Leslie, Vernon (1967) *The Lackawaxan Stemmed Point.* Chesopiean, Vol. 5, No. 4, pp. 11-14.

Lake Erie - first identified by Winsch (1975). It may be part of the technological continuum of Stanly, Kanawha, Fox Valley, Lake Erie types. Type should have a MPRV occurrence, but none were observed; thus, type not used.

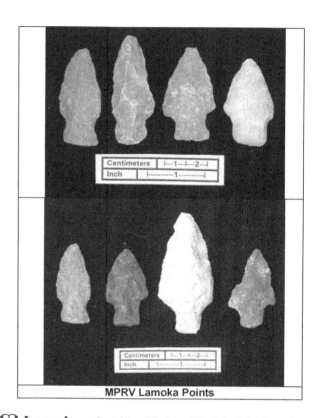

MPRV Lamoka Points

Lamoka – first identified by Ritchie (1961) and named after the site in New York. It is a common point in the MPRV and is a classic narrow-bladed point. Native Americans are using small field or streambed cobbles as their lithic sources. While northern specimens are usually made from flint, local materials are used including rhyolite, quartzite, and quartz. Type is manufactured with bipolar splitting and bifacial antler percussion flaking with pressure flaking to finalize the point. Pressure flaking is used to resharpen a point. It is a macrotypic point, and type validity is traditional. Expention length = 36 mm, study number = 66; general L/W*T ratio: 16.20. **Basic Description**: Stemmed/Notched; it is a small, narrow, thick point. Base is straight or convex. Blade is trianguloid. Shoulders are usually pointed. Unfinished forms are thick and when placed into service, points rarely exceed 50 mm. Type dates 2700 to 4700 BP and is found along the upper Atlantic area. **Modality**: Its primary function is a spearpoint. **Comments**: The Lamoka point may be the Halifax technology of the Northeast. Both types have approximately the same time period. The technology is split into stemmed and notched varieties which creates problems in using the type. This may need further verification, especially since the type continues into the Woodland (Ritchie 1961) and a similar technology, called the Durst (Justice 1987), is found in the Great Lakes area. Ritchie (1961) suggested a Lamoka A and B type because of differences in its cross sections of biconvex and rhomboidal shapes. This distinction is not made here; however, the stem and notched varieties are maintained. The stemmed form is considered here as the basic morphological style. **User Lifeways**: Bands with general foraging strategies. **User Ecology**: Occupied piedmont and coastal environments during a subboreal climate. **Comparative Types**: Dustin (Binford and Papworth 1963) and Mason Neck (Hranicky

1994). **Reference**: Ritchie, William A. (1961) *A Typology and Nomenclature for New York Projectile Points*. Bulletin 384, New York State Museum and Science Service, Albany, NY.

MPRV LeCroy Points

📖 **LeCroy** – first identified by Kneberg (1956), and MPRV typing is based on the St Albans site excavation. The type has one of the highest bifurcate frequencies of all Archaic Period expended points that are found throughout the lower Middle Atlantic area. But, for the MPRV, the type is relatively rare. This absence may be explained by the infrequency of rhyolite usage. Type is manufactured with bifacial antler percussion flaking with pressure flaking to finalize the point. Pressure flaking is used to resharpen a point. Native Americans are using field or streambed cobbles as their lithic sources, which may include quartz quarrying. MPRV material is characteristically made from white quartz, but other local materials are used. It is a macrotypic point, and type validity is traditional. Expention length = 30.11 mm, study number = 87; general L/W*T ratio: 10.43. **Basic Description**: Bifurcate; it is a narrow point, and often has a serrated blade. For nonexpended forms, blades are wide with parallel sides. Bilobes are pointed and sometimes ground on sides. Type dates 9400 to 7200 BP and is found all over the eastern U.S. **Modality**: Its primary function is a knife. **Comments**: The LeCroy point technology is part of a bifurcate continuum for the East (Hranicky and Painter 1988). Bifurcate technology probably originated in the Quad type technology of the Southeast. This technology ranges over time from the Nottoway River, MacCorkle, Culpeper. St Albans, LeCroy, Susquehanna Valley, Lake Erie, and Kanawha types (Hranicky and Painter 1988). Each represents a technological stage in the continuum time period (7200 to 9400 BP). This type has a wide distribution in the East and is generally found in the expended form. The St Albans site (Broyles 1971) produces the best point sample for the MPRV. The LeCroy frequency is light for both sides of the Potomac River; however, in St Mary's County, Maryland, there is a high frequency of occurrence. **User Lifeways**: Highly mobile bands with general foraging strategies. **User Ecology**: Occupied all environments during a boreal climate. **Comparative Types**: MacCorkle (Broyles 1971), St Albans (Broyles 1971), Culpeper (Hranicky and Painter 1988), Nottoway River (Painter 1970), and Lake Erie (Winsch 1975). **Reference**: Kneburg, Madeline (1956) *Some Important Projectile Point Types Found in the Tennessee Area*. Tennessee Archaeologist, Vol. XII, No. 1, pp. 17-28.

Ledbetter – first identified by Kneberg (1956). Type is related technologically to the Koens-Crispin and not used. See Koens-Crispin.

Lehigh – as in Witthoft (1953). It is combined with the Koens-Crispin type and not used.

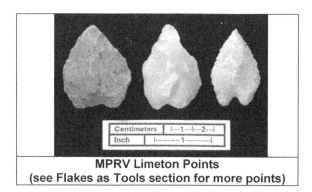

MPRV Limeton Points
(see Flakes as Tools section for more points)

Limeton – first identified by Wilkinson and Leslie (1967) and was named after a city in Virginia. It probably is a member of the bifurcate family. It is found in the Shenandoah River valley and occurs in the MPRV (Hranicky and Painter 1988). The MPRV distribution appears to be above the fall line. Usually, it is made from a flake (Hranicky 1991). No data (especially dates) as it needs more study. Specimens were found at the Thunderbird site in Warren Count. **Reference**: Wilkinson, Elizabeth and Vernon Leslie (1967) *The Limeton Point: A Shenandoah Valley Notched-Base Triangle.* Chesopiean, Vol. 5, No. 1.

Lobate – first identified by Michael Johnson and Larry Moore in the 1980s. The name is a reference to bifurcate technology and does not convey meaning in terms of a specific style or design. St Albans, LeCroy, McCorkle, Nottoway River are all lobate points, but each has a distinctive style in Native Americans' manufacture of them. False type and not used.

Long – Witthoft (1956) named the point after a site in Pennsylvania. Custer (2001) argues it is a regional variant of the Savannah River type. See Custer and Mellin (1986) for analysis and usage of the type. It is not used.

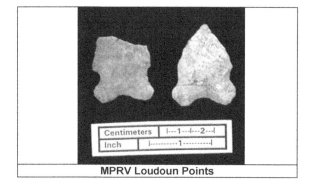

MPRV Loudoun Points

Loudoun – named in Hranicky (2002b) after the county where it was first observed. It has a wide, rectangular stem with a concave base. It is part of the continuum of the Big Sandy type. Specimens were observed but not recorded. Type is conditional with more study needed. Also, type may be the same as Broyles' (1971) Kessell type.

Lucketts – tentative types named after the area where the point was first observed. It is a medium-to-large point with pronounced corner notches. Point has one square-corner, and the other is a rounded-corner. Base is slightly-to-deeply concave. It appears to be a variation of the Big Sandy point. See Projectile Point Typology section for illustration.

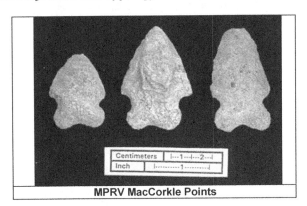

MPRV MacCorkle Points

 MacCorkle – first identified by Broyles (1971) and is based on the St Albans site excavation. Type is manufactured with bifacial antler percussion flaking with pressure flaking to finalize the point. Pressure flaking is used to resharpen a point. Native American lithic sources and procurement methods are unknown, but probably involve local sources. MPRV material is primarily flint, but local stones, such as quartzite and rhyolite, are used. It is a macrotypic point, and type validity is distinct. Expention length = 45 mm, study number = 3; general L/W*T ratio: 15.00. **Basic Description**: Bifurcate; it is a medium point with pronounced bilobes. Lobes are usually ground. Type dates 9200 to 8600 BP and is found in the upper Ohio, Kanawha, and Potomac River valleys. **Modality**: Its primary function is a knife. **Comments**: The MacCorkle point technology is part of a bifurcate continuum for the East (Hranicky and Painter 1988). It probably has a blade technology associated with it, and the point itself may be made off a blade (Hranicky 1993). The bifurcate technology ranges over time from the Nottoway River, MacCorkle, Culpeper, St Albans, LeCroy, Susquehanna Valley, Lake Erie, and Kanawha types (Hranicky and Painter 1988). Each represents a technological stage in the continuum time period (8800 to 8900 BP). This point may be the originating bifurcate technology for all upland provenances. It is a similar type to the Nottoway type (Painter 1970), but they do not occupy the same time and space. **User Lifeways**: Large bands with general foraging strategies. **User Ecology**: Occupied uplands environments during a boreal climate. **Comparative Types**: Culpeper (Hranicky and Painter 1988), LeCroy (Kneberg 1956), St Albans (Broyles 1971), Nottoway River (Painter 1970), and Rice (Bray 1956). **Reference**: Broyles, Bettye (1971) *The St Albans Site, Kanawha County, West Virginia*. West Virginia Geological Survey, Report of Archaeological Investigations, Morgantown, WV.

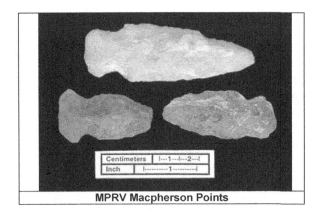

MPRV Macpherson Points

Macpherson – first identified by Kinsey (1972). Type is manufactured with bifacial antler percussion flaking with pressure flaking to finalize the point. Pressure flaking may have been used to resharpen a point. Most specimens that are recovered are expended points (Hranicky 1991). Native Americans are using field or streambed cobbles as their lithic sources. MPRV materials are quartzite and rhyolite. It is a macrotypic point, and type validity is distinct. Expention length = 74 mm, study number = 16; general L/W*T ratio: 26.64. **Basic Description**: Notched; it is a long, narrow point with wide side notches and a rounded base. Type dates 4500 to 3700 BP and is found from New York to Virginia. **Modality**: Its primary function is a spearpoint. **Comments**: The Macpherson point's crudeness easily places it in the Late Archaic Period. As a suggestion, it may be ancestral to the Snyders point and may have had a wider blade. **User Lifeways**: Bands with general foraging strategies. **User Ecology**: Occupied piedmont environments during a subboreal climate. **Comparative Types**: Durst (Wittry 1959). **Reference**: Kinsey, W. Fred (1972) *Archaeology in the Upper Delaware Valley.* Pennsylvania Historical and Museum Commission, No. 2, Harrisburg, PA.

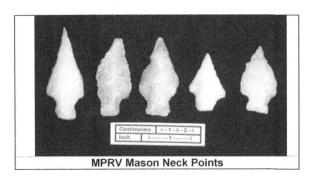

MPRV Mason Neck Points

Mason Neck – first identified by Hranicky (1991). It was named after the area in northern Virginia. The type is probably related to, if not the same, technology as the Lamoka type. Its main attribute is the twist or beveled blade. Type is manufactured with bifacial antler percussion flaking with pressure flaking to finalize the point. Pressure flaking is used to resharpen a point. Native Americans are using small field or streambed cobbles as their lithic sources for bipolar flaking. MPRV point material is commonly made from white quartz. It is a macrotypic point, and type validity is conditional. Expention length = 36 mm, study number = 11; general L/W*T ratio: 16.94. ***Basic Description***: Stemmed; it is a medium point with a twist blade and small squarish stem. It is probably part of the Lamoka Phase in the Middle Atlantic. Type dates 5500 to 4200 BP and is found in Virginia and Maryland. **Modality**: Its primary function is a spearpoint. **Comments**: The Mason Neck point is common in the MPRV. It has a smaller stem than the Lamoka points found here. **User Lifeways**: Small bands with general foraging strategies. **User Ecology**: Occupied piedmont and coastal environments during a subboreal climate. **Comparative Types**: Lamoka (Ritchie 1961). **Reference**: Hranicky, Wm Jack (1991) *Projectile Point Typology and Nomenclature for Maryland, Virginia, West Virginia, and North/South Carolina*. ASV Special Publication Number 26.

\#

McWhinney – named by Heilman for the McWhinney site in Preble County, Ohio and defined in Vickery (1972). It is a thick-stemmed point. The stem is squarish or has a slightly constricted-neck. Base is snapped or rounded (cortex remaining). Type dates 4000 to 1000 BP and is found in the Ohio River valley. It appears to be a valid type and is made primarily from black flint. The type is similar to or the same as the Iddens (Chapman 1981) or Holston (Hranicky and Painter 1989). It is not used.

> Regardless of who types a point, it is always subject to a personal opinion; not everyone will agree. The process is referred to as the scientific observation in archaeology.

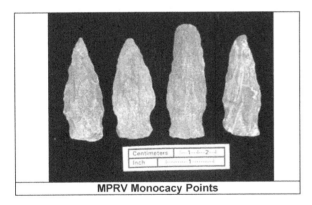

MPRV Monocacy Points

Monocacy – first identified by Kent (1970). MPRV material is rhyolite. It was made by percussion (with minor pressure) flaking, which gives it a crude appearance. It is a microtypic point, and type validity is conditional. Its primary function is a knife. Expention length = 52 mm, study number = 19; general L/W*T ratio: 20.80. ***Basic Description***: Stemmed; it is a medium point with a squarish stem. Stem sides are slightly indented. Base is slightly convex. Type dates to the Late Archaic Period and is only found in the MPRV. **Modality**: Its primary function is a spearpoint. **Comments**: The Monocacy point as originally defined probably does not exist; however, because of the high usage of rhyolite in this area, an attempt was made to define a useable type. **User Lifeways**: Bands with general foraging strategies. Type borders on being a notched point. **User Ecology**: Occupied piedmont environments during a subatlantic climate. **Comparative Types**: Bare Island (Ritchie 1961). **Reference**: Kent, Barry C. (1970) *Diffusion Spheres and Band Territory Among the Archaic Period Cultures of the Northern Piedmont*. Ph.D. dissertation, University Microfilms, Ann Arbor, MI.

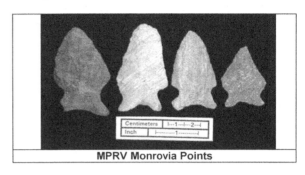

MPRV Monrovia Points

Monrovia – first identified by Hranicky (1991) and named after the area in Maryland where it was first observed. Type is manufactured with bifacial antler percussion flaking with pressure flaking to finalize the point. Pressure flaking is used to resharpen a point. Native Americans are using field or streambed cobbles as their lithic sources. MPRV material is primarily rhyolite with other local materials being used occasionally. It is a microtypic point, and type validity is conditional. Expention length = 42 mm, study number = 11; general L/W*T ratio: 11.76. ***Basic Description***: Side-notched; it is a small point with shoulders sometimes barbed. Notches create horned stem corners. Base is deeply concave. Type dates 4000 to 2500 BP and is only found in the MPRV. **Modality**: Its primary function is unknown. **Comments**: The Monrovia point is not common and appears to be made exclusively from rhyolite. Type may be related technologically to the Susquehanna or Orient types. It is mixed in Ritchie (1961) and illustrated as Brewerton points. **User Lifeways**: Small bands with general foraging strategies. **User Ecology**: Occupied piedmont environments during a subatlantic climate. **Comparative Types**: Paisano (Kelly (1963), Orient (Ritchie 1961), and Brewerton (Ritchie 1961). **Reference**: Hranicky, Wm Jack (1991) *Projectile Point Typology and Nomenclature for Maryland, Virginia, West Virginia, and North/South Carolina*. ASV Special Publication Number 26.

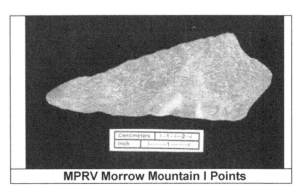

MPRV Morrow Mountain I Points

MPRV Morrow Mountain I Points

Above: Morrow Mountain II point is from Charles County, Maryland
MPRV Morrow Mountain I Points

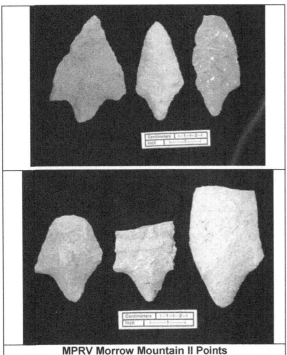

MPRV Morrow Mountain II Points

📖 **Morrow Mountain** – first identified by Coe (1964) and is based on the Hardaway site excavation. It was named after the rhyolite mountain in North Carolina. The mountain was the Native Americans' source for rhyolite for most of prehistory. It is classified as a broadspear. Type was described initially as a Type I and II point. Based on preserved specimens, some of these points exceed 250 mm when they were initially made (Hranicky 1994). Type is manufactured with bifacial antler percussion flaking with percussion (and perhaps pressure) flaking to finalize the point. Pressure flaking is used to resharpen a point. Native Americans are using large field or streambed cobbles as their lithic sources. MPRV material is classically quartzite, but rhyolite is used. It is a macrotypic point, and type validity is traditional. Expention length (I) = 64 mm, length (II) = 70 mm, study number = 36; general L/W*T ratio: 13.39 (I) and (II) 23.33. ***Basic Description***: Broadspear (Type I); it is a wide-bladed point with a short tapering stem. Base is round. Type dates (MM I) 6000 to 7300 BP and (MM II) 5000 to 5500 BP and is found all over the eastern U.S. Stemmed (Type II); it is a narrow-bladed point with a short tapering stem. Base is pointed. Type dates 4500 to 3000 BC and is found all over the eastern U.S. **Modality**: Its primary functions are a knife and spearpoint. **Comments**: The Morrow Mountain I point probably initiates the large knife in the Middle Atlantic area. Of course, this is known as the Broadspear Tradition. The technology represents an influx of new pointmaking traditions in the lower Middle Atlantic area; as suggested here, the Eva technology is the source for the Morrow Mountain I point. Type II probably continues down to the Early Woodland. It could be the Poplar Island, although this style does seem to have a strong northeastern focus. If the type occurs in the Northeast, it may date to 8200 BP. **User Lifeways**: Large bands with general foraging strategies. **User Ecology**: Occupied all environments during an Atlantic climate. **Comparative Types**: For Morrow Mountain I: Almagre (Suhm, Krieger, and Jelks 1954), Garden I (Cleland and Peske 1968), For Morrow Mountain II: Poplar Island (Ritchie 1961), Gary (Newell and Kriger 1949), and Garden II (Cleland and Peske 1968). **Reference**: Coe, Joffre L. (1964) ***The Formative Cultures of the Carolina Piedmont***. Transactions of the American Philosophical Society, New Series, Vol. 54, Part 5, Philadelphia, PA.

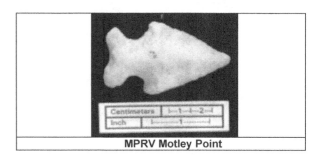

MPRV Motley Point

Motley - as first identified by Ford, Philips, and Haag (1955). This technology is considered the same as the Normanskill type. It only occurs in southwestern Virginia. Type is illustrated but not used.

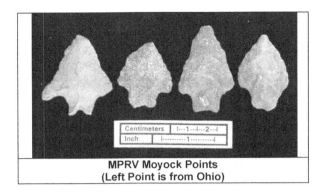

MPRV Moyock Points
(Left Point is from Ohio)

Moyock – named by Painter and Hranicky (1989) after the city in North Carolina. MPRV materials are chert, flint, quartzite, and quartz. It is a macrotypic point, and type validity is distinct. Expention length = 39 mm, study number = 5; general L/W*T ratio: 10.92. **_Basic Description_**: Stemmed; it is a small point with a small square stem. Base is indented or straight. Shoulders are angular. Point is thick for its size. Type possibly dates 5500 to 4500 BP and is found in the lower Middle Atlantic states. **Modality**: Its primary function is a spearpoint. **Comments**: The Moyock point is a distinctive point and has a low MPRV frequency. It has a high frequency in southeast Virginia and northeast North Carolina. Its size distinguishes it from the Stanly type. Surface finds suggest that it may be associated with pottery. **User Lifeways**: Mobile bands with general foraging strategies. **User Ecology**: Occupied piedmont environments during a subboreal climate. **Comparative Types**: None. **Reference**: Painter, Floyd and Wm Jack Hranicky (1989) *The Moyock Point*. Chesopiean, Vol. 27, No. 2, pp. 24-26.

Neville – named by Dincauze (1976). It may be the same as the Buggs Island type (Hranicky 1994). Distribution remains to be established. Type is not used. See Zekiah Swamp.

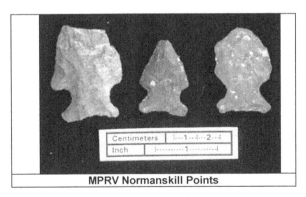

MPRV Normanskill Points

Normanskill – as described in Ritchie (1961). It was named after the area in New York. Type is manufactured with bifacial antler percussion flaking with pressure flaking to finalize the point. Pressure flaking is used to resharpen a point. Native Americans are using field or streambed cobbles as their lithic sources. MPRV materials are chert, flint, quartzite, and rhyolite. It is a macrotypic point, and type validity is distinct. Expention length = 49 mm, study number = 3; general L/W*T ratio: 22.27. **_Basic Description_**: Side-notched; it is a slender, thick prominent wide side-notched point with a straight base. Cross section is biconvex. It rarely has basal grinding. Type dates 2700 to 3300 BP and is found in the Northeast and Middle Atlantic states. **Modality**: Its primary function is a spearpoint. **Comments**: The Normanskill point is a distinctive point and has a low-to-moderate MPRV frequency. Ritchie (1961) suggests that it is a transition between the Lamoka and Brewerton technologies. This is false; the technology origin has not been demonstrated. It is technologically related to the Motley types (as in Justice 1987). Basic type occurs in chert, which was not observed in the MPRV. **User Lifeways**: Mobile bands with general foraging strategies. **User Ecology**: Occupied piedmont environments during a subatlantic climate. **Comparative Types**: Motley (Ford, Phillips, and Haag 1955). **Reference**: Ritchie, William A. (1961) *A Typology and Nomenclature for New York Projectile Points*. Bulletin 384, New York State Museum and Science Service, Albany, NY.

MPRV Nottoway Point
Note: Point is made from Carolina slate.

Nottoway River – first identified by Painter (1970). It does occur this far north from its southern Virginia and North Carolina source. This type is generally made from slate. It is a similar type to the MacCorkle type, but they do not occupy the same time and space. The type is considered here as the beginning technology for the Bifurcate continuum (Hranicky and Painter 1988) and dates to 8500 BP. This technology is probably related to the Quad point technology (Hranicky and Painter 1988). Type is illustrated but not used.

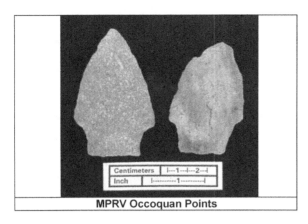

MPRV Occoquan Points

Occoquan – named in Hranicky (2002b) after the river in Virginia where it was first observed. It has a wide, tapering stem with a straight base. It is made from rhyolite and quartzite. It is a conditional type and needs more study. Type may be a variation of the Genesee type of the Northeast. Type is illustrated but not used.

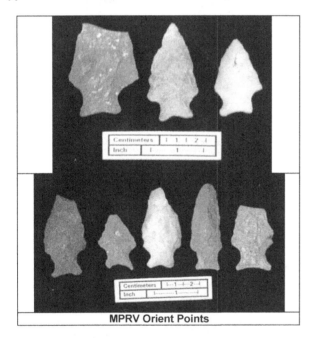

MPRV Orient Points

📖 **Orient** – first identified by Ritchie (1961). It is classified as a narrow-bladed point. Type is manufactured with bifacial antler percussion flaking with pressure flaking to finalize the point. Pressure flaking is used to resharpen a point. Native Americans are using quarry-sourced materials with some pickup stones. MPRV material is usually rhyolite with some occurrence of quartzite. It is a macrotypic point, and type validity is traditional. Expention length = 43 mm, study number = 14; general L/W*T ratio: 15.63. ***Basic Description***: Fishtail; it is a slender, gracefully formed medium point with a narrow waist and flaring stem and deep concave base. Stem is frequently ground. Shoulders are sloping and merge into the stem giving it the fishtail appearance. Type dates 1750 to 4000 BP and is found in the middle Atlantic area. **Modality**: Its primary function is a knife and spearpoint. **Comments**: The Orient point is related to the Susquehanna technology. It probably becomes the Dry Brook type (as in Ritchie 1961). **User Lifeways**: Semipermanent bands with general foraging strategies. **User Ecology**: Occupied piedmont and some coastal environments during a subatlantic climate. **Comparative Types**: Susquehanna (Witthoff 1953) **Reference**: Ritchie, William A. (1961) *A Typology and Nomenclature for New York Projectile Points*. Bulletin 384, New York State Museum and Science Service, Albany, NY.

MPRV Otter Creek Points

Otter Creek – as described in Ritchie (1961). It was named after the creek in New York. Type is manufactured with bifacial antler percussion flaking with pressure flaking to finalize the point. Pressure flaking is used to resharpen a point. Native Americans are using field or streambed cobbles as their lithic sources. MPRV material is primarily flint, but local materials are used. It is a macrotypic point, and type validity is distinct. Expention length = 35 mm, study number = 5; general L/W*T ratio: 12.89. ***Basic Description***: Side-notched; it is a large point with square tangs and a concave base. Cross section is biconvex. Type dates 2500 to 6500 BP and is found in the eastern U.S. **Modality**: Its primary functions are a knife and spearpoint. **Comments**: The Otter Creek point is probably related to early Laurentian phases in New York. Ritchie (1961) suggests a deep concave base, but these are difficult to find. As such, the technological form suggests a carryover from the Big Sandy/Kirk technology continuum; this remains to be proven. However, this side notch has a wide-spread distribution for both time and space. **User Lifeways**: Bands with general foraging strategies. **User Ecology**: Occupied all environments during an Atlantic climate. **Comparative Types**: Cold Springs (Butler 1961), Godar (Perino 1963), Newton Falls (Sofsky 1965), Osceola (Rizenthaler 1946), Raddatz (Wittry 1959), Robinson (Cole and Deuel 1937), Logan Creek (Kivet 1962), and Raccoon (Mayer-Oaks 1955). **Reference**: Ritchie, William A. (1961) *A Typology and Nomenclature for New York Projectile Points*. Bulletin 384, New York State Museum and Science Service, Albany, NY.

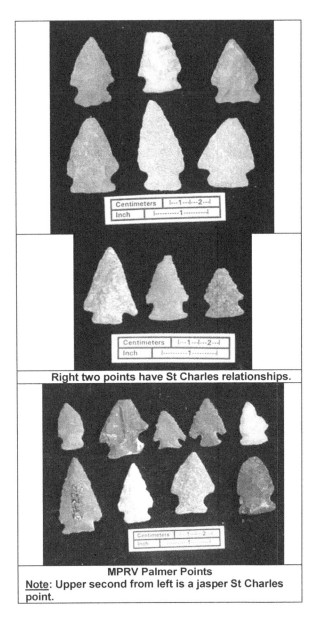

Right two points have St Charles relationships.

MPRV Palmer Points
Note: Upper second from left is a jasper St Charles point.

MPRV Patuxent Points

MPRV Patuxent Points

Palmer type is located between Hardaway and Kirk points. **User Lifeways**: Large bands with hunter/gatherer strategies. **User Ecology**: Occupied all environments during a boreal climate. **Comparative Types**: Kirk (Coe 1964), St Charles (Scully 1951), and Charleston (Broyles 1971). **Reference**: Coe, Joffre L. (1964) *The Formative Cultures of the Carolina Piedmont*. Transactions of the American Philosophical Society, New Series, Vol. 54, Part 5, Philadelphia, PA.

 Palmer – first identified by Coe (1964) and is based on the Hardaway site excavation. Type is manufactured with bifacial antler percussion flaking with pressure flaking to finalize the point. Pressure flaking is used to resharpen a point. Native Americans are using quarry-sourced materials with some pickup stones. MPRV material is usually fine-grain flints or cherts, but rhyolite, quartz, and quartzite do occur. It is a macrotypic point, and type validity is traditional. Expention length = 40 mm, study number = 37; general L/W*T ratio: 12.00. *Basic Description*: Corner-notched; it is a small, well-made, corner-notched point. Shoulders are barbed. Base is straight or slightly convex, which is usually ground. Type dates 9500 to 9000 BP and is found all over the eastern U.S. **Modality**: Its primary function is a spearpoint. **Comments**: Many archaeologists argued that the Palmer point evolved from the Hardaway type. This is especially noted for North Carolina archaeologists and their Hardapalmer type (Daniel 1998). It is related to the St Charles technology, which accounts for its wide-spread distribution and convex base. At the Hardaway site, the

 Patuxent – first identified by Kent (1970) and named after the river in Maryland. Type is manufactured with bifacial antler percussion flaking with pressure flaking to finalize the point. Pressure flaking is used to resharpen a point. Native Americans are using large field or streambed cobbles as their lithic sources. MPRV materials are usually quartzite or rhyolite. It is a macrotypic point, and type validity is conditional. Expention length = 60 mm, study number = 66; general L/W*T ratio: 18.18. *Basic Description*: Stemmed; it is a medium-to-large point with a flaring stem. Base is straight. Type dates 3700 to 3400 BP and is found in the middle Potomac River valley. **Modality**: Its primary functions are a knife and spearpoint. **Comments**: The

Patuxent point is a continuation of the Savannah River technology and probably is the terminal form of this technology. The flaring stem may be a preparatory technology for the Susquehanna pointmakers in the region. **User Lifeways**: Semipermanent bands with general foraging strategies. **User Ecology**: Occupied piedmont environments during a subboreal climate. **Comparative Types**: Savannah River (Coe 1964). **Reference**: Kent, Barry C. (1970) *Diffusion Spheres and Band Territory Among the Archaic Period Cultures of the Northern Piedmont*. Ph.D. dissertation, University Microfilms, Ann Arbor, MI.

MPRV Pequea Points

Pequea – first identified by Kent (1970). Type is initialized by percussion flaking and finalized by pressure flaking. MPRV material is principally quartz. It is a microtypic point, and type validity is conditional. Expention length = 48 mm, study number = 14; general L/W*T ratio: 22.58. *Basic Description*: Stemmed; it is a long narrow point with a small squarish base. Type has not been dated but is considered here as Late Archaic. It is only found from the Potomac River to southern Pennsylvania. It a crudely made point. **Modality**: Its primary function is a spearpoint. **Comments**: The Pequea point does seem to be a true projectile point as numerous specimens have impact fractures. **User Lifeways**: Large bands with general foraging strategies. **User Ecology**: Occupied piedmont and coastal environments during a subboreal climate. **Comparative Types**: Lamoka (Ritchie 1961) and Mason Neck (Hranicky 1991). **Reference**: Kent, Barry C. (1970) *Diffusion Spheres and Band Territory Among the Archaic Period Cultures of the Northern Piedmont*. Ph.D. dissertation, University Microfilms, Ann Arbor, MI.

None were observed in the study collections.

MPRV Perkiomen Points

Perkiomen – first identified by Witthoft (1953). Type is manufactured with bifacial antler percussion flaking with pressure flaking to finalize the point. Probably, the Native Americans are using quarry-sourced materials with some pickup stones. MPRV material is usually jasper, but rhyolite is used. It is a macrotypic point, and type validity is traditional. Expention length = N/A mm, study number = 0; general L/W*T ratio: N/A. Basic Description: Broadspear; it is a medium, asymmetrical-bladed point with a small stem. Stem corners are rounded, and base is straight or slightly convex. Blade is always wide. Type dates 3700 to 3500 BP and is found in the upper middle Atlantic area. Modality: Its primary function is a knife. Comments: The Perkiomen point is a continuation of the Susquehanna technology, with a material change from rhyolite to jasper. A version of this technology is the Dismal Swamp type in Virginia (Painter 1963) in lower tidewater Virginia. This typemarker always used colorful materials. The expended form is always greater than 50 mm. User Lifeways: Large bands with general foraging strategies. User Ecology: Occupied piedmont and coastal environments during a subatlantic climate. Comparative Types: Susquehanna (Witthoft 1953) and Dismal Swamp (Painter 1963). Reference: Witthoft, John (1953) Broad Spearpoints and the Transition Period Cultures in Pennsylvania. Pennsylvania Archaeologist, Vol. XXIII, No. 1, pp. 4-31.

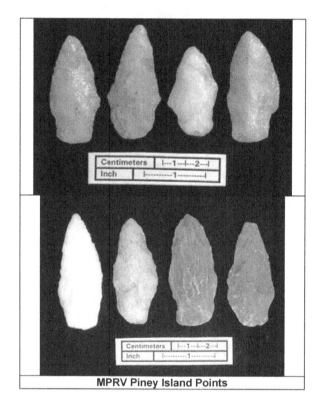

MPRV Piney Island Points

Piney Island – first identified by Kent (1970). MPRV material is quartz, quartzite, and rhyolite. It is a microtypic point, and type validity is distinct. MPRV material is primarily rhyolite. Expention length = 41 mm, study number = 31; general L/W*T ratio: 22.77. *Basic Description*: Stemmed; it is a crudely-made medium point with a squarish stem and convex base. The suggested date is 4200 to 3800 BP. **Modality**: Its primary function is a knife. **Comments**: The Piney Island point is similar to the Bare Island point and is related technologically. It has a high frequency of occurrence in the MPRV area. Custer (1996) suggests the Bare Island type dates to the Middle Archaic Period, but it does not fit the technology that was practiced at that time period. However, the type has origins in the Northeast and represents an early-narrow spear point. **User Lifeways**: Bands with general foraging strategies. **User Ecology**: Occupied piedmont and coastal environments during a subboreal climate. **Comparative Types**: Bare Island (Ritchie 1961), Catoctin (Hranicky and Painter 1988) and Calvert (Stephenson, et al. 1963). **Reference**: Kent, Barry C. (1970) *Diffusion Spheres and Band Territory Among the Archaic Period Cultures of the Northern Piedmont*. Ph.D. dissertation, University Microfilms, Ann Arbor, MI.

MPRV Rappahannock River Points

MPRV Poplar Island Points

Poplar Island – as described in Ritchie (1961) and Kinsey (1959). Type is manufactured with bifacial antler percussion flaking with pressure flaking to finalize the point. Pressure flaking is used to resharpen a point. Native Americans are using field or streambed cobbles as their lithic sources. MPRV materials are rhyolite and quartzite with occasional occurrences of quartz and flint. It is a macrotypic point, and type validity is traditional. Expention length = 74 mm, study number = 23; general L/W*T ratio: 24.66. **Basic Description**: Stemmed; it is a medium-to-large, finely flaked point which has rounded shoulders, a slender-to-wide isosceles blade, constricting stem, and rounded base. Tip is always on the medial axis. Type dates 2500 to 4000 BP and is found in the Middle Atlantic area. **Modality**: Its primary function is a knife. **Comments**: The Poplar Island point is an interesting in-between technology of broadspear and narrow-bladed points. The constricting stem resembles Rossville and Morrow Mountain II types. It has an occasional association with steatite bowls. The MPRV may be the southern boundary for the type, unless the Ebenezer point (Smith and Hodges 1968) is the same technology. **User Lifeways**: Bands with general foraging strategies. **User Ecology**: Occupied piedmont and some uplands environments during a subboreal climate. **Comparative Types**: Ebenezer (Smith and Hodges 1968). **Reference**: Ritchie, William A. (1961) *A Typology and Nomenclature for New York Projectile Points*. Bulletin 384, New York State Museum and Science Service, Albany, NY.

Rappahannock River – first identified by Hranicky (1991) and was named after the river in Virginia. Type is manufactured with bifacial antler percussion flaking with pressure flaking to finalize the point. Pressure flaking is used to resharpen a point. Native Americans are using field or streambed cobbles as their lithic sources. MPRV materials are usually quartzite and quartz. It is a microtypic point, and type validity is conditional. Expention length = 40 mm, study number = 11; general L/W*T ratio: 16.00. **Basic Description**: Stemmed; it is a medium point with beveled, triangular blade. Stems are straight-sided or very slightly constricting with rounded corners and very shallow basal notches. It has a biconvex cross section. Type dates 4500 to 3500 BP and is generally found in Virginia but includes southern Maryland. **Modality**: Its primary function is a spearpoint. **Comments**: The Rappahannock River point may be related to bifurcate technology, but needs further refining. The type has not been identified in an archaeological site context. **User Lifeways**: Bands with general foraging strategies. **User Ecology**: Occupied piedmont environments during a subboreal climate. **Comparative Types**: Southampton (Hranicky and Painter 1988). **Reference**: Hranicky, Wm Jack (1991) *Projectile Point Typology and Nomenclature for Maryland, Virginia, West Virginia, and North/South Carolina*. ASV Special Publication Number 26.

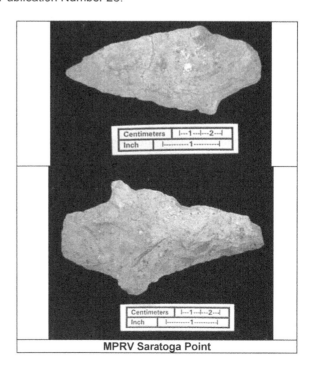

MPRV Saratoga Point

Saratoga – is based on Winters (1963). Type is a slightly tapering, rounded base point that occurs in the MPRV area. The type originates in the Ohio and Illinois valleys, and as such, these illustrated specimens may be local abnormalities. The local varieties appear to be made from rhyolite. It is considered a broad-bladed point (Justice 1988). Like the Genesee type, it is basically a large square-stemmed point; there may be a technological relationship as the type dates overlap. However, few samples were observed; thus, the type is illustrated but not used.

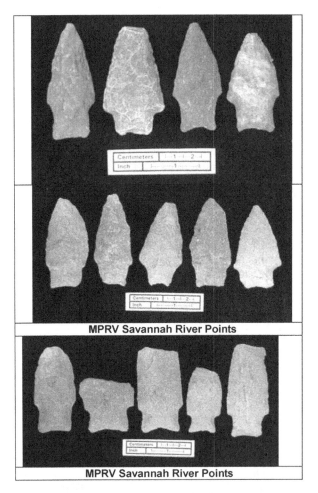

MPRV Savannah River Points

MPRV Savannah River Points

📖 **Savannah River** – first identified by Claflin (1931) and as in Coe (1964). Numerous attempts have been attempted to divide the type into narrow and wide stem varieties. Type is made by percussion flaking. Based on preserved specimens, some of these points exceed 250 mm when they were initially made (Hranicky 1994). Even normally, most point life cycles started with extremely large bifaces, which suggest its primary function is a knife. Its time period lies on the introduction of steatite bowls, which is demonstrated in numerous blade shapes (Hranicky 1990 and 1994). Type is manufactured with bifacial antler percussion flaking. Pressure and percussion (chipping) flaking are used to resharpen a point. Native Americans are using large field or streambed cobbles as their lithic sources. MPRV material is usually quartzite, but rhyolite and quartz also occur. It is a macrotypic point, and type validity is traditional. Expention length = 83 mm, study number = 150+; general L/W*T ratio: 29.45. The expended form averages 50 mm (Coe 1964) **_Basic Description_**: Stemmed; it is a medium-to-large, thick point with a square stem and concave base. Shoulders are sharp but rounded versions occur. Stem is slightly constricted and usually has pointed corners. Type dates 4900 to 2700 BP. **Modality**: Its primary functions are a knife (wide blade) and spearpoint (narrow blade) and late as a multifunctional tool. **Comments**: The Savannah River point is the most common point in the MPRV. The narrow stem form has the highest frequency, and the wide stem usually has the heaviest resharpening. The antecedent for this technology is the Stanly point (Coe 1964). The Patuxent type may be the MPRV termination for this technology. It represents longer occupation of sites and suggests river basin territories. Straight-based forms occur, which makes these difficult to identify in surface materials. These pointmakers made some of the largest bifaces in the U.S.; the large ones are primarily found in the East as they do not occur in western states. **User Lifeways**: Large bands with general foraging basically occupying riverines. **User Ecology**: Occupied all environments during a subboreal climate. **Comparative Types**: Benton and Kays (Kneberg 1956), Arrendondo (Bullen 1968), and Hamilton (Bullen 1975). **Reference**: Chaflin, William H. (1931) *The Stallings Island Mound, Columbia County, Georgia*. Papers of the Peabody Museum of American Archaeology and Ethnology, Vol. 14, No. 1, Cambridge, MA.

Schuylkill – first identified by Kent (1970). It is the same technology as the Morrow Mountain II or Poplar Island types. It is a false type and not used.

MPRV Snook Kill Points

📖 **Snook Kill** – as described in Ritchie (1961). Type is manufactured with bifacial antler percussion flaking with pressure flaking to finalize the point. Type is manufactured with bifacial antler percussion flaking with pressure flaking to finalize the point. Pressure flaking is used to resharpen a point. Native Americans are using field or streambed cobbles as their lithic sources. MPRV material is primarily quartzite, but specimens occur in rhyolite. The northeast specimens are usually made from flint. It is a macrotypic point, and type validity is traditional. Expention length = 65 mm, study number = 2; general L/W*T ratio: 23.06. **_Basic Description_**: Stemmed; it is a large, thick point with a moderately small constricting stem. Base is straight. Cross section is biconvex or plano-convex. Shoulders are often asymmetric. It occasionally has basal grinding. Type dates 2500 to 4100 BP and is found in the Northeast and Middle Atlantic areas. **Modality**: Its primary function is a knife. **Comments**: The Snook Kill point is the same technology as the Lehigh (Witthoft 1953), and the name has survived in the literature (Ritchie 1958). The type is probably related to the Ledbetter type of the Southeast (see Justice 1987). **User Lifeways**: Bands with general foraging strategies. **User Ecology**: Occupied piedmont environments during a subboreal climate. **Comparative Types**: Koens-Crispin and Poplar Island (Ritchie 1961). **Reference**: Ritchie, William A. (1961) *A Typology and Nomenclature for New York Projectile Points*. Bulletin 384, New York State Museum and Science Service, Albany, NY.

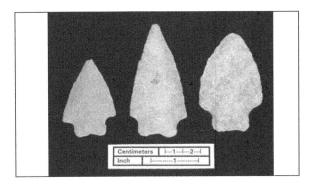

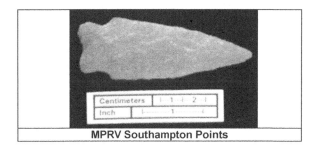

MPRV Southampton Points

Southampton – first identified by Hranicky and Thompson (in Hranicky and Painter 1988 and 1989) and named after the county in Virginia. Type is manufactured with bifacial antler percussion flaking with pressure flaking to finalize the point. Pressure flaking is used to resharpen a point. It appears to be a piedmont point, but it has not been recovered in an archaeological site context. Native Americans are using field or streambed cobbles as their lithic sources. MPRV materials are quartzite, rhyolite, and white quartz. It is a microtypic point, and type validity is conditional. Expention length = 56 mm, study number = 16; general L/W*T ratio: 13.26. **_Basic Description_**: Stemmed; it is a medium-to-large point with rounded basal corners. Type dates 7000 to 6000 BP and is found in Maryland, Virginia, and the Carolinas. **Modality**: Its primary function is a spearpoint. **Comments**: The Southampton point may be related to bifurcate technology, but needs further refining. The type has not been identified in an archaeological site context. **User Lifeways**: Bands with general foraging strategies. **User Ecology**: Occupied piedmont and coastal environments during an Atlantic climate. **Comparative Types**: Rappahannock River (Hranicky 1991) and Kanawha (Broyles 1971). Hranicky, Wm Jack and Floyd Painter (1988) *Projectile Point Types in Virginia and Neighboring Areas*. Special Publication Number 16, Archeological Society of Virginia.

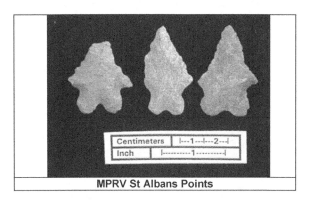

MPRV St Albans Points

📖 **St Albans** – first identified by Broyles (1971) and is based on the St Albans site excavation. The type was named after the St Albans site in Kanawha County, West Virginia (Broyles 1971). Broyles' (1971) A and B varieties have not stood the test of time and have failed as varieties in the literature. Type is manufactured with bifacial antler percussion flaking with pressure flaking to finalize the point. Pressure flaking is used to resharpen a point. Native Americans are using field or streambed cobbles as their lithic sources; there may be some quarrying when available to them. MPRV materials are usually flint or white quartz, but rhyolite, slate, and quartzite are used. It is a macrotypic point, and type validity is traditional. Expention length = 33 mm, study number = 9; general L/W*T ratio: 10.18. ***Basic Description***: Bifurcate; it is a long narrow point with rounded bilobes. Blade is frequently serrated. Type dates 7000 to 6500 BP and is found all over the eastern U.S. **Modality**: Its primary function is a knife. **Comments**: The St Albans point technology is part of a bifurcate continuum for the East (Hranicky and Painter 1988). The bifurcate technology ranges over time from the Nottoway River, MacCorkle, Culpeper, St Albans, LeCroy, Susquehanna Valley, Lake Erie, and Kanawha types (Hranicky and Painter 1988). Each represents a technological stage in the continuum time period (6500 to 10,000 BP). This type has a wide distribution in the East. **User Lifeways**: Bands with general foraging strategies. **User Ecology**: Occupied all environments during a boreal climate. **Comparative Types**: MacCorkle (Broyles 1971), LeCroy (Kneberg 1956), Culpeper (Hranicky and Painter 1988), and Nottoway River (Painter 1970). **Reference**: Broyles, Bettye (1971) ***The St Albans Site, Kanawha County, West Virginia***. West Virginia Geological Survey, Report of Archaeological Investigations, Morgantown, WV.

MPRV St Charles Points

📖 **St Charles** – first identified by Scully (1951). Type is manufactured with blade technology with pressure flaking to finalize the point. Native Americans are using quarry-sourced materials with some pickup stones. MPRV materials are flint, jasper, and possibly quartzite and rhyolite. It is a macrotypic point, and type validity is traditional. Expention length = <50 mm, study number = 2; general L/W*T ratio: 12.99.

Examples of St Charles Stem/Bases (Perino 1985). Left drawing shows the Hardaway-St Charles relationship. Technological continuum: Clovis, Dalton, Dalton-Hardaway, Hardaway, St Charles, Palmer, Big Sandy, and probably Pine Tree, Lost Lake, and Kirk types.

Basic Description: Notched; it is a well-made point with small side-notches. Stem/base is small with sometimes a basal notch. It is often called a dovetail point (drawings). Heavy basal and notch grinding is common. Type dates 10,500 to 9000 BP and is found over most of the lower eastern U.S. **Modality**: Its primary function is a knife. **Comments**: Without a doubt, the St Charles point is the most overlooked type in Virginia, Maryland, West Virginia, and North Carolina (Hranicky and McCary 1996). Justice (1987) shows its distribution as covering piedmont-upland Virginia, western Maryland, and all of West Virginia. Broyles (1971:27, artifact b) shows a St Charles found on a river bank but does not note it as a St Charles. Also, Coe (1964:71, row A) shows a St Charles point. Type may be what is called a Hardapalmer point (Daniel 1998), but this is highly speculative. Also for southern Virginia, failure to recognize this technology is causing wrong interpretations in the Early Archaic. The Hardaway type is the source for the St Charles technology. The Lost Lake (DeJarnette, Kurjack, and Cambron. 1962), Kessell (Broyles 1971), and Big Sandy (Kneberg 1956) technologies succeed this type. The Ice House Bottoms site yields the type a date of 7500 BC (Chapman 1973); it is much earlier for the Southeast. Additionally, Luchterhand 1970 suggests an 8000 BC date for the type. **User Lifeways**: Highly mobile, large bands with hunter/gatherer strategies. **User Ecology**: Occupied all environments during a boreal climate. **Comparative Types**: This type is present in the lower Middle Atlantic area and represents Early Archaic; it has a technological relationship with Hardaway and Palmer types. **Reference**: Scully, Edward G. (1951) ***Some Central Mississippi Valley Projectile Point Types***. Mimeographed paper, Museum of Anthropology, University of Michigan, Ann Arbor, MI.

MPRV Stanly Points

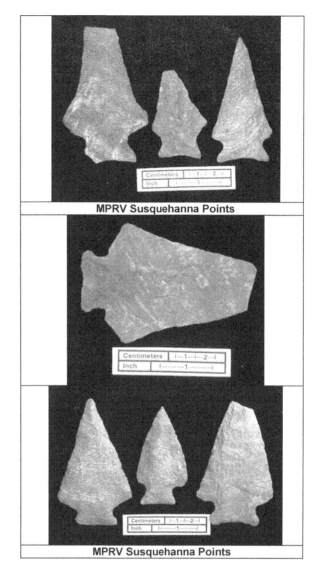

MPRV Susquehanna Points

MPRV Susquehanna Points

📖 **Stanly** – first identified by Coe (1964), was named after the county in North Carolina. Type is manufactured with bifacial antler percussion flaking with pressure flaking to finalize the point. Pressure flaking is used to resharpen a point. Native Americans are using quarry-sourced materials with some pickup stones. MPRV material is principally rhyolite, but other materials do occur. It is a macrotypic point, and type validity is positive. Expention length = 49 mm, study number = 3; general L/W*T ratio: 12.56. **Basic Description**: Broadspear; it is a triangular-shaped, broad-bladed point with a small constricted stem. Its tip is sometimes off the medial axis. Dates 6500 to 7500 BP and is found in the Middle Atlantic area. **Modality**: Its primary function is a knife. **Comments**: The Stanly point is difficult to discern from the Kanawha type. And, Coe (1964) argues: *the Stanly occupation was a continuation of the Kirk horizon*. The MPRV may be the northern boundary for the type. As such, the continuum is Kirk stemmed, Kanawha (?), Stanly, and Savannah River points. As a suggestion, the separation into a distinct type occurs around 3500 BC. **User Lifeways**: Bands with general foraging strategies. **User Ecology**: Occupied piedmont and some uplands/coastal environments during an Atlantic climate. **Comparative Types**: Kanawha (Broyles 1971). **Reference**: Coe, Joffre L. (1964) *The Formative Cultures of the Carolina Piedmont*. Transactions of the American Philosophical Society, New Series, Vol. 54, Part 5, Philadelphia, PA.

📖 **Susquehanna** – first identified by Witthoft (1953) and named after the river in Pennsylvania. It is among the most common points found in the MPRV. Its time period lies on the introduction of steatite bowls and semipermanent village life. Type is manufactured with bifacial antler percussion flaking with pressure flaking to finalize the point. Pressure flaking is used to resharpen a point. Native Americans are using quarry-sourced materials with some pickup stones. MPRV material is principally rhyolite, but other materials do occur. It is a macrotypic point, and type validity is traditional. Expention length = 68 mm, study number = 87; general L/W*T ratio: 11.33. **Basic Description**: Broadspear; it is a triangular-shaped, broad-bladed point with a constricted stem or wide corner notches. It has a trianguloid blade and tip is on the medial axis. Base can be either concave or straight and is usually ground. Dates 3650 to 2700 BP and is found in the upper Middle Atlantic area and the Northeast. Modality: Its primary function is a knife. **Comments**: The Susquehanna point is a transition from the Late Archaic into the Early Woodland. It represents a change from a mobile to semisettled population. This technology may have come from the Ohio Valley, namely the Ashtabula (Mayer-Oakes 1955) and Motley (Ford, Phillips, and Hagg 1955) technologies. The Orient type plays a role in this technology as either a continuation or spin-off technology. Like the Savannah River point, it has steatite bowls associated with it. The MPRV may be the southern boundary for the type. User Lifeways: Large, semipermanent bands with general foraging strategies. User Ecology: Occupied piedmont and some uplands/coastal environments during a subboreal climate. **Comparative Types**: Table Rock (Bray 1956). **Reference**: Witthoft, John (1953) *Broad Spearpoints and the Transition Period Cultures in Pennsylvania*. Pennsylvania Archaeologist, Vol. XXIII, No. 1, pp. 4-31.

MPRV Susquehanna Valley Point

Susquehanna Valley – first identified by Fogelman (in Hranicky 1991). It was renamed from the Susquehanna bifurcate type to the Susquehanna Valley bifurcate type to avoid confusion with the classic Susquehanna type (Hranicky 1991). Type is manufactured with bifacial antler percussion flaking with pressure flaking to finalize the point. Pressure flaking is used to resharpen a point. Native Americans are using field or streambed cobbles as their lithic sources. MPRV materials are flint, quartzite, and rhyolite. It is a microtypic point, and type validity is conditional. Expention length = 36 mm, study number = 1; general L/W*T ratio: 6.67. *Basic Description*: Bifurcate; it is a small point with flaring bilobes that have straight bases. Type dates 8000 to 7000 BP and is found in the Northeast. Modality: Its primary function is a knife. **Comments**: The Susquehanna Valley point technology is part of a bifurcate continuum for the East (Hranicky and Painter 1988). The bifurcate technology ranges over time from the Nottoway River, MacCorkle, Culpeper, St Albans, LeCroy, Susquehanna Valley, Lake Erie, and Kanawha types. However, for this study, it is not placed in the bifurcate technology continuum. User Lifeways: Small bands with general foraging strategies. User Ecology: Occupied uplands and piedmont environments during a subboreal climate. **Comparative Types**: Lake Erie (Winsch 1975). **Reference**: Hranicky, Wm Jack (1991) *Projectile Point Typology and Nomenclature for Maryland, Virginia, West Virginia, and North/South Carolina*. ASV Special Publication Number 26.

Swatara – first identified by Kent (1970). Type is the same as the Koens-Crispin point. It is a false type and not used.

Van Lott – name by Michie (1965) and defined as a coastal type in Hranicky (1991). It probably occurs in the MPRV but not used.

Virginsville Point
Above: point is from Charles County, Maryland

Virginsville – named by Fogelman (1988) after the city in Pennsylvania. It is probably a variation of the Koens-Crispin or Saratoga technology. It is illustrated but not used.

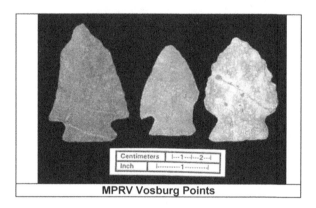
MPRV Vosburg Points

Vosburg – as described in Ritchie (1961). Type is manufactured with bifacial antler percussion flaking with pressure flaking to finalize the point. Pressure flaking is used to resharpen a point. Native Americans are using field or streambed cobbles as their lithic sources. MPRV material is primarily flint. It is a macrotypic point, and type validity is distinct. Expention length = 42 mm, study number = 3; general L/W*T ratio: 9.80. *Basic Description*: Corner-notched; it is a medium point with corner notches and a straight base. Base is usually ground. Blade is slightly serrated. It usually has barbs. Type dates 5200 to 4500 BP and is found in the Middle Atlantic area. **Modality**: Its primary function is a knife. **Comments**: The Vosburg point is in the Laurentian focus (Ritchie 1944). This point is difficult to identify from nonexcavated contexts because it resembles other notched types. **User Lifeways**: Bands with general foraging strategies. **User Ecology**: Occupied all environments during a subboreal climate. **Comparative Types**: Palmer and Kirk (Coe 1964), Brewerton (Ritchie 1963), and Kings (Marshall 1958). **Reference**: Ritchie, William A. (1961) *A Typology and Nomenclature for New York Projectile Points*. Bulletin 384, New York State Museum and Science Service, Albany, NY.

Wading River - first identified by Ritchie (1961). It is probably the antecedent to the Bare Island technology. It is not used.

Warren – first identified by Gardner (1986). False type; it is based on expended Kirk and/or St Charles points. It is not used.

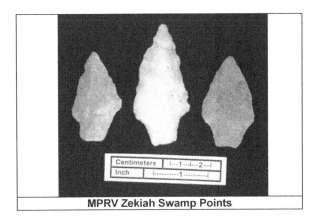

MPRV Zekiah Swamp Points

Zekiah Swamp – first identified by McDaniel (1976). Local point technology that probably has associations in macrotypic constricting stem technologies; however, it is justified as a local type. Native Americans are using field or streambed cobbles as their lithic sources. MPRV materials are rhyolite and quartzite. It is a microtypic point, and type validity is conditional. Expention length = 39 mm, study number = 3; general L/W*T ratio: 14.18. *Basic Description*: Stemmed; it is a medium triangular point with weak shoulders and a tapering stem with a straight base. Type dates 4000 to 3000 BP and is found in Virginia and Maryland. **Modality**: Its primary function is a spearpoint. **Comments**: The Zekiah Swamp point may be an expended form of the constricting stem Snooks Kill, Poplar Island, Buggs Island (Hranicky and Painter 1989) or Neville (Dincauze 1976) types. It has not been recovered from an archaeologically excavated site context, but it is maintained here until proven otherwise. **User Lifeways**: Bands with general foraging strategies. Dates may be earlier than listed. **User Ecology**: Occupied piedmont environments during a subboreal climate. **Comparative Types**: Neville (Dincauze 1976), Swannonoa (Keel 1976), and Buggs Island (Hranicky and Painter 1988). **Reference**: McDaniel, R. E. (1976) *A Zekiah Swamp Projectile Point – A Stemmed Device with Surprisingly Constant Proportions and Some Hypothetical Justifications*. Maryland Archeology, Vol. 12, No. 1.

MPRV Woodland Period

The following points represent the MPRV Woodland Period, which dates approximately 2000-1000 BC to 1600 AD. It is subdivided into the Early Woodland (Adena main type), Middle Woodland (Madison and Levanna main types), and Late Woodland (Potomac main type). Each type is illustrated with specimens that closely match published type descriptions. Types are included that have been published as occurring in the MPRV, but were not used for various reasons as discussed. The following types are presented in BC/AD years:

- Adena Stemmed Point (400 BC – 100 AD)
- Calvert Stemmed Point (1350 BC – 500 AD)
- Capron Triangle Point (1000-1500 AD)
- Carderock Triangle Point (1000-1200 AD)
- Catoctin Notched Point (Early Woodland)
- Chesser Stemmed Point (400-700 AD)
- Duncan's Island Stemmed Point (no date)
- Fox Creek Lanceolate/Stemmed Point (0-800 AD)
- Fulton Turkeytail Point (1000-500 BC)
- Goose Creek Spike Point (500-1000 AD)
- Hellgramite Notched Point (900-800 BC)
- Jacks Reef Notched/Stemmed Point (800-1000 AD)
- Levanna Triangle Point (1000-500 AD)
- Lowes Island Stemmed Point (1500-700 BC)
- Madison Triangle Point (800-1400 AD)
- Meadowood Notched Point (1200-500 BC)
- Merom Stemmed Point (800 BC)
- Nomini Notched Point (880 AD)
- Piscataway Stemmed Point (0-300 AD)
- Pohick Notched Point (Woodland)
- Potomac Triangle Point (1400-1600 AD)
- Potts Notched Point (0-100 AD)
- Robertson Stemmed Point (no date)
- Rossville Stemmed Point (600 BC – 700 AD)
- Snyders Notched Point (200 BC – 400 AD)
- Valina Triangle Point (Woodland)
- Veron Stemmed Point (Late Archaic – Woodland)
- Waratan Stemmed Point (0-100 AD)
- Whites Ferry Lanceolate Point (Early Woodland).

The Adena point technologies are the best made projectile points during the Woodland Period (Figure 7). However, they are not well represented in the MPRV.

Figure 7 – Adena (Robbins) Point from Delaware. It is made from Knife River flint which is found in the Dakotas. It shows long-range travel for both a technology and its material (see Thomas 1970 and 1976).

MPRV Adena Points

 Adena – first identified by Mills (1902). It is the second oldest named type in the U.S. It is generally well made from flint, but local materials are used. Type is manufactured with bifacial antler percussion flaking with pressure flaking to finalize the point. Pressure flaking is used to resharpen a point. Native Americans lithic sources and procurement methods are well known, but probably involve local quarry sources. MPRV material is fine-grain flints, but local materials are used. It is a macrotypic point, and type validity is traditional. Expention length = 39 mm, study number = 6; general L/W*T ratio: 13.56. *__Basic Description__*: Stemmed; it is a large stemmed point. Base is round, and blade is frequently resharpened. Shoulders are angular and usually weak. Cross section is flat or biconvex. Stem varies from square, beaver-tail, and round. Basal grinding is rare. Type dates 1700 to 3000 BP and is found all over the eastern U.S. **Modality**: It is a multifunctional point. **Comments**: The Adena type has numerous variations within the type (Ford 1976). The technology is a continuation of square-stemmed points, such as the Cresap. It generally indicates the Early Woodland. The round-like stem/base represents a later time period for the type (Perino 1985). For the MPRV, it is not well represented; thus, the various stem shapes need study. The eastern shore area of Maryland has a high concentration of the points (Hranicky 2011). **User Lifeways**: Mound builders, village, and local foodstuffs. **User Ecology**: Occupied all environments during a subatlantic climate. **Comparative Types**: Robbins (Dragoo 1963), Cresap (Dragoo 1963), Florence (Perino 1985), Mason (Montet-White 1968), Morhiss (Suhm, Krieger, and Jelks 1954), and Waubesa (Baerries 1953). **Reference**: Mills, William C. (1902) *Excavation of the Adena Mound*. Ohio Archaeological and Historical Quarterly, Vol. X, No. 4.

Bradly – named by Kneburg (1956) after a county in Tennessee. It is called a spike point. Type shown here is associated with pottery and is assigned to the Woodland period. MacCord and Hranicky (1979) use the type for Virginia; however, it remains tentative for the MPRV, and it is not used.

Brandywine – first identified by Kent (1970). It is a false type and is not used.

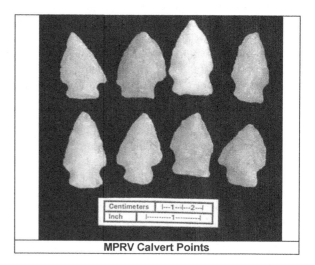

MPRV Calvert Points

Calvert – first identified by Stephenson, et al. (1963) and named after the county in Maryland. It is manufactured with bifacial antler percussion flaking with pressure flaking to finalize the point. Pressure flaking is used to resharpen a point. Native Americans are using field or streambed cobbles as their lithic sources. MPRV materials are quartz, quartzite, and rhyolite. It is a microtypic point, and type validity is site-specific. Expention length = 31 mm, study number = 23; general L/W*T ratio: 12.40. *__Basic Description__*: Stemmed; it is a very short, thick, wide point with rudimentary shoulders, parallel-sided or constricting stem with a straight or slightly rounded base. Type dates 1900 to 3200 BP and is found in Virginia and Maryland. **Modality**: Its primary function is a knife. **Comments**: The Calvert point is most like an expended form of a mixed bag of types. It was not used in Hranicky (1994) for this reason, but is presented here as still being a valid type. Waselkov (1982) reports Bushnell Plain pottery associated with the point. **User Lifeways**: Village and local foodstuffs. **User Ecology**: Occupied piedmont environments during a Scandic climate. **Comparative Types**: Genesee (Ritchie 1961) and Elam (Crook and Harris 1952). **Reference**: Stephenson, R. L., L. L. Ferguson, and G. H. Ferguson (1963) *The Accokeek Creek Site: A Middle Atlantic Seaboard Culture Sequence*. Anthropological Papers No. 20, Museum of Anthropology, University of Michigan, Ann Arbor, MI.

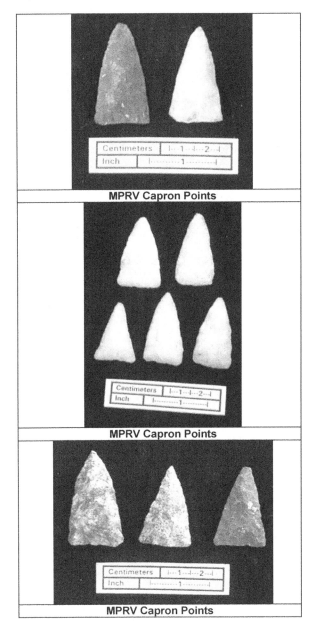

MPRV Capron Points

Capron – named by Smith (1984). Type is manufactured from a percussion biface with pressure flaking to finalize the point. MPRV material is fine-grain flints, rhyolite, quartz, but local materials are used. It is a microtypic point, and type validity is traditional. Expention length = 32 mm, study number = 2; general L/W*T ratio: 9.14. *Basic Description*: Triangle; it is an isosceles point with a straight base. Type dates 3000 to 500 BP and is found in tidewater Virginia through southern Maryland. **Modality**: Its primary function is an arrowpoint. **Comments**: For unknown reasons, the Capron point has not been used in the literature. In southern Virginia, the point occurs in high-quality materials, such as chalcedony, agate, and crystal quartz. **User Lifeways**: Village and local foodstuffs. **User Ecology**: Occupied all environments during a neoboreal climate. **Comparative Types**: Caraway and Clements (Coe 1964). **Reference**: Smith, Gerald P. (1984) *The Hand Site, Southampton County, Virginia*. ASV Special Publication Number 11.

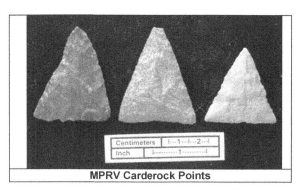

MPRV Carderock Points

Carderock – named here after the area along the Potomac River where it was first observed. Type is thin and well made. MPRV materials are quartz, quartzite, and rhyolite. It is a microtypic point, and type validity is conditional. Expention length = 12 mm, study number = 7; general L/W*T ratio: 7.63 *Basic Description*: Triangle; it is a medium triangle with straight sides and base. Type is often a perfect equilateral triangle and corners are sharp. Type dates 1000 BP and is found from MPRV to New York. **Modality**: Its primary function is an arrowpoint. **Comments**: The Carderock only differs from the Levanna type by a straight base. The straight base may be a piedmont and uplands technology. For the MPRV, specimens were observed only above the fall line. As such, this type may be the same as Geier's (1983) Little Egypt type. **User Lifeways**: Village and local foodstuffs. **User Ecology**: Occupied piedmont environments during a neoboreal climate. **Comparative Types**: Levanna (Ritchie 1961), Madison (Scully 1951), Caraway (Coe 1946), Little Egypt (Geier 1983), Coles Mountain (Geier 1983), Occaneechee (Hranicky 1991), and Yadkin (Coe 1964). **Reference**: None; to be published.

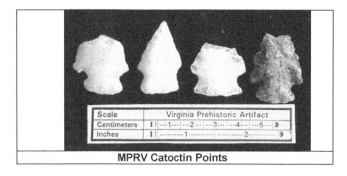

MPRV Catoctin Points

Catoctin – named by Hranicky (in Hranicky and Painter 1988) after a run in Virginia and Maryland. Type is manufactured with bifacial antler percussion flaking with pressure flaking to finalize the point. Pressure flaking is used to resharpen a point. MPRV materials are quartz and rhyolite. It is a microtypic point, and type validity is conditional. Expention length = 44 mm, study number = 16; general L/W*T ratio: 20.17. ***Basic Description***: Notched; it is a long, narrow, thick point with side notches and a convex base. Type dates Early Woodland Period and is found in Maryland and Virginia. **Modality**: Its primary function is a knife. **Comments**: The Catoctin point is crudely made which makes it difficult to identify. Type may be expended Snyder points. **User Lifeways**: General foraging. **User Ecology**: Occupied piedmont environments during a subboreal climate. **Comparative Types**: Excelsor (Brennan 1970), White Tail (Whyte 1979), and Piney Island (Kent 1970) **Reference**: Hranicky, Wm Jack and Floyd Painter (1988). **Projectile Point Types in Virginia and Neighboring Areas**. Special Publication Number 16, Archeological Society of Virginia.

MPRV Chesser Points

Chesser – first identified by Prufer (1967). This type suffers from numerous type names for this technology. Because of this, the point is difficult to classify from field finds. A basic requirement for identification is an association with pottery. Type is manufactured with bifacial antler percussion flaking with pressure flaking to finalize the point. Pressure flaking is used to resharpen a point. Native Americans are using field or streambed cobbles as their lithic sources. MPRV material is basically flint, but local materials are used. It is a macrotypic point, and type validity is conditional. Expention length = 43 mm, study number = 2; general L/W*T ratio: 14.96. ***Basic Description***: Stemmed; it is a medium point with a flaring stem. Base is straight. Shoulders are weak and angular. Stem corners are mildly pointed. Type dates 500 to 700 BP and is found in Ohio, Pennsylvania, West Virginia, Maryland, and Virginia. **Modality**: Its primary function is a spearpoint. **Comments**: The Chesser point is probably a technological style that is found all over the eastern U.S. It is maintained here because of its relationship to the Steuben type. It is probably the same technology as the Lowes point. The Patuxent type may be its ancestral technology. **User Lifeways**: Small bands with general foraging strategies; non-MPRV occupation suggests village associations. **User Ecology**: Occupied all environments during a subatlantic climate. **Comparative Types**: Bakers Creek (DeJarnette, Kurjack, and Cambron 1962) and Edgewood (Suhn, Krieger, and Jelks 1954). **Reference**: Prufer, Olaf H. (1967) *Chesser Cave: A Late Woodland Phase in Southeastern Ohio*. In Studies in Ohio Archaeology, edited by O. Prufer and D. McKenzie, pp. 21-22, Kent State University Press.

Clarksville – first identified by Coe (1964). It is the southern Virginia and North Carolina version of the Potomac type. Type name is not used in the MPRV.

Conewago – first identified by Kent (1970). Type is the same as the Fox Creek point. It is a false type and is not used.

Cresap – first identified by Dragoo (1963). Occupied the Rappahannock River valley, but it has not been reported in the MPRV (Hranicky 1991). For the present, it is not used.

MPRV Duncan's Island Points

Duncan's Island – first identified by Kent (1970). Point is percussion made. MPRV materials are quartz, quartzite, and rhyolite. It is a microtypic point, and type validity is conditional. Expention length = 53 mm, study number = 8; general L/W*T ratio: 21.68. ***Basic Description***: Stemmed, it is a long, narrow point with a small stem. Base is straight or slightly convex. Its primary function is a knife. Type has not been dated. **Modality**: Its primary function is a knife. **Comments**: The Duncan's Island point may be lost in the commonness of rhyolite points in the MPRV area. Type needs to be identified in an archaeological site context. **User Lifeways**: Band with general foraging strategies. **User Ecology:** Occupied piedmont environments during a suboreal climate. **Comparative Types**: Monocacy (Kent 1970), Piney Island (Kent 1970), Bare Island (Ritchie 1961), and Clagett (Stephenson, et al. 1963). **Reference**: Kent, Barry C. (1970) *Diffusion Spheres and Band Territory Among the Archaic Period Cultures of the Northern Piedmont*. Ph.D. dissertation, University Microfilms, Ann Arbor, MI.

MPRV Fox Creek Lanceolate Points

MPRV Fox Creek Stemmed Points

📖 **Fox Creek** – renamed from the Steubenville type by Funk (1976). It is a percussion-flaked point, probably with a wooden billet. It occurs as a stemmed and lanceolate form. The lanceolate form is sometimes mistaken for a Clovis point. Type is manufactured with bifacial antler percussion flaking with pressure flaking to finalize the point. Percussion flaking is used to resharpen a point. Native Americans are using quarry-sourced materials with some pickup stones. MPRV material is principally rhyolite and any other materials are rare. It is a macrotypic point, and type validity is traditional. Expention length (lanceolate) = 67 mm, length (stemmed) = 58 mm, study number = 4 and 38; general L/W*T ratio: 18.48. **Basic Description**: Lanceolate; it is a crudely made point with a straight or concave base. Stemmed; it is the same as the lanceolate form except it has shouldering which produces a stem. Type dates 1000 to 2000 BP. **Modality**: Its primary function is a knife. **Comments**: The Fox Creek point probably suffered from archaeological indifference to the rule of who first named a point and published it should get credit for the name. This type is the Stubenville type which was used by Ritchie (1961) for the technology. It is also known locally as the Selby Bay type (as identified by Mayr 1972). **User Lifeways**: Village and local foodstuffs. **User Ecology**: Occupied piedmont and coastal environments during a Scandic climate. **Comparative Types**: Selby Bay (Mayr 1972) and Stubenville (Mayer-Oaks 1955). **Reference**: Funk, Robert E. (1976) *Recent Contributions to Hudson Valley Prehistory*. Memoir, New York State Museum, No. 22, Albany, NY.

Fort Ancient – generally attributed to Griffin (1966). It occurs in the headwaters of the Potomac River, but no specimens were observed in the MPRV. It is not used.

MPRV Fulton Point (Broken)

Fulton – as identified by Scully (1951). It was reported in southwestern Virginia (Hranicky 1994). Distribution follows northward from West Virginia into Pennsylvania and New York. For its eastern distribution, it is an uplands technology and one quartzite specimen was observed in the MPRV. It is almost exclusively made from flint. Type dates 3000 to 1500 BP. **Other data**: not available for the MPRV. **Comments**: It is a leaf-shaped (bipointed) point with small side notches on the proximal end. Notches are shallow and C-shaped. It is usually well made from flints and cherts. More study is needed; thus, the type is not used here. Along with the Adena, the turkey-tail point is among the older typed points in the U.S. (Brown 1907). **Reference**: Scully, Edward G. (1951) *Some Central Mississippi Valley Projectile Point Types*. Mimeographed paper, Museum of Anthropology, University of Michigan, Ann Arbor, MI.

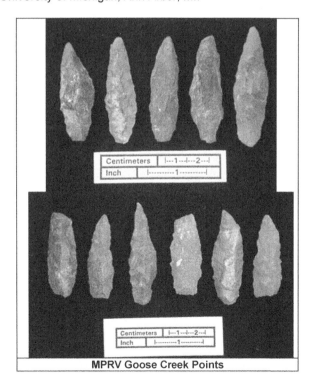

MPRV Goose Creek Points

Goose Creek – first identified by Hranicky and Merry (1991) and named after the creek in Virginia. It may have origins in the Archaic, but most specimens are found with pottery; thus, it dates to the Woodland period (Hranicky 1991). Type is manufactured with bifacial antler percussion flaking. Pressure flaking is used to resharpen a point. Native Americans are using quarry-sourced materials with some pickup stones. MPRV material is primarily rhyolite as no other materials have been observed. It is a microtypic point, and type validity is conditional. Expention length = 42 mm, study number = 34; general L/W*T ratio: 24.23. **_Basic Description_**: Spike; it is a long, narrow point which has a poorly defined stem. It is crudely made, but is very consistent in length of approximately 50 mm. Type dates 500 to 1000 BP and is found in Virginia and Maryland. **Modality**: Its primary function is a drill or perforator. **Comments**: The Goose Creek point is the classic spike point and its function and archaeological context remain to be studied. Type appears to be a local invention that primarily occurs in the MPRV. **User Lifeways**: Village and local foodstuffs. **User Ecology**: Occupied piedmont environments during a subatlantic climate. **Comparative Types**: Nodena (Perino 1985) and Bradley (Kneberg 1956). **Reference**: Hranicky, Wm Jack and Charles W. Merry (1991) *The Goose Creek Spike*. Chesopiean, Vol. 29, No. 1, pp. 16-18.

Hamilton – first identified by Lewis (1955). It occurs in Shenandoah and Page Counties and in southern areas of the Shenandoah Valley and mountainous areas at the headwaters of the Potomac River. However, no specimens were observed in the MPRV. It is not used.

Heck Rockshelter – first identified by Kinsey (1958). MPRV is probably too far south for the type which is found in Pennsylvania. It is not used.

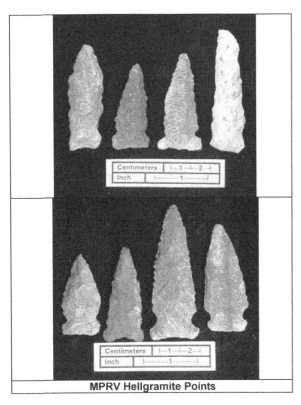

MPRV Hellgramite Points

Hellgramite – first identified by Kinsey (1959). Type is manufactured with bifacial antler percussion flaking with pressure flaking to finalize the point. Pressure flaking is used to resharpen a point. Native Americans are using quarry-sourced materials with some pickup stones. MPRV material is primarily rhyolite. Expention length = 43 mm, study number = 14; general L/W*T ratio: 18.10. It is a macrotypic point, and type validity is positive. **_Basic Description_**: Side-notched; it is a serrated point with small notches. Base is straight. Type dates 2500 to 4300 BP and is found in the lower Susquehanna River valley through to the MPRV. **Modality**: Its primary function is unknown. **Comments**: The Hellgramite point may be an expended form of another side-notched technology. **User Lifeways**: Unknown. **User Ecology**: Occupied piedmont environments during a subatlantic climate. **Comparative Types**: None. **Reference**: Kinsey, W. Fred (1959) *Recent Excavations on Bare Island in Pennsylvania: The Kent-Hally Site*. Pennsylvania Archaeologist, Vol. 29, Nos. 3-4.

MPRV Jacks Reef Pentagonal Points

(Broken – Stem Missing)

MPRV Jacks Reef Notched Points

Jacks Reef – first identified by Ritchie (1961). Type is manufactured with bifacial antler percussion flaking with pressure flaking to finalize the point. Pressure flaking is used to resharpen a point. Native Americans lithic sources and procurement methods are unknown, but probably involve local sources. MPRV materials are primarily jasper and flint, but local rhyolite and quartzite occur occasionally. It is a macrotypic point, and type validity is traditional. Expention length (pentagonal) 37 mm, length (notched) = 41 mm, study number = 1 and 0; general L/W*T ratio: 7.88. ***Basic Description***: Corner-notched; it is a medium, well-made thin point. Shoulders are angular, and base is straight. Notches are narrow and deep. Pentagonal: it is a medium, thin, stemless point that indicates a knife. Sides and base are straight, with occasional grinding. Both types date 1000 to 2700 BP and are found in the Middle Atlantic area. **Modality**: Its primary function is a knife. **Comments**: Both forms of the Jacks Reef share the same technology as the Pee Dee type (Coe 1964) and Afton type (Bell and Hall 1953). This technology has been known for some time (see Mills 1922). This technology probably has Hopewell origins. The tensile strength is low because of its thin cross section. The pentagonal form is the most common in the MPRV. **User Lifeways**: Village and local foodstuffs. **User Ecology**: Occupied all environments during a neoatlantic climate. **Comparative Types**: Pee Dee (Coe 1964), Rabbit (Nelson 1969), and Afton (Bell and Hall 1953). **Reference**: Ritchie, William A. (1961) ***A Typology and Nomenclature for New York Projectile Points***. Bulletin 384, New York State Museum and Science Service, Albany, NY.

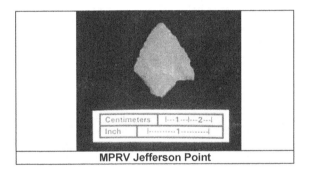

MPRV Jefferson Point

Jefferson – first identified by Hranicky (in Hranicky and Painter 1988). This type needs more study. It may be an expended Piscataway point; however, the Jefferson point is thinner. Type is illustrated but not used. It is defined in Hranicky (2001). **Reference**: Hranicky, Wm Jack and Floyd Painter (1988) ***Projectile Point Types in Virginia and Neighboring Areas***. Special Publication Number 16, Archeological Society of Virginia.

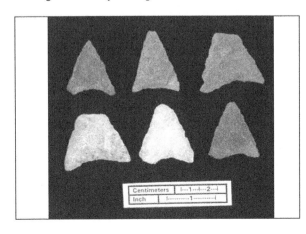

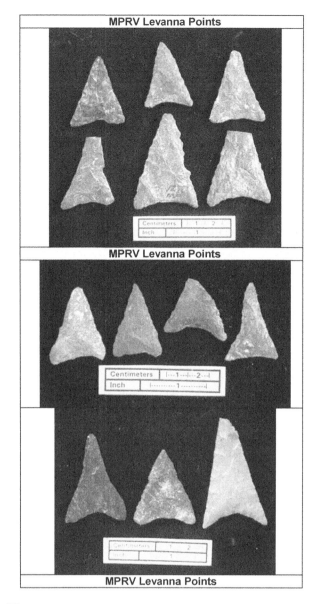

MPRV Levanna Points

Levanna – first identified by Ritchie (1928 and 1961). It was named for the Levanna site in Cayuga County, New York (Ritchie 1928). Type is manufactured with bifacial antler percussion flaking with pressure flaking to finalize the point. Pressure flaking is used to resharpen a point. Native Americans are using field or streambed cobbles as their lithic sources. MPRV materials are rhyolite, flint, jasper, quartzite, and quartz. It is a macrotypic point, and type validity is traditional. Expention length 41 mm, study number = 34; general L/W*T ratio: 8.44. ***Basic Description***: Triangle; it is a medium, thin point with a concave base. Generally, it has an equilateral shape. Blade edges are usually straight, but incurvate edges occur. Type dates 2400 to 600 BP and is found in the Northeast. Base is always deeply-to-moderately concave **Modality**: Its primary function is a spearpoint (arrowpoint?) **Comments**: The Levanna and Yadkin points are the same technology. However, because of regional preferences by archaeologists, two separate types are maintained in the literature. Virginia is in the middle of the type-name usage. From the James River southward, Yadkin should be used. From the James River northward, Levanna should be used. For the James River, either type name can be used. This style may have been replaced by the smaller Madison type, but resharpening confuses this assessment. While Ritchie (1961) reports straight bases, this structure is retyped here as the Carderock triangle type. **User Lifeways**: Village and local foodstuffs. **User Ecology**: Occupied all environments during a neoboreal climate. **Comparative Types**: Yadkin and Roanoke (Coe 1964). **Reference**: Ritchie, William A. (1961) *A Typology and Nomenclature for New York Projectile Points*. Bulletin 384, New York State Museum and Science Service, Albany, NY.

MPRV Lowes Island Points

Lowes Island – described here and named after specimens found near Lowes Island, Maryland. Type is manufactured with bifacial antler percussion flaking with pressure flaking to finalize the point. Pressure flaking is used to resharpen a point. Native Americans are using field or streambed cobbles as their lithic sources. MPRV material is generally quartzite and rhyolite. It is a microtypic point. Expention length = 51 mm, study number = 26; general L/W*T ratio: 16.32. **Basic Description**: Stemmed; a medium-to-large narrow point with a square or rectangular stem. Type dates to the Early Woodland Period and is found in the MPRV area, and perhaps northward to Pennsylvania. **Modality**: Its primary function is a knife. **Comments**: The Lowes Island point may be lost in the commonness of square-stemmed points in the MPRV area. Type needs to be identified in an archaeological site context. **User Lifeways**: Bands with general foraging strategies. **User Ecology:** Occupied all environments during a subatlantic climate. **Comparative Types**: Kays (Kneberg 1956) and Bare Island (Ritchie 1961). **Reference**: Hranicky, Wm Jack (2016) *Arrowheads in Virginia*. Virginia Academic Press, Alexandria, VA.

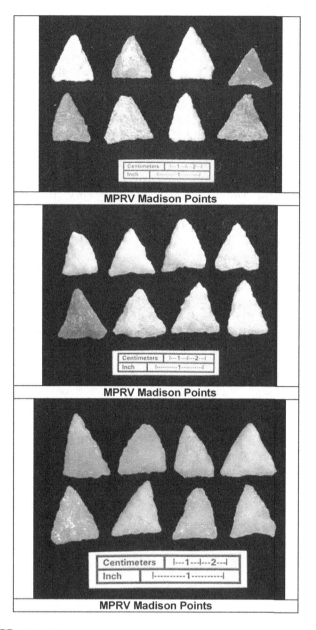

MPRV Madison Points

MPRV Madison Points

MPRV Madison Points

Madison – first identified by Scully (1951). Type is manufactured with bifacial antler percussion flaking with pressure flaking to finalize the point. Pressure flaking is used to resharpen a point. Native Americans are using small field or streambed cobbles as their lithic sources. MPRV materials are rhyolite, flint, quartzite, and quartz. It is a macrotypic point, and type validity is traditional. Expention length = 22 mm, study number = 59; general L/W*T ratio: 9.57. **Basic Description**: Triangle; it is a small-to-medium, well-made point with straight sides. It is either an equilateral, or mostly an isosceles-shaped form. Base ranges from straight to slightly concave. Serrations occur. Type dates 1200 to 800 BP (?) and is found throughout the eastern U.S. **Modality**: Its primary function is an arrowpoint. **Comments**: Some specimens of the Madison point are resharpened forms of larger point types; thus, the Madison may not be a true type. Larger, straight-based triangles are retyped here as the Carderock triangle. The Madison has the largest distribution of any triangle point. However, common style does not mean a related technology. It generally is an excellent timemarker for the Middle Woodland period. Perino (1985) suggests type is a narrow, long triangle. For the MPRV, a major attribute is its thickness; however, Roper (1970) reports the mean thickness at 4.43 mm for the type. The MPRV sample is n=50 @ mean 5.13 mm. As another comparison, Cambron and Hulse (1968) report the type thickness at 4.0 mm. **User Lifeways**: Village and local foodstuffs. **User Ecology**: Occupied all environments during a neoboreal climate. **Comparative Types**: Caraway (Coe 1964), O'Leno (Bullen 1968), and Plains Triangle (Nicholson 1976). **Reference**: Scully, Edward G. (1951) *Some Central Mississippi Valley Projectile Point Types*. Mimeographed paper, Museum of Anthropology, University of Michigan, Ann Arbor, MI.

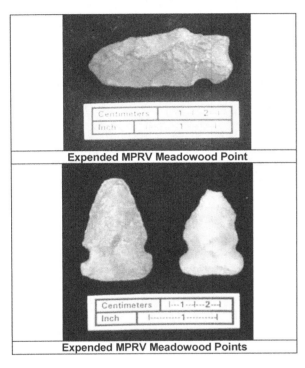

Meadowood – first identified by Ritchie (1958). Native Americans are quarrying but also are using field or streambed cobbles as their lithic sources. Point is flat due to refined flaking. MPRV materials are chert, flint, quartzite, and rhyolite. It is a marcotypic point, and type validity is positive. Expention length = 36 mm, study number = 3; general L/W*T ratio: 12.96. ***Basic Description***: Side-notched; it is a medium-to-large, thin point with small-to-medium side notches and a triangular blade. Base is slightly convex. Stem corners are rounded. Notching is weak; a point may be double side-notched. Approximately 50% have basal grinding. Type dates 3200 to 1500 BP and is found in the Northeast and Middle Atlantic area. **Modality**: Its primary function is a knife. **Comments**: The Meadowood point represents a transition from the Late Archaic to Early Woodland time period. This point style has associations with the turkey-tail point (Perino 1985). The Meadowood point is not well-defined for the MPRV area, but it is used here as a valid point type occurrence. Only expended specimens were observed. **User Lifeways**: Large bands with general foraging strategies. **User Ecology**: Occupied all environments during a subatlantic climate. **Comparative Types**: Logan (Tomak 1983) and Upper Valley (Kneberg 1956). **Reference**: Ritchie, William A. (1961) *A Typology and Nomenclature for New York Projectile Points*. Bulletin 384, New York State Museum and Science Service, Albany, NY.

Merom – first identified by Winters (1969). Type is manufactured with bifacial antler percussion flaking with pressure flaking to finalize the point. Pressure flaking is used to resharpen a point. Native Americans are using field or streambed cobbles as their lithic sources. MPRV material is usually flint but local materials occur. It is a macrotypic point, and type validity is distinct. Expention length = 41 mm, study number = 3; general L/W*T ratio: 12.61. ***Basic Description***: Stemmed; it is a medium point with a round stem. Its primary function is a spearpoint. Type dates 2800 BP and is found all over the lower eastern U.S. **Modality**: Its primary function is a knife. **Comments**: The Merom point is the same technology as the Beacon Island type (Hranicky 1991). Either type name can be used. Justice (1988) classifies the point as an expanding stem type. **User Lifeways**: Bands with general foraging strategies. **User Ecology**: Occupied basically an uplands environment during a to be determined climate. **Comparative Types**: Trimble (Winters 1969). **Reference**: Winters, Howard (1969) *The Riverton Culture*. Illinois State Museum, Report 13, State of Illinois, Springfield, IL.

Morgan - named by Hranicky (1991) after a former ASV president. Type was reported as a piedmont (Virginia and North Carolina) occurrence during the Late Archaic Period; however, it now appears to be a Middle Woodland Period type. Type occurs in slate, rhyolite, and quartzite. It may be associated with the Fox Creek type; but because of it being made from slate and quartzite, this association and date are tentative. It is further defined in Hranicky (2001). It is illustrated but not used.

MPRV Nomini Points

Nomini – first identified by Waselkov (1982). Type is percussion flaked with pressure finishing. Native Americans are using field or streambed cobbles as their lithic sources. MPRV materials are quartz, quartzite, and rhyolite. It is a microtypic point, and type validity is conditional. Expention length = 27 mm, study number = 6; general L/W*T ratio: 10.12. **Basic Description**: Notched; it is a small, broad-bladed point with shallow side notches and a straight or slightly concave base. Blade is thick with straight edges. Type dates 1220 BP and is found in Virginia and Maryland's coastal area. **Modality**: Its primary function is a spearpoint. **User Lifeways**: Village and local foodstuffs. **User Ecology**: Occupied piedmont and coastal environments during a neoatlantic climate. **Comparative Types**: None. **Reference**: Waselkov, Gregory A. (1982) *Shellfish Gathering and Shell Midden Archaeology*. Ph.D. dissertation, University of North Carolina, Chapel Hill, NC.

Pee Dee – first identified by Coe (1964). This type is the same as Jacks Reef and is not used.

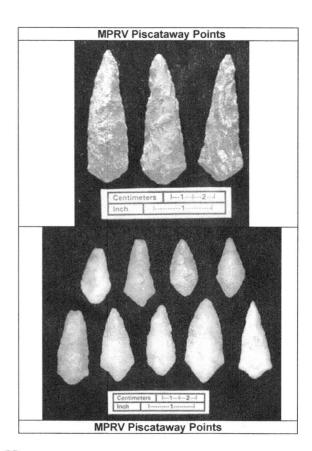

MPRV Piscataway Points

MPRV Piscataway Points

📖 **Piscataway** – named by Stephenson, et al. (1963) after the bay in Maryland. Native Americans are using field or streambed cobbles as their lithic sources. MPRV material primarily quartz, but rhyolite and quartz specimens occur. It is a microtypic point, and type validity is distinct. Expention length = 41 mm, study number = 63; general L/W*T ratio: 23.91. **Basic Description**: Stemmed; it is a small-to-medium, long and narrow point with contracting and pointed stems. Bases are usually pointed but rounded bases do occur. This is the classic definition of the point; however, Figure 8 shows an alternative chassis assembly. The pointed base is the suggested workend.

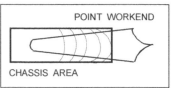

Figure 8 – Suggested Hafting of a Piscataway Point

Type dates 1300 to 4150 BP and is found in Virginia and Maryland. **Modality**: Its primary function is a knife. **Comments**: The Piscataway point is a hafted knife, not a projectile point. Initially, the point was placed into service with lengths over 100 mm. No specimens were observed with impact fractures. **User Lifeways**: Village and local foodstuffs. **User Ecology**: Occupied all environments during a Scandic climate. **Comparative Types**: Bassett (Webb 1948) and Cliffton (Krieger 1946). **Reference**: Stephenson, R. L., L. L. Ferguson, and G. H. Ferguson (1963) *The Accokeek Creek Site: A Middle Atlantic Seaboard Culture*

Sequence. Anthropological Papers No. 20, Museum of Anthropology, University of Michigan, Ann Arbor, MI.

MPRV Pohick Points

Pohick - named here after the bay in Fairfax County. It principally made from rhyolite. Type dates probably to the Middle Woodland Period and is found only in the MPRV. Expention length = 42 mm, study number = 14; general L/W*T ratio: 13.36. ***Basic Description***: Notched: it is a medium, thin point with wide side notches that cause a flaring base. Base is straight. Shoulders are asymmetrical. Blade is triangular. ***Modality***: Its primary function is a knife. **Comments**: The Pohick point has not been identified in a cultural context other than it is suggested as occurring in pottery contexts. **User Lifeways**: Village and local foodstuffs. **User Ecology**: Occupied piedmont environments during a neoatlantic climate. **Comparative Types**: Morgan (Hranicky 1991). **Reference**: None.

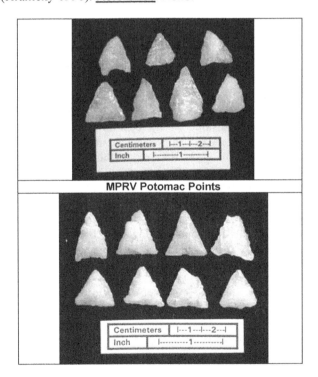
MPRV Potomac Points

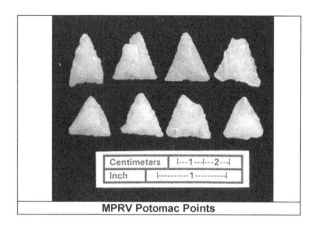
MPRV Potomac Points

📖 **Potomac** – first identified by Stephenson, et al. (1963) after the river. Type is manufactured by pressure flaking a flake into a triangle form. It is rarely resharpened. MPRV materials are quartzite, quartz, flint, and rhyolite. However, the dominant material is white quartz. It is a microtypic point, and type validity is traditional. Expention length = 18 mm, study number = 100+; general L/W*T ratio: 3.37. ***Basic Description***: Triangle; it is a very small, thin point with straight edges and either a straight or concave base. Type dates 400 to 600 BP and is found in Virginia and Maryland. ***Modality***: Its primary function is an arrowpoint. **Comments**: The Clarksville (Coe 1964) and Potomac points are the same technology. However, because of regional preferences by archaeologists, two separate types are maintained in the literature. Virginia is in the middle of the type-name usage. From the James River southward, Clarksville should be used. From the James River northward, Potomac should be used. For the James River, either type name can be used. This type is a true arrowhead. **User Lifeways**: Village and local hunting. **User Ecology:** Occupied piedmont and coastal environments during a neoboreal climate. **Comparative Types**: Clarksville (Coe 1964). **Reference**: Stephenson, R. L., L. L. Ferguson, and G. H. Ferguson (1963) *The Accokeek Creek Site: A Middle Atlantic Seaboard Culture Sequence*. Anthropological Papers No. 20, Museum of Anthropology, University of Michigan, Ann Arbor, MI.

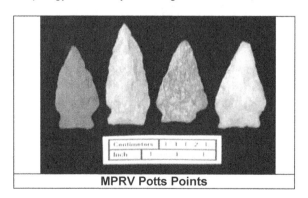
MPRV Potts Points

📖 **Potts** – formalized by MacCord and Hranicky (1979) and is named after the site in Virginia. Type is manufactured with bifacial antler percussion flaking with pressure flaking to finalize the point. Pressure flaking is used to resharpen a point. Native Americans are using field or streambed cobbles as their lithic sources. MPRV materials are quartzite and rhyolite with minor white quartz usage. It is a microtypic point, and type validity is distinct. Expention length = 45 mm, study number = 9; general L/W*T ratio: 24.75. **_Basic Description_**: Corner-notched; it is a medium-to-large triangular point with corners removed and straight base. Blades are triangular. Type dates 2000 to 2400 BP and is found in Virginia, Maryland, North Carolina, and Tennessee. **Modality**: Its primary functions are a knife and spearpoint. **Comments**: The Potts point has a straight base that is in contrast to the Warratan point's concave base. They are both the same point, with the straight-based form having a high frequency of occurrence in the MPRV. Both points have been found together in surface finds, but generally, only one style is found on a site. The type may only occur at or below the fall line, and the MPRV is possibly the northern limits for the type. **User Lifeways**: Village and local foodstuffs. **User Ecology**: Occupied all environments during a Scandic climate. **Comparative Types**: Kittatinny (Kraft 1975), Warratan (Painter 1963), Plott (Lewis and Kneberg 1961), Sykes (as in Keel 1972), and White Springs (Cambron 1964). **Reference**: MacCord, Howard A. and Wm Jack Hranicky (1979) *A Basic Guide to Virginia Prehistoric Projectile Points*. Special Publication Number 6, Archeological Society of Virginia.

Raccoon - first identified by Mayer-Oakes (1956). Type is used in the Ohio River valley and western Pennsylvania. It is the same technology as the Afton, Pee Dee, and Jacks Reef types and dates to the Late Woodland Period. Type is not used.

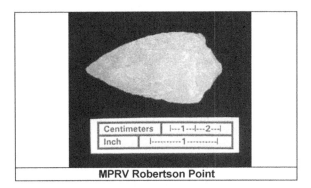
MPRV Robertson Point

Robertson – first identified in Hranicky (2002b) and named after the first president of the Archeological Society of Virginia. Type is manufactured with bifacial antler percussion flaking with pressure flaking to finalize the point. Pressure flaking is used to resharpen a point. Native Americans are using field or streambed cobbles as their lithic sources. MPRV materials are quartzite and rhyolite with minor white quartz usage. It is a microtypic point, and type validity is distinct. Expention length = 48 mm, study number = 1; general L/W*T ratio: 15.36. Type has not been dated but probably dates to the Woodland Period. **Basic Description**: Stemmed; it is a consistently medium point with a pointed stem. **Modality**: Its primary function is a knife. **Comments**: The Robertson point is a new type and its nomenclature remains to be determined. Southern specimens are classically made from white quartz. **User Lifeways**: Village and local foodstuffs. **User Ecology**: Occupied piedmont and coastal environments to be determined climate. **Comparative Types**: The Robertson point is common in southern Virginia; the MPRV may be its northern limit. The technology is similar to the Stark type in the Northeast (see Dincauze 1976), which is an Archaic Period type. The best technology association is the Piscataway point type (Stephenson, et al. 1963). **Reference**: Hranicky, Wm Jack (2001) *Projectile Point Typology for the Commonwealth of Virginia*. Virginia Academic Press, Alexandria, VA.

Robbins – first identified by Dragoo (1963). Occupied the Rappahannock River valley, but it has not been reported in the MPRV. It is classified here as an Adena point type. For the present, it is not used.

MPRV Rossville Points

Rossville – first identified in Skinner (1915) and described in Ritchie (1961). Native Americans are using field or streambed cobbles as their lithic sources. MPRV materials are primarily rhyolite with quartzite and quartz occurrences. It is a macrotypic point, and type validity is traditional. Expention length = 48 mm, study number= 30; general L/W*T ratio: 17.45. **_Basic Description_**: Stemmed; it is a medium, thick, lozenge-shaped point. Stem is contracting and usually forms a point for the base or has rounded base. Shoulders are rounded with some specimens being sharp. Type dates 1600 to 3100 BP and is found in the Middle Atlantic area. **Modality**: Its primary function is a knife. **Comments**: The Rossville point is frequently resharpened to expention which makes it a difficult point to identify. **User Lifeways**: Village and local foodstuffs. **User Ecology**: Occupied all environments during a neoatlantic climate. **Comparative Types**: Chesapeake (Hranicky and Painter 1988). **Reference**: Ritchie, William A. (1961) *A Typology and Nomenclature for New York Projectile Points*. Bulletin 384, New York State Museum and Science Service, Albany, NY.

Selby Bay – first identified by Mayr (1972) who used the type name in place of the Fox Creek type. They are the same point technology, and this type name is not used here. However, Potter (1993) uses the type in his study, but his illustrated points are mistyped. Some archaeologists argue for a side-notched form which is a false type, even if the Selby Bay point is used as a type. It is not used.

Above: Expended Points from Charles County, Maryland. Initially, they were wide points.

MPRV Snyders Points

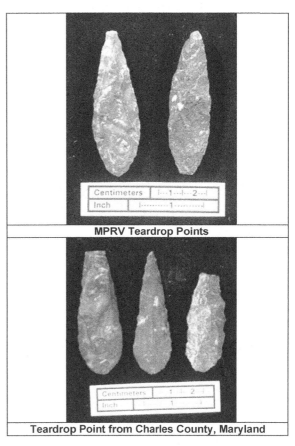

MPRV Teardrop Points

Teardrop Point from Charles County, Maryland

Snyders – first identified by Scully (1951). Type is manufactured with bifacial antler percussion flaking with pressure flaking to finalize the point. This type has a high percentage of expended points which make it difficult to identify. The expended form has a lateral blade reduction which leaves a long narrow point. Pressure flaking is used to resharpen a point. Native American lithic sources and procurement methods are unknown, but probably involve local sources. MPRV material is primarily quartzite, but rhyolite and flint occur. It is a macrotypic point, and type validity is traditional. Expention length = 47 mm, study number = 7; general L/W*T ratio: 10.74. ***Basic Description***: Corner-notched; it is a medium-to-large point with deep-wide corner notches and a round base. Notch is produced by direct percussion (Justice 1988). As such, notch is often wide. Type is a Hopewell point and is found principally in the Ohio and Mississippi River valleys. **Modality**: Its primary function is a knife or spearpoint. Type dates 2200 to 1400 BP and is found in most of the upper eastern states. **Comments**: The Snyders point is difficult to discern in its resharpened, expended form. The expended form has a convex base and wide side notches. Its wide notch on expended forms is often confused with the Halifax type. **User Lifeways**: Village and local foodstuffs. **User Ecology:** Occupied all environments during a Scandic climate. **Comparative Types**: Gibson (Scully 1951), Lafayette (Bullen 1968), Williams (Suhm, Krieger, and Jelks 1954), and Manker (Montet-White 1968). **Reference**: Scully, Edward G. (1951) *Some Central Mississippi Valley Projectile Point Types*. Mimeographed paper, Museum of Anthropology, University of Michigan, Ann Arbor, MI.

Teardrop – various people have identified it in the Middle Atlantic area, but it has not been named (see Mounier and Martin 1994). This point is made by bipolar flaking technique. It occurs in quartzite and rhyolite, but it has its highest frequency in white quartz. Twelve specimens were observed in the study collections; it remains untyped. It is illustrated but not used. **Reference**: Mounier, R. A. and J. W. Martin (1994) *For Crying Out Loud!: News about Teardrops*. Journal of Middle Atlantic Archaeology, Vol. 10, pp. 125-140.

MPRV Valina Point

Valina – first identified by Hranicky (in Hranicky and Painter 1989). Name is a combination of Virginia and Carolina. MPRV materials are quartzite and rhyolite with minor white quartz usage. It is a macrotypic point, and type validity is distinct. Expention length = 46 mm, study number = 4; general L/W*T ratio: 14.15. **Basic Description**: Triangle; it is a small-to-medium point with rounded corners. Its primary function is a knife or scraper. Type dates to the Woodland period and is found in Maryland and Virginia. Type date remains to be determined, and it is found in Maryland, Virginia, and North Carolina. **Modality**: Its primary function is a knife. **Comments**: The Valina point was first observed in southern Virginia collections and now appears to have a macrotypic distribution. **User Lifeways**: Village and local foodstuffs. **User Ecology**: Occupied piedmont and coastal environments during a ? climate. **Comparative Types**: None. **Reference**: Hranicky, Wm Jack and Floyd Painter (1989) *A Guide to the Identification of Virginia Projectile Points.* Special Publication Number 17, Archeological Society of Virginia.

MPRV Veron Points

MPRV Veron Points

Veron – first identified by Stephenson, et al. (1963). Type is manufactured with bifacial antler percussion flaking with pressure flaking to finalize the point. Pressure flaking is used to resharpen a point. Native Americans are using field or streambed cobbles as their lithic sources. MPRV materials are quartz, quartzite, and rhyolite. It is a microtypic point, and type validity is site-specific. Expention length = 35 mm, study number = 62; general L/W*T ratio: 12.72. **Basic Description**: Stemmed; it is a short, thick, wide-bladed point with pronounced shoulders, constricted stem, and expanding, straight base. Type probably dates 5100 to 5900 BP and is found in Virginia and Maryland. **Modality**: Its primary function is a knife. **Comments**: The Veron point is probably a combination of expended types; all of which were used to create the type. The type was not used in Hranicky (1991 and 1994) but is attempted here. It can be classified as a square-stemmed Woodland point. **User Lifeways**: Village and local foodstuffs. **User Ecology**: Occupied piedmont environments during a subatlantic climate. **Comparative Types**: None for its time period. **Reference**: Stephenson, R. L., L. L. Ferguson, and G. H. Ferguson (1963) *The Accokeek Creek Site: A Middle Atlantic Seaboard Culture Sequence*. Anthropological Papers No. 20, Museum of Anthropology, University of Michigan, Ann Arbor, MI.

MPRV Warratan Points

Whites Ferry Points
Left-to-Right: Orange County (Virginia), Fairfax County (Virginia), Granville County (North Carolina), and Sussex County (Virginia).

📖 **Warratan** – first identified by Painter (1963 Type is manufactured with bifacial antler percussion flaking with pressure flaking to finalize the point. Pressure flaking is used to resharpen a point. Native Americans are using field or streambed cobbles as their lithic sources. MPRV materials are quartzite and rhyolite with minor white quartz usage. It is a microtypic point, and type validity is distinct. Expention length = 37 mm, study number = 4; general L/W*T ratio: 23.33. **_Basic Description_**: Corner-notched; it is a medium-to-large triangular point with corners removed and straight base. Blades are triangular. Type dates 2000 to 1800 BP and is found in Virginia, Maryland, North Carolina, and Tennessee. **Modality**: Its primary functions are a knife and spearpoint. **Comments**: The Potts point has a straight base that is in contrast to the Warratan point's concave base. They are both the same point, with the straight-based form having a high frequency of occurrence in the MPRV. Both points have been found together in surface finds, but generally, only one style is found on a site. The type may only occur at or below the fall line, and the MPRV is possibly the northern limit for the type. **User Lifeways**: Village and local foodstuffs. **User Ecology**: Occupied all environments during a Scandic climate. **Comparative Types**: Kittatinny (Kraft 1975), Warratan (Painter 1963), Plott (Lewis and Kneberg 1961), Sykes (as in Keel 1972), and White Springs (Cambron 1964). **Reference**: Painter, Floyd (1963) *The Mussel Eaters of Warratan, Part 2, The Warratan Projectile Point.* Chesopiean, Vol. 1, No. 2, p. 6.

Whites Ferry – named here by Wm Jack Hranicky and Charles W. Merry after types found near the ferry on the Potomac River. Type is manufactured by percussion flaking with pressure flaking finalization. It is a macrotypic point, and type validity is distinct. Expention length = 81 mm, study number = 8; general L/W*T ratio: 21.55. **_Basic Description_**: Lanceolate, it is a medium-to-large biface with excurvate sides and a straight base. Blades are excurvate; no obvious hafting area as no grinding has been observed. Corners are rounded. It is always thin and made from high quality materials. Type dates to Early Woodland Period and is found in the eastern U.S. **Modality**: Its primary function is a knife. **Comments**: This type appears to be similar to the Fox Creek type, only better made. It probably has a distribution all over the eastern U.S. The Bakers Creek (Dejarnette, et al. 1962) is a similar (or same) point that has Hopewell associations (Perino 1991). It is sometimes mistakenly called a Clovis preform. Holmes (1897) was the first to publish (not named) examples that are made from quartz and rhyolite. **User Lifeways**: Village and local foodstuffs. **User Ecology**: Occupied piedmont and coastal environments: to be determined climate. **Comparative Types**: Pandora (Suhm, Kreiger, and Jelks 1954) and Web (Fogelman 1988). **Reference**: Hranicky, Wm Jack (2002) *Lithic Technology in the Middle Potomac River Valley.* Kluwer Academic/Plenum Publishers, NY, NY.

Woodland - identified formally by Petraglia and Knepper (1996). It is not ground; thus, suggesting a later form of the Halifax or variety of the Brewerton. It falls within the Woodland Period; but, if named after a period, then all post-1000 BC points fit the name. It remains to be typed; as named, it is a false type. It is not used.

Yadkin – first identified by Coe (1964). This type is the same as the Levanna point and is not used here. Generally, it refers to southern Virginia and North Carolina triangular points. It may have a deeper concave base than the Levanna, but this has not been tested. It is not used.

MPRV Flakes as Tools
(Native American Stone Debitage and Its Use for Work)

The idea that broken rocks have sharp cutting edges is as old as humanity. As two stones are struck together, chippage occurs. While chippage as a process is a simplified statement for stone tool technology, flakes via chippage are the major products of the toolmaking process; all of which constitute lithic technology's basic concept – flaking. Most flakes constitute debitage; but in many prehistoric settings, pick-up flakes were used (and sometimes modified) as tools and present a group of the edge cutting tool industry – called flake tools. The basic assumption of flake tool usage is that it is a hand-held, short-term tool class.

Archaeological investigations of sites, such as Meadowcroft in Pennsylvania and Cactus Hill in Virginia, have provided a look into preprojectile point technology, which argue - *flakes as tools have considerable antiquity in the Americas*. The study of prehistoric Native American flake tools is now getting a scientific overhaul that promises data about primitive technologies. In addition to the flake, blade technology is considered as having a pre-Clovis (Pleistocene era) origination.

The most common item in lithic technology…
the Flake (Drawing from Crabtree 1972).

There is ample evidence of human occupation in the MPRV before the Paleoindian period. During this period, Native Americans came into the area with a fully developed lithic technology that, in addition to projectile points, included flake and other blade microtools. Many of these tools became basic elements in the Native Americans' toolkit throughout prehistory. Blade tools are rare in the MPRV, and those that are found are usually made from jasper and probably related to the Thunderbird complexes of Warren County, Virginia. However, rhyolite and quartzite flake tools are common and follow styles for particular functions, namely graving, punching, perforating, scraping, and shaving.

This section presents a brief summary of flake tools with annotated illustrations. These types of tools are generally lacking in private collections, as many collectors do not pick up flakes. This is unfortunate since many of them are being destroyed by modern farming disking methods for preparing fields for planting. Since blade-flake tools are found in what appear to be short-term camp sites, the so-called pick-up flake was considered an expedient temporary tool to perform a task. However, the Native Americans would modify a flake to perform one of the functions mentioned previously. Finally, there is evidence that a small number of MPRV flakes were hafted.

Flakes

As a continuation from the Toolmaking Technology section, some flakes are used as tools; they are discussed here as a category, perhaps an industry in the Native Americans toolkit. Other than being sorted and counted by materials, flake analysis is frequently lacking in archaeological survey and site analyses. For flake analysis, see Toolmaking Technology section.

Flakes are everywhere archaeologically speaking. They are most common at quarry and toolmaking sites and generally are present but have low frequencies in village sites. As such, flakes usually indicate tool production areas. When properly analyzed, flakes represent the entire toolmaking and utilization processes. Additionally, flakes are signatures of knappers and can be used to describe how a knapper made a tool. As a suggested hypothesis, flakes can identify individual knappers; of course, this remains to be proven with computer-assisted analysis.

Another aspect of flakes is their usage as tools. Characteristically, most flakes have a sharp edge and can be used as a quick, pick-up tool for a single task requiring a cutting implement. The following definitions of a flake offer an overview of their usefulness in archaeological research.

A **flake** is according to Edmonds (1996):

In simple terms, a flake is a piece of stone that has been removed from a core or tool by percussion or pressure. Flakes occur in a bewildering array of forms, a fact that is reflected in the nomenclature developed by stone tool specialists. Perhaps the most important point to be recognized is that the form, size, and general characteristics of flakes will vary according to the type of production activity being undertaken. The close analysis of flake assemblages often allows us to identify what was being made in a given context, and how a particular episode of production was organized in technical terms.

And flakes, according to Crabtree (1972):

Flakes are cone parts and the fracture angle of the cone is the ventral side of the flake. The apex of the cone (proximal end of the flake) where the force is applied is called the platform part. Examination of the platform angle and the fracture angle of the cone will determine the direction of applied force. Because of the amorphous nature of most raw material, the worker must constantly calculate the fracture angle of the cone to determine the direction of applied force in order to remove flakes at an angle different from the direction of force by the percussor or compressor. Both the position of the material being worked and the direction of the applied force are constantly changing in the initial stages of manufacture. This enables the worker to select the platform area and determine the correct angle of applied force.

And flakes, according to Brennan (1973):

Flakes may be of various shapes. The natural disposition of the cryptocrystalline series and most dense rocks is to break conchoidally, or like a Venus clam shell; that is, the flake tends to be round or squamate, scab-shaped. But this all depends on the topography, as it were, of the block below where the blow is struck, which may have excrescences and bulges in it. The shape also depends on the strength, the follow-through, and the angle of the strike. The right coincidence of these can produce the flake or strip blades with parallel edges like a table knife; or thick, tabular spalls to be used as secondary cores.

A flake or spall that runs the length of the core will thin out to a razor edge on the end opposite the striking platform, and that end will be rounded or sharp. But if the flake does not run the length of the core but breaks off short, it terminates in what is called a "hinge fracture," which is blunt and square across. This happens more often in the making of flake blades than in routine chipping.

About 90 percent of flakes, chips, and spalls are subsumed in the foregoing explanation; the other 10 percent will be atypical in that they show no striking platform or bulb of percussion. These are called "resolved" flakes and there are experts who say they were struck by lucky accident with a baton. "Lucky" is not here a carelessly tossed-off synonym for adventitious. The platform and bulb of percussion very often constitute a nuisance; this thickening seems to have been very difficult to reduce further by chipping and probably always remained an unsatisfactory and awkward factor, although it could be minimized by using a baton instead of a hammerstone.

Flake Tools as a Class

As mentioned, flakes are the most common objects in prehistory; basically, they are the by-products of toolmakage and usage. Most are simply discards, but a small percentage have secondary importance, in that they were used as tools. The primary functions are: cutting, scraping, and perforating. The flake tool constitutes a cutting industry in eastern prehistory and is a minor (but present) class in the technological continuum for pre-Contact Native Americans. The flake tool may be an economic and/or environmental factor in lithic technology, but most likely, it is simply an expedient tool of convenience.

Figure 1 – Limeton Points, Warren County, Virginia. These points are made off flakes.

Most flake tools were never used as projectile points, but the Limeton point type may have been a true point (Figure 1). This point is always made from a flake (Wilkison and Leslie 1967). Nomenclature and statistics are presented in the Projectile Point section. Other flake projectile points also occur, such as the triangle point (Hranicky 1995).

Flake tools in the MPRV are common and probably date to the Late Archaic Period to the end of the Woodland Period. For earlier periods, these tools were made using a blade technology. Either way, they are primarily expedient, short-term tools. They are easy to make; most are made with a percussion flaker. Small deliberate flakes are usually the result of soft flaker flaking. Some flakes were hafted as small knives. This tool was used as a small skinning or gutting tool for small animals, birds, or fish. The flake knife was hafted to a small bone handle with pitch or sinew. It is a short-term knife. Additionally, flake tools served other functions, such as perforators, spokeshaves, scrapers, or saws.

As with other non-projectile point tools, few studies have been made on the so-called utilized flake. It remains the new, unidentified tool for archaeological classification schemas. This publication initializes the study with MPRV flake tools and offers an analysis that should be comparable to other areas in the Middle Atlantic States.

Flake Tool Size

MPRV flake tools average 50 mm in length. Larger flake tools are represented by chance-finds in collections. Also, larger pieces tend to be bifacially flaked. As such, basic sizing data remain to be studied.

Size has a practical function in flake analysis. Most reports contain some type of mass analysis for flakes found in an archaeological context, such as sorted by size and material. This only proves that flakes have size and composition; unless traced back to cores, quarries, etc., these data have little value. Flakes under 25 mm probably can be grouped as utilized or nonutilized flakes. For flakes over 25 mm, utilization (or not) becomes a tool aspect in analysis.

Flake Parts and Attributes

The basic flake is a piece of stone that is removed from another stone that is being manufactured into an artifact; it is any detached stone piece. It generally is considered the opposite of a blade. The following presents the general nomenclature and descriptions for flakes. Flake sources are (Callahan 1979):

1 – Block core
2 – Spheroid core
3 – Biface core
4 – Cobble
5 – Nodule
6 – Tabular plate
7 – Frost spall
8 – Thermal spall
9 – River spall.

Generally, flaking methods or categories are:

1 – Primary (first flake, general flaking)
2 – Secondary (thinning flakes, shaping flakes)
3 – Tertiary (retouch, edge trim, basal thinning, fluting).

Flaking can also be divided into:

1 – Thinning
2 – Edge shaping
3 – Retouch.

Each flake has two faces: inner facet and outer facet. Flake surfaces are:

1 – Dorsal Surface
 - platform
 - preparation scars
 - dorsal ridges
 - dorsal scars
2 – Ventral Surface
 - lip
 - bulb of force
 - hackles

Major attributes are:

1 – Width
2 – Length
3 – Thickness
4 – Material
5 – Flake angle
6 – Bulb size
7 – Overall shape.

Most flakes have the following parts, which are (Figure 2):

1 – Striking platform
2 – Percussion cone
3 – Conchoidal (bulb) of percussion
4 – Splinters
5 – Striations
6 – Undulations
7 – Faces (interior or exterior).

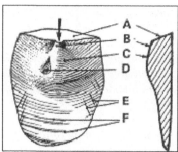

Figure 2 – Parts of a Flake – A: Striking Platform, B: Percussion Cone, C: Conchoidal (Bulb) of Percussion, D: Splinters, E: Striations, and F: Undulations. Arrow indicates the striking point that removed it from the core.

Flake Tool Types

Flake tools are found (Figures 3 and 4) as:

1 – Utilized flake – single-time, pick-up flake used for a single task, usually cutting, then discarded.

2 – Modified flake – thin flake that is modified to perform a specific function, such as scraping, cutting, perforating, shaving, etc.

3 – Hafted flake – sharp-edged flake that was hafted as a small tool.

These two photographs show the deliberate physical change in normal flake structure. Utilized flakes generally have small serrations along one lateral edge, while modified flakes have had the normal shape modified so as to create a specialty tool. These tools follow patterns (or styles) that have not been clearly identified in American archaeology. The user takes advantage of the flake's thinness and natural cutting edge.

Figure 3 – Utilization Jasper Flake. It has retouch on proximal edge. It represents a pick-up flake that was used for a short-term task. Note platform (left).

Figure 4 – Modified Rhyolite Blade-Flake. It has edge retouch; it has no flake modification of shape. Note platform (lower center).

Flake Production

As mentioned, flakes are products of the stone flaking reduction methods. They vary in size and shape that complicates classification. This study assumes deliberate designs that the Native Americans applied to basic small tool functions. The flake is equated to the blade in terms of modification. Flake tools are made from core-flakes.

Note: Burin technology was not performed on a flake; however, this remains to be argued and proven.

If a flake is worked on one face and used, it can be called a uniface tool. Generally, this involves a large flake that has single face reduction.

Figure 5 – Quartzite Flakes That Were Probably Hafted. Left: (L = 51, W = 53, T = 10 mm) and right: (L = 51, W = 41, T = 12 mm). The basal end of both flakes is the bulb scar end.

Flake Hafting

The basic assumption of flake tools is they are hand-held tools. Occasionally, flake modification suggests hafting (Figure 5). The flake tool always implies an expedient tool; thus, hafting suggests a longer lifecycle. This aspect of flake utilization is difficult to assess archaeologically. The discipline has never considered the flake in the same respect as other microtools, namely the projectile point and knife.

This technology is similar to Converse's (1963) hafted shaft scrapers (Figure 6). The biface form probably dates to the Early Archaic Period; however, the flake form is not related. Another hafted form is the Edgefield scraper that is found in the Southeast (Michie 1968). Waller (1971) reports similar hafted flake knives in Florida. These examples offer further study.

Flakes as Multifunctional Tools

As a convenient pick-up tool, the flake has numerous multifunctional purposes in prehistory. While it is considered here as a nonformal or short-term implement, the practice was common and may suggest it was a normal implement in the social setting, especially for the Late Archaic and Early Woodland Periods.

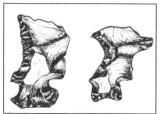

Figure 6 – Hafted Flint Scrapers from the Ohio River Valley (Converse 1963). Drawings show stemmed and notched varieties.

All flake tool technology has several commonalities (functions), such as:

1 – Graving
2 – Scraping
3 – Perforating
4 – Drilling
5 – Shaving
6 – Sawing
7 – Cutting.

Lithic Edges

An edge (share) definition for a lithic tool is lacking in archaeology. One can assume an edge is sharp, dull, etc.; these are subjective estimates and lack scientific validity. As for prehistoric tools, cutting capability was a value that perhaps varied among cultures, but at the same time, it is a factor needed for tool efficiency. From a knapping perspective, lithic uniformity is a priori and is a tacit assumption for the knappability of stone. This is obvious in analyzing Native American tools and implements.

Blade edges are dependent on material and can only be measured in terms of their share's durability. Efficiency of a blade edge is task driven. Longevity of the edge is dependent on work. Each can be measured scientifically, and the Native Americans lithic choice was partly due to stone availability and their cultural perception of stone efficiency, longevity, and perhaps spiritual or traditional worldview factors. Also, lithic mass is not a factor in edge evaluation.

The best stone edge for cutting is obsidian. The worst cutting is sandstone. The sharpest-edged stone in the MPRV is quartz. The correlation suggested between them is that obsidian is 1000 times better for producing cutting edges. As a measurement, all other stones fall between 1 and 1000. As suggested (Hranicky 2002b), mass and hardness are not factors; molecular density is. If 1000 is set to obsidian, then cryptocrystalline is placed in the higher end, for example flint = 900, chert = 850, and jasper = 800. The stone shares tend to be elastic. For more granular materials, the setting would be 300 for rhyolite and 200 for quartzite. These shares tend to be brittle. Quartz could be assigned as the middle of 500 as would be most igneous rocks, for example basalt = 600, greenstone = 550 or hornfeld = 450. Any number above 500 can be considered a culture-selected attribute of the stone's cutting capabilities. These ranges can be classified as a share cutting property of:

1 – Fine = 1000-750
2 – Metafine= 750- 500
3 – Coarse= 500-250
4 – Gravelly = 250-1.

Figure 7 shows flake edge samples. All are fresh breaks. Differences in the cutting edges are obvious.

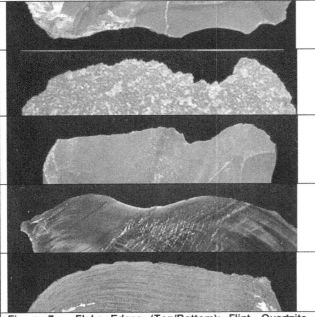

Figure 7 – Flake Edges (Top/Bottom): Flint, Quartzite, Jasper, Obsidian, and Mussel Shell. Obsidian produces the sharpest cutting edge known to mankind. Obsidian is rare in the East; in Virginia, it only occurs on the Potts site (McCary 1953). In New Jersey, see Bello and Cresson (1998).

Pleistocene Blade-Flakes

As well as all of Virginia, the MPRV is divided into two large cultural occupation periods, which are:
- Pleistocene era (blades, namely flake tools)
- Holocene era (bifaces, namely arrowdeads).

Each time period requires a different kind of archaeology, and other than scientific principles, neither really over lap in archaeological practices.

Blade-Flake Archaeology

The Pleistocene blade-flake is generally a 35-40 mm flat flake and still has a platform remnant with one lateral margin being microflaked. These tools were probably only used at the campsite and upon moving, they were discarded. Figure 8 shows the basic tool morphology and properties. It basic properties are:
- Striking platform
- Point
- Microflaked edge.

The basic morphology has:
- Structural axis
- Functional axis.

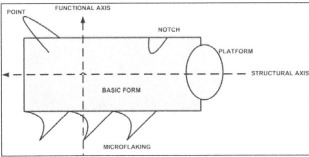

Figure 8 – Basic Blade-Flake Model

While many archaeologists still refer to the time period before Clovis as pre-Clovis, this time period is now being referred to as Early American or PaleoAmerican (Hranicky 2015). The main difference between pre- and post-Clovis is the roll-over of the U.S. environment from the glacial to post-glacial era, or to the contemporary environment.

Otherwise, blade is defined here as any lithic piece struck from a parent rock that is made into a tool. It is called an objective piece. Many archaeologists would simply call them worked flakes. The terminology is up to the reader's vocabulary. Microflaking is defined as very fine chipping on a margin. Any specimen that does not have flake scars or modification evidence is classified as a flake or bulk. The use of the term "blade" has numerous definitions in the literature (Collins 1999). Of course, blades and bifaces occur in each archaeological era. Only earlier than these people and Clovis toolmakers were able to do this "thin" flaking in jasper; it disappears after them and is never seen again in Virginia (Hranicky 2015). Several Higgins artifacts argue thin blade manufacture. This knapping method is a principal factor in a relative date for the site. Again some reviewers will argue these artifacts are modified flakes, the difference between a blade and a flake is:
- Flake has a V-shaped profile (tapers or flairs)
- Blade has a parallel profile (flat)
- However, occasionally both have similar profiles.

Objective piece manufacturing (also called a blank) is the way an ancient knapper started producing a tool class. The basic of the method are 1) starting with a cobble which is bifacially reduced, 2) quarrying a spall which is bifacially reduced, or 3) striking off a parent a long flat and narrow piece which is pressured flaked into a tool.

Blades (Levallois flakes) usually have prepared platforms (see Tool #1). At Higgins, tools generally have a flat profile, with the exceptions of a biface punch. This flatness factor is present in their toolmaking ability. The loss of this technological ability in prehistory may be present in the demise of Paleoindian toolmakers. Certainly, thin blades/flakes disappear in the Holocene, almost if the lack of it was not present in post-Clovis toolkits.

Since all implements are blade technology, can a technology class be described for the collection? No, the sample is too small. However, functional purposes can be attempted for recovered specimens. They are basically knives and perforators.

See Plate 17 for examples of Pleistocene era blade-flake tools.

Figure 9 shows a jasper blade that was found on the Shenandoah River near the confluence of the Potomac River. It does not appear to be Warren County jasper; most likely, it is from Pennsylvania. Measurements: L = 85, W = 29, T = 9 mm. While Clovis does occur in the MPRV, long blades were not reported in this study.

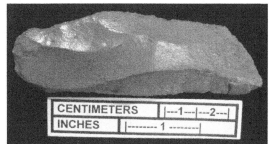

Figure 9 – Basic Blade Example

Plate 17 - MPRV Flake Tools*

#1 – Saw/scraper/spokeshave/graver, quartzite (L = 57, W = 34, T = 8 mm). Bulb is at lower left lateral edge. It has pronounced lateral serrations, worn spokeshave, lower right graver, and distal spoon-like scraper. It was a hand-held tool. Workend is reinforced by a medial axis extending from midtool to tip.

#2 – Punch/graver/spokeshave, jasper (L = 51, W = 33 T = 8 mm). Bulb is at the distal end, strong punch (medial ridge) and spokeshave has heavy retouch. Left protrusion is broken suggesting it may have had dual punch workends. It was a hand-held tool. A short medial axis is used to reinforce the workend.

#3 – Graver/knife/spokeshave, rhyolite (L = 49, W = 29, T = 11 mm). Bulb is probably at the distal end, has pronounced medial ridge to give it added strength. Spokeshave at the distal end is minor, but used. Graver tip is dull because of usage and below the tip is edge retouch. It may have been hafted. Workend is reinforced by a medial axis extending from midtool to tip.

#4 – Knife, flint (L = 60, W = 35, T = 10 mm). It has cortex remaining at both ends. Right middle lateral edge has steep edge flaking and lower left lateral has minor retouch. It has a high medial ridge. It was a hand-held tool.

#5 – Saw-like, spokeshave, quartzite (L = 44, W = 40, T = 10 mm). Bulb is at the proximal end and flake has a curve to it. Left lateral edge has wide serrations and upper right of distal end has a minor, but used spokeshave. It was a hand-held tool.

#6 – Punch/spokeshave, quartzite (L = 55, W = 37, T = 7 mm). Bulb is at the distal end, which was deliberate. Perforator is thicker than the rest of the tool. It has two spokeshaves on the right lateral edge. Lower one is well used. And tip is dull. It was a hand-held tool.

#7 – Graver/Scraper, quartzite (L = 47, W = 39, T = 9 mm). Bulb is at lower left. It has a sharp graver and distal end scraper.

#8 – Knife (or graver or punch), jasper (L = 58, W = 27, T = 12 mm). Bulb is at the proximal end. Punch has medial ridge to give it strength. Distal end has minor edge retouch. It was probably a hand-held tool.

#9 – Spokeshave, rhyolite (L = 47, 32, T = 13 mm). Bulb is at the proximal end. Spokeshave is massive. It has basal grinding at both lower lateral margins. It was definitely a hafted tool.

 #10 – Graver/spokeshave (?), quartzite (L = 50, W = 47, T = 12 mm). It was probably hafted; bulb is at distal end, graver tip is broken, and has minor retouch in the spokeshave.	 #11 – Graver, quartzite (L = 43, W = 42, W = 11). It was probably hafted; bulb is at the proximal end, tip is broken, and has a wide C-shape lateral edge which may have been used.	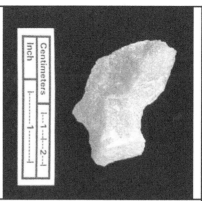 #12 – Graver, quartzite (L = 42, W = 38, T = 11 mm). Bulb is at the distal end and it has straight, wide (9 mm) tip. It was probably hafted and functioned as a fine woodworking tool or engraver.
 #13 – Beaked-graver/spokeshave, quartzite (L = 51, W = 49, T = 9 mm). It was hand-held, has a small spokeshave, and bulb is at the lower left lateral edge.	 #14 – Knife, quartzite (L = 60, W = 43, T = 6 mm). It is essentially a pick-up flake that has small lateral edge and distal end retouch. It was hand held.	 #15 – Graver, quartzite (L = 48, W = 43, T = 11 mm). Graver tip is sharp. It was a hafted, single function tool.
 #16 – Graver/knife, quartzite (L = 50, W = 43, T = 10 mm). It was a hand-held tool, and the platform is at the upper left lateral edge. It has lower right lateral edge retouch.	 #17 – Punch, rhyolite (L = 48, W = 35, T = 8 mm). Bulb is at proximal end which has cortex remaining. Tip is sharp and utilizes a semi-medial ridge. It may be a hafted tool.	 #18 – Graver/perforator, quartzite (L = 32, W = 31, T = 7 mm). Bulb cannot be determined; has flaking hump on other side. It was a multifunctional, hand-held tool.

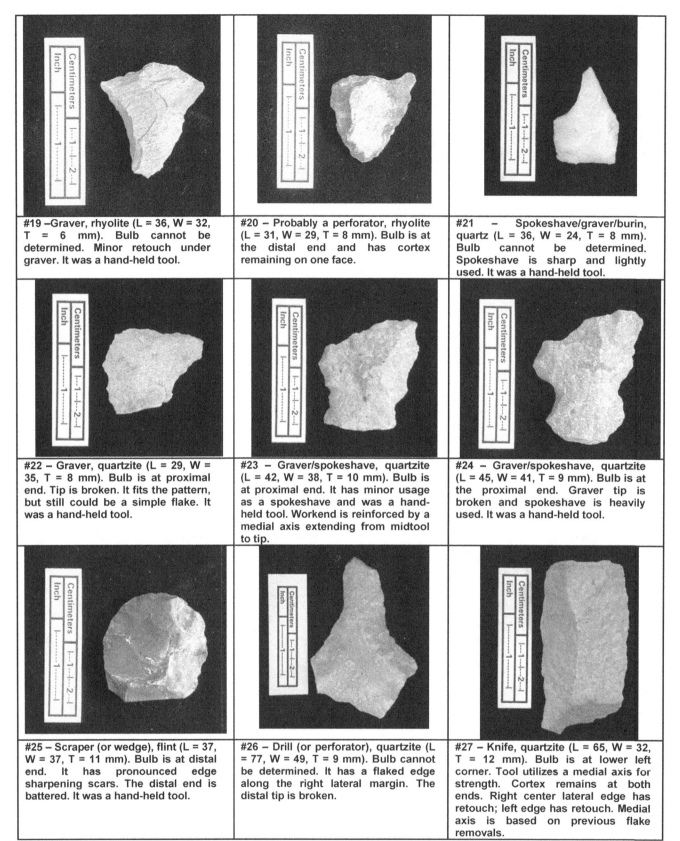

#19 – Graver, rhyolite (L = 36, W = 32, T = 6 mm). Bulb cannot be determined. Minor retouch under graver. It was a hand-held tool.	#20 – Probably a perforator, rhyolite (L = 31, W = 29, T = 8 mm). Bulb is at the distal end and has cortex remaining on one face.	#21 – Spokeshave/graver/burin, quartz (L = 36, W = 24, T = 8 mm). Bulb cannot be determined. Spokeshave is sharp and lightly used. It was a hand-held tool.
#22 – Graver, quartzite (L = 29, W = 35, T = 8 mm). Bulb is at proximal end. Tip is broken. It fits the pattern, but still could be a simple flake. It was a hand-held tool.	#23 – Graver/spokeshave, quartzite (L = 42, W = 38, T = 10 mm). Bulb is at proximal end. It has minor usage as a spokeshave and was a hand-held tool. Workend is reinforced by a medial axis extending from midtool to tip.	#24 – Graver/spokeshave, quartzite (L = 45, W = 41, T = 9 mm). Bulb is at the proximal end. Graver tip is broken and spokeshave is heavily used. It was a hand-held tool.
#25 – Scraper (or wedge), flint (L = 37, W = 37, T = 11 mm). Bulb is at distal end. It has pronounced edge sharpening scars. The distal end is battered. It was a hand-held tool.	#26 – Drill (or perforator), quartzite (L = 77, W = 49, T = 9 mm). Bulb cannot be determined. It has a flaked edge along the right lateral margin. The distal tip is broken.	#27 – Knife, quartzite (L = 65, W = 32, T = 12 mm). Bulb is at lower left corner. Tool utilizes a medial axis for strength. Cortex remains at both ends. Right center lateral edge has retouch; left edge has retouch. Medial axis is based on previous flake removals.

* Bulb indication may be actual bulb or indicate direction from which the flake was struck from core. Most of these flakes have remnant platforms which probably indicates they were created in the Pleistocene era.

Bifaces as Knives
(Native American Cutting Implements)

As Curry, O'Brian, and Timble (1985) noted in their discussion of hafted bifaces, not all projectile points were used in projectiling. As an argument and explanation, the Native American projectile point has other functions, namely the knife function. This function for a projectile point dates to the Clovis point and continues to the post-Contact era.

The prehistoric knife has numerous conditions that are used in classification and explanations. Any projectile point can be a knife, but any knife cannot be a projectile point. The difference is the functional angle that the tool's blade applies to the target area. Secondly, blade weight is a factor because projectile points are only flyable under certain weight conditions. Furthermore, any sharp edge (share), such as on a flake, can be used as a knife. Conversely, any biface or blade can serve in a cutting capacity of a knife and then be made into a tool. While perhaps confusing, the knife and projectile point are different tools, but at the same time, they are the same; only the user makes the difference. In essence, points kill, knives butcher that kill and; of course, both serve other work functions in their usage.

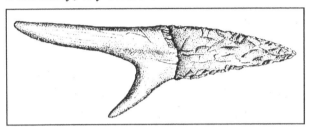

Bone-Handled Knife from Montgomery County, Virginia
(Based on Benthall 1969)

These biface usages offer wear patterns that can be analyzed to determine the tool's function. If a biface form is multifunctional, the problem of functional differences goes back to square-one in archaeology; biface-tool usage is difficult to determine, especially for small (<65 mm) bifaces.

This section offers an overview of MPRV knives with examples from other areas. Since the illustrated specimens are surface finds, no time depth is assumed. Knife classifications and analyses have not been attempted in the Middle Atlantic area. Unlike projectile points, knife morphology is not easily classifiable as each knife is basically unique. The assumed premise is that all knives, by definition, are hafted tools. Size is often the only distinguishing factor between a spearpoint and knife. However, in measuring knife size, expention must be assumed for specimens under study. A knife sample of the study collection artifacts is shown at the end of this section, which includes a basic artifact classification, material, and measurements.

Knife Basics

If the Clovis projectile point is considered a functional cutting implement, then the knife dates to the Paleoindian period in the U.S. (Figures 1 and 2). However, it served a dual function of butchering and projectiling. Also, for the early periods of prehistory, core blade technology was used as a method of producing cutting implements. For point typology, the biface knife form easily dates to the Clovis, Dalton, Hardaway, and St Charles pointmaking periods and was the primary function for these points; impact fractures are extremely rare on these points. These tools were probably hafted knives, but more study is needed of the totality of the knife and its functions. As a possible hypothesis, bone and antler points were the basic form of projectiling in the Paleoindian era and points were used as cutting implements. For a comparative example, a bone knife is shown later.

The knife was probably exempt from environmental and economic factors that influence lithic technology. The knife may simply be an innate tool that early hominid primates did not need to discover; it is derived from natural intelligence. Its antiquity goes back to very basics of social behavior and survival. It was the primary part of all pre-Contact Native Americans toolkits, and its function did not change throughout prehistory. Basically, the knife probably had a multiple usage and performed numerous tasks. And, the knife was the primary tool for survival in human prehistory.

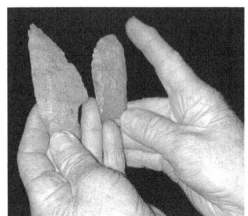

Figure 1 – Clovis Point and Knife in the Charles Merry Collection

Throughout this section, reproduction knives showing various chassis mountings are shown (illustrations Repo-A through Repo-G). These repro-tools (replications) were used experimentally and data were applied to the study collection analyses. Specimens from outside the MPRV are used for discussion. Also, the ulu (an Eskimo-named knife) is discussed in the Miscellaneous Tools/Implements section.

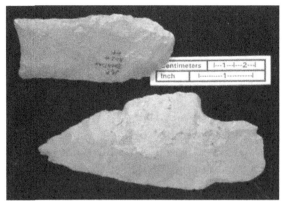

Figure 2 – Paleoindian Knife and Point from Montgomery County, Maryland. Measurements: Top, L = 68, W = 29, T = 8, Flute 25 and 23 mm; Bottom, L = 99, W = 42, T = 10 mm. These tools were found together along the Potomac River and are made from Point-of-Rocks jasper.

A knife is a biface or blade tool with one or multiple cutting edges (workends). The actual cutting edge is called a share. The tip of the knife blade is called the acutus. These terms were defined earlier and are in Hranicky (2002). The knife has basically two forms of manufacture:

1 – Biface knives
2 – Blade (flake) knives.

Eisenberg (1991) suggests two broad functional categories of:

1 – Slicing knife – predominantly ovate or lanceolate forms
2 – Butchering knife – thick biface with sinuous-edge cutting.

There is a functional overlap with these two categories. And, even with wear patterns, assigning a knife to one category remains speculative. Also, it includes an assumption that regular bifaces are used as knives, which, of course, is not generally the case.

Figure 3 – Pick-up Flake Jasper Knife. It still has cortex remaining and was used as a knife and spokeshave (at the arrow). It measures L = 64, W = 51, and T = 10 mm.

In addition to lithic knives, MPRV Native Americans used mussel shell, wooden, bone, and cane knives. Due to preservation factors, these knives are difficult to identify archaeologically, and none was observed in the study collections. The variety of knife materials tends to suggest functional differences, but again, this hypothesis is impossible to prove archaeologically. For this study, lithic forms are the basic focus. See Flakes as Tools section for descriptions of lithic edges.

Pick-up flakes were common knives (Figure 3). See MPRV Flakes as Tools section. However, the hafted biface is the primary knife form (Figure 4).

Knife edges may be beveled or retouched. The knife may be a hand-held or hafted implement and classified as either a micro- or macrotool. Shape varies extensively in both time and space. As suggested, it is the basic implement for all prehistoric toolkits. Operationally, it can be divided into:

1 – Hafted knives
2 – Handheld knives.

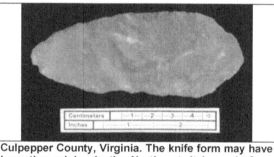

Culpepper County, Virginia. The knife form may have Lauretian origins in the Northeast. It is made from Onondaga chert.

Figure 4 – Rhyolite Biface Knife (Bottom). This form is common in the MPRV; however, flint/chert materials are rare.

A classic knife discovery in Virginia is the knife found in Burial #92 at the Shannon site in Montgomery County, Virginia (drawing shown in introduction). It is a hafted biface in a bone handle. The knife blade was removed when it was placed in the burial; it was ceremonially killed (Benthall 1969). The knife demonstrates dual cutting edges, which is suggested here as a skinning or butchering knife. At present and without standard wear pattern analyses, the single- and dual-edge knives probably have different functions. Naturally, the projectile point is assumed to be a dual edge implement, but many show wear only on one edge.

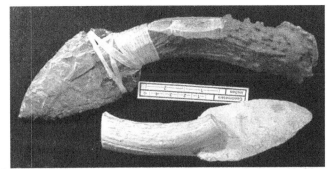

Repo-A – Example Knives Showing Antler Hafting Technique. Top is hafted with Fibers and Bottom is hafted with Pine Tar (Replication with Native Points).

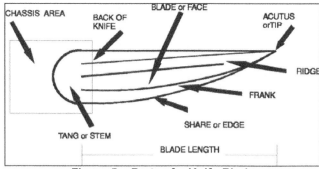

Figure 5 – Parts of a Knife Blade

As a knife population, the MPRV knife rarely shows a complete blade expention or impact fractures. It is a common tool and may have been a community rather than a personal tool. A grainy (coarse) stone was the preference. Due to archaeological preservation of organic materials, the hafted knife can only be suggested. For the MPRV, no basic knife style can be determined least wise with the sample at hand. Both projectile points and knives are found in the same context that complicates assigning them to types based on function and/or structure.

Basic shapes tend to follow the structure of projectile points, namely lanceolate, notched, and stemmed forms. The triangle may not have functioned as a true knife. As mentioned, the projectile point is always assumed to have been a hafted tool.

Aside from any pick-up flakes being used as a cutting implement, knives are generally bifacially produced so as to form at least one cutting (functional) share. Most knives make use of both lateral edges for cutting.

Core blades can be used as cutting implements, but for the MPRV, no pure blade knife technology was observed. However, large flakes (nonbiface) were observed as knives. The blade knife and core blades are discussed below.

Parts of a Knife Blade

The handle is the principal part of a knife as it controls the cutting action angle and direction on a target area. Additionally, it controls the amount of blade pressure, up to the limit of the handle construction and blade mounting. Blade parts (assembly) are shown in Figure 5, which are:

1 – Blade
2 – Share (edge)
3 – Bank (or back)
4 – Blade ridge (not always present)
5 – Frank
6 – Frank shoulder
7 – Acutus (point or tip)
8 – Tang (hafting area).

The acutus (pronounced as *a-cut-us*) is the pointed (distal) end away from the chassis of a knife and is usually part of the workend. The blade consists of:

1 – Share, which is the cutting edge

2 – Frank, which is the taper from the share to the top of the blade (Figure 6).

3 – Blade, which is the part of the tool that forms the cutting edge assembly.

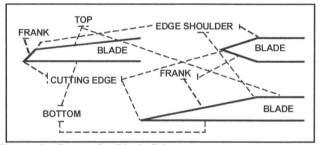

Figure 6 – Parts of a Blade Edge

The blade edge is composed of the share and frank. It has one dimension that can be used to classify the blade; this is the frank angle. While difficult to measure, it is a correlation of sharpness (cutting edge of the share). If the share has dual franks, the edge becomes a bit, such as found on axes, celts, adzes, etc. As a rule, no knife has two cojoining franks.

When studied for their wear patterns, frank angles will provide interesting data that can be interpreted for social knife uses. This approach has not been tested archaeologically.

Bipointed bifaces are either dual acutus implements or, most likely, one point served as a tang that was inserted into a wooden or antler handle. The acutus determines if the knife is used in a saw-like or perforating action. Any nonblade part of a knife is the tang. As such, the knife always has a distal workend that indicates the knife's usage and the way to hold it. The workend is the actual cutting part of a knife blade. And, the blade ridge (usually at the medial axis) is a length-wise flake line that was intended to strengthen the blade.

The basic structure is a stone set-up that permits a cutting edge from the bank to the share. Even if the blade has dual shares, the blade always has part of it designed for a chassis mounting or hand holding. Since no studies are available on knife design and function, this bank-to-share design is suggested here as a means to studying lithic knives. Figure 7 shows the basic knife form for the MPRV.

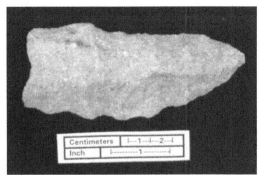

Figure 7 – Savannah River Quartzite Knife (L = 82, W = 38, T = 18 mm). It is a classic knife form which has a hafting area, curved share, pointed acutus, and a structure reinforcing ridge on the knife's blade (face). From this ridge to the blade edge is the part called the share. The original blade was probably a lanceolate shape and is not represented in the expended form.

Knife or Projectile Point

Each projectile point and knife is limited to its size for function. While size is often an argument for a knife, each tool has a weight capacity for its function, and when exceeded, it fails that function. For example, only a limited number of lithic grams are flyable on an arrow or spear. All projectile points, excluding small arrow points, can be used as knives. The main difference is that a projectile point has, as its major workend, the point's tip. Whereas, a knife's major workend is its long blade edge. The chassis is similar for both the small knife and projectile point. In other words, the basic function of both tools is quite similar, which essentially makes it difficult to argue a single function for either tool.

We can assume that larger knives have more torque than smaller ones, but the physics of size versus stone and hafting combinations remains to be studied. The knife class is difficult to separate from the projectile point class.

Case Study on Knives

This case study of six MPRV knives (Figures 8a/8b through 14) offers a definitional argument for the knife form in eastern prehistory. All specimens have basic attributes that can be used to identify the knife in archaeological contexts. However, these attributes occur throughout prehistory and are represented at various times in the technological continuum. Morphology (form) is not representative of a time period. Projectile points can be typed, but most of the other tools in the Native Americans' lithic technology cannot be typed. There are possibilities for regional typing of knives, such as the Savannah River knife. The consequence comes from the fact that the Native Americans' toolkit is Panindian and most of its basic components are found throughout American space and time.

The basic knife form is not one that meets standards of terminology, structure, or function in American archaeology.

The knife may well be a European tool form (philosophy or way of thinking) that has been imposed on the Native American's way of creating a cutting implement. In the other hand, the hafted knife form is universal, and the basic knife structure may have been discovered numerous times all over the world. Figure 8 shows a reverse of workend and hafting area based on normal archaeological thinking concerning parts of a knife. The specimen was selected showing a slightly off-center workend to amplify the argument. This blade form occurs on the Chesapeake and Piscataway points (see Projectile Point section.).

Figure 8a – Quartzite Knife (L = 107, W = 47, T = 12 mm). It is a bipointed knife form. The hafted part is the right end in the pictured specimen. Study knife is from Prince Georges County, Maryland.

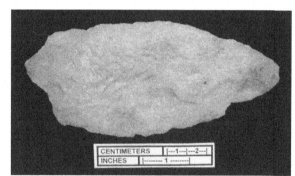

Figure 8b - Paleoknife, quartzite, Warren County, Virginia, L = 142, W = 62, T = 12 mm.

Initially when manufactured, the knife in Figure 8 was probably a bipointed biface of which one end was hafted. The open end was used as a knife or whatever function was needed by the user. When the blade became dull, the user resharpened it; thus, he customized the shape. When the blade was resharpened back to the hafting area, the knife was considered as expended and discarded. Over the years, the hafting material decayed and disappeared. Upon finding it, some archaeologists would consider the small pointed end as the stem and assume that the blade was unused. The microscopic wear patterns are on the left part of the shown knife.

Note: Pointed bases on knives are not always workends. Some of the pointed bases are used as hafting parts of the biface. And, some knives have dual acutuses.

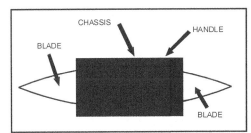

Figure 9 – Suggested Hafting for the Wytheville Point

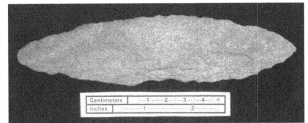

Figure 10 – Rhyolite Bipointed Knife (L = 147, W = 37, T = 9 mm). There is no share wear pattern present which indicates it was never used. The specimen probably dates to the Early Woodland Period. The chassis mount was the left end shown. This bipointed form is called the Wytheville point type (Hranicky 2001). The study knife is from Lancaster County, Pennsylvania.

The bipoint biface is named the Wytheville projectile point type (Hranicky 2001). Expended forms suggest it occurs in the MPRV, but bipointed specimens are rare. Figures 9 and 10 show a classic example. The dual-bladed knife has not been reported archaeologically or ethnographically. The Wytheville point is an excellent candidate for this knife form.

Figures 11 and 12 show two pointed bifaces that also illustrate the knife form.

The knife in Figure 11 could easily fit into the Late Archaic Period toolkit, but for a few special attributes. First, the base is ground and secondly, the base has evidence of the knapper's attempt at removing a flute. This tool most likely shows a form (structure) that originated in the Late Paleoindian Period and continued (off and on) to Contact. While found elsewhere, this form is totally absent during the Middle Archaic Period in the Middle Atlantic area; it comes back during the Late Archaic Period. The argument, of course, is that the lanceolate form is basically a knife and has always functioned as such. The Clovis argument for knife versus spearpoint is an old one (Hranicky 1987).

Figure 11 – Unfluted Clovis Quartzite Point (L = 105, W = 42, T = 18 mm). Resharpening has destroyed the lanceolate shape which is the basic style for the Clovis point? Or: it is too thick for a Clovis point. It is a basic Late Archaic/Woodland knife. The rule is: no flute, no Clovis. It has a small, wide flute. The study knife is from Montgomery County, Maryland.

The knife in Figure 12 illustrates a symmetrical pattern in the early manufacture of knives. The knapper set up a platform (or nipple) on the base from which he was planning to remove a flute. He understruck it and only removed a small chip that essentially destroyed the base. The medial axis was off center as well as having several hinges on the face near the center. For these reasons, the knapper discarded the piece. Of course, this biface could drop into the Woodland Period toolkit (see Web Complex examples in Delaware), but circumstances suggest otherwise. For one more argument, the piece is extremely thin and was pressure flaked (on quartzite).

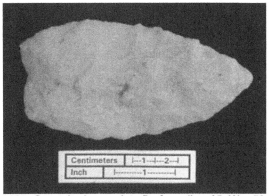

Figure 12 – Quartzite Lanceolate Preform (L = 95, W = 50, T = 8 mm). Paleoindian or Woodland knife? The study knife is from Washington County, Maryland.

These examples show the mechanics of knife making, and suggest the Native American form of a cutting implement was dual edges, thin, and had an overall lanceolate form. While ideally a lanceolate form, the simple elongated blade is the common form as shown by the knives illustrated at the end of the section.

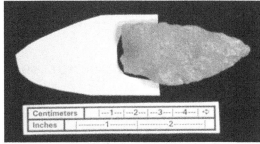

Figure 13 – Quartzite Knife (L = 51, W = 24, T = 10) with an Example of Hafting. The study knife is from St Mary's County, Maryland.

As an aspect of the knife, one factor becomes a defining attribute. This is hafting. As argued, all knives, by definition, are hafted implements. Naturally, pick-up flakes and bifaces could perform temporary cutting functions, but the basic Native American knife was hafted (Figure 13).

The end of a knife's lifecycle is ordinarily the expention of the blade (Figure 14). Aside from breakage, the length of the remaining blade that the Native Americans considered still useable varied culturally. If natural resources were not scarce or difficult to obtain, the blade length could be determined archaeologically based on site-specific specimens.

Figure 14 – Constricted stemmed point (L = 68, W = 48, T = 9 mm). It is often called a broadspear or knife. The knife's workend (right margin in photograph) is traditionally what is called the point's base. This is a classic expended knife, which is often classified as a Morrow Mountain I point. The study knife is from Montgomery County, Maryland.

As previously suggested, the knife was the most basic implement in prehistory. It was the tool that performed most of the daily tasks. While the projectile point served as a knife, other biface forms were also used as a knife and had functions that depended on the Native American's daily circumstances. This leaves the projectile point as being a secondary implement in the Native Americans' toolkit.

Repo-B – Example: Antler Handle with Quartzite Blade (Replication by Scott Silsby)

Percursor Knife/Chopper Forms

While the argument is true that choppers were the first lithic tool for early hominids, separating an object into two or more pieces is among mankind's most primitive behaviors. The chopper accomplished this task, but the sharp-edged flake (knife) was neater and produced a separating method that could be controlled. As such, the knife was the second tool that was developed. It continues as a basic human implement to this day.

For the American Indians, the knife is among the oldest of lithic tools. Pre-Clovis knives were hafted uniface (core) blades (Figure 15). This technology needs to be identified in American contexts; it is beginning to be reported.

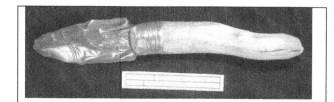

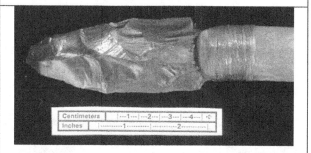

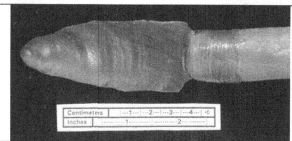

Figure 15 – Top knife (Replication) is an overall view of the knife. Lower, both sides, Errett Callahan's Idea of a Pre-Paleoindian Hafted Knife. It has a flint blade and wooden handle. This form continues into the Paleoindian and Early Archaic Periods. After which, the knife generally became a bifacial-flaked implement. Uniface knives are found in the Woodland and Mesoamerican contexts; however, many of them are large flake knives rather than true core blades.

In addition to lithic knives, the bone knife (or even wooden knife) probably predates the lithic forms. Due to poor bone preservation, bone knives are not well preserved in the archaeological record. Also, this holds true for the MPRV as no bone knives were observed in the study collections. Surely, they did exist. Figure 16 shows a bone knife example from the Plains.

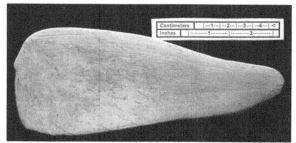

Figure 16 – Bone Knife from Bismarck, North Dakota. It was made from a buffalo scapula.

Core Blades as Knives

The core blade knife is essentially a uniface knife. The knife is made using blade technology (Figure 17). While the technique dates to the Paleoindian Period, there is little evidence of it persisting after the Early Archaic Period. It reappears in some parts of the U.S. during the late periods, which is probably the result from diffusion from Mesoamerica. It is not found in the MPRV unless the Elys Ford point type is a true blade.

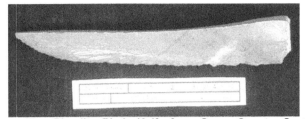

Figure 17 – Rhyolite Blade Knife from Green County, South Carolina (L = 124, W = 22, T = 19 mm). The blade has cortex remaining on the wide end, bulb scar is pronounced, share has retouch, and has a sharp acutus. The knife probably dates from Early Archaic Period back to Paleoindian Period.

Figure 18 shows a blade specimen from Virginia. The same technique was used for both these knives. A heavy blow was delivered to the platform to remove the blade. Next, share retouch was performed and created a lightly serrated edge. This is the largest blade found to date in Virginia. While it is a surface find, it probably can be dated to the Paleoindian Period. It has a well-developed patination.

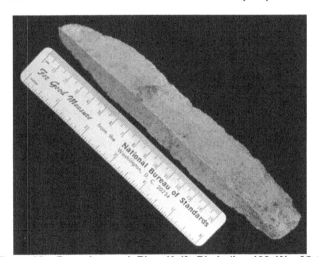

Figure 18 – Rappahannock River Knife Blade (L = 193, W = 35, T = 11 mm). It is made from flint which is found in western Virginia and North Carolina. It has a massive bulb scar and edge retouch. Based on the technology, it is probably a Paleoindian tool.

Flakes as Knives

Any sharp–edged flake can be used as a knife. These forms were probably the so-called pickup flake knife (also utilized flake). Whether they were carried as a basic component of the basic toolkit remains to be proven. Figure 19 shows a flake knife has more usage that what would be called a pickup flake. The difference is flake modification, even resharpening as opposed to simple edge retouch. It may be a class, but more specimens are needed. See Flakes as Tools section.

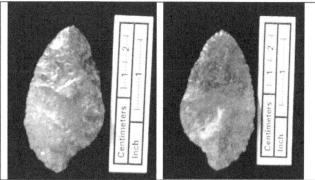

Figure 19 – Flake Knife (L = 49, W = 26, T = 9 mm). It has flake scars on one face (left), bulb scar (right), and edge retouch on both faces. The blade has a taper that make use of flake's natural shape. It is made from Onondaga chert and probably represents the Meadowood phase of the Early Woodland period.

Holding a Stone Knife

There is an assumption the Native American's holding and using a stone knife was the same as the so-called European method. The chassis is different, if only in terms of handle/blade strength is reduced from the metal models. Most people cut with a knife by pulling the blade through the target towards the user. If applied to the prehistoric knife, this method causes stress on the chassis. It cases the blade to be pulled from the handle; losing the hafting. By pushing the knife away from the user, the blade is pushed into the handle. Thus, in cutting a piece of hide, the user would use the acutus to penetrate the hide, then push the blade forward through the hide. This method of knife useability was tested by the author and is suggested here as a hypothesis in Native American stone knife usage (Hranicky 2002a).

Uniangulus Knife Form

The uniangulus knife form is common among eastern biface knives (Figures 20a and 20b). This style is based on one cutting edge (Baker 1995 and Hranicky 2002). Obviously, biface knives can have dual cutting edges, but the Native American preference to only use one suggests a cultural or functional preference. Uni-edge versus dual-edges remains to be studied.

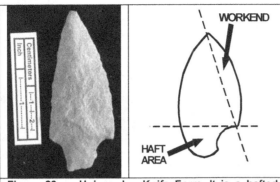

Figure 20a – Uniangulus Knife Form. It is a hafted knife that uses one cutting edge (workend). Left specimen is a MPRV example.

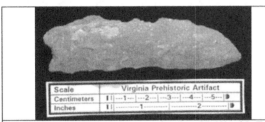

Knife (expended form), quartzite (L = 87, W = 22, T = 11 mm) (Nansemond Cty, VA). It has dual shares and a sharp acutus.

Knife, quartzite (L = 79, W = 24, T = 10 mm). (Sussex Cty, VA). It has dual shares and a sharp acutus.

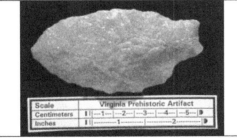

Knife, quartzite (L = 79, W = 40, T = 10 mm) (Princes Anne Cty, VA). It has dual shares and a sharp acutus.

Figure 20b – Non-MPRV Uniangulus Knife Forms

Knife Hafting

Numerous experimental hafting examples are shown in the section. The true Indian way can be surmised from ethnographic specimens that have survived. Figure 21 shows two examples.

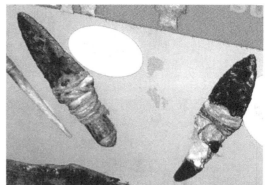

Figure 21 - Ethnographic Knife Examples on Display at the Pamunkey Museum, King William County, Virginia

Knife Materials

Material used for knives varies, and justification by Native American knappers is not obvious. Sample statistics are presented at the end of this chapter. The sharpest edges for MPRV stones is white quartz. For the East, clear quartz was used for knives that date to the Paleoindian Period.

Knife (Blade/Biface) Identification

While most tools could serve as a knife, the hafted functional tool called the knife was established in the early American prehistory, or most likely, this technique was carried into the New World. It can be identified by the following:

1 – Made on a blade with one or more workends
2 – Made on a thin biface with one or more workends
3 – Blade/biface is thin <12 mm
4 – Blade is flat with a taper in thickness
5 – Striations are parallel to the share's edges
6 – May exhibit polish in areas above the workend
7 – Generally has a tang, share, and acutus.

The Distal/Proximal (D/P) ratio for a knife is usually <1.0; however, expended blades may skew this number.

Knife versus Point Continued

While numerous tools exhibit both functions, most points appear to favor a single function. Large points (>50 mm) probably served as a knife, even though this length could easily be hafted as a spear. Edge wear along lateral margins versus impact chippage on the point's tip is the best indicator of function. The blade edge (straight, excurvate, recurvate, and encurvate) offers a functional determination, with straight being preferred for spearing. The acutus (tip) angle also qualifies and as a suggestion:

1 – Acutus (Tip) <45 degrees = projectile
2 – Acutus (Tip) <>35-45 degrees = either
3 – Acutus (Tip) >44 degrees = knife.

There are numerous ways to calculate the acutus angle (see Hranicky 2002a). Figure 22 shows a way to measure the angle. It is called the apex angle. Any use of blade edges to produce the angle has the built-in resharpening bias from the prehistoric user; whereas, the method shown is an angle definition based on the biface maker.

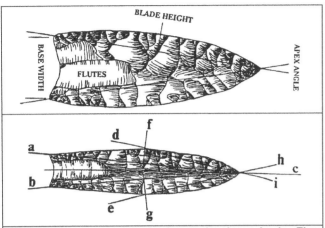

Figure 22 – Base-to-Tip Produces the Apex Angle. The angle can be calculated from length and base width; however, it allows an objective blade height measurement.

The dce angle can be used to determine the cutting part of the blade. These knife measurements and others remain to be established archaeologically.

Figure 23 shows long, narrow blades, but on what would have been long-bladed implements. The blade tip angle is not necessarily an attribute needed for the knife function; it is not part of the cutting operation of the tool.

The prima facia difference between a point and knife class is that the former is a hand-held tool and the latter is a projectiling tool; otherwise, there are usually functional overlaps for both classes.

Figure 23 – Broken Point Tips with Narrow Blades. These blades were percussion-flaked with pressure flaking to shape them. Overall, they were probably made during the Late Archaic or Woodland Periods. They are probably broken knives; none show impact fractures.

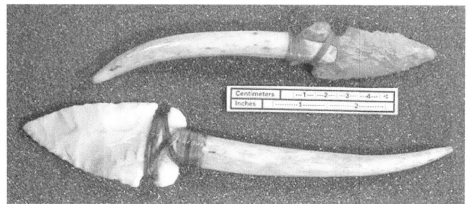

Repo-C – Deer Antler Hafted Knife Examples (Replications with Native Points). Both knives are sinew wrapped with small amounts of pine tar. Blade is set in a notch in the antler handle.

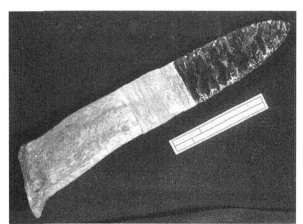

Repo-D – Example of a Bone Handle Knife with an Obsidian Blade (Replication). See experimental section.

The share is the best indicator of function and edge wear is an indication of usage. As shown, a knife can be bipointed; thus, the tip angle is only one of several indicators for the knife function. Basically, the difference between a knife and projectile point is the value of attributes to the researcher. His/her opinion lies on observation of physical properties, but standards for any empirical determination based on metrics remain to be established in archaeology.

Blade Shape and Design

Tool function is often displayed in blade shape. However, blade resharpening may obscure the initial blade functional shape. Additionally for the Native American, subsequent resharpening may have changed the tool's primary function to a new one. This problem presents difficulties in archaeological analyses. The key to studying Native American tool maintenance is their continuing blade edge angles, frank design, tip angles, cross sections, and blade thickness. Even so and repeating, no standards have been developed from which blade changes can be observed and measured.

A major knife form occurs in the Middle Atlantic area that is often mislabeled archaeologically. It is the bipointed knife which was presented previously. This biface was hafted in a wooden or antler handle with the other end becoming the cutting part of the tool. As a consequence, projectile points with pointed bases are frequently knives. The false blade was hafted and the pointed V-shaped end is the share and acutus. Wear patterns on the study collections suggest this focus,

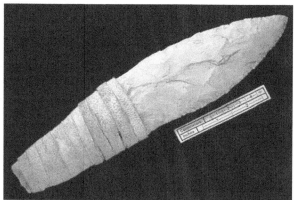

Repo-E – Knife Example – Large Biface with Leather Handle (Replication Using a Native Biface)

One knife attribute totally missing in MPRV and many cases of eastern knives is blade taper. Taper is the gradual change of thickness from one end to the opposite end of a blade (proximal to distal ends). In other words, the acutus is much thinner than the other end of the blade. As a note, blade taper is common on projectile points, which complicates its assessment for knives. Is it not needed for a knife? While variations do occur, the MPRV knife blade is essentially flat. However, plano-convex cross sections do occur. It is present in blade core and large flake (reduction form) knives. These analytical data have not been reported. It is present on MPRV knives in the collections, but the author failed to record it.

Taper is usually the result of blade technology as opposed to biface production. In some cases, the blade is bifacially-flaked; a classic example is the Lerma point (Hranicky and Painter 1988). This point is not found as far north as the MPRV. This is probably the only point that could be called a dagger. Dagger blades always have a blade taper. The D/P ratio is always <1.0.

Most MPRV knife shapes maintain the triangularly-shaped form (wedge). As mentioned, the acutus angle varies, but the blade shape maintains a pointed end. This implies usage such as a tool that sometimes is used to penetrate a target object and then to cut it open, namely butchering tools.

As suggested in this discussion, knife classification in New World archaeology remains open, such as terminology, standards, identifications, physical properties and attributes, useability, life cycles, and numerous other factors. This overview with artifactual examples should prompt future research and better attention analytically to site-context specimens.

Knife Blade Edges

Knife blade edges are the same as discussed in the MPRV Flakes as Tools section. The edge classifications, namely fine, metafine, coarse, and gravelly, are used on knife specimens illustrated here. See blade edges in the MPRV Flakes as Tools.

Knife Size

Most knives that are found in archaeological contexts are expended forms. Any attempt at reconstructing the original size is precarious, at best, or good scientific guessing. Statistical inferences are possible, but the main problem lies with no (very few) MPRV specimens from which statistical regressions can be constructed. This analysis involves curve fitting or linear regression methods that use knife data to calculate (estimate) knife lengths. This method was used in Hranicky and McCary (1996) to estimate blade lengths for expended Clovis points. Additionally, expended forms do not always indicate their original structure; thus, once again, the size problem has no foundation, other than by using comparative data from areas that have produced large knives. There is an assumption that some or all MPRV knives at all time periods were long (>150 mm); data is based on a statistical regression.

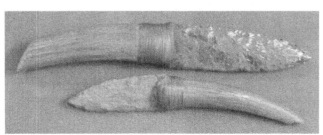

Repo-F – Knives (Replications). Top: Elk horn handle, artificial sinew, and obsidian blade. Bottom: elk horn handle, artificial sinew, native blade. They were made by James C. Gurley (Case City, Virginia).

Knife Measurements

Knife measurements are different than for projectile points. The function and structure dictates the following:

1 – Thickness is a measurement of the thickest part of the knife; it can also be described as minimum and maximum measurements. Thickness profile is based on length and width measurements.

2 – Length is a measurement along the longest axis of the knife.

3 – Height is the width of the blade across the workend of the knife. Blade areas that are not intended as a cutting edge are not measured.

4 – Frank angle as measured from one flat plane. Frank/shoulder angles can also be used.

5 – Chassis-to-blade edge angles are indicators of function, but standards need to be developed for the correlation.

6 – If a backed-bladed knife, the angle from back to edge is measured.

7 – Acutus to share angle which is measured off the medial axis.

Based on the MPRV sample, the average knife thickness is 10-11 mm, and the implement is usually made from quartzite. Aside from the projectile point, most MPRV knives have only one cutting edge.

Knife Styles

While some knife types have been identified and published (see Hranicky 2002), no style (or typology) has been established for knife forms found in the Middle Atlantic area. The specimens and data used in the study are insufficient to perform typological identifications. MPRV specimens are arranged by morphology with an assumption that some of the styles indicate types and have established distributions for both geography and chronology. Basic styles are:

1 – Lunate	2 – Crescent
3 – Stemmed	4 – Notched
5 – Single-sided	6 – Double-sided
7 – Triangle	8 – Flake
9 – Blade	10 – Tanged
11 – Elongated	12 – Oblong
13 – Backed	14 – Beveled
15 – Ovoid	16 – Cortex-backed
17 – Fan (ulu)	18 – Diagonal.

<u>Note</u>: Elongated knives may be hand-held implements.

These morphological categories are used to classify knives in the study area. Specimens are shown in the following pages.

One style found in Virginia is similar to the famous Cody knife of the American Southwest (see Wormington 1957 and Agenbroad 1978). It was found on the Dime site in Virginia (Figure 24). For an overview of the Dime site, see Bottoms (1999). The diagonal blade edges also occur in the Edgefield scraper found primarily in South Carolina (Michie 1968). These blade treatments are assumed here to be knives, but certainly could be used for other functions.

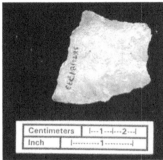

Figure 24 – Cody-Like Knife from the Dime Site (44SK92) in Virginia (L = 35, W = 37.7, T = 11.1 mm). It is made from quartz and has a V-shaped point to its edge. The Dime site has a Paleoindian Period component; thus, it is assumed to be a Paleoindian tool. Reference to the Plains Cody knife may be a parallel invention or accidental by a tool user/maker.

Knife Useability

The knife was the basic tool for performing daily tasks of food processing, shelter preparation and maintenance, clothing design and dress, and numerous human activities. The knife has a lifecycle of useability wherein each Indian society determined what tools were still useable and which tools had reached expention.

When to discard was the Native Americans' choice based on his/her perception of what is the normal length; naturally, breakage is usually an automatic expention, but occasionally the blade is retrofitted.

Most knives found archaeologically are expended implements. This is usually evidenced by dull shares, blunt acutuses, and short blades. However, based on the MPRV sample, no data can be extracted to provide clues to the *what-is* the normal expended knife (see Plate 18).

The expention process involved discarding the knife blade/handle at a time when the blade needed resharpening but was at a length that the user considered the end had come for the tool. The blade may have still had usable life remaining. For expention, the cognitive assessment of usable blade life is based on cultural factors, such as finding materials, time needed to make the tool, toolmaker availability, etc. Also, as a hypothesis, toolmaking was probably a summer activity. Some stones, such as rhyolite are not workable under 45°.

Based on national sampling, the maximum length (average) for knives is 200 mm. It has one acutus and one share; it is usually made from flint (Hranicky 2002a). No MPRV knife was observed that was even close to the national average. MPRV knives when put into service probably averaged 125 mm. Expention appears to be 65 mm. The major lithic material is quartzite. See Table 1 for summary statistics in a MPRV study and following pages are examples.

Useability always implies work. And, work implies efficiency. Efficiency is an interesting concept which is basically measured in time and blade (share) durability. For prehistory, efficiency is simply: does the tool accomplish the task for which it was intended? Prehistoric tool efficiency is an infant in technological analyses. See Useability in Toolmaking Technology section.

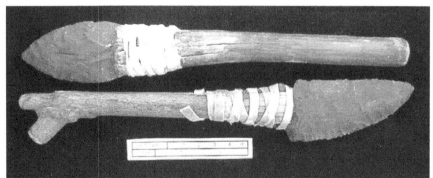

Repo-G – Two Rhyolite Knives with Wooden Handles (Replications). Top is leather wrapped and bottom is fiber wrapped. Blades were inserted and glued with pine pitch and then wrapped to secure the blade. Wood is the worst material in terms of preservation and, as such, is rarely preserved in Middle Atlantic archaeology. Knives were made by Jeffry Tottenham.

Table 1 – Summary Data for MPRV Study Sample *				
Materials	**Length ****	**Width**	**Thickness**	**L/W Ratio**
Rhyolite: 16 (21.3%) Quartz: 3 (4.0%) Quartzite: 46 (61.3%) Flint: 3 (4.0%) Slate: 2 (2.6%) Conglomerate: 1 (1.3%) Jasper: 2 (2.6%) Shale: 2 (2.6%)	Max: 126 mm Min: 47 mm Ave: 80.86	Max: 58 mm Min: 24 mm Ave: 35.84	Max: 30 mm Min: 8 mm Ave: 12.84	Max: 4.30 Min: 5.80 *** Ave: 2.26
Shapes	**Frank**	**Shares**	**Acutus**	**Cortex**
Elongated: 14 (18.7%) Triangle: 1 (1.3%) Stemmed: 29 (38.7%) Oblong: 3 (4.0%) Ovoid: 3 (4.0%) Crescent: 3 (4.0%) Lunate: 3 (4.0%) Hand-held: 1 (1.3%) Flake: 1 (1.3%) Notched: 3 (4.0%) Hafted: 7 (9.3%) Cortex-backed: 1 (1.3%) Tang: 1 (1.3%) Fan: 1 (1.3%) Bipointed: 3 (4.0%)	Shoulder: 54 (72.0%) Taper: 12 (28.0%)	Single: 31 (41.3%) Dual: 44 (58.7%)	Sharp: 32 (42.7%) Dull: 43 (57.3%)	Yes: 8 (10.7%) No: 67 (89.3%)

* Sample is random without any defined selection criteria (see following pages).
** Length has a bias that most of the knives that were recovered in the study collection are expended forms.
*** Thinner knives have better ratios.

Plate 18 - MRPV Knife Specimens

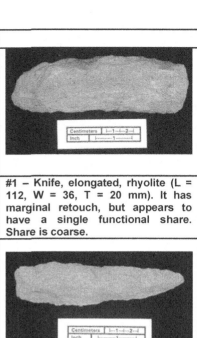	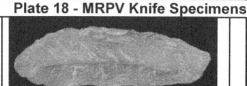	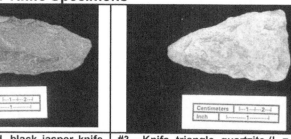
#1 – Knife, elongated, rhyolite (L = 112, W = 36, T = 20 mm). It has marginal retouch, but appears to have a single functional share. Share is coarse.	#2 – Knife, elongated, black jasper knife (L = 114, W = 34, T = 17 mm). It has a flattened bank and straight worn share. Share is coarse. (Warren County)	#3 – Knife, triangle, quartzite (L = 66, W = 38, T = 13 mm). It has dual shares. It is probably an expended knife. Share is coarse.
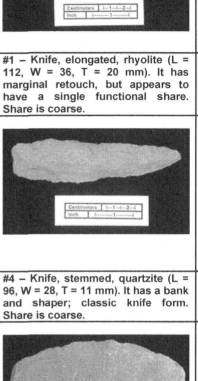		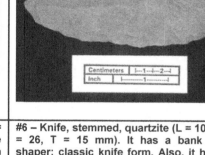
#4 – Knife, stemmed, quartzite (L = 96, W = 28, T = 11 mm). It has a bank and shaper; classic knife form. Share is coarse.	#5 – Knife, oblong, quartzite (L = 72, W = 41, T = 12 mm). Bank and share are difficult to identify. It is probably an expended knife. Share is coarse.	#6 – Knife, stemmed, quartzite (L = 102, W = 26, T = 15 mm). It has a bank and shaper; classic knife form. Also, it has a blade ridge. Share is coarse.
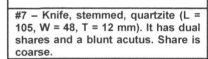		
#7 – Knife, stemmed, quartzite (L = 105, W = 48, T = 12 mm). It has dual shares and a blunt acutus. Share is coarse.	#8 – Knife, stemmed, quartzite (L = 92, W = 39, T = 12 mm). It has a bank and shaper; classic knife form. Share is coarse.	#9 – Knife, ovoid, rhyolite (L = 65, W = 36, T = 11 mm). It can be called a circular share with no bank. It has no acutus. Share is coarse.

#10 – Knife, stemmed, quartzite (L = 84, W = 30, T = 12 mm). It has a bank and shaper; classic knife form. Share is coarse.	#11 – Knife, stemmed, quartzite (L = 91, W = 25, T = 25 mm). It has dual shares and a pointed acutus. Share is coarse.	#12 – Knife, stemmed, quartzite (L = 72, W = 41, T = 15 mm). It may be a biface; otherwise, it is an expended knife. Share is coarse.

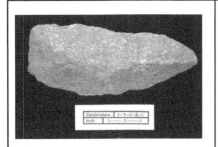 #13 – Knife, stemmed, quartzite (L = 120, W = 49, T = 30 mm). It has a bank and shaper; classic knife form. Also, it has a blade ridge. Share is coarse.	 #14 – Knife, elongated, rhyolite (L = 86, W = 24, T = 9 mm). It has a bank and shaper; classic knife form. Share is coarse.	 #15 – Knife, crescent, quartzite (L = 116, W = 55, T = 17 mm). It has a curved share, ridged blade, and irregular bank. Share is coarse.
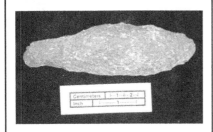 #16 – Knife, stemmed, rhyolite (L = 108, W = 34, T = 12 mm). It has dual shares and is probably an expended knife. Share is coarse.	 #17 – Knife, lunate, quartzite (L = 81, W = 39, T = 20 mm). It has triple shares with no defined chassis area. Shares are coarse.	 #18 – Knife, lunate, quartzite (L = 72, W = 41, T = 16 mm). It has triple shares with no defined chassis area. It is probably an expended knife. Shares are coarse.
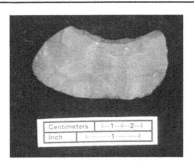 #19 – Knife, crescent, flint (L = 61, W = 29, T = 17 mm). It has a curved share and bank with no acutus. Share is metafine.	 #20 – Knife, hand-held, flint (L = 72, W = 48, T = 13 mm). It has worn but defined share. Part of one share is used for a spokeshave. Share is metafine.	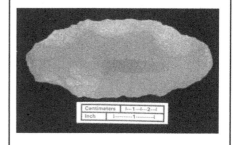 #21 – Knife, flake, quartzite (L = 108, W = 44, T = 12 mm). It has dual shares which were not intended for long term usage. It has no acutus and cortex on one face. Share is coarse.
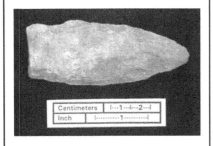 #22 – Knife, notched, slate (L = 69, W = 29, T = 7 mm). It has dual shares and a blunt acutus. Shares are gravelly.	 #23 – Knife, hafted, quartzite (L = 79, W = 34, T = 12 mm). It has a single share and irregular bank. It has a blunt acutus. It is probably an expended knife. Share is coarse.	 #24 – Knife, hafted, rhyolite (L = 74, T = 34, T = 12 mm). It has blade ridge and irregular shares. The acutus is pointed. Shares are coarse.

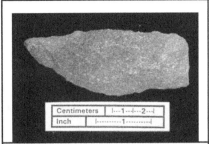 #25 – Knife, stemmed, rhyolite (L = 72, W = 29, T = 12 mm). It has a straight bank and curved share with a pointed acutus. Share is coarse.	 #26 – Knife, stemmed, rhyolite (L = 65, W = 27, T = 9 mm). It has dual shares with a pointed acutus. It is probably an expended knife. Shares are coarse.	 #27 – Knife, stemmed, quartz (L = 54, W = 28, T = 13 mm). It has dual shares forming a V and a pointed acutus. It is probably an expended knife. Shares are metafine.
 #28 – Knife, elongated, quartzite (L = 65, W = 29, T = 11 mm). It has dual acutuses and a curved, single share. It is probably a short-term expended knife. The right end is the chassis end. Shares are coarse.	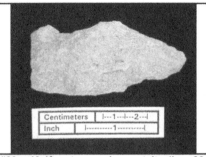 #29 – Knife, stemmed, quartzite (L = 62, W = 29, T = 10 mm). It has dual shares and has a pronounced hafting area. Shares are coarse.	 #30 – Knife, cortex-backed, quartzite (L = 89, W = 46, T = 18 mm). It has a cortex bank and curved share. It does not have an acutus. Share is coarse.
 #31 – Knife, notched, quartzite (L = 76, W = 38, T = 9 mm). It has dual shares and no acutus. Hafting area is small. It could be classified as a saw. Shares are coarse.	 #32 – Knife, lunate, quartzite (L = 126, W = 56, T = 19 mm). It has dual shares (curved and straight) with one acutus. Shares are coarse.	 #33 – Knife, elongated, quartzite (L = 98, W = 39, T = 9 mm). It has triple shares with a hafting area (left pointed end). Shares are coarse.
 #34 – Knife, oblong, quartzite (L = 78, W = 49, T = 11 mm). It has a notched share and curved bank. Acutus is blunt or nonexistent. Share is coarse.	 #35 – Knife, hafted, conglomerate (L = 66, W = 38, T = 16 mm). The right pointed end is the tang. It has poor remaining shares and acutus. It is an expended knife. Share is coarse.	 #36 – Knife, stemmed, rhyolite (L = 48, W = 36, T = 11 mm). It has a curved share and semipointed acutus. It is an expended knife. Share is coarse.

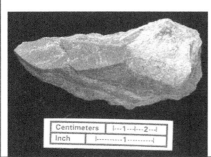 #37 – Knife, stemmed, rhyolite (L = 80, W = 35, T = 25 mm). It is a thick knife that was probably hafted. It has dual shares which are coarse.	 #38 – Knife, tang, jasper (L = 101, W = 42, T = 13 mm). It has a stem haft with dual shares. Acutus is blunt. Share is metafine.	 #39 – Knife, stemmed, quartzite (L = 92, W = 49, T = 8 mm). It has a square hafting area, dual shares, and blunt acutus. It is probably an expended knife. Shares are coarse.
 #40 – Knife, elongated, quartzite (L = 77, W = 31, W = 14 mm). It has dual shares with no acutus. Hafting is difficult to identify. Share is coarse.	 #41 – Knife, elongated, quartzite (L = 77, W = 29, T = 9 mm). It has a ridged-blade, dual shares, and pointed acutus. Shares are coarse.	 #42 – Knife, stemmed, quartzite (L = 59, W = 30, T = 7 mm). It has a ridged-blade, dual shares, and pointed acutus. It is probably an expended knife. Shares are coarse.
 #43 – Knife, stemmed, quartzite (L = 77, W = 33, T = 10 mm). It has a well worn share and straight bank. Acutus is broken. Shares are coarse.	 #44 – Knife, ovoid, quartzite (L = 86, W = 48, T = 12 mm). It has a straight bank and curved share. Acutus is dull. Shares are coarse.	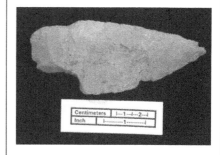 #45 – Knife, stemmed, jasper (L = 99, W = 49, T = 10 mm). It was found with a Paleoindian point. It has dual shares and pointed acutus. Shares are metafine.
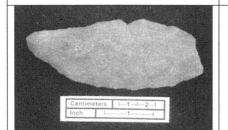 #46 – Knife, elongated, quartzite (L = 84, W = 32, T = 10 mm). It has a single share, bank, and pointed acutus. Share is coarse.	 #47 – Knife, elongated, rhyolite (L = 79, W = 30, T = 11 mm). It has a single share, bank, and pointed acutus. Share is coarse.	 #48 – Knife, stemmed, quartzite (L = 78, W = 34, T = 9 mm). It has dual shares and pointed acutus. Share is coarse.

Artifact Caches
(Native American Hiding Places for Lithic Materials)

Caches have been reported in Virginia, West Virginia, and Maryland (Hranicky and Herndon 1992), (Hranicky 1992, 1990, 1989 and 1987), (Curry 1992), (Wimsatt 1958), (Livesay, et al. 1970), (MacCord 1980 and 1972), (Painter 1964), (Tisdale 1964), (Stevens and Whitted 1976), (Wells 1969), (Geasey 1974), and elsewhere in the Middle Atlantic area. Native American caches represent an isolated artifact or group of artifacts placement usually near a river or major stream. They are probably the result of a young Native American knapper's work, as most Maryland and Virginia caches are composed of poorly made pieces. But, who made them and why will probably never be known. Of course, we maintain the archaeological speculations for all caches.

The placement may be a ceremony or rite for adulthood or graduation as a member of a society's toolmakers. However, numerous caches indicate that their contents were for future usage. A general characteristic for most cache bifaces is that they are made from the same lithic material. The basic purpose of a cache remains to be proven; they may be multipurpose artifact deposits.

Sample of the Duck River Cache, Humphreys County, Tennessee. Based on Fowke (1913), it is probably the most famous cache ever found in America. The flintknapper who made these cache blades was the *best* flintknapper who ever lived in the prehistoric U.S.

This section provides cache examples from throughout the Middle Atlantic area. The purpose was to provide an overview cache distribution and composition so that future studies may reveal the true nature of cache deposits by pre-Contact Native Americans. Cache distributions need further studies. Reference to the MPRV is made, but the focus is caches in general for the Middle Atlantic area.

Cache Blades

The cache blade is a general reference to any unfinished biface found outside of a site. Occasionally, caches are found inside a site's boundaries, but these are rare. They are frequently called blades as opposed to their actual description of biface. Either term is acceptable. Figure 1 shows a biface that would typically be called a cache blade by archaeologists. Figure 2 shows a comparative example of an Adena cache.

Figure 1 – Rhyolite Cache Blade from Adams County, Pennsylvania (L = 154, W = 72, T = 13 mm). It is probably an Adena blade that is common in the Eastern U.S. The D/P ratio is 0.689 which shows a taper to the blade.

The **cache blade** is:
...large, well-made biface made from high quality materials, usually flint.

Cache blade is used sometimes, especially by collectors, to refer to Adena or Hopewell bifaces. Large bifaces are found throughout time and space in prehistoric America. Ceremonial blade refers to an unusually large artifact.

Cache Make-Up

The concept that cache bifaces represent crude unfinished tools has been with archaeologists for years. One of the earliest archaeologists to define the cache is McGuire (1896), as:

The so-called cache tool or lanceolate stones, commonly found in great numbers in a single place, was probably stock material carried from the original source of supply in that shape in which it could best be transported for subsequent specialization into implements.

Figure 2 – Adena Eicholtz Cache from Lawrence County, Pennsylvania. They are made from Flint Ridge flint and were found in 1910 by Iva Price. The blades are presently in the collection of Robert Converse.

For the MPRV, caches are not numerous, but this may be due to under reporting. Holmes (1897) offers:

There can be little doubt that these hoards are deposits of blades produced in the quarry-shops or on sites furnishing supplies of raw material and transported and stored for utilization or trade. Few caches of the quartzite blades have been reported from the tidewater country. It is much more common to find deposits of blades of other materials not obtained in the region, and therefore brought from a distance by quarry workers or traders. At the mouth of South river, Maryland, near the banks of Selby bay, four hoards have been found, and are now for the most part in the collection of Mr. J. D. McGuire. Two are of argillite and one of jasper, brought, no doubt, from workshops in Pennsylvania, some 150 miles away, and one is of rhyolite, probably from the quarries on the head of Monocacy creek, in Pennsylvania.

Note: Holmes may not have been aware of the jasper quarries in Warren County, Virginia.

Montet-White (1997) suggests:

Cached hoards represent single events or moments in time when one or several individuals buried items of value in the hope of retrieving them at a later date when they may be required to perform a task, proceed with a ceremony, or participate in exchange. Caches, therefore, open a window on forms of behavior not visible in the rest of the archaeological record.

The fall line cache reported by Wimstatt (1958) is among the oldest reported MPRV cache. While rhyolite has a high frequency of MPRV usage, few local caches made from it have been discovered. Rhyolite caches are numerous in southern Virginia and North Carolina. These caches appear to be from the Paleoindian and/or Early Archaic Periods. There are no radiocarbon dates from them. Unfortunately, most caches are found by nonarchaeologists and receive little more attention other than picking them up. Once removed in this manner, precise dating and blade placement are impossible.

Another factor that will never be known – is how many caches were buried and later retrieved by the Native Americans. These offer comparative data, as cache interpretations remain somewhat speculative for archaeology. This section covers a wider range of artifact geographies than the other sections because cache data need to be published. MPRV caches are probably under reported; a subjective opinion by the author.

The watershed plays a major role in the location of caches; however, this remains as a primary concern in the study of cache placements (Hranicky 1987 and 1990). As such, it is extremely important that all caches be reported and published.

Cache Purpose

There are as many theories about cache placement and purpose as there are caches; none of which has ever been proven. Peterson and MacCord (1989) write that popular opinions are:

1 – Caches were buried to improve their knappability
2 – Caches belonged to traders who forgot them
3 – Caches were hidden to prevent theft
4 – Caches were buried for future needs
5 – Caches were symbols of power/status.

One argument for caches that has been with archaeology for a number of years is that burial improved workability, namely burial adds moisture to the stone. The poor quality of most caches suggests that this is not the case; however, fresh stone preferences were criteria for ancient knappers.

Hranicky (1987) presents a Social Network Model (SNM) for explaining the reason, source, and location of caches. Since that publication, more cache data and study suggest that ceremony was the principal reason for the cache. Future storage of stone tools is not a viable answer to why the Native Americans created caches. Far too many of the cache blades are so poorly made that they would not be used to make *real* tools. The SNM suggests these factors for cache analyses:

1 – Cache size
2 – Social practices
3 – Toolmaking quality
4 – Near water placement
5 – Buried contexts
6 – Raw material
7 – Trade or exchange gifts
8 – Territory marker.

Caches represent the mystery of deliberate artifact placement by Native Americans for reasons or beliefs known only to them. The overall pattern suggests caches are (Hranicky 1987):

1 – Storage for future use
2 – Ceremonial, such as adulthood
3 – Graduation, such as becoming a flintknapper
4 – Tribute, gods, neighbors, chiefdoms, etc.
5 – Magic, obtain good magic or lose bad magic
6 – Hunting, bring good luck
7 – Unknown reasons.

The ceremonial aspect remains the basic interpretation in this publication. For example, a 2500+ piece Onondaga biface cache was discovered in New York (Ritchie 1955). It was covered with red ocher and is assigned to the Meadowood pointmakers. The cache size suggests a ceremonial purpose. Another Meadowood cache, Lumberton, New Jersey reported in the 1880s suggests a cache purpose was storage for future usage. Granger (1981) provides basic data (see Table 1).

Caches

The following caches are discussed:

1 – Somerset County Cache
2 – Montgomery, North Carolina Bifaces
3 – Waratan Cache
4 – Beaver Cache
5 – C. Merry Cache
6 – Belvoir Cache
7 – Wilkison Cache
8 – Ward Cache
9 – Buckingham County Cache.

Table 1 – Meadowood Cache			
	H/L value	Range	Mean
Blade length	74/33 mm	37 mm	46 mm
Blade width	31/21 mm	10 mm	24.5 mm
Blade width (tip)	21/15 mm	6 mm	17.5 mm
Base width	31/19 mm	12 mm	26 mm
Base height	5/2 mm	3 mm	4 mm
Max. thick	6/4 mm	2 mm	5 mm
Max. length	72/37 mm	37 mm	51 mm
Weight	13.6/5.3 g	8.3 g	9.7 g

Another similar cache was found in the spring of 1995 in Pennsylvania, which has Onondaga bifaces and several other tools (Kemble 1999). These Meadowood caches and other northeast caches indicate a functional ceremonial purpose. The general characteristic here is well-made bifaces. These caches date to the Early Woodland Period.

Middle Atlantic area caches are usually made from the same lithic material and were made using bifacial reduction technology. Overall, most cache bifaces are poorly made. As a suggestion, prehistoric caches are an eastern phenomena. Caches do not have a definite distributional pattern for the MPRV or Middle Atlantic area. Archaeologically, are caches a class of artifacts? If so, is the industry storing?

Sommerset County Cache, Maryland

Recently, a 10-piece rhyolite biface cache was found in Somerset County, Maryland. It has Fox Creek-like flaking; thus, its classification. It was probably made using a wooden billet. Cache data are presented in Table 2, and Figures 3 and 4 show the bifaces. All pieces appear to be quarry blanks that suggest storage for future use. Quarry source may be miles away.

Montgomery County Bifaces, North Carolina

A factor that has not been reported in caches is cache blades that are ceremonially broken. A rhyolite cache from Montgomery County, North Carolina is composed of 12+ bifaces (total not known). Each biface is broken in the center. The discoverer of the cache glued the pieces back together. Table 3 contains cache data, and Figures 5 and 6 show the actual specimens. The North Carolina cache is poorly made and offers a contrast to the Somerset Cache. The bifaces were probably made using a medium billet and probably represent an Early Archaic period toolmaker's effort.

Table 2 – Somerset County Biface Cache				
Biface #	Thickness (mm)	Width (mm)	Length (mm)	L/W*T Ratio	Comments
C1	23.4	75.0	115.2	35.94	Medial ridge on spall
C2	26.4	73.4	110.0	39.56	Hinge fracture, bold flakes
C3	22.5	61.6	125.0	45.66	Medial ridge, well-shaped
C4	21.5	69.4	126.0	39.03	Major hinge scar, well-shaped
C5	17.8	71.2	124.2	29.65	Broad hinge fracture, well-shaped
C6	13.3	68.1	122.4	23.90	Hinge fracture, spall, thin, well-shaped
C7	18.1	63.1	103.4	29.65	Thick, well-shaped
C8	23.0	74.1	124.3	38.58	Best of cache, hinge fracture
C9	16.1	69.0	125.9	30.31	Thin, well-shaped
C10	16.8	61.1	99.2	29.40	Smallest, thick, well-shaped
Averages	18.11	68.60	117.56	---	All bifaces can be worked into tools; overall quality is good.

Figure 3 – Rhyolite Bifaces from the Somerset County Cache, Maryland, Bifaces 1 – 5. All bifaces represent quarry spall bifaces that can be made into an implement.

Figure 4 – Rhyolite Bifaces from the Somerset County Cache, Maryland, Bifaces 6 – 10. All bifaces represent quarry spall bifaces that can be made into an implement.

Table 3 – Biface Data from a Montgomery County, North Carolina Cache *					
Biface #	Thickness (mm)	Width (mm)	Length (mm)	L/W*T Ratio	Comments
C1	10.4	52.1	151.8	30.30	Well made, thin, easily made into a knife or projectile point
C2	13.5	39.4	179.0	61.33	Long, thin, well made, probably intended as a knife
C3	17.9	57.3	215.0	67.16	Thick, minor hinge fractures, may be a knife
C4	12.4	69.1	169.0	30.32	Wide, thin, well made
Averages	10.45	54.48	178.70	---	Cache was probably ceremonially killed. It shows no signs of usage.

* Sample data, total number of bifaces is not known.

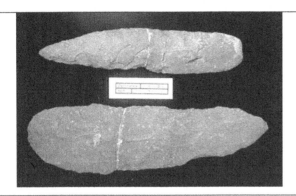

Figure 5 – Examples of Killed Bifaces from a Cache in Montgomery County, North Carolina (2 of 4). These bifaces were ceremonially broken. Their basic shape indicates a knife function.

Figure 6 – Examples of Killed Bifaces from a Cache in Montgomery County, North Carolina (2 of 4). These bifaces were ceremonially broken. Their basic shape indicates a knife function. These cache bifaces are part of a cache of which the total size is unknown.

Warratan Cache, North Carolina

The unpublished Warratan cache (North Carolina) is included because it offers what may be a future storage rhyolite cache of bifaces. Or, it suggests a single and experienced knapper. This cache is typical of the Virginia-North Carolina border caches in rhyolite. The cache data are presented in Table 4, and bifaces are illustrated in Figure 7. For rhyolite cache discussions, see Hranicky (1990 and 1992).

The consistency of the biface manufacture indicates a single knapper; however, this is a subjective assessment. The most obvious structural feature is the rounded corners, which are unusual for Virginia/North Carolina caches.

Figure 7 – Warratan Cache Made of Rhyolite

Table 4 – Warratan Cache Data					
Biface #	Thickness (mm)	Width (mm)	Length (mm)	L/W*T Ratio	Comments
W1	6.5	27.0	46.1	11.10	Two hinge fractures, pressure flaking, rounded corners
W2	7.0	26.0	43.3	11.66	Curved long axis, major hinge
W3	5.8	27.0	---	---	Broken, major hinge, pressure basal flakes, slight concave base
W4	8.1	24.2	56.8	19.01	Well-developed medial ridge, two deep flake scars, bad L/W*T ratio
W5	8.3	26.4	62.1	19.52	Cortex remaining, developed medial ridge, pressure flaking, rounded corners, bad L/W*T ratio

Table 4 – Warratan Cache Data					
W6	9.3	24.6	54.1	20.45	Cortex remaining, major hinge, high medial ridge, rounded corners, slight convex base
W7	5.5	32.4	50.2	8.52	Could be resharpened knife, excellent flaking, developed medial ridge, thin, good L/W*T ratio
W8	6.5	31.9	45.4	9.25	Well-made, pressure flaking, rounded corners
W9	5.8	30.0	43.9	8.49	Well-made, rounded corners, thin, good L/W*T ratio
W10	7.1	27.6	54.2	13.94	Numerous hinges, one good face, one bad face, poor medial ridges, rounded corners
W11	7.9	24.6	49.9	16.02	One polished notch, basal thinning, hinge fracture
W12	7.9	28.5	48.2	13.36	Minor hinge, semi-developed medial ridge, rounded corners, poor knapping
W13	7.9	25.0	44.7	14.13	Bad lateral edge, minor hinge, basal thinning, rounded corners, poorly made
W14	7.1	27.5	48.2	12.44	Minor hinges, high spots, pressure flaking, rounded corners, well-made
W15	7.8	28.8	55.9	15.14	One deep flake scar, well-made, minor hinge, basal thinning, rounded corners
W16	7.3	27.8	48.6	12.76	Thick, tip rework, well-made, rounded corners
W17	7.3	28.1	59.9	15.56	Hump, deep flake scar, well-shaped, rounded corners, slight concave base
W18	7.7	27.8	47.7	13.21	Polished side notch, high spot, well-made, rounded corners
W19	7.6	29.3	52.2	13.54	Well-made and shaped, good medial ridge, basal thinning, rounded corners
Averages	7.28	27.61	53.61	-----	

Beaver Cache, Virginia

The Beaver cache was discovered in Pittsylvania County, Virginia. It is named after its reported finder. Initially, the cache had over 75 pieces, but was broken up on the relic market. It may totally lack credibility, but it does appear to be an authentic cache. There is no data available on the discovery time or location other than the county. Table 5 contains the basic cache data with manufacture comments. Figures 8 through 13 show the cache specimens. The cache was included because it is unpublished, made of rhyolite, and more importantly, it has both flake (blade) and biface pieces. Generally, the cache appears to have been made by inexperienced knappers. The rhyolite is not from the same source. This cache is the first one to be published which indicates more than one knapper. The cache is classified here as Paleoindian.

Table 5 – Beaver Cache Data					
Biface#	Thickness (mm)	Width (mm)	Length (mm)	L/W*T Ratio	Comments
1	10.0	21.0	56.0	26.67	Center hump and several hinges; made on flake or blade
2	6.0	24.2	61.0	15.12	Thin, partial medial ridge
3	9.7	25.5	59.0	22.44	High medial axis, deep hinges, made on flake
4	9.0	25.0	65.0	23.40	Cortex remaining, deep flake scars
5	9.1	27.0	55.0	18.54	Center axis hump, made on a flake
6	7.0	29.9	53.2	12.45	Deep hinges, convex base, biface
7	10.0	34.5	62.1	18.00	Large hump which would cause failure, flake?
8	10.0	21.5	61.0	28.37	Heavily weathered, parallel flaking, hinges, part of this cache?
9	8.5	30.0	56.0	15.87	Triangle shape, high medial axis, biface
10	10.5	29.2	59.5	21.40	Hump, high lower medial axis, hinges
11	9.1	30.5	54.5	16.26	Biface, convex base, deep hinge
12	9.5	29.0	61.3	20.08	Hinges, made on a blade, medial ridge
13	9.0	21.2	60.2	25.56	Biface, narrow, deep hinge
14	8.1	32.5	49.7	12.39	Ovoid-shaped, biface, edge retouch
15	101	25.0	57.0	23.03	High medial ridge, biface
16	8.4	23.0	65.5	23.92	Hinge, deep flake scar, narrow biface
17	10.2	19.2	60.5	32.14	Narrow bifaces, deep scar, almost a black flint
18	8.1	33.0	59.0	14.48	Ovoid-shaped, weathered, well made

					Table 5 – Beaver Cache Data
19	7.0	27.8	55.0	13.85	Cortex remaining, probably made on a flake, hinge
20	7.0	25.2	58.5	16.25	Thin, developed medial ridge, minor hinges
21	11.0	32.0	85.3	29.32	Cortex on tip remaining, developed medial ridge, well made
22	9.4	36.0	67.0	17.49	Minor hinges
23	11.0	40.0	85.2	23.43	Made on large flake, deep hinge, cortex remaining on tip
24	9.2	35.0	65.0	17.09	Made on large flake, minor hinges
25	9.5	31.0	82.0	25.13	Developed medial ridge, edge breakage
26	7.0	31.0	65.0	14.68	Minor hinges
27	11.0	21.1	69.5	36.23	Hump with deep hinge
28	8.0	22.3	61.5	22.06	Tip and corner damage
29	13.1	27.0	81.9	39.74	Large hump, broken, hinges
30	9.0	24.8	61.0	22.14	Cortex remaining, edge retouch, deep flake scars
31	8.0	25.0	79.0	25.28	Cortex remaining, developed medial ridge, well made
32	8.9	27.1	63.0	20.69	Made off core blade, developed medial ridge, well made
33	9.0	34.5	78.0	20.35	Broken, basal thinning, hinges
34	9.9	24.5	79.6	32.16	Deep scars, high area
35	7.0	25.0	61.5	17.22	Cortex remaining, developed medial ridge, best of cache
36	9.5	23.8	63.0	25.15	Broken tip, deep scars, hump, basal thinning
37	9.2	31.3	83.5	24.54	Well-shaped, basal thinning and setup (nipple?), deep scar
38	7.0	33.5	68.7	14.36	Well-made, thin and flat
39	8.8	25.5	71.5	24.67	Very poor medial ridge, overall well made
40	8.3	25.2	61.3	20.19	Off center medial ridge
41	8.3	22.5	57.0	21.03	Deep side hinge, hump
42	9.5	25.1	52.0	19.68	Deep depression, small hump, minor hinges
43	11.5	20.0	61.0	35.08	High medial ridges, long surface fracture
44	8.0	28.0	48.0	13.71	Triangle shape, deep surface depressions
45	10.0	31.0	53.0	17.10	Convex base, flat area, hinges
46	8.9	24.0	56.0	20.77	Heavily patinated, developed medial ridges, cortex remaining
47	8.5	16.0	54.5	28.95	High ridge, hump, hinges
48	7.0	19.0	61.0	22.47	Deep scar, hump, hinges
49	7.5	24.0	51.0	15.94	Deep side scar, flat medial ridge
Averages	8.97	26.92	63.17	21.77	

Figure 8 – Beaver Cache Blades #1 to #9

Figure 9 – Beaver Cache Blades #10 to #19

Figure 10 – Beaver Cache Blades #20 to #25

Figure 11 – Beaver Cache Blades #26 to #32

Figure 12 – Beaver Cache Blades #33 to #39

Figure 13 – Beaver Cache Blades #40 to #49

C. Merry Cache, Maryland

The C. Merry cache consists of five bifaces that were found near Seneca in Montgomery County, Maryland (Hranicky 1988). Two bifaces are made from rhyolite, and three are quartzite. Overall, they are long, narrow bifaces that could have been finished into points or tools. Cache data are presented in Table 6 (Hranicky 1988). The significance of this cache is its use of dual materials. Most caches are composed of a single stone.

Table 6 – C. Merry Cache						
Biface #	Width (mm)	Length (mm)	Thick (mm)	W*L	W*L*T	W/T (ratio)
1	45.0	105.0	15.0	4725	70875	3.00
2	44.0	111.0	16.0	4884	78144	2.75
3	49.0	131.0	21.0	6419	134799	2.33
4	45.0	96.0	8.0	4320	34560	5.62
5	44.0	120.0	10.0	5280	52800	4.40
Averages	45.5	112.6	14.0	5125.6	74235.6	3.62

Belvoir Cache, Virginia

The Belvoir cache is composed of five quartzite bifaces (Hranicky 1987). It was named after and was found at Ft Belvoir, Virginia. The average measurements are width (38.5 mm), length (91.4 mm), and thickness (8.6 mm). The average Width/Thickness (W/T) ratio is 4.17; all of which indicate a well-made cache. As a comparison, the C. Merry quartzite cache is width (45.4 mm), length (112.6 mm), and thickness (14.0 mm) with a W/T ratio of 3.62. The C. Merry cache probably dates to the Late Archaic Period; whereas, the Belvoir cache is possibly Paleoindian or Early Archaic. Neither cache has a datable context. Ft Belvoir has produced another cache (44Fx10) of which Figure 14 shows a broken cache biface.

Figure 14 – Broken Jasper Cache Biface from Ft Belvoir, Virginia.

Figure 15 – Sample Bifaces from the Wilkison Cache. Several pieces still have cortex remaining that suggests these bifaces are first stage shaping after obtaining quarry boulders or blocks. It probably represents a near quarry workstation.

Wilkison Cache, Virginia

The Wilkison cache (Warren County, Virginia) is a partial jasper cache that was part of a reduction station where the Native Americans were making bifaces from quarry bulk (Hranicky 1989). It has poorly-made pieces which suggests biface rejects. Average measurements are length (79.1 mm), width (54.3 mm), and thickness (15.4 mm) with a W/T ratio of 5.13. Figure 15 shows a representative sample of the bifaces. The cache probably dates to the Paleoindian Period.

Meherrin River Cache

The Meherrin River cache was initially found by Floyd Painter in the 1950s (Figure 16). Since its discovery, three more bifaces have been found in the same area (not shown). Basic data are itemized in Table 7. The collection is currently held in public trust by Edward Bottoms. It is well made, probably by a single knapper, and probably dates to the Paleoindian Period. The cache has four white quartzite bifaces; all other bifaces are made from quartzite.

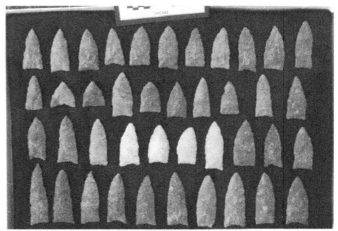

Figure 16 – The Meherrin River Cache

Table 7 – Metric Data on Bifaces in the Meherrin River Cache						
Point Number	Length	Maximum Width	Maximum Thickness	Point Outline	Type Base	Stone Material
MRC-1	52	23	5	Lanceolate	Concave	Blue-Gray Quartzite
MRC-2	60	24	6	Lanceolate	Concave	Grey-Tan Quartzite
MRC-3	50	31	8	Triangular	Concave	Blue-Gray Quartzite
MRC-4	66	26	8	Lanceolate	Concave	Blue-Gray Quartzite
MRC-5	48	25	8	Lanceolate	Straight	Blue-Gray Quartzite
MRC-6	52	21	6	Lanceolate	Concave	Gray-Tan Quartzite
MRC-7	50	21	8	Lanceolate	Concave	Gray Quartzite
MRC-8	49	25	8	Lanceolate	Concave	Gray Quartzite
MRC-9	35	25	7	Lanceolate	Straight	Gray Quartzite
MRC-10	54	25	8	Lanceolate	Straight	Gray Quartzite
MRC-11	52	23	8	Lanceolate	Concave	Gray Quartzite
MRC-12	45	22	9	Lanceolate	Straight	Gray Quartzite
MRC-13	39	22	8	Triangular	Straight	Gray Quartzite
MRC-14	56	25	9	Lanceolate	Concave	Gray Quartzite
MRC-15	45	24	9	Triangular	Concave	Gray Quartzite
MRC-16	51	25	8	Lanceolate	Concave	Blue-Gray Quartzite
MRC-17	49	22	7	Lanceolate	Concave	Gray Quartzite
MRC-18	53	25	9	Lanceolate	Concave	Gray Quartzite
MRC-19	56	21	6	Lanceolate	Concave	Blue-Gray Quartzite
MRC-20	62	23	9	Lanceolate	Straight	Gray Quartzite
MRC-21	63	23	8	Lanceolate	Concave	Gray Quartzite
MRC-22	50	23	7	Lanceolate	Concave	Blue-Gray Quartzite

MRC-23	47	21	7	Triangular	Concave	Tan Quartzite
MRC-24	55	22	8	Lanceolate	Straight	Gray Quartzite
MRC-25	51	22	10	Triangular	Concave	Gray Quartzite
MRC-26	44	34	7	Lanceolate	Straight	White Quartz
MRC-27	45	25	8	Lanceolate	Concave	White Quartz
MRC-28	50	24	8	Triangular	Concave	Tan-White Quartz
MRC-29	74	22	9	Lanceolate	Concave	Gray Quartzite
MRC-30	66	26	9	Lanceolate	Concave	Gray Quartzite
MRC-31	58	22	8	Lanceolate	Concave	White Quartz
MRC-32	53	25	9	Lanceolate	Straight	Gray Quartzite
MRC-33	60	24	9	Lanceolate	Concave	Gray Quartzite
MRC-34	32	28	6	(Resharpened) Pentagonal	Concave	Gray Quartzite
MRC-35	63	25	8	Lanceolate	Concave	Gray Quartzite
MRC-36	41	22	7	Triangular	Straight	Gray Quartzite
MRC-37	51	22	8	Lanceolate	Concave	Gray Quartzite
MRC-38	30	26	8	(Resharpened) Pentagonal	Straight	Gray Quartzite
MRC-39	58	28	10	Lanceolate	Concave	Gray Quartzite
MRC-40	41	23	6	Pentagonal	Concave	Gray Quartzite
MRC-41	65	26	8	Lanceolate	Concave	Gray Quartzite
Average	51.73	24.17	7.85			

Ward Cache, Maryland

The Ward cache was found near Mexico in Carroll County, Maryland (Curry 1992). It consists of 10 well-made, rhyolite bifaces (two are broken). They are long, narrow bifaces which could have been finished into points. One biface was made on a large flake and still retains its curvature. They probably can be attributed to the Fox Creek pointmakers. Table 8 presents measurements.

Table 8 – Ward Cache Data		
Length (cm)	Width (cm)	Thickness
17.9	5.0	N/A
15.8	5.2	N/A
15.7	4.5	N/A
15.5	4.5	N/A
15.0*	5.4	N/A
14.7	5.0	N/A
13.8	4.6	N/A
13.7	5,4	N/A
13.7	5.0	N/A
7.9**	4.9	N/A

* Broken into two pieces
** Proximal half

These cache bifaces were found in a pit of which the top part was plow disturbed. There is little data on the site preparation of caches other than simple dirt burials. This cache is similar to the Sommerset County cache.

Buckingham County Cache, Virginia

The Buckingham County cache, Virginia (tentative name) is a quartz cache that consists of 34 bifaces. It was found near Winginia, Virginia. This cache has not been recorded and published. A sample is shown in Figure 17. It is included because of the rarity of quartz caches in Virginia and Maryland.

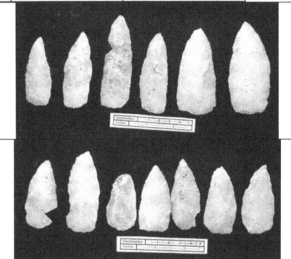

Figure 17 – Buckingham County Quartz Cache. It consists of 34 bifaces which are fair in knapping quality. It has not been published.

Shell Cache

One cache that may simply be a deposit of rejected shells was found on the Maryland side of the Potomac River near Seneca (Figure 18). It was composed of eight different types of shells and numbered 50+ pieces. It may not be prehistoric as no artifacts were found with it. However, shells were traded from the Gulf to the Great Lakes to all of the Atlantic coast from the Late Archaic to Contact (Smith 1987).

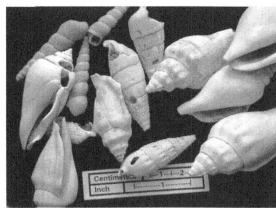

Figure 18 – Maryland Shell Cache

Conclusion

Caches may never be understood in archaeology, as each one offers different information; but they have numerous similarities. This is the best subject in archaeology for *more data are needed*. Caches have a history that goes back to Clovis blades (see Collins 1999) which is somehow a part of the lithic continuum of the American Native American. The practice of cache placement continued to the Contact period. They present themselves as buried treasures from which there is often an endless number of explanations.

From the notebook . . .
Cache Blade – large, well-made biface made from high quality materials, usually flint. Cache blade is used sometimes, especially by collectors, to refer to Adena or Hopewell bifaces. Large bifaces are found throughout time and space in prehistoric America (From: Hranicky 2002). 
Drawing of a Massachusetts Cache Blade (Fowler 1976)

MPRV Prehistoric Pottery

The ceramic era of prehistoric Native Americans in Virginia starts with the excavation of Pope's Creek shell mound by Holmes (1903). Slatery (1946) is given credit with pottery as being synonymous with the Woodland Period in Virginia. His major effort was the excavation at Seldon Island. This work lead to the class known the Marcy Creek Series (Evans 1955). Without a doubt, Clifford Evans 1955 *A Ceramic Study of Virginia Archeology* which was published by the Smithsonian in Washington, DC.

Miscellaneous Virginia Pot Sherds

Virginia pottery was borrowed technology by early Native Americans from the Southeast with fiber-tempered ware originating in Florida (Hranicky 1976 and 1981). Marcy Creek as first defined by Manson (1948) is the oldest type in Virginia. It has a steatite tempering which is generally the argument for this pottery is the transition in early bowls to pottery Woodland ceramics.

Potomac Pottery

The basic studies of Virginia prehistoric pottery are based on the Evans (1955) publication on pottery. Of course, numerous papers have been presented to the profession since. The major problem with these study collections are their collection methods. Pottery sheds were not considered as important; thus, they were not generally maintained by sites or areas. The Merry collection had large boxes of pottery, and it was impossible to truly sort them be types. There needs to be studies outside these private collections to type MPRV ceramics (Potter 1993). Johnson (2009) provides a pottery overview (see Table 1). Stephenson, et al. (1963) is used for type definitions.

Collectors frequently do not pick up pottery sherds or keep them. Charlie Merry kept all his pottery in large boxes which made useful sorting impossible. Whereas, Spencer Geasey kept his pottery by sites which made his ceramic collection a valuable resource.

While the author's copy is not the best, Paul Cresthull 1966 Data Sheet provides an excellent overview of MRVP pottery.

Clifford Evans at the Smithsonian

Table 1 – MPRV Pottery Types (After: Johnson 2009)		
DIAGNOSTIC POTTERY TYPE* (common surface treatment and predominant temper in parentheses)		
V	Marcey Creek (plain/flat base/soapstone)	3,400-3,000
	Selden Island (cordmarked/soapstone)	-3,200
	Accokeek (cordmarked/sand and grit)	3,000-2,400
	Popes Creek (netmarked/coarse sand)	2,600-1,750
	Mockley (netmarked/shell)	1,750-1,200
VI	Shepard (cordmarked/crushed rock)	1,200-650
	Keyser (cordmarked/shell)	650?
	Rappahannock (fabric marked/shell)	1,000-400
	Potomac Creek (cordmarked & plain/sand)	700-350
VII	Cottage-ware or Colonial/historic (plain/various)	390-140** (estimate)

* Partially derived from Egloff and Potter (1982) and Potter (1993).
** Includes dates for indistinguishable slave/tenant cottage industry wares of similar technology. End dates for American Indian manufactured, cottage industry, utilitarian wares are not known.

Various Pottery Dates as Supplied by the DHR:

Mockley Ware (AD 200-900)
Townsend Ware (AD 900-1650)
Croker Landing Ware (as early 1200 BC – coastal plain)
Sand Tempered Ware (500-1000 BC)
Prince George Ware (400 BC – 200 AD)
Potomac Creek Ware (AD 1300-1650)
Camden Ware (ca 1600 AD)
Dan River Ware 1200-1700 AD)
Wright Check and Connestee Ware (AD 1000-?)
Radford Ware (AD 1200-1700)
Southern Appalachian Ware (AD 1400-1700)

Data Sheet No. 5. Courtesy of the Arch. Soc. of Md. Inc. (Harford County Chapter)
SOME POTTERY TYPES IN MARYLAND (After Robert L. Stephensen, Accokeek Creek Site)

	Ware	Temper	Type	Body	Base	Comment	Reported
EARLY WOODLAND	Marcey Creek	Steatite Crushed	Marcey Creek Plain		Flat	Thick Soapy	Ma-1948 St-1963
			Selden Island Cord Marked				Sl-1946 Ev-1955
	Popes Creek	Sand Coarse to Medium	Popes Creek Cord Marked		Conical Semi-Conical	Friable Thick. Inside Scored	St-1963
			Popes Creek Net Impressed				St-1963 Ho-1903
MIDDLE WOODLAND	Accokeek	Sand Medium to Fine	Accokeek Cord Marked		Conical Semi-Conical	Thinner Harder Interior NotScored	St-1963
	Albemarle	Quartz or Other Grit Crushed	Albemarle Cord Marked		Rounded Semi-Conical	Hard. Angular Fracture Compact Clayey Texture	Ev-1955 St-1963
			Albemarle Net Impressed				
			Albemarle Fabric Impressed				
	Mockley	Shell Unburned Crushed	Mockley Plain		Semi-Conical Rounded	Laminated Texture Thick Clayey Soft & Crumbly	St-1963
			Mockley Cord Marked				
			Mockley Net Impressed				
LATE WOODLAND	Townsend	Shell Unburned Crushed	Rappahannock Fabric Impressed		Rounded Semi-Conical	Lamellar Texture Thin Crumbly	Bl-1950 Ev-1955 St-1963
			Rappahannock Incised				
	Potomac Creek	Quartz orOther Grit Crushed	Potomac Creek Plain		Rounded Some Flat or Semi-Conical	Hard Thin	St-1963
			Potomac Creek Cord Impressed				
	Moyoane	Sand Fine	Moyoane Plain		Rounded	Gritty & Friable Feel. Smooth Texture	St-1963
			Moyoane Cord Impressed				
			Moyoane Incised				

Ma(Manson)   St(Stevensen)   Sl(Slattery)   Ho(Holmes)   Ev(Evans)   Bl(Blaker)

Paul Cresthull, August 1966

MPRV Rockart

Rockart is an above-ground prehistoric resource that is often difficult to date. Virginia has over 20 sites that are both pictograph and petroglyph forms. For the MPRV, there are six known rockart sites which have been recorded by the Virginia Rockart Survey (Hranicky 2015). Called glyphs, Virginia has numerous designs and patterns that involve painting glyphs on stone, engraving glyphs into rock, or making actual human/animal figurines. Virginia rockart does not have a single style and covers thousands of years. We attempt to find all of their sites, but Mother Nature does a good job of hiding them. The Survey report represents nearly 50 years of finding and recording rockart sites in Virginia (Hranicky 2015). All rockart glyphs have three factors:

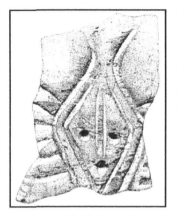

Bald Friar Glyph, Maryland

- The image and its color
- Its boundary and its color
- Image texture or base material
- If possible, cultural contexts.

The glyph classification from most Virginia and surrounding sites can be divided into:
- Realistic - forms or images of living creatures.
- Abstract - forms that are graphic (non-living creatures).

Virginia Rockart Survey

The Virginia Rockart Survey was started in 1983 by Wm Jack Hranicky to record outdoor inscriptions in prehistory. Later, then State Archaeologist, Allen Outlaw asked him to continue, and he became its director for survey operations. For many years, Dale Collins was the assistant Survey Director. The Survey has investigated numerous reported sites as possible rockart sites, but few actually turned out to be valid sites. However, the public has been the major source for information which has produced rockart sites. With acid rain being so common in the uplands, pictographic sites are disappearing in Virginia. The Survey is the only active organization finding and recording Virginia sites. The recording of Virginia sites depends on the Survey and its volunteers. An up-to-date publication on all Virginia rockart sites is available in Hranicky (2015 – on Amazon).

Bull Run Petroglyph Site

The Bull Run glyph (44FX###) is an incised stick figure with pecking around the head and upper chest. Hands are claw-like, with no fingers. Glyph has no feet; only legs. The glyph is weathered suggesting a considerable antiquity. It was placed inside a small rockshelter on a flat wall. Shelter wall has graffiti which does not affect the glyph.

Reported (independently) by: John Lombardo and John Lockard. Recorded: 7-23-2013 by the Virginia Rockart Survey and Virginia Department of Historic Resources. Location: Bull Run River Drainage, Fairfax County, Virginia

Bull Run Petroglyph

Difficult Run Petroglyph Rockart Site

Petroglyph Site (44FX2380) is an ethnographic example of a tool assembly of the atlatl (hook and board) and spear (point and shaft). For a site report, see Hranicky (2001). Rockart sites are another example of Native American sacred places. Glyphs are very difficult to photograph. The panel is composed of four glyphs.

Gary Eyler (Alexandria) found the site in 1983. He reported it to the National Park Service in 1986, The Survey became involved with shortly the after.

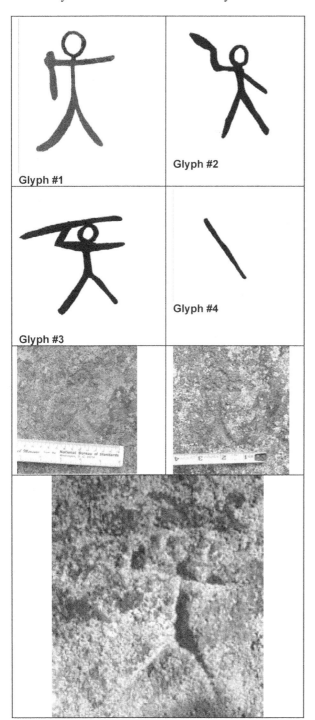

Boulder Face Containing the Glyph Panel in 2008

Fish Glyph in the Potomac

The Fish Glyph is located on the Maryland side of Great Falls in the Potomac River. It was investigated by the Virginia Rockart Survey (Hranicky, et al. (2014), and was published in National Geographic by George Stuart (Garrett 1987).

Palisades Museum of Prehistory

Gulf Branch Petroglyph Site

This petrographic site is located at the area identified as (44AR6) on the Potomac River. It lies approximately 35 meters south of the confluence of Gulf Branch and the Potomac River. The site was first reported to Scott Silsby by his father in the 1950s. The area was used for quarrying stone for buildings in the early days of the federal city. Since its location and age remain to be studied, the site has not been named or given a state site number.

Gulf Branch Petrogyyph, Arlington County, Virginia

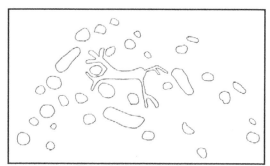
Petroglyphs on boulder

Silsby's Boulder

Silsby's Boulder

This rockart boulder was named after its finder – Scott Silsby who has spent many years studying and publishing Native American lifeways in the Middle Atlantic area. It was found at Pimmit Run on the Virginia side of the Potomac River. It is the property of the National Park Service. The designs were pecked into the boulder's surface. The boulder is micaschist, and due to this material's surface weakness or poor weather resistance, the boulder surface probably dates to the Late Woodland. The anthropomorphic design showing three-fingered hands(?) does occur in versions of eastern rockart (Wellman 1979). Rockart-associated cupules are common.

The boulder has been moved the Great Falls Park's Visitors Center and is maintained by the National Park Service.

General Display View

Miscellaneous Tools/Implements
(Various Native American Stone Tools and Implements)

Within the MPRV area and study collections, numerous archeological contexts and artifacts are found that offer insights to Native American manufacture of basic implements in their toolkits. This study of them provides a wide range of examples of both micro- and macrotools that can be used for comparative data for other tool geographies. Tool manufacture, useability, and maintenance are presented which have some inferences based on experimental archeology. A sample of the study collection artifacts is shown throughout this section, which includes artifact measurements and materials. Axes and celts are grouped together.

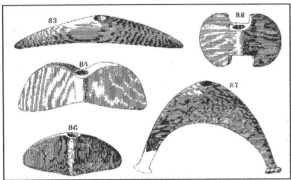

Bannerstones. Thomas Wilson (1888) was the first to call these implements *bannerstones*. He probably got the name from New York collectors.

This section contains a broken bannerstone study that is based on specimens from Pennsylvania, Maryland, and Virginia. Its basic conclusion is broken bannerstones were the result of being deliberately killed by the Native Americans upon the death of the former owner or killed by the owner for bad magic.

The macrotool part of the study collections had the largest bias, in that, these artifacts are larger, and thus were field-collected years ago. Recent collections do not contain as many of them as would be expected. Also, numerous tool classes are not readily identifiable by collectors, and again were not picked up and kept in collections. All of which produce a built-in sampling bias. Aside from this condition, this study still demonstrates a wide variety of Native American macrotools. This section has microtools which are not illustrated elsewhere and uses illustrative specimens from outside the MPRV.

> As a special note: non-MPRV tools and implements are used here to amplify what should be present in the Potomac River valley and offer comparative specimens for general analyses. The overall assumption is that the MPRV is part of the pre-Contact Native Americans' lithic technology continuum and most of the Native Americans' U.S. toolkit items are found in the MPRV.

In his book, ***Man the Tool-Maker***, Kenneth Oakley (1952) of the British Museum states:

Man is a social animal, distinguished by "culture": by the ability to make tools and communicate ideas. Employment of tool appears to be his chief biological characteristic, for considered functionally they are detachable extensions of the forelimb ... relying on extra-bodily equipment of his own making, which could be quickly discarded or changed as circumstances dictated, man has become the most adaptable of all creatures.

Stone Tools and Implements

This section contains nonpoint MPRV tools and implements. It provides a summary of micro- and macrotools, which were in the study collections. The term tool and implement are used interchangeably, but an implement is basically not a typeable tool; whereas, the term tool always implies an industry of which some (all) may be typeable. Some typing is discussed in this section. Since implements are discussed, the definition is:

Any lithic object that has a workend and is used to perform a work task. It does not have to have a consistent structure (type) within a class or industry. An implement is usually a multifunctional tool.

And, according to Bradley (1975):

... any piece of lithic material that has been modified to an intended stage of lithic reduction sequence in a specified assemblage. It must be demonstrable that it is the final stage and is not intended for further modification (other than by use). The method of its manufacture is not important to its initial identification.

The basic definition for a tool is:

A manually-operated object designed to perform work in order to accomplish a task or group of tasks which have a predetermined outcome in a social setting. The tool has a traditional design, established behavioral usage, and conforms to constraints imposed by nature.

This section is not necessarily inclusive of all tools/implements in the Native American toolkit at various times in MPRV prehistory. Where site data are available, study collection analyses incorporate them. If particular tools were absent (but expected) from the study collection, they are noted throughout this publication. Table 1 presents tool classes used in this section.

Table 1 – Tool Classes	
Abradingstone	Flesher
Adz	Gamestone
Anchor	Gorget
Antler Tools	Gouge
Anvilstone	Graver
Arrow	Hammerstone
Atlatl	Hoe
Atlatl Hook	Knife
Axe (Pecked and Polished, Flat Cobble, and Chipped)	Maul
	Netsinker
	Nuttingstone
Ball	Peckingstone
Bannerstone (Bannerstone Hole Study)	Perforator
	Pestle and Mortar
Bead	Pick
Birdhead Graver	Pin
Birdstone	Pipe
Boilingstone	Projectile Point
Bola	Pump Drill
Bone Tools	Punch
Bow	Quarry Digging Tool
Burin	Rubbingstone
Celt	Saw
Charmstone or Magicstone	Sharpener or Saw Abrader
Chisel	Sinewstone/Sharpener
Chopper	Spatula and Spud
Concretion Container	Split Cobble Abrader
Crescent	Splitter
Depilator	Spokeshave
Discoidal	Ulu
Disk	Wedge
Drill	Whetstone
Flake Tools	

Industry Function and Classification

Each tool class is classified to a basic modality that is the primary function within an industry. In some cases, these tools are multifunctional, but only the primary function is given, which assumes the basis of usage or work. The approximate functional angle is listed. The bit angle for each macrotool was not measured due to periodic sampling in collectors' homes, and time was usually a factor in recording specimens. Tool function and angles were discussed in the Toolmaking section.

Industry Ecoscene

Each tool industry is classified for its MPRV ecoscene. This appraisal is more subjective than objective as it is based on general observations of the study collection provenances. This distribution is very tentative. In some cases, (+) and (-) are used to indicate high/low frequencies. The ecoscenes used are uplands, piedmont, and coastal plain. They are discussed in the MPRV Environment section.

The nature of the collected data precludes tool assignments of evaluations using a watershed perspective. Based on general observations, macrotool distribution is uniform throughout the MPRV.

Typing/Classing Macrotools

Once past projectile point typology, typing and/or classing lithic artifacts tends to disappear in macrotool (nonpoint) archeology. There are several established axe and celt types, but rarely are other tools typed. Other methods are used to group them, namely tool functions based on class within an industry. Even here, analysis and classification fails because of the failure to clearly define tools within industries. The workend, namely the bit, is the key to classifying macrotools. There is no standard in archeology for defining/classifying macrotool bits. Bit angles were used for classifying macrotool functions. See Toolmaking Technology section.

Macrotools are presented in this section; however, they are not well represented in the MPRV artifact sample. Figure 1 shows macrotool basic examples. The atlatl is discussed; no actual atlatl specimen survives from the MPRV. Thus, it is based on experimental and ethnographic archeology. Additionally, the bow and arrow is discussed here and is based primarily on experimental archeology. Since no bow or arrows have been found in a MPRV archeological context, experimental data is offered as an insight to their prehistoric usage.

All tool classes are listed alphabetically with illustrated specimens. All specimens have provenance identifiers or otherwise are MPRV specimens. As mentioned in the Toolmaking Technology section, pecking and grinding (smoothing) is a primary technique in manufacturing macrotools. It is discussed and illustrated where appropriate.

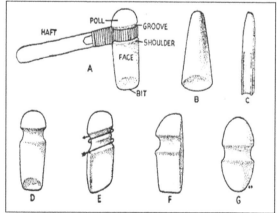

Figure 1 – Stone Tools: A = Hafted Axe, B = Celt, C = Gouge, D = Full Grooved Axe, E = Spiral-Groove Axe, F = Three-Quarter Grooved Axe, and G = Full Grooved Axe

Abraderstone
Modality (Industry): rubbing.
Useability: generalized.
Ecoscene (Environments): all.
Functional Angle: 170° to 180°
Bit Angle: N/A.
General Climate: glacial and postglacial.

The abraderstone is any large (>50 mm) soft stone that shows evidence of rubbing or being used to smooth another surface (Figure 2). It was used to sharpen or polish axes, celts, and other marcotools. In knapping, it is used for platform preparation by abrading a flaking edge. It is usually made from sandstone. This tool has a similar (or same) function as the whetstone; perhaps, hand versus ground/lap usage. Whetstone does require more pressure on its surface.

Figure 2 – Abraderstone, sandstone (L = 89, W = 56, T = 27 mm, 8.5 oz)

Adz

Modality (Industry): cutting.
Useability: specialized.
Ecoscene (Environments): all, piedmont (+).
Functional Angle: 60° to 75°
Bit Angle: >20° & <35°
General Climate: postglacial.

The adz is an implement that has a narrow cutting bit that is beveled with one flat face (Figure 3). It is a long narrow tool that usually has a thick cross section. It is not usually grooved; however, grooving does occur. Figure 4 shows a miniature adz. Specimens do occur with one irregular face, which are called humpback adzes. Another type is the beveled adz, which has one face divided into three flat facets. Adzes are usually made from fine-grain igneous rocks or flint. Major parts are:

1 – Butt or Poll   2 – Shoulder
3 – Workend   4 – Bevel
5 – Blade.

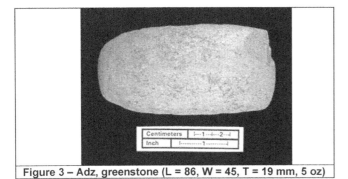

Figure 3 – Adz, greenstone (L = 86, W = 45, T = 19 mm, 5 oz)

For the eastern U.S., the adz bit has four basic styles:

1 – Triangular   2 – Trapezoidal
3 – Square   4 – C-Shaped.

Figure 4 – Miniature Grooved Adz (or axe) from Long Island, New York (L = 65, W = 41, T = 21 mm). It was found in the early 1940s. (Formerly in the Geasey collection, now in the Southold Indian Museum in New York.) It does not have an axe bit angle.

The adz is not adequately defined in archeology, namely the bit angle and face. The suggested angle was presented previously. The bit has a flat face. However, this same structure applies to the hoe.

The adz is used with a chopping action (not stripping) on wood. The cutting angle is approximately 80 degrees. It works best on wet or green wood. Also, hardwoods, as opposed to softwoods, are better for this tool. The MPRV adz has been reported as being grooved. The adz is shown in the Experimental Archeology section.

Anchor (Canoe)

The anchor is a large boulder that sometimes has notches. It was used to anchor canoes near shorelines. None were observed in the study collections. It is larger (>75mm) than a netsinker.

Antler Tools

Antlers, especially deer, were used for numerous tools. The antler was probably a very common projectile point throughout prehistory. It could be sharpened with an abrader and easily attached to a shaft by drilling out the base, then gluing it to the shaft. If the point/shaft missed its intended target and struck a hard surface damaging the point's tip, a pocket abrader could resharpen it. Retrofitting could be done during the hunt and put the spear back into service.

The antler was also used as a flaking implement. Different antlers have different effects when used to flake stone. Some flakers have been preserved in archeological contexts; however, most have disappeared because they have little endurance when buried. None were observed in the MPRV collections. Native examples are shown in the Toolmaking Technology section and new flakers are shown in the Experimental Archeology section.

Charles Pettit, mentioned in the Introduction section as a contributing amateur, studied antler (tines) specimens from the Winslow site (18MO9) (in Slattery and Woodward 1992:67) and commented:

The cut antler fragments are interesting in that two distinct methods were used in removing the tips. Seventy-three percent had been cut with an encircling groove perpendicular to the axis of the antler. Twenty-seven percent were removed by a series of cuts or nicks obliquely oriented (10 to 20 degrees) to the long axis. Two or three cuts were employed in essentially equal frequency; and one specimen showed four cut marks.

Figure 5 – Quartzite Anvilstone from Williamson Site, Dinwiddie County, Virginia

Anvilstone
Modality (Industry): holding.
Useability: specialized.
Ecoscene (Environments): all.
Functional Angle: 85° to 100°
Bit Angle: N/A.
General Climate: postglacial.

The anvilstone is a small boulder with a flat surface that was used to place a core or biface on to remove flakes. It is frequently associated with the bipolar flaking method. The flat face shows small indentations in the center of the surface. The anvilstone usually had surface modification on one face. If both faces show center indentations, it may have functioned as a peckingstone. Note: large, cup-like indentations indicate that the stone was used as a nut-cracking stone, crushing, or pump-drill capstone. There is overlap for the classification based on function. Anvilstone is used for all three classifications, but a knapper's stone is preferred. For the MPRV, quartzite is the primary material (Figures 5 and 6).

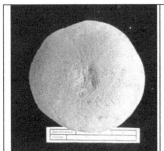

Multitool, quartzite (L = 55, W = 32, T = 9 mm)	Anvilstone/abrader, quartzite (L = 98, W = 96, T = 40 mm)

Figure 6 – MPRV Anvilstones

Arrow
Modality (Industry): penetrating.
Useability: specialized.
Ecoscene (Environments): all, coastal plain(+).
Functional Angle: 120° to 180°
Bit Angle: N/A.
General Climate: postglacial.

Generally, the arrow is considered a bow-launched weapon; however, sling-thrown references do occur. This is a key tool in the Late Woodland and merits a greater discussion of its components. Also, see discussion on bow.

Figure 7a – Pueblo Arrows from New Mexico. Arrow shafts are cane, points are flint and stemmed and notched, and bound with sinew.

It is a straight, wooden or cane shaft which is launched from a bow. It has a pointed end and the opposite end has flight-stabilizing feathers (Figures 7a and 7b). Examples of newly-made arrows are shown in Figure 8. The following are parts of an arrow (Hranicky 2002a):

1 – Head	2 – Shaft
3 – Foreshaft	4 – Shaftment
5 – Feathering	6 – Nock.

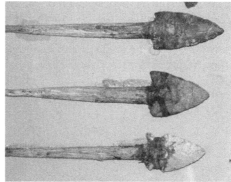

Figure 7b – Pamunkey Arrows (19th century). Pamunkey Museum, King William County, Virginia, W. P. Miles is Chief.

Arrow (manufacture), according to Mason (1894):
The continent of America furnishes excellent facilities for the study of the arrow. Every variety of climate, material, and land or water game are here, to create an indefinite diversity of structures.

In its simplest form, the arrow is a straight rod pointed at one end, perhaps in the fire, and notched at the other end for the bow-string. But such a missile would be of little worth; and so the arrow has undergone many modifications in answer to the demands of the hunter. The parts of a highly developed arrow are the following:

(1) The shaft; of which it is necessary to study the material, the technique, the form, the length, the grooves, and the ornamentations.

(2) The shaftment; which is that part of the shaft upon which the feather is fastened. This section of the arrow varies in length, in form, and greatly in ornamentation, because it is the part of the weapon upon which bands and other ornamental marks are usually placed.

(3) The feathering; or the strips of feather or other thin material laid on at the butt of the arrow to give it directness of flight. The study of this feature includes the method of seizing; the attaching to the shaftment; the position of the feather, whether flat or perpendicular to the shaft; the manner of trimming the plume; the line, whether straight or spiral, upon which each feather is laid, and the glue or cement.

Figure 8 – Newly-Made Arrows by Jeffrey P. Tottenham (2001 Primitive Technology Weekend at Oregon Ridge, Maryland)

(4) The nock; or the posterior end of the arrow, seized by the fingers in releasing. This is a very important feature in the study of this weapon. For instance, the Eskimo arrows have flat nocks, while all other arrows in the world seem to be more or less cylindrical or spherical. In some the form is top-shaped; in others, bulbous; in others, cylindrical; and in others, spreading, like the tail of a fish or swallow. In modern arrows a footing is added to the nock.

(5) The notch; or cut made at the end of the arrow to receive the bowstring. Each stock of aborigines has its own way of making this cut at the end of the arrow; and this characteristic, born of the material, though seemingly unimportant, is frequently helpful to the student in deciding upon the tribe to which the arrow belongs.

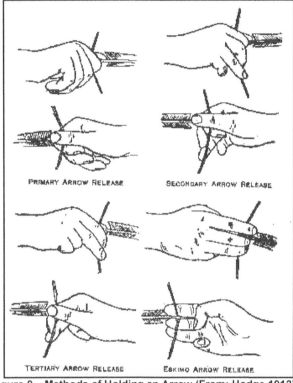

Figure 9 – Methods of Holding an Arrow (From: Hodge 1912)

(6) The foreshaft; or that piece of hard wood or bone or ivory or antler laid into the anterior portion of the shaft and trimmed to a symmetrical shape. It serves the double purpose of making the front of the arrow heavier than the rear, and also affords a better means of attaching arrowheads or harpoon barbs of special form.

(7) The head; or that anterior part of an arrow which makes the wound or produces the result. Before contact with the white race, aborigines were wont to make their arrow-heads of stone, bone, wood, shell, and even of cold hammered metal. The study of the arrow-head involves the point or blade, the faces of the blade, the facettes and serrations and notches of the expanding blade, the butt or tang for attachment, the barbs, and sometimes the barb piece, which is an extra bit of bone or other substance fastened to the posterior end of the stone head to multiply the number of barbs.

There are numerous ways to hold the arrow nock in the bow string (Figure 9). A newly-made arrow is shown in the Experimental Archeology section.

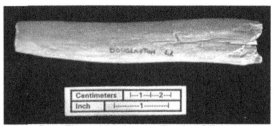

Figure 10 – Deer Tine which has its Tip Cut Off. It was found in the early 1940s. (Formerly in the Geasey collection, now in the Southold Indian Museum in New York.) The tip was probably used as an arrowhead.

Deer tine tips were used as arrow tips. Figure 10 shows the remainder of a tine that was probably cut for its tip. Antler arrowheads were probably common in the Woodland Period giving rise to the argument that the bow and arrow may date to the beginning of the period.

Arrow Straightener

See Shaft Straightener.

Atlatl
Modality (Industry): throwing.
Useability: specialized.
Ecoscene (Environments): all.
Functional Angle: 45° to 180°
Bit Angle: N/A.
General Climate: postglacial.

The atlatl was probably brought into the New World (Hranicky 2002a) and was a primary hunting tool. It easily dates from the Paleoindian period and was used through to the Woodland period. Cressman and Krieger (1940) were among the first to suggest that the atlatl was found in various places around the world; their study is based on Oregon atlatls. This study provides Oregon specimens that indicate a widespread distribution in the Western Hemisphere. Also, they argue that dart points used on atlatl spears were not used on arrows for the bow.

Figure 11– Atlatl Demonstration. Ray Olachia, an Apache from Texas, explaining the use of the atlatl at the 2001 Boy Scouts of America's Jamboree at Camp A. P. Hill in Virginia. He is a well-known expert on Native American tools and weapons.

Stirling (1960) reports a 1944 trip with Richard Stewart (National Geographic) to the State of Michoacan to study the Tarascan Indians who were still using the spear/atlatl for duck hunting from canoes. He provides an excellent account of atlatl usage. Early writings on atlatls are Nuttall (1891) and Saville (1925). Figure 11 shows a modern example. See Experimental Archaeology section.

The tool was used to launch spears and had an accuracy of 75 to 100 meters (Figure 8). A newly-made atlatl example is shown in the Experimental Archeology section. The word is credited to being an Aztec word meaning spear thrower. When the Spanish reached the 16th century New World, the tool was used principally in Middle America and Peru as the bow and arrow had become the more common tool in northern areas of the New World (Stirling 1960).

Figure 12 – Atlatl Usage (Drawing by Floyd Painter)

Early ethnographers describe the tool combination as:

...*long spears made of cane stalks and tipped with obsidian, which they threw with a certain implement called atlatl.*

And a Cortez recorder speaks (Stirling 1960):

...*spears thrown by a crossbow made of another piece of wood.*

Atlatl Hook
Modality (Industry): hooking.
Useability: specialized.
Ecoscene (Environments): uplands ?
Functional Angle: N/A.
Bit Angle: N/A.
General Climate: postglacial.

Only one atlatl hook has been reported in Virginia (Figure 13). It is made of basalt. The hook may have been a separate piece that was attached to the atlatl board or designed as part of it.

The atlatl hook was made from stone, bone, wood, or antler. The hook can also be incorporated in the atlatl board. The Hardaway site produced an atlatl made from antler, but associated materials were lacking; thus, no date. A wooden example is shown in the Experimental Archeology section.

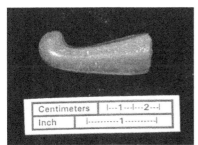

Figure 13 – Virginia Atlatl Hook Made from Basalt. The tool is broken along the long axis.

Awl

There is no evidence that awls were made from stone. However, the perforator or long narrow drill may have served this function. See Bone Tools.

Axe
Modality (Industry): felling.
Useability: specialized.
Ecoscene (Environments): all, piedmont+).
Functional Angle: 90° to 180°
Bit Angle: >35° & <50°
General Climate: postglacial.

An axe is a large, thick implement with a wide blade and cutting edge. Axes are usually hafted and have grooving that facilitated hafting. They occur as nongrooved, double grooved, notched and grooved, such as full grooved (4/4), and three quarter grooved (3/4) axes. Bit can be wide or narrow, and blades can be fluted (Great Lakes area only). Usually both faces (sides) taper toward the bit; however, flat-sided specimens do occur. It was made by pecking/polishing or chipping stone and was usually made from a fine- or coarse-grain igneous rock. The trophy, felling, fluted, barbed, ceremonial, battle-axe (metallic in protohistory - not used), and monolithic axe are example categories of the axe class. Axe parts are:

1 – Poll
2 – Groove
3 – Bit
4 – Body
5 – Tressel
6 – Band (raised flat area on each side of the groove).

Most prehistoric axes are made from igneous rocks, which can be divided into:

I. Light-colored materials
    <> coarse grained
    - granite
    - quartzite
    <> fine grained
    - rhyolite
    - felsite
II. Dark-colored materials
    <>   coarse grained
    - diorite
    - gabbro
    <> fine grained
    - andesite
    - basalt.

The axe is the heavy-duty form of the celt. It is used on trees with diameters >100 mm. The mass of the axe transfers enough energy to cut through the tree. The celt is a light-weight tool and does not transfer enough energy for large trees. Consequently, the bit bounces off a large tree rather than penetrate it; however, it works well on trees with diameters <100 mm. The axe is shown in the Experimental Archeology section.

Figure 14 – MPRV 3/4 Groove Greenstone (L = 129, W = 76, T = 32 mm) It has minor raised grooving. As a postulate here, this axe form is the forerunner to the 3/4 groove flat tressel form.

As used for the study collections, grooving is classified as:

4/4 (or full grooved) groove goes completely around the axe and separates the poll and blade. The groove edge may be raised. Groove width and depth varies.

3/4 groove goes around the axe but stops at the base (tressel). It also may have raised grooving.

2/2 groove is usually restricted to chipped axes. It occurs like notches on both sides of the axe.

1/1 groove is rare but does occur. It generally refers to a notched celt.

Nongrooved axes do occur, but as a form is usually referred to as a large celt.

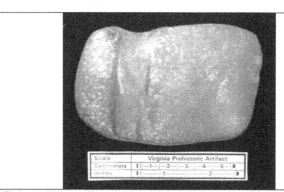

Figure 15a – Basalt Axe Found on the Pamunkey Reservation in 1968 (Formally B. Pirabby Collection). It has a curved tressel with probably indicates a Woodland Period type.

The tressel (bottom) often had a groove running lengthwise that was used to tighten the chassis (Hranicky 1995). It was created by pecking and only appears on pecked and polished axes.

The MPRV axe may show a dating sequence for axes. The 4/4 groove axe is the earliest form of the tool. Around 2500 BC, the 3/4 groove axe becomes popular. As a suggestion here, the flat cobble axe with a 3/4 groove and a round tressel occurs before the flat 3/4 groove axe (Figure 14).

Grooving provides the mechanics for hafting. There are numerous ways to haft an axe in the literature, but no single way or ways is known for the MPRV. Figures 15a and 15b show Pamunkey examples from Virginia. See Plate 19 for MPRV axes. Plate 20 shows more specimens.

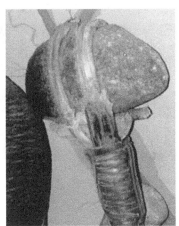

Figure 15b – **Axe Hafting Example. Pamunkey Museum, King William County, Virginia. W. P. Miles is Chief.**

Another form of axe occurs that has a widespread distribution in the East; this is the miniature axe (Figure 16).

Text continued on page 256.

Plate 19 – MPRV Axes

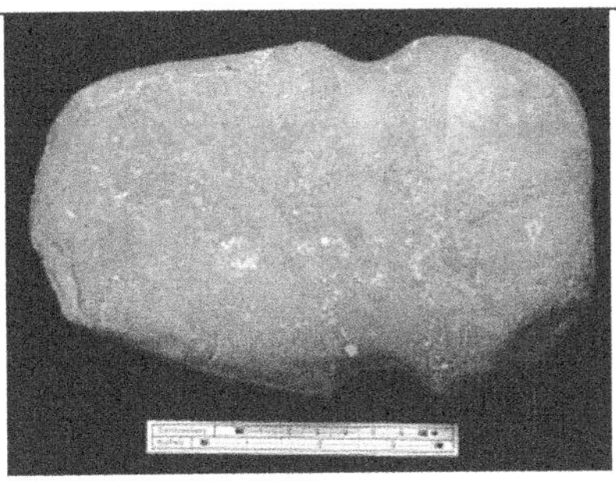

#1 – Axe, 4/4 groove, greenstone (L = 193, W = 127, T = 24, 60 oz)

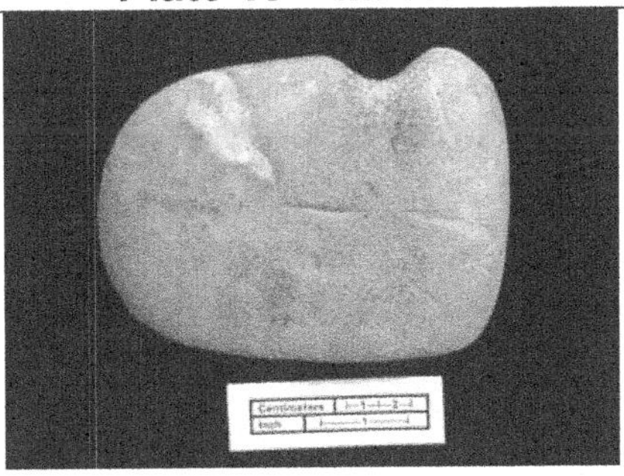

#2 – Axe, pecked/polished, 3/4 groove, quartzite (L= 105, W = 80, T = 15 mm, 13 oz)

#3 – Axe, pecked/polished, 3/4 groove, quartzite (L = 125, W = 80, T = 27 mm, 20 oz)

#4 – Axe, pecked/polished, 4/4 groove, greenstone (L = 82, W = 70, T = 27 mm)

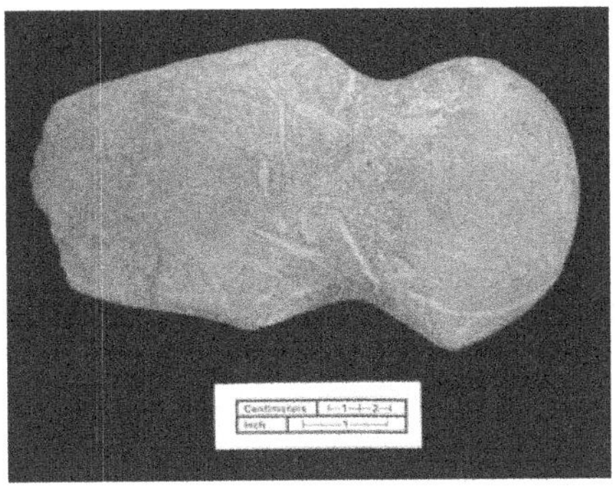

#5 – Axe, pecked/polished, 1/2 groove, quartzite (L = 150, W = 80, T = 35 mm, 22+ oz)

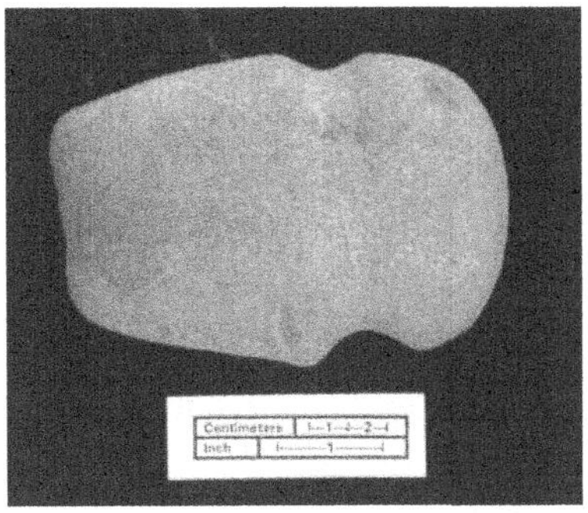

#6 – Axe, pecked/polished, 4/4 groove, quartzite (L = 98, W = 67, T = 27 mm, 11.5 oz)

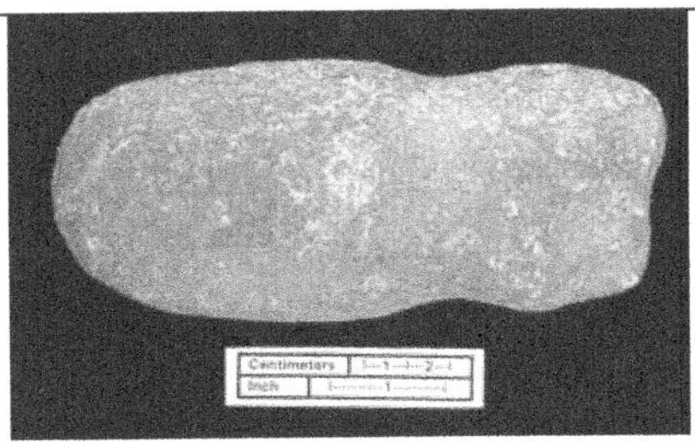

#7 – Axe, pecked/polished, 4/4 groove, greenstone (L = 112, W = 47, T = 27 mm, 13 oz)

#8 – Axe, chipped, 4/4 groove, quartzite (L = 140. W = 90, T = 20 mm)

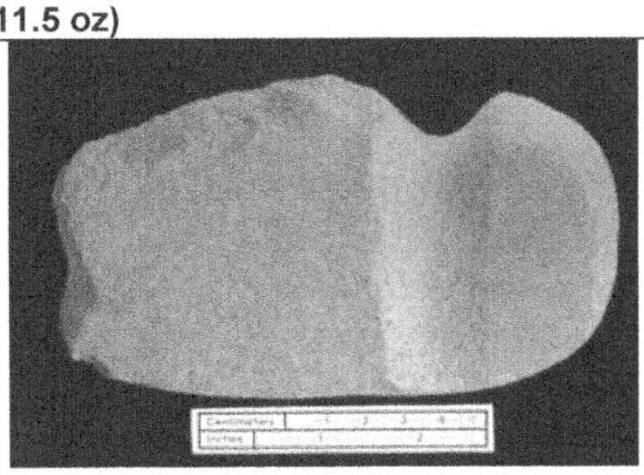

#9 – Axe, pecked/polished, 3/4 groove, quartzite (L = 144, W = 77, T = 29 mm, 22 oz)

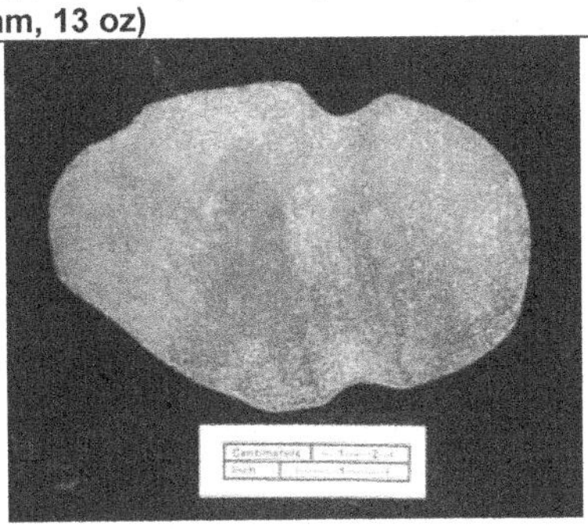

#10 – Axe, pecked/polished, 4/4 groove, basalt (L = 117, W = 82, T = 34 mm, 22 oz)

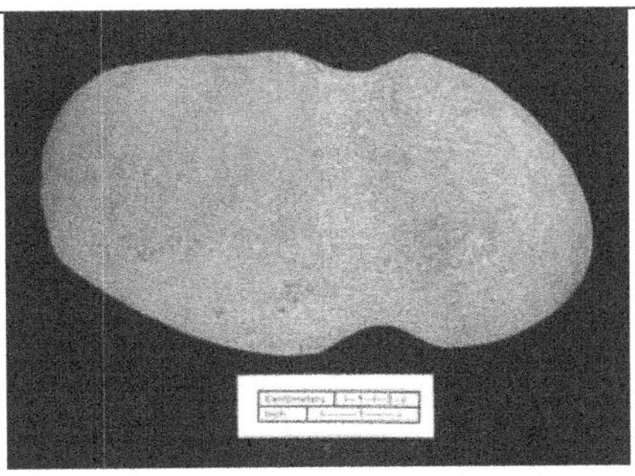

#11 – Axe, pecked/polished, 4/4 groove, greenstone (L = 156, W = 88, T = 40 mm, 31 oz)

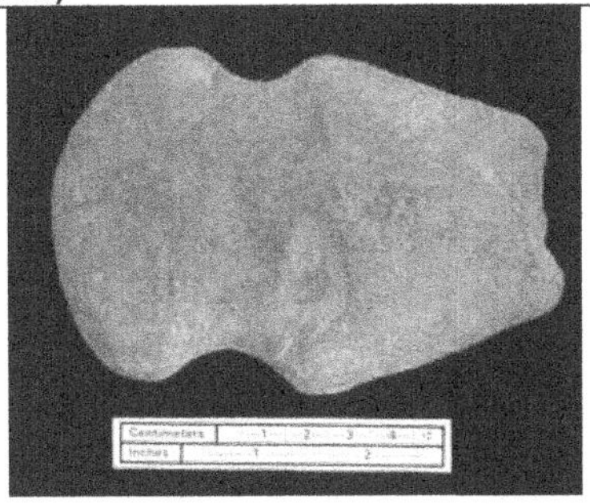

#12 – Axe, pecked/polished, 4/4 groove, basalt (L = 113, W = 75, T = 28 mm, 18 oz)

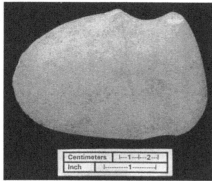

Figure 16 – MPRV Miniature 4/4 Grooved Axe (L = 87, W = 61, T = 29 mm). It is made from greenstone and has minor raised grooving.

The ungrooved axe is a celt-like implement that may be a separate industry of artifacts (Figure 17). It neither fits the celt nor axe industry, but has attributes of both. If part of both industries, then mass is the criteria for separating it. The mass for the implement must be >500 grams.

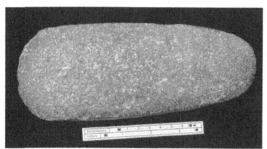

Figure 17 – Large Granite Celt or Ungrooved Axe? It has flat sides, measures L = 211, W = 83, T = 42 mm, and is from Washington County, Virginia.

Experimental archeology has provided a tremendous amount of information for the prehistoric axe. Cole (1979) is a pioneer in experimental archeology as well as data on axes. Mill (1993) provides a study on wear patterns. Carneiro (1979) provides ethnographic data for Native American axe usage.

Figure 18 – Raised Groove Axes from Washington County, Virginia (C. W. (Bill) Nye Collection)

The raised groove axes are among the best prehistoric artifacts found in the Americas (Figure 18). This form of grooving allowed heavy duty service and is the best form of macrotool hafting.

Ball
Modality (Industry): gaming.
Useability: to be determined.
Ecoscene (Environments): all, coastal plain(+).
Functional Angle: N/A.
Bit Angle: N/A.
General Climate: postglacial.

The small ball (<25 mm) was probably a gaming implement, but its function has not been defined (Figure 19). It is usually made from hardstone. Unless found in an archeological context, they are difficult to distinguish from Colonial marbles. Several were observed in the study collections that came from areas with no Colonial association. They do occur as balls made from fired clay which give rise to their validity as a prehistoric implement. Its function remains open. It could have been used as a flesher, boilingstone, bola, or hide softener, but due to their perfect symmetry, a gamestone is offered.

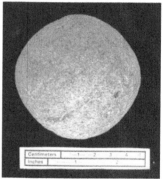

Figure 19 – Quartzite Game Ball or Bola. It is perfectly round and has a diameter of 68 mm. It was found on the Kanawha River in Mason County, West Virginia. It is usually found in Adena-mound contexts. Similar balls (40-50 mm) are found in Southwest Virginia. It functions remains speculative.

Bannerstone
Modality (Industry): weighting.
Useability: specialized.
Ecoscene (Environments): all, uplands(+).
Functional Angle: 45° to 180°
Bit Angle: N/A.
General Climate: postglacial.

Holmes (1897) was the first to report MPRV bannerstones, which he called atlatl weights. Bannerstone is a tool term that may be attributed to Thomas Wilson (1888), who may have gotten the name from New York collectors. The classic publication on bannerstones is Bryon W. Knoblock's (1939) *Bannerstones of the North American Indian*, which has remained the standard for classification. For Virginia, see the study by McCary (1975); for a New Jersey study, see Regensburg and Bello (1997).

The earliest date for the Middle Atlantic area bannerstones is approximately 4500 BC. Based on the Hardaway site excavation, Coe (1964) called it the Stanly-type atlatl weight. A nearby classic study is ***Birdstones, Boatstones and Bar Amulets from the Susquehanna Drainage*** (Smith 1972). It needs more refining for the early date and associated materials.

The bannerstone is usually a well-made, perforated tool probably used as an atlatl weight; however, none were observed in the MPRV. Center or midrib containing the perforation is usually thicker than outer wings. Major parts are:

1 – Midrib   2 – Knob
3 – Center hole   4 – Wing edge
5 – Wing.

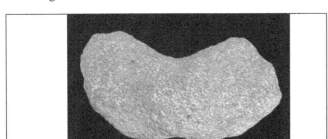
Bannerstone blank, micaschist (L = 135, W = 57, T = 33 mm, 20 oz)

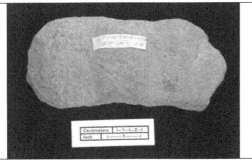
Bannerstone, unfinished (Hanover, PA), quartzite (L = 132, W = 63, T = 31 mm, 13 oz)

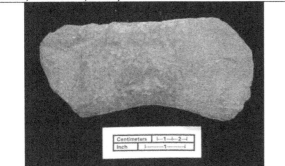
Bannerstone, unfinished, rhyolite (L = 122, W = 57, T = 19 mm, 10 oz)

Figure 20 – Bannerstone Preforms.

It also occurs in an endless variety (Knoblock 1939). The major types are:

1 – Tabular   2 – Square
3 – Reel-shaped   4 – Axe-shaped
5 – Butterfly   6 – Oval
7 – Crescent   8 – Double crescent
9 – Knobbed   10 – Bayonet
11 – Pick-shaped   12 – Boat-shaped
13 – Geniculate   14 – Curved Pick
15 – Hinged   16 – Bottle-shaped
17 – Lunate   18 – Humped
19 – Shield-shaped
20 – Shuttle   21 – Barreled
22 – Triangular   23 – Bottle
24 – Hourglass   25 – Paneled.

Very little data occur for the MPRV, and for that matter, the Middle Atlantic area, to determine the usage of the above styles (see Cresthull 1972). Overall for the MPRV, the bannerstone has what appears to be a normal usage, but lacks the high quality bannerstones found elsewhere. It only has dateable contexts in Woodland Period associations.

Bannerstone usage is often attributed to the atlatl as a weight; it could also have been used as a pendant. The addition of weight to the atlatl for the purpose of increasing spear throwing distance has varying acceptance in the archeological community.

<u>Note</u>: The assumption that only one bannerstone is used on an atlatl is a false assumption in archeology. The actual number can be one to three bannerstones per atlatl, but one was the most common.

It is usually made from slate, granite, syenite, mica schist, porphyry, quartzite, basalt, greenstone, steatite, and other minor materials (Figure 20). The most common (preferred) material is banded-slate from eastern North Carolina and along the shores of Lake Heron. However, exotic stones do not occur in the MPRV specimens; also, large bannerstones are absent from the collections.

The MPRV bannerstone was made using the peck and polish method.

There are basically three classes:

1 – Utilitarian - (small <100 mm and throwing weight)

2 – Status - (medium >99 <200 mm and nonthrowing weight)

3 – Ceremonial (large >199 mm and nonthrowing weight).

Extremely large bannerstones were made which were too heavy to have functioned as atlatl weights; thus, they probably were status symbols.

<u>Note</u>: Size is relative, but small is suggested here as actually being approximately 50 mm for any dimension. Any size over this has a negative effect on throwing.

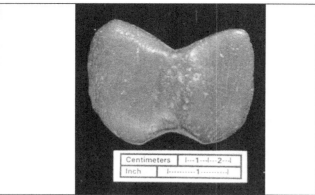

Figure 21 – MPRV Bannerstone, slate (L = 65, W = 46, T = 22 mm)

For the MPRV, complete bannerstones are rare (Figure 21). The materials are usually hardstones, but softstones, namely steatite and schist, are used. Large bannerstones are not common; the average width of MPRV specimens is approximately 100 mm. The primary source is local quarries, southeastern Virginia, and northeastern North Carolina.

The MacCord Bipoint

MacCord (1967) found a resharpened bipoint in the area (44WR5) that was to become the Thunderbird complex (Figure 22). It was made off a blade with bifacial flaking. It is the longest blade-made implement found to date in Virginia. Judging by its morphology, it dates to the Pleistocene era. It is presently lost; new photograph to be supplied.

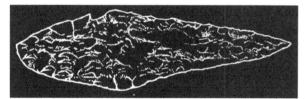

Figure 22 – Jasper Bipoint, L = 170, W = 50, T = 6 to 10 mm

Because many of them were resharpened, they are the most frequently mis-classified artifact in lithic technology.

Figure 23 – Sample of Broken Bannerstone Study Collection

Bannerstone Center Hole Study

The diameter of the center hole on bannerstones has not been studied to determine the drilling methods, size, etc. This study examined 60 broken bannerstones from North Carolina, Virginia, Maryland, and Pennsylvania. Broken bannerstones allowed study of the interior of the center hole.

Figure 24 – Examples of Mid-Ridge Breaks on Bannerstones. Break usually occurs in the center and shows evidence of being struck by a heavy hammerstone.

The bannerstone was probably a life-time personal object presumably for male Native Americans. It was made during adolescence and carried until the user could no longer hunt. A replacement was needed only if the current one had *bad magic*. The killed bannerstone is the result of a stone having bad magic and/or the death of the owner. It was killed by striking it with a heavy boulder on its mid-ridge.

Figure 25 – Two Wing Hole Drilling Examples. Holes are started from both sides. This practice follows the original making of a bannerstone by drilling the hole from both sides.

Bannerstones are rarely placed in graves that suggests that they had a life cycle for the user. This aspect remains to be studied. Figures 23 and 24 show samples of broken bannerstones used in the study. In some cases, broken parts were drilled and used as pendants. Figure 25 shows examples of drilling broken bannerstones, and Figure 26 shows examples of pendants. After the broken bannerstone pieces were made into pendants, even then, they were also killed after usage (Figure 27).

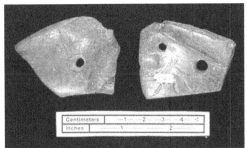

Figure 26 – One- and Two-Hole Pendant Examples. They follow the same pattern as gorgets. Holes always drilled from two sides.

Figure 27 – Examples of Re-breakage after made into Bannerstone Pendants. Re-breaks may show bannerstone retirement (user) or replacement and keeping the old bannerstone as a pendant.

Study Technique

Each broken bannerstone was weighed and measured. The hole was measured by the cord method in geometry. A small piece of tape was placed across the broken hole and then measured using digital calipers. Leaving the tape in place, a measurement was taken from the tape to the center of the outside. These measurements were used to calculate the hole's estimated diameter.

Bannerstone Study Summary

This sample of bannerstones provided data on the hole, breakage, and materials. No large, winged bannerstones were observed. With the exception of one specimen of shale, the remaining bannerstones were made from local stones. Steatite was used in the MPRV, but no broken specimens were observed. The basic style is the winged or butterfly form; the tabular form is less common, but used.

The northern specimens have larger holes than southern counterparts; however, this is a statistical estimate from a small sample. Table 2 presents data from the study. Table 3 presents a statistical summary.

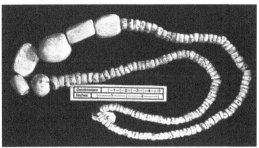

Figure 28 – Mississippian Shell Necklace from Buckingham County, Virginia

Bead

Modality (Industry): decorating.
Useability: none.
Ecoscene (Environments): all.
Functional Angle: N/A.
Bit Angle: N/A.
General Climate: postglacial.

The stone bead is a small pebble that has been drilled completely through. It is usually made from hard stones and polished. Color does not seem to have been a factor. Most Native American beads were made from seashells, animal bones and teeth, and other organic materials. Stone beads are rare and none were observed in the study collections. For the MPRV, drilled squirrel scapulas were common for necklaces. Another form of beads is drilled shell pieces; they date to the Late Woodland Period (Figure 28).

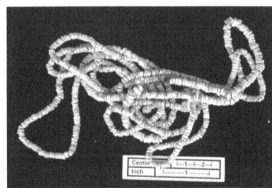

Figure 29 – Shell Beads from the Potomac Creek Site, Maryland (Hugh Stabler Collection). The beads average 2.7 mm in diameter.

Figure 29 shows typical Virginia beads. In most Late Woodland sites, these beads number in the thousands. The hole was probably drilled with a lithic graver. It was a time-consuming task to make several thousand beads. They are assumed here to be status beads.

Table 2 – Broken Bannerstone Sample Data

#	ORIGIN	MATERIAL	COLOR	WIDTH	HGHT	THICK	WGT	CORD	HGHT	DIA	OBSERVATION
PA1	Penn	Shale	Gray	55	49	21	71	10.52	5.61	10.5	Hole is smooth with parallel to wall striations
PA2	Penn	Diabase	Gray	55	44	23	69	12.93	5.99	13.0	Smooth hole; has two partially drilled holes on wing edges
PA3	Penn	Greenstone	Gray	37	42	24	33	13.63	8.32	13.9	Polished hole; small notches on wing edge
PA4	Penn	Diabase	Gray	52	54	23	55	11.36	4.86	11.5	Polished hole; vertical shaft not parallel
PA5	Penn	Basalt	Grayish black	33	57	20	40	12.56	4.87	13.0	Hole is polished; well-made specimen
PA6	Penn	Basalt	Dark gray	55	41	20	30	12.14	5.17	12.3	Hole is polished; has hole drilled in wing
PA7	Penn	Rhyolite	Blackish	68	50	24	82	15.14	7.67	15.1	Hole not completely drilled; pecking shows on wing; unfinished
PA8	Penn	Greenstone	Dark gray	45	47	27	61	10.14	4.49	10.2	Hole is rough and irregular
PA9	Penn	Greenstone	Gray	39	65	19	81	9.17	3.06	9.9	Hole is narrow and irregular; has a small hole drilled into the hole wall
PA10	Penn	Gypsum	Tan	65	41	14	41	14.56	7.03	14.6	Hole smooth; has parallel to hole striations
PA11	Penn	Diabase	Dark gray	51	46	20	31	12.11	5.11	12.3	Hole is poorly drilled; hole drilled in wing
PA12	Penn	Greenstone	Gray	27	60	25	57	11.92	7.84	12.4	Hole is rough; wing edge has two notches
PA13	Penn	Greenstone	Gray	30	46	11	23	8.29	2.47	9.4	Hole smooth; has groove cut from hole to tip of wing
PA14	Penn	Diabase	Gray	58	38	23	42	11.29	7.17	11.6	Hole is smooth
PA15	Penn	Greenstone	Gray	57	51	23	61	13.06	4.75	13.7	Hole is polished; wing has two partially drilled holes
PA16	Penn	Andesite	Gray	53	38	14	37	8.81	3.5	9.0	Hole is polished
PA17	Penn	Basalt	Blackish	44	49	24	35	16.43	7.65	16.5	Hole is polished; has two holes drilled in wing; edge may be notched
PA18	Penn	Greenstone	Gray	107	46	24	102	14.81	8.5	15.5	Hole is smooth; partially broken
PA19	Penn	Basalt	Black	51	55	23	60	13.96	7.66	15.0	Hole is smooth; has dark stain
PA20	Penn	Greenstone	Light brown	72	47	25	62	15.33	6.33	14.0	Hole is very rough; shows drill rings
PA21	Penn	Greenstone	Gray	50	54	23	43	15.49	7.05	15.6	Hole is rough and is uneven; wing tip is battered
PA22	Penn	Andesite	Brown	31	54	24	50	13.03	4.39	15.6	Hole rough; has groove cut from hole to tip of wing
PA23	Penn	Basalt	Dark gray	29	64	24	53	14.13	6.26	14.1	Hole rough; has groove cut from hole to tip of wing
PA24	Penn	Greenstone	Gray	35	63	22	63			14.2	Hole is smooth; drilled from both ends
******	Averages			50.0	50.0	21.7	53.4			13.0	
9085	Maryld	Gypsum	Tan	38	80	27	83	12.37	8.74	13.1	Hole is smooth and tapers to one end
9083	Maryld	Diabase	Gray	34	43	28	44	12.75	6.32	12.8	Hole is smooth

- 262 -

#	ORIGIN	MATERIAL	COLOR	WIDTH	HGHT	THICK	WGT	CORD	HGHT	DIA	OBSERVATION
9086	Maryld	Greenstone	Light gray	22	59	24	36	13.69	5.93	13.8	Hole is polished and tapers to one end
9081	Maryld	Basalt	Dark gray	51	61	24	64	12.88	5.07	13.3	Hole is smooth and shows drill rings
9101	Maryld	Rhyolite	Light gray	50	36	20	30	12.06	3.94	13.2	Hole is smooth; has drilled hole (broken) in wing
9082	Maryld	Andesite	Dark brown	45	45	21	38	11.34	8.34	12.2	Hole is polished
9100	Maryld	Gypsum	Light gray	20	57	17	28	11.16	7.21	11.5	Hole is smooth
9084	Maryld	Greenstone	Gray	38	40	28	53	12.65	9.67	13.8	Hole is rough
******	Averages			37.3	52.6	23.6	47.0			13.0	
2737	Virginia	Marble	Dark yellow	84	28	22	92			11.04	Complete hole, well defined
2742	Virginia	Andesite	Black	81	52	24	77			12.86	Completed, broken wing
3495	Virginia	Greenstone	Dark gray	61	48	28	149	12.52	7.54	12.7 half	Irregular hole; drilled from both ends; broken in half
3496	Virginia	Quartzite	Gray	58	49	39	102	11.71	4.86	11.9	Rough; no rings showing
3497	Virginia	Granite	Gray	33	56	26	48	14.64	9.73	15.2	Hole completely polished
6487	Virginia	Slate	Gray	53	45	13	28	9.21	3.27	9.8	Hole has scratches end to end; wing drilled
6950	Virginia	Quartzite	Brown	48	41	25	54	14.09	8.57	14.4	Rough; no rings showing
9074	Virginia	Quartzite	Gray-brown	35	45	24	47	11.61	4.58	11.9	Hole irregular, drilled both ends; wing notched
9075	Virginia	Schist	Gray	15	43	12	17	8.15	3.07	8.5	Small bannerstone, drill rings, rough
9073	Virginia	Greenstone	Dark gray	34	48	18	33	11.73	4.12	12.5	Hole has top/bottom scratches, but drilled; has hole polish
9102	Virginia	Greenstone	Dark gray	52	60	16	59	7.28	3.16	7.4	Hole has top/bottom scratches, not drilled
9103	Virginia	Quartzite	Light gray	48	39	15	36	11.1	4.16	11.6	Drill rings, drilled both ends
9104	Virginia	Schist	Gray	52	45	12	34	5.08	1.6	5.6	Thin bannerstone; hole smooth
9105	Virginia	Slate	Gray	69	42	21	45	12.45	4.41	13.2	V-shaped hole, drill rings
9106	Virginia	Basalt	Dark Gray	45	37	18	28	10.72	4.18	11.1	Small bannerstone, hole semismooth
9107	Virginia	Slate	Light black	39	30	13	13	8.97	2.83	9.9	Complete polish
9108	Virginia	Basalt	Dark gray	34	42	22	35	10.04	2.79	11.8	Hole irregular, drilled both ends; drill rings
9109	Virginia	Rhyolite	Gray	45	32	20	24	11.65	4.58	12.0	Hole smooth, funneled end
9110	Virginia	Basalt	Dark gray	53	45	19	39	12.81	10.93	14.7	Hole polished; funneled end
9111	Virginia	Basalt	Light black	50	50	23	48	17.62	6.83	18.2	Drilled both ends, drill rings, little polished area
9113	Virginia	Basalt	Light black	49	60	24	42	17.09	9.37	17.2	Hole polished; drill rings showing
9114	Virginia	Basalt	Dark gray	22	55	17	26	11.73	3.63	13.1	Hole has polish, drill rings, drilled wing
9115	Virginia	Greenstone	Dark gray	47	41	13	32	7.74	2.27	8.9	Hole drilled both ends, drill rings
9116	Virginia	Greenstone	Light gray	55	53	16	38	8.58	3.0	9.1	Drill rings, drilled both ends, polish

9117	Virginia	Greenstone	Dark gray	45	46	18	27	7.02	1.5	9.7	End-to-end scratches, small notch
9118	Virginia	Greenstone	Dark gray	51	30	20	18	10.71	2.51	13.9	End-to-end scratches, no drill rings
9120	Virginia	Greenstone	Gray	22	38	9	8	8.82	1.99	11.8	Irregular hole, drill rings
9112	Virginia	Basalt	Dark gray	50	40	18	28	7.8	1.99	9.6	Polished hole
Average				47.5	44.3	19.5	43.8			11.8	
9024	N Carolina	Shale	Tan	35	35	18	26				Failure and hole incomplete
No Average											

Table 3 – Summary of Bannerstone Study

Pennsylvania Bannerstones				Maryland Bannerstones				Virginia Bannerstones			
Sample	Max Diameter	Min Diameter	Average Diameter	Sample	Max Diameter	Min Diameter	Average Diameter	Sample	Max Diameter	Min Diameter	Average Diameter
24	16.5	9.0	13.0	8	13.8	11.5	13.0	28	18.2	7.4	11.8

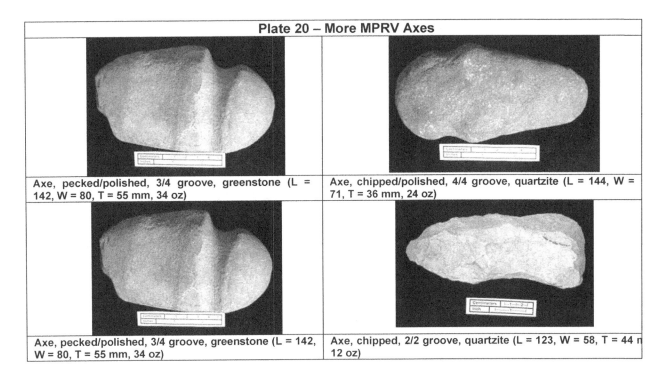

Plate 20 – More MPRV Axes	
Axe, pecked/polished, 3/4 groove, greenstone (L = 142, W = 80, T = 55 mm, 34 oz)	Axe, chipped/polished, 4/4 groove, quartzite (L = 144, W = 71, T = 36 mm, 24 oz)
Axe, pecked/polished, 3/4 groove, greenstone (L = 142, W = 80, T = 55 mm, 34 oz)	Axe, chipped, 2/2 groove, quartzite (L = 123, W = 58, T = 44 m 12 oz)

Copper was used to make beads, and they were common all over the U.S. Copper is easily traceable to its source; thus, trade routes can be established. Since no copper beads were observed in the study collections, Figure 30 shows examples. They make an excellent example of Panindian technology.

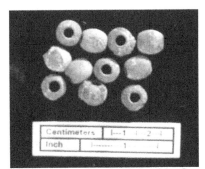

Figure 30 – Copper Beads (Columbia, Oregon)

Bedrock Mortar
Modality (Industry): grinding.
Useability: generalized.
Ecoscene (Environments): uplands.
Functional Angle: 80° to 100°
Bit Angle: N/A.
General Climate: postglacial.

The bedrock mortar has not been reported in the MPRV. An example is shown in Figure 31. The mortar is probably ceremonial because it was used to process large amounts of foodstuffs at one time. There is a wide-spread use of them, and their dates are probably late. It is classified as an above-ground resource which is impossible to date precisely. The lithic mortar has a wooden counterpart that includes a wooden pestle. See Prehistoric MPRV Chronology.

Figure 31 – Bedrock Mortar. It is U-shaped (D =315, W = 223 mm) in limestone on the Holmans Creek, Shenandoah County, Virginia. It probably dates to the Early Woodland.

Bipoints – bipoints are found worldwide and date to 75,000 years ago in Africa where it was invented (Hranicky 2007 and 2012). Virginia bipoints have not been dated archaeologically in land-based sites.

The classic bipointed implement is often suggested as being Solutrean; however, few New World specimens have been found and, more importantly, no dateable context can be assigned to them. The bipoint is found all over the Western Hemisphere. The eastern shore area has produced numerous specimens (Figure 32).

Figure 32 - Flint, Dorchester County, Maryland. It has minor resharpening (left).

Birdshead Graver
Modality (Industry): graving.
Useability: specialized.
Ecoscene (Environments): uplands.
Functional Angle: to be determined.
Bit Angle: N/A.
General Climate: postglacial.

The birdshead graver (Hranicky 2002b) was initially discovered during rockart surveying at Short Mountain in Shenandoah County, Virginia. Figures 32 and 33 show specimens. It is a flake tool which has the striking bulb at the proximal end. The graver is on the upper lateral side; the bulb scar is on the back side if graver is viewed on the right side. The beak flake is often a normal flake during removal. The energy traveling through the stone fans out favoring a side of least resistance. This causes the pointed edge. The difference between the normal flake and birdshead is the reinforcing ridge on one face; it indicates intentional shaping.

Its shape resembles a bird's head; thus, its name. The graver tip is sharp, but not structurally strong. Sometimes, it has supporting flake ridge(s) to reinforce the tip. It has short-term usage, and its function is suggested here as possibly a woodworking tool, namely spear and arrow shafts. But as a major suggestion, the tool was used for body adornment, namely tattooing. It occurs as a biface and uniface (flake) tool. Several specimens are shown in the Flake as Tools section which are classified as occurring during the Pleistocene era.

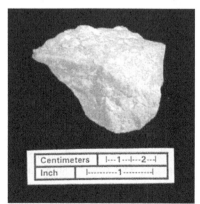

Figure 32 – Classic Birdshead Graver. The graver is reinforced with a medial ridge extending to its tip. It is made from quartzite and has a right and left lateral margin spokeshave.

Figure 33 – Birdshead Gravers from Shenandoah County, Virginia. Left-to-right, material is quartzite, jasper, and flint. The jasper tool probably dates to the Paleoindian period.

Birdstone
Modality (Industry): weighting.
Useability: specialized.
Ecoscene (Environments): ?
Functional Angle: N/A.
Bit Angle: N/A.
General Climate: postglacial.

The birdstone is a polished stone artifact that looks like a bird; sitting bird; pop-eyed birdstone (Figures 34). It is often drilled with two or four holes that suggest that it was an atlatl weight. Ethnographically, the object was used for a variety of reasons, such as indicating pregnancy, readiness for marriage (women), worn in the hair as a symbol of office (badge of office of clan), but most likely, it has an unknown prehistoric purpose. For birdstones examples, see Hranicky (1994), Smith (1972), and Lowery (1988). It probably serves the same function as the barstone.

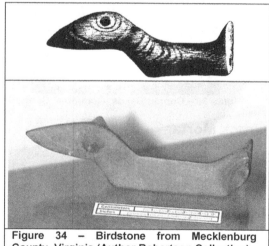

Figure 34 – Birdstone from Mecklenburg County, Virginia (Author Robertson Collection)

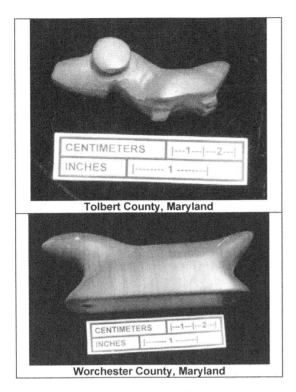

No birdstones were observed in the study collections; however, they do occur in the MPRV (see Lowery 1988).

Blowgun

Since it is a Panindian tool that is found all over the prehistoric U.S., it is assumed to be found in the MPRV. It was made of cane and probably averaged 2-3 meters in length. It was used on small game. For overview, see Swanton (1946). See Experimental Archaeology section for an ethnographic example.

Boilingstone
Modality (Industry): heating.
Useability: generalized.
Ecoscene (Environments): all, piedmont(+).
Functional Angle: N/A.
Bit Angle: N/A.
General Climate: postglacial.

The boilingstone is rarely recognized in archeological contexts or field surveys. It is considered a normal small river cobble that usually shows no wear usage (Figure 35), and as such, it is not classified as a tool. The MPRV specimens are always made from quartzite. Due to fire-heating, the surface patination is often flaked off. It is a spherical object measuring approximately 35–50 mm. The boilingstone dates to the Late Archaic Period and was no longer used when steatite vessels and pottery came into the social scene. Their ceramic pots made excellent cooking (and baking) utensils. It was heated in a hearth and then placed into a skin/wooden container to heat its contents.

Figure 35 – Boilingstones from a Hearth at the Tuscarora Rockshelter, Frederick County, Maryland. They probably date to the Late Archaic Period.

Bola
Modality (Industry): throwing.
Useability: specialized.
Ecoscene (Environments): all, coastal plain(+).
Functional Angle: to be determined.
Bit Angle: N/A.
General Climate: postglacial.

The bola has escaped archeology's site contexts for years. The tool is found all over America, especially where there are migratory ducks and geese. The tool is not common in the MPRV and appears to be an Archaic tool (Figure 36). It is usually made from hardstones, but quartzite and rhyolite specimens do occur. The MPRV bola is spherically-shaped and averages 25 to 30 mm in diameter. It is usually polished, but weathering may have obscured this attribute. For usage, it was placed in a piece of leather which had the edges punched for straps. Three or four bolas were held by their straps and swung around the head, then released at the target, usually low flying birds.

<u>Note</u>: It is sometimes grooved and some specimens have a neck, which is called a plummet. It has also been suggested as having a bola function. Overall, classification of balls, bolas, and boilingstones is difficult.

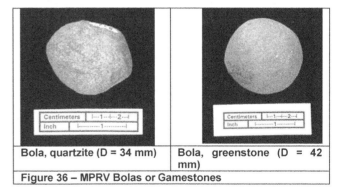

Bone Tools

All prehistoric societies used bone, antler, and wooden tools (Figures 37, 38, and 39). This study leaves this aspect of technology to another study elsewhere. Due to preservation factors, bone tools from archeological contexts that date prior to the Woodland Period are extremely rare, especially in the eastern U.S. The major material for Woodland bone tools is deer bone. Bone served as handles for knives, small celts and adzes. For the MPRV, bone tools include:

1 – Fishhook   2 – Harpoon
3 – Knife   4 – Perforator
5 – Arrow   6 – Depilator
7 – Flesher   8 – Hoe.

These tools probably extend back to Paleoindian times, but are only preserved in Woodland site contexts. An example of a bone adz is shown in the Experimental Archeology section, and a bone-handled knife is in the Bifaces as Knives section.

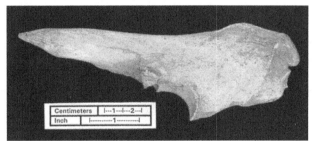
Figure 37 – Deer Ulna Awl (or Knife). It was found on the Mendota Site, Washington County, Virginia in the 1950s.

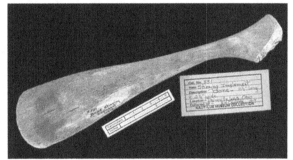
Figure 38 – Bone Stirring Implement. It is from Drainsville, Ohio and was found in 1917.

Figure 39 – Sample of Bone Tools from North Dakota. Top/down: beamer, fishhook, and awl. Note: a bone Plains knife was shown in the Bifaces as Knives section.

Bow (and Arrow)
Modality (Industry): projectiling.
Useability: specialized.
Ecoscene (Environments): all.
Functional Angle: 120° to 180°
Bit Angle: N/A.
General Climate: postglacial.

Since MPRV ethnographic data for the bow and arrow is lacking and, of course, no actual specimens have been preserved, the study becomes one of comparative ethnography from elsewhere, basic bow and arrow studies, and inference from the archeological record (Figure 40). While Saxton (1918), Rogers (1940), and Laubin and Laubin (1980) are classic references in the study of the bow and arrow, the primary reference is T. M. Hamiton's (1982) *Native American Bows* published by the Missouri Archaeological Society. One of the earliest ethnographic sources is Hakluyt's (1851) translation of de Soto's conquest of Florida written by Elvas. See Arrow in this section.

The bow and arrow is a tool combination that uses the tension of wood with ends tied with sinew and a feathered, stone tipped shaft that it launches (Figure 41). It was a major hunting implement that was probably invented around 1000 BP for the New World. However, Bradbury (1997) suggests a Late Archaic origin for this technology. The efficiency of the bow and arrow can be measured in foot-pound-second forces, velocity, and impact on a target.

Figure 40 – From North Carolina, this is John White's drawing from which Theodore de Bry made this engraving in 1590. It has become a classic illustration in the Middle Atlantic area.

For bow and arrow usage, see Nassaney and Pyle (1999) and Bettinger and Eerkens (1999). Bow usage, according to Waldrof (1985), is:

The advent of the compound bow has dealt a cruel blow to traditional archery and to some, using a bow with training wheels is a sacrilegious act. To me, shooting a beautiful Plains bow that has had its back covered with sinew and rattlesnake skin or mastering the power of a yew longbow stirs ancient memories in a primitive soul. I am not Indian, but archery is as much a part of early Europe as well as the Americas. One only has to look at the 5000-year-old Levantine rock paintings to realize how much a part of our heritage archery is.

For bow/arrow efficiency analysis, the heavier (denser shaft) arrow and a faster bow generally equal greater hunting efficiency. Their accuracy according to Bourne (1904), a chronicler of the de Soto expedition, who wrote:

They never remain quiet, but are continually running, traversing from place to place, so that neither crossbow nor arquebuse can be aimed at them. Before a Christian can make a single shot with either, an Indian will discharge three or four arrows; and he seldom misses of his object. Where the arrow meets with no armour, it pierces as deeply as the shaft from a crossbow. Their bows are very perfect; the arrows are made of certain canes, like reeds, very heavy, and so stiff that one of them, when sharpened, will pass through a target. Some are pointed with the bone of a fish, sharp like a chisel; others with some stone like a point of diamond; of such the great number, when they strike upon armour, break at the place the parts are put together; those of cane split, and will enter a shirt of mail, doing more injury than when armed [wearing armor].

Figure 41 – Scott Silsby at the 1999 Oregon Ridge Knapp-In Demonstrating Shooting a Prehistoric-Designed Bow and Arrow

Bow strength, according to Van Buren (1974), is:

I have found through review of a broad sample of North American bows that the average strength (pull weight) was approximately 47 pounds. Pope (1923) states as follows concerning the strength of the average North American bow: "The average Indian bow, however, is obviously constructed to draw less than 28 inches. This fact, and the study of their arrows and the bend capacity of their bows will convince any archer that 25 or 26 inches is the average draw of most natives." If the average pull weight of North American bows was in the neighborhood of 47 pounds and if the average draw of most North American natives was 25 or 26 inches, then the average weight of arrows used, including the arrowhead, must have been in the vicinity of 1 ounce to 1-1/4 ounces. The weight of the average arrowhead would be expected to be approximately one-seventh of the total weight of the arrow. Therefore, from the standpoint of the strength of the average North American bow, the weight of the arrowheads most probably used would be within a range of 2 grams to 5 grams. The probable top weight, 17.8 grams, must be considered to be within the usage range, and consideration must be given to arrowheads of weights as high as 100 grams for short-range hunting.

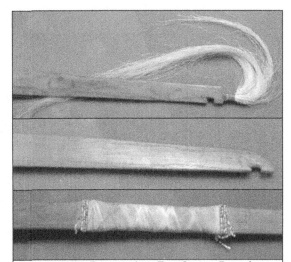

Figure 42 – Reservation Era Osage Bow from Oklahoma Dating Around 1880. Top photographs show the nocks, one of which has a horse-hair attachment. The bottom photograph shows a leather-wrapped handle. The bow is decorated with colorful trade beads. While bow shape varied, it is composed of three parts: 1) handle, 2) upper nock, and 3) lower nock.

And, based on a 19th century Sioux oak bow from Hamilton (1991), which had a 13/16-inch pine board associated with it, the board had been shot with metal arrowheads which penetrated it. A historic bow example is shown in Figure 42.

Bowl (Stone)

Large bowls in the MPRV were made from steatite. No complete specimens were observed in the study collections. However, complete specimens are stored at the Smithsonian Institution, Washington, DC. Figure 42 shows and example that also is in the form of a bird effigy.

Figure 43 – Steatite Effigy Bowl from Washington County, Virginia (Hranicky and Bartlett 1996)

Burin
Modality (Industry): graving.
Useability: specialized.
Ecoscene (Environments): all, uplands(+).
Functional Angle: to be determined.
Bit Angle: N/A.
General Climate: postglacial.

A burin is a pointed flake that was used to engrave bone, antler, or stone (Figure 44). The burin has numerous functions, such as creating starter holes for drills or perforators or graving. According to Collins (1999):

It is a specialized, chisel-like tool, the working edge of which is formed by the acute intersection of two planes, at least one (but usually both) of which was formed by the removal of a prismatic flake (the burin spall).

As demonstrated by the Williamson site in Virginia, burin technology starts with the Paleoindian period. Based on types by Bordes (1968), they occur as:

1 – Straight dihedral burin
2 – Canted dihedral burin
3 – Angular dihedral burin
4 – Multiple dihedral burin
5 – Busqued burin
6 – Burin on straight truncation
7 – Burin on oblique truncation
8 – Multiple burins on double truncations
9 – Borer burin (straight dihedral)
10 – Burin spall.

Figure 44 – Burin on a Biface, quartzite (L = 82, W = 44, T = 15 mm)

The range of burin types for the Middle Atlantic area needs more archeological study. The tool is often overlooked in surveys and archeological site excavations. No MPRV specimens were observed. The following offers a brief overview of the burin.

<u>Major Middle Atlantic area burin styles</u> are:

1 – Dihedral - has two or more facets so that a point is formed.

2 – Burin from break - fracture where a protrusion on one edge remains.

3 – Burin on truncation - fractured edge has been retouched to form the burin.

4 – Multiple burin - blade with two or more protrusions.

<u>Another opinion for burin types</u> are (Miller 1962):

1 – Bec-de-flute burin - has either a single or double workend, via single- or double-faceted flaking

2 – Faceted angle burin - similar to a polyhedric burin; it occurs on broken flakes

3 – Flat burin - facet runs down the cutting edge of the flake and encroaches on the flake bulb

4 – Polyhedric burin - made from a thick flake with parallel facets on one side of the working edge and are opposed by a single facet.

Burin technology, according to Mobley (1991), is:
Burin technology involves the process of removing the edge of a piece of stone, using force applied parallel rather than perpendicular to the edge. Almost any sort of chipped stone artifact (excluding large blocky specimens) can be subjected to burination, but the most common burins are made on flakes and bifaces. Burination creates two classes of artifacts: burins and burin spalls.

Burins are those specimens which have had an edge removed through burination. They are identified by a long negative flake scar forming the specimen's edge, with undulations indicating that force was applied in a direction parallel to the specimen's edge. These burin facets, as they are called, are distinct from simple breaks, whether accidental or intentional, although it may be difficult to determine whether the facets result from intentional or accidental burination. Burination is similar to microblade production, in that the force is applied parallel to the specimen's edge, and a long thin spall is removed that thereby removes the "edge" of the parent specimen, which now becomes a burin. In this analysis burins are generally distinguished from microblade cores in that:

1 – Burins are less wide than microblade cores

2 – Burins have one burin facet per edge, and no more than two

3 – Prepared platforms on burins consist of a slight notch formed by unifacial retouch, whereas prepared platforms on most microblade cores are formed by a single flake scar often struck perpendicular to the blade face.

Celt
Modality (Industry): felling.
Useability: specialized.
Ecoscene (Environments): all, piedmont(+).
Functional Angle: 90° to 180°
Bit Angle: >25° & <40°
General Climate: postglacial.

A celt is a small-to-large V-shaped tool that is not usually grooved and is much smaller than an axe. It is thick with a tapering face that forms a sharp bit. Poll is usually small, pointed, and flat. The basic style is usually highly polished and shows high quality workmanship and is assumed to have been a hafted tool. However, battered polls exist which implies hand holding and poll with a wooden hammer. However, these celts may simply have unfinished polls from production. Hafting examples are shown in Figure 45, and it is discussed in the Experimental Archaeology section.

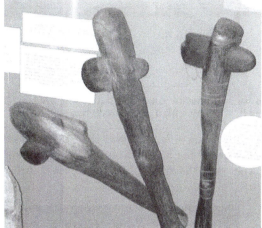

Figure 45 – Pamunkey Celts. Pamunkey Museum, King William County, Virginia. W. P. Miles is Chief.

Three basic types are tapered, square, and flint celts. Grooved celts are sometimes called miniature axes. Another category is the crude, chipped celt which was probably first identified in Virginia by Holland (1960). It occurs in both the Woodland Period but with higher frequencies in the Late Archaic Period.

Most celts are usually made from fine-grain igneous rocks. For the MPRV, greenstone is the most common material. Double bitted celt occurs, but it is rare. There is no limit on the length of a celt; however, specimens over 200 mm are often classified as ungrooved axes. Parts are:

1 – Bit
2 – Blade
3 – Body
4 – Poll
5 – Side.

A celt style occurs in Virginia that merits consideration as a type. It has a wide bit and a very narrow body which comes to a very narrow (almost pointed) poll. Bit often flares and is curved. The body is flattish and has a V-shape. Figures 46, 47, and 48 show specimens. The pointed poll allowed the celt to be inserted into a wooden handle; repeated use of the celt droved (secured) the celt in the handle. It could be removed for transport or making a new handle. See Plate 21 for more MPRV celts.

Like the axe, the celt was made by the pecking to surface into shape and then polishing the surface smooth. There is evidence for both the axe and celt that the preform was flaked into a celt form, then pecked until the surface was smoothed, and finally polishing it (Figure 46).

Figure 46 – Andesite Chipped Celt (King William County, Virginia (L = 176, W = 67, T = 43 mm). It has water wear.

Figure 47 was first published in Hranicky (1995) and is named here as the Shenandoah celt. Hafted examples of other celts are shown in the Experimental Archeology section.

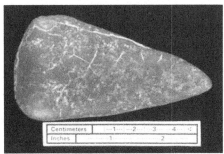

Figure 47 – Shenandoah Celt, chlorite (L = 97, W = 51, T = 14 mm) (Washington County, Virginia). It is a V-shaped implement with a pointed poll.

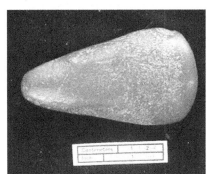

Figure 48 – Shenandoah Celt, greenstone (L = 96, W = 57, T = 18 mm) (Frederick County, Maryland)

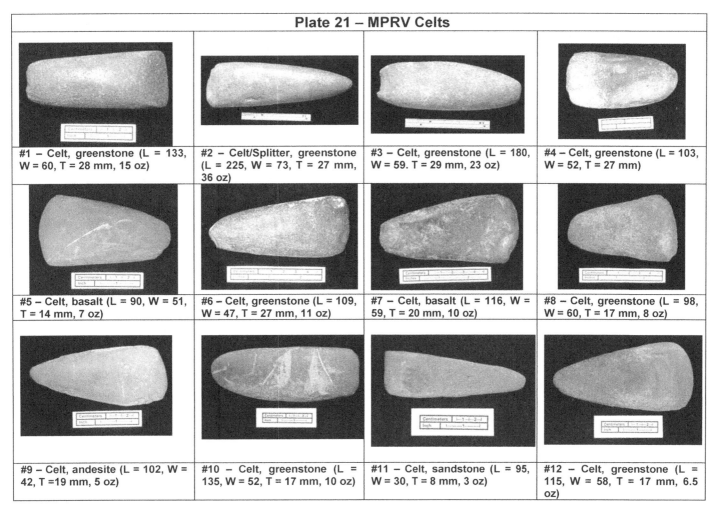

Charmstone or Magicstone
Modality (Industry): spiriting.
Useability: specialized.
Ecoscene (Environments): all.
Functional Angle: N/A.
Bit Angle: N/A.
General Climate: postglacial ?

Charmstone is a human-modified stone that does not exhibit an apparent function or purpose archaeologically. It is usually a small object that is made from special materials, such as quartz, chlorite, or colorful flints. It can have grooving, notching, or reshaping. It is assumed to be a shaman's object for religious ceremonies. Tallystones and engraved stones are included as charmstones. Quartz crystals are often found on Native American sites and probably had a magic property. One specimen was observed in the study collections and is shown in Figure 49.

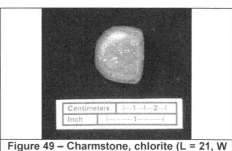

Figure 49 – Charmstone, chlorite (L = 21, W = 23, T = 11 mm)

Chisel
Modality (Industry): planning.
Useability: specialized.
Ecoscene (Environments): all.
Functional Angle: 90° to 145°
Bit Angle: >20° & <35°
General Climate: postglacial.

The chisel is difficult to identify because of its similar shape with the celt and adz. It always assumes some degree of poll battering. The main difference is the frank angle for the bit. It is a medium-to-large, cylindrically- or rectangularly-shaped implement with a beveled bit. Poll is usually round. It also served as a scraper or wedge. The bit may need defining, as some chisels indicate pick functions

(Hranicky 1995). The chisel is rare in the MPRV (Figure 50). However, this is probably a sampling bias.

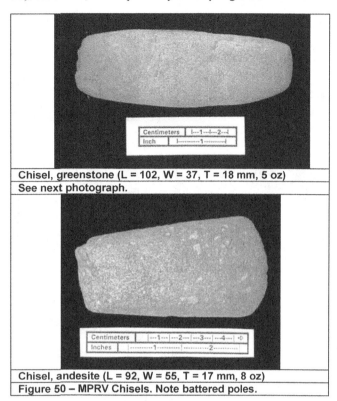

Chisel, greenstone (L = 102, W = 37, T = 18 mm, 5 oz)
See next photograph.

Chisel, andesite (L = 92, W = 55, T = 17 mm, 8 oz)
Figure 50 – MPRV Chisels. Note battered poles.

Chopper
Modality (Industry): chopping.
Useability: generalized.
Ecoscene (Environments): all.
Functional Angle: 80° to 110°
Bit Angle: >20° & <50°
General Climate: postglacial.

The chopper is among the oldest tools associated with human beings (Figures 51 and 52). It is classified here as a member of the hammerstone industry (two classes: blunt and wedge). It is a heavy, hand-held implement with a single cutting workend. For the MPRC, it is primarily made from quartzite, with minor occurrences in rhyolite. Early prehistoric choppers were made from igneous stones.

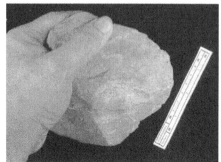

Figure 51 – MPRV Greenstone Hand-Held Chopper

The backed chopper is one that still has cortex remaining on the side/end that is opposite the workend. This backing fits the hand and cushions the chopper.

Figure 52 – MPRV Quartzite Hand-held Chopper. It has a cortex backing opposite the workend.

Concretion Container
Modality (Industry): containing.
Useability: generalized.
Ecoscene (Environments): piedmont and coastal plain.
Functional Angle: 85° to 100°
Bit Angle: N/A.
General Climate: postglacial.

The concretion container is a small bowl made naturally by nature. It was used for pigments for special ceremonies or purposes (Figures 53, 54, and 55).

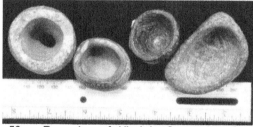

Figure 53 – Examples of Virginia Concretion Containers (Hranicky 1990)

The basic archeological assumption has been the paint pot (Hranicky 1990). For an early writing on the use of red paint, see Willoughby (1915). Logan and Fratt (1993) provide comparative data for pigment making.

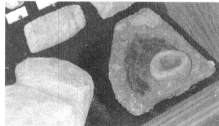

Figure 54 – Small Paint Pot (no measurements) (Loudoun County)

Crescent
Modality (Industry): cutting.
Useability: specialized.
Ecoscene (Environments): uplands and piedmont.
Functional Angle: 180° ?
Bit Angle: N/A.
General Climate: glacial and postglacial.

No crescents were observed in the study collection; however, it probably does occur in the MPRV. It is a C-shaped implement that has antiquity going back to the Paleoindian Period. The Paleoindian crescent is made off a blade; whereas, the Woodland form is a biface. Tool was not used during the Middle Archaic Period. There is a technological relationship between it and the spokeshave. See Spokeshave.

Figure 55 – Paint Pots and Associated Pieces of Red Hematite from Long Island, New York. They were found in the early 1940s. (Formerly in the Geasey collection, now in the Southold Indian Museum in New York.)

Discoidal
Modality (Industry): gaming.
Useability: specialized.
Ecoscene (Environments): all, coastal plain(+).
Functional Angle: to be determined.
Bit Angle: N/A.
General Climate: postglacial.

No discoidals were observed in the study collections; however, they are found in sites (as in MacCord and Hranicky 1992). It is a circular object that has indented faces. Edges are sometimes grooved or flat (Figure 56). Specimens occur with a center hole through both faces. It was used as a gamestone.

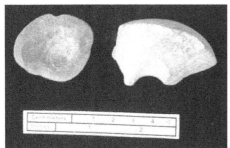

Figure 56 – Left: Concretion Container, Right: Broken Discoidal (Shenandoah County, Virginia)

Disk
Modality (Industry): unknown.
Useability: specialized.
Ecoscene (Environments): all.
Functional Angle: to be determined.
Bit Angle: N/A.
General Climate: postglacial.

The disk is a circular, flat implement made of stone or fired-clay. The purpose is assumed to be a gaming object, but it could have been used to work hides in the tanning process. None were observed in the MPRV study collections, but an example is shown in Figure 57. Especially in the U.S. Southeast, it has a wide-spread distribution (Hranicky 1995). The perforated style could have been a netsinker. See Rubbingstone.

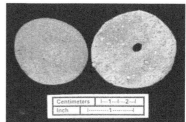

Figure 57 – Virginia Disks. Left is from Green County, Virginia (quartzite, L = 39, W = 34, T = 10 mm) and right is from Shenandoah County (pottery, D = 44, T = 7 mm)

Drill
Modality (Industry): penetrating.
Useability: specialized.
Ecoscene (Environments): all.
Functional Angle: 80° to 110°
Bit Angle: N/A.
General Climate: postglacial.

The drill is a long narrow implement that usually has a square stem (Figures 58, 59, and 60). However, point blades were often made into drills or punches. The difference between a drill and punch/perforator is the drill was rotated while the punch was pushed through materials. All three implements were used in the MPRV; they are primarily Late Archaic and Woodland Period tools but earlier versions do occur. The predominant MPRV materials are rhyolite and quartzite.

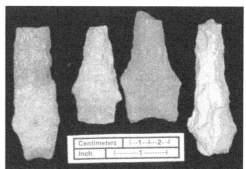

Figure 58 – Various Examples of MPRV Drills

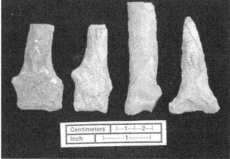

Figure 59 – Miscellaneous MPRV Drills. Drill shape indicates hafting.

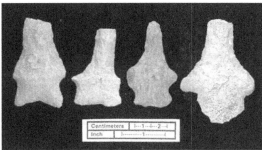

Figure 60 – Miscellaneous MPRV Drills. Drill shape indicates hafting. The MPRV collections did not contain an unbroken drill; tool life cycle may have been limited to a few work applications.

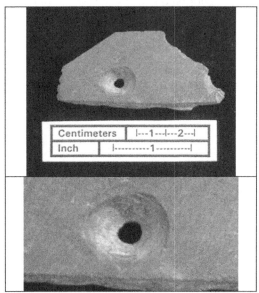

Figure 61 – Broken Pendant Showing Drill Hole. Hole drilling was often performed from both sides, which met when drilled through.

Figure 61 shows a drilled hole. Holes are often drilled from both faces towards the center. Drills were either reeds (used with water and sand) or stone.

The number of different shapes found in the MPRV suggests that they are typeable; however, one attempt was made at classification based on morphology.

The Potomac Valley drill is named here after a sample found in the MPRV. It is a large drill, usually made from quartzite, and has a pronounced hafting area (Figure 62). The stem sides are incurvate, and the base is concave. No unbroken specimens were observed in the study collections.

Figure 62 – Examples of Potomac Valley Drills

Did prehistoric Native American technology survive into the Colonial Period?

Figure 65 – MPRV Fish Weirs. Left: Weir is located between the Maryland shore and Shepherds Island. Photograph date is 7/30/99. Right: Weir located on the Potomac River between Snyders and Taylors landings. Photograph date is 9/4/98. Photographs are courtesy of Dan Guzy (1999). They probably date less than 100 years, but the technology was carried over from the Native Americans.

Ear Plug

Lithic ear plugs were not observed in the study collections or published literature. See Hranicky (1995) for description.

Effigy Objects

No effigy objects were observed in the study collections. For effigy examples, see Cresthull (1981 and 1982), Fowler (1974), Robbins (1963), Thomas (1972), and MacCord (1966). This artifact class includes hand-held to boulder-size stone engraved or carved objects (Figure 63).

Figure 63 – Effigy Stone from Mecklenburg County, Virginia (Arthur Robertson Collection)

Engraved Artifacts

Modality (Industry): decorating.
Useability: specialized.
Ecoscene (Environments): all.
Functional Angle: N/A.
Bit Angle: N/A.
General Climate: postglacial.

Engraved artifacts are a catch-all grouping for any small tool or implement that has incising on its surface. Also, it includes notched and sculptured artifacts. Israel (1996) refers to these items as miniature art, and examples are shown in Figure 64. None were observed in the study collections. Israel (1996) provides a list of possibilities:

1 – Carved faces
2 – Face effigies
3 – Animal effigies
4 – Carved birdstone
5 – Stone maskette
6 – Pendant effigies.

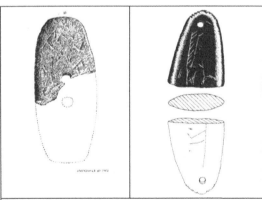

Figure 64 – Left: Engraved Gorget (Holmes 1897) and right: Pendant (Israel 1996) from Calvert County, Maryland

Fish Weirs

Modality (Industry): trapping.
Useability: generalized.
Ecoscene (Environments):
                       piedmont(+), coastal plain(-).
Functional Angle: N/A.
Bit Angle: N/A.
General Climate: postglacial.

Fish weirs are aquatic stone structures which are numerous in the MPRV above the fall line (Hobbs 1964-1967, Holland 1983, and Guzy 1999). For comparison, Bushnell (1930) describes fish weirs on the James River in Virginia. Snyder (1967) shows an aerial view of Heaters Island that shows fish weirs in the Potomac River. Figure 65 (top of page) shows two examples of a MPRV fish weir. The main question is: *Are they Indian?* Guzy (2001) comments:

As I discussed in Guzy (1999), there were considerable efforts between 1768 and 1828 to destroy fish weirs that obstructed river navigation, and from the mid-1800's to about 1930 to destroy fish weirs assumed to be hurting sport fishing (pollution was the more likely culprit). As these weirs were being destroyed, white settlers kept illegally erecting more.

Floods and other natural forces also knock down loose stone weirs or cover them with sediment. I found several weirs documented in the 1960's to have now disappeared and two on the Monocracy that have been greatly destroyed in the past 15-20 years.

Given this historical and physical evidence, it seems to me that the Potomac fish weir ruins we find today are more likely to be a hundred or so years old, not thousands. While I have no doubt that there were prehistoric fish weirs on the Potomac, I would guess that few have survived, although many people choose to believe that they all did.

Figure 66 – Fish Trap. Pumunkey Museum, King William County, Virginia – W. P. Miles is Chief.

Potomac River islands provided natural channels for fish. The Indians and early settlers ported large boulders and placed them in the channel in V-shaped formations. This practice made fish capture very easy. While not easily dateable, fish weir technology probably dates to the Middle to Late Woodland Period when population densities were increasing; thus, a need for increased foods, and weirs provided abundant supplies of fish. While Guzy (1999) reports numerous weirs, he does state that the Maryland General Assembly ordered them destroyed in 1768. This probably reduced the number of existing weirs. Mother Nature probably removed the rest before the modern age. The actual count will never be known.

Beverley (1705) offers a fish weir comment:

...At the Falls of the Rivers, where the Water is shallow, and the Current strong, the Indians use another kind of Weir, thus made. They make a Dam of loose Stone, where of there is plenty at hand, quite across the River, leaving One, Two, or more Spaces or Trunnels, for the Water to pass thro'; at the Mouth of which they set a Pot of Reeds, wove in Form of a Cone, whose Base is about Three Foot, and in perpendicular Ten, into which the Swiftness of the Current carries the Fish, and wedges them in fast, that they cannot possibly return.

In addition to fish weirs, the Native Americans spear fished, used fishhooks, and fish traps (Figure 66). Engineering attributes, volume, capture rate, structure, etc. for weirs remain to be studied and published archaeological.

Flesher, Tanningstone, and Depilator

The flesher, tanningstone, and depilator are bone/stone tools used in hide tanning. They probably occur in the MPRV, but none were observed in the study collections.

Flake Tools

Modality (Industry): numerous.
Useability: specialized.
Ecoscene (Environments): all.
Functional Angle: Cannot be determined.
Bit Angle: N/A.
General Climate: glacial and postglacial.

Flake tools are made from specific types of flakes, as:

1 – Controlled flaking and usually still has the bulb scar
2 – Thickness is usually 10-11 mm
3 – Designed for short-term usage.

They primarily functioned as knives, scrapers, drills, and perforators. The knife flake can also be called a utilized flake or pick-up tool. The flake tool can also be called a uniface tool. See Flakes as Tools section.

Gamestone

Modality (Industry): gaming.
Useability: specialized.
Ecoscene (Environments): all.
Functional Angle: Cannot be determined.
Bit Angle: N/A.
General Climate: postglacial.

Small object that does not have an obvious function (Figure 67). It is an object with a flat surface, ball, disk-shaped, cone-shaped, spherically-shaped, or irregularly-shaped object. It is not easily identified; thus, it is frequently lacking in surface collections. See Disk.

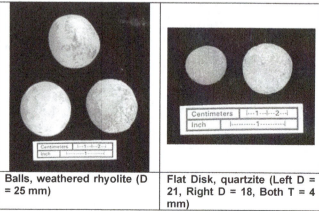

Balls, weathered rhyolite (D = 25 mm)	Flat Disk, quartzite (Left D = 21, Right D = 18, Both T = 4 mm)

Figure 67 – MPRV Gamestones

Gorget

Modality (Industry): decorating.
Useability: unknown.
Ecoscene (Environments): all.
Functional Angle: N/A.
Bit Angle: N/A.
General Climate: postglacial.

The gorget is a personal adornment item made from high quality materials. While stone was the preferred material, Hariot or Harriot (1893) mentions copper gorgets along the North Carolina coast. It is a rectangularly-shaped implement with perforations of one or more holes at perforal ends. The MPRV specimens tend to be two-hole gorgets. Holmes (1987) reported several types (Figure 68). Figure 69 shows MPRV specimens.

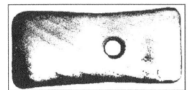

Figure 68 – MPRV Gorget as Reported by Holmes (1897)

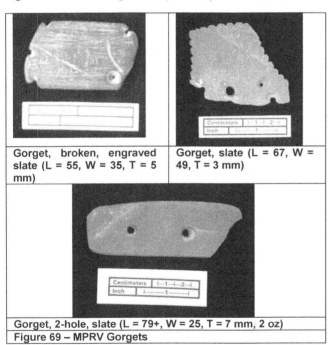

Gorget, broken, engraved slate (L = 55, W = 35, T = 5 mm)	Gorget, slate (L = 67, W = 49, T = 3 mm)
Gorget, 2-hole, slate (L = 79+, W = 25, T = 7 mm, 2 oz)	

Figure 69 – MPRV Gorgets

The shell gorget occurs throughout the Southeast including Virginia. None were observed in the study collections or have been reported in site reports. The shell gorget was engraved with designs that can be dated. Some gorget have dots and bars which probably represent a time period. See Hoffman (2001) for a discussion.

Figure 70 – Shell Gorget with Rattlesnake Motif. It dates 1450 to 1750 AD and is from the Thompson Site, Gordon County, Georgia (Jim Maus Collection, North Carolina).

The rattlesnake shell gorget probably represents the serpent at ceremonial events and shows the true aesthetic qualities of the southeastern Native Americans during the Dallas phase (Figure 70).

Gouge

Modality (Industry): grooving.
Useability: specialized.
Ecoscene (Environments): all.
Functional Angle: 30° to 65°
Bit Angle: >20° & <30°
General Climate: postglacial.

The gouge is a long or short, narrow implement with a hollowed-out face which extends the full or half the length of the tool (Figure 71). It is usually U-shaped. It occurs as grooved or knobbed. Full lengths are called channel gouges. Its primary function was woodworking. The gouge is rare in the MPRV. However, this may be a sampling bias, but most likely, the gouge is associated with the maritime Archaic of the Northeast (see Snow 1980 and Willoughby 1935) and not found in the MPRV because of this reason. Function is probably the same as the adz.

Figure 71 – Gouge from Scottsville, New York. This specimen is the faceted (flat channel edges) type. It is made from felsite.

Graver

Modality (Industry): engraving.
Useability: specialized.
Ecoscene (Environments): all.
Functional Angle: 30° to 65°
Bit Angle: N/A
General Climate: glacial/postglacial.

A graver is a blade or biface tool with a sharp protrusion that is used to engrave pottery, wood, or stone with designs (Figure 72). See Birdshead Graver.

Graver/Knife, weathered rhyolite (L = 67, W = 30, T = 8 mm). Note platform at bottom of the specimen.	Graver/spokeshave/scraper, quartzite (L = 45, W = 36, T = 8 mm)
Figure 72 – MPRV Gravers	

Hammerstone

Modality (Industry): pounding.
Useability: generalized.
Ecoscene (Environments): all.
Functional Angle: 20° to 150°
Bit Angle: N/A.
General Climate: glacial/postglacial.

A hammerstone is a round stone, usually fist size (ellipsoidal) that is used to peck, strike, pound, abrade, or grind on other materials (Figure 73). It shows battered edges. It is classified here as a member of the hammerstone industry (two classes: blunt and wedge). The hammerstone may have been grooved and used as a net sinker, club, or bola. Large, probably single-use, stones are called poundingstones. It is usually made from local cobbles with quartzite being a favorite material (Hranicky 1995). Parts are:

1 – Edge - side
2 – Face - surface.

Hammerstone, quartzite (L = 75, W = 68, T = 45 mm, 13 oz)	Hammerstone, quartzite (D = 85, T = 85 mm, 19 oz)
Figure 73 – MPRV Hammerstones.	

For knapping, there are:

1 – Hard, oval hammer (igneous rock)
2 – Soft, cylindrical (nonigneous rock)
3 – Abrader, smoothing (sedimentary rock).

In the MPRV, hammerstones are made from almost every hardstone, with basalt and diabase (see Geasey and Ballweber 1999 and Ballweber 1991) being primarily used for quarrying. The quartzite hammerstone is the most common and is a primary tool in hard billet flaking. See Peckingstone.

On some hammerstones, the center of the flat face has an indention. Hranicky (1995) argues that these facial intentions were fingerrest for holding it while striking another stone. However, Barber (2001) argues that these indentions functioned as a place for holding stone to remover flakes or blades – the anvilstone.

Hand Drill

The hand drill is a shaft-operated device (Figure 74). It is placed in both hands that are rubbed back-and-forth to cause the device to spin. Pine resin is put in the hands to enhance the grip. The hand drill probably has considerable antiquity. See Pump Drill.

Figure 74 – Using the Hand Drill to Start a Fire. Daniel Abbott (Martinsville, Virginia) at Archeology Day (October 7, 2000), MacCallum-More Museum and Gardens, Chase City, Virginia. The tool's functional angle is illustrated. His expertise shows insight into the traditional Native American way of using tools.

Smith (1907) confirms this method by recording:

Their fire they kindle presently by chafing a dry pointed sticke in a hole of a little square peece of wood, that firing it selfe, will so fire mosse, leaves, or anie such like drie thing will quickly burne.

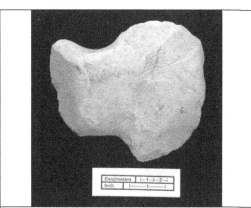

Figure 75 – MPRV Hoe, greenstone (L = 100, W = 88, T = 26 mm). Hranicky (2002b) suggests this tool is a Native American copy of a metal ax.

Hoe

Modality (Industry): tilling.
Useability: generalized.
Ecoscene (Environments): uplands(-), piedmont, Coastal plain(+).
Functional Angle: 85° to 100°
Bit Angle: >30° & <40°
General Climate: postboral.

The hoe was the Native Americans' digging tool in the practice of horticulture (Figures 75 and 76). It is an implement with a wide bit and is usually made from hardstones. The hoe in the MPRV was made from organic materials, such as wood and antler; lithic implements are rare. Specimens indicate that the hoe was also hafted. Based on archeological site contexts and ethnographic evidences, there was a high frequency of wooden hoes. The hoe may have been the last adaptive tool developed in prehistoric America. See Prehistoric Chronology section.

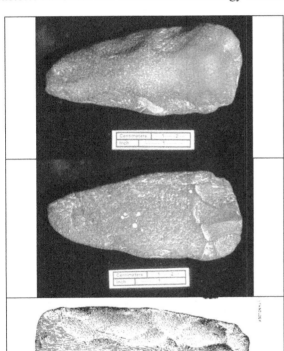

Figure 76 – Hoe (both faces), greenstone (L = 125, W = 60, T = 25 mm). It was found in Shenandoah County, Virginia. It has a D-shaped cross section suggesting bipolar manufacture; it has fingerrest on its sides suggesting it was hand held. The bit is highly polished. Drawing is an example from Holmes (1897).

Knife

Modality (Industry): cutting.
Useability: generalized.
Ecoscene (Environments): all.
Functional Angle: Varies by design, but 60° to 150°
Bit Angle: N/A.
General Climate: glacial and postglacial.

See section on knives. The knife is the most common implement in the MPRV. It has hundreds of styles, but all predominately average 14 mm in thickness. Quartz and rhyolite are the major stones. Neither provides sharp cutting edges when compared to quartz or the western U.S. stone obsidian (Figure 77). White quartz is used, but not with the frequencies of rhyolite and quartzite. See Bifaces as Knives section.

Figure 77 – Clear Quartz Knife from Southeastern Virginia

Quartz has the hardest (but sometimes brittle) edge of any lithic material; material was common for knives and points.

Knob Splitter

The knob splitter has an area used for hand-holding the implement. Poll is not battered which indicated it was probably used in a chopping action. See Splitter.

Lapstone

The lapstone may be another term for anvilstone, but it is often used for the term nuttingstone. It dates to the Archaic Period. See Nuttingstone.

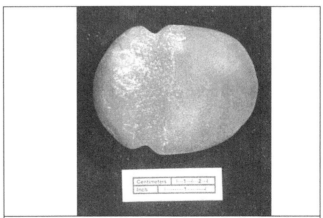

Figure 78 – MPRV Maul, andesite, pecked/polished, 4/4 groove (L = 96, W = 72, T = 22 mm, 11.5 oz)

Maul

Modality (Industry): pounding.
Useability: specialized.
Ecoscene (Environments): all.
Functional Angle: 90° to 180°
Bit Angle: N/A.
General Climate: postglacial.

The maul is a large grooved implement with a round bit or workend (Hranicky 1995). The primary attribute is that it is a round (cross-section) tool (Figure 78). It is usually made from an igneous stone. It is sometimes called a grooved hammerstone. One pointed bit maul was recorded. It has a pointed bit, flat tressel, and flat poll. It is shown here for convenience (Figure 79).

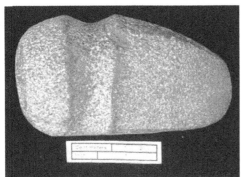

Figure 79 – An Unusual Maul; however, it could be an unusual axe. It is made from greenstone, 3/4 groove, and measures L = 109, W = 60, T = 60 mm. The basic shape is circular as is the classic maul.

The maul needs further refining in archeology; it is defined here as a macrotool with a circular cross section (Figure 80).

Figure 80 – Examples of Virginia Maul Designs (Hranicky 1995)

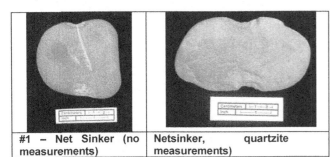

#1 – Net Sinker (no measurements)	Netsinker, quartzite measurements)

Figure 81 – MPRV Netsinkers

Netsinker
Modality (Industry): sinking.
Useability: generalized.
Ecoscene (Environments): all, piedmont(+).
Functional Angle: N/A.
Bit Angle: N/A.
General Climate: postboral.

The netsinker is a notched flat tool that most archeologists assume was used to anchor fish nets to the bottom of rivers and streams. The primary material is quartzite. This microtool has the largest distribution of any tool; basic style is found everywhere (Figures 81 and 82). Most netsinkers are made from a flat disk; the dual notching style has a wide distribution. The basic material is quartzite. Gorall (2000) provides a New York fishing activity study that has comparative data for the MPRV. For a netsinker study, see Kraft (1992). Bello (1993) reports perforated specimens from New Jersey. Netsinkers may date to the Middle Archaic Period (Barber 1980).

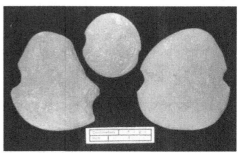

Figure 82 – Netsinkers. Left is from Columbia County (Pennsylvania), center is from Goose Lake (Oregon), and right is from Chemung County (New York).

While the common form has two notches, some Pennsylvania specimens have four notches (Figure 83). The extra set of notches suggests differences in securing the sinker to nets.

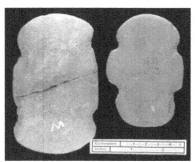

Figure 83 – Quartzite Netsinkers from Forest County, Pennsylvania. Left (Broken): L = 110, W 67, T = 18 mm; right: L = 91, W = 61, T = 9 mm.

Nuttingstone
Modality (Industry): holding.
Useability: generalized.
Ecoscene (Environments): uplands.
Functional Angle: to be determined.
Bit Angle: N/A.
General Climate: postglacial.

A nuttingstone is a flat cobble or boulder that is used to crack nuts. It has one or more (up to 10) indentations (Figure 84). The nuttingstone is probably a Woodland Period addition to the Native Americans' toolkit as its portability is restrictive to long distances.

Figure 84 – Nuttingstone, quartzite (L = 165, W = 130, H = 95 mm). It was found in Shenandoah County, Virginia in a village context. The reverse side was used as an anvilstone. The largest indentation is D = 32 with depth at 21 mm.

The multiple indentations suggest mass production of cracked nuts. Another function is suggested, the oilstone. By using the nuttingstone to crack/press numerous nuts at one time, the oil that they contain can be pressed out (see Native American use of oils in Hudson 1976). This process was tested experimentally and is offered as an alternative hypothesis for the use of the nuttingstone.

A third explanation suggested here is from a Pennsylvania collector. He suggests that a flint flake can be rotated in the limestone or sandstone that produces a fine powder. This powder was used in polishing stone, shell, wood, etc. for smooth surfaces. Figure 85 shows an example of the Pennsylvania stone that easily suggests this hypothesis.

Figure 85 – Pennsylvania Example of Stone with Indentations. The use of the stone was to obtain jewelry-like rouge for polishing. The explanation accounts for the numerous indentations.

Figure 86 shows nutting indentations on a large boulder. It is referred to here as a nutting station; it is located at the Harrison County petroglyph (46H51) site in West Virginia. The site is located 50 meters from the pictograph site (Hranicky and Collins 1997). None have been reported in the MPRV. However, nutting stations are extremely difficult to find.

Figure 86 – Nutting Station, Harrison County, West Virginia. It is located next to the Harrison County petroglyph site which dates to the Mississippian era (Hranicky and Collins 1997).

Oilstone

See Nuttingstone.

Ornaments (Ear and Nose)

No lithic ornaments (ear and nose rings etc.) are assumed since ethnographic data suggest copper, bead strings, and natural objects (bird claws or feathers) were used. Strachey (1849) in his reference to the Powahatans writes:

Their eares they boare with wyde holes, commonly two or three, and in the same they doe hang chaines of stryned pearle bracelets, of white bone or shreds of copper, beaten thinne and bright, and wound up hollowe, and with a greate pride, certaine fowles'leggs, eagles, hawks, turkeys, etc., with beasts' clawes, beares, arrahacounes, squirrels, etc.

Peckingstone
Modality (Industry): pecking.
Useability: specialized.
Ecoscene (Environments): all.
Functional Angle: 85° to 95°
Bit Angle: N/A.
General Climate: postglacial.

A peckingstone is basically a rectangularly-shaped or circularly-shaped hammerstone with side indentations (Hranicky 1995). The indentations were used for the fingers to hold it so that when the stone struck another stone, the fingers would release it. This prevented the striking energy from traveling back into the hand (Hranicky 1995). Hand-holding a stone while striking another stone causes the hand to become numb. By holding it with two fingers and releasing it just before hitting the target area, this is avoided. The primary materials are igneous rocks, but softer stones do occur. See Abraderstone.

Pendant
Modality (Industry): decorating.
Useability: unknown.
Ecoscene (Environments): all.
Functional Angle: N/A.
Bit Angle: N/A.
General Climate: glacial and postglacial.

The pendant is an ornament that was worn around the neck. Holmes (1897) illustrates several, but none were observed in the study collections (Figures 87 and 88). For pendant examples, see Hranicky (1995 and 2002b), Cresthull (1982), and Kraft (1975).

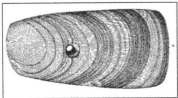

Figure 87 – MPRV Slate Pendant from Holmes (1897)

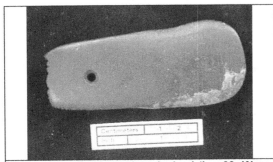

Figure 88 – Pendant, slate, incised (L = 93, W = 40, T = 10 mm) (Beckley Springs, West Virginia)

Perforator
Modality (Industry): penetrating.
Useability: specialized.
Ecoscene (Environments): all.
Functional Angle: open.
Bit Angle: N/A.
General Climate: postglacial.

The perforator is one of four classes of pointed implements that are used to push through a target causing a small hole, which are:

1 – Projectile Point
2 – Perforator
3 – Punch
4 – Drill.

The bit of the perforator sometimes has a medial ridge from the body to the acutus (Figure 89). The body sometimes is extra thick that suggests heavy-duty work.

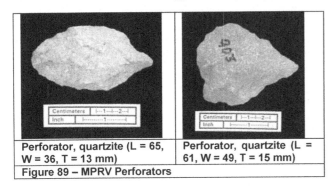

| Perforator, quartzite (L = 65, W = 36, T = 13 mm) | Perforator, quartzite (L = 61, W = 49, T = 15 mm) |

Figure 89 – MPRV Perforators

The projectile point and drill are hafted tools; whereas, the perforator and punch are hand-held tools. Excluding projectile points, the main differences are the bit angles.

1 – Punch has a bit (acutus) angle >45 degrees

2 – Perforator has a bit (acutus) angle >30 degrees but <45 degrees

3 – Drill has a bit (acutus) angle <30 degrees.

The projectile point often shows blade modifications that match one of the angle requirements. Naturally, there is functional overlap of each tool. See Toolmaking section.

Pestle and Mortar
Modality (Industry): grinding.
Useability: generalized.
Ecoscene (Environments): all.
Functional Angle: 80° to 100°
Bit Angle: N/A.
General Climate: postglacial.

The Middle Atlantic stone mortar tends to be small boulders (>150 CM) that are made from sandstone or metaquartzite. Indentation is usually shallow suggesting that it was used for a short time and not carried from village to new village sites. It was used to grind or mix foodstuffs, namely corn, acorns, and nuts. The associated part of the mortar is the pestle that is usually made from a hard stone.

Some archeologists suggest that the ratio between hunter tools (points, knives, and scrapers) and gatherer tools (mortars, pestles, and grinding slabs) indicates a change in subsistence. This may be measurable from the Middle Archaic through Late Woodland Periods.

The mortar and pestle are combination tools that are used to process food, namely grains (Figure 90). The mortar is a hollowed-out or bowl-shaped object in which the pestle is used to grind grain. The mortar is usually made from granular stone. It is sometimes called a cupstone and bedrock mortars do occur in the Middle Atlantic area. The wooden version is sometimes called a log mortar. The large, movable boulder mortars are sometimes called slabstones.

The pestle has several other names: mano, millingstone, and muller. It is a long, cylindrically-shaped implement with a flat end. The workend surface usually is larger than the diameter of the handle part. It is made from various stones that range in hardness from sandstone to basalt. The basalt implements probably functioned as crushers rather than grinders. This pestle is used vertically on the mortar.

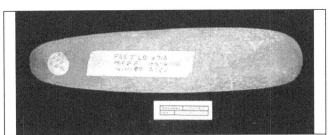

Pestle, andesite (L = 261, W = 57, T = 40 mm, 32+ oz)

Mortar, greenstone (L = 450, W = 312, T = 162) and Pestle, quartzite (L = 250, W = 110, T = 81 mm)

Figure 90 – MPRV Mortar and Pestles

Another type of pestle is the horizontal or roller pestle. It is relatively common in the MPRV. It is a long (>400 mm) cylindrically-shaped implement with round ends. It was used to roll over grains on a large flat surface. It produces less grit than the vertical type. These tools tend to be self-polishing during usage. There is no evidence of resurfacing pestle workends.

These tools were often made from hardwoods; thus, they are not preserved archeologically in buried contexts. There is ethnographic evidence to support wooden implements. See Chronology section.

Pick
Modality (Industry): pounding.
Useability: specialized.
Ecoscene (Environments): all, uplands(+).
Functional Angle: 90° to 180°
Bit Angle: >40°
General Climate: postglacial.

Large, heavy macrotool with a pointed bit. It is usually grooved and made from igneous rocks. The pick is defined here as a rectangularly-shaped marcotool with a pointed bit. The pick and maul probably have similar functions. It was a quarry tool. None were observed in the study collections. See Hranicky (2002b).

Pin
Modality (Industry): fastening.
Useability: specialized.
Ecoscene (Environments): all.
Functional Angle: N/A.
Bit Angle: N/A.
General Climate: postglacial.

The pin or fastener is generally made from bone and is not well preserved in the archeological record. Figure 91 shows a stone pin. It was pushed through overlapping pieces of rawhide; it could have been a stone awl or drill.

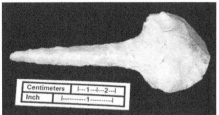

Figure 91 – Pin, awl, or drill, chert (L = 93, W = 38, T = 10). It was found in the MPRV, but was not made from local stone. The white chert is common in the Southeast; thus, the specimen is probably from that area. It is a late Woodland object and probably associated with the Mississippian culture.

Pipe
Modality (Industry): smoking.
Useability: generalized.
Ecoscene (Environments): all.
Functional Angle: N/A.
Bit Angle: N/A.
General Climate: postboral.

The pipe was invented to inhale smoke from burning grasses, but mainly tobacco in its bowl. The eastern variety of tobacco was Nicotianna rustica. There are two pipe classes (Figure 92):

1 – Ceramic
2 – Stone.

The stone pipe was the common form. Timberlake (1765) comments on a peace pipe:

...*was of red stone, curiously cut with a knife, it being very soft, tho extremely pretty when polished.*

Wooden pipes may have existed, but this remains to be proven archeologically. Both manufacturing methods often had decorations or engravings. Stone versions were sometimes carved in effigies, namely animals. These pipes are probably high status pipes. For the southeastern U.S., these pipes are often large and well made (Figure 92). Pipes were not represented in the study collections.

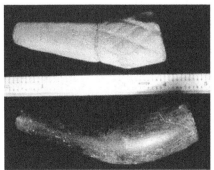

Figure 92 – Virginia Pipes: Top, Ceramic and Bottom, Stone

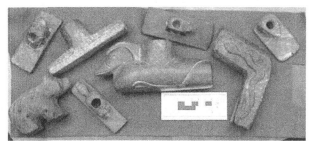

Figure 93 – Mississippian Pipes. Display at the Wolf Creek Museum, Bastian, Virginia. There may have been creditably problems with these specimens. The effigy pipe is a frequently counterfeited artifact.

Figure 94 shows a pipe preform. Stone pipes were made by the peck and polish method of shaping stone. A graver was used to carve effigy figures on the pope.

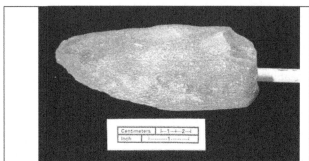

Figure 94 – Pipe blank, rhyolite (L = 115, D = 49) unfinished, hole is drilled to 45 mm

Plummet
Modality (Industry): Remains to be determined.
Useability: unknown.
Ecoscene (Environments): all ?
Functional Angle: Cannot be determined.
Bit Angle: N/A.
General Climate: postglacial.

The plummet is a tear-shaped implement that is found all over the East. It is usually made from hard stones and averages 75 mm in length. While some archeologists suggest it was used as a bola or netsinker, basically it is a problematic implement (Figure 95). Grooved shell columellae occurs in Florida (Walker 2000), which suggest the plummet served the same function as netsinkers. However, the method of securing them to a net remains to be proven. No specimens were observed in the MPRV study collections. See Bola.

Figure 95 – Plummet Examples from Virginia

Projectile Point
Modality (Industry): projectiling.
Useability: probably generalized.
Ecoscene (Environments): all.
Functional Angle: varies depending on function.
Bit Angle: N/A.
General Climate: postglacial. See Projectile Point section.

The projectile point is defined as (Hranicky 1994):
... any lithic object that is bifacially- or unifacially-flaked, has a pointed end, two cutting edges, and a shaft mounting area.

MPRV points are presented in the Projectile Points section. Also, see Hranicky (2002b). Points were made either from quarry materials or field/riverbed pick-up cobbles. Figure 96 shows a generalized lithic reduction sequence for a point.

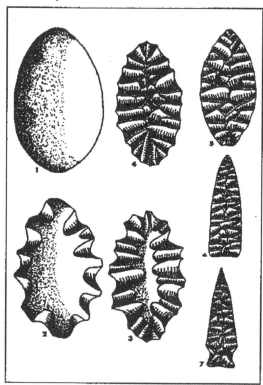

Figure 96 – A Generalized Sequence for Cobble Reduction to Make a Projectile Point (Hranicky and Painter 1989)

Pump Drill
Modality (Industry): drilling.
Useability: specialized.
Ecoscene (Environments): all.
Functional Angle: 80° to 110°
Bit Angle: N/A.
General Climate: postglacial.

The pump drill was used for drilling holes and starting fires. It is a device that uses leverage to rotate a shaft. It has no reliable starting date for its invention. Figure 97 shows the drill and its operations. If natural fibers are used for the pump string, the pump must be held at a slight angle to keep the string from excessively rubbing together which shortens its life. The thumb can be used to control the string tension. See Hand Drill.

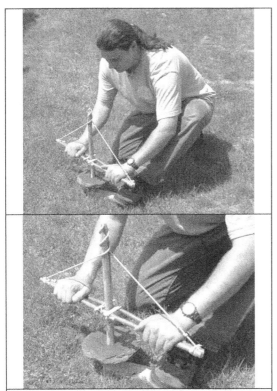

Figure 97 – Use of a Fly-Wheel Pump-Drill on a wooden fireblock by Tim MacWelch at the 2000 Oregon Ridge Knapp-In, Cockysville, Maryland. The tool's functional angle is illustrated.

<u>Note</u>: the pump drill was not used in Virginia and Maryland until the protohistoric period.

Punch

See Perforator.

Quarry Digging Tool

The quarry digging tool is a hoe-like, hafted implement made from a hardstone. None were observed in the study collections. It is used in pit quarrying rhyolite; other stones remain to be proven.

Reamer

Tool class is not used. See Perforator.

Roller Pestle
Modality (Industry): grinding.
Useability: generalized.
Ecoscene (Environments): all.
Functional Angle: 170° to 180°
Bit Angle: N/A.
General Climate: postglacial.

The roller pestle, also called a rod, may date to the Early Archaic Period (Bolian 1980). It is a cylindrically-shaped pestle which is square or pointed on both ends (Figure 98). It is used to grind foods by rolling it over them. Length is usually greater than 25 cm.

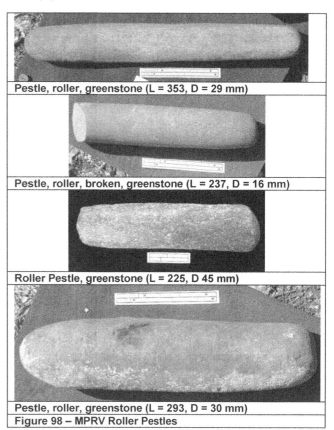

Figure 98 – MPRV Roller Pestles

Rubbingstone
Modality (Industry): smoothing.
Useability: generalized.
Ecoscene (Environments): all.
Functional Angle: N/A.
Bit Angle: N/A.
General Climate: postglacial.

The rubbingstone is a small (<35 mm) cobble that has a flat surface from rubbing it on another surface (Figure 99). It was used to smooth pottery and other surfaces. It was not intended as an abraderstone. It could have been used in the tanning process. Also, it was used to smooth pottery surfaces. See Disk.

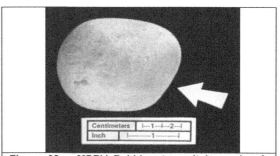

Figure 99 – MPRV Rubbingstone. It is made of quartzite and has a flat place (arrow). Tool has not been washed and will be tested for residue.

Saw
Modality (Industry): cutting.
Useability: specialized.
Ecoscene (Environments): uplands?
Functional Angle: 170° to 180°
Bit Angle: N/A.
General Climate: glacial and postglacial.

The saw is a rare tool in the East. Specimens that do occur are small, hand-held tools usually made from abrasive stones like quartzite (Figures 100 and 101). It is a rectangularly-shaped tool with one share having large tooth-like serrations. The bank (back or nonworkend) is smooth so that the index finger can rest on it and apply even pressure to the share.

Figure 100 – Quartzite Saw (San Diego County, California). It is made on a blade using a medial ridge for strength. It has a snap break, but was probably 100 mm in length. Dates to the Lake Mojave phase (9000 BC) and suggests this tool class has western origins.

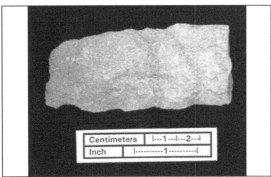

Figure 101 – MPRV Saw, quartzite (L = 68, W = 31, T = 11 mm)

Scraper-Plane
Modality (Industry): cutting.
Useability: specialized.
Ecoscene (Environments): all.
Functional Angle: 170° to 180°
Bit Angle: N/A.
General Climate: postglacial.

The scraper-plane was identified and named by Echard (2000). It is a large scraper-like tool (rabot) made from quartzite. The base is flat with edge flakes creating the workend. It was not observed in the MPRV, but could possibly exist.

Figure 102 – Sharpener, limestone (L = 150, W = 115, T = 89), Baltimore County, Maryland (Hranicky 1987)

Shaft Straightener/Sharpener
Modality (Industry): smoothing.
Useability: specialized.
Ecoscene (Environments): all, piedmont(+).
Functional Angle: N/A.
Bit Angle: N/A.
General Climate: postglacial.

The function of grooved stones for abrasive, sharpening, and polishing is poorly defined in archeology (Figure 102). Figure 103 shows a sandstone specimen that suggests its function was to shape arrow shafts.

Figure 103 – Arrow Shaft Straightener. Artifact has Middle Atlantic area provenance and measures approximately 40 mm.

This implement dates back to the Dalton pointmakers, as Goodyear (1974) reports 56 abraders (straighteners) at the Brand site in Arkansas. Morse (1997) reports 35 at the Sloan site, also a Dalton era site in Arkansas. Madonia (2000) reports an Arkansas find shown in Figure 104. All these references illustrate a technological continuity and widespread distribution.

Figure 104 – Shaft Straightener Drawing from Arkansas (Madonia 2000)

Sharpener or Saw Abrader

Modality (Industry): scraping.
Useability: specialized.
Ecoscene (Environments): all.
Functional Angle: N/A.
Bit Angle: N/A.
General Climate: postglacial.

The sharpener is a small-to-medium size cobble-boulder with grooves cut into its surface. These grooves are usually on the lateral margins.

This implement is confusing because of the failure to understand its function. It is seen as a shaft straightener, edge sharpener, and general abrading. Very few specimens have been recovered, and as such, class remains open for the present.

Sinewstone

Modality (Industry): storing.
Useability: unknown.
Ecoscene (Environments): piedmont.
Functional Angle: N/A.
Bit Angle: N/A.
General Climate: postglacial.

The sinewstone is used to work sinew into cords and/or store cords for future usage. It is a flat stone with long narrow grooves cut into the edges. Holmes (1897) was the first to report the implement in the MPRV, which he called an abraderstone.

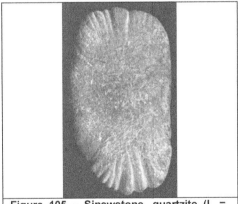

Figure 105 – Sinewstone, quartzite (L = 110, W = 57, T = 27 mm)

It was wrapped with sinew and placed in water; then, it was used (Figures 105, 106, and 107) for storage. Its function is suggested here and remains to be proven. Only one sinewstone was observed in the study collections, which was made from quartzite (Hranicky 1995). Another stone was observed in Pennsylvania by the author several years ago. The tool may be unique to the Middle Atlantic area. Figure 108 offers a comparative specimen. Note: this tool is still problematic in archeology. It is used here as suggested by Brennan (1975) and Fowler (1976), but the true function is suspect.

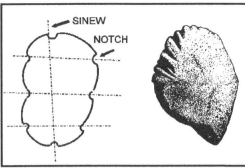

Figure 106 – Parts of a Sinewstone (Hranicky 2000) and Drawing Example (Fowler 1976)

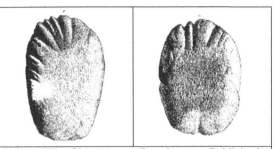

Figure 107 – Sinewstones Drawings as Published by Holmes. He called them abradingstones (Holmes (1897).

Figure 108 – Quartzite Sinewstone (L = 103, W = 56, T = 25 mm). It was found on the North River, Pembroke, Massachusetts.

Spatula and Spud

None were observed in the study collections. For the moment, they do not occur in the MPRV. See Hranicky (2002b) for definitions.

Splitter

Modality (Industry): separating.
Useability: specialized.
Ecoscene (Environments): all.
Functional Angle: 80° to 100°
Bit Angle: >15° & <30°
General Climate: postglacial.

It is a forest environment tool for splitting wood, namely bark for shingle centers for planking (Figure 109). It is a long, narrow tool with a V-shaped bit (Figure 110). It was hand held, and poll was usually struck with a hammerstone (Hranicky 2002b). The tool dates to the Woodland Period; however, this date is tentative. It resembles the celt but is much thinner, and body usually tapers toward the bit. Another possible function is the flesher. It is similar to the

Pueblo tool called *teamahia* that was first identified by Fewkes (1909). As shown, there are two types:

1 – Circularly-shaped
2 – Square/rectangularly-shaped.

Figure 109 – Oak Bark Being Sun Dried. Bark was stripped for use as shingles for shelters by using a splitter. Examples are from the Monacan village reconstruction at Natural Bridge, Virginia.

For a discussion of the splitter class, see Hranicky (2002b). Notably, it is difficult to discern from the celt class.

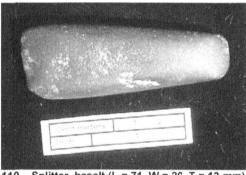

Figure 110 – Splitter, basalt (L = 71, W = 26, T = 13 mm). It was found in Shenandoah County, Virginia in a village context. The specimen has dual bits. The tool tapers toward the smaller bit. This specimen has dual bits; however, most polls are battered.

Two varieties exist that amplify its functions that are: dual bit (Figure 111) and the knob splitter (Figure 112).

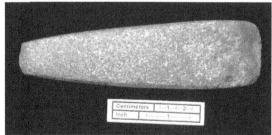

Figure 111– Bi-bitted Greenstone Splitter (L = 130, W = 32, T = 19 mm) from Washington County, Virginia

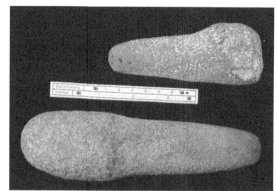

Figure 112 – Greenstone Splitters from Washington County, Virginia. Top: L= 114, W = 49, T = 34 mm; Bottom: L = 173, W = 49, T = 34 mm.

Figure 113 reports for the first time a Kentucky splitter (or pestle). It is a rectangularly-shaped splitter (workend) with a V-shaped bit. The bit function may have been in extracting stone for grinding (by the pestle) into powder.

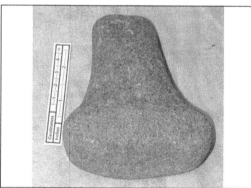

Figure 113 – Chisel-Pestle (Paris, Kentucky). It has a rectangular workend and a V-shaped pole (Dan Isgrig collection).

Split-Cobble Scraper

The split cobble scraper is an invention that occurs during the Woodland Period. These probably occur in the MPRV, but none were observed in the study collections. It is a product of bipolar reduction method in lithic reduction for tools.

Spokeshave
Modality (Industry): shaving.
Useability: specialized.
Ecoscene (Environments): all, piedmont(+).
Functional Angle: to be determined.
Bit Angle: N/A.
General Climate: postglacial.

The spokeshave dates to the Paleoindian Period and was used to shape wooden shafts. It is made on a biface or large flake. It is a C-shaped indentation that has an interior sharp edge. Many spokeshaves are combination tools that serve multipurpose. The distal part of the shave area was sometimes used as a graver. Numerous examples are shown in the Flakes as Tools section.

One major question archeologically is: Do spokeshaves have specific shaving characteristics? There is a tremendous variation in basic style and share design. Each tool appears to have been made for a specific shaft diameter. We assume that the main use was for arrows and spear shafts. The next page shows a spokeshave study that estimates the shaft size for each tool (Plate 22, after next page). Theses specimens are assigned to the Late Archaic Period.

Barber and Tolley (1999) present comparative quartzite spokeshaves from Southwest Virginia. They present no measurements, but shape or form is similar for the MPRV specimens. Their specimens are also made on flakes or bifaces, sometimes one or more spokeshave on the tool, and sometimes have another tool function, such as graver. Tool similarities and materials suggest the Late Archaic Period toolkit has a widespread distribution.

Sword

The use of a wooden sword with flint inserts comes from ethnographic data from Smith (in Tyler 1907). Harriot (1590) shows both men and women wearing a sword (Figure 114). It has a parallel in Garcilaso (1723) that is made of copper with flint inserts. Obviously, none were observed in the study collections. The Virginia/North Carolina Indians probably saw Spanish sailors with them and copied them.

Figure 114 – From Harriot (1590): ... *as for the rest the dyd carye fuche waeppens as the men did, and wear as good as the men for the warre (Harriot 1590). This quote shows the use of the weapons by both sexes.* The use of the sword is significant because it probably was adopted, not invented, from the Spanish who were in the Atlantic coastal waters nearly 50 years before the British. The sword is made of wood; an imitation of a European implement.

Ulu

Modality (Industry): cutting.
Useability: generalized.
Ecoscene (Environments): all, piedmont(+).
Functional Angle: to be determined.
Bit Angle: N/A.
General Climate: postglacial.

The ulu (also ulos) is attributed to and/or named by the Eskimos. It is a half-moon-shaped knife/chopper (Figures 115 and 116). It was reported as a semilunar knife by Abbott (1876); it was an ulu. Probably the first identification was by Mason (1892). It is also called the semi-lunar knife (Brennan 1975). Based on MPRV specimens, the Potomac River is not its southern boundary; additionally, it is found in Canada, New England, Southeast, and Great Lakes states (Hranicky 2002b).

Figure 115 – Historic Ulu Example (c. 1850-1860). It is made from slate with a wooden back (W = 89, H = 51, T 5 mm). It is from St Lawrence Island.

The ulu has three basic styles:

1 – Cone-backed
2 – Plain-backed
3 – Line-backed.

The cone across the top (back) slides into a groove that was cut into a wooden handle. Blades are sometimes grooved or perforated. The share is typically V-shaped. The primary material is ground slate, but chipped quartzite forms occur. It dates to the Laurentian tradition (4000-2500 BC) of the northeast, namely as a tool with the Vosburg pointmakers. Its origin is the Archaic Maritime which established it as a fish knife used probably by women.

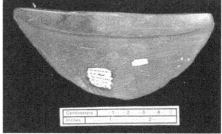

Figure 116 – Broken Ulu from Pennsylvania. It was expertly restored by Gary Fogelman (Indian Artifact Magazine)

Note: Restoration is primarily a museum function, but many collectors have broken artifacts restored to enhance their display.

The MPRV ulu has only been observed in quartzite (Figure 117). Specimens have been observed as wide as 150 mm. For an overview, see Turnbaugh (1977) and Rainey (2000).

Figure 117 – Ulu, quartzite (L = 119, W/H = 59, T = 19 mm)
Fairfax County Archaeological Survey, Virginia

Wedge
Modality (Industry): dividing.
Useability: specialized.
Ecoscene (Environments): uplands.
Functional Angle: Open, to be determined.
Bit Angle: Open, to be determined.
General Climate: glacial and postglacial.

The wedge or slotting tool is a square-shaped tool that was used for felling trees or splitting wood (Figure 118). It is found in the Paleoindian through Woodland toolkits. Another term for it is piece esquillee. It is a double inclined plane used to separate a soft material. The larger the ratio of length to thickness, the greater the mechanical advantage. The wedge averages 50 mm square and 10-15 mm thick. The basic concept of the wedge is present in most tool classes, namely splitter, celt, axe, etc.

Wedge, rhyolite (L = 50, W = 40, T = 11 mm)	Wedge, jasper (L = 52, W = 51, T = 13 mm)

Figure 118 – MPRV Wedges

Adair (1775) gives us an ethnographic account of the wedge, as:

To make planks they merely indented the section of a tree at one end and then split it with a maul and a hard wooden wedge.

Whetstone
Modality (Industry): polishing.
Useability: generalized.
Ecoscene (Environments): piedmont.
Functional Angle: N/A.
Bit Angle: N/A.
General Climate: postglacial.

The whetstone is a flat usually fine stone, such as limestone, which was used to abrade hardstone tool's bit. It is very poorly reported in the eastern archeological literature. Figure 119 shows an experimental whetstone that was used to create bits on newly-made axes and celts.

Figure 119 – Modern Example of a Whetstone.
The tool's functional angle is illustrated.

Plate 22 – MRPV Spokeshaves

These MPRV spokeshaves are a sample to demonstrate a method of estimating their usage on a target, presumably wood (Hranicky 2002b). There are two possible stages, debarking and shaping operations. There are at least five possible products, namely arrowshafts, spearshafts, dartshafts, insert shafts, and cylindrical tool handles. The geometry formula is (1/2 C) * (1/2 C) / (H) + (H), whereas:(C = cord and H = height). It is used to estimate the diameter of the target object (Hranicky 2002b). Naturally, a scraper could be used, but the spokeshave controlled the curve in scraping the wood and offered a better tool for shaping curved surfaces. As a note, MPRV spokeshaves are predominantly quartzite, but rhyolite specimens do occur. One quartz specimen was observed in the study collections.

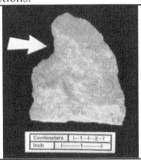	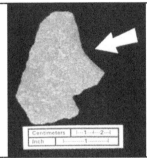	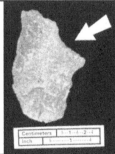
#1 – Spokeshave, quartzite, biface (L = 68.40, W = 54.83, T = 15.50 mm, wgt 60 g). Calculation: cord = 26.93, height = 7.24, shaft = 32.28 mm diameter. It is a heavy duty, hand-held implement. Spokeshave shows high polish.	#2 – Spokeshave, quartzite, flake (L = 58.60, W = 47.76, T = 11.04 mm, wgt 24 g). Calculation: cord = 25.93, height = 4.72, shaft = 40.33 mm diameter. It is a hand-held implement that was possibly used for de-barking a shaft.	#3 – Spokeshave, quartzite, flake (L = 64.84, W = 41.56, T = 12.18 mm, wgt 29 g). Calculation: cord = 26.03, height = 4.04, shaft = 45.97 mm diameter. It is a hand-held implement that was possibly used for de-barking a shaft.
	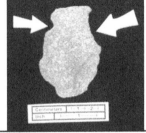	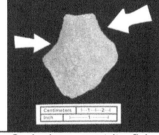
#4 – Spokeshave, quartzite, biface (L = 59.39, W = 40.24, T = 10.28 mm, wgt 26 g). Calculation: cord = 20.54, height = 6.00, shaft = 23.57 mm diameter. It is a hand-held implement that was used to shape a shaft, probably an arrow shaft.	#5 – Spokeshave, quartzite, flake (L = 58.51, W = 42.12, T = 9.13 mm, wgt 29 g). Calculation: (1) cord = 8.96, height = 3.45, shaft = 9.27 mm, cord = 25.06, height = 4.01, shaft = 43.16 mm diameter. It is a double spokeshave. It is a hand-held implement that was used to work two different size shafts.	#6 – Spokeshave, quartzite, flake (L = 52.45, W = 46.06, T = 9.75 mm, wgt 23 g). Calculation: (1) cord = 28.81, height = 3.88, shaft = 57.36 mm, (2) cord = 20.65, height 2.00, shaft = 55.20 mm diameter. It is a double spokeshave. It is a hand-held implement that was used to work two different size shafts. One shave could have been used for debarking.
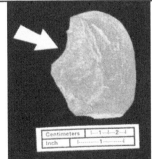		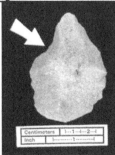
#6 – Spokeshave, quartzite, flake (L = 59.39, W = 40.24, T = 10.28 mm, wgt 26 g). Calculation: cord = 20.54, height = 6.00, shaft = 23.57 mm diameter. It is a hand-held implement that was used to shape a shaft, probably an arrow shaft.	#7 – Spokeshave, quartzite, biface (L = 59.39, W = 40.24, T = 10.28 mm, wgt 26 g). Calculation: cord = 20.54, height = 6.00, shaft = 23.57 mm diameter. It is a hand-held implement that was used to shape a shaft, probably an arrow shaft.	#8 – Spokeshave, quartzite, biface (L = 59.39, W = 40.24, T = 10.28 mm, wgt 26 g). Calculation: cord = 20.54, height = 6.00, shaft = 23.57 mm diameter. It is a hand-held implement that was used to shape a shaft, probably an arrow shaft.

Experimental Archaeology
(Experimenting with Native American Tools and Living Conditions)

Flintknappers, many of whom are archaeologists, have been experimenting with and replicating Native American stone tools for several decades in the MPRV and Middle Atlantic area. Work has yielded insights into Indian ways for making and using stone tools. While some MPRV ethnographic data do occur for tools, most of the functions for basic tools have been learned by replication (living archaeology) and laboratory analyses (wear patterns). Also, analysis of Native tools in archaeological contexts has provided a tremendous amount of information on tool useability. Actual field testing of tools has also added to this database. These combinations provide the basis for classification, class (work domains), industry/toolkit analyses, and typology. Experimental examples of tool chassis and stone implements are shown at the end of this section. Experimental knives and their hafting (chassis) were shown previously in the Bifaces as Knives section.

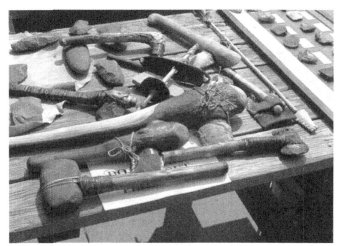

Experimental tools made by Scott Silsby and displayed at the 2000 Primitive Technology Weekend, Oregon Ridge, Maryland.

MPRV experimental archaeology began with the Middle Atlantic Knapp-In which was started in the early 1980s in Arlington, Virginia. The organizers were Errett Callahan, Jack Cresson, Michael Johnson, and Scott Silsby. Their flintknapping investigations and findings are used throughout this publication. In the early 1990s, the knapp-in was moved to Oregon Ridge Nature Center in Cockeysville, Maryland and is now organized by Kirk Drier of the Baltimore County Department of Recreation and Parks. The event is now called Primitive Technology Weekend, and flint-knappers come in from states as far away as Connecticut and Kentucky to practice, compare, study, and discuss toolmaking.

Experimental archaeology goes beyond stone toolmaking; it involves living the way the Native Americans did. It provides a tremendous insight into ancient ways.

Based on John White's drawings, an ancient camp fire is preserved. Ancient meal (corn, bean, and meat stew) is replicated by Daniel Abbott (Nanticoke descendant) at the 2001 Indian Day at the MacCallum More Museum, Chase City, Virginia.

While academic training provides the philosophical understanding of toolmaking and its usage, archaeologists who make and use stone tools have a better comprehension of the reality of tools in Nature's wild environment in which the Native Americans lived. Quite simply, if an archaeologist cannot make and use a Clovis point, why listen to him/her tell you how the Native Americans made the point. Of course, there is always an intellectual understanding of all archaeological topics.

Basic Experimental Approaches

As presented, hands-on analysis of stone tools (Native tools/implements) provides the experience with antiquity – touching prehistory. This is one way to see the past, another way is to make replication tools and implements the way Native Americans did. Then, use them like they did. All of which provides an explicative way to preform archaeology. This section contains numerous examples of hands-on archaeology via experimental archaeology.

Starting with **Prehistoric Axes, Celts, Bannerstones, and Other Large Tools in Virginia and Various States** (Hranicky 1995), the author has maintained that the elementary understanding of stone tools comes from being able to make and use them as the Native Americans did. This approach (and perhaps philosophy) is called experimental archaeology. It can be justified with statements, such as:

Without experimentation, it would have been impossible to develop an understanding of how the lithic assemblages examined in this analysis were generated (Pecora 1995).

The earliest published study of stone tools based on an experimental approach is Warren's (1914) **The Experimental Investigation of Flint Fracture and Its Application to Problems of Human Implements.** It at least starts the 20th century scientific inquiry to stone toolmaking. It is followed by Pond's (1930) **Primitive Methods of Working Stone, Based on Experiments of Halvor L. Skavlem.**

One who rarely receives credit as one of America's earliest experimental archaeologists is H. Holmes Ellis of the Ohio Historical Society's Lithic Laboratory. In 1957, he published **Flint-Working Techniques of the American Indians: An Experimental Study.** Based on strong use of ethnographic data, it is among the best studies ever made in those early (beginning) days of lithic technology. He addressed every form of flintknapping that is regularly published today. Or, as he concludes (1957):

For many years there have been some rather peculiar ideas in the minds of the general public, among others, as to the exact manner in which the common arrowhead was fashioned. It is the sincere hope of the Lithic Laboratory that this outline of the procedures followed has tended to throw some light on the problems connected with aboriginal flint working.

The purpose of experimental archaeology is to discover the nature of prehistoric tools by actually making and using them; it offers a true evaluation of the behavior of stone tools. According to Coles (1979):

One way in which archaeology can reach back and experience some parts of ancient life is through attempts to reproduce former conditions and circumstances. By trying to make and use some of the weapons and tools of the past we can often gain an insight into the importance of those objects to their original inventors and owners.

Or, experimentation according to Crabtree (1972):

There is nothing as potent as an experiment for verifying techniques. It allows the worker to record all the stages of manufacture, to study the characteristics of the debitage flakes, and to prove or disprove the theory. The analyst can best verify his theories by experiment. He need not become proficient at flintknapping but even a try will familiarize him with the mechanical and physical problems involved in the manufacture, and emphasize the importance of preparation and force. Different tool types with like characteristics are pertinent to individual assemblages so even experiment remains empirical until the worker has produced an exact replica of the aboriginal artifact. Experiment is the end result of hypothesis based on theory but not supported by fact even though, in this instance, the aboriginal approach may parallel or vary slightly.

Experimental archaeology for American lithic technology was initiated by Holmes Ellis in the 1950s and fathered by Don Crabtree in the early 1970s. Since then, it has become a major factor in identifying and understanding pre-Contact Native American tools. There are three basic categories, which are:

1 – Flintknapping (generalized term) – techniques needed to make micro- and macrotools

2 – Tool supplies and processes – materials for and mechanics of producing tools

3 – Tool usage – living and surviving with tools.

The major scientific value that is applied to archaeology is the workability and durability of various stones that the Native Americans used. Experimental archaeologists frequently know stone materials by region, easily recognize them in archaeological contexts, and assess the stone's capability in tool flintknapping and manufacturing.

While beneficial to archaeology, caution is needed, as Whittaker and Stafford (1998/2000) point out:

In addition to archeologists who make stone tools for experimental purposes, there is a growing number of flintknappers who make lithic artifacts for fun and for profit. The scale of non-academic knapping is little known to archeologists and is connected to a flourishing market for antiquities, fakes, replicas, and modern lithic art. Modern stone tools are being produced in vast numbers, and are inevitably muddling the prehistoric record. Modern knappers exploit some material sources heavily and their debitage creates new sites and contaminates old quarry areas. Modern knapping is, however, a potential source of archeological insights, and a bridge between the professional community and the interested public. Modern knapping also is creating a "twentieth-century stone age," and archeologists working with lithic artifacts need to be aware of the problems and potentials.

Tool experimentation in living exercises provides tool usage data that can be used as comparative data for tools recovered in archaeological contexts. Recently, Stieber (2000) reports Bruce Hackell's lithic experiments with a recently deceased elephant on which tests were made for spear penetration. He commented:

We wanted to better understand how effective thrusting spears would be as weapons for hunting.

Furthermore, experimental archaeology can provide data for defining and clarifying tool industries, classes, and types by providing concrete attributes and traits based on actual usage of replicated stone tools. Both the scientific and Native ways can be defined. The two are the same, but for reasons beyond this study, they are not necessarily compatible.

This study provided hands-on experience with using a spear to penetrate an animal hide. And, these data, as well as other research, provide insights for tool hafting and types of work tasks that the tool was used for by the Native Americans. Experimental tools provide:

1 – Tool durability data by chassis and material
2 – Task utilization data by tool class and industry
3 – Structure variation data for latitudes in tool function
4 – Skill assessments data by toolmaking techniques
5 – Useability methods
6 – Bit/blade wear pattern data for usage identification on Native tools.

Not all archaeologists agree on using experimental data; they prefer Native tool data. The advantages and disadvantages of experimental archaeology are:

Major disadvantages are:

1 – Artificial environment - method is not always used in actual living environments

2 – Experimenter effect - range or variation among experimenters

3 – Lack of control - difficulty in controlling natural elements, such as temperature, moisture, etc.

4 – Sample size - experiments produce small populations as opposed to real-world large populations

5 – Experimental logic - different ways and methods of producing and recording similar data

6 – Comparative data - lack of standards to regulate data acquisitions

7 – Reliability - experimenters are frequently not trained archaeologists

8 – Validity of experiments – professional individual to monitor actual experiments.

Major advantages are:

1 – Discovery - various knapping methods that produce the same tools or expected results

2 – Wear patterns - various tool usages are measured and analyzed

3 – Longevity – estimates of tool lifecycles

4 – Production economies – resource requirements and expenditures

5 – Lithic materials - understanding differences in stone workability

6 – Tool replication - morphology studies and analyses needed to reproduce tools

7 – Identification - curation elements and practices for specific tool classes and industries

8 – Creation of new methods - producing test data that are otherwise not available to archaeology.

Cultural Factors

One aspect of the experimental method for tool technology is a cultural perspective that few archaeologists make any attempt at identifying in archaeological contexts. It is the Native American way of making and using tools as opposed to Anglo (others) way of doing the same thing. Two factors are noticeably different: timing and spacing. While probably not observable contexts using today's methods, space utilization and movement (timing) is culturally determined. If for no other reasons, Native Americans should be consulted when practicing experimental archaeology. Of course, the basic argument to this is: both groups are too far removed from the prehistoric world in order to perform *like it once was*. The argument is: it is better if it is Native.

Figure 1 – Monacan Village Reconstruction at Natural Bridge, Virginia. Victoria DiProsperis is a site interpreter. The village project is ongoing and will show how they lived in the early 1700s. The Monacans once occupied most of central Virginia and were organized into a Confederacy that consisted of the Tutelo, Saponi, and Mannahoac tribes. The village was an excellent example of authentic living history. Display has been discontinued.

Figure 2 shows a dewelling reconstruction at the Bluemont Fair's Indian village in September 2016.

Chris White
Figure 2 – Dewelling by Chris White

Indian Village Life Replications

Another form of prehistoric studies is the practice by numerous Native American groups in replicating villages and performing Native ways of living in them. They often provide Native American interpreters with all material culture being made by that group. The ongoing village construction by the Monacans at Natural Bridge, Virginia is an excellent example (Figure 1). They are better able (qualified) to reconstruct a village, especially space utilization that is purely Indian. The Native American village was a polite mixture of nature and humanity. The Wolf Creek village replication was shown in the Prehistoric MPRV Chronology section.

> *The Power of Old Ways* written by Beth Py Lieberman (2001) reports Native American concern for their historic past. As archaeologists, we must be mindful of this in our dealing with prehistoric artifacts and authentic replications. This article reports a study by the National Museum of the American Indian (NMAI), formerly the George Heye Foundation, of Plains Indian painted shirts. Joseph D. Horse Capture commented, *we believe that many of the shirts still retain some of the power and the spirituality of the old ways.* There is a world of reasoning for working with them; there is still a tremendous amount of prehistory to be discovered.

Lithic Identification for Tools

For most flintknappers, the preferred stones are the ones that Native Americans used. However, stone workability is often a factor that involves modern knapper's skill and ability; thus, Native stones are not always used. All stones discussed here are described in the MPRV Environment section. Any stone not used by the Native Americans is not considered for authentic reproductions and replications.

Figure 3 – Monacan Village Reconstruction at Natural Bridge, Virginia. These quartzite boulders could be used in hearths, supports, or for tools.

An aspect of the village which has received little attention in archaeology other than a *bunch of rocks* is the supply of usable stone boulders, which were used for supports, hearths, and toolmaking (Figure 3). Some basic questions are: How many site reports contain an inventory of miscellaneous boulders found on a site floor? Were the boulders there when the Native Americans set up the village, or did they bring in specific stones for particular usage? Additionally, most microtools were made outside the village; however, some villages in archaeological contexts do contain numerous debitage and flakes. Tool resharpening was usually a village or camp site practice; thus, evidence should be present.

Figure 4 – Scott Silsby Demonstrating the Use of an Adz at the 2000 Primitive Technology Weekend at Oregon Ridge in Maryland. Note the use of safety glasses.

Learning Flintknapping

Both prehistoric and modern toolmakers learn flintknapping be actual practice based on two dimensions: process and performance. The dimensions are learned in stages, thus, the assumption here of knapping stages (Hranicky 2002a). Perhaps, they could be called units of knowledge and experience.

While one can start with no knowledge of stone reduction, most have someone show him/her the basics. The first dimension is learning the procedures and principles for reducing stone into tools. The second dimension involves the mechanical processes of performing the first dimension. The overall toolmaking procedures involves stone mechanics, rules for flaking, observing examples of flaking, flaking practice, and finally, developing a skill or experience with the process. There is no difference between the pre-Contact or contemporary Native Americans making stone tools or modern knappers (non-Native American) making tools. Style and technique usually varies among these toolmakers, but the overall, piles-and-piles of flakes coming off during tool production is the same worldwide. See Toolmaking Technology section for biface stages and Figure 4.

Safety Considerations

No one would be allowed to work in a chemistry or physics laboratory without wearing safety clothing and protective gear (Figure 3). However, the knapping laboratory seems to defy safety considerations. Perhaps it's the *abo* nature of the Native American way of life, but few flintknappers wear safety gear. The following procedures are highly recommended here:

1 – Safety glasses
2 – Gloves
3 – Protective covering for the lap and legs.

And, always mark knapping debris with a historic object so that future archaeologists will not confuse the site with a Native site. Leave historic objects in the debris to mark it as being non-Native American.

Figure 5 – Oregon Ridge 1999 Primitive Technology Weekend, Errett Callahan demonstrating flake removal. His book *The Basics of Biface Knapping in the Eastern Fluted Point Tradition* (1976) has become a standard reference in flintknapping.

Knapp-Ins

Knapp-ins are held all over the U.S. It is a meeting of flintknappers and other students of Native American prehistory. Most of the MPRV experimental material and data come from the Oregon Ridge Knapp-In that is held in Maryland (Figures 5 and 6). It has now been discontinued. Another flintknapping example is shown in Figure 7.

As an example of research based on knapp-ins and laboratory experiments, Tsirk and Parry (2000) argue that liquids on the surface of obsidian during fracture leave distinctive markings. Numerous research designs and testing have come out of knapp-ins. Figure 7 is an example of Tsirk's work.

Figure 6 – Oregon Ridge 1999 Primitive Technology Weekend, Jack Cresson flintknapping. His publications on *bipolar flintknapping* are well-quoted in the archaeological literature. After 20+ years, the Oregon Ridge Knapp-in has been discontinued.

Figure 7 – Example of Jack Cresson's Work in New Jersey Rhyolite (L = 93, W = 40, T = 7 mm). The D/P profile is perfectly flat and cross section is slightly lens shaped. It is an example of expert flaking. D/P ratio = .867 which low compared to below specimen; knife function.

A major purpose of knapp-ins as well as general lithic archaeology is to educate the general public and students about prehistoric tools (Figures 8a and 8b). As such, an educated public (prehistorically speaking) is more likely to support public archaeology, especially funding for continuing research and site preservations. Figure 8c shows a point with full-face fluting by Callahan.

Figure 8 – Examples of Flintknapping by Are Tsirk (2001 Primitive Technology Weekend at Oregon Ridge, Maryland).

Figure 8a – Errett Callahan lecturing on the use of copper knapping tools used by the Native Americans. This presentation was made at the 2000 Primitive Technology Weekend at Oregon Ridge in Maryland. He has lectured at numerous universities all over the U.S.

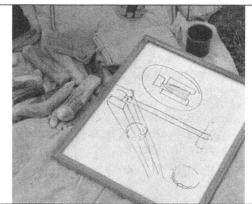

Figure 8b – Drawing board used for instruction.

Figure 8c – Early Callahan. Point was made in the 1960s and is made from Texas alibate flint.

Flintknapping

Flintknapping is a catch-all term for making stone tools, namely bifaces. It involves making stone implements in various ways and testing them against Native tools to determine Native American production and usage. We have limited U.S. ethnography for toolmaking and, as such, most of our understanding comes from tool replication and experimentation in actual living environments. Flintknapping is becoming a science specializing in the actual production methods used by pre-Contact American Indians.

Experimental archaeology is assumed here to be the pre-Contact Native American way; this means no metal tools and no precut slabs of stone. This form of flintknapping is what Callahan (2000) calls *traditional flintknapping*, or as he comments:

All in all, I would encourage students to undertake their basic training exclusively by traditional means. Stick to the old tools and techniques and practice strict replication. Learn how to copy the ancient originals accurately until you can do it with your eyes closed. Then and then only consider taking up where the elders left off and enter unexplored territory.

Thermal Alteration of Stone

Experiments on heat treating of knappable stone have been going on for over 35 years, as in Ellis (1957), Crabtree and Butler (1964), Luedtke (1992), Purdy and Brooks (1971), Moore (1999), or Katz (2000). The basic argument is heating stone improves its workability. The process usually causes a change its color. One answer to color change, besides heat treating, is forest fires. Stone is usually heated 500° to 900° for any time period from one to eight hours. The general premise is that the Native Americans heat-treated stones. Several possible heat-treated stones were found in the MPRV study collections. However, there was no evidence of it being used extensively, especially on rhyolite and quartzite. This aspect of lithic technology remains wide open for more study.

Theoretically, ΔH is the temperature at which lithic material changes its structure so that the crystal lattice is better subjected to fracture as:

$$\Delta H = M \times S \times \Delta T$$

whereas:
 ΔH = structural change at X temperature
 M = mass in grams
 S = specific heat of the lithic material
 ΔT = change over time (initial and final).
thus:

$$\text{Calories} = g \times (cal/g\,^\circ C) \times {}^\circ C$$

If the specific heat or atomic weight is known for a lithic material, their relationships can be determined by the Law of Dulong and Petit, as:

$$S_m \times \text{Atomic Weight} = 6.3 \text{ cal/mole } ^\circ C$$

<u>Note 1</u>: In conduction thermal alteration, all lithic material has a ΔH max, which can really be considered as lithic destruction, such as material either sublimates or evaporates.

Heat treatment probably causes stress planes in stone's outer area. Thus, this area fractures easily. For the moment, heat treated stone probably has only an outer layer of softness. The internal molecular lattice probably remains unchanged during the heat treatment, regardless of nonmetling temperatures (Hranicky 2002a).

<u>Note 2</u>: As a practical rule, stone plasticity increases with heat; what effects remain after cooling need more study, especially effect on brittleness.

Lithic materials which differ in their properties respond differently to heat treatment (see Pagoulatos 1992 for a study example).

Hampton (1999) describes a quarrying process that includes heating the boulder before striking it with a large hammerstone to remove large pieces. These pieces were reduced to smaller cores (spalls); next they are worked into biface blanks. Casual measurements were made of: L = 30.5 to 14, W = 10 to 5.0, T = 6.5 to 4.0 cm. These bifaces are transported away from the quarry to an area near the village. This probably avoids chippage in the village. In his study, toolmaking and usage are a male activity.

Stone Temperature and Workability

Quartzite and rhyolite are not workable in temperatures less than 40 degrees (Hranicky 2002a). Do we have seasonality in flintknapping for the Native Americans? This aspect of working stone has not been tested and published in archaeology.

Standard References

The following are standard references in experimental archaeology, replication, and authentic presentations of prehistoric tools.

1 – *Flint-Working Techniques of the American Indians: An Experimental Study* (1957) by H. Holmes Ellis (The Ohio Historical Society, Columbus, Ohio).

2 – *An Introduction to Flintworking* (1972) by Don E. Crabtree (Idaho State University Museum, Pocatello, Idaho).

3 – *The Basics of Flintknapping in the Eastern Fluted Point Tradition* (1996) by Errett Callahan (Pitdown Productions, Inc., Lynchburg, Virginia).

4 – *Flintknapping – Making and Understanding Stone Tools* (1994) by John C. Whittaker (University of Texas Press, Austin, Texas).

5 – *Lithics – Macroscopic Approaches to Analysis* (1998) by William Andrefsky, Jr. (Cambridge University Press, Cambridge, England).

6 – *Experimental Determination of Stone Tool Uses* (1980) by Lawrence H. Keeley (University of Chicago Press, Chicago, Illinois).

7 – *Stone Tool Analysis – Essays in Honor of Don E. Crabtree* (1985) edited by Mark G. Plew, James C. Woods, and Max G. Pavesic (University of New Mexico Press, Albuquerque, New Mexico).

8 – *Stone Tools – Theoretical Insights into Human Prehistory* (1996) edited by George H. Odell (Plunum Press, New York, New York).

9 – *Culture of Stone – Sacred and Profane Uses of Stone among the Dani* (1999) by O. W. Hampon (Texas A&M University Press, College Station, TX).

10 – *Lithic Debitage – Context and Form* (2001) edited by William Andrefshy (University of Utah Press, Salt Lake City, UT).

11 – *Lithics – Macroscopic Approaches to Analysis* (1998) by William Andrefsky (Cambridge University Press, England).

12 – *Experimental Archaeology* (1979) by John Coles (Academic Press, San Francisco, CA).

Coles (1979) was also among the early pioneers in experimental archaeology. His primary contribution is his experimentation in prehistoric arts and crafts.

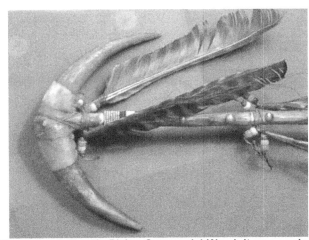

Figure 9 – Authentic Plains Ceremonial Wand. It was made in the late 19th century by Sioux Indians.

Ethnographic Sources

Major museums, especially smaller Native American museums, are excellent sources for examining and studying historic artifacts. While early historic artifacts may (and probably do) have European influences in tool design and usage, they still make excellent copy-items for replications. This source is especially useful for obtaining information on macrotool chassis designs. Figures 9 and 10 show historic examples that maintain traditional methods of making ceremonial objects. These items are often replicated by contemporary Native Americans for sale to the general public.

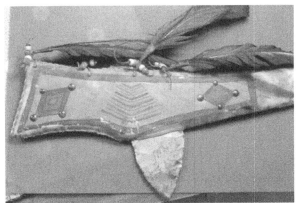

Figure 10 – Authentic Wooden War Club. It is also called a gunstock club. Plains Indians made this specimen in the late 19th century.

The Island of New Guinea has produced numerous ethnographic studies; among which, a recent study by O. W. (Bud) Hampton produced a tremendous amount of stone working and tool usage that provides a basic insight to American prehistoric stone tools. His publication (1999) **Culture in Stone** will become a classic reference. He measured actual specimens, namely axes and adzes. Recorded hafting methods, tool decorations for trading and sacred ceremonies, and tool usage in actual living settings. The people in his study, the Dani, only use four ground tools: axe, adz, gouge, and chisel. The biface is also present in their toolkit.

Another study that merits mentioning is Carneiro's (1979) work among the Yanomano Indians of Venezuela. It provides ethnographic methods in felling trees.

Modern ethnography via oral histories still provides insights to tools and weapons. For example, Sharpe (1970) lists hand-made weapons of the Cherokee:

- Shields (hickory or buffalo hide)
- Breastplates (buffalo hide)
- Helmet (three-inch strip of buffalo hide)
- Bowstring guard (buffalo hide)
- War club (sycamore with stone ball)
- Battle axe (stone axe commonly called tomahawk)
- Bow (sycamore or hickory, shaped, dipped in bear oil, and heat treated)
- Arrow (shaft of cane, heads of flint, feathers from eagle)
- Quiver (buffalo skin)
- Spear (wooden shafts sometimes tipped with flint)
- Knife (flint, in sheath fastened to a belt)
- Blowgun (small game, not for war)
- Dart (made of locust and feathered with thistle-down).

In some cases, deer skins were used in place of buffalo skins. Apparently, the buffalo disappeared near Contact times in Virginia.

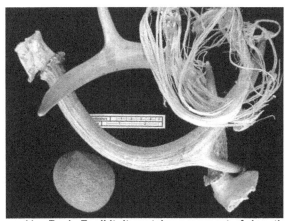

Figure 11 – Basic Toolkit. It contains a new set of deer tines, strands of deer sinew, and a small quartzite cobble; from something like this millions of years ago led to the modern age. It started by working silicon (stones with quartz crystals) and comes down to 21st century's computers that are based on silicon (quartz crystals, mostly early radio, but stones). In some ways, things never change.

While other members of the animal kingdom make and use simple tools, only mankind has mastered the process of toolmaking – from a simple rock to a simple transistor. Based on this history, what are the very basic items needed for survival anywhere? While this varies among archaeologists, the basics would certainly include: hardstone hammer, firemaking apparatus, sinew and cordage, an antler flaker, sharp-edged object, and perhaps glue (Figure 11). Development of tools from this basic toolkit lead to empires. See Toolmaking Technology section.

Toolmaking as a Technoculture

Toolmaking is the social practice, procedures, and methods of producing tools, namely hafted tools. Also, it is culture-bound based on learned behavior and shared traditions. This form of technology can be called a technoculture providing the technology can be separated from other forms in the same industry, such as the Savannah River technology as compared to the Koens-Crispin technology; both are technocultures.

Modern flintknappers can learn the cultural ways of pre-Contact Indians and replicate modern tools based on these traditions or technocultures. It requires years of study of the American Indian. For example, the most famous technoculture is Clovis. Only a few modern knappers can replicate these points.

It is this argument that presents the case for anthropological and archaeological advanced degrees. It does not totally exclude personal efforts to become a master.

Hafting

The hafting process creates the chassis mounting for the tool, of which the basic elements are the stone tool and wooden/bone handle. The handle or shaft secures the tool for the performance of work. In experimental archaeology, various stone tools are hafted to experimental handles and then used to perform work that the Native Americans did with their tools. As there are few preserved eastern ethnographic tool examples, we assume that chassis mounts varied throughout prehistory.

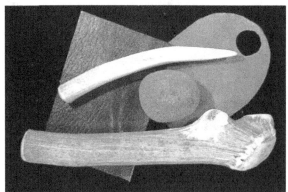

Figure 12 – Knapper's Basic Toolkit: Pads, Pointed Antler, Round Abrader, and Deer Billet

Flintknapper's Toolkit

Flintknapping in experimental archaeology follows the Native American ways in making tools and using them in constructing shelters, toolmaking, pottery manufacture, and food processing; all of which involve numerous stone tool classes. Replicating tools that are associated with flintknapping are shown in Figures 12 through 18. The following is a summary of tools needed for flintknapping.

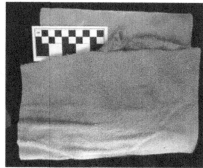

Figure 13 – Knee Pad. Most knappers use a piece of deer hide to place on the knee while knapping. It is called a deer sheet.

The billet (antler or wood) is a soft hammer method used for striking tool preforms to remove flakes in the process of making stone tools; a club-like rod that is made of anything but stone. Callahan (1979) recommends the following billets for experimental knapping:

1 – <u>Heavy Billet</u> - usually an elk antler weighing approximately 650 grams. It is used on all lithic materials and for secondary thinning.

2 – <u>Medium Heavy Billet</u> - usually a moose antler weighing approximately 400 grams. It is used on all lithic materials except coarse quartzite, coarse rhyolite, felsite, and common basalt.

3 – <u>Heavy Wooden Billet</u> - usually made from boxwood-like wood and weighs approximately 480 grams. It is used on obsidian, basalt, and some quartzites; it is used for secondary thinning.

4 – <u>Medium Billet</u> - usually a white-tailed deer antler and weighs approximately 260 grams. It is used on all materials except coarse quartzite, coarse rhyolite, felsite, and common basalt.

5 – <u>Medium Light Billet</u> - usually a white-tailed deer antler weighing approximately 180 grams. It is used on all materials except coarse quartzite, coarse rhyolite, felsite, and common basalt.

6 – <u>Light Billet</u> - usually a white-tailed deer antler weighing approximately 80 grams. It is used on all materials except coarse quartzite, coarse rhyolite, felsite, and common basalt.

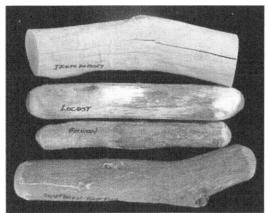

Figure 14 – Wooden Billets (top down) Ironwood, Locust, Boxwood, and Southern Red Oak

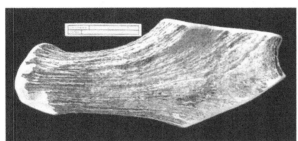

Figure 15 – Moose Billet. It is used for coarse materials such as rhyolite and quartzite. Since it is not usually preserved archaeologically, there is no way to assume that the Native Americans used it; however, by inference, we assume they did.

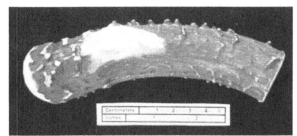

Figure 16 – Mule Deer Billet. It is a medium flaker and works well.

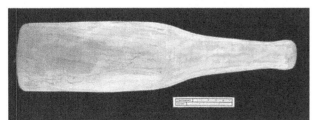

Figure 17 – Wooden Mallet. This mallet is made of sycamore and works well on quartzite when initializing a preform. It also can be used as a quarry tool.

A few newcomers in lithic technology believe that they discovered wooden billet flaking. It has been reported ethnographically for over a hundred years (for example, Roth 1904 and 1921), and according to Leakey (1935) flaking:

... that a suitably shaped piece of stone will serve the purpose equally well. The essential thing ... is that if this so-called "wood technique" is to be produced the blows must be struck with some object that imparts the force of the blow in quite a different way from an ordinary hammer stone... What I want to stress here is that the value of a wooden bar lies not in the stone itself, but in the shape of the wooden bar. A piece of stone shaped like a wooden bar, or even a limb bone of an animal will serve equally well.

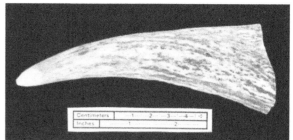

Figure 18 – Elk Punch. It is used to drive off blades, narrow flakes, and flutes.

Some knappers argue that the wooden mallet (large billet) works quartzite and rhyolite better than classic antler billets. The argument is valid and may apply to stone work by the Fox Creek pointmakers. The basic idea is that the larger, but softer, wooden striker transfers energy more slowly into the stone which produces better controlled flaking. The mallet has also been argued as a quarrying tool. The method has not been tested other than at knapp-ins, or by the author, and remains open for acceptance. For billets, we simply need more published data.

Basic Microtool Making Process

The following are basic operations in the toolmaking process and tool usage. These operations vary depending on the intended function and structure of the manufactured tool. These operations are based on Crabtree (1972), Whittaker (1994), Callahan (1996), Andrefsky (1998), and Hranicky (2002a).

Operation I - Obtaining raw materials: raw material is either a single piece of flint, a small nodule, a spall from a nodule, or a prepared core.

Operation II - Edging: removing the round, square, or thin edges by flaking with a hammerstone or billet.

Operation III - Primary thinning: the edge is thinned and prominent humps and ridges are removed.

Operation IV - Secondary thinning: edge is ground with an abrader, or a striking platform is prepared below the center line of the preform, whichever is necessary for the removal of thinning flakes.

Operation V - Shaping: edge is further straightened by light blows with a small antler or pressure flaking.

Operation VI - Finishing: preform is finished by notching, fluting, basal grinding, and minor retouching.

Operation VII - Reworking: when a tool gets dull or broken, billet flaking can be used to redo the defective tool into a new one.

These operations are expanded from stages listed in the Toolmaking Technology section. These stages are used to produce data collecting methods on toolmaking processes. This outline is expanded in the Toolmaking Technology section.

Notching and Grinding

Two finishing processes were often added to microtools, namely:

1 – Notching
2 – Grinding.

Notching is a procedure of flaking small indentations into the stem area of a projectile point and other small bifaces. Notching allowed better securing of the point to the shaft. Examples of notching were illustrated in the Toolmaking Technology section.

A small pointed flaker (deer antler, beaver tusk, or K-9 tooth) is used to pressure flake a small narrow or wide channel into the stem side, corner, or basal area. Each flake is taken off on reverse sides. The finished notch is usually ground.

Grinding is a procedure of using an abraderstone to smooth the stem area of a projectile point. By smoothing the stone, it was less likely to cut into the sinew wrapping. The stem sides are ground, and the base was frequently ground. Grinding is usually classified rather subjectively as light, medium, or heavy. Grinding is called polishing as a surface treatment on macrotools.

As a research design, the hafting process can be measured to produce a hafting index. For example, the notch depth or length divided into the base (stem) width of a projectile point produces a coefficient that can be used for comparison to other points. When these point indexes are made for the type, the coefficient becomes an attribute of the type. Grinding also provides the same index; measure the lateral grinding height into the base (stem) width which produces the index. For nonground and nonnotched points, lateral stem height and base width are used. This coefficient is directly related to function and tool efficiency (Hranicky 2002a).

Fluting

Basically, fluting is the process of removing long thinning basal flakes from a biface. The technologies vary, but major techniques are pressure flaking and percussion. See Waldorf (1984 and 1987).

Feathering

In prehistory, the dart, arrow, and light spear were probably feathered. The method offered accuracy and increased distance. The following are suggested (Hranicky 2002a):

Arrow Feathering - based on ethnographic drawings and descriptions, the arrow had three feathers, was approximately 50 to 75 mm in length, and the most common feather was turkey or eagle.

Arrow (Feather Positions) - for a three-feather arrow, no feather is placed on the bow side as this tends to strip the feather off during launching. The three feather positions are:

1 – Cock feather (top feather)
2 – Leveler (horizontal or middle feather)
3 – Rudder (bottom feather).

The feather is attached with small amounts of glue and securing the feather ends with sinew. The feather is weather proof, and there is no evidence that anything else was used. We do not know how far back in time feathering goes.

While turkey feathers are the most common in ethnographic descriptions, we can assume that other feathers were used. The goose feather has more oil in it and makes a more durable shaft feather (Figure 19).

<u>Note</u>: Do not sell arrows or tools made with parts from migratory birds and game. It is a violation of federal laws.

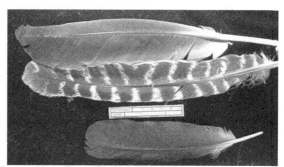

Figure 19 – Top: Goose, Middle: Turkey, Lower: Blackbird Feathers. Also, Eagle feathers (not shown) were popular.

Tool Useability and Efficiency

Two ideal tool analyses that can be accomplished by experimental archaeology are tool useability and efficiency. Hranicky (2002b) provides an overview for both factors, and they are discussed in this text. Standards and procedures need to be developed in order to produce valid scientific data. These experiments were beyond the scope of this study.

Tool Wear Pattern Analyses

Laboratory analysis of experimental tools provides data that can be used in analyses of Native tools. Basic techniques are defined in Keeley (1980), Plew, et al. (1985), Andrefsky (1998 and 2001), and Odell (1996).

This publication does not present methodologies for these analyses. However, as a suggestion these guidelines should be used:

Processes:
1 – Records. Record manufacturing techniques and material.

2 – Usage. Perform tests by using tools on different target materials. Examples are:

- Whittling wood
- Sawing wood
- Chopping wood
- Drilling wood
- Scraping wood
- Adzing wood
- Splitting wood
- Graving wood.

These examples are based on wood, but other materials should be tested, such as butchering, hide processing, and any other material found in Native American living environments.

3 – Time. Record length of time tool was used on the target. Also, amount of pressure, functional angles, and other factors are used. Table 1 presents a recording example:

Table 1 – Wear Patterns					
No.	Tool	Material	Target	Action	Time/Temp
#51	Flake	Flint	Wood	Scarping	10min/80°
#83	Axe	Granite	Wood	Chopping	15min/85°

Observation:
1 – Cleaning. If tool edges are analyzed optically, the workends should be cleaned. Grease, fat, and mineral deposits obscure visual inspections. To remove them, soak the specimen in warm solution of HCl (15% solution) and follow it with a NaOH solution (25% solution). The HCl removes lithic/mineral deposits and cleans striations. The NaOH removes organic remains.

2 – Record measurements. Measure physical properties, weigh tool, and photograph workends before and after testing.

3 – Make optical observations preferably with a digital camera.

Results:
Publish results and ensure data can be replicated by other archaeologists.

Nonlithic Experimentation

While lithic technology experimentation is the most popular, nonlithic (organic) experimentation also produces data that can be used for site context materials and their interpretation (Figure 20). Figures 21 and 22 show examples of Virginia Native American hide processing. Animal hides provided basic clothing, but culture determined clothing styles and decorations

The Native Americans are an excellent source for providing information on Native ways of life. When this information is coupled with experimental archaeology and field/site collected data, the opportunity of high quality and accurate interpretations about the Native Americans' history becomes a practical reality.

Figure 20 – Native American Basketry (Display at the 2000 Virginia State Fair, Richmond, Virginia). Various native plants and trees are used for basketry and dyes.

Animal skins composed most of the MPRV Native Americans' clothing, namely deer, bear, rabbit, and fox garments (Figure 24). Color dyes were applied and well as shell beads were attached. There does not appear to be a sexual distinction between clothing, but this remains to be proven.

Adair (1775) comments on the Chickasaw that provides a model for MPRV dress:

They formerly wore shirts, made of drest deer-skins, for their summer visiting dress; but their winter-hunting clothes were long and shaggy, made of the skins of panthers, bucks, bears, beavers, and otters; the fleshy sides outward, sometimes doubled, always softened like velvet-cloth, though they retained their fur and hair.

Figure 21 – Bear Hide Processing (Display at the 2000 Virginia State Fair, Richmond, Virginia)

For the eastern Siouan, Lawson (1860) comments:

The Indian men have a match coat of hair, furs, feathers, or cloth, as the women have...Their feather match coats are very pretty, especially some of them, which are made extraordinary charming, containing several pretty figures wrought in feathers, making them seem like a fine flower silk shag; and when new and fresh, they become a bed very well, instead of a quit. Some of another sort are made of hair, raccoon, beaver, or squirrel skins, which are very warm. Others again are made of the green part of the skin of a mallard's head, which they sew perfectly well tigeather, their thread being either the sinews of a deer divided very small, or silk grass.

Figure 22 – Deer Hide Processing (Display at the 2000 Virginia State Fair, Richmond, Virginia)

Cordage

Cordage is probably the oldest nonlithic industry for mankind. There is not a lot of archaeological evidence, but the assumption is well-noted based on opinion. One of the main sources for cordage in the MPRV is dogbane (Milkweed). The bark is removed by first cracking a branch with a small hammerstone and then breaking it open long ways. The interior woody substance is removed without breaking the fibers (hemp). Next, the bark is removed from the fibers.

Once the fibers are removed, they are woven into long cords. They can vary in thickness depending on the cordage need. The Dogbane fiber is strong; for example, a bow string (cord) of 40 pounds. Also, it is durable and is resistant to rotting. Figure 23 shows the cordage process. This cordage can be woven into small purses, even shirts and trousers.

Figure 23 – Cord Making Process. Top: splitting dogbane bark, middle: weaving it into cordage, bottom: roll of cordage. Cordage maker is Daniel Abbott (Archaeology Day October 6, 2001, MacCallum More Museum and Gardens, Chase City, Virginia).

Textiles

Textiles are not common in the archaeological record of the East. Most examples come from ethnographic sources (Figure 24). Most data come from the American Southwest. Miner (1936) was among the first to argue their significance in archaeology. Jakes and Ericksen (2001) and Peterson (1996) offer overviews on production of textiles, including plant dye usage. While somewhat dated, Bliss' (1981) ***A Handbook of Dyes from Natural Materials*** is an excellent basic reference for sourcing and identification of dyes. Experimentally, this industry is wide open in archaeology.

Figure 24 – Winter Dress (based on Harriot 1590). Clothing be Contact time probably already has culture contact, namely the Spanish sailing the waters of the Middle Atlantic area. Adair (1775) comments on made and female Chickasaws:... *wrap a piece of cloth round them, that has a near resemblance to the old Roman toga or praetexta.*

The eastern basket is made with strips of wood, such as pine. These strips are about 3-4 mm thick and 16-20 mm wide. Color was usually added. As suggested here, shellac was used to seal the wood. It was probably with pine resin that was mixed with a vegetable oil. Figure 25 shows experimental basketmaking, and Figure 26 shows experimental baskets. Table 2 presents a summary of basket materials and color dyes.

Figure 25 – Experimental Basketmaking at the 2001 Primitive Technology Weekend at Oregon Ridge, Maryland. Basket maker is Michael Sottosanti – and he makes excellent bows.

Table 2 – Basketry Materials and Dye Sources	
Material	Dye Source
Honeysuckle vines	Blood root
White oak splints	Yellow root
Pine splints	Oak, walnut, birch, dogwood, hickory and maple bark
Rivercane	
Bark	
Wild hemp	
	Poison ivy root
	Poppy root
	Sassafras root
	Butterfly root
	Charcoal
	Hemitite
	Sumac
	Bedstraw

Figure 26 – New Baskets by Michael Sottosanti. They were made at the 2001 Primitive Technology Weekend at Oregon Ridge, Maryland.

The stick basket is probably the oldest container known to mankind (Figure 27). The skin container also has a considerable antiquity. The stick basket is made by weaving green sticks or small branches (51 mm in diameter). While not waterproof like skins, it can be used to carry fruits, berries, nuts, etc. from field collections by the Native Americans.

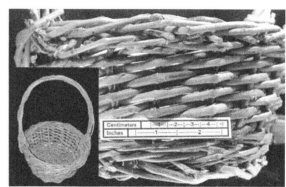

Figure 27 – Modern Example of a Stick Basket. Any type of branches from small bushes can be used to weave it. It was made by local Native Americans.

The stick container is made without any fasteners or straps. Each stick is wrapped around a support post in the basket wall. The stick is alternated between posts which are spaced 20-25 mm apart. The earlier forms probably had pointed bases which is also found in early pottery vessels. This process is similar to birds making a nest; it became refined over time. The handle is made from sticks that are twisted together. They probably had a color appliqué. The durability of the container is excellent, but depends on the amount of weight carried in it. Archaeologically, it is not preserved in the ground more than a few years; thus, we never see it in archaeological contexts.

Body adornment is considered a cultural universal. It includes hair length, clothing, bracelets, necklaces, shoes, gloves, ear/noserings, tattooing, etc. Native Americans wore jewelry/ornaments in their hair, around necks and ears, wrists, and ankles. They used feathers, shells, bones, teeth, stone, and other small objects. One interesting experimental archaeology focus deals with drilling beads; naturally, other adornment items are replicated. Figure 28 shows bracelet and necklace examples.

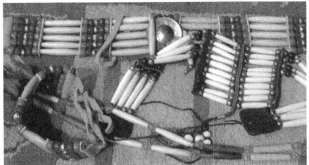

Figure 28 – Example of Bracelets and Necklaces Made by Jim Roane (2001 Primitive Technology Weekend at Oregon Ridge, Maryland)

Bone Handle Tools

A bone handle knife was shown previously in the Bifaces as Knives section and bone examples were shown in the Miscellaneous Tools/Implements section. We can assume that the Native Americans used bone for tool handles, but due to poor preservation, we may never know how extensive it was. The marrow in bones was eaten, which is a factor in broken bone abundance in site contexts. The following is an experiment creating a bone-handled adz (Figure 29). It had durability, but transferred very little energy into the target area of wood.

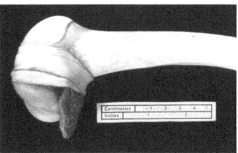

Figure 29 – Adz (Reproduction). Deer Femur (Bone) with a rhyolite biface. Blade is glued with pine tar and leather wrapped.

As a contrast, a small adz was mounted in a pine board (Figure 30). It is not as efficient as a large adz, but it works as well as the shown bone adz.

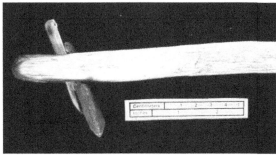

Figure 30 – Adz (Reproduction). Blade is set in a pine board with wedges to support it. Hole was made by burning the blade slot.

Animal Processing

Experimental archaeology provides insights into animal killing, butchering, and processing animal parts for tools (Figure 31). Since deer was the most common meat in the MPRV, this aspect is often found among abo practicing primitive lifeways. Another use for butchering data is in Early Man(woman) studies, especially Mammoth-associated sites with no bifaces. This type of testing can discern between animal knawing versus bone scraping by humans.

Deer provided the Native Americans with meat (consumption), hides (clothing and strapping), antlers (tools and points), bones (marrow consumption and tools), sinew (wrapping), and hooves (glue). As with today, they are quite plentiful during the MPRV Woodland Period.

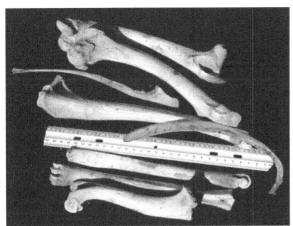

Figure 31 – Deer Bones that are Ready for Processing. A number of bone tools can be made from the long bones, scapula, or ribs. Deer bones are common in Woodland Period contexts and actual bones can be used to train students of archaeology.

A Clovis Case Study

Michael F. Johnson and Wm Jack Hranicky teamed to produce a classic Clovis. Johnson used Knife River flint and produced a high quality point (Figures 32 and 33). Hranicky patinated the point and added use wear (Figures 34 and 35).

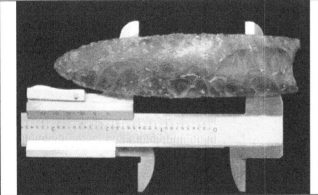

Figure 32 – Newly-Made Clovis Paleoindian Projectile Point. It was made from Knife River Flint (Dakotas) by Michael F. Johnson. This point was never hafted.

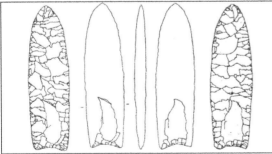

Figure 33 – Drawings of the Johnson Point Shown Above. Detailed flake scars can be compared with Native points to determine workmanship and methods.

The point was made by replicating eastern Clovis fluting traditions. Flaking style, general outline, and size would be identified by Clovis pointmakers as one of theirs. Patination copied nature's surface alteration by exposure to the natural elements.

Figure 34 – Patination Process for Aging the Clovis Point. The solution created by Wm Jack Hranicky is quite caustic. It creates 10,000 years of patination in about 10 minutes.

The point passed several relic shows as an authentic Clovis point. It was never represented as a Native point. The study proved that Native American points and tools can be made which can be represented as *real* points. The relic world has more fake Clovis points than the Native Americans ever could have made. The study also provided point test data (based on several new flint points) that offer an answer to the wear pattern question – how long did the Native American have to use a tool before striations would appear on the blade edge? Additionally, can these striations be identified as to what caused them? Yes, and this study offers an estimate on tool usage by material. See Wear Patterns in the Toolmaking Technology section. These materials will also leave microscopic residues on blade edges. As such, excavated artifacts with sharp work edges should not be washed.

Figure 35 – Adding Edge Wear to the Clovis Point. Several one-inch pine boards were used.

Another factor of Native points is oxidation under the hinges. If no oxidation is present, the point is usually a fake. Thus, fakers always oxidize their points. This step is easy. Place the point in a water solution containing several rusty nails (Figure 36).

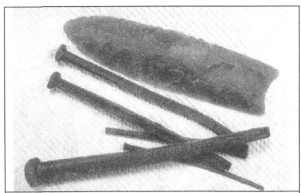

Figure 36 – Clovis Point in Oxidizing Solution. Point is placed in a solution with rusty nails for a week. This process leaves oxidization under hinges.

The final factor that is often overlooked by a faker is impact fractures. Whether the point was used as a knife or spear, the point's tip frequently shows microscopic impact fractures. Thus, to fake a point, these impact flake scars can be added with a small hammer (Figure 37).

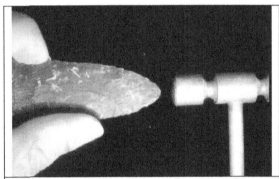

Figure 37 – Creating Impact Fractures. Impact fractures show usage.

This study shows one of numerous studies being performed by archaeologists, flintknappers, and other interested scientists who believe that we can gain a tremendous insight to prehistoric stone tools by replicating them and using them in actual living archaeology settings. At the same time, it shows how replication can be used to create fake points.

Unfortunately, this information aids fakers and, as the above example illustrates, fake points are difficult to identify. However, the basic key to authentication is patination. As an ethical practice, all replications must be marked in such a way that they cannot be presented as Native points or tools. The best way to mark Clovis points is a name and date in the flute channel.

Patination Replication

The purpose of this example is not to teach how to fake patination surfaces on newly-made tools, but to illustrate that it can be done. While 99.99% of all points that come from private collections are the *genuine article*, this source is not always reliable because many collectors buy points and various tools and implements. This non-finder source presents a problem for both archaeological analysis and museum acquisitions (Hranicky 1996). High-value artifacts, such as Clovis points, Adena-Hopewell mound artifacts, large axes and celts, and more, are frequently replicated and sold to the collector. Most collectors do not have the skill to identify the fakes; therefore, their collection is tainted with a few bad artifacts.

There are several patination analysis tools/methods that are available and/or currently being developed which can be used to detect fake points (Hranicky 2002a). One new method is to determine the ionization of the surface salts on a point and compare it to known patinated surfaces of authentic points. Other methods include patination measuring depths that are compared to known point environments and examining layering (or striations) within patination (Hranicky 2002a). Even with scientific detection methods, fake points get into the archaeological database.

The Blowgun

There has been little attention in the American literature on the prehistoric usage on the blowgun. The eastern variety is made from cane that varied in length from 2 to 4 meters. The effective range was close, 15 to 20 meters. However, longer blowguns have ranges of 50+ meters. It was used almost exclusively on small game, such as squirrels and birds (Speck 1909). Its method of manufacture is found in Speck (1938); his description is for the Catawba blowgun.

The tool is Panindian for the whole U.S. and has neither a date for its beginning nor geographical source. However, it is found worldwide. Figure 38 shows an ethnographic example of a blowgun.

Figure 38 – Ethnographic Example of a Blowgun from Brazil. Blowgun is made of split halves of wood that were carved to make the channel for the dart. They were joined back together with glue. It was then wrapped with wood bark. The mouthpiece is an hour glass-shaped wooden piece and attached with pitch. The darts are made of palmwood. The hand-woven bag holds fiber for the dart. Example and demonstration provided by Charlie Martin (2001 Primitive Technology Weekend at Oregon Ridge, Maryland).

Living Archaeology

Tool usage, namely tool useability, is the study of tool work or replicating tools and using them in actual living environments. It is sometimes called living archaeology. Structural analyses are performed to determine tool durability and performance for specific tasks, such as felling trees, hide processing, butchering, etc. The bow/arrow and atlatl/spear are common test tools (Figure 39).

Making tools to study Indian methodology is an important aspect of experimental archaeology, but unless experimental tools work in living test environments, the study has little merit in modern archaeology. Figures 40 through 46 show actual tool usage. Figure 43 shows an example of handle wrapping with a leather strip. It was used it the next two photographs.

Usage has two effects on tools:

1 – Depletion of the blade (workend)
2 – Stress or breakdown of the chassis system (hafting).

Figure 39 – Michael F. Johnson (Fairfax County Archaeologist) demonstrating the atlatl and spear throwing at the 1986 ASV Fieldschool in Fairfax County, Virginia.

While chassis deterioration is not readily observable microscopically on a tool, workend reduction and wear is. This type of study allows interpretation as to how the tool was used and its efficiency as a tool. Comparative data come directly from experimental archaeology. See Toolmaking Technology section.

Figure 40 – Adz Usage (Replication Tool). Scott Silsby using an adz that he made on the end of an oak limb.

Figure 41 – Adz Usage (Replication Tool). Close-up view of using the adz. The tool's functional angle is illustrated.

Figure 42 – Axe Usage (Replication Tool). Close up view of an axe striking a piece of oak timber. The tool's functional use is illustrated.

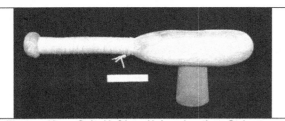

Figure 43 – Celt Hafting Using Leather Strip to Wrap the Handle. Celt was made of greenstone and has a pine chassis. Celt was made by pecking a river cobble and then polishing it. Bit was shaped by using a whetstone and forms a 45° angle.

Figure 44 – Celt Usage (Replication Tool). Jack Hranicky using a celt. The tool's functional angle is illustrated.

Figure 45 – Celt Usage. Close up view of using a celt to fell a tree. The celt has a celt/slot form, which keeps the celt secure with each strike that drives the celt into the wood.

Figure 46 – Using a similar axe as above. Daniel Abbott (Nanticoke descendant) chops a piece of hickory. He notes that when the bit strikes the wood, pull the axe towards you the increase the cutting action.

Replication versus Reproduction

A major focus of experimental archaeology is its presentation of results based on testing of replicated tools. These tools are frequently used in living archaeological demonstrations and artifact displays. Basically, there are two types of newly-made tools and implements:

1 – Replication - making a tool or implement the way that the Native Americans did. A replication toolmaker never uses metal knapping tools. A replication is an exact copy of a Native tool that is made using Native American methodologies. As a formal definition of **replication**:

...producing a tool type that can be observed in several cultural settings.

For comparative analysis, types are replicated in similar situations found elsewhere. Replication is a test of other scholar's works. And, it is a form of experimental tool parameters based on prehistoric Native American methodologies.

Note: Native American methods (and ways) varied and/or most of their techniques are known; but still, there may not be an *all true* replication.

2 – Reproduction - artificially copying of Native American tools using modern tools to make them. As a formal definition of **reproduction:**

...the process of making a tool or implement by any means available to produce a copy of an Indian tool or implement.

Methods may use metal tools, especially for initial size of lithic materials and producing bulk materials for the reproduction. Reproduction tools are often cast of authentic Native tools.

As mentioned, one major problem with replications is that these tools often get into the public realm as authentic Native artifacts. Again, each replication must be marked as a modern tool (Figure 47).

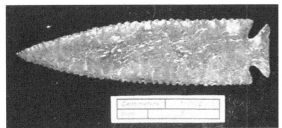

Figure 47 – Good, Bad, but not Ugly. Is this a real Native point from Maryland? It is made from flint, a field find, and extremely thin.

As an example of replication, the prehistoric canoe was cited here as being a major part of the MPRV Native Americans' communication system. The basic styles are known ethnographically and several Native American groups still make the classic wooden canoe today. Figures 48 to 51 show the recovery of a prehistoric canoe in North Carolina. It provides evidence of style (shape) and method of manufacture. It shows John White's drawing (1590 engraving) of canoe making. Finally, it shows the modern replication by Cherokee Native Americans. The problem of its replication is not style, but method of manufacture. While the modern example is truly Native American, it fails as an authentic replication because it was made with steel tools. While this may be a small point to argue, replication must incorporate history and people; why bother if the replication is not a true historical presentation.

Tool Replications

On the following pages (Plates 23 and 24), macrotool examples are shown. There are numerous chassis mounts in prehistory for large stone tools, and these examples represent possible ways the Native Americans hafted their celts, axes, and adzes.

Flintknapping is a common form of replication. Most knappers spend years studying and practicing making stone tools. Figure 48 shows xx at the 2016 Bluemont Fair in Virginia.

Figure 48 – Jason Drevenak from the North American Bushcraft School (Hedgesville, WV) Flintknapping at the Bluemont Fair's Indian Village in September 2016.

Chassis Mounting

Chassis mounting is the process of hafting a newly-made tool to a shaft or handle (Hranicky 2002a). The following pages illustrate tool hafting based on experimental techniques.

Figure 48 – Archaeological recovery of a dugout canoe. Canoe being loaded onto a Corps of Engineers truck which transported it to the Underwater Branch at Ft Fisher, North Carolina.

Figure 49 – Ethnographic drawing of dugout canoe making. Engraving based on John White's watercolors of North Carolina Native Americans.

Figure 50 – Burning a Log to Make a Canoe by Virginia Native Americans (2000 Virginia State Fair, Richmond, Virginia)

Figure 51 – Canoe Making Simulation at Historic St Mary's City, Maryland. At Contact (1634), the residents of the area were the Yaocomaco.

Bone Knives

Large bone knives could have been made from large game, such as buffalo's ribs. Figure 52 shows two modern knives made from cow ribs.

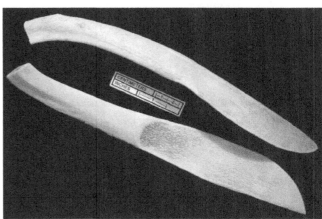

Figure 51 – Newly-Made Bones Knives

Plate 23 - Examples of Experimental Stone Tools and Hafting

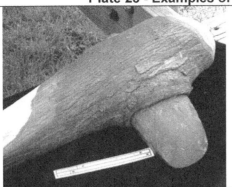

#1 – Description: Axe has a bitternut hickory handle with a greenstone blade. Celt was placed in a slot in the tree and the bark grew around it; then it was cut and used. It was made by Scott Silsby.

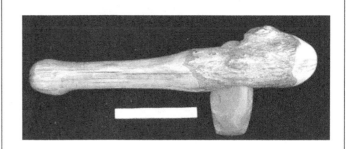

#2 – Description: Celt has an ironwood handle and greenstone blade. The bit is beveled. It was made by Scott Silsby.

#3 – Description: Axe has deer leg bone handle with a bi-blade. The handle and axe were wrapped with deer hide which still has hair on it. Then it was wrapped with sinew. The hair may have been used for chassis protection. This axe was tested on deer kills for obtaining sinew. It was made by Scott Silsby.

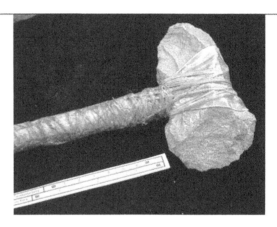

#4 – Description: Celt has deer leg bone handle with a bi-blade. The handle and axe were wrapped with deer hide which did not have hair on it. Then it was wrapped with sinew. It was made by Scott Silsby.

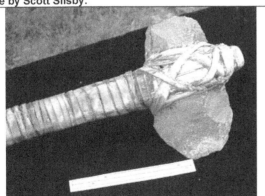

#5 – Description: Celt has a split crotch elm branch handle and greenstone blade. Blade/handle was wrapped with rawhide and sinew. Rosin was used for waterproofing. It was made by Scott Silsby.

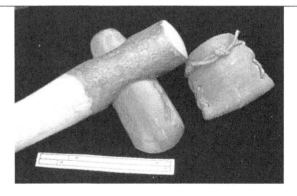

#6 – Description: Celt has a dogwood handle with a greenstone blade. It is called by Scott Silsby, who made it, - a hatchet. It has a leather pouch for its blade.

Plate 24 - Examples of Experimental Stone Tools and Hafting

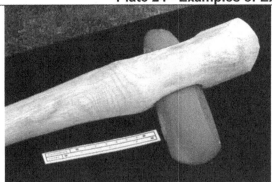

#7 – Description: Celt has an ash handle with a greenstone blade. It is another experiment in slot-celt hafting. It was made by Scott Silsby.

#8 – Description: Maul has a wooden handle with a 3/4 groove greenstone head. It was wrapped with rawhide and cross bound with sinew. It was made by Scott Silsby.

#9 – Description: Atlatl, wood with bone atlatl hook. It shows the placement of a feathered spear for throwing.

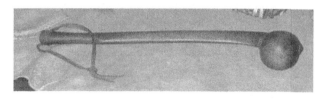

#10 – Ball Club. Made by Daniel Abbott (Nanticoke descendant). These wooden clubs are often carved with human/spirit faces (see Kraft 1989 and 1995). The style probably originated with the Iroquoian people.

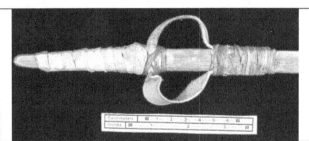

#11 – Description: Handle of Basketmaker atlatl (Reproduction). It is made on a pine platform which has the hook carved into the platform. The handle is made from leather tongs in which the fingers are placed. It is a copy of a Basketmaker culture atlatl in the Southwest.

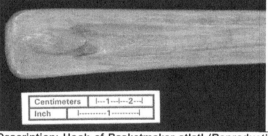

#12 – Description: Hook of Basketmaker atlatl (Reproduction). It is the hook for the atlatl shown left. The hook was cut with stone graving tools. Bear grease has been applied to keep the thrower flexible. The thrower is efficient, but keeping the spear (dart) in the hook requires practice. This atlatl is fluted on the spear side for better guidance in loading the spear.

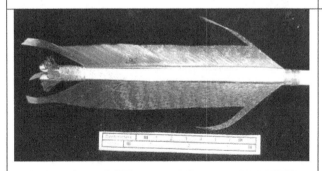

#13 – Description: Cane Arrow showing stone point. The feathers are turkey tail and the point is flint. The feathers were soaked before mounting; after they dry, they shrink and tighten the sinew wrapping. Each feather is tied at its ends. The point is a serrated Levanna type. It was made by Scott Silsby.

Appendix A – Broadspear Examples

Plate 7 – Examples of Virginia and North Carolina Broadspears
(Formerly in the Fred Morgan Collection)

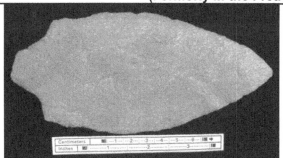

#1 – Koens-Crispin broadspear, quartzite (L = 164, W = 76, T = 11 mm). It is well made, thin, and has a flat profile. (Prince George County, Virginia)

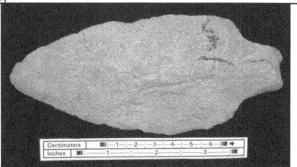

#2 – Savannah River broadspear, quartzite (L = 142, W = 64, T = 14 mm) (Sussex County, Virginia)

#3 – Savannah River broadspear, quartzite (L = 130, W = 44, T = 16 mm) (King William, County, Virginia)

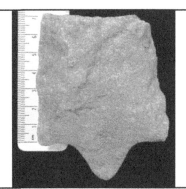
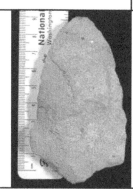

#4 – Morrow Mountain II broadspear, quartzite (L = broken, W = 75, T = 18 mm) (Nansemond County, Virginia)

#5 – Morrow Mountain I broadspear, quartzite (L = 99, W = 57, T = 15 mm) (Stokes County, North Carolina)

#6 – Koens-Crispin broadspear, rhyolite (L = 103, W = 44, T = 16 mm) (Stokes County, North Carolina)

#7 – Savannah River broadspear, weathered rhyolite (L = 151, W = 53, T = 12 mm). It probably had a wide blade, but resharpening has reduced its width. (Giles County, Virginia)

Appendix B - Tribute to William Henry Holmes

Tribute to William Henry Holmes

William Henry Holmes (1846-1933) was born in Cadiz, Ohio into a farming family. While his life-time devotion was art, he did not receive formal training in it. He did receive a teaching certificate in 1865 and graduated from McNeedly Normal School in 1870. By chance in a Cadiz bookstore, he met a War Department clerk who suggested

to him that he should go to Washington City to study art. He moved to the city in 1871 to study with the painter Theodore Kaufmann. He soon met Mary Henry, daughter of Joseph Henry, the first Secretary of the Smithsonian. This led him to become a scientific illustrator for the institution. Holmes actually lived in one of the Smithsonian's towers. His skill made him numerous friends, namely Ferdinand V. Hayden who had successfully lobbied Congress to establish the United States Geological Survey of the Territories (became the USGS). Holmes became an artist for the Survey. He worked with Hayden in his 1872 survey of Yellowstone. During these surveys, Holmes would be forever influenced by his visit to Anasazi ruins in the San Juan Valley of New Mexico and Arizona. Also, while working at Yellowstone, he noticed that they worked nodules of obsidian, where he wrote: *It occurred to [me] that the various Indian tribes of the neighboring valleys had probably visited this locality for the purpose of procuring material for arrow points and other implements.*

Photograph permission: Smithsonian Institution, Washington, DC.

Holmes exhibited the romance of the past in America as seen by the Native Americans. He lived in a time when he could actually see, talk to, and spend time with Native Americans while the land was still theirs.

Holmes, with the assistance of William Jackson, took on the task of displaying a Puebloan cliff house for the 1876 Centennial Exposition in Philadelphia. In 1879, he toured European museums and lived in the artist colony in Munich. He returned to the U.S. and again worked for the USGS and found himself out west. While working in this capacity, he was appointed honorary curator of aboriginal pottery at the United States National Museum (USNM). From 1880 to 1889, he published numerous collections of shell, ceramic, and stone objects and worked throughout the country, especially the Southwest. Under the Bureau of American Ethnology (BAE), he performed archaeological investigations in the Mexico and Jamez Valley of New Mexico. During times between investigations, he exercised his artwork abilities with exhibits in New Orleans, Louisville, and Cincinnati. All of which produced over 30 publications.

Holmes earned his reputation the hard way by climbing mountains, mapping unknown territories, and drawing antiquities from American prehistory. Later, Ph.D.s from European universities would consult with him on the American Indians and geology of America. He would combine this interest into a natural history of archaeology.

In 1889, Powell appointed Holmes to take over the BAE's fieldwork. He would then become involved in the question of America's Paleolithic. Holmes came up against Frederick W. Putnam's (Salem Museum) so-called American paleoliths. He differed with Thomas Wilson (Smithsonian) about these artifacts.

To settle the argument, he selected a site on Piney Branch in Washington City that contained artifacts in what was considered as being Tertiary and Cretaceous ages. Holmes' excavation (1889-1890) established that the Cretaceous was the age of the gravels at the site. He argued the artifacts were recent and virtually started the end of the great American debate over paleolithics. However, not everyone was convinced; such as Charles C. Abbott of the Trenton gravels fame who was unconvinced by the Piney Branch evidence. Holmes would eventually discredit Abbott's Trenton Paleoliths. The Piney Branch site may be considered the beginning of American archaeology as it is today.

Holmes' philosophy was to view observations as the consequence of natural history. The observation became the abstraction that he used in his methodology; archaeology was to him a science. For him, science was based on empirical observations. These observations were frequently made on Native Americans, which allowed him to deduce prehistoric peoples' lives and their tools.

Holmes' path would cross with Franz Boas of the Field Museum in Chicago. He *out-did, with help of others,* Boas in competing for the job of curator, and their relationship would reverberate over the next three decades. He still continued to complete his research in the Potomac River valley, which climaxed with the publication of ***Stone Implements of the Potomac-Chesapeake Tidewater Province*** in 1897. This work would award him with the Loubat Quinquennial Prize – a prize of $1,000. While his work in Chicago was rewarding, such as a trip to the ruins of the Yucatan, in 1897 he would return to Washington City as head curator of the Department of Anthropology of the USNM. Under this position, he would formulate and publish ***Aboriginal Pottery of the Eastern United States***. Once into the 20th century, Holmes would become the chief (not choosing director's title) of the BAE. He oversaw the compilation of the two-volume work entitled ***Handbook of American Indians North of Mexico*** in 1907 and 1910. The author was Frederick Webb Hodge. Another one of Holmes' major contributions to American archaeology was his role in the passage of the Antiquities Act of 1906. Nonfederal archaeologists were upset by the Act because they resented their practice being regulated by the Smithsonian. He greatly increased the USNM's collections and established the Department of Physical Anthropology and appointed Ales Hrdlicka to head it. This appointment would lead to a fruitful period in American anthropology.

From this time on, Holmes would publish little and had little time for fieldwork. But he still was recognized for his work in archaeology. In 1905, he was elected into the National Academy of Sciences. In 1910, he retired as head of the BAE and became head of the Division of Anthropology and became curator of the American Gallery of Art. He would write his substantial works entitled ***Handbook of Aboriginal American Antiquities*** in 1919. He received another Loubat Prize for this effort.

Holmes would be party to events that would brand anthropologists as being spies. Boas gained control of the American Anthropologist and subsequently published a letter called ***The Nation*** in 1919 in which he accused unnamed anthropologists as being spies. This led to Boas' resignation from the American Anthropological Association. After which, Holmes resigned from the USNM and returned once again to art – he helped establish the journal Art and Archaeology. He would continue for the remainder of his life at the Gallery. On April 20, 1933, he died. William Henry Holmes and his wife are buried in Rock Creek Cemetery in Washington, DC – just two miles from the Piney Branch site that launched his career.

Photograph of Holmes' Family plot in Rock Creek Cemetery, Washington, DC.

No matter whether archaeologist or Native American, their lives become the buried past. We are only temporary custodians of humanity's material cultural remains.

Appendix C – Potomac Crossroads Projectile Points

Potomac Crossroads Projectile Points (continued):

While most of the points are not classifiable in established types, many are boarder-line types. Depending on the observer's viewpoints, there may be new types here. Never force a point into a type; it is either a named type or it is not. There is **no** such thing as a type variant in archaeology. The following specimens are all surface-collected points. Private collections in the MRPV use to contain thousands of point; most are gone.

Appendix D Potomac Valley Clovis Site

Reprinted with permission from:

Hranicky, Wm Jack
(2015) Quartzite Legacy Among the Paleoindians of Virginia. Journal of Middle Atlantic Archaeology, Vol. 31, pp. 129-142.

Quartzite Legacy among the Paleoindians of Virginia
Wm Jack Hranicky

Abstract: This paper discusses the Paleoindian stone usage of quartzite in Virginia. A paleo-workstation on the Potomac River was discovered, which is classified as a Paleoindian site. Various preforms are analyzed with metric data. While preform data are lacking in Virginia, the various reduction models are argued for quartzite paleopoints, such as parallel-sided and ovate preforms in quartzite. The source for the quartzite is suggested as Potomac River cobbles. Point maintenance for the type style is discussed. The paper argues that the true lithic paleo-stone preference in Virginia was quartzite.

* * * * * * * * *

This paper presents a study of quartzite specimens that were collected on a plow-disturbed second terrace in Loudoun County, Virginia at the confluence of Maryland's Monocracy River and the Potomac River. This area above the fall line separating the piedmont and coastal areas of the river basin. They were discovered during the author's Potomac River survey in the 1990s (Hranicky 2002). Flakes and debitage were not collected because the area was going to be further investigated with test pits with a possible excavation; however, the site-area was developed, and it is now all modern housing. The site was classified as a Paleoindian knapping station for the replenishment of this particular group of people's toolkit, and in this case, they left only quartzite artifacts. The source of their quartzite is suggested as being from cobbles in the Potomac River. One complete fluted point was found (#5) which was beveled. This specimen was probably replaced by then a newly-made specimen. These materials are all surface finds; thus, a more extensive range of artifacts is, of course, not available. All specimens were precussion flaked for mass morphologies, and there was evidence of pressure flaking for thinning and edge preparation for final point shapes. There is an assumption that finalizing was successful at the site. Lack of evidence for this stage is probably a sampling error.

The collected site sample total was 63 specimens. These quartzite artifacts were made by hard- and soft-hammer percussion which is common to most quartzite technologies (Figure 1). They are classified as production material as the result of manufacturing quartzite fluted points. The site's sample analysis was based on Bradley, et al. (2010), Andrefsky (2001), Odell (1996), Hall and Larson (2004), and Plew, et al. 1985). The overview for quartzite usage was Ebright (1987). Hranicky (2015) argues for a quartzite preference on the Middle Atlantic coast. This study approach involved identifying common attributes, classifying a typology, and aggregate analysis (artifact completeness).

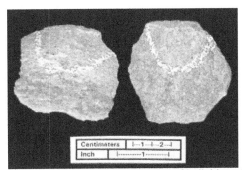

Figure 1 - Hard Hammer Percussion Quartzite Flakes. Chalk Lines Show Percussion Bulbs.

The major problem using surface recovered materials (nonsite) is distinguishing between Clovis, Morrow Mountain, and Savannah River broken quartzite pieces/debitage. Many archaeologists cannot classify these type specimens between Paleoera and Archaic era production materials. Additionally for geologic distribution, there are two types: orthroquartzite and metaquartzite. The scope of these topics is beyond this paper, other than noting the archaeological problems. And, the most dominant quartzite broken pieces in Virginia are Savannah River materials; thus, again complicating field recovery diagnosis. For paleo quartzite usage, what are the criteria that are used for identifying quartzite-worked forms by the Paleoindians? For broad paleo analytical categories that were used, Hranicky (2015a) suggests:

- Presence of fluting
- Cross-face flake scars
- Broad, but thin flakes scars
- Lanceolate form (<7mm thin)
- Biface reduction of preforms
- Thin/flat cross sections
- High-quality stone materials
- Symmetrical lateral margins
- Presence of blades and microtools.

The Virginia Paleoindians used every workable stone to make their points and tools, which included among other stones, greenstone (7 points in the McCary Survey) and petrified wood. The most popular stone by point count is the chalcedony of south central Virginia. Because of its quarry location, the Williamson site produced the most recovered paleopoints. If only numbers were used, then this stone would be the preferred stone. But, when the lithic distribution is examined statewide, the picture suggests an entirely different lithic preference in the paleoera. This picture is complicated by a paleo chronology that has not been defined for Virginia; for that matter, there are no reliable Paleoindian dates in Virginia. The basic question is: Do lithic preferences determine individual population occupations or are these people using various stones depending on availability? This is the "lithic determinism" as argued by Gardner (1979 and 1989) many years ago for the jasper usage at the Thunderbird site in Warren County, Virginia.

If the site's artifacts were Savannah River preforms, they are generally thicker and have a biconvex cross section. Also, they lack cross-face flake scars. Basically, Savannah River well-made preforms average 12-20 mm in thickness; whereas, Clovis preforms are usually under 8-12 mm (Hranicky 2015a). One specimen (#1) was recovered with a fluting nipple, which is identical to jasper preforms found on the Thunderbird site (Hranicky 2015c). The nipple was created by removing two flakes on each side of the proposed nipple. The nipple setup was reported at the Plenge site in New Jersey (Kraft 1973). None of the specimens could be retrofitted; however, this is probably a small sample problem.

Quartzite has numerous qualities depending on where it is found. The best material is the fine-grain stone found in southern Virginia (Bottoms 1968), but the Potomac basin has numerous outcrops which were used throughout prehistory. The Rappahannock River valley/basin has the poorest quality quartzite due to ancient geological formations (as in Sibley and Blatt 1976). Basically, the material from this site is defined as:

> **Quartzite** = Quartz group (silicified sandstone). It has a hardness of 7 and a specific gravity at 2.5-2.8. It has a tan to white color. It has rough conchoidal fracture. Fracture surface granular, slightly lumpy. This quartzite is a metamorphosed sandstone. Frequently, the individual grains of sand have been cemented by the introduction of secondary silica, producing a rock stronger than the original deposit. Workability is 9.7 (as in Callahan 1979). The quality of quartzite ranges from fine- to course-grain material. The site material is mostly orthoquartzite showing an almost pure cemented sandstone.

This site probably represents a small Paleoindian band whose flintknappers were using quartzite cobble to manufacture fluted points as there is no large close-by quartzite boulders or outcrops. Since no cobble reduction debris was found at the site, blanks were created on the river bank. Then, these were transported to the site for final processing. The artifacts represent a mid-range in the production of fluted points. There is no way to determine the number of successful points; but judging by the biface failures, the number was substantial. There was no indication that they produced any other tools except points; however, two tools were found which were probably not made at the site. As a note, cobble reduction was used at the nearby Paw Paw Cove Paleoindian site in Maryland (Lowery 1989). Holmes (1897) reported on quartzite quarries in the Piney Branch region in Washington, DC which involved cobble exploitation.

The term "high-quality lithic materials" is commonplace when referring to Paleoindian stone usage, namely the Clovis pointmakers. These materials are classified as cryptocrystalline stones which are argued as having the best workability for microtool production in Virginia (Callahan 1979). For Virginia, they are chert, chalcedony, quartz, quartzite, jasper, shale/slate, and rhyolite. Other minor stones occur. Figure 2 shows the generalized lithic distribution in Virginia of major stones (Hranicky 2008). It is based on recovered fluted points in the McCary (MC) Fluted Point Survey of Virginia. Can they be considered regional lithic preferences in Virginia (Figure 1)? No, because the collected data is skewed by complete points vs. a failure by collectors to pick up broken paleo-points, namely paleo-blade tips.

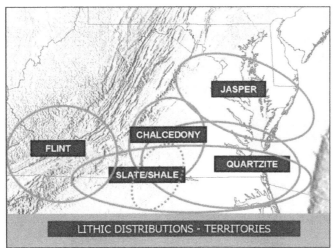

Figure 2 – Lithic Stone Clusters in Virginia Based on the McCary Fluted Point Survey (Hranicky 2008)

Clovis artifact distributions represent settlement and mobility, subsistence and technological strategies, hunting/collecting areas, and the overall human adaptation to specific environments. Hranicky (2008a) argued for Virginia lithic distributions based on data from the McCary Survey (as in Hranicky 2008b). The chalcedony points are clustered in a 100+ mile radius of the Williamson site. The distribution of jasper suggests northern Virginia and adjacent states, such as Delaware and eastern Maryland. Numerous other stones in the Survey have a wide geography among the neighboring states, which includes West Virginia, Maryland, and North Carolina. The question remains: do these stone geographies represent population movement, stone availability, preference, and/or chronology?

Further, Callahan (1979) discovered and introduced the basic preform to Virginia archaeology. It was based on materials from the Thunderbird and Williamson sites. This model applies to points made from jasper and chalcedony, including quartzite (Figure 3). This model has been a standard in eastern archaeology for years but, as specimens below show, the parallel-sided preform (as in Collins 1999) was used. The parallel-sided preform appears to be the main reduction style at the site, but one ovate-shaped biface was also found. Thus, two methods of stone reduction were used at the site. The parallel-sided specimens shown are flat and average 11.85 mm in thickness.

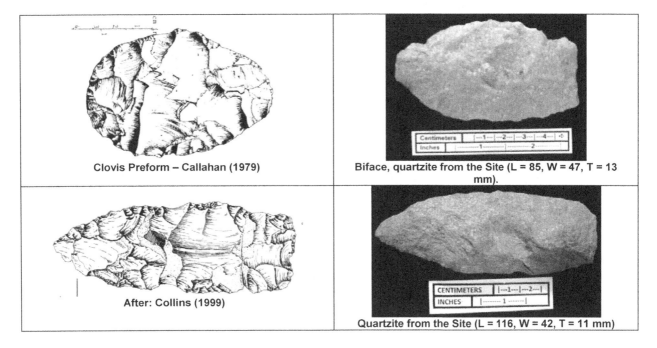

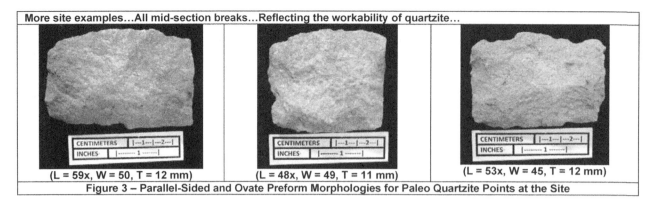

Figure 3 – Parallel-Sided and Ovate Preform Morphologies for Paleo Quartzite Points at the Site

(L = 59x, W = 50, T = 12 mm) (L = 48x, W = 49, T = 11 mm) (L = 53x, W = 45, T = 12 mm)

More site examples...All mid-section breaks...Reflecting the workability of quartzite...

Several early stage specimens were recovered which reflect a local source for the stone (Figure 4). There are no quartzite boulders on the terrace nor is there an outcrop of quartzite. Thus, there was a first reduction area. The suggestion is cobbles in the Potomac River. Two specimens had cortex remaining on one face. To divide the assemblage into stages is difficult because of the sample size. The number of perverse fractures argues that they were having difficulty working the material, either by lack of skill or hardness of the stone. Attempts at early stage fluting (or basal thinning) was only on one face of the recovered specimens showing basal thinning. The site materials had no evidence of heat treating.

Figure 4 – Broken Quartzite Early Stage Reduction Piece (L = 77x, W = 53, T = 14 mm)

Based on these specimens, point style was maintained by the use of parallel-sided preforms. The broken specimen (# 2) shows type maintenance through to fluting. Since quartzite is the only production stone, the question becomes – is this stone a requirement for this type style? Would flint/chert pointmakers manufacture their points the same way? The answer may be a cross-cutting social maintenance that is dependent on Clovis geography and chronology by specific bands. Obviously, the site's sample cannot be appraised for social requirements and their conditions in the production processes.

While the literature overly stresses that Clovis and other paleopoints were made from cryptocrystalline stones, Virginia paleopoints have strong evidence of the Native American tradition for using quartzite for prehistoric points/knives. It is argued here that in the Middle and Late Archaic the predominant stone was quartzite. Flint and cherts do have their high patterns of usage across the U.S. But, Virginia Paleoindians made heavy usage of quartzite, among other stones. See Johnson (1989), and Hranicky and McCary (1995). Hranicky (2006) and Ebright (1987) argue that quartzite has a regenerative property. As a blade edge cuts into a material, the edge breaks down. Small microchips break off, and leave another ragged cutting edge. Whereas, flints and cherts tend to self-polish, thus, leaving a smooth edge. This may have been a factor in selecting quartzite, but flints and cherts areas are not readily available in eastern Virginia. To some extent, rhyolite has the regenerative edge property, see McCary and Hranicky (2008). All of which still leaves jasper, and because of Thunderbird, it is the generally cited for Virginia. Also, the 400+ known chalcedony points from the Williamson site contribute to this discussion in the literature. Stone selection and its justification are a cultural factor that requires more quartzite paleosites.

Paleoindian broken specimens are found all over the state without major concentrations; thus, collecting data on them has and is a problem for Virginia archaeology. Also, museums, societies, and state agencies are making little effort to record private collections. Even the Archeological Society of

Virginia's members do little in surface surveys today. They used to have an annual award for the chapter which found the most sites. And, field surveys are difficult because they are no longer deeply-plowed. As a result, quartzite concentrations will be difficult to find. Basically, this stone is a nonsite study problem.

The entire collection has a thinness of 11.79 mm (average and n=63). Due to breakage, other metric data was not attempted. However, for one example, Figure 5 shows a well-made biface and, because of its ratios, it is argued as Paleoindian. The biface has an attribute (characteristic) called a flat profile. It has a constant thickness from distal to proximal ends. The sign of experienced knapping is the flat profile, but additionally, the distal/proximal profile (D/P) may indicate the knapper's intended function. This profile was measured. Using a digital caliper, the biface measures L = 82.65, W = 50.52, T = 11.25 mm. Taking a measurement at 5 mm on each end at the medial axis: distal = 10.66 and proximal = 10.41 mm. By using these measurements as D/P as a ratio, a well-made biface should always equal 1.0; in this case, D/P = 1.0240. This number indicates the minor rise in the biface's center. The D/P ratio is argued as Paleoindian. The specimen was probably a knife not an intended point.

Figure 5 – White Quartzite Biface (L = 82, W = 50, T = 9 mm)

Figure 6 show a quartzite biface that has a burin-like tip. It has minor wear. This specimen has a broad basal thinning flake on one face. These quartzite specimens do not match the quartzite found at the site. No wear analysis was performed on any of the specimens. The other specimen also had a pointed tip and a spokeshave. It was made off a flat blade-like piece (uniface) which was probably not made at the site. It has a medial ridge which tapers off to form the pointed tip. The reason for the discard is the tip became dull or was broken. While speculative, these people were using quartzite as their basic stone from elsewhere in Virginia.

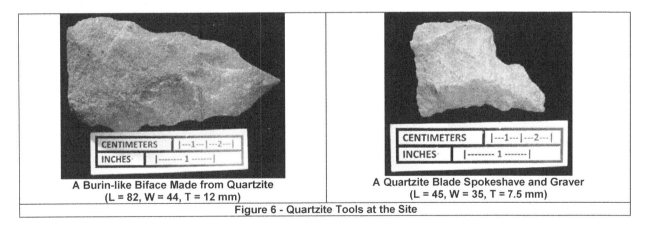

Most of the site's specimens are made from a fine-grain quartzite (orthroquatzite) cobbles while a few were from granular stones. These were probably river-bank tested before they were transported to the site for initial-to-final reduction. Two specimens still had the cortex remaining, thus quarrying a large boulder was not the source for their material. A color range occurs in the collection: was color a consideration? This sample is too small to make this assessment.

Figure 7 shows a sample of the quartzite forms collected in the field survey. As mentioned, the surface was disturbed and only a limited sample was collected. The sample shows various production stages. One microtool was observed but still it argues for the site being a knapping station for points. Most of these broken lanceolate forms do not show fluting attempts which argues that fluting was a late stage process. While most breakage occurred horizontally, three diagonal fractures occur. All of these specimens are considered discards, and the successful points were carried off the site. No complete site-manufactured fluted point was found.

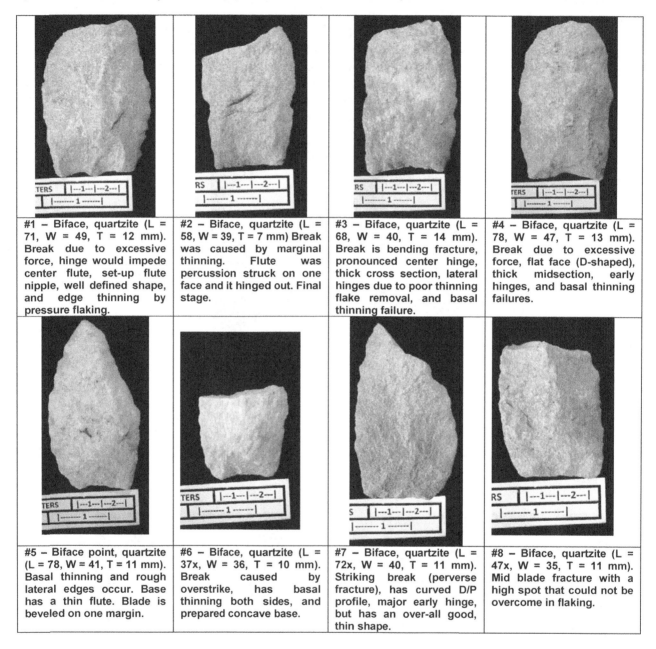

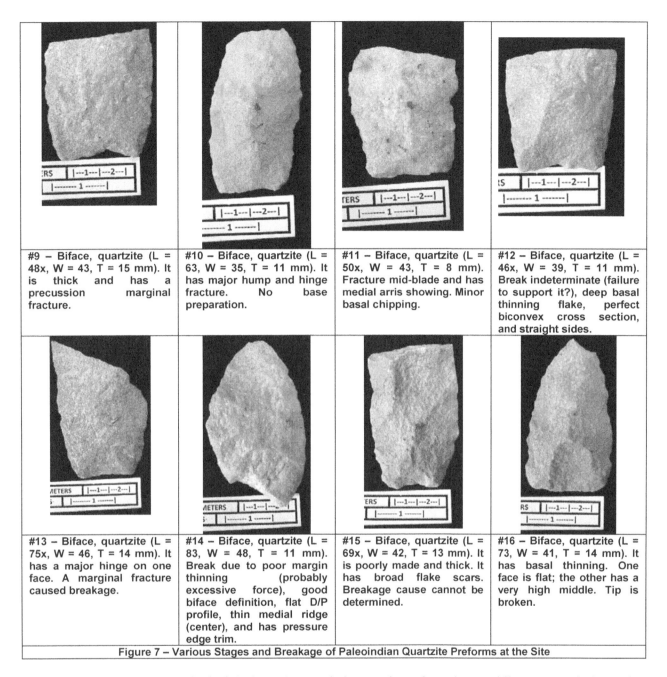

Figure 7 – Various Stages and Breakage of Paleoindian Quartzite Preforms at the Site

The McCary Survey of Virginia has 98 recorded quartzite paleopoints. While not a topic here, there are 122 recorded quartz points. Most Survey points only have surface rubbings, but the author attempted to find each and re-record and photograph them. As a database problem, flaking patterns are difficult to discern. And, many of the Survey's points can no longer be found in the state. Figure 8 shows a fluted point sample from the MC Survey. The relationship between, if any, quartz and quartzite has not been analyzed archaeologically in Virginia. These two stones constitute nearly 20% of the Survey specimens.

Figure 8 – Examples of Quartzite Paleopoints in Virginia

The large paleoknife is often misinterpreted in Virginia archaeology. Even Ben McCary rejected them as being too large. To compound this problem, the Paleoindians used and subsequently resharpened them, which often left small, irregularly-shaped points. In field-surface collections, they would, of course, be next to impossible to identify as Clovis – especially when made from quartzite. At least, thickness becomes a question for quartzite specimens.

In paleotimes, did stone preferences cause quarries or did quarry preferences cause stone tools? Regardless of the answer, quarries are an important topic in the study of Paleoindians. This topic provides interesting discussions among archaeologists but will not be furthered here, other than stating its significance (Figure 9 and 10). No quartzite paleo-quarry has been identified and published in Virginia. However, the Magothy quartzite quarry site is an archaeological site near Pasadena in Anne Arundel County, Maryland may have paleo debitage (Source: Maryland Historic Trust). For Clovis basics again, high-quality stone was the most common among these pointmakers so why look for a quartzite quarry. This study sample reflects poorly made preforms, but these were the discards. There is no way to determine the successful number of points. They assume a lithic preference by these people.

Modern experienced flintknppers will argue that the point size is not material dependent (Hranicky 2008). If Paleoindians could manufacture a fluted point out of greenstone, then these knappers could work any stone. While not in the survey, a basalt Clovis is in a private collection. One of the largest Virginia quartzite fluted points is MC 1000 which is named the McCary fluted point (Figure 9). It was made from a dark tan quartzite and shows size was not a factor in working quartzite. These large points were probably common in the paleoera, but resharpening-to-expended forms is what we find in surface surveys. The preforms suggest 50-60 mm for the length of the points at this site. This average length was suggested by Hranicky and McCary (1995) for all fluted points in Virginia.

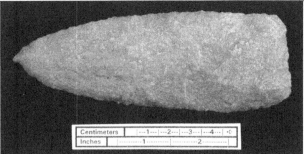

Figure 9 - Quartzite Point/Knife from Sussex County, Virginia. It measures L = 126, W = 46, T = 17 mm and has a bold flute.

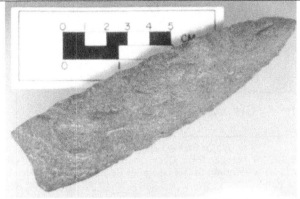

Figure10 - MC 1000 Quartzite Paleopoint. It measures L = 136, W = 37, T = 10 mm and is from Dinwiddie County, Virginia.

While the jasper quarries of Thunderbird and the chalcedony quarrying at the Williamson sites receive all the "press" in the literature, they are not dominant stones in the paleoera of Virginia (Figure 11). These two stones are often classified as Paleoindian. After chalcedony used by knappers at the Williamson site for points, quartzite takes second place. And, the initial stone study by Hranicky (2008) was skewed because private collectors basically only have complete Clovis points. Broken points are seemingly absent. However, broken quartzite points are numerous in surface surveys by the author. And, quartzite debitage has the highest frequency in Virginia for all archaeological periods. The author has made an effort to select and record the paleo materials; thus, the adjustment here for lithic distribution for state-wide use of quartzite.

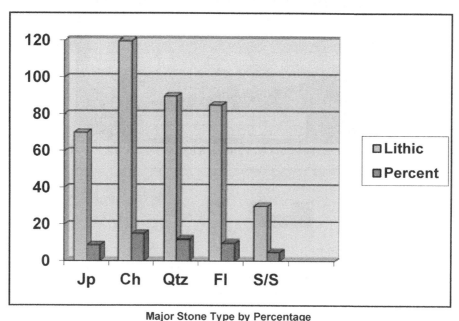

Major Stone Type by Percentage
Jp = jasper, Ch = chalcedony, Qtz = quartzite, Fl = flint, S/S = shale/slate
Figure 11 – Paleoindian Stone Usage in Virginia (McCary Survey Data).

Continuing, the next question: Does Clovis technology initiate a quartzite legacy that continues throughout Virginia prehistory? The author argues for an affirmative YES. And, this legacy probably has older origins in the so-called pre-Clovis era. The subsequent cultural major types are the Morrow Mountain and Savannah River points. As suggested, Clovis, regardless of its stone, initiates projectile point technology in the U.S. (Hranicky 2015). Biface origins by stone remain to be established in the Southeast. For an example, when one examines the North Carolina Clovis population, there is an abundance of shale/slate paleopoints and paleo materials. Each state's geography has Clovis stone preferences probably based on stone availability and geography, such as riverines.

For one comparative example from South Carolina, Goodyear (2014) reports a Clovis study on the usage of raw materials for tools. As expected, chert usage was 51.3% vs. quartzite at 20.5% out of the 100% sample (n=39). Yet, by Dalton times, chert was 21.2% as compared with 33.3% in quartzite out of the 100% sample (n=66). When bifurcates were examined, quartzite totaled the highest at 38.6% vs. chert at 15.7% (n=70). The data suggest a movement from chert to quartzite from the Paleoindian era to the Archaic era.

In concluding, Figure 12 shows an ovate biface which was found near the site cluster. Its quartzite material does not match the site's basic quartzite. It has a thickness that suggests either a failure or a non-paleo specimen. It illustrates the difficulty identifying nonsite finds. It is argued as being a Morrow Mountain preform or possibly a Savannah River preform. Its flaking pattern is not Clovis.

Figure 12 – An Ovate Biface from the Virginia Fall Line on the Potomac River

The data collected by the McCray Fluted Point Survey has been used for years by scholars from around the world. Unfortunately, the Executive Board of the Archaeological Society of Virginia in the early 2000s voted to stop the Survey. Their argument was there were too many fakes in the database. Nonsense! Also, this board was dominated by state employees, a few amateurs, all of whom had little knowledge of paleo-stone materials and their paleo-processes. The author was the last Survey director, but still continues to collect paleodata and information. The main location of Virginia's Survey/records of paleodata is now in the Virginia Museum of Natural History. The author estimates that there are 2500+ fluted points in Virginia. Only 1055 have been recorded (Hranicky 2008). There were three Survey directors: Ben C. McCary, Michael F. Johnson, and Wm Jack Hranicky.

Since many early state-wide survey publications and the computation of Eastern States Archaeological Federation's (Brennan 1982) fluted point survey, the Paleoindian Database of the Americas (PIDBA) was organized and has become the standard Paleoindian point database for archaeological Paleoindian research. The count for the U.S. is now 28,000+ points. It is housed at the University of Tennessee, Knoxville, and David G. Anderson and Michael K. Faught are Project Directors. However, more state surveys are needed to fill-in missing database points and their data. At least Virginia's paleodata are included in the PIDBA.

References:

Andrefsky, William
(2001) Lithic Debitage – Context, Form, Meaning. University of Utah Press, Salt Lake City, UT.

Bottoms, Edward
(1968) Bertie County Oolithic Quartzite and its Aboriginal Utilization in Eastern Virginia and North Carolina. Cheopiean, Vol. 6, pp. 32-43.

Bradley, Bruce A., Michael B. Collins, and Andrew Hemmings
(2010) Clovis Technology. International Monographs in Prehistory, Archaeological Series 17.

Brennan, Louis A. (ed.)
(1982) A Compilation of Fluted Points of Eastern North America by Count and Distribution: An AENA Project. Archaeology of Eastern North America, Vol. 10, pp. 27-46.

Callahan, Errett
(1979) The Basics of Biface Knapping in the Eastern Fluted Point Tradition - A Manual for Flintknappers and Lithic Analysis. Archaeology of Eastern North America, Vol. 7, No. 1, pp. 1-179.

Collins, Michael B.
(1999) Clovis Blade Technology. University of Texas Press, Austin, TX.

Ebright, Carol A.
(1987) Quartzite Petrography and its Implication for Prehistoric Use and Archeological Analysis. Archaeology of Eastern North America, Vol. 17, pp. 29-45.

Gardner, William A.
(1989) Pleistocene and Early Holocene (circa 9200 to 6800 BC) In: Paleoindian Research in Virginia – A Synthesis, eds. J. Wittkofski and T. Reinhart, ASV Special Publication No. 19.
(1979) Typology and Chronology of Fluted Points from the Flint Run Area. Pennsylvania Archaeologist, Vol. 49, No. 1, pp. 13-45.

Goodyear, Albert C.
(2014) Paleoindian in Cowasee: Time, Typology, and Raw Material Selection. Chesopiean, Vol. 52, No. 4, pp. 1-28.

Hall, Christopher and Marry Lou Larson
(2004) Aggregate Analysis in Chipped Stone. University of Utah Press, Salt lake City, UT.

Holmes, William Henry
(1887) Stone Implements of the Potomac-Chesapeake Tidewater Province. 15th Annual Report of the United States Bureau of Ethnology, Washington, DC.

Hranicky, Wm Jack
(2015a) Recording Clovis Points. AuthorHouse, Bloomington, IN.
(2015b) Personal examination of Thunderbird artifacts at the Smithsonian. No Thunderbird official site report has been published.
(2008a) Lithic Distribution for Paleopoints in Virginia. ASV Quarterly Bulletin, Vol. 64, No. 2, pp. 49-64.
(2008b) McCary Fluted Point Survey of Virginia – Point Numbers 1-1055. AuthorHouse, Bloomington, IN.
(2007) Experimental Archaeology - A Science for Studying Native American Prehistoric Technology. AuthorHouse, Bloomington, IN.
(2002) Lithic Technology in the Middle Potomac River Valley of Maryland and Virginia. Kluwer/Plenum Publishers, New York, NY.

Hranicky, Wm Jack Hranicky and Ben C. McCary
(1995) Clovis Technology in Virginia. ASV Special Publication Number 31, Pt. 1.

Johnson, Michael F.
(1989) Paleoindian Chronology for Virginia. In: Paleoindian Research in Virginia – A Synthesis, eds: J. Wittkofski and T. Reinhart, ASV Special Publication No. 19.

Kraft, Herbert C.
(1973) The Plenge Site: A Paleo-Indian Occupation Site in New Jersey. Archaeology of Eastern North America, Vol. 1, pp. 56-117.

Lowery, Darrin
(1989) The Paw Paw Cove Paleoindian Site Complex, Talbot County, Maryland. Archaeology of Eastern North America, Vol. 17, pp. 143-164.

Odell, George H.
(1996) Stone Tools – Theoretical Insights into Human Prehistory. Plenum. New York, NY.

Plew, Mark G., James C. Woods, and Max G. Plaveic
(1985) Stone Tool Analysis Essays in Honor of Don Crabtree. University of Utah Press, Salt Lake City, UT.

Sibley, Duncan F. and Harvey Blatt
(1976) Intergranular Pressure Solution and Cementation of the Tuscarora Orthoquartzite. Journal of Sedimentary Petrology, Vol. 46, No. 4, pp. 881-896.

References

The following references are listed as MPRV source literature. Not all of these references were used in the text but were included to create a general bibliography for the reader. These references only partly include Contract archaeology literature at Virginia or Maryland state agencies. Reports are also on file at the Fairfax Archaeological Survey and Alexandria Archaeology Museum.

Abbott, Charles C.
(1885) The Use of Copper by the Delaware Indians. The American Naturalist, Peabody Academy of Science, Salem, MA.
(1876) The Stone Age of New Jersey. Annual Report of the Smithsonian for 1875, pp. 246-380.

Adair, James
(1775 as in 1930 Reprint) The History of the American Indians. Watauga Press, Johnson City, TN.

Adams, William Y.
(1991) Archaeological Typology and Practical Reality. Cambridge University, Cambridge, England.

Adney, Edwin T. and Howard I. Chappelle
(1964) The Bark and Canoes and Skin Boats of North America. Bul. 230, United States National Museum, Washington, DC.

Agenbroad, Larry D.
(1978) The Hudson-Meng Site: An Alberta Bison Kill in the Nebraska High Plains. Caxton Printers, Ltd., Caldwell, ID.

Ahler, Stanley A.
(1989) Mass Analysis of Flaking Debris: Studying the Forest Rather Than the Trees. In: Alternative Approaches to Lithic Analysis, ed. D. Henry and G. Odell, pp. 85-118, American Anthropological Association Archaeological Papers 1.

Anderson, David G.
(1994) The Savannah River Chiefdoms – Political Change in the Late Prehistoric Southeast. University of Alabama Press, Tuscaloosa, AL.
(1991) The Bifurcate Tradition in the South Atlantic Region. Journal of Middle Atlantic Archaeology, Vol. 7, pp. 91-106.
(1990) The Paleoindian Colonization of Eastern North America: A View from the Southeastern United States. Research in Economic Anthropology, Supplement 5, pp. 163-216, JAI Press, Greenwich, CT.

Anderson, David G. and Kenneth E. Sassaman
(1996) The Paleoindian and Early Archaic of the Southeast. University of Alabama Press, Tuscaloosa, AL.

Andrefsky, Jr., William
(2001) Lithic Debitage – Context, Form, and Meaning. W. Andrefsky, ed., University of Utah Press, Salt Lake, UT.
(1998) Lithics - Macroscopic Approaches to Analysis. Cambridge University Press, New York, NY.
(1997) Thoughts on Stone Tool Shape and Inferred Function. Journal of Middle Atlantic Archaeology, Vol. 13, pp. 125-44.
(1995) Cascade Phase Lithic Technology: An Example for the Lower Snake River. North American Archaeologist, Vol. 16, pp. 95-115.
(1994) Raw Material Availability and the Organization of Technology. American Antiquity, Vol. 59, pp. 21-35.
(1991) Inferring Trends in Prehistoric Settlement Behavior from Lithic Production Technology in the Southern Plains. North American Archaeologist, Vol. 12, pp. 129-44.
(1986) Numerical Types and Inspectional Types: Evaluating Shape Characterization Procedures. North American Archaeologist, Vol. 7, pp. 95-112.

Arber, Edward (ed)
(1910) Travels and Works of Captain John Smith, President of Virginia and Admiral of New England, 2 vols. John Grant, Edinburgh.

Atkinson, T. C., K. K. R. Briffa, and G. R. Coope
(1987) Seasonal Temperatures in Britain During the Past 22,000 Years Reconstructed Using Beetle Remains. Nature, Vol. 325, pp. 587-592.

Ayers, Harvard G. and J. Glenn Little
(1967) 18FR100, A Woodland Site in Piedmont Maryland. ASV Quarterly Bulletin, Vol. 22, No. 1, pp. 26-38.

Baerries, David
(1953) Blackhawk Village Site. Journal of Iowa Archaeological Society, Vol. 2, No.4.

Bahn, Paul
(1991) Archaeology – Theory, Method, and Practice. Thames and Hudson, Ltd., London.

Baird, S. F.
(1879) Report to the Secretary, Annual Report, Smithsonian Institution, pp. 7-64, Washington, DC.

Baker, Winston H.
(1995) A Hypothetical Classification of Some of the Flaked Stone Projectiles, Tools and Ceremonials from the Southeastern United States. Williams Printing, Inc., Quincy, MA.

Ballweber, Hattie L.
(1996) Archaeology. Maryland Historical Press, Lanham, MD.
(1991) The Burall Site (18FR628): A Rhyolite Processing Site in Frederick County, Maryland. Maryland Archeology, Vol. 27, No. 2, pp. 3-30.

Barber, Michael B.
(2001) Pitted Hammerstones: Form and Function. ASV Quarterly Bulletin, Vol. 56, No. 2, pp. 60-66.

Barber, Michael B. and George A. Tolley
(1999) Lithic Utilization Patterns in the Blue Ridge of Virginia: Site Types and Site Boxes. Journal of Middle Atlantic Archaeology, Vol. 15, pp. 187-200.

Barber, Russell J.
(1980) Post-Pleistocene Anadromous Fish Exploitation at the Buswell Site, Northeastern Massachusetts, In: Early and Middle Archaic Cultures in the Northeast, ed. D. Starbuck and C. Brian, pp. 97-110, Occasional Publications in Northeastern Anthropology, No. 7, Department of Anthropology, Franklin Pierce College, Rindge, NH.

Bartram, William
(1853) Observations on the Creek and Cherokee Indians, 1789. Reprint: Transactions of American Ethnology, Vol. 3, Pt 1. New York.

Bass, William M.
(1987) Human Osteology. Missouri Archaeological Society, Columbia, MO.

Bastian, Tyler
(1980) The Early Pursuit of Archaeology in Maryland. Maryland Historical Magazine, Vol. 75, pp.1-7.

Baugh, Timothy G. and Jonathan E. Ericson (eds.)
(N.D.) Prehistoric Exchange Systems in North America. Plenum Press, New York, NY.

Beauchannys, W. M.
(1902) Metallic Implements of the New York Indians. New York State Museum, Bul. 55, University of State of New York, NY.

Bell, Robert E.
(1958/60) Guide to the Identification of Certain American Indian Projectile Points. Special Bulletin Nos. 1-2, Oklahoma Anthropological Society.

Bell, Robert E. and Roland S. Hall
(1953) Selected Projectile Point Types of the United States. Bulletin of the Oklahoma Anthropological Society, No.1.

Bello, Charles A.
(1993) Three Unusual Stone Weights from Gloucester County, New Jersey. Bulletin of the Archaeological Society of New Jersey, Vol. 48, pp. 37-38.

Bello, Charles A. and John H. Cresson
(1998) An Obsidian Biface from the Lower Delaware Valley. Bulletin of the New Jersey Archaeological Society Vol. 53, pp. 127-128.

Benthall, Joseph L.
(1969) Archeological Investigation of the Shannon Site, Virginia State Library, Richmond, VA.

Benyus, J. M.
(1989) The Field Guide to Wildlife Habitats of the Eastern United States. Fireside, Simon & Schuster, Inc., New York, NY.

Beverley, Robert
(1705) The History and Present State of Virginia (Four Parts). Reprinted 1947, University of North Carolina Press, Chapel Hill, NC.

Binford, Lewis R.
(1980) Willow Smoke and Dogs' Tails: Hunter-Gatherer Settlement Systems and Archaeological Site Formation. American Antiquity, Vol. 45, pp 4-20.

Binford, Lewis R. and Mark L. Papworth
(1963) The Eastport Site, Antrim County, Michigan. In: Miscellaneous Studies in Typology and Classification by Anta M. White, Lewis R. Binford, and Mark L. Papworth. Museum of Anthropology, University of Michigan, Anthropological Papers No. 19, pp. 71-123.

Birkeland, Peter W.
(1984) Soils and Geomorphology. Oxford University Press, New York, NY.

Bjerrum, L., A. Casagrande, R. B. Peck, and A. W. Skempton
(1960) From Theory to Practice in Soil Mechanics. John Wiley & Sons, New York, NY.

Black, David W. and Lucy A. Wilson
(1999) The Washademoak Lake Chert Source, Queens County, New Brunswick, Canada. Archaeology of Eastern North America, Vol. 27, pp. 81-108.

Blackman, M. James
(1976) The Geochemical Analysis of Jasper Artifacts and Source Materials from Delaware and Pennsylvania. In: Transactions of the Delaware Academy of Science, ed. John C. Kraft, pp. 5-6 and 37-48, Newark, DE.

Blake, Leonard W. and Hugh C. Cutler
(2001) Plants from the Past. University of Alabama Press, Tuscaloosa, AL.

Blanton, Dennis B.
(1992) Middle Woodland Settlement Systems in Virginia. In: Middle and Late Woodland Research in Virginia – A Synthesis, eds. T. Reinhart and M. Hodges, Special Publication Number 29, Archeological Society of Virginia.

Blanton, Dennis B., Stevan C. Pullins, and Veronica L. Deitrick
(1999) The Potomac Creek Site (44ST2) Revisited, Virginia Department of Historic Resources, Research Report Series, No. 10, Richmond, VA.

Bliss, Anne
(1981) A Handbook of Dyes From Natural Materials. Scribner & Sons, New York, NY.

Bolian, Charles E.
(1980) The Early and Middle Archaic of the Lakes Region, New Hampshire. In: Early and Middle Archaic Cultures in the Northeast, ed. D. Starbuck and C. Brian, pp. 115-134, Occasional Publications in Northeastern Anthropology, No. 7, Department of Anthropology, Franklin Pierce College, Rindge, NH.

Bondar, Gregory H.
(2000) Prehistoric Distribution and Use of Metarhyolites in Eastern North America. Paper presented at the 65th SAA Meeting in Philadelphia, PA

Booth, D.
(1991) Urbanization and the Natural Drainage System-Impacts, Solutions and Prognoses. Northwest Environmental Journal, Vol. 7, No. 1, pp. 03-118.

Bloomfield, Leonard
(1946) Algonquian: In Linguistics Structures of Native Americans. Viking Fund Publications in Anthropology, No. 6, ed. Cornelius Osgood, pp. 85-129. Reprint by Johnson Reprint Company, New York, NY.

Bordes, Francois
(1970) The Old Stone Age. McGraw-Hill Publishers, New York, NY.

Bormann, F. H. and F. E. Likens
(1994) Pattern and Process in a Forested Ecosystem. Springer-Verlag, New York, NY.

Bottoms, Edward
(1999) Summary Report on the Dime Site (44SK92), Suffolk, Virginia. ASV Quarterly Bulletin, Vol. 54, No. 3, pp. 166-171.

Boyce-Ballweber, Hettie L.
(1988) Geophysical Applications in Archeology and Their Use in Maryland. Maryland Archeology, Vol. 24, No. 1, pp. 1-9.
(1987) Cultural Manifestations at the Friendsville Site in Garrett County, Maryland. Pennsylvania Archaeologist Vol. 57, No. 2, pp. 61-63.

Boyd, C. Clifford, Jr.
(1989) Paleoindian Paleoecology and Subsistence in Virginia. In: Paleoindian Research in Virginia – A Synthesis, eds. M. Wittkofski and T. Reinhart, Special Publication Number 19, Archeological Society of Virginia.

Boyd, V. G., E. A. Moore, and R. J. Dent
(1990) Phase III Archaeological Investigations of 18AN572, Anne Arundel County, Maryland. Potomac River Archeological Survey, Washington, DC.

Bradbury, Andrew P. and Jay D. Franklin
(2000) Raw Material Variability, Package Size and Mass Analysis. Lithic Technology, Vol. 25, pp. 62-78.

Bradbury, Andrew P and Philip J. Carr
(1999) Examining Stage and Continuum Models of Flake Debris Analysis: An Experimental Approach. Journal of Archaeological Science, Vol. 26, pp. 105-116.

Bradley, Bruce A.
(1975) Lithic Reduction Sequences: A Glossary and Discussion. In: Lithic Technology – Making and Using Stone Tools, ed. E. Swanson, Aldine Press, Chicago, IL.

Bray, Robert
(1956) The Culture-Complexes and Sequences at the Rice Site (23SN200) Stone County, Missouri. Missouri Archaeologist, Vol. 18.

Brennan, Louis A.
(1975) Artifacts of Prehistoric America. Stackpole Books, Harrisburg, PA.
(1974) The Lower Hudson: A Decade of Shell Middens. Archaeology of Eastern North America, Vol. 2, pp. 81-93.
(1970) The Twombly Landing Site. Bulletin, New York State Archaeological Association, No. 49.
(1970) American Dawn: A New Model of American Prehistory. Macmillan, New York, NY.

Brew, John O.
(1946) Archaeology of Alkali Ridge, Southwestern Utah. Papers, Vol. XXI, Peabody Museum of American Archaeology and Ethnology.

Bromberg, Francine Weiss
(1987) Site Distribution in the Coastal Plain and Fall Zone of the Potomac Valley from ca 6500 BC to 1400 AD. M.A. Thesis, Catholic University of America, Washington, DC.

Brose, D.
(1975) Functional Analysis of Stone Tools: A Cautionary Note on the Role of Animal Fats. American Antiquity, Vol. 40, pp. 86-94.

Brown, Larry N.
(1997) A Guide to the Mammals of the Southeastern United States. University of Tennessee, Knoxville, TN.

Brown, Lois
(n.d.) The Distribution of Paleo-Indian Projectile Points in Maryland. M.S. Division of Archaeology, Maryland Geological Survey, Baltimore.

Broyles, Bettye
(1971) The St Albans Site, Kanawha County, West Virginia. West Virginia Geological Survey, Report of Archaeological Investigations, Morgantown, WV.
(1966) Preliminary Report: The St Albans Site (46Ka27), Kanawha County, West Virginia. West Virginia Archeologist, No. 19, pp. 1-43.

Brunner, D. B.
(1897 2nd ed) The Indians of Berks County, PA., Being a Summary of All the Tangible Records of the Aborigines of Berks County, with Cuts and Descriptions of the Varieties of Relics Found within the County. Eagle Book Point, Reading, PA.

Brush, G.
(1986) Geology and Paleoecology of Chesapeake Estuaries. Journal of the Washington Academy of Science, Vol. 76, No. 3, pp. 146-160.
(1982) An Environmental Analysis of Forest Patterns. American Scientist, Vol. 17, pp. 18-25.

Bullin, Ripley P.
(1975) A Guide to the Identification of Florida Projectile Points. Kendall Books, Gainesville, FL.
(1968) A Guide to the Identification of Florida Projectile Points. Florida State Museum, University of Florida, Gainesville, FL.
(1958) Six sites Near the Chattahoochee River in the Jim Woodruff Reservoir Area, Florida. River Basin Surveys Papers, No. 14, Smithsonian Institution, Bureau of American Ethnology, Washington, DC.

Bushnell, David I.
(1937) Indian Sites Below the Falls of the Rappahannock, Virginia. Smithsonian Miscellaneous Collections, Vol. 98, No. 4.
(1935) The Manahoac Tribes in Virginia, 1608. Smithsonian Miscellaneous Collections, Vol. 94, No. 8.
(1930) Five Monacan Towns in Virginia, 1607. Smithsonian Miscellaneous Collections, Vol. 82, No. 12.
(1920) Native Cemeteries and Forms of Burial East of the Mississippi. Bureau of American Ethnology, Smithsonian Institute, Washington, DC

Butler, B. Robert
(1961) The Old Cordilleran Culture in the Pacific Northwest. Occasional Papers of the Idaho State College Museum, No. 9.

Butzer, Karl W.
(1971) Environment and Archaeology: An Ecological Approach. Aldine, Chicago, IL.

Byers, Douglas S.
(1959) The Eastern Archaic: Some Problems and Hypotheses. American Antiquity, Vol. 24, No. 3, pp. 233-256.

Cadzow, Donald A.
(1936) Archaeological Studies of the Susquehannock Indians of Pennsylvania. Pennsylvania Historical Commission, 3, Harrisburg, PA.

Callahan, Errett
(2001) Personal communication (2001 Primitive Technology Weekend, Oregon Ridge, Maryland).
(2000) What is Traditional Flintknapping? Bulletin of Primitive Technology, No. 20, p. 11.
(1995) Functional Motions - Working Wood with Stone Tools. Bulletin of Primitive Technology, No. 9, pp. 50-57.
(1987) An Evaluation of the Lithic Technology in Middle Sweden During the Mesolithic and Neolithic. Societas Archaeologica Upsaliensis, Uppsala, Sweden.
(1981) Pamunkey Housebuilding: An Experimental Study of Late Woodland Construction in the Powhatan Confederacy. Ph.D, dissertation, Catholic University, Washington, DC.
(1979) The Basics of Biface Knapping in the Eastern Fluted Point Tradition - A Manual for Flintknappers and Lithic Analysis. Archaeology of Eastern North America, Vol. 7, No. 1, pp. 1-179.
(1976) The Pamunkey Project, Phase I and II. The Ape, Experimental Archaeology Papers, Vol. 4, Virginia Commonwealth University of Virginia, Richmond, VA.

Calver, J. L.
(1963) Geologic Map of Virginia: 1:500,000. Commonwealth of Virginia, Department of Conservation and Economic Development, Division of Mineral Resources.

Cambron, James W.
(1964) Handbook of Alabama Archaeology, Part I, Point Types, ed. David DeJarnette. Archaeological Research Association of Alabama, Inc.
(1962) The Stanfield-Worley Bluff Shelter Excavations. Journal of Alabama Archaeology, Vol. 8, Nos. 1-2.
(1957) Some Early Projectile Point Types from the Tennessee Valley. Journal of Alabama Archaeology, Vol. 3, No 2, pp. 17-19.
(1956) The Pine Tree Site – A Paleo-Indian Habitation Locality. Tennessee Archaeologist, Vol. XII, No. 2.

Cambron, James W. and David C. Hulse
(1975) Reprint. Handbook of Alabama Archaeology, Part 1, Point Types. Archaeological Research Association of Alabama, Inc., Mound State Monument, Moundville, AL.
(1968) Handbook of Alabama Archaeology, Part 1, Point Types. Archaeological Research Association of Alabama, Inc., Mound State Monument, Moundville, AL.

(1960) The Transitional Paleo-Indian. Journal of Alabama Archaeology, Vol. VI, No. 1.

Cameron, Laurie Dale
(1976) Prehistoric Hunters and Gatherers of the Upper Chesapeake Bay Region: A Study of the Use of a Predictive Model for the Analysis of Subsistence Settlement Systems. B.A. Thesis, Department of Anthropology, University of Michigan, Ann Arbor, MI.

Campbell, B. U.
(1906) Early Mission among the Indians in Maryland. Maryland Historic Magazine, Vol. 1, pp. 293-316.

Carbone, Victor A.
(1982) Environment and Society in Archaic and Woodland Times. In: Practicing Environmental Archaeology: Methods and Interpretations, R. Moeller (ed.), Occasional Paper No. 3, American Indian Archaeological Institute, Washington, CT, pp. 39-52.
(1976) Environment and Prehistory in the Shenandoah Valley. Ph.D. Dissertation, Department of Anthropology, The Catholic University of America, Washington, DC.

Carneiro, Robert L.
(1979) Tree Felling with a Stone Axe: An Experiment Carried Out Among the Yanomamo Indians of Southern Venezuela. In: Ethnoachaeology, ed. C. Kramer, pp. 21-58, Columbia University Press, New York, NY.

Carr, Christopher, and Herbert Haas
(1996) Beta-Count and AMS Radiocarbon Dates of Woodland and Fort Ancient Period Occupations in Ohio, 1350 BC – AD 1650. West Virginia Archeologists, Vol. 48, Nos. 1-2, pp. 19-53.

Carr, Kurt W. and Roger W. Moeller
(2015) First Pennsylvanians. Pennsylvania Historical & Museum Commision, Harrisburg, PA.

Chapman, Carl H.
(1980) The Archaeology of Missouri, II. University of Missouri Press, Columbia, MO.
(1975) The Archaeology of Missouri, I. University of Missouri Press, Columbia, MO.
(1948) A Preliminary Survey of Missouri Archaeology. Missouri Archaeologist, Vol. 10, Pt. 4, pp. 135-164.

Chapman, Jefferson
(1979) The Howard and Calloway Island Sites. Tennessee Valley Authority Publications in Anthropology Number 23. The University of Tennessee Department of Anthropology, Report of Investigations Number 27.
(1975) The Rose Island Site and the Cultural and Ecological Position of the Bifurcate Point Tradition in Eastern North America. Ph.D. Dissertation, Department of Anthropology, University of Tennessee.
(1973) The Icehouse Bottom Site 40MR23. Department of Anthropology, University of Tennessee, Report of Investigation, No. 14, Knoxville, TN.

Case-Dunn, Christopher, and Thomas D. Hall
(1999) The Chesapeake World: Complexity, Hierarchy and Pulsations of Long Range Interaction in Prehistory. Paper presented International Studies Association, Washington, DC.
(1997) Rise and Demise: Comparing World-Systems. Westview Press, Boulder, CO.

Chrysler, M.A.
(1910) The Ecological Plant Geography of Maryland; Coastal Zone; Western Shore District. In: The Plant Life of Maryland by F. Shreve, M., A. Chrysler, F. H. Blodgett, and F. W. Besley. The Johns Hopkins Press, Baltimore, MD.

Cissna, Paul B.
(1986) The Piscataway Indians of Southern Maryland: An Ethnohistory from Pre-European Contact to the Present. Ph.D. Dissertation, American University, Washington, DC.

Clark, Charles B.
(1950) The Eastern Shore of Maryland and Virginia. Lewis Historical Publishing Company, New York, NY.

Clark, Wayne E.
(1980) The Origins of the Piscataway and Related Indian Cultures. Maryland Historical Magazine, Vol. 75, No. 1, pp. 8-22.
(1976) The Application of Regional Research Designs to Contract Archaeology: The Northwest Transportation Corridor Archaeological Survey Project. M.A. Thesis, Department of Anthropology, American University, Washington, DC.
(1975) Controlled Surface Investigations of an Archaic Period Hunting Camp. Maryland Archeology, Vol. 11, No. 1.
(1974) A Grooved Axe from the Piedmont Province of Maryland. Maryland Archeology, Vol. 10, Nos. 1-2.

Clark, Wayne E. and W. Dana Miller
(1975) Projectile Points. In: Report on the Excavation at UMBC Site 18-BA-71, ed. K. Vitalli. Archaeological Society of Maryland, Miscellaneous Papers, Vol. 10, pp. 27-52.

Claassen, C.
(1991) Normative Thinking and Shell-Bearing Sites. Archaeological Method and Theory, Vol. 3, pp. 249-298).

Clayton, Sarra
(1973) The Potomac (Patawomeke) Indians, ASV Quarterly Bulletin, Vol. 26, No. 3, pp. 136-44.

Cleland, Charles E.
(1976) The Focal-Diffuse Model: An Evolutionary Perspective on the Prehistoric Cultural Adaptations of Eastern North America. Midcontinental Journal of Archaeology, Vol. 1, pp. 59-75.

Cleland, Charles E. and Richard Peske
(1968) The Spider Cave. In: The Prehistory of Burnt Bluff Area. Ed. James E. Fitting. Museum of Anthropology, University of Michigan, Anthropological Papers, No. 34.

Cliflin, William H., Jr.
(1931) The Stallings Island Mound, Columbia, Georgia. Papers of the Peabody Museum of American Archaeology and Ethnology, Vol. 14, No. 1, Cambridge, MA.

Cloos, Ernest and C. H. Broedle
(1940) Geologic Map of Howard County, Maryland: 1:62,500. Maryland Geological Survey, Baltimore, MD.

Cloos, Ernest and C. W. Cooke
(1953) Geologic Map of Montgomery County, Maryland and District of Columbia. Maryland Geological Survey, Baltimore, MD.

Cloud, Ron
(1969) Cache River Side-Notched Points. Central States Archaeological Journal, Vol. 16, No. 3.

Clyde, V.
(1959) The Shepard Barrack Site. Archeological Society of Maryland, Miscellaneous Papers, No. 1, pp. 8-9.

Coe, Joffre L.
(1970/90s) Personal communications at early Middle Atlantic Archaeological Conferences and Southeastern Archaeological Conferences. In 1994, he was the author's guest in Virginia; he received the ASV Out-of-State Award for outstanding archeology.
(1964) The Formative Cultures of the Carolina Piedmont. Transactions of the American Philosophical Society, New Series, Vol. 54, Part 5, Philadelphia, PA.
(1952) The Cultural Sequence of the Carolina Piedmont. In: Archaeology of Eastern United States, ed. James B. Griffin, pp. 301-311.
(1937) Keyauwee - a Preliminary Statement. Bulletin of the Archaeological Society of North Carolina, Vol. 3, No. 2, Chapel Hill, NC.

Cole, Fay-Cooper and Thorne Deuel
(1937) Rediscovering Illinois: Archaeological Exploration In and Around Fulton County. University of Chicago Press, Chicago, IL.

Coles, John
(1979) Experimental Archaeology. Academic Press, London, England.
(1979) An Experiment with Stone Axes. In: Stone Axe Studies, ed. T. McClough and W. Ciemmirs, pp. 106-107, Council for British Archaeology, Report No. 23, London.

Collings, Frances d'A.
(1988) The Discovery of the Chesapeake Bay: An Account of the Explorations of Captain John Smith in the Year 1608. Chesapeake Bay Museum. St. Michaels, MD.

Collins, Michael B.
(1999) Clovis Blade Technology. University of Texas Press, Austin, TX.

Connaway, John M.
(1957) The Denton Site: A Middle Archaic Occupation in the Northern Yazoo Basin, Mississippi. Mississippi Department of Archives and History, Jackson, MS.

Converse, Robert N.
(1963) Ohio Flint Types. Special Publication, Archaeological Society of Ohio.

Cook, Thomas G.
(1976) Broadspear: Culture, Phase, Horizon, Tradition, or Knife. Journal of Anthropological Research, Vol. 32, No. 4, pp. 337-357.

Corliss, F. R. and H. T. Wright
(1967) A Preliminary Analysis of Recent Excavations in the Upper Potomac Valley. Maryland Archeology, Vol. 3, pp. 145-153.

Cowan, C. Wesley and Patty Jo Watson
(1992) The Origins of Agriculture. Smithsonian Press, Washington, DC.

Cowan, Frank L.
(1999) Making Sense of Flake Scatters: Lithic Technological Strategies and Mobilities. American Antiquity, Vol. 64, No. 4, pp. 593-607.

Cowin, Verna L.
(1991) The Middle Archaic in the Upper Ohio Valley. Journal of Middle Atlantic Archaeology, Vo. 7, pp. 43-52.

Crabtree, Don E.
(1975) Comments on Lithic Technology and Experimental Archaeology. In: Lithic Technology, Making and Using Stone Tools, ed. E. Swanson, pp. 105-114, Mouton Publishers, Chicago. IL.
(1972) An Introduction to Flintworking. Occasional Papers of the Idaho State Museum, No. 28, Pocatello, ID.
(1966) A Stone-Worker's Approach to Analyzing and Replicating the Lindenmeier Folsom. Tebiwa, No. 9, pp. 3-39.
(1970) Flaking Stone Tools with Wooden Implements. Science 169:3941:146-153.
(1968) Mesoamerican Polyhedral Cores and Prismatic Blades. American Antiquity 33:446-478.
(1967) Notes on Experiments in Flintknapping: 3. A Flintknapper's Raw Materials. Tebiwa 10:1:8-24.
(1967) Notes on Experiments in Flintknapping: 4. Tools Used for Making Flaked Stone Artifacts. Tebiwa 10:1:60-73.
(1966) A Stoneworker's Approach to Analyzing and Replicating the Lindenmeier Folsom. Tebiwa 9:1:3-39.

Crabtree, Don E. and B. Robert Butler
(1964) Notes on Experiments in Flintknapping: 1 Heat Treatment of Silica Materials. Tebiwa, Vol. 7, pp. 106.

Creasman, Steven D.
(1995) Upper Cumberland Archaic and Woodland Period Archeology at the Main Site (15BL35), Bell County, Kentucky, Cultural Resource Analysis, Inc., Lexington, KY.

Cressman, L. S. and Alex D. Krieger
(1940) Atlatls and Associated Artifacts from Southcentral Oregon. Reprint from: Early Man in Oregon, University of Oregon Monographs, Studies in Anthropology, No. 3.

Cresson, Jack
(1990) Broadspear Lithic Technology: Some Aspects of Biface Manufacture, Form, and Use History with Insights Towards Understanding Diversity. In: Experiments and Observations on the Terminal Archaic of the Middle Atlantic Region. R. Moeller ed., Archaeological Services, Bethlehem, CT.

Cresthull, Paul
(1985) A Stone Weeping Eye Face from Harford County, Maryland. Maryland Archeology Vol. 21, No. 1: cover photo.
(1982) Prehistoric Antler Effigy Pendant. Maryland Archeology Vol. 18, No. 2; cover photo.
(1981) Prehistoric Human Face Effigy. Maryland Archeology Vol. 17, No. 2; cover photo.
(1978) Projectile Point Chronology in Maryland: Late Archaic-Woodland Period. Maryland Archeology, Vol. 14, Nos. 1-2.
(1976) C-14 Dates for Early Archaic Point Traditions and Types. Maryland Archeology, Vol. 12, No. 2.
(1975) A Sample of Early Archaic Notched Points. Maryland Archeology, Vol. 11, No. 2.
(1974) Typology of Human Head Petroglyphs from Bald Friar, Cecil County. Maryland Archeology, Vol. 10, Nos. 1 and 2.
(1972) Fishtail and Related Points in Maryland. Maryland Archeology, Vol. 8, No. 1.
(1972) A Sample of Bannerstones from Northern Maryland. Maryland Archeology, Vol. 8, No. 1.
(1972) Chance 18PO5: A Major Early Archaic Site, Pt. 2. Maryland Archeology, Vol. 8, pp. 40-53.
(1971) Chance 18PO5: A Major Early Archaic Site. Maryland Archeology, Vol. 7, pp. 51-52.
(1969) Bifurcate Base & Other Early Archaic Points in Northern Maryland. Maryland Archeology, Vol. 5, No. 2.

Crook, Jr., Wilson W., and R. K. Harris
(1952) Trinity Aspect of the Archaic Horizon: The Carrollton and Elam Foci. Bulletin of the Texas Archaeological Society, Vol. 20.

Cronin, Thomas M.
(1999) Principles of Paleoclimatology. Columbia University Press, NY.

Cross, Dorothy
(1941) Archaeology of New Jersey. Archeological Society of New Jersey and New Jersey State Museum, Vol. 1, Trenton, NJ.

Crowley, Thomas J. and Gerald R. North
(1991) Paleoclimatology. Oxford Monographs on Geology and Geophysics No. 18, Oxford University Press, New York, NY.

Curry, Dennis C.
(2000) Mysteries of Mass Graves. Discovering Archaeology, Vol. 2, No. 3, pp. 40-45.
(1999) Feast of the Dead – Aboriginal Ossuaries in Maryland. Archeological Society of Maryland, Inc. and Maryland Historical Trust, Crownsville, MD.

Curry, Dennis C. (with Douglas and Barbara Ward)
(1992) Ward Cache (18CR198), Near Mexico, Carroll County, Maryland. Maryland Archeology, Vol. 28, No. 1, pp. 33-34.

Curry, Dennis C. and Maureen Kavanagh
(1992) Excavating Rosenstock 1992: Stone Maskette from the Sheet Midden. ASM Ink Vol. XVIII, No. 8, p. 4.
(1991) Carved Bone Figure from Rosenstock Village. Maryland Archeology Vol. 27, No. 2; cover photo.

(1991) The Middle to Late Woodland Transition in Maryland. North American Archaeologist, Vol. 12, pp. 3-28.

Curry, Marianne, Michael J. O'Brian, and Michael K. Timble
(1985) The Classification of Pointed, Hafted Bifaces. Missouri Archaeologist, Vol. 46, pp. 77-187.

Curry, Dennis C. and Jay F, Custer
(1982) Holocene Climatic Change in the Middle Atlantic Area: Preliminary Observations from Archaeological Sites. North American Archaeologist, Vol. 3, pp. 275-286.

Custer, Jay F.
(2001) Classification Guide for Arrowheads and Spearpoints of Eastern Pennsylvania and the Central Middle Atlantic. Pennsylvania Historical and Museum Commission, Harrisburg, PA.
(1996) Prehistoric Cultures of Eastern Pennsylvania. Pennsylvania Historical and Museum Commission, Harrisburg, PA.
(1996) A Guide to Prehistoric Arrowheads and Spear Points of Delaware. Center for Archaeological Research, Department of Anthropology, University of Delaware, Newark, DE.
(1990) Early and Middle Archaic Cultures of Virginia: Culture Change and Continuity. In: Early and Middle Archaic Research in Virginia - A Synthesis., eds. T. Reinhart and M. Hodges, Special Publication Number 22, Archeological Society of Virginia.
(1987) Core Technology at the Hawthorn Site, New Castle County, Delaware: A Late Archaic Hunting Camp. In: The Organization of Core Technology, eds. J. Johnson and C. Morrow. Westview Press, Boulder, CO.
(1982) A Reconstruction of the Middle Woodland Cultures of the Upper Delmarva Peninsula. In: Practicing Environmental Archaeology: Methods and Interpretations, R. Moeller (ed.), Occasional Paper No. 3, American Indian Archaeological Institute, Washington, CT, pp. 29-37.
(1984) Delaware Prehistoric Archaeology. University of Delaware Press, Newark, DE.
(1984) The Paleoecology of the Late Archaic: Exchange and Adaptation. Pennsylvania Archaeologist, Vol. 54, Nos, 3-4, pp. 32-47.

Custer, Jay F. and Glen S. Mellin
(1986) Analysis of "Broadspears" from Delaware: Form, Function, and Distribution. Bulletin of the Archaeological Society of Delaware, Number 22, pp. 1-29.
(1984) Delaware Prehistoric Archaeology. University of Delaware Press, Newark, DE.

Dabbs, Denton S.
(1969) Salvaging the Long Branch Creek Site near Annandale, Fairfax County, Virginia. ASV Quarterly Bulletin, Vol. 24, No. 2, pp. 127-132.

Daniel, Jr., I. Randolph
(2001) Stone Raw Material Availability and Early Archaic Settlement in the Southwestern United States. American Antiquity, Vol. 66, No. 2, pp. 237-265.
(1998) Hardaway Revisited. University of Alabama Press, Tuscaloosa, AL.

Davis, D. D.
(1975) Pattern of Early Formative Subsistence in Southern Mesoamerica, 1500-1100 BC. Man, Vol. 10, pp. 41-59.

deBlij, A. J. and Peter O. Muller
(1998) Physical Geography of the Global Environment. John Wiley & Sons, Inc., New York, NY.

DeJarnette, David, Edward Kurjack, and James Cambron
(1962) Stanfield-Worley Bluff Shelter Excavations. Journal of Alabama Archaeology, Vol. 8, No. 2.

De LaBarre, Reamor Robin
(1958) Chesapeake Bay India Population. M.A. Thesis, Johns Hopkins University, Baltimore, MD.

Deller, D. Brian and Christopher J. Ellis
(2001) Evidence for Late Paleoindian Ritual from the Caradoc Site (AfHj-104), Southwestern Ontario, Canada. American Antiquity, Vol. 66, No. 2, pp. 267-284.

Dent, Richard J.
(2009) Excavations at the Hughes Village Site: Life on the Middle Potomac Valley Bottomland. Maryland Archeology, Vol. 45, Nos. 1&2, pp. 1-28.
(2000) Accokeek Creek: Chronology, the Potomac Creek Complex, and Piscataway Origins. Paper presented at the ESAF meeting in Solomons, MD.
(1995) Chesapeake Prehistory – Old Traditions, New Directions. Plenum Press, New York, NY.
(1993) Paleoindian Occupation of the Potomac River Valley. Current Research in the Pleistocene, Vol. 10, pp. 12-14.
(1991) Deep Time in the Potomac River Valley – Thoughts on Paleoindian Lifeways and Revisionist Archaeology. Archaeology of Eastern North America, Vol. 19, pp. 23-41.
(1979) Ecological and Sociocultural Reconstruction in the Upper Delaware Valley. Ph.D. Dissertation. The American University, Washington, DC.

Deppe, Helen B.
(1972) The Donaldson Site, Arlington County, Virginia. ASV Quarterly Bulletin, Vol. 27, No. 2, pp. 101-113.

Didier, M. A.
(1975) The Argillite Problem Revisited: An Archaeological and Geological Approach to a Classical Archaeological Problem. Archaeology of Eastern North America Vol. 3 pp. 90-100.

Dillehay, Thomas D.
(2000) The Settlement of the Americas. Basic Books, New York, NY.

Dincauze, Dena Ferran
(1976) The Neville Site. Peabody Museum Monographs, No. 4, Harvard University, Cambridge, MA.
(1971) An Archaic Sequence for Southern New England. American Antiquity, Vol. 36, No. 2, pp. 194-198.

Dincauze, Dena L.
(1981) Paleoenvironment Reconstruction in the Northeast: The Art of Multi-disciplinary Science. In: D. R. Snow, ed., Foundation of Northeast Archaeology, pp. 51-96, Academic Press, New York, NY.

Dobyns, Henry F.
(1966) Estimating Aboriginal American Population: An Appraisal of Techniques with a New Hemispheric Estimate. Current Anthropology, Vol. 7, pp. 395-416.

Donn, William L
(1975) Meteorology, 4th edition. Mc Graw-Hill, New York, NY.

Dragoo, Don W.
(1976) Some Aspects of Eastern North American Prehistory: A Review 1975. American Antiquity, Vol. 41, pp. 3-37.
(1963) Mounds for the Dead. Annals, Vol. 37, Carnegie Museum, Pittsburgh, PA.

Drake, Avery Ala, Jr., Scott Southworth, and K. Y. Lee
(1999) Geologic Map of Seneca Quadrangle, Montgomery County, Maryland, and Fairfax and Loudoun Counties, Virginia. USGS, Reston, VA.

Duncan, Gwenyth
(1999) Faunal Analysis of the Potomac Creek Site (44ST2). In: The Potomac Creek Site Revisited, authors, D. Blanton, S. Pullins, and V. Deitrick, Virginia Department of Historic Resources, Research Report Series, No. 10, Richmond, VA.

Eames, Frank
(1915) The Fashioning of Flint. Ontario Provincial Museum Reports, No. 27, p. 70.

Eastman, Jane M., Loretta Lautzenheiser, Mary Ann Holm, and Thomas J. Padgett
(1998) 31DH614: A Prehistoric Lithic Workshop in Durham County, North Carolina. North Carolina Archaeology, Vol. 47, pp. 83-108.

Ebright, C. A.
(1992) Early Native American Prehistory on the Maryland Western Shore: Archaeological Investigation at the Higgins Site, Vols. 1-3. Maryland State Highway Administration and Department of Natural Resources, Baltimore, MD.

Eckard, Christopher S.
(2000) Scraper-Planes of the Coastal Plain of Virginia. ASV Quarterly Bulletin, Vol. 55, No. 3, pp. 170-180.

Echo-Hawk, Roger C.
(2000) Ancient History in the New World: Integrating Oral Traditions and the Archaeological Record in the Deep Time. American Antiquity, Vol. 65, No. 2, pp. 267-290.

Edler, Robert W.
(1990) Early Archaic Indian Points and Knives. Collector Books, Paducah, KY.

Edmonds, Mark
(1996) Stone Tools and Society. B.T. Batsford, Trafalgar Sq., North Pomfret, VT.

Egloff, Keith T.
(1999) Virginia Radiocarbon Database. Virginia Department of Historic Resources, Richmond, VA.
(1991) The Late Archaic and Early Woodland Periods in Virginia: Interpretation and Explanation within an Eastern Context. In: Late Archaic and Early Woodland Research in Virginia – A Synthesis, eds. T. Reinhart and M. Hodges, Special Publication Number 23, Archeological Society of Virginia.

Egloff, Keith and Deborah Woodward
(1992) First People: The Early Indians of Virginia. University of Virginia Press, Charlottesville, VA.

Egloff, Keith T. and Joseph M. McAvoy
(1990) Chronology of Virginia's Early and Middle Archaic Period. In: Reinhart, Theodore R. and Mary Ellen N. Hodges (eds.), Middle and Late Woodland Research in Virginia – A Synthesis. Special Publication Number 29, Archeological Society of Virginia.

Egloff, Keith T. and Stephen R. Potter
(1982) Indian Ceramics from Coastal Plain Virginia. Archaeology of Eastern North America, Vol. 10, pp. 95-117.

Eisenberg, Leonard
(1991) The Mohonk Rockshelter: A Major Neville Site in New York State. In: The Archaeology and Ethnology of the Lower Hudson Valley and Neighboring Regions: Essays in Honor of Louis A. Brennan, ed.: H. Kraft, Occasional Publications in Northeast Anthropology, No. 11, pp. 159-176.

Ehrlich, Paul and Anne Ehrlich
(1981) Extinction. Random House, New York, NY.

Elliott, Daniel T. and Kenneth E. Sassaman
(1995) Archaic Period Archaeology of the Georgia Coastal Plain and Coastal Zone. Georgia Archaeological Research Design Paper No. 11, University of Georgia, Athens, GA.

Ellis, H. Holmes
(1957) Flint-Working Techniques of the American Indians: An Experiment Study.

Evans, Clifford
(1955) A Ceramic Study of Virginia Archeology. Bureau of American Ethnology, Bul. 160, Washington, DC.

Feest, Christian F.
(1978) Nanticoke and Neighboring Tribes. In: Handbook of North American Indians, Vol. 15: The Northeast, ed. Bruce G. Trigger, pp. 240-252. Smithsonian Institution, Washington, DC.
(1973) Seventeenth Century Virginia Algonquian Estimates. ASV Quarterly Bulletin, Vol. 28, No. 3, pp. 66-79.

Ferguson, Alice L. L.
(1940) An Ossuary Near Piscataway Creek. American Antiquity 6(1):4-18.
(1937) Burial Area in Moyaone. Journal of the Washington Academy of Sciences, Vol. 27, No. 6, pp. 261-7.
(1932) Moyaone and the Piscataway Indians. National Capital Press, Washington, DC.

Ferguson, Alice L. and Henry G. Ferguson
(1960) Piscataway Indians of Southern Maryland. Alice Ferguson Foundation. Accokeek, MD.

Fewkes, Jesse Walker
(1909) Antiquities of the Mesa Verde National Park. Bul. 41, Bureau of American Ethnology, Smithsonian Institution, Washington, DC.

Fiedel, S.
(1995) Blood from Stones? Some Methodological and Interpretive Problems in Blood Residue Analysis. Journal of Archaeological Science, Vol. 23, pp. 139-147.

Fischler, Beb
(1978) A Preliminary Analysis of the Projectile Points at the Jeffery Rock Shelter. B.A. thesis, Department of Anthropology, American University, Washington, DC.

Fitting, James E.
(1965) A Quantitative Examination of Virginia Fluted Points. American Antiquity, Vol. 30, pp. 480-491.

Fitzhugh, William
(1972) The Eastern Archaic: Commentary and Northern Perspective. Pennsylvania Archaeologist, Vol. 42, pp. 119.

Flannery, Regina
(1939) An Analysis of Coastal Algonquian Culture. Catholic University of America Press, Washington, DC.

Fleming, Anthony H., Avey Ala Drake, Jr., and Lucy McCartain
(1994) Geologic Map of Washington West Quandral, District of Columbia, Montgomery and Prince Georges Counties, Maryland, and Arlington and Fairfax Counties, Virginia. USGS, Reston, VA

Fogelman, Gary L.
(2001) Artifacts and Early Cultures on the Susquehanna's West Branch. Fogelman Publishing Co., Turbotville, PA.
(1991) Glass Trade Beads of the Northeast. Booklet No. 70, Fogelman Publishing Company, Turbotville, PA.
(1988) A Projectile Point Typology for Pennsylvania and the Northeast. Fogelman Publishing Company, Turbotville, PA.

Ford, Richard I.
(1979) Paleoethnobotany in American Archaeology. In: Advances in Archaeological Method and Theory, Vol. 2, ed. M. Schiffer, Academic Press, New York, NY.
(1974) Northeastern Archaeology: Past and Future Directions. Annual Review of Anthropology, pp. 385-413.

Ford, T. Latimer
(1976) Adena Sites on Chesapeake Bay. Archaeology of Eastern North America, Vol. 4, pp. 63-88.

Ford, James A. and Clarence H. Webb
(1956) Poverty Point, A Late Archaic Site in Louisiana. American Museum of Natural History, Anthropological Papers, Vol. 46, Pt. I.

Ford, James A., Philip Phillips, and William G. Haag
(1955) The Jaketown Site in West Central Mississippi. American Museum of Natural History, Anthropological Papers Vol. 46, No. 1, pp. 1-136.

Foster, Robert J.
(1988) General Geology. Merrill Publishing Company, Columbus, OH.

Fowke, G.
(1894) Archaeologic Investigations of the James and Potomac Valleys. Bureau of American Ethnology, Bulletin 23.

Fowler, William S.
(1976) A Handbook of Indian Artifacts from Southern New England. Massachusetts Archaeological Society.
(1974) Figured Art: Its Presence in Stone Age New England. Bulletin of the Massachusetts Archaeological Society Vol. 24, No. 1, pp. 20-24.

Franklin, Katherine A.
(1979) A Late Woodland Occupation Site on Lower Mason Island, Montgomery County, Maryland. M.A. Thesis, Department of Anthropology, American University, Washington, DC.

Frink, Douglas S.
(1996) Asking More Than Where: Developing A Site Contextual Model Based on Reconstructing Past Environments. North American Archaeologist, Vol. 17, No. 4, pp. 307-336.

Frison, George
(1968) A Functional Analysis of Certain Chipped Stone Tools. American Antiquity, Vol. 33, pp. 149-155.

Frye, Keith
(1990) Roadside Geology of Virginia. Mountain Press Publishing Company, Missoula, MT.

Funk, Robert E.
(1991) The Middle Archaic in New York. Journal of Middle Atlantic Archaeology, Vol. 7, pp. 7-18.
(1978) Post-Pleistocene Adaptations. In: Handbook of North American Indians, Vol. 15, Smithsonian Institution, Washington, DC.
(1976) Recent Contributions to Hudson Valley Prehistory. Memoir 22, New York State Museum, Albany, NY.

Funk, Robert E. and Beth Wellman
(1984) Evidence of Early Holocene Occupations in the Upper Susquehanna Valley, New York State. Archaeology of Eastern North America, Vol. 12.

Galke, Laura J.
(2000) Inferring Prehistoric Settlement Patterns Using Phase I Archeological Data from the Naval Air Station, Patuxent River. Maryland Archeology, Vol. 36, No. 2, pp. 1-10.

Gall, Daniel G. and Vincas P. Steponaitis
(2001) Composition and Provenance of Greenstone Artifacts from Moundville. Southeastern Archaeology, Vol. 20, No. 2, pp. 99-117.

Gallivan, Martin D.
(2016) The Powhatan Landscape: An Archaeological History of the Algonquian Chesapeake. University Press of Florida, Tallassee, FL.

Galloway, Patricia (ed.)
(1989) The Southeastern Ceremonial Complex: Artifacts and Analysis. University of Nebraska Press, Lincoln, NB.

Garcilaso de la Vega
(1723) La Florida del Inca. 2nd ed, Madrid.

Gardner, William M.
(1989) An Examination of Cultural Change in the Late Pleistocene and Early Holocene (Circa 9200 to 6800 BC). In: Paleoindian Research in Virginia – A Synthesis, eds. M. Wittkofski and T. Reinhart, Special Publication Number 19, Archeological Society of Virginia.
(1987) Comparison of Ridge and Valley, Blue Ridge, Piedmont, and Coastal Plain Archaic Site Distribution: An Idealized Transect (Preliminary Model). Journal of Middle Atlantic Archeology, Vol. 3, pp. 49-80.
(1986) Lost Arrowheads & Broken Pottery. Thunderbird Museum Publication, Front Royal, VA.
(1985) The Paleoindians of the Shenandoah Valley, Virginia. Archaeology. Vol. 39, pp. 28-34.
(1995) A Chisel-Pick from Jackson County, North Carolina. ASV Quarterly Bulletin, Vol. 50, No. 3, p. 47.
(1983) Stop Me If You've Heard This One Before: The Flint Run Complex Revisited. Archaeology of Eastern North America, Vol. 11, pp. 49-64.
(1982) Early and Middle Woodland in the Middle Atlantic: An Overview. In: Practicing Environmental Archaeology: Methods and Interpretations, R. Moeller (ed.), Occasional Paper No. 3, American Indian Archaeological Institute, Washington, CT, pp. 53-86.
(1981) Paleoindian Settlement Pattern and Site Distribution in the Middle Atlantic. In: Anthropological Careers: Essays Presented to the Anthropological Society of Washington during its Centennial Year 1979, ed. R. Landman, pp. 51-73, Anthropological Society of Washington, Washington, DC.
(1978) Comparison of Ridge and Valley, Blue Ridge, Piedmont, and Coastal Plain Archaic Site Distributions: An Idealized Transect. Paper, American Anthropological Association Meeting, Washington, DC.
(1977) Flint Run Complex and Its Implications for Eastern North American Prehistory. In: Amerinds and Their Paleoenvironments in Northeastern North America, eds. S. Newman and B. Salwen, Annals of the New York Academy of Science, No. 288, pp. 257-263.
(1975) Early Pottery in Eastern North America: a Viewpoint. In Proceedings of the 6th Middle Atlantic Archaeology Conference, pp. 13-26, Lancaster, PA.
(1974 – editor) The Flint Run Paleo-Indian Complex: A Preliminary Report 1971-1973 Seasons. Occasional Publication Number 1, Archeology Laboratory, Department of Anthropology, Catholic University, Washington, DC.

Gardner, William M. and Charles W. McNett, Jr.
(1971) Early Pottery in the Potomac. First Middle Atlantic Archaeological Conference, pp. 42-52.
(1970) Problems in Potomac River Archaeology. Proposal to the National Science Foundation. American University, Washington, DC.

Gardner, William M. and Robert A. Verrey
(1979) Typology and Chronology of Fluted Points from the Flint Run Area. Pennsylvania Archaeologist, Vol. 49, Nos. 1-2, pp. 13-46.

Gardner, William M., S. Gluckman, E. McDowell, and C. McNett
(1969) A Report of Excavations at the Stout Site. ASV Quarterly Bulletin, Vol. 24, No. 2, pp. 133-143.

Geasey, Spencer O.
(1993) A Comparative Analysis of Flaked Lithic and Ceramic Assemblages from Three Rock Shelters in Frederick County, MD. Vol. 29, Nos. 1-2, pp. 43-53.
(1975) The Log Cabin Rock Shelter (18FR27). Maryland Archeology, Vol. 11, No. 2, pp. 6-12.
(1974) Types of Rhyolite Cache Blades Found in Frederick County, Maryland. Maryland. Archeology, Vol. 10, No. 1-2, pp. 1-6.
(1974) Everhart Rockshelter. Pennsylvania Archaeologist, Vol. 42, No. 3, pp. 16-30.
(1973) Albert's Cave (18FR5). Maryland Archeology, Vol. 9, Nos. 1-2, pp. 3-9.
(1972) Everhart Rockshelter. Pennsylvania Archaeologist, Vol. 42, No. 3, pp. 16-30.
(1971) The Stevens Rock Shelter (Site 18FR101). Maryland Archeology, Vol. 7, No. 2, pp. 23-28.

(1971) The Tuscarora Rock Shelter (Site 18FR9). Maryland Archeology, Vol. 7, No. 1, pp. 1-16.
(1968) The Boyers Mill Rock Shelter (Site 18FR6). Maryland Archeology, Vol. 4, No. 2, pp. 25-37.
(1965) Two Small Rock Shelters in Frederick County, Maryland. Maryland Archeology, Vol. 1, No. 2, pp. 31-38.

Geasey, Spencer O., and Hettie L. Ballweber
(1999) A Study of Two Prehistoric Sites Associated with the Highland Metarhyolite Quarry, Frederick County, Maryland. Maryland Archeology, Vol. 35, No. 2, pp. 9-26.
(1992) Archeological Investigations at the Shelter Rock Rock Shelter (18FR431) Frederick County, Maryland. Maryland Archeology, Vol. 28, No. 2, pp. 1-16.
(1991) Prehistoric Utilization of the Highland Metarhyolite Outcrop in the Maryland Blue Ridge Province. Archaeology of Eastern North America, Vol. 19, pp. 75-114.

Geier, Clarence R.
(1996) The Cattle Run Variant of the Savannah River Projectile Point Type. Quarterly Bulletin, Archeological Society of Virginia, Vol. 51, No. 4, pp. 154-177.

Geier, Clarence R. and Warren R. Hofstra
(1999) Native American Settlement in the Middle and Upper Drainages of Opequon Creek, Frederick County, Virginia. ASV Quarterly Bulletin, Vol. 54, No. 3, pp. 154-165.

Gilbert, Jr., William Harlen
(1943) The Eastern Cherokees. Bul. 133, Nos. 19-26, Bureau of American Ethnology, Smithsonian Institution, Washington, DC.

Gilsen, L.
(1979) The Environmental Ecology of Calvert County, Maryland. Maryland Archeology Vol. 15, Nos. 1-2, pp. 1-30.

Gingerich, Joseph A. M. (ed.)
(2013) In the Eastern Fluted Point Trdition. University of Utah Press, Salt Lake City, UT.

Goddard, Ives
(1978) Eastern Algonquian Languages. In: Northeast, ed: B. Trigger, Vol. 15, pp. 70-77, Handbook of North American Indians, W. Sturtevant, ed., Smithsonian Institute, Washington, DC.

Godsal, Frederick W.
(1915) The Fashioning of Flint. Ontario Provincial Museum Reports, No. 27, pp. 65-66.

Gold, Debra L.
(2000) Utmost Confusion Reconsidered: Bioarchaeology and Secondary Burial in Late Prehistoric Interior Virginia. In: Bioarchaeological Studies of Life in the Age of Agriculture, P. M. Lambert ed., University of Alabama Press, Tuscaloosa, AL.

Goodchild, Peter
(1999) Survival Skills of the North American Indians. Chicago Review Press, Inc., Chicago, IL.

Goodyear, Albert
(1979) A Hypothesis for the Use of Cryptocrystalline Raw Materials Among Paleo-Indian Groups of North America. Research Manuscript Series Number 156. Institute of Archaeology and Anthropology, University of South Carolina, Columbia.
(1974) The Brand Site: A Techno-functional Study of a Dalton Site in Northeast Arkansas. Arkansas Archeological Survey, Research Series 7.

Gorall, Robert J.
(2000) The Ancient Shoreline at Hunter's Home. Bulletin, New York State Archaeological Association, No. 116, pp. 1-24.

Gould, R. A.
(1980) Living Archaeology. Cambridge University Press, London.

(1978) Explorations in Ethnoarchaeology. University of New Mexico, Albuquerque, NM.

Gould, R., D. Koster, and A. Sontz
(1971) The Lithic Assemblage of the Western Desert Aborigines of Australia. American Antiquity, Vol. 36, pp. 149-169.

Graham, William J.
(1935) The Indians of Port Tobacco River, Maryland, and Their Burial Places. Published by the author. Washington, DC.

Gramly, R. M.
(1997) Selections from The Sirkin Collection of North American Indian Flakes Stone Points, Knives and Drills, Persimmon Press, Buffalo, NY.

Granger, Joseph
(1981) The Seward Site Cache and a Study of the Meadowood Phase "Cache Blades" in the Northeast. Archaeology of Eastern North America, Vol. 9, pp. 63-103.

Griffith, Daniel R.
(1981) Prehistoric Ceramics of Delaware: An Overview. Archaeology of Eastern North America, Vol. 10, pp. 46-68.
(1974) Ecological Studies of Prehistory. Transactions of the Delaware Academy of Sciences Vol. 5, pp. 63-81.

Griffin, James B.
(1967) Eastern North American Archeology: A Summary. Science, Vol. 156, pp. 175-191.
(1966) The Fort Ancient Aspect. Anthropological Papers, No. 28, Museum of Anthropology, University of Michigan, Ann Arbor, MI.
(1952) Archeology of the Eastern United States. University of Chicago Press, Chicago, IL.
(1945) An Interpretation of Siouan Archaeology in the Piedmont of North Carolina and Virginia. American Antiquity, Vol. 10, pp. 321-330.
(1943) The Fort Ancient Aspect, Its Cultural and Chronological Position in Mississippi Valley Archaeology. University of Michigan Press, Ann Arbor, MI.

Gruhn, Ruth
(1961) The Archaeology of Wilson Butte Cave, South-Central Idaho. Occasional Papers of the Idaho State College Museum, No. 6.

Gulliford, Andrew
(2000) Sacred Objects and Sacred Places – Preserving Tribal Traditions. University Press of Colorado, Boulder, CO.

Guzy, Dan
(2001) Personal communication.
(1999) Fish Weirs in the Upper Potomac River. Maryland Archeology, Vol. 35, No. 1, pp. 1-24.

Haile, Edward W.
(1998) Jamestown Narratives – Eyewitness Accounts of the Virginia Colony – The First Decade: 1607-1617. Round House, Champlain, VA.

Hakluyt, Richard
(1851) The Discovery and Conquest of Terra Florida by Don Ferdinando de Soto, written by Elvas. A 1611 reprint edition by William B. Rye, London.

Hampton, O. W.
(1999) Culture of Stone. Texas A & M University Press, College Station, TX.

Hamilton, T. M.
(1972) Native American Bows. G. Shumway, York, PA. Also, (1982) Special Publication No. 5, Missouri Archaeological Society, Columbia, MO.

Hancock, James E.
(1927) The Indians of the Chesapeake Bay Section. Maryland Historical Magazine, Vol. 22, pp. 23-40.

Handsman, Russell G.
(1977) The Bushkill Complex as an Anomaly: Unmasking the Ideologies of American Archaeology. Ph.D. Dissertation. American University, Washington, DC.
(1970) Catoctin Creek: A Multi-Component Site in the Upper Potomac Valley. Manuscript: Department of Anthropology, American University, Washington, DC.

Hantman, Jeffrey L.
(1990) Virginia in a North American Perspective. In: Early and Middle Archaic Research in Virginia - A Synthesis, eds. T. Reinhart and M. Hodges, Special Publication Number 22, Archeological Society of Virginia.
(1990) Between Powhatan and Quirank: Reconstructing Monacan Culture and History in the Context of Jamestown. American Anthropologist, Vol. 92, No. 3, pp. 676-90.

Hantman, Jeffrey L. and Michael J. Klein
(1992) Middle and Late Woodland Archaeology in Piedmont Virginia. In: Middle and Late Woodland Research in Virginia – A Synthesis, eds. T. Reinhart and M. Hodges, Special Publication Number 29, Archeological Society of Virginia.

Hantman, Jeffrey L., Karenne Wood, and Diane Shields
(2000) Writing Collaborative History. Archaeology, Vol. 53, No. 5, pp.56-61.

Hariot [Harriot], Thomas
(1893) Narrative of the First English Plantation of Virginia. Reprint, London. Earlier versions are 1588 and 1590.
(1590; reprint 1972) A briefe and true report of the new found land of Virginia. Dover Publications, Inc., New York, NY.

Harrington, John P.
(1955) The Original Stracy Vocabulary of the Indian Language. Anthropological Papers, No. 46, Bur of American Ethnography, Bul. 157, pp.189-202.

Harris, Marvin
(1968) The Rise of Anthropological Theory. Thomas Y. Crowell Company, New York, NY.

Hassan, Fekri A.
(1981) Demographic Archaeology. Academic Press, New York, NY.

Hastings, Jerry
(1970) The Grumman Site (44LD20): An Archaic Surface Site in Loudoun County, Virginia. ASV Quarterly Bulletin, Vol. 25, No. 1, pp. 46-48.

Hawks, E. W. and Ralph Linton
(1916) A Pre-Lanape Site in New Jersey, University of Pennsylvania, University Museum Anthropological Publications, Vol. 6, No. 3.

Hayden, Brian
(1993) Archaeology - The Science of Once and Future Things. W.H. Freeman and Company, New York, NY.
(1987) Lithic Studies Among the Contemporary Highland Maya. University of Arizona Press, Tucson, AZ.
(1982) Interaction Parameters and the Demise of Paleoindian Craftsmanship. Plains Anthropologist 27(96):109-123.
(1979) Lithic Use-Wear Analysis. Academic Press, New York, NY.

Haynes, Jr., C. Vance
(1993) Clovis-Folsom Geochronology and Climate Change. In: From Kostenki to Clovis – Upper Paleolithic-Paleoindian Adaptations, eds. O. Soffer and N. Praslov, Plenum Press, New York, NY.

Heizer, Robert and Adam Treganya
(1944) California Indian Mines and Quarries. California Journal of Mines and Geology, Vol. 40, No. 3.

Hester, Thomas R. and Robert Heizer
(1973) Arrow Points of Knives? Comments on the Proposed Function of Stockton Point. American Antiquity, Vol. 38, pp. 220-221.

Hickey, Joseph Vincent
(1970) The Prehistory of Southeastern Charles County, Maryland: An Archaeological Reconnaissance of the Zekiah Swamp. M.A. Thesis, Department of Anthropology, George Washington University, Washington, DC.

Hill, J. N. and R. K. Evans
(1972) A Model for Classification and Typology. In: Models in Archaeology. D. L. Clarke, ed., pp. 231-273. Duckworth. London, England.

Hobbs, Horace P.
(1967) Rock Dams on the Potomac River. National Park Services Magazine, August, pp. 14-19.
(1966) Rock Dams in the Upper Potomac (Conclusion?). ASV Quarterly Bulletin, Vol. 21, No. 1, pp. 21-23.
(1965) Rock Dams in the Upper Potomac (Continued) ASV Quarterly Bulletin, Vol. 19, No. 4, pp. 96.
(1965) Rock Dams in the Upper Potomac, III. ASV Quarterly Bulletin, Vol. 20, No. 2, pp. 51-53.
(1964) Rock Dams in the Upper Potomac. ASV Quarterly Bulletin, Vol. 18, No. 3, pp. 55-60.

Hobson, C. A.
(1964) The Crystalline Rocks of Howard and Montgomery Counties. In: The Geology of Howard and Montgomery Counties, Maryland. Maryland Geological Survey, Baltimore, MD.

Hodges, Mary Ellen
(1993) The Archaeology of Native American Life in Virginia in the Context of European Contact: Review of Past Research. In: The Archaeology of 17th Century Virginia, eds. T. Reinhart and D. Pogue, ASV Special Publication No. 30, pp. 1-66.

Hoffman, Darla S.
(2001) Late Woodland Engraved Shell Gorgets from Virginia, West Virginia, and Beyond. ASV Quarterly Bulletin, Vol. 56, No. 2, pp. 68-76.

Holland, C. G.
(1983) Dams. ASV Quarterly Bulletin, Vol. 38, No. 2, pp. 80-107.
(1970) An Archeological Survey of Southwest Virginia. Smithsonian Contributions to Anthropology, No. 12.
(1960) Preceramic and Ceramic Cultural Patterns in Northwest Virginia, Smithsonian Institution, Bureau of American Ethnology, Bul. 173, pp. 1-263.
(1955) An Analysis of Projectile Points and Large Blades. In: A Ceramic Study of Virginia Archeology by Clifford Evans, pp. 165-195. Smithsonian Institution Bureau of American Ethnology Bulletin 160.

Holmes, William H.
(1919) Handbook of Aboriginal American Antiquities. Bureau of American Ethnology, Bul. 30, Washington, DC.
(1907) Aboriginal Shell Heaps of the Middle Atlantic Tidewater Region. American Anthropologist Vol. 9, No. 1, pp. 113-128.
(1903) Aboriginal Pottery of the Eastern United States. 20th Annual Report of the Bureau of American Ethnology, Washington, DC.
(1897) Stone Implements of the Potomac-Chesapeake Tidewater Province. Bureau of American Ethnology Annual Report, 1893-94, pp. 13-152.
(1890) A Quarry Workshop of Flaked Stone Implement Makers in the District of Columbia. American Anthropologists, Vol. 3, pp. 1-26.
(1891) Manufacture of Stone Arrow-points. American Anthropologist, Vol. 4, pp. 49-58.

(1883) Art in Shell of the Ancient Americans. 2nd Annual Report of the Bureau of American Ethnology, pp. 179-305.

Holzapfel, Elaine
(2001) Fluted Point Survey of the Darke County, Ohio Area. Ohio Archaeologist, Vol. 51, No. 2, pp. 6-10.

Howard, Edgar B.
(1935) Evidence of Early Man in North America. Museum Journal, University of Pennsylvania, Vol. 24, Nos. 2-3.

Howell, David H.
(1939) Comment Concerning Certain Mineralogical Terminology. Notebook, Society for American Archaeology, pp. 42-45.

Hranicky, Wm Jack
(2016) The Arrowhead in Virginia. Virginia Academic Press, Alexandria, VA.
(2015) North American Projectile Points. AuthorHouse, Bloomington, IN.
(2015) Virginia Fixed and Portable Artworks. Virginia Academic Press, Alexandria, VA.
(2015) The Arrowhead in Virginia. Virginia Academin Press, Alexandria, VA.
(2015) Quartzite Legacy Among the Paleoindians of Virginia. Journal of Middle Atlantic Archaeology, Vol. 31, pp. 129-140.
(2012) Bipoints Before Clovis. Universal-Publishers, Boca Raton, FL.
(2011) The Adena Culture of the Sandy Hill Area, Dorchester County, Maryland. AuthorHouse, Bloomington, IN.
(2010) Pre-Clovis in Virginia: A Matter of Antiquity. Archaeology of Eastern North America, Vo. l38, pp. 53-62.
(2008) Lithic Distribution for Paleopoints in Virginia. ASV Quarterly Bulletin, Vol. 64, No. 2, pp. 49-64.
(2008) the Eastern U.S. Continental Shelf: A Late Pleistocene and Early Holocene Focus in Virginia. Journal on Middle Atlantic Archaeology, Vol. 24, pp. 45-55.
(2007) A Solutrean Landfall on the U.S. Atlantic Coast? Middle Atlantic Journal of Archaeology, Vol. 23, pp. 1-15.
(2007) Experimental Archaeology - A Science for Studying Native American Prehistoric Technology. AuthorHouse, Bloomington, IN.
(2007 - Revised) Prehistoric Projectile Points Found Along the Atlantic Coastal Plain. Universal Publisher, Boca Raton, FL.
(2002) Lithic Technology in the Middle Potomac River Valley of Maryland and Virginia. Kluwer Academic/Plenum Publishers, New York, NY.
(2002a) Analytical Concepts for Prehistoric Stone Tools. To be published.
(2002b) Indian Stone Tools for the Commonwealth of Virginia. Virginia Academic Press, Alexandria, VA.
(2001) Projectile Points for the Commonwealth of Virginia. Virginia Academic Press, Alexandria, VA.
(2001) Difficult Run Petroglyphs (44FX2380): A Solar Observatory in the Potomac River Valley of Virginia. ASV Quarterly Bulletin, Vol. 56, No. 2, pp. 37-50.
(1997) ASV Backlog Project. ASV Quarterly Bulletin, Vol. 52, No. 2, pp. 90-91.
(1996) Arrowheads, Antiques, Relics, and Junque. ASV Quarterly Bulletin, Vol. 51, No. 3, pp. 118-138.
(1996) Prehistoric Technology as a Continuum. Paper presented at the Middle Atlantic Archaeological Conference, Ocean City, MD.
(1995) Clovis Technology in Virginia. ASV Special Publication Number 31, Pt. 1.
(1995) Prehistoric Axes, Celts, Bannerstones, and Other Large Tools in Virginia and Various States. ASV Special Publication Number 34.
(1995) Flake Points. ASV Quarterly Bulletin, Vol. 50, No. 3, p. 37.
(1994) Middle Atlantic Projectile Point Typology and Nomenclature. ASV Special Publication Number 33.
(1993) Bannerstones: The Broken Ones. Central States Archaeological Journal, Vol. 40, No. 2, pp. 74-76.
(1993) An Early Archaic Toolkit from Virginia. North American Archaeologist, Vol. 14, No 4, pp. 333-339.
(1993) Late Archaic Tools for Working Steatite in the Middle Atlantic Area. Central States Archaeological Journal, Vol. 40, Nr. 3, pp. 150-151.
(1992) Patination: A Poor Determinant of Age. Ohio Archaeologist, Vol. 42, No. 4, pp. 13-15,
(1992) A Dan River Cache. Central States Archaeological Journal, Vol. 39, No. 4, pp. 1278-180.
(1991) Projectile Point Typology and Nomenclature for Maryland, Virginia, West Virginia, and North/South Carolina. ASV Special Publication Number 26.
(1991) Macpherson Side-Notched Points. Maryland Archeology, Vol. 27, No. 2, pp. 41-42.
(1990) Ammonium-Chloride Treatment of Artifacts. Popular Archaeology, Vol. 19, N0. 1, pp. 6-7.
(1990) Possible Prehistoric Steatite Working Tools. ASV Quarterly Bulletin, Vol. 45, No. 4, pp. 236-240.
(1990) Virginia Paint Pots: Concretion Containers and Small Pots of Ceramic and Stone. Chesopiean, Vol. 28, No. 1, pp. 5-11.
(1990) The Loy Carter Biface Cache from Mecklenburg County, Virginia. ASV Quarterly Bulletin, Vol. 45, No. 2, pp. 84-92.
(1989) Do's and Don't's of Collecting and Displaying Projectile Points. Ohio Archaeologist, Vol. 39, No. 2, pp. 31-32.
(1989) The Lake Mohave Knife. Ohio Archaeologist, Vol. 39, No. 3, pp. 32-33.
(1989) The McCary Survey of Virginia Fluted Points: An Example of Collector Involvement in Virginia Archeology. ASV Quarterly Bulletin, Vol. 44, No. 1, pp. 20-34.
(1989) Wilkinson Biface Cache. ASV Quarterly Bulletin, Vol. 44, No. 3, pp. 170-176.
(1988) The C. Merry Cache. Maryland Journal of Archeology, Vol. 24, No. 1, pp. 10-17.
(1988) Catalog of Virginia Quartz Projectile Points, Part 2. Chesopiean, Vol. 26, No. 2, 1988.
(1988) The Bare Island Point. ASV Quarterly Bulletin, Vol. 43, No. 2, pp. 80-96.
(1987) Suggested Dates for Twenty-eight Middle Atlantic Projectile Points. ASV Quarterly Bulletin, Vol. 42, No. 4, pp. 188-192.
(1987) The Classic Clovis Point: Can It Be Defined? Chesopiean, Vol. 25, No. 1, pp. 18-28.
(1987) The Belvoir Cache of Bifaces. ASV Quarterly Bulletin, Vol. 42, No. 3, pp. 159-170.
(1987) Catalog of Virginia Quartz Projectile Points, Part 1. Chesopiean, Vol. 25, No. 3, pp. 2-16.
(1987) The Single Light Method (SLM): A New Technique in Photographing Artifacts. Florida Anthropologist, Vol. 40, No. 3, pp. 215-220.
(1987) The Quantum Projectile Point Classification. Ohio Archaeologist, Vol. 37, No. 4, pp. 28-29.
(1987) An Edge Trimming Artifact from Maryland. Central States Archaeological Journal, Vol. 34, No. 4, pp. 194-195.
(1986) Dictionary of Terms for American Prehistoric Projectile Points. ASV Special Publication Number 15.
(1986) The Hardaway Point Makers: Big Game Hunters and the River Cobble Tradition? ASV Quarterly Bulletin, Vol. 41, No. 6, pp. 192-205.
(1985) Virginia's Amateur Certification Program. Archaeology of Eastern North America, Vol. 13, pp. 176-177.
(1985) Defining Prehistoric Indian Art. ASV Quarterly Bulletin, Vol. 40, Nos. 3-4, pp. 112-122.
(1984) Virginia Paleoindians: A Perspective on Origins. Chesopiean, Vol. 22, No. 4, pp. 15-19.
(1984) Three in a Crowd in Archaeology. Chesopiean, Vol. 21, No. 3, pp. 32-33.
(1982) History, Objectives, and Goals of the Archaeological Society. ASV Special Publication Number 10.
(1981) Linguistic Sources for the Timucua. Chesopiean, Vol. 19, Nos. 5-6, p.81.
(1981) We Say and Write What We Think – Not What We Mean. Proceedings: 28th International Technical Communication Conference, pp. E-44 to E-47, Pittsburgh, PA.
(1979) Spanish Influences on Pre-Colonial Virginia. ASV Quarterly Bulletin, Vol. 33, No. 4, pp. 160-167.
(1975) A Paleodemographic Study of Prehistoric Virginia Skeletons. ASV Quarterly Bulletin, Vol. 30, No. 1, pp. 1-17.

(1976) Origins for the Fishtailed Fluting Tradition of South America. Chesopiean, Vol. 14, Nos. 1-2, pp. 19-25.
(1976) Timucua Linguistic relationship to the Orinoco Delta of South America with an Archaeological Perspective: Fiber-tempered Ware. ESAF Meeting in Richmond, VA.
(1976) The Ammonium-Chloride Treatment of Artifacts for Photographic Purposes. Chesopiean, Vol. 14, Nos. 5-6, p. 101.
(1975) A Paleodemographic Study of Prehistoric Virginia Skeletons. ASV Quarterly Bulletin, Vol. 30, No. 1, pp. 1-17.
(1974) A Framework of Virginia Prehistory. ASV Quarterly Bulletin, Vol. 28, No. 4, pp. 201-214.

Hranicky, Wm Jack and L. Dale Collins
(1997) Harrison County Petroglyph Site (46H51) West Virginia. ASV Quarterly Bulletin, Vol. 52, No. 1, pp. 23-28.

Hranicky, Wm Jack and Charles S. Bartlett
(1996) A Bird-Effigy Bowl from Southwest Virginia. ASV Quarterly Bulletin, Vol. 51, No. 2, pp. 59-63.

Hranicky, Wm Jack and Ben C. McCary
(1996) Clovis Technology in Virginia. ASV Special Publication Number 31.

Hranicky, Wm Jack and Charlie S. Herndon
(1992) The Cornelius Site Cache (54-s). Quarterly Bulletin, Archeological Society of Virginia, Vol. 47, No. 2, pp. 100-103.

Hranicky, Wm Jack and Charles W. Merry
(1991) The Goose Creek Spike. Chesopiean, Vol. 29, No. 1, pp. 16-18.

Hranicky, Wm Jack and Floyd Painter
(1989) A Guide to the Identification of Virginia Projectile Points. Special Publication Number 17, Archeological Society of Virginia.
(1988) Projectile Point Types in Virginia and Neighboring Areas. Special Publication Number 16, Archeological Society of Virginia.
(1988) Bifurcate Technology in Prehistoric Virginia. ASV Quarterly Bulletin, Vol. 43, No. 4, pp. 172-192.

Hranicky, Wm Jack and Howard A. MacCord
(2000) The Trittipoe Site (44LD10), Loudoun County, Virginia. ASV Quarterly Bulletin, Vol. 55, No. 2, pp. 87-96.

Hranicky, Wm Jack, Scott Silsby, and Doug Dupin
(2013) Two Rockart Sites on the Potomac River Fall Line. ASV Quarterly Bulletin, Vol. 68, No. 1, pp. 18-24.

Hudak, Joseph
(1990) Trees for Every Purpose. McGraw-Hill Book Company, New York, NY.

Hudson, Charles
(1976) The Southeastern Indians. University of Tennessee Press. Knoxville, TN.

Hughes, Richard B.
(1979) A Preliminary Cultural and Environmental Overview of the Prehistory of Maryland's Lower Eastern Shore Based Upon a Survey of Selected Artifact Collections from the Area. Maryland Historical Trust Manuscript Series 26.

Humphery, Robert L and Mary Elizabeth Chambers
(1977) Ancient Washington, American Indian Cultures of the Potomac Valley. GW Washington Studies 6, Washington, DC.

Hurley, G. A.
(1980) A Tribute to Turkey Tayac. Maryland Archeology, Vol. 16, No. 1.

Inashima, Paul Y.
(2012) A Chronological Summary of the Prehistory of the Clark's Branch Site (44FX3226). Quarterly Bulliten, Vol. 67, No. 4, pp. 133-141.
(2011) A Seldon Island Component in the Eastern Piedmont of Fairfax. ASV Quaterly Bulletin, Vol. 66, No. 4, pp. 147-154.
(2011) Supplement No. 1 to "Establishing a Radio Carbon Date Based Framework for Northeastern Virginia Archaeology." ASV Quarterly Bulletin, Vol. 66, No. 3, pp. 89-140.
(2008) Establishing a Radiocarbon Date Base Framework for Northeastern Virginia Archaeology, ASV Quarterly Bulletin, Vol. 63, No, 4, pp. 187-290.
(1999) Establishing a Radiocarbon Date Based Framework for the Northeastern Virginia Archaeology. ASV Quaterly Bulletin, Vol. 63, No. 4, pp. 187-276.
(1992) Radiocarbon Dates Compiled by the National Park Service Eastern Applied Archaeology Center, 1983-1992. ASV Quarterly Bulletin, Vol. 47, No. 4, pp. 162-166.
(1992) A Preliminary Summary of Organic Residues Studies and Their Application on Lithic Materials from the Northern Blue Ridge. ASV Quarterly Bulletin, Vol. 47, No. 4, pp. 179-102.
(1990) Prehistoric Subsistence, Settlement, and Seasonality in the Northern Blue Ridge. ASV Quarterly Bulletin, Vol. 45, No. 4, pp. 227-234.
(1989) Notes on a Randolph Stemmed Projectile Point (?) from the Northern Blue Ridge. ASV Quarterly Bulletin, Vol. 44, No. 1, pp. 47-48.

Ingbar, Eric E.
(1994) Lithic Material Selection and Technological Organization. In: The Organization of North American Prehistoric Chipped Stone Tool Technology, ed. P. Carr, pp. 45-46, International Monographs in Prehistory, Archaeological Series 7, Ann Arbor, MI.

Israel, Stephen
(1998) Archeological Investigations at the Clipper Mill Road Rockshelter (18BA32), Baltimore County, Maryland. Maryland Archeology, Vol. 34, No. 1, pp. 15-32.
(1996) Artifacts. Maryland Archeology, Vol. 32, No. 1, pp. 32-34.
(1996) Preliminary Assessment of the Betty Griswold Fisher Prehistoric and Historic Archeological Surface Collections from Baltimore, Calvert, and Dorchester Counties. Draft manuscript.
(1995) Prehistoric Turtle Effigy on Full-Grooved Axe. Maryland Archeology, Vol. 31, Nos. 1-2.
(1993) Artifacts. Maryland Archeology, Vol. 29, Nos. 1-2, p. 69.

Israel, Stephen S. and J. M. Davis
(1992) The Emge Site (18BA177): Preliminary Report on a Quartz Lithic Workshop in Central Baltimore County. Maryland Archeology, Vol. 28, No. 2.

Israel, Stephen and Randy Whitlock
(1989) Prehistoric Bird Effigy on Small Black Polished Celt. Maryland Archeology Vol. 25, No. 2, pp. 33-34.

Jakes, Kathryn A. and Annette G. Ericksen
(2001) Prehistoric Use of Sumac and Bedstraw as Dye Plants in Eastern North America. Southeastern Archaeology, Vol. 20, No. 1, pp. 56-66.

Jenkins, Ned J., David H. Dye, and John A. Walthall
(1986) Early Ceramic Development in the Gulf Coastal Plain. In: Early Woodland Archaeology, ed. K. Farnsworth and T. Emerson, pp. 546-563, Center for American Archaeology, Kampsville Seminars in Archaeology, No. 2, Kampsville, IL.

Jirikowic, Christine A.
(1995) The Hughes Village Site: A Late Woodland Community in the Potomac Piedmont. Ph.D. Dissertation. American University, Washington, DC.
(1990) The Political Implications of a Cultural Practice: A New Perspective on Ossuary Burial in the Potomac Valley. North American Archaeologist, Vol. 11, pp. 353-374.

Johnson, Andrew
(1999) Powhatan Population Distribution as an Artifact of Contact. ASV Quarterly Bulletin, Vol. 54, No. 4, pp. 236-247.

Johnson, Frederick

(1946) Man in the Northeastern North America. Papers of the Robert S. Peabody Foundation for Archaeology, Philips Academy Andover, MA.

Johnson, Michael F.
(2009) Early Archaic through Woodland Occupations at the Gateway Site (44FX1994). Quarterly Bulletin, Vol. 64, No. 3, pp. 105-138.
(2000) Fairfax County Archeologist, personal communication.
(1996) Americandian Life in Fairfax County – 10,000 BC to AD 1650. Heritage Resources Information Series, No. 3, Falls Church, VA.
(1989) The Lithic Technology and Material Culture of the First Virginians: An Eastern Clovis Perspective. In: Paleoindian Research in Virginia – A Synthesis, eds. M. Witikofsi and T. Reinhart, Special Publication Number 19, Archeological Society of Virginia.

Jonas, A. I.
(1928) Geologic Map of Carroll County, Maryland. Maryland Geological Survey, Baltimore, MD.

Jonas, A. I. and G. W. Stose
(1938) Geologic Map of Frederick County and Adjacent Parts of Washington and Carroll Counties, Maryland: 1:62,500. Maryland Geological Survey, Baltimore, MD.

Jones, V. C.
(1966) The Story of Turkey Tayac. Maryland Archeology, Vol. 2, No. 1.

Jordan, Francis
(1906) Aboriginal Fishing Stations on the Coast of Middle Atlantic States. New Era Printing, Lancaster, PA.

Joukowsky, Martha
(1980) A Complete Manual of Field Archaeology. Prentice-Hall, Inc., Englewood Cliffs, NJ.

Judd, N. M.
(1940) Progress in the Southwest. In: Essays in Historical Anthropology, Misc. Col., Vol. C, pp. 417-444, Smithsonian Institution, Washington, DC.

Justice, Noel D.
(1987) Stone Age Spear Points of the Midcontinental and Eastern United States. Indiana University Press, Bloomington.

Kalin, J.
(1981) Stem Point Manufacture and Debitage Recovery. Archaeology of Eastern North America, Vol. 9, pp. 134-75.

Karklins, Karlis
(1982) Glass Beads. No. 59, History and Archaeology, Natural Historic Parks and Sites Branch, Parks and Environment, Canada.

Katz, Gregory M.
(2000) Heat Treatment and Characterization of Pennsylvania's Stony Ridge Chert. Journal of Middle Atlantic Archaeology, Vol. 16, pp. 143-153.
(2000) Archaic Period Triangular Bifaces in the Middle Atlantic Region: Technological and Functional Considerations. Masters Thesis, Temple University, Philadelphia, PA.

Kavanagh, Maureen
(2001) Late Woodland Settlement in the Monocacy River Region. Maryland Archeology, Vol. 37, No. 1, pp. 1-12.
(1982) Archaeological Resources of the Monocacy River Region. Maryland Geological Survey, Division of Archaeology, File Report #164.

Keel, Bennie C.
(1976) Cherokee Archaeology. University of Tennessee Press, Knoxville, TN.

(1972) Woodland Phases of the Appalachian Summit Area. Ph.D. dissertation, Department of Anthropology, Washington State University.

Keeley, Lawrence H.
(1980) Experimental Determination of Stone Tool Uses A Microwear Analysis. University of Chicago Press, Chicago, IL.

Klein, Michael J. and Thomas Klatka
(1991) Late Archaic and Early Woodland Demography and Settlement Patterns. In: Late Archaic and Early Woodland Research in Virginia – A Synthesis, eds. T. Reinhart and M. Hodges, Special Publication Number 23, Archeological Society of Virginia.

Kelly, Thomas C.
(1963) Roark Cave. Bulletin of the Texas Archaeological Society, Vol. 33.

Kemble, Allen
(1999) A Pennsylvania Meadowood Cache. Indian Artifact Magazine, Vol. 18, No. 3, pp. 10-11.

Kempe, D. R. and J. A. Templeman
(1983) Techniques. In: The Petrology of Archaeological Artefacts, ed. D. Kempe and A. Harvey, pp. 26-53, Clarendon Press, Oxford.

Kent, Barry C.
(1996) Piney Island and the Archaic of Southeastern Pennsylvania. Pennsylvania Archaeologist, Vol. 66, No. 2, pp. 1-42.
(1970) Diffusion Spheres and Band Territory Among the Archaic Period Cultures of the Northern Piedmont. Ph.D. dissertation, University Microfilms, Ann Arbor, MI.

Kent, Barry C., Ira F. Smith, III, and Catherine McCann
(1971) Foundations of Pennsylvania Prehistory. Number 1, Pennsylvania Historical Commission, Harrisburg, PA.

Kidder, Alfred V.
(1936) Introduction and Discussion. In: The Pottery of Pecos, Vol. II, by A. V. Kidder and A. O. Shepard, Papers, No. 7, Southwestern Expedition, New Haven, CT.

Kinsey, W. Fred
(1977) Patterning in the Piedmont Archaic: A Preliminary View. Annals, New York Academy of Sciences, No. 288, pp. 375-91.
(1972) Archaeology of the Upper Delaware Valley. Anthropological Series, Pennsylvania Historical and Museum Commission, No. 2, Harrisburg, PA.
(1971) The Middle Atlantic Culture Province. Pennsylvania Archaeologist, Vol. 41, pp. 1-8.
(1959) Recent Excavations on Bare Island in Pennsylvania: The Kent-Hally Site. Pennsylvania Archaeologist, Vol. 29, Nos. 3-4.

Kivet, Marvin F.
(1962) A Report on the Logan Creek Complex. Paper presented at the Plains Conference, Lincoln, NB.

King, Frances B.
(1999) Plant Remains from the White Fort Site. In: White Fort and Middle Sandusky Tradition Occupation of the Black River Valley of Northern Ohio. Archaeology of Eastern North America, Vol. 27, pp. 149-156.

Kinsey, W. Fred III
(1974) Early to Middle Woodland Cultures on the Piedmont and Coastal Plain. Pennsylvania Archaeologist Vol. 44(4), pp. 9-19.
(1972) Archaeology of the Upper Delaware Valley. Number 2, Pennsylvania Historical Commission, Harrisburg, PA.
(1959) Recent Excavations on Bare Island in Pennsylvania, The Kent-Halley Site. Pennsylvania Archaeologist, Vol. XXIX, Nos. 3-4.
(1958) An Early Woodland Rock Shelter in South Central Pennsylvania. Pennsylvania Archeologist, Vol. XXVIII, No. 1.

Klein, R.
(1972) Urbanization and Stream Quality Impairment. American Water Resources Association, Water Resources Bulletin, Vol. 15, No. 4.

Kneburg, Madeline
(1956) Some Important Projectile Point Types Found in the Tennessee Area. Tennessee Archaeologist, Vol. XII, No. 1, pp. 17-28.

Knecht, Heidi (ed.)
(1997) Projectile Technology. Plenum Press, New York, NY.

Knoblock, Bryon W.
(1939) Bannerstones of the North American Indian. Privately published, La Grange, IL.

Knox, James C.
(1983) Responses of River Systems to Holocene Climates. In: Late Quaternary Environments of the United States, Vol. II, ed. H. Wright, pp. 26-41, University of Minnesota Press, Minneapolis, MN.

Kraft, Herbert C.
(1995) Lenape and/or Susquehannock Treasures in Skokloster Castle, Sweden. Bulletin of the Archaeological Society of New Jersey, Vol. 50, pp.1-18.
(1992) Of Fish, Nets, and Sinkers. Bulletin of the Archaeological Society of New Jersey, Vol. 47, pp. 11-19.
(1986) The Lenape - Archaeology, History, and Ethnography. Volume 21, New Jersey Historical Society, Newark, NJ.
(1975) Upside-down Pendants. Bulletin of the Archaeological Society of New Jersey No. 32, p. 33.

Krieger, Alex D.
(1960) Archaeological Typology in Theory and Practice. In: Men and Culture, University of Pennsylvania Press, pp. 141-151, Philadelphia, PA.
(1946) Culture Complexes and Chronology on Northern Texas. University of Texas Publication, No. 4640.

Krogman, W. Marion
(1978) The Human Skeleton in Forensic Medicine. Charles C. Thomas, Springfield.

Johnson, Arthur F.
(1968) New Dates for the Archaic. ASV Quarterly Bulletin, Vol. 22, No. 4, p.172.

Ladoo, Raymond B. and W. M. Myers
(1951) Nonmetallic Minerals. McGraw-Hill Book Company, Inc., New York, NY.

Lafarge, Oliver
(1956) A Pictorial History of the American Indian. Crown Publishing, Inc., New York, NY.

Langland, M. J., P. L. Lietman, and Scott Hoffman
(1995) Synthesis of Nutrient and Settlement Data for Watersheds within the Chesapeake Bay Drainage Basin. U.S. Geological Survey, Water-Resources Investigations Report 95-4233.

Lantz, Stanley W.
(1989) Age, Distribution and Cultural Affiliation of Raccoon Notched Point Varieties in Western Pennsylvania and Western New York. Bulletin of the Carnegie Museum of Natural History, No. 28.

Laubin, Reginald and Gladys Laubin
(1980) American Indian Archery. University of Oklahoma Press, Norman, OK.

Lawson, John
(1860) History of Carolina. Raleigh, NC. Editions are: 1714 London and 1937 Richmond, VA.

Leakey, L. S. B.
(1935) Adam's Ancestors. Longmans, Green, and Company, New York, NY.

Leedecker, C. H.
(1991) Excavation of the Indian Creek V Site (18PR94) Prince Georges County, Maryland. Louis Berger and Associates, Washington, DC.

Leedecker, Charles H. and Cheryl A. Holt
(1991) Archaic Occupations at the Indian Creek V Site (18PR94), Prince Georges County, Maryland. Journal of Middle Atlantic Archaeology, Vol. 7, pp. 67-90.

Leslie, Vernon
(1967) The Lackawaxen Stemmed Point. Chesopiean, Vol. 5, No. 4, pp. 11-14.
(1967) The Milanville Ground Side-Notched Projectile Point. Chesopiean, Vol. 5, Nos. 5-6.

Lewis, Clifford M. and Albert J. Loomie
(1953) The Spanish Jesuit Mission in Virginia, (1570-1572). University of North Carolina Press, Chapel Hill, NC.

Lewis, Thomas M. N.
(1954) The Cumberland Point. Bulletin of the Oklahoma Anthropological Society, Vol. II, pp. 7-8.

Lewis, Thomas M. N. and Madeline Kneberg Lewis
(1961) Eva - An Archaic Site. University of Tennessee Press, Knoxville, TN.
(1960) Editors Notes. Aaron B. Clement Collection, Tennessee Archaeologist, Vol. 16, No. 1.

Lieberman, Beth Py
(2001) The Power of the Old Ways. Smithsonian Magazine, Vol. 31, No. 10, p. 22.

Lippson, Alaice Jane
(1973) The Chesapeake Bay in Maryland: An Atlas of Natural Resources. Johns Hopkins University Press, Baltimore, MD.

Little, Barbara J.
A Chronological Overview for Middle Atlantic Archeology and Some Thoughts of Issues. Maryland Archeology, Vol. 32, pp. 11-29.

Livesay, J. A., James A. Livesay, Jr., and David M. Livesay
(1970) A West Virginia Quarry Blade Cache. ASV Quarterly Bulletin, Vol. 24, No. 3, pp. 198-200.

Logan, Erick N. and Lee Fratt
(1993) Pigment Processing at Homol'ovi III: A Preliminary Study. Kiva, Vol. 58, No. 3, pp. 415-428.

Logan, Wilfred
(1952) Graham Cave, An Archaic Site. Missouri Archaeological Society, Memoir No. 2.

Looker, R. B. and Carl Manson
(1960) Preliminary Survey – Zekiah Swamp. Archaeological Society of Maryland, Miscellaneous Papers 3:11-13.

Loney, Helen C.
(2000) Society and Technological Control: A Critical Review of Models of Technological Change in Ceramic Studies. American Antiquity, Vol. 65, No. 4, pp. 646-668.

Lowery, Darrin
(2001) Archaeological Survey of the Chesapeake Bay Shorelines Associated with Accomack County and Northampton County, Virginia. Virginia Department of Historic Resources, Survey and Planning Report Series No. 6, Richmond, VA.
(1990) Recent Excavation at the Paw Paw Cove Site: A Maryland Coastal Plain Paleoindian Habitation. Current Research in the Pleistocene, Vol. 7, pp. 29-30.

(1988) A Birdstone from Talbot County, Maryland. Maryland Archeology, Vol. 24, No. 2.

Lowery, D. and J. R. Custer
(1990) Crane Point: An Early Archaic Site in Maryland. Journal of Middle Atlantic Archaeology, Vol. 6, pp. 75-120.

Lowie, R. H.
(1917) Oral Tradition and History. Journal of American Folklore, Vol. 30, (116). Pp. 161-167.

Luchterhand, Kubert
(1970) Early Archaic Projectile Points and Hunting Patterns in the Lower Illinois Valley. Illinois State Museum Report of Investigations, No. 19.

Luckenbach, Alvin H., Wayne E. Clark and Richard Levy
(1987) Rethinking Cultural Stability In: Eastern North American prehistory: Linguistic Evidence from Eastern Algonquian. Journal of Middle Atlantic Archaeology, Vol. 3, pp. 1-33.

Luedtke, Barbara
(1992) An Archaeologist's Guide to Chert and Flint. University of California, Los Angeles, CA.

MacCord, Howard A., Sr.
(2001) How Crowded was Virginia in A.D. 1607? ASV Quarterly Bulletin, Vol. 56, No. 2, pp. 51-59.
(1999) Cultural Periods and Transitions: Virginia Prehistory as a Continuum. ASV Quarterly Bulletin, Vol. 54, No. 2, pp. 130-136.
(1996) The Fout Site, Frederick County, Virginia. ASV Quarterly Bulletin, Vol. 51, No. 1.
(1995) The Wilkerson Site, Westmoreland County, Virginia. ASV Quarterly Bulletin, Vol. 50, No. 3.
(1991) The Indian Point Site, Stafford County, Virginia. ASV Quarterly Bulletin, Vol. 46, No. 3.
(1989) The Intermontane Culture: A Middle Appalachian Late Woodland Manifestation. Archaeology of Eastern North America, Vol. 17, pp. 89-108.
(1986) The Lewis Creek Mound Culture in Virginia. Privately printed.
(1984) Evidence for a Late Woodland Migration from Piedmont to Tidewater in the Potomac Valley. Maryland Archeology, Vol. 20, No. 2.
(1980) The Hammarstyom Caches, Prince Georges County, Virginia, Vol. 35, No. 2, pp. 109-110.
(1971) The Brown-Johnson Site. ASV Quarterly Bulletin, Vol. 25, No. 4, pp. 230-272.
(1972) The Mothershed Cache. ASV Quarterly Bulletin, Vol. 26, No. 4, pp. 203-204.
(1970) The Shenandoah Farm Site, Clarke County, Virginia. ASV Quarterly Bulletin, Vol. 24, No. 3.
(1968) The Sours Site, Warren County, Virginia. ASV Quarterly Bulletin, Vol. 23, No. 2.
(1967) An Unusual Jasper Knife from Warren County, Virginia. ASV Quarterly Bulletin, Vol. 22, No. 2.
(1966) Miniature Human-Effigy Heads in Virginia. Quarterly Bulletin Vol. 20, No. 3, Part 1, pp. 66-76.
(1964) The Bowman Site, Shenandoah County, Virginia. ASV Quarterly Bulletin, Vol. 19, No. 2, pp. 43-49.
(1959) Early 19th Century Archeology in Virginia. ASV Quarterly Bulletin, Vol. 14, No. 1-2.
(1958) Indians at Fort Belvoir. ASV Quarterly Bulletin, Vol. 12, No. 3.
(1957) Archeology of the Anacostia Valley of Washington, DC and Maryland. Journal, Washington Academy of Sciences, Vol. 47, No. 12.
(1947) A Bundle Burial from the Keyser Farm Site. ASV Quarterly Bulletin, Vol. 1, No. 4.

MacCord, Howard A. and C. Lanier Rogers
(1966) The Miley Site, Shenandoah County, Virginia. ASV Quarterly Bulletin, Vol. 21, No. 1, pp. 9-20.

MacCord, Howard A., Karl Schmitt, and Richard G. Slattery
(1957) The Shepard Site Study. Archeological Society of Maryland, Bulletin 1.

MacCord, Howard A. and Olier D. Valliere
(1965) The Lewis Creek Mound, Augusta County, Virginia. ASV Quarterly Bulletin, Vol. 20, No. 2.

MacCord, Howard A. and Carl P. Manson
(1952) A Shenandoah Valley Burial Cave. ASV Quarterly Bulletin, Vol. 6, No. 4.

MacCord, Howard A. and Wm Jack Hranicky
(1992) The Fisher Site, Loudoun County, Virginia. In: Richard Slattery and Douglas Woodward - The Montgomery Focus. Maryland Archeological Society, Bulletin Number 2.
(1979) A Basic Guide to Virginia Prehistoric Projectile Points. Special Publication Number 6, Archeological Society of Virginia.

Madonia, Joe
(2000) A Shaft Smoother from Philips County. Field Notes, No. 297, p. 9

Magne, Martin
(1985) Lithics and Livelihood: Stone Tool Technologies of Central and Southern Interior B. C. Archaeological Survey of Canada, Mercury Series 133, Ottawa, ON.

Mason, Otis T.
(1892) The Ulu, or Women's Knife, of the Eskimo. USNM Report for 1890, pp. 411-416, Washington, DC.

Mason, Ronald J.
(2000) Archaeology and Native American Oral Traditions. American Antiquity, Vol. 65, No. 2, pp. 239-266.

McCary, Ben C.
(1982) Obsidian Artifact Found in Virginia. ASV Quarterly Bulletin, Vol. 23, No. 2, pp. 88-89.
(1981) An Uncommon Paleo-Indian Artifact. ASV Quarterly Bulletin, Vol. 37, No. 4, pp. 210-211.
(1975) Bannerstones from the Dismal Swamp Area and Nearby Counties in Virginia and North Carolina. ASV Quarterly Bulletin, Vol. 30, No. 1, pp. 30-39.
(1957) Indians in Seventeenth-Century Virginia. Virginia 350th Anniversary Celebration Corporation, Williamsburg, VA.
(1953) The Potts Site, Chickahominy River, New Kent County, Virginia. ASV Quarterly Bulletin, Vol. 8, No. 1.
(1947) A Survey and Study of Folsom-Like Points Found in Virginia, Nos. 1-131. ASV Quarterly Bulletin, Vol. 2, No. 1.

McDaniel, R. E.
(1976) A Zekiah Swamp Projectile Point. A Stemmed Device With Surprisingly Constant Proportions and Some Hypothetical Justifications. Maryland Archeology, Vol. 12, No. 1, pp. 10-21.

McMillan, Barbara Ann
(1972) An Archaeological Survey of St. Mary's County, Maryland. M.A. Thesis, Department of Anthropology, American University, University Microfilms, Ann Arbor, MI.

McNett, Charles W., Jr.
(1979) The Cross-Culture Method in Archaeology. In: Advances in Archaeological Method and Theory, Vol. 2, ed. M. Schiffer, Academic Press, New York, NY.
(1975) Excavations at the Spring Branch Site. ASV Quarterly Bulletin, Vol. 29, No. 3, pp. 97-123.

McNett, Charles W., Jr. and Ellis E. McDowell
(1974) An Archaeological Survey of Swan Point Neck, Maryland. Archaeological Society of Maryland, Miscellaneous Papers 9.

McNett, Charles W., Barbara A. McMillan, and Sydney B. Marshall
(1977) The Shawnee-Minisink Site. In: Amerinds and Their Paleoenvironment in Northeastern North America, ed. by W. S. Newman and B. Salwen, pp. 382-396. Annals of the New York Academy of Sciences 288.

McNett, Charles W. and Wm Jack Hranicky
(1973) Archeological Survey of Douglas Point, Maryland. ASV Quarterly Bulletin, Vol. 28, No. 3, pp. 157-161.

McNett, Charles W., Jr. and William M. Gardner
(1971) Shell Middens of the Potomac Coastal Plain. First Middle Atlantic Archaeological Conference, pp. 21-31.

McDonald, George F.
(1968) Debert, A Paleo-Indian Site in Central Nova Scotia. National Museum of Canada, Anthropological Papers, No. 16.

McGuire, Joseph D.
(1896) Classification and Development of Primitive Implements. American Anthropologist, Vol. IX, No. 7, pp.227-236.

McKnight, Justine Woodard
(1999) Potomac Creek Archaeobotantical: Analysis of Flotation-Recovered and Hand-Collected Plant Remains from the Potomac Creek Site (44ST2). In: The Potomac Creek Site Revisited, authors, D. Blanton, S. Pullins, and V. Deitrick, Virginia Department of Historic Resources, Research Report Series, No. 10, Richmond, VA.

McLaughlin, R. J. W.
(1977) Atomic Absorption Spectroscopy. In: Physical Methods in Determinative Mineralogy, ed. J. Zussman, pp. 371-89, Academic Press, London.

Manson, Carl
(1948) Marcy Creek Site: An Early Manifestation in the Potomac Valley. American Antiquity, Vol. 12, pp. 223-227.

Manson, Carl P., Howard A. MacCord, and James B. Griffin
(1944) The Culture of the Keyser Farm Site. Papers, Michigan Academy of Science, Arts, and Letters, Vol. 29, pp. 375-418.

Marshall, Richard A.
(1958) The Use of Table Rock Reservoir Projectile Points in Delineation of Cultural Complexes and Their Distribution. M.A. Thesis, University of Missouri, Columbia, MO.

Martin, Paul S. and Richard G. Klein, eds.
(1984) Quaternary Extinctions – A Prehistoric Revolution. University of Arizona Press, Tucson, AZ.

Maslowski, Robert F., Charles M. Niquette, and Derek M. Wingfield
(1995) Kentucky-Ohio-West Virginia Radiocarbon Database. West Virginia Archeologist, Vol. 47, Nos. 1-2.

Maxwell, Hu
(1910) The Use and Abuse of Forest by the Virginia Indians. William and Mary Quarterly Historical Magazine, Vol. 19, pp. 73-104.

Mayr, Thomas
(1972) Selby Bay in Retrospect. Maryland Archeology, Vol. 8, No. 1, pp. 2-5.
(1966) Notched and Grooved Axes in Southern Maryland. Maryland Archeology, Vol. 2, No. 2.

Mason, Ottis. T.
(1895) Origin of Invention. Charles Scribner's Sons, London.
(1889) The Aborigines of the District of Columbia and the Lower Potomac – A Symposium. American Anthropologist, Vol. 2, pp. 225-268.

Mayer-Oakes, William J.
(1955) Prehistory of the Upper Ohio Valley. Anthropological Series No. 2, Annals of Carnegie Museum, Vol. 34, pp. 38, Pittsburgh, PA.

Meeks, Scott C.
(2000) The Use and Function of Late Middle Archaic Projectile Points in the Midsouth. Report of Investigation 77, University of Alabama Museums, Moundville, AL.

Meggers, Betty J.
(1972) Prehistoric America. Aldine Publishing Company, New York, NY.
(1954) Environmental Limitation on the Development of Culture. American Anthropologist Vol. 54, pp. 800-23.

Mercer, Henry C., Edward D. Cope, and R. H. Harte
(1897) Researches upon the Antiquity of Man in the Delaware Valley and Eastern United States. University of Pennsylvania Publications in Philosophy, Literature, and Archaeology, No. 6, Ginn Publications, Boston, MA.

Metzgar, R. G.
(1973) Wetlands in Maryland. Maryland Department of State Planning Publication No. 157. Baltimore, MD.

Michie, James L.
(1970) The Broad River Point. Chesopiean, Vol. 8, No. 1.
(1968) The Edgefield Scraper. Chesopiean, Vol. 6, No. 2.
(1966) The Taylor Point. Chesopiean, Vol. 4, Nos. 5-6.
(1965) The Van Lott Point. Chesopiean, Vol. 3, No. 6.

Mills, Peter R.
(1993) An Axe to Grind: A Functional Analysis of Anasazi Stone Axes From Sand Canyon Pueblo Ruin (5MT765), Southwestern Colorado. Kiva, Vol. 58, No. 3, pp. 393-413.

Mills, William C.
(1922) Exploration of the Mound City Group. Ohio Archaeological and Historical Quarterly, Vol. XXXI, No. 4, pp. 422-584.
(1902) Excavation of the Adena Mound. Ohio Archaeological and Historical Quarterly, Vol. X, No. 4.

Miner, Horace
(1936) The Importance of Textiles in the Archaeology of the Eastern United States. American Antiquity, Vol. 1, No. 3, pp. 181-192.

Mix, A. C. and W. F. Ruddiman
(1985) Structure and Timing of the Last Deglaciation: Oxygen-Isotope Evidence. Quarterly. Science. Review, Vol. 4, pp. 59-108.

Moeller, Roger W.
(1991) A New Interpretation of Late Woodland Features. Journal of Middle Atlantic Archaeology, Vol. 7, pp. 107-126.
(1982) Practicing Environmental Archaeology: Methods and Interpretations, Occasional Paper No. 3, American Indian Archaeological Institute, Washington, CT.

Moerman, D.
(1986) Medical Plants of Native Americans. Technical Report No. 19, University of Michigan Museum of Anthropology, Ann Arbor, MI.

Montet-White, Anta
(1997) Caches. In: The Paleoindians of the North American Midcontinent, edited A. Montet-White. Musee Departemental de Prehistoire de Solutre.
(1968) The Lithic Industries of the Illinois Valley in the Early Middle Woodland Period. Museum of Anthropology, University of Michigan, Anthropological Papers, No. 35.

Mooney, James
(1928) The Aboriginal Population of America North of Mexico. J. Swanton ed., Smithsonian Miscellaneous Collections 80(7), Washington, DC.
(1907) The Powhatan Confederacy, Past and Present. American Anthropologist, Vol. 9, pp. 29-52.

(1890) The Powhatan Indians. American Anthropologist, Vol. 3, p. 132.
(1889) Indian Tribes of the District of Columbia. American Anthropologist, Vol. 2, pp. 259-66.

Moore, Elizabeth A.
(1994) Prehistoric Economies During the Late Woodland Period of the Potomac Valley: An Examination of Animal Resource Utilization. Ph.D. dissertation, Department of Anthropology, American University, Washington, DC.
(1994) Bone and Antler Tools and Decorative Objects from the Rosenstock Site (18FR18). Maryland Archeology, Vol. 30, No. 1.

Moore, Joseph V.
(1999) Thermal Alteration Technology in a Historic Native American Village: Implications and Explanations from Playwicki. Journal of Middle Atlantic Archaeology, Vol. 15, pp. 67-75.

Morlot, A.
(1860) General Views on Archaeology. Annual Report of the Board of Regents of the Smithsonian Institution, Washington, DC.

Morse, Dan F.
(1997) Dalton. In: The Paleoindians of the North American Midcontinent, ed. Anta Montel-White, Musee Departemental de Prehistorire de Solutre.
(1997) The Sloan Site: A Paleoindian Dalton Cemetery in Arkansas. Smithsonian Press, Washington, DC.

Moorehead, Warren K.
(1938) A Report on the Susquehanna River Expedition. Museum of the American Indian, Heye Foundation.
(1910) The Stone Age in North America (Vols. 1-2). Houghton Mifflin Co., New York, NY.

Morrow, Juliet E.
(1995) Clovis Projectile Point Manufacture: A Perspective from the Ready/Lincoln Hills Site, 11JY46, Jersey County, Illinois. Midcontinental Journal of Archaeology, Vol. 20, No. 2, pp. 167-191.

Mouer, L. Daniel
(1991) The Formative Transition in Virginia In: Late Archaic and Early Woodland Research in Virginia – A Synthesis, eds. T. Reinhart and M. Hodges, Special Publication Number 23, Archeological Society of Virginia.
(1990) The Archaic to Woodland Transition in the Piedmont and Coastal Plain Sections of the James River Valley, Virginia. Ph.D. dissertation, University of Pittsburgh, Pittsburgh, PA.

Mounier, R. A. and J. W. Martin
(1994) For Crying Out Loud!: News about Teardrops. Journal of Middle Atlantic Archaeology, Vol. 10, pp. 125-140.

Munford, B. A.
(1982) The Piney Branch Quarry Site: An Analysis of a Lithic Workshop in Washington, DC. Manuscript., George Washington University, Washington, DC.

Munson, Patrick J.
(1966) The Sheets Site: A Lake Archaic-Early Woodland Occupation in West-Central Illinois. Michigan Archaeologist, Vol. 12, No. 3.

Murdock, G. P.
(1949) Social Structure. Macmillan, New York, NY.

Myer, William E.
(1928) Indian Trails of the Southeast, Bureau of American Ethnology, 42nd Annual Report, 1924-1925, pp. 727-857.

Neidley, John W.
(1996) The Archeology of Three Sites of the Goose Creek Watershed in Northern Virginia. ASV Quarterly Bulletin, Vol. 51, No. 2, pp. 49-58.

Neill, Wilfred T.
(1963) Three New Florida Projectile Point Types Believed to be Early. Florida Anthropologist, Vol. 14, No. 4.

Nelson, Charles M.
(1969) The Sunset Creek Site (45Kt28) and Its Place in Plateau History. Report of Investigations, No. 47, Washington State University Laboratory of Anthropology, Pullman, WA.

Nelson, M. C.
(1991) The Study of Technological Organization. In: Archaeological Method and Theory, Vol. 3, ed. M. Schiffer, pp. 57-100. University of Arizona Press, Tucson, AZ.

Nelson, Nels Christian
(1916) Flint Working by Ishi. Holmes Anniversary Volume, pp. 397-402, Washington, DC.

Nemecek, Sasha
(2000) Who Were the First Americans? Scientific American, Vol. 283, No. 3, pp. 80-87.

Newell, H. Perry and Alex D. Krieger
(1948) The George C. Davis Site, Cherokee County, Texas. American Antiquity, Vol. 14, No. 4.

Newman, M.
(1994) Immunological Analysis of Artifacts from Two Sites in Clinton County, Pennsylvania. In: Archaeological Excavations on Kettle Creek: Investigations at 36CN165 and 36CN199, Clinton County, Pennsylvania (appendices), by M. Petraglia and D. Knepper, on file, Pennsylvania Bureau for Historic Preservation, Harrisonburg, PA.

Newman, Walter S. and Bert Salwen
(1977) Amerinds and Their Paleoenvironments in Northeastern North America, eds. W. Newmand and B. Salwen. Annals of the New York Academy of Sciences, Vol. 288, New York, NY.

Nicholson, B. A.
(1976) A Study of Projectile Point Typology at the Stott Site (DlMa1) and Some Observations on Basal Attrition. Archaeology of Montana, Vol. 17, Nos. 1-2.

Nuttall, Zelia
(1891) The Atlatl or Spear Thrower of the Ancient Mexicans. Archaeology and Ethnography. Papers, Peabody Museum, Harvard University, Vol. 1, No. 3.

Oakley, Kenneth P.
(1952) Man the Tool-Maker. British Museum (Natural History), London, Eng.

Odell, George H.
(1996 – ed.) Stone Tools – Theoretical Insights into Human Prehistory. Plenum Press, New York, NY.
(1981) The Morphology Express Function Junction: Searching for Meaning in Lithic Tool Types. Journal of Anthropological Research, Vol. 37, pp. 319-42.
(1980) Toward a More Behavioral Approach to Lithic Concentrations. American Antiquity, Vol. 45, pp. 404-31.
(1975) Micro-wear in Perspective: A Sympathetic Response to Lawrence H. Keeley. World Archaeology, Vol. 7, pp. 226-240.

Opperman, Anthony F.
(1980) A Study of the Prehistoric Ceramics from Maycocks Point, Prince George County, Virginia. Senior Thesis, College of William and Mary.

Orndorff, Randall C., Jack B. Epstein, and Robert C. McDowell
(1999) Geologic Map of the Middletown Quadrangle, Frederick, Shenandoah, and Warren Counties, Virginia. USGS, Reston, VA.

Ortman, Scott G.
(2000) Conceptual Metaphor in the Archaeological Record: Method and an Example from the American Southwest. American Antiquity, Vol. 65, No. 4, pp. 613-645.

Pagoulatos, Peter
(1992) The Re-Use of Thermally Altered Stone. North American Archaeologist, Vol. 13, No. 2, pp. 115-129.

Painter, Floyd
(1991) The Faison Projectile Point. Chesopiean, Vol. 29, No. 1, pp. 22-25.
(1988) Two Terminal Archaic Cultures of SE and NE North Carolina. Journal of Middle Atlantic Archaeology, Vol.4, pp. 25-28.
(1970) The Nottoway River Projectile Point. Chesopiean, Vol. 8, No. 1, pp. 2.
(1964) The Meherrin River Cache. Chesopiean, Vol. 2, No. 2, p. 5.
(1963) The Mussel Eaters of Warratan, Part 2, The Warratan Projectile Point. Chesopiean, Vol. 1, No. 2, p. 6.
(1963) The Dismal Swamp Point. Chesopiean, Vol. 1, No. 3, p. 16.

Painter, Floyd and Wm Jack Hranicky
(1989) The Moyock Point. Chesopiean, Vol. 27, No. 2, pp. 24-26.
(1989) The Lerma Projectile Point Type in Virginia. Chesopiean, Vol. 26, Nos. 3-4, pp. 16-23.
(1988) The Lerma Point Type in Virginia. ASV Quarterly Bulletin, Vol. 43, No. 1, pp. 40-88.

Parfit, Michael
(2000) Hunt for First Americans. National Geographic, Vol. 198, No. 6, pp.41-67.

Parkes, P. A.
(1986) Current Scientific Techniques in Archaeology. Croom Helm, London.

Patton, Bob
(1999) Old Tools – New Eyes. Stone Dagger Publications, Denver, CO.

Patterson, LeLand W.
(1990) Characteristics of Bifacial Reduction Flake Size Distribution. American Antiquity, Vol. 55, pp. 550-558.

Peck, D. W.
(1975) Discriminate Functions for Maryland Projectile Point Types. Maryland Archeology, Vol. 11, No. 2.

Peck, D. W. and T. Bastian
(1977) Test Excavations at the Devilbis Site, Frederick County. Maryland Archeology, Vol. 13, No. 2.

Pecora, Albert M
(1995) Appendix D: Technological Analysis of The Main Site Lithic Assemblage. In: Upper Cumberland Archaic and Woodland Period Archeology at the Main Site (15BL35), Bell County, Kentucky by S. D. Creasman, Cultural Resource Analysis, Inc., Lexington, KY.

Perino, Gregory
(1991) Selected Preforms, Points, and Knives of the North American Indians, Vol. 2, Points and Barbs Press, Idabel, OK.
(1985) Selected Preforms, Points, and Knives of the North American Indians, Vol. 1, Points and Barbs Press, Idabel, OK.
(1968/71) Guide to the Identification of Certain American Indian Projectile Points. Special Bulletin Nos. 3-4, Oklahoma Anthropological Society.
(1969) North Points or Blades. Central States Archaeological Journal, Vol. 16, No. 4.
(1963) Tentative Classification of Two Projectile Points and One Knife from West-Central Illinois. Central States Archaeological Journal, Vol. 10, No. 3.

Peterson, James B.
(1996) A Study of Native Fiber Industries from Eastern North America: Resume and Retrospect. In: A Most Indispensable Art, pp. 1-29, University of Tennessee Press, Knoxville, TN.

Peterson, Torsten E. and Howard A. MacCord
(1989) The Peterson Cache, Prince George County, Virginia. ASV Quarterly Bulletin, Vol. 44, No. 3, pp. 163-169

Petraglia, Michael
(1994) Reassembling the Quarry: Quartz Procurement and Reduction Along the Potomac. North American Archaeologist, Vol. 15, No. 4, pp. 283-319.
(1993) Small Sites Not Forgotten: Investigations of a Temporary Manufacturing Station in Maryland, Journal of Middle Atlantic Archaeology, Vol. 9, pp. 97-116.

Petraglia, Michael and Dennis Knepper
(1996) Assessing Prehistoric Chronology in Piedmont Contexts. North American Archaeologist, Vol. 17, No. 1, pp. 37-59.

Petraglia, Michael, Dennis Knepper, and John Rissetto
(1998) The Nature of Prehistoric Activities on Kettle Creek, an Upland Tributary of the West Branch of the Susquehanna. Journal of Middle Atlantic Archaeology, Vol. 14, pp. 14-38.

Petraglia, Michael, Dennis Knepper, John Rutherford, Philip LaPorta, Kathryn Puseman, Joseph Schulderein and Noreen Turos
(1998) The Prehistory of Lums Pond: The Formation of an Archaeological Site in Delaware (2 vols.). Delaware Department of Transportation Archaeology Series No. 155, Delaware Department of Transportation, Dover, DE.

Petrides, George A.
(1958) A Field Guide to Trees and Shrubs. Houghton Mifflin Company, Boston, MA.

Pike, K.
(1954) Language in Relation to a Unified Theory of the Structure of Human Behavior, vol. 1. Summer Institute of Linguistics, Glendale.

Plew, Mark G., James C. Woods, and Max G. Pavesic
(1985) Stone Tools Analysis – Essays in Honor of Don E. Crabtree. University of New Mexico Press, Albuquerque, NM.

Pond, A. W.
(1930) Primitive Methods of Working Stone, Based on Experiments of Halvor L. Skavlem. Logan Museum, Beloit College, Beloit.

Pope, Saxton
(1923) A Study in Bows and Arrows. University of California Publications in American Archaeology and Ethnology.

Porter, Frank W., II
(1979) The Foundations of Archaeology and Anthropology in Maryland: A Summary Essay. Man in the Northeast, Vol. 21, pp. 61-73.
(1979) Indians in Maryland and Delaware – A Critical Bibliography. Indiana University Press, Bloomington, IN.

Potter, Stephen R.
(1993) Commoners, Tribute, and Chiefs – The Development of Algonquian Culture in the Potomac Valley. University Press of Virginia, Charlottesville, VA.

Pousson, John F.
(1983) Archaeological Excavations at the Moore Village Site, Chesapeake and Ohio Canal National Historical Park, Allegany County, Maryland. National Park Service, Denver Service Center, Eastern Team, Seneca, MD.

Powell, John
(1990) Points and Blades of the Coastal Plain. American Systems of the Carolinas, West Columbia, SC.

Powell, John Wesley
(1895) Stone Art in America. American Anthropologist, Vol. 8, No. 1, pp. 1-2.

Procudfit, S. V.
(1889) Ancient Village Sites and Aboriginal Workshops in the District of Columbia. American Anthropologist, Vol. 2, pp. 241-246.

Prufer, Olaf A.
(1967) Chesser Cave: A Late Woodland Phase in Southwest Ohio. In: Studies of Ohio Archaeology, ed. Olaf A. Prufer and Douglas H. McKenzie, Western Reserve University Press, Cleveland, OH.
(1963) Paleo-Indians of Ohio. Ohio Historical Society, Columbus, OH.

Purdy, Barbara A.
(1996) How to Do Archaeology the Right Way. University Presses of Florida, Gainesville, FL.
(1981) Florida's Prehistoric Stone Technology. University Presses of Florida, Gainesville, FL.

Purdy, Barbara A. and H. K. Brooks
(1971) Thermal Alteration of Silica Minerals: An Archaeological Approach. Science, Vol. 173, pp. 322-325.

Purrington, Burton L.
(1983) Ancient Mountaineers: An Overview of the Prehistoric Archaeology of North Carolina's Western Mountain Region. In: Prehistory of North Carolina, eds. M. Mathis and J. Crow, pp. 83-160, North Carolina Division of Archives and History, Raleigh, NC.

Raber, Paul A., Patricia E. Miller, and Sarah M. Neusius, eds.
(1998) The Archaic Period in Pennsylvania. Recent Research in Pennsylvania Archaeology, Number 1, Pennsylvania Historical and Museum Commission, Harrisburg, PA.

Rainey, Mary Lynne
(2000) An Historic Perspective on Contemporary Classification Systems: The Case of the Ground Stone Ule. Bulletin of the Massachusetts Archaeological Society, Vol. 61, No. 2, pp. 34-44.

Ramous, Maria and David Duganne
(2000) Exploring Public Perceptions and Attitudes about Archaeology. Harris/Interactive.

Rapp, Jr. George and Christopher L. Hill
(1998) Geoarchaeology – The Earth-Science Approach to Archaeological Interpretation. Yale University Press, New Haven, CT.

Redman, Charles L.
(1999) Human Impact on Ancient Environments. University of Arizona Press, Tucson, AZ.

Reeve, S. A.
(1992) Changes in Time: A Seriation Chronology for Southern Maryland. Journal of Middle Atlantic Archaeology, Vol. 8, pp. 107-137.

Regensburg, Richard and Charles A. Bello
(1997) A Selection of Spearthrower Weights from the Savich Farm. Bulletin of the New Jersey Archaeological Society, Vol.52, pp.107-112.

Reinhart, Theodore R. and Mary Ellen N. Hodges (eds.)
(1992) Middle and Late Woodland Research in Virginia – A Synthesis. Special Publication Number 29, Archeological Society of Virginia.
(1991) Late Archaic and Early Woodland Research in Virginia – A Synthesis. Special Publication Number 23, Archeological Society of Virginia.
(1990) Early and Middle Archaic Research in Virginia - A Synthesis. Special Publication Number 22, Archeological Society of Virginia.

Reiter, Paul
(1938) Review of "Handbook of Northern Arizona Pottery Wares by H. S. Colton and L. L. Hargrave." American Anthropologist, n.s., Vol. XL, pp. 480-491.

Reynolds, Elmer R.
(1883) Ossuary at Accotink. Smithsonian Miscellaneous Collections, Vol. 25, pp. 92-94.
(1880) Aboriginal Soapstone Quarries in the District of Columbia. In: Twelfth Annual Report of the Trustees of the Peabody Museum of American Archaeology and Ethnology, Vol. 2, pp. 526-35.

Richerson, Peter J., Robert Boyd, and Robert L. Bettinger
(2001) Was Agriculture Impossible During the Pleistocene But Mandatory During the Holocene? A Climate Change Hypothesis. American Antiquity, Vol. 66, No. 3, pp. 387-411.

Rinaldo, John and P. S. Martin
(1941) Review of "Winona and Ridge Ruin, Part I by J. C. McGregor." American Anthropologist, n.s. Vol. XLIII, pp. 654-656.

Ritchie, William A.
(1969) The Archaeology of Martha's Vineyard. Natural History Press, Garden City, New York, NY.
(1961) A Typology and Nomenclature for New York Projectile Points. Bulletin 384, New York State Museum and Science Service, Albany, NY.
(1955) Recent Discoveries Suggesting an Early Woodland Burial Cult in the Northeast. New York State Museum and Science Service, Circular 40, Albany, NY.
(1958) An Introduction to Hudson Valley Prehistory. New York State Museum and Science, Bulletin 358, Albany, NY.
(1940) Two Prehistoric Village Sites at Brewerton, New York. Rochester Museum of Arts and Sciences, Research Records No. 5, Rochester, NY.
(1945) An Early Site in Cayuga County, New York. Rochester Museum of Arts and Sciences, Research Record No. 7, Rochester, NY.
(1944) The Pre-Iroquoian Occupations of New York State. Rochester Museum of Arts and Sciences, Memoir No. 1, Rochester, NY.
(1932) The Lamoka Site: The Type Station of the Archaic Algonkuin Period in New York. Researches and Transactions of the New York State Archaeological Association, Vol. 7, pp. 79-134.
(1928) An Algonkian Village Site near Levanna, N.Y. Research Records of Rochester Municipal Museum, No. 1.

Ritzenthaler, Robert E.
(1961) Truncated Barb Points from Dodge County. Wisconsin Archaeologist, Vol. 42, No. 2.
(1946) The Osceola Site, Wisconsin Archaeologist, Vol. 27, New Series.

Robbins, Maurice
(1963) A Porpoise Effigy. Bulletin of the Massachusetts Archaeological Society Vol. 24, No. 3-4, pp. 49-50.

Robertson, Victoria Emery
(1976) The Newtown Neck Site: A Surface Collection. M.A. Thesis. George Washington University, Washington, DC.

Rogers, C. Lanier
(1968) The Harbon Site, Warren County, Virginia. ASV Quarterly Bulletin, Vol. 23, No. 2, pp. 90-98.

Rogers, Spencer L.
(1940 The Aboriginal Bow and Arrow in North America and Eastern Asia. American Anthropologist, Vol. 42, No. 2.

Roper, Donna C.
(1970) Statistical Analysis of New York State Projectile Points. M. A. thesis, Indiana University, Bloomington, IN.

Rose, C. B.
(1966) The Indians of Arlington. Arlington Historical Society, Arlington, VA.

Rose, Fred
(2001) Stream Protection Strategy – Baseline Study. Stromwater Management Branch, Department of Public Works and Environmental Services, Fairfax County, VA.

Rosen, Steven A.
(1997) Lithics After the Stone Age: A Handbook of Stone Tools from the Levant. AltaMira Press, Walnut Creek, CA.

Roth, Edmund Walter
(1921) Pressure Fracturing Process: An Omission. American Anthropologist, Vol. 23, p. 239.
(1904) Domestic Implements, Arts, and Manufactures. Brisbane, Australia.

Rountree, Helen C.
(1995) Young Pocahontas in the Indian World. J & R Graphic Services, Inc., Yorktown, VA.
(1993 ed.) Powhatan Foreign Relations, 1500-1722. University of Virginia Press. Charlottesville, VA.
(1993) The Powhatans and Other Woodland Indians as Travelers. In Rountree (ed.), pp. 21-52.
(1993) Summary and Implications. In: Rountree (ed.) 1993a., pp. 206-228.
(1990) Pocahontas's People: the Powhatan Indians of Virginia Through Four Centuries. University of Oklahoma Press. Norman, OK.
(1989) The Powhatan Indians of Virginia. University of Oklahoma Press, Norman, OK.

Rountree, Helen C. and Thomas E. Davidson
(1997) Eastern Shore Indians of Virginia and Maryland. University of Virginia Press. Charlottesville, VA.

Rue, David J.
(1991) Contemporaneity of Late Archaic Piedmont Projectile Point Forms: The Woodward Site (36CH374), Chester County, Pennsylvania. Journal of Middle Atlantic Archaeology, Vol. 7, pp. 127-154.

Saville, Marshall H.
(1925) The wood carver's art of ancient Mexico. Museum of the American Indian, Heye Foundation, Contributions, Vol. 9.

Scharf, John Thomas
(1882) History of Western Maryland. Vol. 2, Louis H. Everts, Philadelphia, PA.

Schmitt, Karl
(1952) Archeological Chronology of the Middle Atlantic States. In: Archeology of Eastern United States, ed. J. Griffin, pp. 59-70, University of Chicago Press, Chicago, IL.

Schock, Jack M. and Terry Weis Langford
(1979) A Guide to Some Prehistoric Projectile Points from Southern Kentucky. Kentucky Archaeological Association, Inc., Bul. 11.

Scully, Edward G.
(1951) Some Central Mississippi Valley Projectile Point Types. Mimeographed paper, Museum of Anthropology, University of Michigan, Ann Arbor, MI.

Sears, William H.
(1954) A Late Archaic Horizon on the Atlantic Coastal Plain. Southern Indian Studies, Vol. 6, pp. 28-36.
(1948) What is the Archaic. American Antiquity, Vol. 2, pp. 122-124.

Sharpe, J. Ed
(1970) The Cherokees – Past and Present. Cherokee Publications, Cherokee, NC.

Shore, B.
(1996) Culture in Mind: Cognition, Culture, and the Problem of Meaning. Oxford University Press, Oxford, Eng.

Skinner, Alanson
(1915) Chronological Relations of Coastal Algonquian Culture. Nineteenth International Congress of Americanists, Proceeding, pp. 52-58, Washington, DC.

Shott, Michael J.
(2000) The Quantification Problem in Stone-Tool Assemblages. American Antiquity, Vol. 65, No. 4, pp. 725-738.
(1994) Size and Form in the Analysis of Flake Debris: Review and Recent Approaches. Journal of Archaeological Method and Theory, Vol. 1, pp. 69-110.

Siebert, Frank T.
(1975) Resurrecting Virginia Algonquian from the Dead. In: Studies in Southeastern Indian Languages, ed. J. Crawford. University of Georgia Press, Athens, GA.

Slattery, Richard G.
(1946) A Prehistoric Indian Site on Selden Island, Montgomery County, Maryland. Journal of the Washington Academy of Sciences, Vol. 36, pp. 262-266.

Slattery, Richard G. and Douglas R. Woodward
(1992) The Montgomery Focus: A Late Woodland Potomac River Culture. Archeological Society of Maryland, Inc., Bul. 2.

Slattery, Richard G., William A. Tidwell, and Douglas R. Woodward
(1966) The Montgomery Focus. ASV Quarterly Bulletin, Vol. 21, No. 2.

Small, Lawrence M.
(2000) A Passionate Collector. Smithsonian Magazine, Vol. 31, No. 8, p.18.

Smith, Bruce D.
(1993) Rivers of Change, Essays on Early Agriculture in Eastern North America. Smithsonian Institution Press, Washington, DC.
(1993) Rivers of Change, Essays on Early Agriculture in Eastern North America. Smithsonian Press, Washington, DC.
(1992) Prehistoric Plant Husbandry in Eastern North America. In: The Origins of Agriculture, ed. W. Cowan and P. Watson. Smithsonian Press, Washington, DC.
(1986) The Archaeology of the Southeastern United States: From Dalton to de Soto, 10,500-500 BP. In: Advances in World Archaeology, Vol. 5, eds. F. Wendorf and A. Close, pp. 1-92, Academia Press, New York, NY.

Smith, D. C. and Frank M. Hodges
(1968) The Rankin Site, Cocke County, Tennessee. Tennessee Archaeologist, Vol. 12, No. 2.

Smith, Gerald P.
(1984) The Hand Site, Southampton County, Virginia. ASV Special Publication Number 11.

Smith, Ira F., III
(1972) Birdstones, Boatstones, and Bar Amulets from the Susquehanna Drainage. Pennsylvania Archaeologist Vol. 41, Nos. 1-2, pp. 63-70.

Smith, Marvin T.
(1987) Archaeology of Aboriginal Culture Change in the Interior Southeast: Depopulation During the Early Historic Period. University Presses of Florida, Gainsville, FL.

Smith, M. T. and J. B. Smith
(1989) Engraved Shell Masks in North America. Southeastern Archaeology, Vol. 8, No. 1, pp. 9-18.

Smith, John
(1986 – original 1624) The General Historie of Virginia. Ed. Philip L. Barbour, University of North Carolina Press, Chapel Hill, NC.
(1986 – original 1612) A Map of Virginia. Ed. Philip L. Barbour, University of North Carolina Press, Chapel Hill, NC.
(1907) Works, 1608-1625. by Lyon Gardiner Tyler, in: Narratives of Early Virginia, 1608-1625, New York, NY.

Snow, Dean R.
(1980) The Archaeology of New England. Academic Press, New York, NY.

Snyder, IV, J. J.
(1967) Heaters Island Site, Frederick County – A Preliminary Report. Maryland Archeology, Vol. 3, No. 2.

Soday, Frank J.
(1954) The Quad Site, A Paleo-Indian Village in Northern Virginia. Tennessee Archaeologist, Vol. X, No. 1, pp. 1-20.

Sofsky, Charles
(1965) The McKibben Site (33Tr57), Trumbull County, Ohio: A Contribution to the Paleo-Indian and Archaic Phases of Ohio. Michigan Archaeologist, Vol. 11, No. 1.

Sollas, W. J.
(1924) Ancient Hunters and Their Modern Representatives. Macmillan Company, New York, NY.

Speck, Frank G.
(1938) The Cane Blowgun in Catawba and Southeastern Ethnology. American Anthropology, Vol. 40, No. 2, pp. 198-204.
(1928) Chapters on the Ethnology of the Powhatan Tribes of Virginia. In: Indian Notes and Monographs, Museum of the American Indian, Heye Foundation, Vol. 1, No. 5, New York, NY.
(1925) The Rappahannock Indians of Virginia. Contributions from the Museum of the American Indian, Heye Foundation, Indian Notes and Monographs, 5.
(1915) The Nanticoke Community of Delaware. Contributions from the Museum of the American Indian, Heye Foundation, Indian Notes and Monographs, 2.
(1909) Ethnology of the Yuchi Indians. Anthropology Publications, University Museum, University of Pennsylvania, PA.

Speck, Frank G. and Claude E. Schaeffer
(1950) The Deer and Rabbit Hunting Drive in Virginia and the Southeast. Southern Indian Studies, Vol. 2, No. 1, pp. 3-20.

Spiess, Arthur and Mark Hedden
(2000) Avon: A Small Paleoindian Site in the Western Maine Foothills. Archaeology of Eastern North America, Vol. 28, pp. 63-79.

Southworth, C. Scott
(1995) Geologic Map of Purcellville Quadrangle, Loudoun County, Virginia. USGS, Reston, VA.
(1994) Geologic Map of the Bluemont Quadrangle, Loudoun and Clarke Counties, Virginia. USGS, Reston, VA.
(1991) Geologic Map of Loudoun County, Virginia, Part of the Harpers Ferry Quadrangle. USGS, Reston, VA.

Speiden, Sandra
(2000) The Thunderbird Site Preservation Project – A History. ASV Newsletter, No. 156, pp. 5-6.

Staats, F. Dayton
(1998) A Hardaway Side-Notched Point from Warren County. Bulletin of the Archaeological Society of New Jersey, No. 53, pp. 114-115.

Stangeski, Andrew J.
(1996) Agate Basin and Dalton in a New Home: 28BU214 in New Jersey. Archaeology of Eastern North America, Vol. 24, pp. 59-80.

Stephenson, R. L., L. L. Ferguson, and G. H. Ferguson
(1963) The Accokeek Creek Site: A Middle Atlantic Seaboard Culture Sequence. Anthropological Papers No. 20, Museum of Anthropology, University of Anthropology, University of Michigan, Ann Arbor, MI.

Stearns, Richard E.
(1965) Indian Village Sites of the Patuxent River. Maryland Archeology, Vol. 1, No. 2.
(1943) Some Indian Village Sites of Tidewater Maryland. Proceedings of the Natural History Society of Maryland, Vol. 9.
(1940) The Hughes Site. Proceedings, Natural History Society of Maryland, Vol. 6, pp. 1-20.

Steponaitis, Laurie Cameron
(1983) An Archeological Study of the Patuxent Drainage, Vol. I. Maryland Historic Trust Manuscript Series No. 34.
(1980) A Survey of Artifact Collections from the Patuxent River Drainage, Maryland. Maryland Historical Trust Monograph Series Number 1, Annapolis, MD.
(1979) A Survey of Artifact Collections from the Patuxent River Drainage, Maryland. Maryland Historical Trust and Department of Natural Resources.

Stevens, J. Sanderson
(1991) A Story of Plants, Fire, and People: The Paleoecology and Subsistence of the Late Archaic and Early Woodland in Virginia. In: Late Archaic and Early Woodland Research in Virginia – A Synthesis, eds. T. Reinhart and M. Hodges, Special Publication Number 23, Archeological Society of Virginia.

Stewart, R. Michael
(1998) Thoughts on the Origins of Ceramic Use and Variation. Journal of Middle Atlantic Archaeology, Vol. 14, pp. 1-12.
(1992) Observations on the Middle Woodland Period of Virginia: A Middle Atlantic Region Perspective. In: Reinhart, Theodore R. and Mary Ellen N. Hodges (eds.) Middle and Late Woodland Research in Virginia – A Synthesis. Special Publication Number 29, Archeological Society of Virginia.
(1989) Trade and Exchange in Middle Atlantic Prehistory. Archaeology of Eastern North America, Vol. 17, pp. 48-78.
(1987) Rhyolite Quarry and Quarry-Related Sites in Maryland and Pennsylvania. Archaeology of Eastern North America, Vol. 15, pp. 47-57.
(1982) The Middle Woodland of the Abbott Farm: Summary and Hypothesis. In: Practicing Environmental Archaeology: Methods and Interpretations, R. Moeller (ed.), Occasional Paper No. 3, American Indian Archaeological Institute, Washington, CT, pp. 19-28.
(1981) Prehistoric Burial Mounds in the Great Valley of Maryland, Maryland Archeology, Vol. 17, No. 1, pp. 1-16.

Stewart, T. Dale
(1939) Excavations at the Indian Village of Potawomeke (Potomac). Excavation and Field-Work of the Smithsonian Institution in 1939, pp. 87-90, Washington.

Stewart, T. Dale and Waldo R. Wedel
(1937) The Finding of Two Ossuaries on the Site of the Indian Village of Nacotchtanke (Anacostia). Journal of the Washington Academy of Sciences, Vol. 27, No. 5, pp. 213-19.

Stewart, Michael and John Cavallo
(1991) Delaware Valley Middle Archaic. Journal of Middle Atlantic Archaeology, Vol. 7, pp. 19-42.

Stevens, Tom and George Whitted
(1979) Two Caches from Southside Virginia. ASV Quarterly Bulletin, Vol. 30, No. 4, pp. 187-189.

Stieber, Tamar
(2000) Obsessed with Old Technology. American Archaeology, Vol. 4, No. 2, pp. 19-25.

Strass, Alan E. and O. Don Hermes
(1996) Anatomy of a Rhyolite Quarry. Archaeology of Eastern North America, Vol. 24, pp. 159-171.

Stirling, M. W.
(1960) The Use of the Atlatl on Lake Patzcuare, Michoacan. Smithsonian Institution, Bureau of American Ethnology, Bul. 173, pp. 265-268.

Stromberg, B.
(1985) Revision of the Late-Glacial Swedish Varve Chronology. Boreas, Vol. 14, pp. 101-105.

Suhm, Dee Ann, Alex D. Krieger, and Edward B. Jelks
(1954) An Introductory Handbook of Texas Archeology. Bulletin of the Texas Archeological Society, No. 25.

Sullivan, Alan P. and Kenneth C. Rozen
(1985) Debitage Analysis and Archeological Interpretation. American Antiquity, Vol. 50, pp. 755-779.

Swanton, John R.
(1952) The Indian Tribes of North America. Bul. 145, Bureau of American Ethnology, Smithsonian Institution, Washington, DC.
(1946) The Indians of the Southeastern United States. Bul. 137, Bureau of American Ethnology, Smithsonian Institution, Washington, DC.
(1931) Source Material for the Social and Ceremonial Life if the Choctaw Indians. Bul. 103, Bureau of American Ethnology, Smithsonian Institution, Washington, DC.

Tankersley, Kenneth B.
(2000) The Puzzle of the First Americans. Discovering Archaeology, Vol. 2, No. 1, pp. 31-33.

Taylor, Colin and William C. Sturtevant, eds.
(2000) The Native Americans – The Indigenous People of North America. Salamander Books, Ltd., London.

Thomas, Ronald A.
(1976) A Brief Survey of Prehistoric Man on the Delmarva Peninsula. Transactions of the Delaware Academy of Science – 1974 and 1975. Newark, DE.
(1976) Webb Phase Mortuary Customs at the Island Field Site. In: Transactions of the Delaware Academy of Science, ed. John C. Kraft, pp. 49-61, Newark, DE.
(1974) A Brief Survey of Prehistoric Man on the Delmarva Peninsula. Paper for the Delaware Academy Science.
(1972) Two Small Stone Effigies from Cecil County, Maryland. Maryland Archeology Vol. 8, No. 1, pp. 10-12.
(1970) Adena Influences in the Middle Atlantic Coast. In: Adena: The Seeking of an Identity, ed B. K. Swartz, pp. 56-87. Ball State University Press, Muncie, IN.
(1966) Paleoindian in Delaware. Delaware Archaeology, Vol. 2, pp. 1-11.

Thomas, Ronald A., Daniel R. Griffith, Cara L. Wise, and Richard E. Artusy, Jr.
(1975) Environmental Adaptation on Delaware's Coastal Plain. Archaeology of Eastern North America Vol. 3, pp. 35-89.

Tidwell, Willam A.
(1967) The Montgomery Focus. Archeological Society of Maryland, Miscellaneous Papers, Vol. 6, pp. 11-15.
(1959) Artifact Typology in the Potomac Area. Archeological Society of Maryland, Miscellaneous Papers, No. 1.

Tilley, C.
(1999) Metaphor and Material Culture. Blackwell, London.

Timberlake, Henry
(1765) The Memoirs of Lieut. Henry Timberlake. London.

Tisdale, John W.
(1964) The Daniel Cache, Mecklenburg County, Virginia. ASV Quarterly Bulletin, Vol. 19, No. 2, p.35.

Tomak, Curtis H.
(1983) A Proposed Prehistoric Cultural Sequence for a Section of the West Fork of the White River in Southwestern Indiana. Tennessee Anthropologist, Vol. 8, No. 1.

Torquemada, Juan de
(1615) Monarquia Indians, Seville, Spain.

Torrence, Robin (ed)
(1989) Time, Energy, and Stone Tools. Cambridge University Press, Cambridge.

Trimble, C. C.
(1996) Paleodiet in Virginia and North Carolina as Determined by Stable Isotope Analysis of Skeletal Remains. M.A. thesis, Department of Environmental Sciences, University of Virginia, Charlottesville, VA.

Truncer, James J.
(1989) Steatite Source Characterization in Eastern North America: New Results Using Instrumental Neutron Activation Analysis. Archaeometry, Vol. 49, No. 1, pp. 23-44.
(1990) Perkiomen Points: A Study in Variability. In: Experiments and Observations on the Terminal Archaic of the Middle Atlantic Region, R. Moeller editor, Archaeological Services, Bethlehem, CT.

Tsirk, Are and William J. Perry
(2000) Fractographic Evidence for Liquid on Obsidian Tools. Journal of Archaeological Science, Vol. 27, pp. 987-991.

Tuereian, Karl K.
(1996) Global Environment Change – Past, Present, and Future. Prentice-Hall, Inc., Upper Saddle River, NJ.

Turnbaugh, William A.
(1977) An Archaeological Perspective of the Ulu or Semi-Lunar Knife in Northeastern North America. Archaeology of Eastern North America, Vol. 5, pp. 86-94.
(1975) Toward an Explanation of the Broadspear Dispersal in Eastern North American Prehistory. Journal of Anthropological Research, Vol. 31, No. 1, pp. 51-68.

Professionally collected. West Virginia Clovis Point with Associated Scraper – Site was excavated. (Photograph Credit: National Park Service)

Turner, E. Randolph
(1989) Paleoindian Settlement Patterns and Population Distribution in Virginia. In: Paleoindian Research in Virginia – A Synthesis, eds. M. Wittkofski and T. Reinhart, Special Publication Number 19, Archeological Society of Virginia.

(1978) Population Distribution in the Virginia Coastal Plain, 8000 BC to AD 1600. Archaeology of Eastern North America, Vol. 6, pp. 60-72.

Tylor, Sir Edward Burnett
(1861) Anahuac: or Mexico and the Mexican, Ancient and Modern. Longman, Green, Longman, and Roberts, London.

Ubelacker, Douglas H.
(1989) Human Skeletal Remains. Taraxacum, Washington, DC.
(1974) Reconstruction of Demographic Profiles from Ossuary Skeletal Samples: A Case Study from Tidewater Potomac. Smithsonian Contributions to Anthropology, Vol. 18, Washington, DC.

USDA
(1971) Selected Weeds of the United States. U.S. Government Printing Office, Washington, DC.

USGS
(1967) Engineering Geology of the Northeast Corridor – Washington, DC to Boston, Massachusetts: Bedrock Geology. U.S. Geological Survey, Reston, VA.

VanDerwarker, Amber M.
(2001) An Archaeological Study of Late Woodland Fauna in the Roanoke River Basin. North Carolina Archaeology, Vol. 50, pp. 1-46.

Vickery, Kent D.
(1972). Projectile Point Type Description: McWhinney Heavy Stemmed. Paper presented at the Southeastern Archaeological Conference, Morgantown, WV.

Vogel, Virgil J.
(1970) American Indian Medicine. University of Oklahoma Press, Norman, OK.

Waldrof, D.C.
(1984) The Art of Flintknapping. Privately published by the author.
(1987) Story in Stone. Mound Builder Books, Branson, MO.

Walker, Karen J.
(2000) The Material Culture of Precolumbian Fishing: Artifacts and Fish Remains from Coastal Southwest Florida, Southeastern Archaeology, Vol. 19, No. 1, pp. 24-45.

Wall, Robert D.
(1993) Archeological Investigations at the Millersville Site, 18AN803, Anne Arundel County, Maryland. Maryland Archeology, Vol. 29, Nos. 1-2, pp. 1-30.
(1991) Early to Middle Archaic Period Occupations in Western Maryland: A Preliminary Model. Journal of Middle Atlantic Archaeology, Vol. 7, pp. 53-65.

Waller, Ben I.
(1971) Hafted Flake Knives. Florida Anthropologist, Vol. 24, pp. 173-174.

Wanser, J. C.
(1982) A Survey of Artifact Collections from Central Southern Maryland. Maryland Historical Trust, Manuscript Series No. 23, Annapolis, MD.

Warashina, T.
(1992) Allocation of Jasper Archaeological Implements by Means of ESR and XRF. Journal of Archaeological Science, Vol. 19, pp. 357-73.

Ward, H. Henry
(1988) Prehistoric Utilization of Ironstone in the Central Middle Atlantic. Pennsylvania Archaeologist, Vol. 58, No. 1, pp. 7-25.

Warren, S. Hazledine
(1914) The Experimental Investigation of Flint Fracture and Its Application to Problems of Human Implements. Journal of the Royal Anthropological Institute, Vol. 44, pp. 416-440.

Waselkov, Gregory A.
(1987) Shelfish Gathering and Shell Midden Archaeology. In: Advances in Archaeological Method and Theory, Vol. 10, pp. 92-210.
(1982) Shellfish Gathering and Shell Midden Archaeology. Ph.D. dissertation, University of North Carolina, Chapel Hill, NC.
(1982) Two Buried Early Woodland Components in the Lower Potomac Valley, Virginia. In: Practicing Environmental Archaeology: Methods and Interpretations, R. Moeller (ed.), Occasional Paper No. 3, American Indian Archaeological Institute, Washington, CT, pp. 13-18.

Washington, W. M. and C. L. Parkinson
(1986) An Introduction to Three Dimensional Climate Modeling. University Science Books, Mill Valley, CA.

Waters, Michael R.
(1992) Principles of Geoarchaeology – A North American Perspective. University of Arizona Press, Tucson, AZ.

Watts, W. A.
(1983) Vegetational History of the Eastern United States 25,000 to 10,000 Years Ago. In: Late-Quaternary Environment of the United States, ed. H. E. Wright, University of Minnesota Press, Minneapolis, MN, pp. 294-310.

Webb, Clarence H.
(1948) Caddoan Prehistory: The Bossier Focus. Bulletin of the Texas Archaeological and Paleontological Society, No. 19.

Weed Science Society of America
(1966) Weeds. Vol. 14, pp. 347-386.

Weiner, Michael A.
(1972) Earth Medicine-Earth Foods. Collier Books, New York, NY.

Wells, G. L.
(1983) Late-Glacial Circulation over Central North America Revealed by Aeolian Features. In: Variations in the Global Water Budget, eds. A. Stree-Perrott, et al. D. Reidel, Dordrecht, Neatherlands, pp. 317-330.

Wells, John H.
(1969) The Witt Cache. ASV Quarterly Bulletin, Vol. 23, No. 4, pp. 157-159.

Wendland, W. and R. A. Bryson
(1974) Dating Climatic Episodes of the Holocene. Quaternary Research Vol. 4, pp. 9-24.

Werner, David J.
(1972) Type description. In: Archaeology in the Upper Delaware Valley, by Fred W. Kinsey III, Pennsylvania Historical and Museum Commission, Harrisburg, PA.

Whittaker, John C.
(1994) Flintknapping - Making and Understanding Stone Tools. University of Texas Press, Austin, TX.

Whittaker, John C. and Michael Strafford
(1998/2000) Replicas, Fakes, and Art: The Twentieth Century Stone Age and Its Effects on Archaeology. Arkansas Archeologist, Vol. 39, pp. 19-30.

Whyte, Tom
(1979) Cultural Resource Mitigation Activities at the McClintic Bridge Site Complex. The Gathright Reservior, Bath County, Virginia. Occasional Papers in Anthropology, No. 4, James Madison University, Harrisburg, VA.

Wilke, Steve and Gail Thompson
(1977) Prehistoric Archaeological Resources in the Maryland Coastal Zone: A Management Overview. Maryland Department of Natural Resources, Annapolis, MD.

Wilkinson, Elizabeth and Vernon Leslie
(1967) The Limeton Point: A Shenandoah Valley Notched-Base Triangle. Chesopiean, Vol. 5, No. 1.

Willoughby, Charles C.
(1935) Antiquities of the New England Indians. Peabody Museum of Harvard University, Cambridge.
(1915) The Red Paint People of Maine. American Anthropologist, Vol. 17, pp. 406-409.

Wilmsen, E. N.
(1968) Functional Analysis of Flake Stone Artefacts. American Antiquity, Vol. 32, pp. 383-388.

Wilson, Thomas
(1889) Chipped Stone Classification. In: Report of the United States National Museum for 1887. U.S. National Museum, Washington, DC.
(1889) The Paleolithic Period in the District of Columbia. American Anthropologist, Vol. 2, pp. 235-241.
(1888) A Study of Prehistoric Anthropology – Hand-Book for Beginners. Smithsonian Institution Report for June 30, 1888, Washington, DC.

Wimsatt, W. K., Jr
(1958) A Cache of Blades near the Great Falls of the Potomac. Archaeology, Vol. 11, No. 2, pp. 87-92.

Winsch, John
(1975) Identifying Flint Artifacts, No. 6 of a Series, LeCroy or Lake Erie Bifurcated Points. Artifacts, Vol. 5, No. 3.

Winters, Howard D.
(1969) The Riverton Culture. Illinois State Museum, Reports of Investigation No. 13, Springfield, IL.
(1967) An Archaeological Survey of the Wabash Valley in Illinois. Illinois State Museum, Report of Investigations, No. 10.
(1963) An Archaeological Survey of the Lower Wabash Valley in Illinois. Report of Investigations, No. 10, Illinois State Museum.

Witthoft, John
(1959) Notes on the Archaic of the Appalachian Region. American Antiquity, Vol. 25, pp. 79-85.
(1953) Broad Spearpoints and the Transition Period Cultures in Pennsylvania. Pennsylvania Archaeologist, Vol. XXIII, No. 1, pp. 4-31.
(1949) An Outline of Pennsylvania Prehistory. Pennsylvania History, Vol. 16, No. 3, pp. 3-15.

Wittkoski, J. Mark and Theodore R. Reinhart
(1989) Paleoindian Research in Virginia – A Synthesis. Special Publication Number 19, Archeological Society of Virginia.

Wittry, Warren L.
(1959) Archaeological Studies of Four Wisconsin Rock Shelters. Wisconsin Archaeologist, Vol. 1, No. 4.

Wolf Creek Indian Village and Museum, Bastian, Virginia

Wood, W. R. and R. B. McMillan
(1976) Prehistoric Man and His Environments. Academic Press, New York.

Wood, Peter H., Gregory A. Waselkov, and M. Thomas Hatley
(1989) Powhatan's Mantle – Indians in the Colonial Southeast. University of Nebraska Press, Lincoln, NE.

Woodland Conference
(1943) The First Archaeological Conference on the Woodland Pattern. American Antiquity, Vol. 8, pp. 383-400.

Woodward, D. R.
(1968) Farmington Landing Site, Prince Georges County. Archeological Society of Maryland, Miscellaneous Papers, No. 7.

Woodward, D. R. and W. A. Tidwell
(1967) Progress Report, Piscataway Site, Prince Georges Co. – The Montgomery Focus. Archeological Society of Maryland, Miscellaneous Papers, No. 6.
(1963) Hypothesis Concerning Archaic Settlement of Zekiah Swamp, Charles Co., Based on Analysis of Projectile Points. Archeological Society of Maryland, Miscellaneous Papers, No. 5.

Wormington, Marie
(1957) Ancient Man in North America. Popular Series No. 4, Denver Museum of Natural History.

Wright, Henry E.
(1987) Synthesis: The Land South of the Ice Sheets. In: North American and Adjacent Oceans During the Last Deglaciation, eds. W. F. Ruddiman and H. E. Wright, The Geology of North America, Vol. K-3, Geological Society of America, Boulder, CO.

Wright, Henry T.
(1973) An Archaeological Sequence in the Middle Chesapeake Region, Maryland. Archaeological Studies No. 1, Department of Natural Resources, Maryland Geological Survey, Baltimore, MD.

Yanovsky, Elias
(1936) Food Plants of the North American Indians. Misc. Pubs. No. 237, United States Department of Agriculture, Washington, DC.

Yerkes, Richard W.
(1987) Prehistoric Life on the Mississippi Floodplain: Stone Tool Use, Settlement Organization, and Subsistence Practices at the Labras Lake Site, Illinois. University of Chicago Press, Chicago, IL.

From an old notebook . . .

H. Holmes Ellis was among the earliest archaeologists to use the experimental method, or as he said: *...to critically appraise the work which has been accomplished in the investigation of flint fracture and the specific methods utilized by the aborigines in working of stone; and to record the experimental results achieved by the Lithic Laboratory.*

The following are examples from his studies...

The Lithic Laboratory for the Eastern United States was established at the Ohio State Museum in January, 1938, for the study of lithic materials of Native Americans --- and more importantly, their economy, methods and techniques for making tools, and their utilization.

Topics:

Character of Flint
Mechanics of Flint
Percussion Flaking
Direct Rest vs. Free-Hand
Pressure Flaking
Thermal Processes.

Note: Shown below, he was the first to experiment with a hafted, hard hammerstone. None have published the technique since.

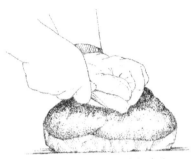

Fig. XVII. Rest pressure with unhafted antler tip.

Fig. XI. Indirect rest percussion with antler tip.

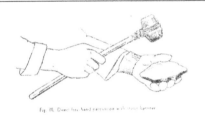

Fig. III. Direct free-hand percussion with stone hammer.

Fig. IX. Indirect free-hand percussion with one man.

Major publication: *Flint-Working of the American Indians: An Experimental Study.* The Ohio Historical Society, Columbus, Ohio (1957).

Note: This book is a mimeographed publication and very few copies still exist.

Index

1/1 groove, 267
2/2 groove, 267
3/4 groove, 267
4/4 groove, 267
Abiotic framework, 40
Abraderstone, 261
Abrading an edge, 160
Absorption, 64
Accokeek site, 32
Acutus, 226
Acutus, 22
Acutus (tip) angle, 231
Adena, 12, 200
Adena cache, 241
Adena influences, 100
Adornment, 321
Adz, 262
Agate (onyx), 47
Air motion, 64
Algonquian studies, 1
Alluvial sediments, 46
Amateur archaeological, 8
Amateur archaeologist, 7
American public, 8
American wayfarers, 68
Amos, 174
Anchor, 262

Andesite, 49
Animal killing, 321
Animal skins, 318
Antler tools, 115
Antler tools, 262
Anvilstone, 263
Apex angle, 232
Appalachian plateau, 26
Aquatic stone structures, 288
Archaeological resources management, 34
Archaic broadspear, 86
Archaic native americans, 91
Archaic period, 69, 72
Archaic period divisions, 84
Archaic summary, 91
Argillite, 48
Arm-chair listener, 7
Arrow, 264
Arrow straightener, 265
Artform, 12
Artifact collections, 34
Artifacts, study of, 10
Artwork, 12
Ashtabula, 174
Assumptions, 7
Atlantic coastal plain, 26

Atlatl, 266
Atlatl, 265, 329
Atlatl hook, 266
Atlatl/spear, 324
Atmosphere, 64
Atomic absorption spectroscopy (aas), 52
Awl, 266
Axe, 266, 328
Axe grooves, 267
Bald friar, 13
Ball, 269
Ball club, 329
Band, 22
Bannerstone, 269
Bannerstone study, 272
Bare island, 174
Barium-56, 65
Basalt, 49
Basic design principle, 149
Basic framework, 5
Basic knife form, 227
Baskets, 102, 103
Battle axe, 314
Bead, 272
Beans, 99
Beaver cache, 247

Bec-de-flute burin, 282
Bedrock mortar, 276
Behavioral property, 152
Belief system, 94
Belvoir cache, 250
Beveled edge, 133
Bibliographic overview, 1
Biface, 120, 122, 130, 136, 163
Biface, 22
Biface core, 217
Biface hump, 133
Biface knives, 230
Biface mistakes, 132
Biface nomenclature, 114
Biface technology, 134
Bifaces, 118, 123, 127, 312
Bifaces, 114, 134
Bifurcate form, 149
Bifurcate point, 89
Big sandy, 174
Big sandy auriculate, 175
Big sandy ii, 175
Billet, 315
Billet flaking, 118
Bimodality, 159
Bipoint biface, 228
Bipoints, 276
Bipolar flaking, 135
Birdshead graver, 277
Birdstone, 277
Bit, 22
Bit wear down, 110
Blade, 23, 226
Blade configurations, 139
Blade edge, 226
Blade edges, 138, 322
Blade function, 153
Blade modification, 160
Blade modification, 162
Blade parts, 226
Blade technology, 133
Blade tools, 215
Blank, 118
Blank, 111
Block core, 217
Blowgun, 323
Blowgun, 278, 314
Blue ridge, 26
Body adornment, 321
Boilingstone, 278
Bola, 278
Bone handle adz, 321
Bone knife, 229
Bone knives, 327
Bone tools, 278
Botany, 62
Bottle neck, 175
Boulders and outcrops, 115
Bow (and arrow), 279
Bow and arrow, 93, 279
Bow and arrow usage, 280
Bow strength, 280
Bow/arrow, 324
Bow/arrow efficiency, 280
Bowstring guard, 314
Bracelet, 321

Bradly, 201
Brandywine, 201
Brewerton, 176
Broad river, 175
Broadspear model, 147
Broadspear technology, 87, 88
Broadspear technology, 134
Broadspear tradition, 87
Broadspears, 135
Broken points, 137
Brown-johnson site, 95
Broyles, bettye, 32
Buck mountain, 61
Buckingham county cache, 252
Buggs island, 176
Burin, 281
Burin styles, 281
Burin technology, 218
Burin types, 281
Butchering, 321
C. Merry cache, 250
Cache bifaces, 241, 242, 252
Cache blade, 241
Cache placement, 242
Cache purpose, 242
Caches, 244
Caches, 241, 243
Cactus hill, 215
Cactus hill site, 68
Calvert, 201
Cane arrow, 329
Cane shaft, 264
Canoe, 326
Capron, 201
Captain john smith, 1, 68
Carderock, 202
Catchment, 23
Catchment utilizations, 14
Catoctin, 202
Catoctin creek site, 32
Cattle run, 176
Cause/effect climatical, 65
Celt, 282, 328
Ceramic pipe, 297
Ceremonial bannerstone, 270
Ceremonial caches, 243
Ceremonially broken, 121
Ceremonially killed, 225
Chalcedony, 48
Change, 14
Charles w. Mcnett, 30
Charleston, 176
Charmstone, 284
Chassis, 20, 129
Chassis deterioration, 324
Chassis mounting, 326
Cherokee native americans, 326
Cherokee warfare, 101
Chert, 48
Chesapeake, 177
Chesapeake bay, 1, 26, 68
Chesser, 202
Chevron trade bead, 38
Chiefdom form, 102

Chippage, 215
Chippage, 23
Chipped stone, 109
Chisel, 284
Chlorite, 49
Chopper, 285
Chopper/knife, 229
Chuchatuck, 177
Circular biface, 121
Circular bifaces, 121
Clagett, 178
Clarksville, 203
Classification, 145
Classification methodology, 144
Classifying stone debris, 133
Clear quartz, 59
Clifford evans', 29
Climate, 40, 64
Climate causes, 64
Climatic conditions, 63
Climatical conditions, 64
Climatologic factors, 64
Clothing, 318
Clovis, 12, 167, 322
Clovis fluting, 129, 322
Clovis fluting, 129
Clovis knife, 224
Clovis pointmakers, 322
Clovis points, 168
Coarse edge, 219
Coastal plain, 45
Coastal plain, 44
Coastal plain, 26
Coastal plain soils, 66
Coastal sediments, 47
Cobble, 135
Cobble axis, 135
Cobble modification, 135
Cobble scraper, 302
Cody-like knife, 235
Coe, joffry, 9
Cognitive behavior, 155
Collecting, 37
Collecting/hunting, 92
Collector, 6
Collectors, 6
Colonial marbles, 269
Concretion container, 285
Condensation, 64
Conditional point, 148
Condoquinet, 178
Conewago, 203
Conglomerate, 49
Contact period house, 93
Container revolution, 91
Continuum, 13
Copper beads, 276
Copper gorgets, 291
Copper usage, 102
Cordage, 129
Core, 111
Core, 23
Core blade, 224
Core blade knife, 229
Corn, 99

Cortex, 119
Cortex, 117
Cresap, 203
Crescent, 285
Cross-over electrophoresis, 62
Cryptocrystline technologies, 85
Crystal structure, 108, 166
Culluvial sediments, 46
Culpeper, 178
Cultural continuum, 13
Cultural divisions, 69
Cumberland, 170
Curation, 23
Cutting implement, 228
Cutting implements, 226
D/p ratio, 127, 231
Dalton, 73, 170
Dart, 314
Debitage, 136
Debitage classification, 135
Deciduous forest, 44
Decortation, 23, 117
Deer antler, 262
Deer antler tools, 115
Deer flaker, 129
Deer hooves, 129
Demographics, 72
Depilator, 289
Deposits - soils, 65
Diabase, 49
Diorite, 49
Discoidal, 286
Disk, 286
Display tray, 37
Distal/proximal (d/p) index, 121
Distal/proximal (d/p) index, 120, 121
Distal/proximal index, 118
Distinct point, 148
Drill, 286
Drilled hole, 287
Drybrook, 178
Dual-edges, 230
Duncan's island, 203
Dye usage, 319
Ear ornaments, 295
Ear plug, 288
Ecoregion approach, 43
Ecoscene approach, 43
Ecoscenes, 91
Edged blank, 119
Edgefield scraper, 235
Edging, 316
Edible foodstuffs, 40
Efficiency, 140, 317
Efficiency, 152
Effigy objects, 288
Elderly knappers, 109
Electron microprobe analysis (empa), 52
Elys ford, 170
Emic, 105
Engraved artifacts, 288

Environment, 40
Environmental livability, 14
Eolian sediments, 46
Erb, 178
Ethnographic data, 38
Ethnographic observation, 158
Etic, 105
European technology, 34
Eva, 178
Everhart rockshelter site, 33
Evidences of knowledge, 10
Excavation, 10
Excelsor, 179
Expended forms, 138
Expention, 38
Expention, 23, 116
Expention types, 138
Experimental archaeology, 306
Experimental archaeology, 307
Experimental material, 311
Experimental stone tools, 328
Extraction of stone, 57
Fairfax stone, 26
Faison, 179
Fakes, 323
False point, 148
Feather, 117
Feathering, 317
Felsic soils, 66
Felsite, 48
Fiber-tempered pottery, 92
Field and riverbed cobbles, 115
Field cobbles, 86
Final manufacture stage, 137
Fine edge, 219
Finished biface, 121
First europeans, 68
First virginians and marylanders, 68
Fish net, 99
Fish trap, 289
Fish weirs, 288
Fisher site, 33
Fishhook, 279
Flake, 23
Flake attributes, 217
Flake knife, 230
Flake sources, 217
Flake technology, 134
Flake tool usage, 215
Flake tools, 215, 217
Flake tools, 218, 289
Flaked implement, 112
Flakes, 215
Flaking methods, 217
Flat burin, 282
Flat-cobble, 109
Flesher, 289
Flint, 48
Flint celts, 282
Flintknapper's toolkit, 115
Flintknappers, 309
Flintknapping, 307, 312

Flintknapping tools, 315
Fluting, 129, 317
Food sources, 25
Food sourcing and processing, 63
Foodstuff data, 62
Force, 135
Forces in nature, 106
Forest or camp fires, 108
Form and shape, 155
Fort ancient, 204
Fox creek, 203
Fox valley, 179
Frank, 23, 226
Front royal jasper, 55
Full grooved, 266
Fulton, 204
Function, 156, 159, 219
Function, 23, 158
Function of length, 139
Functional axis, 140, 153
Functional work axis, 154
Funerary objects, 148
Gabbro, 49
Gameherds, 25
Gamestone, 269
Gamestone, 289
Generalized usage, 139
Genesee, 179
Geoarchaeology, 25
Geologic divisions, 63
Geological settings, 46
Georeferencing, 5
Glacial sediments, 47
Glaciation, 25
Glottochronology, 69
Glue, 130
Glues, 129
Gneiss, 49
Goals, 2
Goose creek, 204
Gore site, 33
Gorget, 291
Gouge, 291
Granite, 49
Grassland environments, 65
Gravelly edge, 219
Graver, 291
Greenstone, 49
Griffin, james, 29
Grinding or polishing, 109
Groove, 267
Groove styles, 110
Grooved celts, 282
Grooved stones, 300
Guilford, 180
Haft dimension, 20
Hafted bifaces, 224
Hafting, 117
Hafting index, 316
Halifax, 89, 180
Hamilton, 204
Hammering stone, 117
Hammerstone, 59, 60
Hammerstone, 292
Hand drill, 292

Hands of the past, 2
Hard hammer flaking, 117
Hard hammerstone, 118
Hardaway, 73, 171
Hardaway-dalton, 170, 171
Harpers ferry, 26
Harpoon, 99
Heat treating, 312
Heating stone, 278
Heat-treated stones, 312
Heavy billet, 315
Heavy wooden billet, 315
Heavy-duty celt, 267
Heck rockshelter, 204
Hellgramite, 205
Heye foundation, 6
Hides, 321
Hinge, 117
Historian, 7
Historic examples, 313
Hoe, 93
Hoe, 293
Holding a knife, 230
Holmes, 181
Holocene, 11, 44, 65
Hornfel, 49
Horticultural ceremonies, 95
Horticulture, 65
Houses, 94
Hubbard brook ecosystem, 43
Hughes site, 33
Human behavior, 10
Human-wave theory, 69
Humpback adzes, 262
Hunting verses cutting implements, 89
Hunting/gathering, 107
Ice age, 25, 68
Ice-covered areas, 65
Identify toolmaking, 145
Ideological-religious, 12
Impact fractures, 323
Implement, 23
Improperly-flaked bifaces, 130
Indian relationships, 32
Indian ways, 306
Infant mortality, 103
Isolate point, 148
Jacks reef, 205
Jasper, 48
Jefferson, 205
Jeffrey rockshelter, 33
Joffre l. Coe, 29
Kanawha, 181
Kerns site, 33
Kessell, 182
Kinsey, fred, 30
Kirk, 183
Knapper, 105
Knapping, 23
Knapping debris, 310
Knapping errors, 123, 127, 130
Knapping mistakes, 137
Knapp-ins, 316
Knapp-ins, 311
Knife, 224

Knife, 293
Knife dimensions, 234
Knife edges, 225
Knife function, 224, 225
Knife holding, 230
Knife length, 234
Knife measurements, 234
Knife on flake, 230
Knife or knife, 227
Knife river flint, 322
Knife size, 234
Knife taper, 233
Knife types, 234
Knife, parts of, 226
Knives and drills, 138
Knob splitter, 293
Koens-crispin, 87, 183
Labeling artifacts, 103, 161
Lackawaxan, 184
Lacustrine sediments, 46
Lake erie, 184
Lamoka, 184
Lanceolate form, 149
Land, 64
Land space, 64
Lapstone, 293
Large game herds, 85
Latent shape, 154
Lecroy, 185
Ledbetter, 185
Lehigh, 185
Lenapes, 13
Length, 139
Levanna, 101, 206
Lifecycle, 138, 153, 218, 228
Lifecycle, 21
Lifeways, 141
Light billet, 315
Limestone, 49
Limeton, 185
Limeton, 217
Limonite, 48
Lithic edges, 219
Lithic hardness, 142
Lithic knives, 225
Lithic materials, 47, 308, 312
Lithic reduction, 118
Lithic sourcing, 51
Lithic technology, 315
Lithic technology, 19
Lithic testing, 117
Lithics, 23
Little catoctin creek, 112
Living archaeology, 36
Living archaeology, 36
Living archaeology, 36
Living history, 309
Lobate, 185
Local prehistories, 1
Long, 185
Longevity, 219, 308
Looter, 6
Loudoun, 186
Lowes island, 206
Lucketts, 186
Lumpers and splitters, 145

Maccord bipoint, 271
Maccord, howard, 30
Maccorkle, 89, 186
Macpherson, 186
Macrotool, 23
Macrotool bits, 110
Macrotool chassis, 20
Macrotool lengths, 23
Macrotoolmaking, 108
Macrotools, 261
Macrotypic, 151
Madison, 101, 207
Mafic soils, 66
Magicstone, 284
Maize, 99
Making bifaces, 118
Mano, 296
Manufacturer, 105
Manufacturing, 105
Marble, 49
Marcy creek, 33
Mask, 95
Mason island site, 33
Mason neck, 187
Material culture, 11
Maul, 293, 329
Mccary fluted point survey, 82
Mcwhinney, 187
Meadowcroft, 215
Meadowcroft site, 68
Meadowood, 207
Meadowood caches, 243
Mechanical advantage, 106
Medium bifaces, 163
Medium billet, 315
Medium heavy billet, 315
Medium light billet, 315
Mental template, 153
Merom, 208
Metafine edge, 219
Metal axe, 34
Metal technology, 34
Microscopic thin sections, 50
Microtool, 23
Microtool lengths, 23
Microtoolmaking, 108
Microtypic, 151
Middle atlantic knapp-in, 306
Millingstone, 296
Miniature axe, 267
Mini-ice age, 101
Mississippian axe, 144
Mobility, 23
Modality, 261
Modality, 23
Modality operation, 159
Modality operations, 159
Model of ʃ l, 139
Modern knapping, 307
Modified flake, 218
Mohawks, 13
Monacans, 13
Monocacy, 187
Monrovia, 187
Montgomery county cache, 244

Morgan, 208
Morphology, 107
Morrow mountain, 188
Mortar, 276
Mortar, 296
Mortuary practices, 1, 100
Motley, 189
Moyock, 189
Mprv, 3
Mprv bifurcates, 89
Mprv ecoscene, 261
Mprv environment, 25, 45
Mprv knife, 226
Mprv quarries, 56
Mprv sites, 32
Mprv timemarkers, 69
Mprv tools and implements, 260
Mprv's lithic materials, 45
Muller, 296
Multifunctional operations, 159
Multifunctional tool, 160
Multimodality, 159
Multiple cutting edges, 225
Multiple types, 145
Museum, 28
Museum acquisitions, 323
Museumologist, 7
Museums, 8
Narrow blades, 232
Narrowspear tradition, 89
Native american artifacts, 37
Native american concern, 309
Native american flintknapping, 19
Native american habitation, 43
Native american hamlet, 94
Native american technology, 34, 163
Native american toolkit, 260
Native american tools, 307
Native american villages, 102
Native americans, 7, 34, 38, 95
Native americans created caches, 243
Native americans' toolkit, 146
Native artifacts, 326
Native point, 322
Native points, 322
Natural law, 11
Necklace, 321
Need artifacts, 10
Negative point, 148
Net fishing, 99
Netsinker, 294
Neutron activation analysis (naa), 51
Neutron activator, 53
Neville, 189
Nomini, 208
Nonflake debris, 130
Nongrooved axes, 267
Nontypeable microtools, 163
Normanskill, 189
North branch, 26

North carolina cache, 244
Northumberland, 171
Notched form, 149
Notched stones, 294
Notching, 137, 316
Nottoway river, 89, 190
Nuttingstone, 294
Obsidian, 49
Occoquan, 190
Ocean, 64
Off-center workend, 227
Off-centered stems, 114
Oilstone, 295
Onyx, 47
Operational functions, 153
Operations, 116
Orient, 190
Ornaments, 295
Otter creek, 190
Overkill theory, 69
Owasco, 101
Oxidation, 322
Paint pot, 285
Paleoethnobotany, 62
Paleoindian period, 44, 69, 71
Paleoindian summary, 84
Paleoindian technology, 83
Palmer, 191
Pamunkey museum, 4
Panindian borrowing, 146
Panindian knowledge, 13
Panindian tools, 7
Paraprofessional archaeologist, 7
Patination, 149
Patination measuring, 323
Patination process, 148
Patination replication, 323
Patination surfaces, 323
Patuxent, 192
Paw model, 68
Paw summary, 73
Pecked-polished, 109
Pecking and grinding, 108
Pecking and grinding, 117
Peckingstone, 295
Pee dee, 208
Pendant, 295
Pequea, 192
Percussion chipping, 160
Perforator, 296
Peridotite, 49
Perkiomen, 192
Pestle, 299
Pestle, 296
Physical environment, 40
Physical function, 153
Pick, 297
Pick-up flakes, 225
Piedmont, 44
Piedmont plateau, 26
Pin, 297
Piney island, 193
Pipe, 297
Piscataway, 209
Pit(s), 99

Plant dye, 319
Plants, 62
Plasma emission spectroscopy (pes), 52
Pleistocene blade, 220
Plum nelly, 33
Plummet, 298
Pohick, 209
Point, 23
Point chronology, 93
Point classification, 144
Point distribution, 151
Point lookout, 26
Point or knife, 227
Point shapes, 149
Point technologies, 85
Point typology, 4, 63, 144, 261
Pointed flake, 281
Pointed flaker, 316
Polish time-line, 142
Polish wear, 141
Political control, 102
Poll, 23, 266
Poorly-made bifaces, 130
Poplar island, 193
Population numbers, 72
Positive point, 148
Pothunter, 6
Potomac, 101, 210
Potomac creek site, 101
Potomac river, 25
Potomac river basin, 1
Potomac river basin, 44
Potomac valley drill, 287
Pottery, 92
Potts, 210
Powhatan chiefdom, 1
Precipitation, 64
Pre-clovis knives, 229
Pre-jamestown contact, 38
Preparatory biface, 122
Pressure flaking, 117, 160
Prima facia evidence, 145
Primary axis, 141
Primary preform, 111
Primitive technology, 306
Principles, 20
Private collections, 4, 38
Process (technology, 23
Processing, 116
Processual analysis, 14
Procurement, 116
Production economies, 308
Production, process, and tool attributes, 134
Professional archaeologist, 7
Projectile point, 298
Projectile point, 23
Protohistory, 1
Psychic unity, 11
Public opinion, 8
Pump drill, 298
Punch, 299
Qcm, 149
Quantum classification method, 149

Quarry analyses, 57
Quarry bulk, 251
Quarry extraction, 58
Quarry maul, 59
Quarry processes, 56
Quarry rejects, 58
Quarry spall, 58
Quarry spalls, 121
Quarry testing, 58
Quarry tool, 58
Quarry tool, 58
Quartz crystal, 48
Quartz crystals, 284
Quartz sources, 60
Quartz usage, 59
Quartzite, 48
Quartzite bifaces, 123
Quartzite hammerstone, 59
Quiver, 314
Raccoon, 210
Radiocarbon database, 68
Radioisotopic example, 53
Rainfall, 65
Raised groove, 269
Rappahannock river, 193
Raw materials, 146
Raw materials, 47
Rawhide, 130
Reamer, 299
Reduction area, 116
Reduction methodologies, 106
Reduction methods, 121
Reduction model, 116
Reduction process, 116
Relic hunter, 7
Relic miner, 7
Replacement, 116
Replication, 326
Replication, 21, 325
Reproduction, 325
Reproduction, 325
Reproduction knives, 224
Resharpening, 115, 153
Retouched, 112
Retrofitting, 115, 160
Retrofitting, 262
Reworking, 316
Rhodolite, 49
Rhyolite, 49
Rhyolite bifaces, 127
Rhyolite caches, 242
Richard j. Dent, 32
Ritchie, william, 8
River cobble tradition, 86
River transportation, 100
Riverine cultures, 101
Riverways, 44
Robbins, 211
Robert stephenson, 29
Robertson, 211
Rockart, 25
Rockshelter sediments, 47
Roller pestle, 297
Roller pestle, 299
Rossville, 211
Rough out, 111

Rubbingstone, 299
Rule in typology, 147
Safety clothing, 310
Safety gear, 310
Sandstone, 49
Saratoga, 194
Savannah river, 87, 194
Saw, 300
Saw abrader, 301
Schists, 49
Schuylkill, 195
Scraper, 302
Scraper-plane, 300
Secondary preform, 111
Seed domestication, 91
Selby bay, 211
Serrated blade edge, 133
Serrations, 133
Settlement pattern, 83
Settlement patterns, 1, 27, 66
Shaft and socket method, 130
Shaft straightener, 300
Shaft/socket, 130
Shale, 49
Shall cache, 252
Share, 233
Share, 23, 226
Sharp–edged flake, 230
Sharpener, 300, 301
Shell beads, 272
Shellac, 320
Shelter, 94
Shepard site, 33
Shields, 314
Short-term implement, 219
Signatures, 3
Simpson, 171
Sinew, 129
Sinew (wrapping), 321
Sinewstone, 301
Site specific point, 148
Skill, 148, 158
Slash-and-burn method, 99
Slate, 49
Smith point, 26
Smith's first bay expedition, 68
Smithsonian, 27
Snapped biface, 120
Snook kill, 195
Snyders, 100, 212
Social network model, 242
Social norms, 155
Social style, 158
Social system, 23
Social systems, 14
Soft hammer flaking, 117
Soil formation, 66
Soils, 65
Solar radiation, 64
Somerset county cache, 244
Sourcing jasper, 54
Sourcing rhyolite, 53
Southampton, 195
Spatula, 301
Specialized usage, 139

Split shaft, 130
Split-cobble scraper, 302
Splitter, 301
Spokeshave, 286
Spokeshave, 302
Spokeshaves, 305
Spring sediments, 46
Spud, 301
Squash, 99
St albans, 196
St charles, 196
St charles technology, 88
Stage 0, 118
Stage 1, 119
Stage 2, 119
Stage 3, 120
Stage 4, 121
Stages of manufacture, 134
Standard references, 313
Stanly, 197
Status bannerstone, 270
Steatite, 49, 90
Stemmed form, 149
Step, 117
Stick basket, 320
Stone, 24
Stone bead, 272
Stone benification, 57
Stone milling, 57
Stone pipe, 297
Stone processing, 57
Stone refinement, 57
Stoneworking techniques, 117
Stored maize, 94
Striations, 141, 323
Strontium-38, 65
Structural analysis, 152
Structure, 107, 152, 155
Structure (point), 24
Structure and function, 147
Structure and function, 152, 163
Structure properties, 154
Structure/design, 153
Study assumptions, 7
Style, 158
Susquehanna, 12, 87, 198
Susquehanna valley, 89, 198
Suwannee, 172
Swatara, 198
Sword, 303
Syenite, 50
Symmetry, 114
Synchronic versus diachronic, 68
T. Dale stewart, 29
Talc, 49
Target, 24
Teamahia, 302
Teardrop, 212
Technique, 21
Technoculture migrations, 88
Technological continuum, 14, 73, 87, 106, 107, 166
Technology, 36, 106
Technology, 24, 158

Technology continuum, 13
Technology divisions, 69
Technology experimentation, 318
Technology maintenance, 13
Technology overview, 78
Technology philosophy, 19
Technology processes, 107
Terminal archaic, 89
Terminal pleistocene, 82
Textiles, 319
Thermal alteration, 312
Thermal alteration, 312
Thermal spall, 217
Thickness, 122
Thin sections, 50
Thinning flake, 217
Three-feather arrow, 317
Thunderbird paloindian site, 68
Thunderbird site, 32, 82
Time crime, 38
Timemarkers, 69
Tomahawk, 314
Tool, 24
Tool analyses, 20
Tool assembly, 24
Tool classes, 261
Tool definition, 260
Tool durability, 308
Tool efficiency, 140, 158
Tool expention, 138
Tool experimentation, 307
Tool function, 141, 158, 233
Tool handles, 12
Tool industries, 261
Tool maintenance, 14
Tool modification, 114
Tool operation, 159
Tool operations, 159
Tool operations, 107
Tool production, 105
Tool structure, 154
Tool usage, 307
Tool usage, 117, 141, 307, 324
Tool usages, 138
Tool's lifecycle, 114
Tool's physical assembly, 154
Toolkit classes, 74
Toolkit replenishment, 59
Toolkits, 260
Toolmaking, 107, 108, 306

Toolmaking, 105, 314
Toolmaking procedures, 310
Toolmaking process, 145, 316
Toolmaking processes, 316
Toolmaking technology, 89
Tools, artform, 12
Topper site, 68
Trachyte, 50
Traditional point, 148
Transitional archaic, 89
Transportable bifaces, 59
Treasure hunter, 7
Tressel, 267
Triangle biface, 136
Triangle form, 150
Triangle technology, 100
Trimodality, 159
Trittipoe site, 33
Trolling equipment, 99
Tundra, 65
Type descriptions, 166
Type validity, 148
Typologists, 145
Typology, 146
Typology, 144, 163
Ulos, 303
Ulu, 303
Ungrooved axes, 282
Uniangulus knife, 230
Uniangulus knife, 231
Uni-edge, 230
Uniface tool, 114, 218
Unimodality, 159
Unique point, 148
Uplands, 44
Urban archaeology, 35
Use wear, 20
Useability, 153, 317
Useability, 138, 235
Utilitarian bannerstone, 270
Utilized flake, 230
Utilized flakes, 218
Validity, 148
Valina, 212
Valley and ridge, 26
Valley and ridge soils, 66
Value of collectors, 6
Van lott, 198
Variation, 14, 158
Variety, bannerstone, 270
Veron, 213
Village, 309

Virginsville, 198
Vosburg, 199
V-shaped celt, 282
Wading river, 199
Ward cache, 252
Warming phase, 65
Warratan, 213
Warratan cache, 246
Warren, 199
Water, 63
Water supply, 63
Watershed, 27, 44
Watershed approach, 43
Watersheds, 84
Wear out, 20
Wear pattern analysis, 142
Wear patterns, 141, 227
Wear patterns, 139
Wedge, 304
Wedge-advantage, 114
Weeds, 62
Whetstone, 304
Whites ferry, 214
Wilkison cache, 251
William a. Gardner, 32
William a. Ritchie, 29
William j. Graham, 29
Williamson, 61
Winged bannerstone, 87
Winslow site, 33
Wisconsin glaciation, 25
Wood carvers, 95
Wooden mallet, 316
Wooden mortars, 102
Wooden pipes, 297
Wooden shaft, 264
Wooden sword, 303
Wooden tools, 278
Woodland, 214
Woodland geoscene, 46
Woodland period, 69, 72, 91
Woodland summary, 102
Work, 24
Workend, 20
Workends, 225
Wrapped - notch, 129
X-ray emission analysis (xrea), 51
X-ray fluorescence spectrometry (xrfs), 51
Yadkin, 214
Zekiah swamp, 199

Made in the USA
Coppell, TX
21 September 2023

21821264R00208